Living the Country ~~Life~~
All-in-One For D~~ummies~~

M000199145

Gardening Do's and Don'ts

Mary, Mary, quite contrary. How does your garden grow? Pretty darn well, if you follow these tips from Book III:

DO:

- Make sure the growing season where you live is long enough for your plants to reach maturity.
- Sketch out a diagram for your garden before you start to dig.
- Make sure your plants have good air circulation, both above and under the ground.
- Prepare the soil to a depth of 6 to 8 inches, and incorporate lots of organic matter.
- Allow plenty of easy access to your plants for weeding and harvesting.
- Rid your garden of weeds before planting, and diligently weed out new sprouts as they appear.
- Make sure your plants receive about 1 inch of water per week.

DON'T:

- Toss a packet of seeds on some dirt and expect your "garden" to prosper.
- Use soil that's lousy or too thin.
- Plant seedlings without hardening them off first.
- Sow in cold or soggy soil.
- Plant seedlings too close together.

Handy Outdoor Cooking Equipment

You need more than an appetite and a recipe. For successful outdoor cooking, you also need these things, described in Book I, Chapter 5:

- A cast-iron camp oven and/or a cast-iron skillet with a lid (flanged lids and legs are plusses)
- Charcoal
- An ash brush
- Oven gloves
- Long utensils
- Heavy-duty aluminum foil or a metal trash can lid
- A lid hook or lid lifter
- A spyder if your cookware is lacking legs
- A charcoal chimney starter

Oh, and don't forget to pack matches or a lighter to get that fire started!

For Dummies: Bestselling Book Series for Beginners

Tips for Managing Bad Animal Behavior

If your animals are behaving badly (not George Orwell badly, of course), you can keep the peace and avoid an animal revolution with these tactics from Book V, Chapter 3:

- Make sure your animals are properly socialized and used to human interaction.
- Avoid overcrowding — even animals need their space.
- Remove horns from animals that otherwise use them as weapons.

- Castrate aggressive males.
- Separate aggressive animals — experiment with different "roommate" combinations to determine what works best.

Yarn Weights at a Glance

Yarns come in different *weights,* or thicknesses (see Book II, Chapter 2 for more knitting info). The following table gives a quick list of symbols, needle sizes, stitches per inch, and common uses for common yarn weights.

Yarn Weight	Symbol	Needle Size	Stitches Per Inch	Common Uses
Lace	0 LACE	000–1	8–10	Lace knitting
Superfine, fingering, or baby weight	1 SUPER FINE	1–3	7–8	Light layettes, socks
Fine or sport weight	2 FINE	3–6	5–6	Light sweaters, baby things, accessories
DK (double-knitting) or light worsted	3 LIGHT	5–7	5–5½	Sweaters and other garments, lightweight scarves
Medium, worsted, afghan, aran	4 MEDIUM	7–9	4–5	Sweaters, blankets, outdoor wear (hats, scarves, mittens, and so on)
Chunky	5 BULKY	10–11	3–3½	Rugs, jackets, blankets
Bulky	6 SUPER BULKY	13–15	2–2½	Heavy blankets, rugs, sweaters

Living the Country Lifestyle
ALL-IN-ONE
FOR DUMMIES®

Tracy L. Barr, Compilation Editor

Wiley Publishing, Inc.

Living the Country Lifestyle All-in-One For Dummies®

Published by
Wiley Publishing, Inc.
111 River St.
Hoboken, NJ 07030-5774
www.wiley.com

Copyright © 2009 by Wiley Publishing, Inc., Indianapolis, Indiana

Published simultaneously in Canada

For general information on our other products and services, please contact our Customer Care Department within the U.S. at 877-762-2974, outside the U.S. at 317-572-3993, or fax 317-572-4002.

For technical support, please visit www.wiley.com/techsupport.

Wiley also publishes its books in a variety of electronic formats. Some content that appears in print may not be available in electronic books.

Library of Congress Control Number: 2008943503

ISBN: 978-0-470-43061-3

Manufactured in the United States of America

10 9 8 7 6 5 4 3 2 1

WILEY

About the Author(s)

Pam Allen, coauthor of *Knitting For Dummies,* 2nd Edition, is creative director at Classic Elite Yarns. She's also the author of *Scarf Style* and co-author of *Wrap Style, Lace Style, Bag Style,* and *Color Style* (all published by Interweave Press). Her work has appeared in *Knitting in America* (published by Artisan) and numerous magazines and knitting books.

Tracy L. Barr, author of *Cast-Iron Cooking For Dummies,* has been part of the For Dummies phenomenon for almost a decade. An avid cook, she was introduced to cast iron as a young girl when her mother inherited a few pieces, and she has since made cast iron the workhorse of her own kitchen.

Howland Blackiston, author of *Beekeeping For Dummies,* has been a backyard beekeeper for nearly 20 years. He's written many articles on beekeeping and appeared on dozens of television and radio programs. He has been a keynote speaker at conferences in more than 40 countries. Howland is cofounder and president of `bee-commerce.com`, an online superstore offering supplies and equipment for the hobbyist beekeeper.

Kelly Ewing, author of *Making Candles & Soaps For Dummies,* is a writer and editor. She has coauthored, ghostwritten, and edited more than 75 books on a variety of topics. In her spare time (when she can find it), she enjoys spending time with her kids, reading, walking, writing, scrapbooking, cooking, and doing crafts.

Steven A. Frowine, author of *Gardening Basics For Dummies,* has a bachelor's and a master's degree in horticulture from Ohio State University and Cornell, respectively. He has served on boards of various professional organizations, including the National Gardening Association. He is now president of his own horticultural consulting firm, where he works with various companies in the green industry on writing, photography, marketing, and public relations issues.

Christopher Hobbs, L.Ac., author of *Herbal Remedies For Dummies,* is a fourth-generation herbalist and botanist — his grandmother and great-grandmother were professional herbalists, and his father and great-uncle were botany professors — with over thirty years experience with herbs. In 1985, he cofounded the American Herbalists Guild, the only national U.S. organization for professional herbalists.

Michael Hodgson, author of *Camping For Dummies,* works as a content editor for Planet Outdoors and is a founding partner in GearTrends, LLC (`www.GearTrends.com`). Michael's articles have appeared in *Backpacker, Outside, Men's Journal, Adventure Journal, Field & Stream, Outdoor Life,* and *The Christian Science Monitor,* among other periodicals. He has published 18 books on the outdoors.

Theresa A. Husarik, author of *Hobby Farming For Dummies,* is a writer, photographer, crafter, fiber person, and animal lover who lives on a small plot far away from the heart of the city. When she is not tending to her brood, (which includes llamas, alpacas, angora goats, cats, dogs, peacocks, and chickens), she can usually be found either behind the computer writing something or in the craft room making something.

Peter Kaminsky, author of *Fishing For Dummies,* caught his first fish, a 30-pound grouper, on a party boat in the Florida Keys. It was the first time he went fishing, and that grouper won him $45 for the big fish of the day. Kaminsky was hooked. He was Managing Editor of *National Lampoon* at the time. Soon after, he began to write for *Outdoor Life, Field & Stream,* and *Sports Afield.* In 1985, he began his regular contributions to *The New York Times* "Outdoors" column.

Leslie Linsley, author of *Crafts For Dummies,* is the author of more than 50 books on crafts, decorating, and home style. Her work has appeared regularly in national magazines and in newspapers throughout the country.

Jan Saunders Maresh, author of *Sewing For Dummies,* 2nd Edition, is a nationally known sewing and serging journalist and home economist. After graduating from Adrian College in Michigan, she became the education director of one of the largest sewing machine companies in the country, and then the director of consumer education for the largest fabric chain in the country. Both professional experiences gave her a solid foundation in the home sewing industry, which she continues to serve with her many writing, marketing, and industry consulting projects.

Charlie Nardozzi, author of *Vegetable Gardening For Dummies,* graduated from the University of Vermont in 1981 with a degree in plant and soil science. Charlie then spent three years in the Peace Corps in Thailand, helping farmers. He returned to the United States and received a master's degree in education. After working as a landscaper, he served as a horticulturist at the National Gardening Association for more than 10 years.

Shannon Okey, coauthor of *Knitting For Dummies,* 2nd Edition, is the author of nearly a dozen books on knitting and other fiber arts, a columnist for *knit.1* magazine, and a frequent contributor to other craft magazines. She hosts a call-in podcast about knitting and has appeared on many television shows, including *Knitty Gritty, Uncommon Threads,* and *Crafters Coast to Coast.* You can find her online at www.knitgrrl.com.

Molly Siple, author of *Healing Foods For Dummies,* has a Master of Science in Nutritional Science and is also a registered dietician. Her other books include two on female health, coauthored with Lissa DeAngelis, *SOS for PMS* and *Recipes for Change: Gourmet Wholefood Cooking for Health and Vitality at Menopause,* a Julia Child Cookbook Awards nominee. She also lectures on nutrition and is a nutrition consultant to food companies.

Karen Ward, author of *Canning & Preserving For Dummies,* is a life-long home canner, as well as a cookbook author, culinary teacher, and home economist. In addition to judging preserved food at the San Diego County Fair each year, Karen teaches canning and preserving to men and women of all ages to foster the knowledge, skill, and techniques of these ancient and modern-day arts.

Publisher's Acknowledgments

We're proud of this book; please send us your comments through our Dummies online registration form located at `http://dummies.custhelp.com`. For other comments, please contact our Customer Care Department within the U.S. at 877-762-2974, outside the U.S. at 317-572-3993, or fax 317-572-4002.

Some of the people who helped bring this book to market include the following:

Acquisitions, Editorial, and Media Development

Compilation Editor: Tracy L. Barr

Senior Project Editor: Christina Guthrie

Acquisitions Editor: Mike Baker

Copy Editors: Christy Pingleton, Jennifer Tebbe

Assistant Editor: Erin Calligan Mooney

Editorial Program Coordinator: Joe Niesen

Editorial Manager: Christine Meloy Beck

Editorial Assistants: David Lutton, Jennette ElNaggar

Cover Photos: ©Jason Price/Alamy

Cartoons: Rich Tennant
(`www.the5thwave.com`)

Composition Services

Project Coordinator: Katie Key

Layout and Graphics: Samantha K. Allen, Reuben W. Davis, Sarah Philippart, Christin Swinford, Christine Williams

Special Art: Liz Kurtzman

Proofreaders: Melissa Cossell, John Greenough, Toni Settle

Indexer: Broccoli Information Mgt.

Special Help: Alicia South

Publishing and Editorial for Consumer Dummies

Diane Graves Steele, Vice President and Publisher, Consumer Dummies

Kristin Ferguson-Wagstaffe, Product Development Director, Consumer Dummies

Ensley Eikenburg, Associate Publisher, Travel

Kelly Regan, Editorial Director, Travel

Publishing for Technology Dummies

Andy Cummings, Vice President and Publisher, Dummies Technology/General User

Composition Services

Gerry Fahey, Vice President of Production Services

Debbie Stailey, Director of Composition Services

Contents at a Glance

Table of Contents

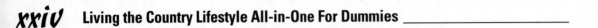

Introduction

• •

*M*odern technology and technological processes are great. Take, for example, the sewing machine. Before its invention, people made clothing by hand. After its invention, the sewing machine enabled women everywhere to make a garment in a fraction of the time it took previously. Now consider the additional advancement of the assembly line and the precision and speed with which thousands of garments can be made in a single day.

What was gained? Speed, efficiency, consistency of outcome. And what was lost? Tedious, eye-straining, finger-pricking labor. And a connection to a traditional, and in many ways, simpler and more meaningful way of doing things. The pricked fingers are gone, but so is the feeling of satisfaction that comes with self-sufficiency and accomplishment. This is just one example, but the lesson — that traditional ways of doing things have value, even if it can't be tallied on a ledger or articulated as time saved — is applicable to many other areas as well.

Living the Country Lifestyle All-in-One For Dummies helps you rediscover the joy and satisfaction that come when you get back to the basics. Whether you long to rediscover what mealtimes can be like when the food you prepare is that which you've grown or preserved yourself; or seek to reawaken the joy of spending time outdoors; or have decided that a natural approach to caring for your health is the best approach, this book can put you on the right track.

About This Book

In a world that seems to grow more fast-paced every day, what do you do if you want to slow life down and get back to the basics — beyond turning back the clocks and tossing out the Cuisinart, that is? You find a resource that's chock-full of information on how to apply traditional, down-home approaches to the activities you have to do or want to do. Lucky you, that's just the kind of information that *Living the Country Lifestyle All-in-One For Dummies* provides. In this book, you can find out how to

✔ Prepare traditional meals, using traditional cookware, indoors or out.

✔ Put up (read *preserve*) fresh fruits and vegetables.

✔ Spin your own wool and knit it up into gorgeous apparel.

✔ Make quilts and other hand-sewn favorites.

✔ Plant and harvest your own fruits, vegetables, and herbs.

✔ Raise your own farm animals.

✔ Experience the great outdoors.

✔ Incorporate the healing power of foods and herbs into your health regimen.

That's a lot of information for one book, but like all *For Dummies* books, the info here is easy to find so you can focus your attention only on the topics that interest you. After reading this book, you may not be an expert, but you'll have a new confidence that may spur you on to discovering even more ways to embrace a country lifestyle.

Conventions Used in This Book

To help you navigate through the text and easily identify different components, this book uses the following conventions:

✔ Web addresses appear in a special font (which looks like this: `www.wiley.com`) so you can easily pick them out.

✔ New terms appear in *italics* and are closely followed by an easy-to-understand definition.

✔ **Bold** highlights the action parts of numbered steps or keywords in bulleted lists.

A special note about the recipes in this book: As is true of most traditional cooking, the recipes have been handed down from one generation to the next and passed from cook to cook. Many recipes have made it to this book in just that way. A typical characteristic of these types of recipes is that they often don't use precise measurements or give specific time guidelines. Instead, they tell you to "Add just a smidgeon of salt," or "Simmer the sauce until it's nice and thick." So that anyone from the culinary novice to the seasoned cook can have success with the recipes in this book, the impreciseness is kept to a minimum. All temperatures are Fahrenheit.

✔ **Measurements:** The recipes largely give precise measurements (a half teaspoon of this or $1^1/_2$ tablespoons of that, for example) or indicate a range ($^1/_2$ to 1 teaspoon, for example).

✔ **Times:** The recipes also indicate approximate prep and cooking times, as well as times for the tasks within individual recipe steps.

But, at the end of the day, to be true to the heritage of traditional cooking, some ingredient amounts are occasionally left to your cooking judgment. Continuing a long-standing kitchen tradition, as soon as you make a recipe, that recipe becomes yours to do with as you please. Take advantage of this flexibility and feel free to adjust any of these recipes to suit your own tastes and cooking style.

And now just a few more quick words about the ingredients. Unless otherwise noted,

  ✔ **Butter** is unsalted.

  ✔ **Milk** is whole.

  ✔ **Eggs** are large.

  ✔ **Salt** is common table salt, and **pepper** is freshly ground black pepper.

  ✔ **Fruits and vegetables** are washed under cold running water before using.

Finally, when you see ☺ before a recipe title, that's an indication that the recipe doesn't contain any meat.

What You're Not to Read

Like all *For Dummies* books, this one makes it easy for you to recognize non-essential information. Feel free to skip these bits without worrying about impairing your understanding of the topic at hand:

  ✔ **Paragraphs beside the Technical Stuff icons:** These paragraphs contain interesting, albeit tangential, info — think background information or technical details that go beyond what the average person would be interested in.

  ✔ **Sidebars:** These are entertaining or informative asides that add to the discussion but don't contain vital, need-to-know information.

  ✔ **Anything that doesn't strike your fancy:** Hey, it's a *For Dummies* book. If you have no interest in beekeeping, for example, feel free to skip that entire chapter. No hard feelings.

Foolish Assumptions

Not every book is for every person. In fact, most books are written for a very *specific* person — obviously one who would be interested in the info the book contains. So here are the assumptions we made about you, our reader:

> ✔ You want easy-to-understand information about how to get back to doing and enjoying the simpler things in life.
>
> ✔ Although you may have an interest in particular topics already and know something about them, you're not an expert and you don't want to be. You just want to know how to get started and how to make a successful go of your attempts — whatever the task at hand is.
>
> ✔ You may not buy into a romanticized "everything was better back then, and we all need to sell our cars and unplug our appliances" mindset, but you do believe there's value in working with your hands and getting back to nature.

If these statements sound like you, then you've got the right book.

How This Book Is Organized

Living the Country Lifestyle All-in-One For Dummies is divided into six books, each one focusing on a particular topic or activity related to living a country lifestyle. Each book is further divided into chapters that relate to that book's topic. So, for example, the book that covers country kitchen skills includes chapters on country cooking, canning and pickling, and so on. This structure allows you to find info whether you're looking for a general area of interest or something more specific.

Book 1: Country Kitchen Skills

Want to know how to cook a down-home meal? Book I includes indoor and outdoor cooking techniques and a collection of recipes that will have you hankerin' to ring the dinner bell. Another traditional skill that's coming back into vogue (for a variety of reasons, including money savings, healthy living, and the desire to support local farmers) is "putting up" produce. To help you do that, this book includes chapters covering how to can, pickle, or dry fruits, vegetables, and herbs.

Book II: Traditional Crafts

Many of the skills required to run a home of yesteryear — candle-making, knitting, spinning, hand-sewing, quilting, and more — have turned into today's crafts. You do them not because you have to, but because you want to. (Believe us, the "wanting to" part is what makes the difference between a chore and a hobby.) Book II gets you started.

Book III: Edible Gardening

Become a gardener and not only do you end up, literally, with the fruits (and veggies) of your labor but also with a connection to the land that goes back to the days when humankind first began cultivating the soil for sustenance. By following the advice and instructions in Book III, you'll end up with a garden that's both beautiful and bountiful.

Book IV: Getting Outdoors

Everyone needs to get outside more. Why? Because life outdoors is simplified and pure. Among the mountains, rivers, woods, and open spaces, city-bound inhibitions and lifestyle complications slip away like excess baggage. The key to truly enjoying nature, rather than just passing through it, is to do so without being insulated by a barrier of technology. Book IV shares basic camping and survival skills, as well as activity ideas that the whole family can enjoy.

Book V: Raising Farm Animals

So many people dream of moving into the country and away from the hustle and bustle of city life — the traffic and smog and long lines and crowds. A key draw of country living? Being able to raise your own farm animals. Whether as pets, food sources, laborers, or sources of fun, animals are a farm institution. In Book V, you discover types of animals available, where you can buy your livestock, how to provide for critters' basic needs, and what to do when an animal gets sick or injured.

Book VI: Natural Health

Long before there was any such thing as an urgent care clinic or a prescription pad, there were natural remedies, many of which have been proven to have actual health benefits. Book VI tells you what these healing foods and herbs are and how to make your own tinctures, salves, infusions, and more.

Icons Used in This Book

To help you identify certain types of information, *Living the Country Lifestyle All-in-One For Dummies* places icons — graphical images — beside particular paragraphs. Here's what the different icons mean:

This icon appears beside little gems of information that you may not have known but that help you perform the particular task more efficiently or easily.

Although this is a reference book that you can jump into whenever you need your memory jogged, this icon appears to denote a particular bit of content that's important enough to store in your own gray matter.

You see this icon wherever you need to take extra care because a mistake could be dangerous or costly.

This icon identifies information that's interesting, but nonessential. Feel free to skip the bits with this icon attached.

Where to Go from Here

Of course, we'd love for you to read this book from cover to cover, but you certainly don't have to — especially given the wide range of topics included. Start with whatever topic interests you. If that's traditional crafts, then head to Book II. Planning a camping trip? Go directly to Book IV.

Don't know where you want to begin? Then why not start at the beginning and work your way through. You're bound to find lots of ideas that'll inspire and motivate you. Or you can look at the Table of Contents for broad categories of information and turn to the Index to look up more specific items.

Bottom line: Where you go from here is wherever you *want* to go.

Book I
Country Kitchen Skills

The 5th Wave   By Rich Tennant

"..and here's what we canned from the garden this year. Beets, carrots, cucumbers...oh, there's that glove I couldn't find."

In this book . . .

Before the twentieth century, food packaging as we know it today didn't exist. There were no straight-from-the-microwave-to-the-table meals in a minute. No snack packs separated into compartmented plastic trays to be thrown in a book bag or briefcase and called lunch. No ready-made pouches of vegetables with "gourmet" sauces. No TVs and no TV dinners.

If your primary criteria for food prep is that it take the least amount of effort and time, these culinary "advancements" are great. But if you long to get back to basics, to reconnect with simpler and, as many would argue, more wholesome foods, then this book is for you. It helps you say good-bye to overprocessed, overpriced foodstuffs and hello to natural foods you put up and prepare yourself.

Chapter 1

Cast-Iron Cooking

In This Chapter

▶ Getting acquainted with basic cast-iron pieces

▶ Preparing your cast-iron cookware for its debut

▶ Following a few easy cleaning and storage rules

▶ Developing your cast-iron cooking know-how

▶ Making traditional cast-iron favorites

Cast iron has a nostalgic appeal. Watch reruns of old TV Westerns or pick up any book chronicling America's past, from colonial times and the settling of the West to more modern portrayals of cowboy roundups, and you're bound to find at least one domestic scene that features a cook, a fire, and a cast-iron pot. If you're trying to get back to basics, the idea of cooking the same way that your ancestors did may persuade you that cast iron is for you.

In addition to its rough-around-the-edges charm, cast iron is also conducive to healthy eating, easy to use and care for, suitable for a wide range of cooking methods, and able to withstand the use and abuse that occurs in a busy kitchen. More importantly, many who use cast iron vouch that food cooked in it tastes better than food cooked in anything else.

This chapter explains what you need to know to become a cast-iron cook yourself.

Selecting Cast-Iron Cookware

Cast iron is easy to find and relatively inexpensive. It also comes in all sorts of shapes and sizes, from the traditional cast-iron skillets and camp ovens to specialty items, such as Bundt pans, loaf pans, and specially shaped cornbread or muffin pans. Fortunately, you don't need a variety of pans to enjoy all the pleasures of cast-iron cooking.

One or two pans are really all you need to begin as a cast-iron cook, and you can't go wrong with a skillet and a lid. With a plain old 10-inch skillet, which is big enough for main-dish meals for most families, you can perform just about any cooking task your heart desires. If your family is a little larger (say six or more), a 10-inch skillet may not be big enough for main dishes, such as casseroles or roasted meats with vegetables. In that case, you may want to add a 12-inch skillet, a fryer (which is like a skillet but with deeper sides), or a Dutch oven to your collection. But go ahead and keep the 10-inch skillet for other dishes, such as cakes, breads, biscuits, and cobblers.

Identifying the cast of characters

You can find both new and used cast-iron cookware in a variety of shapes and sizes. The most popular pieces are skillets and Dutch ovens, but you can find all sorts of other basic pans and pots, too, as well as specialty items.

When you talk about cast iron, you have to talk about *versatility*. Although some items are designed with a special purpose in mind (the *camp oven,* for example, is designed for use outside), you can use cast-iron cookware in a variety of ways and for several different purposes. Use it indoors or out. Put it on the stove or in the stove. Bake a pie in a Dutch oven or roast a chicken in a fry pan. The following sections explain what these pans are *generally* used for. How *you* use them depends on your own cooking style and needs.

Skillets

Cast-iron skillets (shown in Figure 1-1) come in a variety of sizes, from very small (approximately 6 inches in diameter or less) to very large (more than 15 inches in diameter). With average depths between $1\frac{1}{4}$ inches and $2\frac{1}{2}$ inches (depending on the size of the pan), cast-iron skillets are great for a number of cooking tasks, on the stove or in the oven.

Figure 1-1:
Cast-iron skillets are good, all-purpose cooking utensils.

Photograph courtesy of Lodge Manufacturing Co.

Fry pans

Fry pans are similar to skillets except that the sides of fry pans are deeper (usually 3 inches or more) so that the grease doesn't splatter as much when you're frying (see Figure 1-2). You can perform many of the same cooking tasks in these pans that you can in skillets. However, because of the depth of the pan, you can also use fry pans for deep-frying, simmering stews and soups, and slow-cooking on the stovetop or in the oven.

Figure 1-2:
The deeper sides of a fry pan mean less splattering and less mess.

Photograph courtesy of Lodge Manufacturing Co.

Dutch ovens

Dutch ovens are deep-sided pots with lids that you can use on the stovetop or inside the oven. They're the original slow cookers. Put in the food, slap on a lid, set the oven to a low or medium temperature, and then come back a few hours later to a tender, delicious meal. But you can also use your versatile Dutch oven for more cooking activities, such as baking, deep-frying, pan-frying, and simmering. You name it — a Dutch oven can probably do it.

If you go looking for a Dutch oven, keep in mind that this piece of cast-iron cookware falls into two categories: Dutch ovens designed primarily for indoor cooking and Dutch ovens designed for outdoor cooking (see Figure 1-3). The differences between the two are as follows:

- ✔ **The lid:** An indoor Dutch oven has a domed lid. The lid of an outdoor Dutch oven is generally flatter and *flanged* (meaning it has a lip around the rim) so that you can put coals on the top.

- ✔ **The bottom:** Indoor Dutch ovens have flat bottoms; outdoor Dutch ovens have three short legs to keep the oven above the heat source.

✔ **What they're called:** Indoor Dutch ovens are typically called *Dutch ovens,* but some people call them *bean pots.* Outdoor Dutch ovens are called *camp ovens* or, less frequently, *cowboy ovens.* You, however, may call yours anything you want.

For more information about cooking in the great outdoors (including camp oven info) and some recipes to go with it, head to Book I, Chapter 5.

Figure 1-3:
A Dutch oven for indoor use (left) and a camp oven, designed for cooking outdoors (right).

Photograph courtesy of Lodge Manufacturing Co.

REMEMBER

Just because camp ovens are for outdoor use, don't assume your regular old Dutch oven can't be used for outdoor cooking. It can. The outdoor ovens just have a few little amenities built right in to make outdoor cooking that much easier.

Griddles and grill pans

Griddles can be round, square, or rectangular (long enough to fit across two burners on your stovetop), and they come in various sizes, as shown in Figure 1-4. The smooth surface and shallow sides (usually $1/2$ inch or less) are perfect for making pancakes and hot sandwiches; frying eggs, bacon, and anything else; roasting vegetables; and making foods of the hand-held variety, such as quesadillas, fajitas, and pizza.

Figure 1-4:
A sampling of griddles.

Photograph courtesy of Lodge Manufacturing Co.

Grill pans, shown in Figure 1-5, are exactly what they sound like: Pans that you use to grill food (vegetables, seafood, poultry, meat, and so on), either on the stovetop or over a campfire. The ribbed bottom keeps the food out of the drippings and leaves nice sear marks, much like you'd get from cooking on an outdoor grill.

Figure 1-5:
The ribbed bottom of a grill pan keeps your food up and out of any drippings.

Photograph courtesy of Lodge Manufacturing Co.

Because of the ribbed bottom, grill pans aren't suitable for anything other than grilling. If you don't believe it, try stirring a stew in one or getting corn-bread to pop out of one!

Evaluating quality

Whether new or used, cast-iron pans are made from iron and steel formed in sand casts (or molds) — hence the name *cast iron.* The process itself and the materials used give cast iron its texture. If you're used to shiny, smooth aluminum or stainless steel, you may not realize that new cast iron is supposed to feel rough and be a dull, gray color like, well, metal.

The quality of a cast-iron pan directly impacts how well the pan takes seasoning, how efficiently it heats, how long it lasts, and how safe it is to use. When you shop for cast iron, take a close look at the following:

- **Surface texture:** The cast iron should be uniformly rough (like a cat's tongue) and even. It shouldn't be jagged, pitted, chipped, cracked, or obviously scratched. When you run your hand along the interior, you shouldn't feel waves or dips.

- **Width of sides:** The thickness of the sides of the cast iron should be the same all the way around. Uneven width causes hot spots and makes the pan more prone to breaking.

✔ **Metallurgy:** The metals that go into a cast-iron pan must be mixed and heated appropriately. Unfortunately, you can't tell how sound the metallurgy is just by looking. Occasionally, however, you may notice something is obviously wrong, like discolorations or blotchiness in the metal. Avoid cast iron with these flaws, which can result in breaks, hot spots, or uneven heating.

✔ **Where it's made:** American manufacturers must meet government-mandated safety requirements regarding the product itself, the materials that go into it, and the manufacturing process. These safeguards protect both consumers and employees. Manufacturers in other countries may or may not have to abide by similar requirements.

Used cast iron — especially when it comes free from Grandma and includes a bunch of recipes to boot — is great. In fact, if you have a choice between a new cast-iron pan and an old one that's been well used and cared for, go for an old one. Still, as wonderful as an old pan is, you need to evaluate its quality as well. In addition to looking for the characteristics mentioned in the preceding list, pay attention to

✔ **How well it has been cared for:** Although you can refurbish many abused pieces of cast iron, some pieces aren't worth salvaging. Avoid those that are warped, cracked, pitted, or chipped. Although fine for hanging as a wall decoration, these pans are no longer suitable for cooking.

✔ **Whether the item has any paint spots on it:** Dishonest dealers often repair holes and cracks with *epoxy resin* (an adhesive that hobbyists use in abundance when they build model airplanes and cars) and then paint over the repair to hide it.

Epoxy resin is a great adhesive: strong, durable, long-lasting . . . but it's poisonous if swallowed. It can also damage skin on contact and irritate eyes, and must be used in a well-ventilated area.

Prepping Your Cast Iron for Use

Getting your cast iron in ready-to-use shape is essential because new cast iron is porous. It has a slightly rough texture and microscopic pores that you have to fill before you can use the pan. *Seasoning* (which is also called *curing*) is the process of filling these pores and smoothing the rough texture with oil, thus creating a smooth, nonstick surface and protecting your iron pan from rust. The next two sections show you how to season cast iron and keep your efforts from disappearing too quickly.

If you try to cook in cast iron that hasn't been seasoned, you're going to end up with a burned, sticky mess. The pores in your hot pan (which expand slightly when you cook) will absorb whatever you put in it.

Seasoning your cast iron

Seasoning a pan requires little more than an oven, a bit of vegetable oil or melted shortening, and a little time. With these supplies in hand, just follow these steps:

1. **Preheat your oven to 350 degrees.**

2. **While your oven's preheating, wash and dry the pan thoroughly.**

   New cast-iron pans come from the factory with a protective coating that you must remove before you can season them. Simply scrub the pan using the hottest water you can stand, a mild dish detergent or soap, and a stiff-bristled (not wire) brush or a scouring pad (not steel wool).

   This is the only time you'll ever use soap or a scouring pad on your cast iron — unless, that is, you're reseasoning it because of some disaster, culinary or otherwise. (Want to know why soap is a major no-no? Check out the "Rub-a-dub-dub, removing the grub" section later in this chapter.)

3. **Oil all surfaces of the cast iron.**

   Using about a tablespoon of melted shortening or vegetable oil and a paper towel or sponge, wipe the oil over the pan's entire surface — tops, bottoms, handles, legs, and so on. (If you're using shortening, don't dirty another pan just to melt it; instead, melt it in the cast iron you're seasoning.)

   Don't try seasoning your cast iron with lard, bacon grease, butter, or other animal products. If you don't use your cast iron regularly, these seasonings can turn rancid; then you're left with the job of cleaning the seasoning off yourself and reapplying it. Fun, fun, fun.

4. **Place the cookware upside down in the oven and bake for 1 hour.**

   You place the pan upside down so that any excess shortening or oil drips off instead of pooling inside the pan and carbonizing.

   Cover the area underneath your cast iron. Spread aluminum foil on the rack beneath the one your cast iron will be on, or place your cast iron on a baking sheet. Either method serves to catch any excess shortening or oil that may drip off.

   While the cast iron cooks, you may notice a slight smell and perhaps some smoke. That's normal, so don't rush to call the fire department. Just know that the more shortening or oil you use, the more pronounced the smoke and the smell.

5. **When the hour's up, turn the oven off and leave the cookware in there until the oven cools down.**

   Now you can pat yourself on the back for a job well done.

Didn't get the shiny black surface you were expecting? Don't worry. It comes as you use your pan. What you've just done in this process is the *initial* seasoning. Every time you cook with your cast iron, the cure deepens, and in a few months time, you'll have the deep black, satiny finish that you want.

To save time, season multiple pieces in one fell swoop. If your pan has a lid, season the lid when you season the pan. Your only limit is the amount of cast iron you can fit into your oven.

Protecting your seasoning

Now that your pan is seasoned, you can protect and deepen the seasoning and create the nonstick surface you're aiming for by following these suggestions:

- **Use your cast iron frequently.** Every time you cook with your cast iron, you're essentially reseasoning it, deepening its cure.

- **The first six or seven times you cook in your cast iron, use it to cook foods that have plenty of fat.** Fry hamburgers, fry chicken, make bacon, bake pies, and so on.

- **The first few times that you use the pan, avoid cooking acidic foods (such as tomato-based dishes) and alkaline foods (such as beans).** The acid and alkali react with the iron and mess up the seasoning.

- **After cleaning your cast iron, wipe a small amount of vegetable oil around the pan.** Doing so puts back any seasoning that was lost during cleaning. For cleaning instructions, head to the next section.

Occasionally, your seasoning may break down. If you don't use your pan for a long period of time, if you cook food with liquid (steaming vegetables or deglazing the pan with wine, for example), or if you cook acidic foods, such as tomatoes, in it, you may have to reseason your pan. How do you know that you need to reseason your cast iron? The signs are pretty easy to recognize.

- Rust forms.
- Food begins to stick to the pan.
- Your food tastes like metal — not exactly your intended culinary objective.

If you notice these signs, first get rid of any rust (by using a rust eraser) and whatever's burned on. Then follow the seasoning steps outlined in the preceding section.

Cleaning and Storing Cast Iron

It never fails — the joy of cooking inevitably meets up with the chore of caring for your cookware. Fortunately, cast iron is easy to clean and store. You just need to know what to use (and not use — hint: soap) and where to put it to keep moisture or humidity from wreaking havoc.

Rub-a-dub-dub, removing the grub

When you clean cast iron, your aim is two-fold: Clean off whatever remains of dinner and do so without destroying your pan's seasoning. Contrary to what you may expect, you can do that with nothing more than hot water and elbow grease.

Never ever wash cast iron in an electric dishwasher. Dishwasher detergent strips the seasoning you've lovingly applied, the rinse cycle throws water on the newly stripped pans, and then the pans are left to essentially drip dry during the dry cycle.

Here's how to clean your cast iron properly:

1. **Remove any stuck-on bits of food.**

   Scrape the sides and bottom with a spoon — the same task that you do to get the last bit out for leftovers. If your stuck-on bits are a bit more stuck on, try these suggestions:

   - Heat the pan to a temperature that's still safe to touch in order to open the pores and make it easier to clean.

   - Scrub the problem spots with table salt moistened with either oil or water.

   - Use really hot, almost boiling, water and scrub the spot with crumpled-up aluminum foil.

2. **Using hot water and a nonwire scrub brush, scrub the cooking surface.**

   Let the hot water flow over the pan as you scrub with a natural-bristled or stiff plastic brush. (You want the bristles to be about as stiff as the bristles on a medium or hard toothbrush.)

   Don't use soap to wash your cast iron. Soap effectively cuts through oil and grease, and if you consider that *that's* what your seasoning is — oil and grease baked into your pan through possibly years of cooking — you can understand why soap is forbidden. If not using soap makes you worry about what sort of germs may be lingering, pour boiling water into and over the pan after you're done brushing it.

3. **Immediately and thoroughly dry the cast iron with a towel.**

   Put the cast iron on a burner or in a heated oven for a few minutes to make sure that all the moisture is gone.

   Never *ever* let cast iron air-dry. And don't leave it sitting on top of anything or touching anything — like the towel you dried it with — that has moisture. Any remaining moisture — whether it's on your pan or on the item that your pan is sitting on — will cause your cast iron to rust.

4. **Coat the cast iron with a thin layer of vegetable oil while it's still warm and wipe it dry with a paper towel.**

   Doing so helps preserve the seasoning and replaces any that was removed during the cleaning process.

When you use your cast iron to cook bakery-type foods — such as breads, biscuits, and cakes — you don't really need to clean it at all. Simply turn the bread or cake out of the pan to cool, wipe the surface with a clean paper towel, and apply a light layer of vegetable oil. Your pan is then good to go for your next round of cooking.

Storing your cast iron

You have two options for storing your cast iron: stack it in a cabinet or hang it from a hook or pan rack. If you only use your cast iron on camping trips, leave it in the box that it came in. Wherever you plan to keep (or arrange) your cast iron, follow these suggestions:

- ✔ **Make sure that you store your cast iron in a cool, dry place.** Remember, moisture is the enemy.

- ✔ **Store your cast iron with the lid off or ajar.** Cast-iron lids fit fairly tightly, and if any moisture is in the pan, a closed lid won't let it escape, and you'll end up with a rusty pan. If you want to leave the lid on, place a folded-up paper towel between the lid and the pan and place a crumpled-up paper towel inside the pan to absorb any moisture.

- ✔ **If you hang your cast iron from the wall, be sure that the hook or nail is anchored in a stud and can bear the weight of your pan(s).** The same goes if you're hanging your cast iron from the ceiling. And never hang it — even purely decorative cast iron — over a doorway unless you're really, *really* sure it won't fall.

Hitting the road with your cast iron

Many people never take their cast iron anywhere other than potluck dinners, family reunions, or Thanksgiving get-togethers. They then have a tendency to transport it on their lap, between their feet, or safely surrounded by towels in the trunk of their car. Not to protect the cast iron, mind you, but to protect whatever delectable dish is inside it. Many other people, those who take their kitchens outdoors, consider their cast iron a transportable tool, something that they pack with the rest of their gear.

If you belong to the latter group and plan to take your cast iron with you when you head out for

an adventure in the great outdoors, the trick is to keep the pan from bouncing and banging around too much. Put it in the box it came in, wrap it in a towel or burlap sack, or wedge it securely against your mountain-climbing gear or other paraphernalia. If you're feeling particularly protective, you can always cradle the cast iron in your lap — but you don't need to. If cast iron could survive being carted thousands of miles west in covered wagons, it can probably survive your trip into the next county for a cook-off.

Getting Familiar with Cast-Iron Cooking Techniques

Making good food in a cast-iron skillet or pot isn't rocket science. All you need is a well-seasoned pan (explained in the earlier section "Seasoning your cast iron") and a few simple cooking techniques. The following sections describe everything you need to know. Of course, having a few recipes doesn't hurt either. You can find those later in this chapter.

Out of the frying pan and into the fire: Heat and temperature control

Cast iron is a great heat conductor because it absorbs heat quickly and distributes it evenly. Still, if you're not used to cooking with cast iron, the heating properties that make it such good cookware may be exactly what trip you up. The next couple sections give tips on overcoming some of the issues you may face as a new cast-iron user.

When you cook outdoors over an open fire or hot coals, the rules for controlling your cooking temperatures are quite different than those for indoor cooking. For outdoor cooking, you basically control your temperatures by the placement and number of coals. More coals closer to the pan mean higher temperatures; fewer coals farther from the pan mean lower temperatures. Still, getting and maintaining the right temperature when you cook outside is a little more complicated than simply counting coals. You also have to adjust for the weather: air temperature, humidity level, wind speed, and so on. Book I, Chapter 5 explains all about outdoor cast-iron cooking and includes several easy and delicious recipes for the outdoor cook.

Getting the temperature and cooking time right

Cast iron absorbs and retains heat so well that your temperature setting may need to be lower than what's specified in recipes not geared toward cast-iron cookware. Simply set the temperature as the recipe indicates and then adjust it downward as needed. If you notice, for example, that your stew's soft simmer is actually more of a preboil, simply turn the heat setting down until you get the result you want. Eventually, you'll know what setting to use to get the appropriate cooking temperature.

As far as cooking times go, the actual cooking times on many recipes may be slightly less when you cook in cast iron. (***Note:*** The recipes in this chapter are based on cast-iron cooking, so you don't need to worry about this issue here.)

Warming up to the advantages of preheating

Cast iron works best when the heat source is the same size as the bottom of the pan, but burners on modern electric and gas ranges are usually smaller than that. To eliminate this problem, simply preheat the pan when you're going to cook on top of the stove. You can preheat your cast iron on the stovetop or in the oven. If you choose to preheat

- ✔ **On the stovetop:** Set your burner on low and let the cast iron warm up slowly. After the entire pan is warm, turn the heat up to the temperature you want.

- ✔ **In the oven:** Set your cast iron in a warm oven set to low (225–250 degrees). When the pot or pan is heated, take it out of the oven, put it on the stovetop, and turn the burner to the appropriate temperature.

Unless the recipe indicates otherwise, you don't need to preheat your cast iron when roasting in the oven, because the oven heats the cast iron evenly. If you do need to preheat the cast iron, simply put the cool iron in the cool oven and let it warm up as your oven does.

Many cast-iron recipes include preheating instructions. Recipes that aren't specific to cast iron may or may not include such instructions. If you're using a recipe that doesn't include preheating instructions for your cookware, use this rule as your guide: You almost always preheat your cast iron when you're making foods — like cornbreads, pancakes, muffins, quick breads, and any seared dishes — that you want to be crispy or browned on the outside and tender or moist on the inside.

Ending the exile of your metal utensils

Although cast iron does require some care, it isn't particularly persnickety about the type of utensils you use. You can use wooden utensils, plastic utensils, or (believe it or not) the frequently banned pariah of a Teflon-coated kitchen — metal utensils! That's right: Dust off your wire whisk and polish up that metal spoon. They're back in business, baby.

In fact, if you find yourself facing a chunk of food that seems to have permanently attached itself to your cast-iron cookware, you can even scrape it with a putty knife (preferably a clean one, of course). If you're so inclined — or so desperate — just remember that you may need to reseason the spot you scratched at.

Other tips for successful cast-iron cooking

Seasoning and temperature control, more than anything else, can determine whether you become a fan or a foe of cast iron. To nudge you farther over to the fan side, read on for some other cooking tips to keep in mind.

- **Never put a cold pan on a hot burner, pour cold liquid into a hot pan, and so forth.** If you do, you run the risk of shocking your cast iron to the breaking point — literally. Let your pan heat up as the burner heats up, and if you have to add water to a hot pan, make sure that the water is warm or hot. (The same rule applies when you clean cast iron, as explained in the earlier section "Rub-a-dub-dub, removing the grub.")

  All metal cookware is susceptible to *thermal shock,* a drastic and quick change in temperature. Cast iron, being the most brittle of all metal cookware, is more likely to break; aluminum cookware is more likely to warp. Whether the result of thermal shock is a broken or warped pan, the outcome is the same — a pan that's no good for cooking anymore.

- **Don't store food in cast iron.** The acid in the food breaks down the seasoning, and the food takes on a metallic taste. When you're done serving the food, transfer what's left to another container.

- **Although you shouldn't use your cast iron to store your food, you can use it to serve food.** Follow these suggestions:

  - Keep the food simmering until you're ready to eat.

  - Be sure to put a hot pad or trivet under the pan. Cast iron stays hot for a long time, and it can burn or mar your tabletop.

  - To keep food warm for second helpings, cover the pan while you eat.

- **Move your cast iron off an electric burner after you turn the burner off if you want the dish to stop cooking.** Unlike a gas flame, which goes out as soon as you turn the burner off, an electric burner takes a while to cool off. Because cast iron retains heat in proportion to that emitted by the heat source, a dish left on a cooling burner continues to cook. This fact may not present a problem when you're fixing a stew (where a little extra simmer time isn't an issue), but it can be a problem when you're thickening a sauce and don't want it to caramelize.

✓ **Before you cook with cast-iron cake pans, cornstick pans, muffin pans, and other bakeware, oil them or spray them with nonstick cooking spray.** Even the fat-free kind can do the trick. Although these pans should be nonstick if they're properly seasoned, why take a chance if you're going for presentation in addition to taste?

Cooking Up Cast-Iron Classics

The Pilgrims brought cast iron from the Old World to the New, and the pioneers took it westward. Heavy, dark, and rustic, cast iron has a nostalgic appeal that modern-day cookware lacks. It's the cookware of choice for countless outdoor enthusiasts, and no cattle drive would be complete — even today — without a cook, a cast-iron pot, and a campfire.

Although you can cook just about any highbrow dish in cast iron, down-home favorites and comfort foods are what cast iron built its reputation on. These are also the foods that many modern cast-iron cooks still like to prepare in their black iron pans. The following sections contain several of the old standards — the foods that your ancestors may have once been inclined to make but that you and your family can enjoy just as much today.

Main dishes and sides

Of all the many entrees and sides you can create in cast-iron cookware, this section highlights those that, for whatever reason, just aren't the same prepared in anything other than cast iron. Each specific recipe indicates what type of cast-iron cookware it calls for.

Southern Fried Chicken

This recipe is simple, delicious, and easy to prepare. Just be sure to make enough for dinner and still have a few pieces leftover.

Preparation time: 30 minutes

Cooking time: About 35 minutes

Yield: 4 servings (2 pieces each)

3 pounds chicken pieces

11/2 cups buttermilk or milk

Salt and pepper

Paprika

About 1 cup all-purpose flour for dredging

Peanut oil or shortening to fill skillet 1-inch deep

1 Wash the chicken pieces and pat dry.

2 Dip the chicken pieces in milk and then lay them on wax paper. Sprinkle both sides of the pieces with salt, pepper, and paprika and then dredge them in the flour. Let the chicken stand for 20 minutes and dredge in flour again.

3 While the chicken is resting, heat the oil or shortening in a deep cast-iron skillet or a Dutch oven on medium-high heat to 375 degrees. (The oil will be hot but not smoking.) Use an instant-read thermometer to test the temperature now and throughout cooking.

4 Add 4 to 5 pieces of chicken to the skillet, browning both sides. Be careful not to add so much chicken at one time that the oil temperature drops significantly. Turn and move the chicken as necessary to ensure even browning. (Use tongs so that you don't pierce the meat.)

5 Move the chicken to a platter to allow room for the next 4 to 5 pieces. Add the next 4 to 5 pieces of chicken and cook until all are brown.

6 When the second batch of chicken is about brown, return all chicken to the skillet, reduce the heat to low or medium-low, and cover. At this point, it may be necessary to stack the chicken in the skillet. Cook slowly and gently for about 20 minutes, or until fork tender. Check several times and turn or move the pieces as necessary to keep all the chicken browned evenly.

7 Remove the cover and return the heat to medium-high to recrisp the chicken, about 5 minutes after the skillet is hot again. While recrisping, watch the chicken carefully and turn the pieces so that all sides are crisp, taking care not to burn the bottom pieces of chicken.

8 Drain and move to a serving platter, or place on a rack in the oven to keep warm.

Per serving: Calories 664 (From Fat 332); Fat 37g (Saturated 9g); Cholesterol 182mg; Sodium 1,392mg; Carbohydrate 29g (Dietary Fiber 1g); Protein 51g.

Country Captain

This recipe came from the late Mrs. W. L. Bullard of Columbus, Georgia. She once served it to a distinguished guest, Franklin Roosevelt, and it soon became a specialty of the house.

Preparation time: *15 minutes*

Cooking time: *10 to 12 minutes per piece of chicken; 45 minutes in oven*

Yield: *8 to 10 servings*

4 pounds of your favorite chicken pieces, skinned

Salt and pepper

2 cups all-purpose flour

Shortening or peanut oil to fill skillet 1-inch deep

2 medium onions, finely chopped

1 clove garlic, minced

1 bell pepper, seeded and finely chopped

2 teaspoons curry powder

1½ teaspoons salt

½ teaspoon pepper

1 can (28 ounces) whole tomatoes with liquid

1 can (14 ounces) diced tomatoes with liquid

2 tablespoons chopped fresh parsley

½ teaspoon dried thyme

8 cups hot cooked rice

¼ cup currants

½ pound sliced almonds, toasted

1 Preheat your oven to 350 degrees. Wash the chicken and pat dry. Lay the pieces on wax paper; salt and pepper both sides of the chicken. Dredge the pieces in flour until all sides are well coated with flour.

2 Meanwhile, heat 1 inch of shortening or peanut oil in a 12-inch cast-iron skillet over medium-high heat.

3 Fry the chicken pieces a few at a time in the skillet, turning over until golden brown on both sides. You may need to reduce the heat as the chicken cooks, but also raise it when adding uncooked chicken pieces. As the chicken pieces are cooked (about 10 to 12 minutes per piece), remove them to a 5-quart cast-iron Dutch oven.

4 Drain most of the oil from the skillet, leaving 2 tablespoons behind. Add the onions, garlic, and bell pepper to the skillet. Cook until tender. Add the curry powder, salt, pepper, tomatoes, 1 tablespoon parsley, and thyme, and bring to a boil. Pour the mixture over the chicken in the Dutch oven. Bake in the oven for about 45 minutes.

5 Place the chicken pieces around the rim of a large serving platter and mound rice in the center. Stir the currants and half of the almonds into the sauce and immediately pour the sauce over the rice. Garnish with remaining almonds and parsley.

Per serving: Calories 592 (From Fat 224); Fat 25g (Saturated 4g); Cholesterol 60mg; Sodium 651mg; Carbohydrate 63g (Dietary Fiber 7g); Protein 31g.

Pan-Fried Catfish

Once considered a "junk" fish, catfish has gained popularity recently. You can now find it served in many restaurants. When you prepare your catfish fillets, remove any skin and the dark fatty tissue that's directly underneath it. This tissue has a strong fishy taste.

Preparation time: *25 minutes*

Cooking time: *5 minutes*

Yield: *4 servings*

4 catfish fillets (about 1½ pounds)	*Cajun seasoning*
1 cup buttermilk, or enough to cover the fillets	*1 cup cornmeal*
Salt and pepper	*Canola oil to fill skillet ¼-inch deep*

1 In a flat dish, soak the fish fillets in the buttermilk for about 20 minutes.

2 Lay the fish on wax paper. Discard the buttermilk. Season both sides of the fish with the salt, pepper, and Cajun seasoning. Dredge in the cornmeal.

3 Heat the oil in a 12-inch cast-iron skillet over slightly higher than medium-heat. Place fillets in the skillet and brown on both sides, about 2 minutes on each side, turning carefully with a spatula.

4 After the fish browns, reduce the heat to medium or lower to finish cooking if your fillets are thick. Serve with tartar sauce.

Per serving: Calories 427 (From Fat 196); Fat 22g (Saturated 4g); Cholesterol 78mg; Sodium 348mg; Carbohydrate 30g (Dietary Fiber 3g); Protein 31g.

Tartar sauce

I suggest serving tartar sauce in this chapter. You can easily whip up a batch with this recipe. Mix all of the following ingredients together and refrigerate until you're ready to serve:

- 1 cup mayonnaise
- 1½ tablespoon finely chopped cornichons, plus 1 teaspoon cornichon juice
- 1 tablespoon finely chopped green onions — only the green part
- 1 tablespoon Dijon mustard
- ½ to 1 teaspoon minced garlic

Note: *Cornichons* are tart pickles made from tiny little gherkin cucumbers. If you can't find cornichons, you can substitute the same amount of any other pickle you like.

Fried Frog Legs

You can find fresh frog legs in the fish section in gourmet food markets, where they're usually sold in connected pairs. Look for legs that are plump and slightly pink. Fresh frog legs are available from spring through summer; you can buy frozen frog legs year-round. To store fresh frog legs, wrap them loosely and place them in the refrigerator for up to two days. You can also freeze frog legs so long as you thaw them in the refrigerator overnight before trying to cook them. Either way, be sure not to overcook your frog legs — doing so makes them tough.

Preparation time: *2 hours*

Cooking time: *5 minutes*

Yield: *3 servings*

12 small frog legs	*¹/₂ to 1 teaspoon Cajun seasoning*
1 egg	*Vegetable oil for deep-frying*
1 cup buttermilk	*¹/₂ cup self-rising flour*
1 teaspoon salt	*¹/₂ cup self-rising cornmeal mix*
1 teaspoon pepper	

1 Rinse the frog legs and pat dry.

2 In a large bowl, beat the egg, buttermilk, salt, pepper, and Cajun seasoning together. Add the frog legs and soak for up to 2 hours.

3 Heat 5 inches of the oil in a Dutch oven (or cast-iron deep fryer, if you have one) to 375 degrees.

4 In a medium bowl, combine flour and cornmeal. Dredge the frog legs in the flour mixture. Drop into the hot oil without crowding. Fry until golden brown, 4 to 5 minutes. Serve with tartar sauce.

Per serving: *Calories 552 (From Fat 161); Fat 18g (Saturated 2g); Cholesterol 219mg; Sodium 1,652mg; Carbohydrate 38g (Dietary Fiber 2g); Protein 57g.*

◔ Skillet-Fried Potatoes

The secrets to perfect fried potatoes are a heavy skillet (cast iron is perfect), even heat, and self-control. You have to let the potatoes cook long enough to brown and become crispy before you turn them. Also, use a spatula rather than a spoon to turn the potatoes so the slices retain their shape and don't get all mushed together.

Preparation time: *15 minutes*

Cooking time: *30 to 35 minutes*

Yield: *4 to 6 servings*

*6 small Yukon gold potatoes, or 3 russets
(about 2 pounds)*

1 medium onion

2 tablespoons vegetable shortening

2 tablespoons butter

Salt and pepper

1 Wash, peel, and slice the potatoes. Chop the onion.

2 Heat the shortening in a 10-inch cast-iron skillet until a drop of water skips and sizzles in the pan.

3 Arrange $^1/_3$ of the potatoes in a layer in the bottom of the pan, sprinkle $^1/_3$ of the onion over the potatoes, and then sprinkle with the salt and pepper. Dot with $^1/_3$ of the butter. Repeat this step two more times, forming three potato layers.

4 Cover and cook for 20 minutes over medium heat. Don't lift the lid and don't turn the potatoes.

5 Remove the lid and continue to cook, turning the potatoes once or twice, until crispy and done, about 10 to 15 minutes.

Vary It! *For a complete meal, include smoked sausage or cubed ham in the layers and reduce the amount of salt that you use.*

Per serving: *Calories 204 (From Fat 73); Fat 8g (Saturated 3g); Cholesterol 10mg; Sodium 106mg; Carbohydrate 30g (Dietary Fiber 3g); Protein 3g.*

Cornbread and biscuits

Cornbread and biscuits are easy to make. They don't require you to assemble a long list of ingredients, spend much time preparing them, or master hard-to-learn cooking methods. In fact, from start to finish, you can get a version of either to the table in less than 30 minutes.

Generally, southern folks prefer unsweetened cornbread with a crisp crust. They like white cornmeal. Northerners prefer sweeter cornbread with a more cakelike consistency. They go with yellow cornmeal. Whatever kind of corn-meal you use, always preheat your skillet or pan with shortening in it. The hot skillet and melted shortening give your cornbread a crispier, tastier crust.

☞ Real Southern Cornbread

Real southern cornbread isn't sweet. In fact, it uses little or no sugar. The tang in the buttermilk and the bacon grease give this cornbread its flavor.

Preparation time: *10 minutes*

Cooking time: *30 to 40 minutes*

Yield: *8 slices*

3 tablespoons bacon grease or vegetable oil

2 cups white self-rising cornmeal mix

½ teaspoon baking soda

2 eggs, beaten

2 cups buttermilk

1 Preheat your oven to 450 degrees.

2 Put the bacon grease into a 9-inch cast-iron skillet and place it in the oven to get really hot.

3 Blend the cornmeal mix, baking soda, eggs, and buttermilk in a bowl, using a spoon or fork.

4 When the skillet and bacon grease are really hot, carefully remove the skillet from the oven and pour the hot bacon grease into the batter. Quickly stir the bacon grease into the batter.

5 Pour the batter into the hot skillet. It should sizzle and may splatter. Bake for 30 to 40 minutes, or until golden brown.

6 Remove from the oven and let cool 5 to 10 minutes. Invert onto a plate, revealing a crispy brown crust. Cut into wedges and serve hot (with plenty of butter).

Per serving: *Calories 204 (From Fat 58); Fat 6g (Saturated 2g); Cholesterol 60mg; Sodium 692mg; Carbohydrate 29g (Dietary Fiber 2g); Protein 7g.*

Yankee Cornbread

This recipe is for folks who like their cornbread yellow and sweet. You can influence how sweet your cornbread is by experimenting with the amount of sugar you add. If this recipe is just a touch too sweet, add less sugar — 2 tablespoons rather than ¼ cup, for example.

Preparation time: *10 minutes*

Cooking time: *20 to 25 minutes*

Yield: *8 slices*

2½ cups yellow self-rising cornmeal mix

¼ cup sugar

1 cup milk

¼ cup vegetable oil

2 eggs, slightly beaten

1 Preheat your oven to 425 degrees. Grease a 10-inch cast-iron skillet.

2 In a large bowl, combine the cornmeal mix, sugar, milk, oil, and eggs and blend well with a spoon; pour into skillet.

3 Bake for 20 to 25 minutes, or until a toothpick inserted in the center comes out clean.

Vary It! *For corn muffins, grease muffin cups, fill with batter about ²/₃ full, and bake for 15 to 20 minutes.*

Per serving: *Calories 290 (From Fat 94); Fat 10g (Saturated 2g); Cholesterol 57mg; Sodium 491mg; Carbohydrate 43g (Dietary Fiber 2g); Protein 6g.*

◌ Hoecakes (Johnnycakes)

The precursor to pancakes, *hoecakes*, which are sometimes called *Johnnycakes*, go back to colonial times. These tasty cakes resemble thin-ish cornmeal pancakes. Not as common as they once were, hoecakes are still a hit with outdoor enthusiasts because they don't require an oven. Indoors, you can serve them as bread for dinner just like you would cornbread. And you can serve them for breakfast with honey or jam in place of pancakes, toast, or biscuits.

Preparation time: *5 minutes*

Cooking time: *3 minutes*

Yield: *24 cakes*

1 cup white cornmeal	*1 teaspoon salt*
½ cup all-purpose flour	*1 tablespoon sugar*
1¼ teaspoons baking powder	*About 1⅓ cups buttermilk*
¼ teaspoon baking soda	

1 Heat your cast-iron griddle to medium-high heat on your stovetop.

2 In a medium bowl, combine cornmeal, flour, baking powder, baking soda, salt, and sugar. Add buttermilk to the desired consistency — think of a thin, cornmeal pancake batter.

3 Grease a hot griddle with solid vegetable shortening. Test the griddle for correct temperature by splashing a few drops of water onto the surface. If the water dances in beads, the griddle is hot enough.

4 Pour ¼ cup of the batter onto the hot griddle. Turn when the surface is full of bubbles. Fry until the second side is golden brown as well. Keep griddle well greased and hot with each batch. Serve hot with butter.

Per serving: Calories 43 (From Fat 7); Fat 1g (Saturated 0g); Cholesterol 1mg; Sodium 144mg; Carbohydrate 8g (Dietary Fiber 1g); Protein 1g.

☉ *Buttermilk Biscuits*

Buttermilk is a key ingredient in many biscuit recipes. It adds flavor and makes a lighter, airier biscuit than regular milk does.

Preparation time: *10 minutes*

Cooking time: *12 minutes*

Yield: *12 to 14 biscuits*

2 cups all-purpose flour	*2 teaspoons baking powder*
¹/₂ teaspoon salt	*4 tablespoons vegetable shortening*
¹/₂ teaspoon baking soda	*1 cup buttermilk*

1 Preheat oven to 450 degrees.

2 In a large bowl, sift together the flour, salt, baking soda, and baking powder. Work in the shortening with a pastry blender or your fingers, until the mixture resembles coarse meal. Slowly stir in the buttermilk until the dough pulls away from the bowl.

3 Turn the dough onto a lightly floured surface, knead for about 30 seconds, and roll to ¹/₂-inch thickness. Cut with a floured biscuit cutter and place on a cast-iron griddle or skillet coated with cooking spray.

4 Bake for about 12 minutes until golden brown on top.

Per serving: *Calories 104 (From Fat 36); Fat 4g (Saturated 1g); Cholesterol 1mg; Sodium 201mg; Carbohydrate 15g (Dietary Fiber 1g); Protein 2g.*

Chapter 2

Canning and Preserving

- -

In This Chapter

▶ Knowing the proper processing procedures for both water- and pressure-canning

▶ Looking at recipes for canning common fruits and vegetables

▶ Taking food safety into consideration

- -

*O*ver the years, because of our busy lifestyles and the convenience of refrigeration and supermarkets, the art of canning and preserving has declined and almost been forgotten. But today, many people have a renewed interest in taking up these arts. Producing canned and preserved food in your kitchen is fun and easy. This chapter gives you an overview of water-bath canning and pressure canning, as well as easy step-by-step instructions for each technique. If you're new to canning and preserving, don't be over-whelmed or scared off by the rules. After you understand the basic proce-dures for a method, like water-bath canning, you can focus your attention on preparing your recipe.

Before You Begin

Home-canning is a safe and economical way to preserve large or small quanti-ties of high-quality food. Taking the time to select your recipe, choosing and preparing your food, and packaging and processing it for safety are fulfilling and a source of pride for you, the home-canner. Before you begin, though, you need to know a few things about how to make your canning experience successful and safe.

Knowing the acidity levels in foods

Knowing the acidity level of the food you're processing is important because the *pH factor,* the measure of acidity, determines which method you'll use: water-bath or pressure canning. For canning purposes, food is divided into two categories based on the amount of acid the food registers.

✔ **High-acid foods:** These are naturally high in acid, with a pH factor of 4.6 or lower. These foods include fruits, tomatoes, and pickled vegetables, which are actually low-acid foods that have had an acid added to them, converting them to high-acid foods and making them safe for water-bath canning. Processing these foods in a water-bath canner destroys harmful microorganisms.

You can change the acid level in low-acid foods by adding an acid, such as vinegar, lemon juice, or *citric acid* — a white powder extracted from the juice of acidic fruits such as lemons, limes, or pineapples. Some examples of altered low-acid foods are pickles made from cucumbers, relish made from zucchini or summer squash, and green beans flavored with dill.

✔ **Low-acid foods:** Foods in this group contain little natural acid. Their pH level is higher than 4.6. Process these foods in a pressure canner, which superheats your food and destroys the more heat-resistant bacteria, such as botulism.

Water-bath canning and pressure-canning methods aren't interchangeable because the temperature of a water bath only reaches 212 degrees, whereas the temperature of a pressure canner reaches 240 degrees. So always use the canning method called for in a given recipe.

If your recipe doesn't tell you which processing method (water-bath canning or pressure canning) is appropriate for your food, don't guess. Instead, use litmus paper to test the pH level of your food: Simply insert a strip of litmus paper into your prepared food and compare the color to the pH chart of colors that accompanies the litmus paper. If your food has a pH of 4.6 or lower, use the water-bath canning method; if it has a pH of 4.7 or higher, use the pressure-canning method. You can buy litmus paper at teacher- or scientific-supply stores.

Eyeing the all-important headspace

Headspace is the air space between the inside of the lid and the top of the food or liquid in your jar or container (see Figure 2-1). Because proper headspace is important to the safety of your preserved food, always use the headspace stated in your recipe. If your recipe doesn't give you a headspace allowance, use these guidelines:

✔ For high-acid foods (fruits and tomatoes), leave a headspace of ¹/₂ inch.

✔ For low-acid foods (such as vegetables), leave a headspace of 1 inch.

Too little headspace in your canning jars restricts your food from expanding as it boils and can result in some of the food being forced out of the jar and under the lid, leaving particles of food between the seal and the jar rim. If this scenario occurs, your jar won't produce a vacuum seal. Leaving too much headspace may cause discoloration in the top portion of your food. It can also keep your jar from producing a vacuum seal if the processing time isn't long enough to exhaust the excess air in the jar.

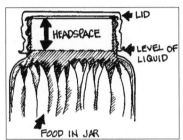

Figure 2-1:
Headspace
in a canning
jar.

Canning Fruits via the Water-Bath Method

Water-bath canning, sometimes referred to as the *boiling-water method,* is the simplest and easiest method for preserving high-acid foods, primarily fruit, tomatoes, and pickled vegetables. Water-bath canning destroys any active bacteria and microorganisms in your food, making it safe for consumption at a later time. It's accomplished by using boiling water to raise the temperature of the food in the jars and creating a vacuum seal.

Your water-bath canning equipment list

The equipment for water-bath canning is fairly inexpensive. Water-bath canning kettles cost anywhere from $25 to $45. In some instances, you may purchase a starter kit that includes the canning kettle, the jar rack, a jar lifter, a wide-mouth funnel, and jars for about $50 to $60. The following sections outline the basic water-bath canning supplies.

A water-bath canner
The water-bath canner consists of a large kettle, usually made of porcelain-coated steel or aluminum. It holds a maximum of 21 to 22 quarts of water, has a fitted lid, and uses a rack to hold the jars (see Figure 2-2).

WATER-BATH CANNING KETTLE

RACK

LID

BASE

Figure 2-2:
A water-bath canning kettle with the rack hanging on the edge of the kettle.

The jar rack

The jar rack for a water-bath canner is usually made of stainless steel and rests on the bottom of your canning kettle. It keeps your jars from touching the bottom of the kettle or each other, while holding the filled jars upright during the water-bath processing period. The rack has lifting handles for hanging it on the inside edge of your canning kettle (refer to Figure 2-2), allowing you to safely transfer your filled jars into and out of your kettle.

Home-canning jars

To ensure safe home-canning, use only jars approved for home-canning and made from tempered glass. *Tempering* is a treatment process for glass that allows the jars to withstand the high heat (212 degrees) of a water-bath canner, as well as the high temperature (240 degrees) of a pressure canner, without breaking.

Home-canning jars come in many sizes — 4-ounce, half-pint, 12-ounce, 1-pint, and 1-quart — and with two different width openings: regular-mouth (about $2^1/_2$ inches in diameter) and wide-mouth (about $3^1/_8$ inches in diameter). Use the jar size recommended in your recipe.

Two-piece caps

Two-piece caps consist of a lid and a metal screw band and are made specifically for use with modern-day home-canning jars. These lids and screw bands create a vacuum seal after the water-bath processing period, preserving the contents of the jar for use at a later time and protecting your food from the reentry of microorganisms.

Jar lifter

This odd-looking, rubberized tonglike item (shown in Figure 2-3), grabs the jar around the *neck* (the area just below the threaded portion at the top of the jar) without disturbing the screw band. This is one tool you don't want to be without.

JAR LIFTERS

Figure 2-3:
Jar lifters.

Foam skimmer

A foam skimmer is a slightly curved, not-quite-flat, large disk with small holes in it attached to a long handle. Its angle makes foam removal from the top of hot jelly, jam, or marmalade easy, while leaving any pieces of fruit or rind in the hot liquid.

Lid wand

A lid wand has a magnet on one end of a heat-resistant stick, enabling you to take a lid from the hot water and place it on the filled-jar rim without touching the lid or disturbing the sealing compound.

Wide-mouth canning funnel

A canning funnel is just like a regular funnel except that the wide mouth fits into the inside edge of a regular- or wide-mouth canning jar. Use this tool for quickly and neatly filling your jars.

Preparing your fruit, glorious fruit

When selecting your fruit, think fresh, fresh, fresh! The best fruit for this canning method is freshly picked, ripe fruit. If you grow your own fruit or have a friend who shares hers with you, great! If not, consider going to a "pick your own" farm. If these aren't options for you, buy your fruit at a farmers' market or at a grocery store that sells quality produce.

The sooner you process your fresh fruit, the better the texture and flavor of your final product. Your fruit can wait a few hours or overnight before you process it, but be sure to refrigerate it until you're ready.

Determining ripeness

To determine the ripeness of fruit, hold it in the palm of your hand and apply gentle pressure with your thumb and fingers. The fruit should be firm to the touch. If there's an impression in the fruit that doesn't bounce back, it's over-ripe and shouldn't be canned. If the fruit is as hard as a rock, leave it. Then smell it. Ripe fruit has a rich, full fruit aroma. A peach should smell like a peach; an apple should smell like an apple. The fragrance should be strong enough to entice you to devour the fruit on the spot.

If you're picking your fruit, always use fruit picked directly from the bush or tree. Fruit collected from the ground (referred to as *dropped fruit* or *ground fruit*) is over-ripe. Don't use it.

Skin on or skin off?

Sometimes leaving the skin on your fruit is optional. Other times, the peel must be removed. Always follow your recipe for specific guidelines.

Whole or sliced?

The fruit you select dictates using it whole or cutting it into pieces. For example, fitting whole apples into a canning jar is difficult, but peeled apples cut into slices easily pack into a jar. Leave small fruit, like berries, whole.

Avoiding discoloration

There's probably nothing less attractive than a piece of perfectly ripe, cut fruit that's *oxidized* or *discolored*, turned dark or brown. Protect your fruit from oxidation by slicing it directly into one of the following *antioxidant solutions*, a liquid to keep your fruit from darkening. Rinse and drain your fruit before packing it into your prepared jars.

✔ **An ascorbic or citric acid solution:** Make a solution with 1 teaspoon of lemon or lime juice in 1 cup of cold water, or use a commercial product, like Ever-Fresh or Fruit-Fresh, available in most supermarkets. When using one of these products, follow the instructions on the container.

✔ **Vinegar, salt, and water:** Make this solution with 2 tablespoons of vinegar (5 percent acidity), 2 tablespoons of salt (pickling or kosher), and 1 gallon of cold water. Don't leave your fruit in this solution longer than 20 minutes, because the solution extracts nutrients from your fruit and changes its flavor.

Packing: Hot versus raw

With a few exceptions, most fresh fruits may be packed raw or hot. Always start with clean, ripe fruit, and follow your recipe's instructions.

✔ **Raw pack:** A raw pack is the preferred method for fruits that become delicate after cooking, such as peaches and nectarines. This method is what it says: packing raw fruit into hot jars.

✔ **Hot pack:** Hot packing heats your fruit in a hot liquid before packing it into your prepared jars.

Lining your jars with liquid

You always add liquid when canning fresh fruit. Your options are boiling water, sugar syrup, or fruit juice.

✔ **Sugar syrup:** Sugar syrup, which comes in five concentrations (see Table 2-1), is simply a mixture of sugar and water. It adds flavor to your canned fruit, preserves its color, and produces a smooth, firm texture. Other sweeteners, such as honey, may be added in addition to or in place of the sugar. To make sugar syrup, bring your syrup ingredients to a boil in a saucepan over high heat; stir to dissolve the sugar.

✔ **Water or fruit juice:** Packing fresh fruit in boiling water or fruit juice produces fruit with a soft texture. Two good choices for fruit juices are unsweetened pineapple juice or white grape juice. Use water you like to drink, without minerals (don't use the sparkling variety). Always use the hot-pack method (see the preceding section for more on this method) when using water or unsweetened fruit juice for your canning liquid.

Determining which liquid to use is up to you, but consider the final use for your canned fruit. For instance, if you're using your canned berries in a fruit cobbler, boiling water may be the better choice because you'll add sugar to the cobbler. If you'll be eating your canned fruit out of the jar, use a sugar syrup or fruit juice.

Table 2-1	Sugar Syrup Concentrations			
Syrup Strength	*Description*	*Granulated Sugar*	*Water*	*Approximate Yield*
Super-light	Sweetness level closest to the natural sugar level in most fruits	1/4 cup	5 3/4 cups	6 cups
Extra-light	Good for sweet fruit, such as figs	1 1/4 cups	5 1/2 cups	6 cups
Light	Best with sweet apples and berries	2 1/4 cups	5 1/4 cups	6 1/2 cups
Medium	Best for tart apples, apricots, nectarines, peaches, and pears	3 1/4 cups	5 cups	7 cups
Heavy	Best for sour fruit, such as grapefruit	4 1/4 cups	4 1/4 cups	7 cups

Always prepare your hot liquid before you prepare your fruit. The liquid should be waiting for you; you shouldn't be waiting for your liquid to boil.

Canning fruit, step by step

Every aspect of the canning procedure is important, so don't skip anything, no matter how trivial it seems. When your food and canning techniques are in perfect harmony and balance, you'll have a safely processed product for use at a later time. This section guides you through the step-by-step process for creating delicious, high-quality, homemade treats for your family and friends. See the next section for recipes for different fruits.

1. **Check and wash all of your equipment and utensils in warm, soapy water, rinsing well to remove any soap residue.**

   Check the jar edges for any nicks, chips, or cracks in the glass, discarding any jars with these defects. If you're reusing jars, clean any stains or food residue from them.

Make sure your screw bands aren't warped, corroded, rusted, or *out of round* (bent or not completely round). Discard any bands that are defective.

Examine new lids (lids aren't reusable) for imperfections, scratches, and dents and check the sealant on the underside of each lid for evenness. Discard lids with imperfections (defective lids don't produce a vacuum seal).

2. **Fill your canning kettle one-half to two-thirds full of water and fill a saucepan one-half full of water. Begin heating the water.**

   Heat extra water in a teakettle or a second saucepan as a reserve (see Step 10).

3. **Submerge your clean jars and lids in hot, not boiling, water for a minimum of 10 minutes.**

   Use your canning kettle for the jars and a saucepan for the lids. You don't need to keep your screw bands hot, but they do need to be clean. Place them where you'll be filling your jars.

4. **Prepare your food exactly as instructed in your recipe.**

   Always use food of the highest quality when you're canning. If you settle for less than the best, your final product won't have the quality you're looking for. Carefully sort through your food, discarding any bruised pieces or pieces you wouldn't eat raw. Follow the instructions in your recipe for preparing your food, like removing the skin or peel or cutting it into pieces.

   Don't make any adjustments in ingredients or quantities of ingredients. If you don't follow the recipe instructions to the letter, your final results won't be what the recipe intended. Worse, any alteration may change the acidity of the product, requiring pressure canning rather than water-bath canning to kill microorganisms.

5. **Transfer your prepared food into the hot jars, adding hot liquid or syrup as dictated by your recipe. Be sure to leave the proper headspace.**

   Use a wide-mouth funnel and a ladle to quickly fill your jars. You'll eliminate a lot of spilling and have less to clean from your jar rims.

6. **Release any air bubbles with a nonmetallic spatula or a tool made for freeing air bubbles.**

   Add more prepared food or liquid to the jar after releasing the air bubbles to maintain the recommended headspace.

7. **Wipe the jar rims with a clean, damp cloth.**

   If there's even one speck of food on a jar rim, the sealant on the lid edge won't make contact with the jar rim, meaning your jar won't seal.

8. **Place a hot lid onto each jar rim, sealant side touching the jar rim, and hand-tighten the screw band.**

9. **Place the jar rack in your canning kettle, suspending it with the handles on the inside edge of the kettle.**

10. **Place the filled jars in the jar rack, making sure they're standing upright and not touching each other. Then unhook the jar rack from the edge of the kettle, carefully lowering it into the hot water.**

    Air bubbles coming from the jars are normal. If your jars aren't covered by at least 1 inch of water, add boiling water from your reserve (see Step 2).

    Unless your recipe calls for the same processing times for half-pint and pint jars, never process half-pint or pint jars with quart jars because the larger amount of food in quart jars requires a longer processing time to kill any bacteria and microorganisms.

11. **Cover the kettle and heat the water to a full rolling boil, reducing the heat and maintaining a gentle rolling boil.**

    Start your processing time after the water boils. Maintain a boil for the entire processing period.

12. **Upon completion of the processing time, remove your jars from the kettle with a jar lifter, placing them on a clean towel or paper towels, away from drafts, with 1 or 2 inches of space around them.**

    Don't attempt to adjust the bands or check the seals.

13. **Completely cool the jars.**

    The cooling period may take 12 to 24 hours.

14. **Test the seals on the cooled jars by pushing on the center of the lid.**

    If the lid feels solid and doesn't indent, you have a successful vacuum seal. If the lid depresses in the center and makes a popping noise when you apply pressure, the jar isn't sealed. Immediately refrigerate unsealed jars, using the contents within two weeks, or as stated in your recipe.

15. **Remove the screw bands from your sealed jars.**

16. **Wash the sealed jars and the screw bands in hot, soapy water.**

    Doing so removes any residue from the jars and screw bands.

17. **Label your filled jars, including the date processed.**

18. **Store your jars, without the screw bands, in a cool, dark, dry place.**

Adjusting your processing times at high altitudes

When you're canning at an altitude higher than 1,000 feet above sea level, you need to adjust your processing time. Because the air is thinner at higher altitudes, water boils below 212 degrees. As a result, you need to process your food for a longer period of time to kill any microorganisms that can make your food unsafe.

Altitude (In Feet)	Increase in Your Processing Time
1,001–3,000	5 minutes
3,001–6,000	10 minutes
6,001–8,000	15 minutes
8,001–10,000	20 minutes

Fresh fruit canning recipes

Almost all fresh fruits can well with these exceptions: bananas, lemons, limes, melons, persimmons, and strawberries. In the following sections, the quantity guide for each fruit fills a one-quart jar. If you're using pint jars, cut the quantity in half.

Always prepare whatever type of hot liquid your recipe calls for before you prepare your fruit. The liquid should be waiting for you; you shouldn't be waiting for your liquid to boil.

Apples

Choose apples suitable for eating or making pies. Peel the skin with a vegetable peeler and remove the core from your apples. Cut the apples into slices or quarters. Treat the fruit with an antioxidant to prevent discoloring (see the earlier section on "Avoiding discoloration").

- ✔ **Quantity guide:** $2^{1}/_{2}$ to 3 pounds for a 1-quart jar.
- ✔ **Hot pack preferred:** Add your rinsed fruit to your hot syrup or other hot liquid and cook for 3 to 5 minutes. Transfer the fruit to your prepared jars and fill the jars with the hot liquid. Allow headspace of $^{1}/_{2}$ inch.
- ✔ **Processing time:** Pints and quarts (20 minutes).

Apricots, nectarines, and peaches

Peel the fruit, cut it in half, and remove the pits. Treat the fruit with an anti-oxidant to prevent discoloring (refer to the earlier section on "Avoiding discoloration").

- ✔ **Quantity guide:** 2 to 2½ pounds for a 1-quart jar.

- ✔ **Raw pack:** Pack your fruit into your prepared jars, cut side down. Add your hot liquid. Allow headspace of ½ inch.

- ✔ **Hot pack:** Add your fruit to your hot syrup or other hot liquid and bring the liquid to a boil. Pack the fruit into your prepared jars, cut side down. Fill the jars with the hot liquid. Allow headspace of ½ inch.

- ✔ **Processing time:** Raw pack: pints, 25 minutes; quarts, 30 minutes. Hot pack: pints, 20 minutes; quarts, 25 minutes.

Berries (except strawberries)

Select perfect, not soft or mushy, berries. Leave them whole. Wash and drain the berries (handling them as little as possible); remove any stems or hulls.

- ✔ **Quantity guide:** 1½ to 3 pounds for a 1-quart jar.

- ✔ **Raw pack (preferred for soft berries, like blackberries, boysenberries, and raspberries):** Fill the prepared jars with the berries, gently shaking the jar to compact the fruit. Fill the jars with the hot liquid. Allow headspace of ½ inch.

- ✔ **Hot pack (preferred for firmer berries, such as blueberries, cranberries, and huckleberries):** Measure the berries into a saucepan, adding ½ cup of sugar for each quart of berries. Bring the mixture to a boil over medium-high heat; stir to prevent sticking. Ladle the hot berries and liquid into your prepared jars, adding boiling water if there isn't adequate liquid to fill the jars. Allow headspace of ½ inch.

- ✔ **Processing time:** Raw pack: pints, 15 minutes; quarts, 20 minutes. Hot pack: pints and quarts, 15 minutes.

Figs

Ripe figs have a short shelf life — about two or three days. Pick fruit that's firm to the touch. Use canned figs as an ice-cream topper or a sweet-roll filling.

- ✔ **Quantity guide:** 2½ pounds for a 1-quart jar.

- ✔ **Hot pack preferred:** Cover washed, whole figs with water. Bring to a boil and cook for 2 minutes; drain. Place the figs in a boiling syrup and cook for 5 minutes longer. Add bottled lemon juice to your prepared jars, 1 tablespoon per 1-pint jar and 2 tablespoons per 1-quart jar. Fill the jars with the hot figs and the hot syrup. Allow headspace of ½ inch.

- ✔ **Processing time:** Pints, 45 minutes; quarts, 50 minutes.

Grapefruit and oranges

Mix grapefruit and oranges for a sweet and tart flavor. Use white grape juice for your filling liquid in place of sugar syrup.

- ✔ **Quantity guide:** 2 to $2^1/_2$ pounds for a 1-quart jar.
- ✔ **Raw pack preferred:** Remove the peel from the fruit. Use a paring knife and carefully remove each fruit section from the membrane. Fill the jars with your fruit and add the hot liquid. Allow headspace of $^1/_2$ inch.
- ✔ **Processing time:** Pints and quarts, 10 minutes.

Pears

All varieties of pears can well. After cutting and peeling the pears, treat your fruit with an antioxidant to prevent discoloring (see the earlier section on "Avoiding discoloration").

- ✔ **Quantity guide:** 2 to 3 pounds for a 1-quart jar.
- ✔ **Hot pack preferred:** Cut the peeled and cored pears into halves or slices. Cook them in boiling syrup for 5 to 6 minutes, or until the pears are hot. Transfer the fruit and the hot syrup to the prepared jars. Allow headspace of $^1/_2$ inch.
- ✔ **Processing time:** Pints, 20 minutes; quarts, 25 minutes.

Rhubarb

Rhubarb, usually mixed with strawberries for a pie filling, is delectable when combined with tart apples. Although rhubarb is a vegetable, it's treated as a fruit because its acid level makes the rhubarb safe for water-bath canning.

- ✔ **Quantity guide:** $1^1/_2$ to 2 pounds for a 1-quart jar.
- ✔ **Hot pack preferred:** Remove and discard any leaves, which are toxic. Wash the rhubarb. Cut the stalks into 1-inch pieces and measure them into a bowl, adding $^1/_2$ cup of granulated sugar for each quart of rhubarb. Stir to coat the pieces with the sugar. Let the mixture stand in a cool place until juice appears, about 3 to 4 hours. Transfer the rhubarb and the juice to a saucepan; bring the mixture to a boil over low heat. Stir once and fill the prepared jars with rhubarb and liquid. Allow headspace of $^1/_2$ inch.
- ✔ **Processing time:** Pints and quarts, 15 minutes.

Tomatoes

A ripe tomato is red all the way to the stem with no soft spots and a strong tomato aroma. Each tomato variety has its own flavor and texture. Ensure the proper acidity level (4.6 or lower) for water-bath canning your variety by adding an acid, like bottled lemon juice or powdered citric acid.

- **Quantity guide:** 2¹/₂ to 3¹/₂ pounds for a 1-quart jar.

- **Hot pack preferred:** Peel your tomatoes. Leave whole or cut into halves or quarters. Place them in a 5- to 8-quart pot and cover them with water. Bring to a boil; gently boil for 5 minutes.

    Add 2 tablespoons of bottled lemon juice to each quart jar, or 1 table-spoon to each pint jar. (**Note:** For citric acid, add ¹/₂ teaspoon to each quart jar and ¹/₄ teaspoon to each pint jar.) Add your hot tomatoes and the hot cooking liquid to the jars; release any air bubbles, adjusting the liquid level to maintain headspace of ¹/₂ inch.

- **Processing time:** Pints, 40 minutes; quarts, 45 minutes.

Pressure Canning Your Veggies

Pressure canning is a process for preserving food with a low acid content by exposing the food to a high temperature (240 degrees) under a specific pres-sure for a specific period of time in a pressure canner. Vegetables fall into the low-acid category. And only one form of canning — pressure canning — and only one piece of equipment — a pressure canner — are approved for safely processing these foods.

To reach a temperature of 240 degrees and superheat your filled jars of low-acid food, use a pressure canner that's approved for pressure canning by the U.S. Department of Agriculture (USDA).

Not all vegetables are suitable for pressure canning. The following should be taken off your pressure-canning list: broccoli, Brussels sprouts, cabbage, cau-liflower, cucumbers, eggplant, onions, parsnips, rutabagas, and turnips. Many of these veggies are suitable for pickling, though. Go to Book I, Chapter 3 for pickling instructions.

The lowdown on pressure canners

In addition to canning jars, two-piece caps, a jar lifter, and a wide-mouth funnel (see the section "Your water-bath canning equipment list" earlier in this chapter for more on these tools), pressure canning requires a specific piece of equipment for safe food preservation — namely, a pressure canner with an accurate gauge, shown in Figure 2-4. These heavy kettles are made for processing home-canned food. They include a locking, tight-fitting cover that makes the kettle airtight, and they come in many sizes and prices.

No matter which type or size of pressure canner you choose, the goal is always the same: to superheat and process low-acid food at a high temperature (240 degrees) that destroys hard-to-kill microorganisms, especially the bacteria that cause botulism.

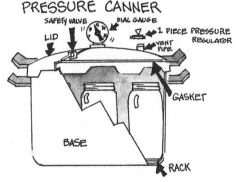

Figure 2-4:
A pressure
canner.

Each pressure canner has a locking cover, a pressure gauge, and an over-pressure plug. Manufacturers of pressure canners, however, slightly vary the same features and add accessories in much the same way car manufacturers add extras to a basic car model. All pressure canners — regardless of extra features or the lack thereof — safely process your filled jars of low-acid food in the same manner.

Don't confuse pressure canners with pressure cookers; they are *not* interchangeable. You use a pressure canner to process and sterilize home-canned, low-acid foods. You use a pressure cooker to cook food fast. Check out *Pressure Cookers For Dummies,* by Tom Lacalamita (Wiley), for information on pressure cooking.

Picking and preparing your vegetables

Whether harvesting your vegetables from the garden or shopping at a farmers' market or your local supermarket, follow these guidelines when selecting your vegetables:

- ✔ **Select vegetables that are free of bruises and imperfections.** These marks could encourage the growth of bacteria in your food.

- ✔ **Process the vegetables the day of harvesting or purchasing — the sooner the better.** If you need to wait a day, store the items in your refrigerator to preserve the quality and prevent deterioration of your food. Don't make your vegetables wait longer than one day!

Properly cleaning your vegetables is important to your finished product. Vegetables growing above the ground usually have a thinner, tenderer skin than vegetables grown in the ground. Remove any stems and leaves. Run water over them; gently rub the skin with your fingers and remove any dirt. Shake off the excess water and place your food on clean kitchen or paper towels. *Root vegetables,* those that grow in the ground (think carrots and beets), may require soaking to loosen any clinging soil. After first rinsing the vegetables, immerse them in a basin of cool water. Using a stiff brush (a new toothbrush works well), scrub the surface of the vegetables, removing any clinging soil. Rinse thoroughly with running water, placing the vegetables on clean kitchen or paper towels to drain.

You can prepare your clean vegetables for filling your jars in two ways: raw or hot, as the following sections explain. Keep in mind, though, that not all vegetables are suited for both methods. Follow your recipe instructions or check out the "Vegetable canning recipes" section later in this chapter.

Raw (cold) packing

The *raw packing* method uses raw, unheated vegetables for filling your prepared jars. Filling the jars with raw vegetables keeps them firm without being crushed during processing. Refer to your recipe instructions to decide whether to remove the skin or cut the vegetables into pieces. To fill your jars using a raw packing method, you simply prepare the hot liquid according to your recipe, fill the prepared jars with the raw vegetables, and then add the hot liquid, being sure to leave the required headspace.

Hot packing

Hot packing is precooking or heating your vegetables prior to placing them in your prepared canning jars. It's the preferred method for the majority of vegetables, particularly firm ones, such as carrots and beets. Using precooked vegetables improves the shelf life of the processed food by increasing the vacuum created in the jar during the pressure-canning period. To prepare your vegetables for hot packing and add them to your canning jars, simply precook the vegetables as directed in your recipe and then immediately fill the prepared jars with the hot vegetables, pouring the hot cooking liquid in and leaving the required headspace.

Pressure-canning instructions

In this section, you find out how to pressure-can low-acid foods. Avoid any temptation to omit any portion of any step in the process. Each step is important to produce safe, home-canned foods.

1. **Check and wash your equipment and utensils in warm, soapy water, rinsing well to remove any soap residue.**

   Make sure your pressure canner is in good working order and examine your jars for nicks or chips, the screw bands for proper fit and corrosion, and the new lids for imperfections and scratches. Discard any damaged items immediately.

2. **Place your clean jars and lids in a kettle of hot — not boiling — water until you're ready to fill them.**

   Never boil the lids because the sealant material may be damaged and won't produce a safe vacuum seal.

3. **Ready your canner by filling it with 2 to 3 inches of water and heating the water.**

   Refer to your owner's manual for specific instructions.

4. **Prepare the food, following your recipe precisely.**

5. **Fill the jars, packing the food into one jar at a time so that the food is snug, yet loose enough for liquid to circulate into the open spaces; then ladle boiling water (or the liquid from precooking the vegetables) into the jars.**

   Refer to your recipe for instructions or head back to the sections "Raw (cold) packing" and "Hot packing" for guidance. Be sure to leave the amount of headspace specified in your recipe.

   Use only one size jar (pint or quart) for each batch of food. Doing so allows you to complete the correct processing time required to evenly heat the jars and destroy microorganisms.

6. **Release any air bubbles with a nonmetallic spatula or a tool to free bubbles.**

   If the headspace drops, add additional food and liquid to the jar.

7. **Wipe the jar rims with a clean, damp cloth; then place a lid on the jar (seal side down) and secure the lid in place with a screw band.**

   Hand-tighten the band without overly tightening it.

8. **Place the jars on the rack in the bottom of the canner, making sure you have the recommended amount of simmering water in the bottom of the canner.**

   Don't crowd the jars or place more jars in the canner than is recommended for your size of pressure canner. Place them so that they're stable, won't tip, and don't touch each other or the side of the canner.

Unlike water-bath canning (refer to the earlier section "Canning Fruits via the Water-Bath Method"), you can process a second layer of pint or half-pint jars at the same time as long as your canner accommodates the height of the two layers. To build the second layer, place a second rack on top of the first layer of jars. Stagger the second layer of jars so they aren't directly above the bottom layer. Doing so permits proper air circulation for achieving the correct pressure and temperature.

9. **Following the instructions in the owner's manual, lock the cover.**

10. **Allow a steady stream of steam to escape from the pressure canner for 10 minutes, or the time recommended in your manual; then close the vent, bringing the pressure to the amount specified in your recipe.**

    Processing time starts when your canner reaches the required pressure. The pressure must remain constant for the entire processing time.

    If the pressure drops at any time during processing, so will the temperature. To remedy this problem, return the pressure to the specified amount by increasing the heat. After the pressure has been regained, start your processing time from the beginning.

11. **After the processing time has passed, turn the heat off and allow the pressure to return to zero.**

    Allowing the pressure to return to zero may take as long as 30 minutes. Don't disturb the canner; jars that are upset may not seal properly.

    Running water over your pressure canner to reduce the pressure is a definite no-no. The sudden change in temperature can cause the jars to burst.

12. **Approximately 15 minutes after the pressure returns to zero, or at the time stated in the manual, remove the lid, opening the cover away from you and allowing the steam to flow away from you.**

13. **After 10 minutes, remove the jars from the pressure canner with a jar lifter, placing them on a clean towel, away from drafts, with 1 to 2 inches of space around the jars.**

    Don't adjust the bands or attempt to check the seals.

14. **Completely cool the jars.**

    Cooling the jars may take 12 to 24 hours.

    As your jars cool, you'll hear a popping noise coming from them, indicating a vacuum seal. This is a good thing. Consider it *canning music.*

15. **Test the seals on completely cooled jars by pushing on the center of the lid.**

    If the lid feels solid and doesn't indent, you've produced a successful seal. If the lid depresses when you apply pressure, the jar isn't sealed. Refrigerate any unsealed jars immediately, using the contents within two weeks, or the period stated in your recipe.

16. **Remove the screw bands of the sealed jars.**

    Storing your sealed jars without the bands allows you to see any signs of food seepage, which indicates a potentially spoiled product.

17. **Remove any residue by washing the jars, lids, and bands in hot, soapy water.**

18. **Label your jars, including the date processed. Then store them, without the screw bands, in a cool, dark, dry place.**

Vegetable canning recipes

This section provides instructions and guidelines for pressure-canning some of the more common fresh vegetables. It also includes tips for selecting your vegetables and determining the approximate amount of fresh vegetables needed to yield 1 quart of finished product.

Asparagus

Select firm, bright-green stalks with tightly closed tips. Stalks with small diameters indicate a young, tender vegetable. Cut stalks into 1-inch pieces or can them whole, placing the tips of the stalks toward the top of the jar.

- **Quantity guide:** 3 to 4 pounds for a 1-quart jar.

- **Hot pack preferred:** Submerge asparagus in boiling water for 2 to 3 minutes. When the food is cool enough to handle, pack the food into the prepared jars.

- **Headspace:** 1 inch for asparagus and liquid.

- **Processing time:** At 10 pounds for 30 minutes (pints), 40 minutes (quarts).

Beans, dried (kidney, navy, pinto, split peas, and so on)

Rinse the beans before you soak them to remove any dust or dirt particles. You can easily accomplish this by placing the beans in a colander and running cold water over them while stirring them with your hands or a spoon.

- **Quantity guide:** 1 to $1^{1}/_{4}$ pounds dried beans for a 1-quart jar.

- **Hot pack preferred:** Place the beans in a large pot. Fill the pot with enough cold water to cover the beans. Place a cover on the beans, allowing them to soak, undisturbed, for 12 to 18 hours. Drain the beans, adding fresh cold water to the pot to cover the beans by 2 inches. Bring the liquid to a boil and continue boiling for 30 minutes. Pack the hot beans into your prepared jars, adding the boiling cooking liquid.

- **Headspace:** 1 inch for beans and liquid.

- **Processing time:** At 10 pounds for 1 hour and 15 minutes (pints), 1 hour and 30 minutes (quarts).

Pressure canning at high altitudes

If you're canning at an elevation higher than 1,000 feet above sea level, adjust the pounds of pressure used during processing according to the following table. Your pressure-canner processing time will remain the same.

Altitude (In Feet)	Weighted Gauge	Dial Gauge
0–1,000	10	11
1,001–2,000	15	11
2,001–4,000	15	12
4,001–6,000	15	13
6,001–8,000	15	14
8,001–10,000	15	15

Beans, green (pole or bush), string, Italian, or wax

Choose tender, small beans. Remove the ends and strings from the beans. Can them whole or cut them into 1- to 2-inch pieces.

- **Quantity guide:** $1\frac{1}{2}$ to 2 pounds for a 1-quart jar.
- **Raw pack:** Place the washed beans into your prepared jars, packing them tightly and covering them with boiling water.
  - **Headspace:** $\frac{1}{2}$ inch for beans and liquid.
  - **Processing time:** At 10 pounds for 20 minutes (pints), 25 minutes (quarts).
- **Hot pack:** Add the beans to boiling water; continue boiling for 5 minutes. Pack the beans into the prepared jars, adding the boiling cooking liquid.
  - **Headspace:** $\frac{1}{2}$ inch for beans and liquid.
  - **Processing time:** At 10 pounds for 20 minutes (pints), 25 minutes (quarts).

Beans, lima or butter

Purchase beans in the shell to ensure freshness, discarding any beans showing signs of rust or mushiness.

- **Quantity guide:** 4 to 5 pounds for a 1-quart jar.
- **Hot pack preferred:** Shell the beans by popping open the casing and placing the loose beans in a colander for washing. Add the beans to boiling water, removing them after 3 minutes. Pack the hot beans into the prepared jars, filling with boiling cooking liquid.

✔ **Headspace:** 1 inch for beans and liquid.

Use a wire or bamboo strainer to quickly remove the beans from the boiling water.

✔ **Processing time:** At 10 pounds for 40 minutes (pints), 50 minutes (quarts). Increase the processing time for beans over $^3/_4$ of an inch in diameter by 10 minutes for pints and quarts.

Beets

Select beets with a deep red color. A beet with a diameter of 1 to 2 inches is the most desirable size for pressure canning. Larger-size beets are best pickled (see Book I, Chapter 3 for pickling instructions).

You can preserve the bright, red color of the beet by adding 1 tablespoon of vinegar (with an acidity of 5 percent) to each quart of liquid.

✔ **Quantity guide:** $2^1/_2$ to $3^1/_2$ pounds for a 1-quart jar.

✔ **Hot pack preferred:** Remove all but 2 inches of the stem, leaving the *taproot* (the main root growing downward into the ground from the bottom of the beet) intact. Scrub any clinging dirt from the beet with a stiff brush. Add the beets to boiling water, cooking them until they're easily pierced with a fork (about 10 to 20 minutes, depending on the size of the beet) and the skins peel off easily. Slice, dice, or leave the beets whole before filling your prepared jars. Add clean, boiling water.

✔ **Headspace:** 1 inch for beets and liquid.

✔ **Processing time:** At 10 pounds for 30 minutes (pints), 35 minutes (quarts).

Bell peppers (green, red, orange, yellow)

Sweet, firm bell peppers produce the best results. Because of the extremely low acid level in this vegetable, you must adjust the acidity level of the bell peppers by adding bottled lemon juice. Use only pint or half-pint jars for this extremely low-acid vegetable.

✔ **Quantity guide:** 1 pound for a 1-pint jar.

✔ **Hot pack preferred:** Remove the bell pepper stem, core, and seeds. Cut the bell peppers into large (about 2- to 3-inch), uniform pieces. Boil the bell peppers for 3 minutes, draining and packing them immediately after cooking. (You can remove the skin by plunging the cooked bell peppers into cold water and peeling off the loose skins, but you don't have to.) Pack the bell peppers into your prepared jars. Add 1 tablespoon of bottled lemon juice to each jar and then fill with the boiling cooking liquid.

✔ **Headspace:** 1 inch for bell peppers; $^1/_2$ inch for liquid.

✔ **Processing time:** At 10 pounds for 35 minutes (pints).

Carrots

Use carrots with a diameter of 1 to $1^1/_2$ inches. Remove clinging dirt from carrots with thin, tender skins by rinsing and scrubbing with a brush. If you prefer carrots without the skin, remove the outer layer with a vegetable peeler. Always remove the tops.

✔ **Quantity guide:** $2^1/_2$ to 3 pounds (cleaned and peeled, if desired, with tops removed) for a 1-quart jar.

✔ **Hot pack preferred:** Slice, dice, or keep the carrots whole. Simmer the carrots in boiling water for 5 minutes. Pack the hot carrots into your prepared jars, using the cooking liquid to fill the jars.

✔ **Headspace:** 1 inch for carrots and liquid.

✔ **Processing time:** At 10 pounds for 25 minutes (pints), 30 minutes (quarts).

Corn, whole kernel

Starting with corn that has the husks on and the silk attached allows you to assess the freshness of the corn. Choose ears with brightly colored husks that are free of spots and moisture; silks should be golden, not matted or brown.

If you want to have better luck selecting corn that's always sweet and tender, try this method: Slightly peel back the husk to check for any pests. If all is clear (no bugs or mold), use your thumbnail to depress a kernel about an inch below the top of the corn. If the ear has adequate moisture, liquid will squirt out, sometimes hitting you in the eye. Buy this ear! If no spitting occurs, select another ear and repeat the test.

✔ **Quantity guide:** 4 to 5 pounds (weighed with husks on) for a 1-quart jar.

✔ **Hot pack preferred:** Remove and discard the husks and silk. Using a sharp knife, cut the kernels from each ear. Measure the corn to calculate water for cooking: For each pint of corn, add 1 cup of boiling water; for each quart of corn, add 2 cups of boiling water. Bring the measured corn and water to a boil, cooking for 5 minutes. Transfer the corn to your prepared jars, adding the boiling cooking liquid.

✔ **Headspace:** 1 inch for corn and liquid.

✔ **Processing time:** At 10 pounds for 55 minutes (pints), 1 hour and 25 minutes (quarts).

Greens (beet, collard, kale, mustard, spinach, Swiss chard, turnip)

Select tender stems and leaves to produce a superior product after cooking and pressure canning. Large, older stems and leaves tend to produce a strong-tasting or stringy product.

- **Quantity guide:** 3 to 4 pounds for a 1-quart jar.
- **Hot pack preferred:** After washing, wilt the greens in batches by immersing them in just enough boiling water in a pot to prevent sticking. Wilting times vary from 2 to 5 minutes because of the size of the leaf and the quantity in each batch. Turn the leaves to cook evenly. Slice the wilted leaves before filling the prepared jars for a tight pack — doing so eliminates trapped air bubbles. Add boiling water, including any left from the wilting process.
- **Headspace:** 1 inch for greens and liquid.
- **Processing time:** At 10 pounds for 1 hour and 10 minutes (pints), 1 hour and 30 minutes (quarts).

Okra

Fresh okra is a pod that's best used when under 4 inches in length.

- **Quantity guide:** About $1^{1}/_{2}$ pounds for a 1-quart jar.
- **Hot pack preferred:** Remove the stems, leaving the caps on for precooking and packing whole. Cover the okra with boiling water, cook for 1 minute, and drain. If you're cutting the pods into 1-inch pieces, remove the caps before packing. Fill your prepared jars, adding the boiling cooking liquid.
- **Headspace:** 1 inch for okra and liquid.
- **Processing time:** At 10 pounds for 25 minutes (pints), 40 minutes (quarts).

Peas

Use peas with a diameter smaller than $^{1}/_{3}$ inch. If you use peas larger than $^{1}/_{3}$ inch, add an additional 10 minutes of processing time for pints or quarts.

- **Quantity guide:** 4 to 5 pounds for a 1-quart jar.
- **Hot pack preferred:** After removing the peas from the pods, add them to boiling water, cooking as follows: small peas (diameter smaller than $^{1}/_{4}$ inch) for 3 minutes, medium peas (with a diameter of $^{1}/_{4}$ to $^{1}/_{3}$ inch) for 5 minutes. Remove the peas from the boiling water and place them in a colander, rinsing them with hot water. Pack the peas in your prepared jars, adding the boiling cooking liquid.
- **Headspace:** 1 inch for peas and liquid.
- **Processing time:** At 10 pounds for 40 minutes (pints and quarts).

Potatoes

These potatoes are round and white with a thin skin. Peel the potatoes prior to precooking. Small potatoes (2 to 3 inches in diameter) may be left whole; cut larger potatoes into quarters before precooking.

- **Quantity guide:** About 5 pounds for a 1-quart jar.

- **Hot pack preferred:** Cover the potatoes with water in a large pot, bring the contents to a boil, and boil for 10 minutes. Drain the potatoes, reserving the cooking liquid. Pack the cooked potatoes into your prepared jars, adding the reserved boiling cooking liquid.

- **Headspace:** 1 inch for potatoes and liquid.

- **Processing time:** At 10 pounds for 35 minutes (pints), 40 minutes (quarts).

Summer squash

Summer squash include crookneck, zucchini, and patty pan, to name a few. The skins are thin and edible, eliminating the need to peel them.

- **Quantity guide:** 2 to 2$\frac{1}{2}$ pounds for a 1-quart jar.

- **Hot pack preferred:** Cut the squash into even-sized slices or cubes. Steam or boil the squash for 2 to 3 minutes. Pack the hot pieces into your prepared jars, filling the jars with boiling water, including any leftover from precooking.

- **Headspace:** $\frac{1}{2}$ inch for squash and liquid.

- **Processing time:** At 10 pounds for 30 minutes (pints), 40 minutes (quarts).

Winter squash and pumpkins

Other types of squash that are good for canning include banana, butternut, Hubbard, spaghetti, and turban squash. Because pumpkins are similar in texture, you can use these instructions for them, too. This process is a bit labor intensive, but the rewards are oh so good!

- **Quantity guide:** 2 to 3 pounds for a 1-quart jar.

- **Hot pack preferred:** Cut the squash into pieces (about 1 inch by 3 inches), scraping out the fiber and the seeds. Place the pieces in a large pot, adding just enough water to cover the pieces. Boil the squash until it's soft and easily pierced with a fork, about 10 to 30 minutes depending on the variety you're using. Scrape the pulp from the softened skin and mash it or run it through a food mill. Return the squash to the pot and bring the contents to a boil, stirring constantly to keep it from sticking. Upon boiling, transfer the squash to your prepared jars.

- ✔ **Headspace:** 1 inch.
- ✔ **Processing time:** At 10 pounds for 55 minutes (pints), 1 hour and 30 minutes (quarts).

Yams and sweet potatoes

Yams are tubers, and sweet potatoes are roots — so they're actually from two different plant species. Even though sweet potatoes and yams are unrelated, they're suitable for the same uses.

Small potatoes may be left whole; cut larger ones into quarters before removing the skins.

- ✔ **Quantity guide:** $2^1/_2$ to 3 pounds for a 1-quart jar.
- ✔ **Hot pack preferred:** Precook vegetables in boiling water until the peels can be rubbed off, about 5 to 15 minutes. Pack hot food into your prepared jars, adding clean boiling water or a boiling sweet syrup ($2^1/_2$ cups granulated sugar and $5^1/_4$ cups water brought to a boil, yielding about $6^1/_2$ cups of liquid).
- ✔ **Headspace:** 1 inch for potatoes and liquid.
- ✔ **Processing time:** At 10 pounds for 1 hour and 5 minutes (pints), 1 hour and 30 minutes (quarts).

Making Sure Your Food Is Still Good to Eat

Although you may follow all the proper steps and procedures for canning foods, you still have a chance for spoilage. The following sections show you how to ensure your food is safe to eat, recognize spoiled food, and dispose of it properly.

Ensuring food safety

There's no guarantee that your home-canned foods will always be free from spoilage, but your chances for spoiled food are greatly reduced when you follow the precise guidelines for each preserving method. In addition to your specific canning procedures, follow these guidelines to guard against food spoilage:

✔ **Don't experiment or take shortcuts.** Use only tested, approved methods.

✔ **Use fresh, firm (not over-ripe) food.** Wash it thoroughly. Can fruit and vegetables as soon as possible after they're picked.

✔ **Use jars and two-piece caps made for home-canning.** Discard any jars that are cracked or nicked.

✔ **Don't over-pack foods.** Trying to cram too much food into a jar may result in under-processing because the heat can't evenly penetrate the food.

✔ **Never use sealing lids a second time.** Always use new lids. The sealant on the underside of the lid is good for only one processing.

✔ **Test your pressure canner before you use it.** Have your dial gauge tested annually to verify its accuracy. (Weighted gauges don't require testing.)

✔ **Process your food for the full amount of time stated in your recipe.** Make adjustments to your processing time and pressure for altitudes over 1,000 feet above sea level. (See the sidebars, "Adjusting your processing times at high altitudes" and "Pressure canning at high altitudes" for more details.)

✔ **Test each jar's seal and remove the screw band before storing your food.** Removing the screw bands from your cooled, sealed jars before storing them allows you to easily detect any broken seals or food oozing out from under the lid, which indicates spoilage.

✔ **Never use or taste any canned food that exhibits signs of spoilage.** Discard it immediately.

Identifying food gone bad

The best way to detect food spoilage is by visually examining your jars. Review the following checklist. If you can answer "true" for each of the following statements, your food should be safe for eating:

✔ The food in the jar is covered with liquid and fully packed, and proper headspace has been maintained.

✔ The food in the jar is free from moving air bubbles.

✔ The jars have good, tight seals. When you rotate the jar, you don't see any seepage or oozing from under the lid.

✔ The food has maintained a uniform color and isn't broken or mushy.

✔ The liquid in the jar is clear, not cloudy, and free of sediment.

✔ When you open the jar, no liquid spurts out, you notice no unnatural or unusual odors, and you see no cottonlike growths on top of the food's surface or on the underside of the lid.

Botulism poisoning can be fatal. Because botulism spores have no odor and can't be seen, you can't always tell which jars are tainted. If you suspect that a jar of food is spoiled, *never, never, never* taste it.

Disposing of spoiled food safely

What you never want to do with spoiled food is pour it into a water source, a sink or garbage disposal, or down the toilet, because it may come into contact with humans or animals through a water-reclamation process. Instead, follow the guidelines in the next sections.

If your jar is still sealed

If the jar has the seal intact, you can simply discard the unopened container in the trash or bury it deeply in the soil. Doing so keeps the product from coming in contact with any human or animal and eliminates the transfer of bacteria.

If your jar has a broken seal

If your jar has a broken seal, you need to take extra precautions to make sure you don't contaminate any other food or surface. Follow these steps:

1. **Boil the jar, lid, screw band, and contents in a covered pot for 30 minutes.**

   Place everything in a deep cooking pot and cover the items with 1 to 2 inches of water, taking care not to splash any of the contents outside of the pot.

2. **Turn off the heat and let the contents cool while remaining covered.**

3. **Discard the contents in a sealed container in the trash, or bury them deeply in the soil.**

4. **Using a solution made up of one part household chlorine bleach to four parts lukewarm water, thoroughly wash everything that came into contact with the jar or spoiled food.**

   This includes all equipment, work surfaces, clothing, and body parts.

5. **Dispose of the jar, the lid and screw band, and any sponges or dishcloths used in any phase of this process by wrapping the items in a trash bag, sealing the bag, and placing it in the trash.**

Chapter 3

Preserving by Way of Pickling

Pickling is used for a wide range of foods, including fruits and vegetables. Although pickling isn't practiced much today, don't overlook this rewarding process. This chapter gives you an overview of pickling, describing the ingredients, the utensils, and the methods used. In no time, you'll be making easy-to-prepare pickled food and condiments to wow your taste buds.

The Art of Pickling

Pickling preserves food in a *brine solution,* a strong mixture of water, salt, vinegar, herbs and spices, and sometimes sugar or another sweetener, such as corn syrup. The perfect balance of these ingredients safely preserves your pickled food. You can achieve this balance by precisely measuring your ingredients and following each step in your recipe.

The ingredients

The four basic ingredients for pickling are salt, vinegar, water, and herbs and spices. Use high-quality ingredients for the best results.

Salt

Salt is used as a preservative. It adds flavor and crispness to your food, especially pickles. Use a pure, additive-free, granulated salt. (Additives in salt cause cloudy liquid. Always read the ingredient label on your salt container to ensure it's additive-free.) The following table lists which salts are acceptable for pickling and which ones aren't.

Acceptable salts	Unacceptable salts
Pickling and canning salt	Table and iodized salt
Most kosher salt	Rock salt
Sea salt	Salt substitutes

Vinegar

Vinegar is a tart liquid that prevents the growth of bacteria. The preferred vinegar for pickling is distilled white vinegar with a sharp, tart flavor. It maintains the color of your food and is relatively inexpensive. Use apple cider vinegar for a milder flavor.

Always use a vinegar with an acidity level of 5 percent. If the level of acidity isn't on the label, don't use the vinegar — the strength of the acid may not be adequate for safe food preservation.

Never dilute or reduce the amount of vinegar in a recipe. If the flavor's too tart, add $1/4$ cup of granulated sugar for every 4 cups of vinegar. Treating flavors in this manner won't upset the balance of your vinegar. If you don't like the flavor when you make the recipe a second time, try another recipe.

Water

Soft water is the best water for your brine solution. *Distilled water,* water with all minerals and other impurities removed, is also a good choice. If you use tap water, make sure it's of drinking quality; if it doesn't taste good straight from the tap, it won't taste better in your food. Also, avoid sparkling water.

To soften tap water, boil it in a large kettle for 15 minutes. Cool the water and allow it to stand for 24 hours. Remove any scum on the surface with a foam skimmer. Ladle the water into a measuring cup without disturbing the sediment on the bottom of the kettle. Add 1 tablespoon of vinegar to each gallon of water.

Herbs and spices

Use the exact amount of herbs or spices called for in your recipe. If your recipe calls for a fresh herb, use the fresh herb. If your recipe calls for a dried spice, use one with a strong aroma. Sometimes recipes call for *pickling spices.* These are blends of many spices, including allspice, bay leaves, cardamom, cinnamon, cloves, coriander, ginger, mustard seeds, and peppercorns. They're mixed by the manufacturer and vary in flavor.

The equipment and the utensils

In addition to the basic equipment for water-bath canning (refer to Book I, Chapter 2), you need nonreactive utensils and equipment for handling, cooking, and brining your food. *Nonreactive* items are usually made of stainless steel, enamelware, or glass.

Stoneware crocks are excellent choices for brining food. You can find them at specialty cookware stores or where canning supplies are sold.

Items made from — or containing — zinc, iron, brass, copper, or galvanized metal and enamelware with chips or cracks in the enamel react with the acids and salt during the pickling process. This reaction alters the color of your food — copper turns your pickles a funny green; iron makes the food black — and produces a finished product that tastes bad. More importantly, galvanized items produce a poison when the acid and the salt touch the zinc. This poison is transferred to your food, causing serious illness (or worse).

Getting an Education in Brining

Brining is part of the pickling process and requires the use of an acid, usually vinegar, to safely convert your low-acid foods (those with a pH level over 4.6) to high-acid foods (with a pH level of 4.6 or less). The brining solution extracts juice and sugar from your food, forming *lactic acid,* a bitter-tasting, tart acid. Lactic acid is the preservative in your pickled food. Preparing your recipe as it's written makes processing your food in a water-bath canner safe.

Preparation methods for your pickled food include the following:

- ✔ **Long brine:** This process is primarily used for making pickles from cucumbers. The brine solution is quite heavy with salt and may contain some vinegar and spices. In a long brine, you submerge the food in the brine solution where it *ferments* (stays in the solution) for anywhere from five days to six weeks. (Your recipe gives you the details.) After fermenting, follow your recipe and make a fresh brine solution for filling your jars.

- ✔ **Short brine:** The soaking period for this method is 24 hours or less. Follow your recipe for the correct proportions in your brine solution. Prepare a fresh solution for filling your jars.

- ✔ **Complete precooking:** In this method, you cook your food completely before filling your jars.

- ✔ **A fresh (or raw) pack:** In this method, fresh raw vegetables are placed in prepared jars and then covered with hot, flavored liquid — usually a spicy vinegar — and processed in your water-bath canner.

Old-time canning recipes may instruct you to "soak your pickles in salt brine strong enough to float an egg." This equates to a 10-percent brine mixture of 1 pound (about $1\frac{1}{2}$ cups) of salt dissolved in 1 gallon of water.

When you're brining, keep these pointers in mind:

- ✔ Keep your food completely submerged in the brine solution, whether it's for a few hours or longer, by placing a sealed, water-filled glass jar on top of your food. The jar applies pressure to keep the foods submerged when you cover your brining container.

- ✔ To maintain crispness, crunchiness, and firmness in your vegetables, add ice, preferably crushed ice, to your soaking solution during the soaking period. This technique works best for short brine soaking. ***Note:*** In older pickling recipes, you may see the addition of alum or pickling (slaked) lime. The recipes in this chapter don't add either of these products because they aren't necessary when you're using modern canning methods.

- ✔ After the soaking period, drain your vegetables in a colander, following your recipe instructions for any rinsing. Some recipes instruct you to roll the drained food in clean kitchen towels to dry it. Doing so works well for larger pieces of food, but it doesn't work with finely chopped relishes.

Packing and Filling Your Jars

The most important thing to do when you're filling your jars is to release air bubbles that are trapped between the food pieces. Using a nonmetallic spatula, press back gently on the contents, going all the way around the jar (see Figure 3-1).

Releasing air bubbles may seem unimportant, but they can play havoc with your final product.

✔ **Jar seals:** Too much air in the jar from trapped air produces excessive pressure in the jar during processing, which interferes with sealing.

✔ **Liquid levels:** When air is trapped between your food pieces before sealing the jars, the liquid level in the jars drops as the food is heated, leaving too much *headspace* (the air space between the inside of the lid and the top of the food or liquid in your jar). Without the proper amount of liquid in the jars, the food floats and becomes discolored.

REMEMBER

Never skip the step of releasing air bubbles. No matter how carefully you pack and fill your jars, you'll always have some hidden bubbles.

RELEASING AIR BUBBLES

USE A NONMETALLIC SPATULA TO PRESS BACK GENTLY ON THE CONTENTS. GO ALL THE WAY AROUND THE JAR.

Figure 3-1: Releasing air bubbles from your filled jars.

Making a Pickled Topper

Use this pickled treat anytime you'd use a relish: on a hamburger or hot dog, in tuna salad, or anytime you want to add flavor to a sandwich.

☞ Sweet Pickle Relish

One advantage of homemade relish is mixing flavors you don't find in commercially produced relishes. You may even wind up with a treat that your family prefers to the store-bought kind.

Preparation time: 25 minutes (not including soaking time)

Cooking time: 30 minutes

Processing time: 10 minutes

Yield: 7 half-pints or 3 pints

5 to 6 medium cucumbers	3 cups granulated sugar
3 to 4 green and/or red bell peppers	2 cups apple cider vinegar
3 to 4 medium onions	2½ teaspoons celery seeds
¼ cup kosher or pickling salt	2½ teaspoons mustard seeds
Cold water, about 4 to 6 quarts	½ teaspoon turmeric

1 Peel the cucumbers and remove the seeds. Finely chop them in a food processor fitted with a metal blade to measure 6 cups.

2 Remove the stems and seeds from the bell peppers. Finely chop them in a food processor fitted with a metal blade to measure 3 cups.

3 Remove the skin of the onions. Finely chop them in a food processor fitted with a metal blade to measure 3 cups.

4 Combine the vegetables in a 5- to 6-quart bowl. Sprinkle them with salt and add cold water to cover the veggies. Cover the bowl; let the veggies stand at room temperature for 2 hours. Rinse the veggies with running water in batches in a colander. Drain well.

5 Combine the sugar, vinegar, celery seeds, mustard seeds, and turmeric in a 5- to 6-quart pot. Bring the liquid to a boil over high heat, stirring occasionally to dissolve the sugar. Add the drained vegetables and return the mixture to a boil. Reduce the heat to medium-high and simmer, uncovered, stirring occasionally, for 20 to 30 minutes, or until most of the excess liquid has evaporated.

6 While your relish is cooking, prepare your canning jars and two-piece caps (lids and screw bands) according to the manufacturer's instructions. Keep the jars and lids hot. (For the full scoop on water-bath canning and detailed instructions on preparing and filling your jars and testing the seals, see Book I, Chapter 2.)

7 Spoon and lightly compact the hot relish into the prepared jars. Release any air bubbles (refer to Figure 3-1); then add more relish and liquid to maintain a headspace of ¹/₂ inch.

8 Wipe the jar rims; then seal the jars with the two-piece caps, hand-tightening the bands. Process your filled jars in a water bath for 10 minutes from the point of boiling. Remove the jars from the boiling water with a jar lifter. Place them on a clean kitchen towel or paper towels, away from drafts. After the jars cool completely, test the seals. If you find jars that haven't sealed, refrigerate them and use them within 2 months.

Pickled Cucumbers Are Just Pickles

Not all cucumbers are the same or can be pickled in the same way. The common salad cucumber, for example, has a dark-green, waxy skin that's so thick the brine solution can't penetrate the waxy coating. Use this cucumber when your recipe doesn't specify "pickling cucumbers," like the recipe for Mixed Pickled Veggies in this chapter. When you want pickles, use a *pickling cucumber*. The skin of a pickling cucumber is thin, not waxy, and is left on the cucumber. Pickling cucumbers are about 4 inches in length — smaller than salad cucumbers. Don't eat pickling cucumbers raw; their flavor is extremely bitter.

For a few of these recipes, you need to seed a cucumber. To do so, peel the cucumber, cut it in half lengthwise, and then scoop out the seeds with a small spoon. Easy enough, huh?

⟳ Speedy Dill Pickles

This recipe makes an old-fashioned dill pickle in almost the blink of an eye.

Preparation time: 30 minutes (not including soaking time)

Cooking time: 5 minutes

Processing time: Quarts, 15 minutes; pints, 10 minutes

Yield: 3 quarts or 6 pints

4 pounds pickling cucumbers	*1 tablespoon whole mixed pickling spices*
6 tablespoons kosher or pickling salt	*18 black peppercorns*
3 cups distilled white vinegar	*3 tablespoons dill seed*
3 cups water	*Fresh dill sprigs (optional)*

1 Wash your cucumbers. Leave them whole if they're smaller than 4 inches in diameter. For larger cucumbers, cut them into slices or cut them lengthwise, in halves or quarters.

2 Prepare your canning jars and two-piece caps (lids and screw bands) according to the manufacturer's instructions. Keep the jars and lids hot. (For information on water-bath canning and detailed instructions on preparing and filling your jars and testing the seals, see Book I, Chapter 2.)

3 Combine the salt, water, and vinegar in a 3- to 4-quart saucepan. Bring the liquid to a boil over high heat, stirring occasionally to dissolve the sugar. Keep the liquid hot.

4 Snuggly pack the cucumbers into your prepared jars. To each quart jar, add 1 teaspoon of pickling spices, 6 peppercorns, and 1 tablespoon of dill seed. To each pint jar, add $1/2$ teaspoon of pickling spices, 3 peppercorns, and $1^1/2$ teaspoons of dill seed. If you're using fresh dill, add a sprig or two to each quart or pint jar in between the inside edge of the jar and the cucumbers.

5 Ladle the hot liquid into your filled jars, leaving a headspace of $1/2$ inch in the quart jars and a headspace of $1/4$ inch in the pint jars. Completely submerge the cucumbers in the liquid. If they protrude from the jar, adjust them until you have the proper headspace; otherwise, internal pressure may prevent the lids from properly sealing. Release any air bubbles with a nonreactive tool (refer to Figure 3-1). Add more liquid to the jar if the level drops after releasing the air bubbles.

6 Wipe the jar rims; then seal the jars with the two-piece caps, hand-tightening the bands. Process your filled jars in a water bath — 15 minutes for quart jars; 10 minutes for pint jars — both from the point of boiling. Remove the jars with a jar lifter. Place them on a clean kitchen or paper towel, away from drafts. After the jars cool completely, test the seals. If you find ones that haven't sealed, refrigerate and use within 2 months.

Vary It! For kosher-style dill pickles, add 2 cloves of peeled, halved garlic to each jar of pickles.

⌒ Bread and Butter Pickles

Wait until you try these tartly sweet pickles. The onion pieces are an added bonus of flavor. These pickles certainly aren't what you find at your supermarket.

Preparation time: 30 minutes (not including the soaking time)

Cooking time: 5 minutes

Processing time: 15 minutes

Yield: 4 to 5 pints

4 pounds pickling cucumbers

4 small to medium onions

½ cup kosher or pickling salt

Ice water, about 4 to 6 quarts

5 cups granulated sugar

4 cups distilled white vinegar

2 tablespoons mustard seed

2½ teaspoons celery seed

1½ teaspoons turmeric

1 Slice the cucumbers into ¼-inch-thick rounds. Peel the onions and cut them in half lengthwise from the tip to the bottom core. Lay them on a cutting board, cut side down, and slice them, starting at the top of the onion, to a thickness of ¼ inch. Place the cucumber and onion slices in a pickling crock or two 5- to 6-quart bowls. Sprinkle them with salt. Add ice water to cover the vegetables. Stir them once; then cover the bowl and let the veggies stand at room temperature for 3 hours. Transfer the veggies to a colander and rinse them thoroughly with running water (you may need to do this in more than one batch). Drain well. Roll the pieces in a clean, dry kitchen towel to partially dry them.

2 Prepare your canning jars and two-piece caps (lids and screw bands) according to the manufacturer's instructions. Keep the jars and lids hot. (For the full scoop on water-bath canning and detailed instructions on preparing and filling your jars and testing the seals, see Book I, Chapter 2.)

3 Combine the sugar, vinegar, mustard and celery seed, and turmeric in an 8- to 10-quart pot. Bring the liquid to a boil over high heat, stirring occasionally to dissolve the sugar and mix the spices. Add the vegetables and return the mixture to a boil. Reduce the heat to medium-high and simmer, uncovered, for 5 minutes.

4 Pack the hot pickles into the prepared jars, leaving a headspace of ¼ inch. Add the hot liquid, leaving a headspace of ¼ inch. Release any air bubbles with a nonreactive tool (refer to Figure 3-1). Add more pickles and liquid to the jar, maintaining ¼ inch of headspace for both the pickles and the liquid.

5 Wipe the jar rims; then seal the jars with the two-piece caps, hand-tightening the bands. Process your filled jars in a water bath for 15 minutes from the point of boiling. Remove the jars with a jar lifter. Place them on a clean kitchen or paper towel, away from drafts. After the jars cool completely, test the seals. If you find jars that haven't sealed, refrigerate them and use them within 2 months.

Pickling Veggies

Pickled vegetables are delicious additions to green salads or a relish plate. Enjoy these treats for a change of pace from plain, raw vegetables.

 *Spiced Pickled Beets*

Use beets that are small and tender, not larger than 2 inches in diameter. Purchase beets with the top leaves attached. If the leaves are wilted and quite dark, the beets aren't fresh; continue your search for fresher beets.

Preparation time: 1 hour and 10 minutes

Cooking time: 25 minutes

Processing time: 30 minutes

Yield: 4 to 5 pints

4 pounds beets	*1 tablespoon mustard seeds*
3 cups thinly sliced white or yellow onions (about 3 medium)	*1 teaspoon kosher or pickling salt*
2½ cups apple cider vinegar	*1 teaspoon whole allspice*
1½ cups water	*1 teaspoon whole cloves*
2 cups granulated sugar	*3 cinnamon sticks, broken into pieces*

1 Trim your beets, leaving the taproots and 2 inches of the stems. Wash and drain the beets, using a stiff brush to remove any clinging soil. Cover the beets with water in a 5- to 6-quart pot. Bring the water to a boil over high heat and cook the beets until they pierce easily with a fork, about 20 to 30 minutes. Drain the beets. Run cold water over them and remove the skin. Remove the stem and taproot. Slice the beets into ¼-inch-thick slices. Place the beets in a bowl; set them aside.

2 Prepare your canning jars and two-piece caps (lids and screw bands) according to the manufacturer's instructions. Keep the jars and lids hot. (For information on water-bath canning and detailed instructions on preparing and filling your jars and testing the seals, see Book I, Chapter 2.)

3 Place the onions, vinegar, water, sugar, salt, mustard seeds, allspice, cloves, and cinnamon sticks in a 5- to 6-quart pot. Bring the liquid to a boil over high heat; reduce the heat and simmer the mixture for 5 minutes. Add your beet slices and simmer the mixture to heat the beets, about 3 to 5 minutes. Remove the cinnamon stick pieces.

4 Pack the hot beets and onions into the hot jars, leaving a headspace of ¹/₄ inch. Ladle the hot liquid over the beets, leaving a headspace of ¹/₄ inch. Release any air bubbles (refer to Figure 3-1); then add more beets and liquid to maintain a headspace of ¹/₄ inch.

5 Wipe the jar rims; then seal the jars with the two-piece caps, hand-tightening the bands. Process your jars in a water bath for 30 minutes from the point of boiling. Remove the jars with a jar lifter. Place them on a clean kitchen or paper towel, away from drafts. After the jars cool completely, test the seals. If you find ones that haven't sealed, refrigerate and use within 2 months.

Mixed Pickled Veggies

The vibrant colors and the variety of vegetables in this recipe are sure to please all tastes. Prepare your vegetables and get them soaking the night before you can them. After putting them into the brine solution, forget about 'em until the next day!

Preparation time: 30 minutes (not including overnight soaking)

Cooking time: 15 minutes

Processing time: 15 minutes

Yield: 6 pints

4 quarts water, at room temperature

1 cup kosher or pickling salt

4 cups (1 small) cauliflower, cut into florets

4 cups (about 2 large) cucumbers, peeled, seeds removed, cut into 1-inch-thick slices, then quartered

2 cups (about 4) carrots, cut into 1¹/₂-inch pieces

2 cups (³/₄ to 1 pound) green beans, cut into 1¹/₂-inch slices

2 cups (about 10 ounces) pearl onions, peeled

1 each green, red, and yellow bell peppers, cut into wide strips

6¹/₂ cups distilled white vinegar

2 cups granulated sugar

¹/₄ cup mustard seeds

2 tablespoons celery seeds

7 spicy, dried red chile peppers (one for the vinegar mixture and one for each jar)

1 On the first day, dissolve the salt in the water in a 5- to 6-quart bowl. After the salt dissolves, add the vegetables. Cover the bowl; leave it in a cool place for 12 to 18 hours. On the second day, thoroughly drain your vegetables in a colander. Don't rinse them.

2 Prepare your canning jars and two-piece caps (lids and screw bands) according to the manufacturer's instructions. Keep the jars and lids hot. (For the full scoop on water-bath canning and detailed instructions on preparing and filling your jars and testing the seals, see Book I, Chapter 2.)

3 Combine the vinegar, sugar, mustard seeds, celery seeds, and one chile pepper in an 8-quart pot. Bring the liquid to a boil over high heat, boiling for 3 minutes to dissolve the sugar and soften the seeds and the chile. Add your vegetables; then return the liquid to a simmer, heating the veggies until they're hot throughout — about 5 minutes, depending on the size of your vegetables.

4 Pack your hot vegetables into the prepared jars, leaving a headspace of $1/4$ inch. Add one dried red chile to each jar, gently sliding it between the veggies and the inside of the jar so it can be seen. Ladle the hot liquid over the vegetables, leaving a headspace of $1/4$ inch. Release any air bubbles with a nonreactive tool (refer to Figure 3-1), adding more vegetables and liquid to maintain a headspace of $1/4$ inch.

5 Wipe the jar rims; then seal the jars with the two-piece caps, hand-tightening the bands. Process your filled jars in a water bath for 15 minutes from the point of boiling. Remove the jars from the boiling water with a jar lifter. Place them on a clean kitchen towel or paper towels, away from drafts. After the jars cool completely, test the seals. If you find jars that haven't sealed, refrigerate them and use them within 2 months.

Chapter 4

Drying Fruits and Other Foods

Drying — a preserving method that dates back to ancient times — is the oldest method known for preserving food. This process removes moisture from food by exposing it to a low temperature. Good air circulation assists in evenly drying the food.

Although you can use an electric dehydrator for dehydrating food, this chapter focuses on oven drying or sun-drying — methods everyone has access to.

Drying Fruit

Dried fruit has many uses — from snacks to sauces, dessert toppings to baked-good fillings. Many of the best fruits for this method oxidize and brown easily when their flesh is exposed to air, but you have some options for preventing any color change in your fruit.

Using the best, perfectly ripened fruit for drying is important for a dried fruit that's worthy of high marks and rave reviews. Most fruit is suited for drying. Fruits *not* recommended for drying include avocados, citrus fruits (except for the peel), crab apples, guavas, melons, olives, pomegranates, and quinces.

The time required for drying fruit ranges from a few hours to many days. As you may expect, an electric dehydrator gives you the shortest drying time, whereas sun-drying gives you the lengthiest (and it requires a lot of your attention and perfect weather conditions to boot). Oven-drying falls in between the two.

Drying time is determined by the moisture in your fruit, the size of your fruit pieces, the moisture in the air (even if you're using an oven), and the pre-treating method you choose. Larger pieces of fruit take longer to dry than smaller pieces of the same fruit. Consequently, the smaller you cut your peaches or the thinner you slice your bananas, the less time you'll need to produce a safely preserved dried product.

Pre-treating fruit

Pre-treating, which retards the enzyme activity in the fruit that causes it to ripen, makes your fruit look good by preventing *oxidation* and *discoloration,* the darkening of the fruit flesh after it's exposed to air. Using a pre-treating method before drying your fruit isn't as important as when you're canning fresh fruit. In fact, it's not necessary at all, but it does shorten the drying time.

Your pre-treating choices are as follows:

- **Water blanching:** This method is the best for maintaining a fruit's bright color. Immerse the fruit in boiling water for a short period of time and then immediately plunge it into ice water to stop the cooking process. Drain the fruit well.

- **Steam blanching:** This method, which is the most common for fruit, helps the fruit retain more of its water-soluble vitamins and minerals than the water-blanching method does. The steam quickly heats the fruit, shortens the drying and rehydrating times, sets the color and flavor, and slows down the enzyme activity, in some cases killing micro-organisms.

  Hang a colander on the inside edge of a pot of boiling water, making sure the colander doesn't touch the water. Place your fruit in the colander and heat it as directed in your recipe. Cool your fruit quickly in a bowl of ice water; then drain the fruit well.

- **Dipping:** In this process, you immerse your fruit into a liquid or a solution to control the darkening. Dipping helps the fruit retain vitamins A and C, which are lost during the oxidation process. You can use any of these liquids:

  - **Lemon or lime juice:** Fresh citrus juice is the most natural of the dipping solutions. Mix 1 cup of juice with 1 quart of water. Soak the fruit no longer than 10 minutes; drain thoroughly before drying.

  - **Ascorbic acid:** This white, powdery substance is available in drugstores. Its common name is vitamin C. Dissolve 1 tablespoon of powder in 1 quart of water. Don't soak your fruit longer than 1 hour; drain it well before drying.

  - **Commercial antioxidants:** You can find these products in supermarkets or wherever canning supplies are sold. Some common brand names are Fruit-Fresh and Ever-Fresh. Follow the directions on the product package for making your solution and determining the soaking time.

At one time, sulfuring fruit was popular for preserving fruit color and vita-mins in dried fruit. Sulfur is unsafe for any drying method other than sun-drying because the sulfur produces dangerous fumes of sulfur dioxide when it's heated, as it would be if you used an oven. People with asthma or other allergies should avoid this product.

Evaluating dryness

Knowing when your fruit is properly dried is important. Normally, touching and tasting a cooled piece of fruit gives you the answer, but when you're in doubt and you positively, absolutely need to know the moisture in your fruit has reduced enough, follow these basic steps:

1. **Prepare your fruit and weigh the portion you'll be drying.**

   Suppose, for example, that you have 20 pounds of prepared peaches.

2. **Look up the amount of moisture (water content) in your fruit from the fruit list in this chapter.**

   According to the fruit list, you know that the water content of peaches is 89 percent.

3. **Determine the total water weight of your fruit.**

   Multiply the weight of your prepared fruit before drying by the water content percentage from the fruit list in the section "Drying recipes, fruit by fruit." For the peach example that's

   20 pounds of peaches × 0.89 water content = 17.8 pounds of water.

4. **Calculate the amount of water (by weight) that needs to be removed from the fruit during the drying process.**

   Multiply your total water weight (your answer from Step 3) by 0.8 (the minimum amount of water you want to remove from your fruit during the drying process). Continuing with the example, that's

   Total water weight of 17.8 × 0.8 = 14.24 pounds of water to remove.

5. **Weigh your fruit when you think it's done; then subtract the amount of the water you want removed (your answer from Step 4) from the total weight of the fruit you prepared for drying (your answer from Step 1).**

   If your fruit weighs this amount or less, your processing is successful. If your fruit weighs more than this amount, return it for more drying. For the peach example:

   20 pounds of prepared fruit − 14.24 pounds of water to remove = 5.76 pounds of dried fruit as your goal.

Properly dried fruit has 80 to 95 percent of its moisture removed.

Oven-drying fruit

If you have an oven — gas or electric — that maintains a temperature between 130 and 150 degrees with the door propped open, you're ready to start drying.

To test your oven's temperature, put an oven thermometer in the center of your oven with the door propped open. Your oven must maintain a temperature of 130 to 150 degrees for one hour to safely dry food. Higher temperatures cook — rather than dry — the food.

This procedure for oven-drying is simple. Here's a summary for drying fruit in an oven:

1. **Preheat your oven to the temperature setting in your recipe.**

2. **Wash and prepare your food as directed in your recipe.**

3. **Place your food on the tray.**

   Leave spaces between the pieces of food so that they're not touching each other or the edge of the tray.

4. **Place your filled trays in the oven.**

   Leave the door propped open to allow moisture to escape from the oven.

5. **If you're using baking sheets or other trays without holes or openings in the bottom, turn your drying fruit.**

   Turning your fruit ensures that it dries evenly. After the first side of the fruit has absorbed all the liquid on the top of the food, turn it over and repeat for the other side. After you've done so on both sides, turn the food occasionally until it's done.

6. **When your fruit appears to be done, completely cool one piece and test it for the level of doneness stated in your recipe.**

7. **Store your cooled food in plastic bags, glass containers, or rigid plastic containers with airtight seals.**

8. **Label your bags or containers.**

Don't add fresh fruit to partially dried trays of fruit. The fresh fruit increases the humidity in the drying chamber and adds moisture back to your drying fruit. This adjustment in the humidity level affects drying and increases the drying time for both fruits.

Sun-drying fruit

Sun-drying lets you dry large quantities of food at one time but can take days — compared to hours in a conventional oven. In addition, you need perfect weather conditions — 85 degrees or warmer and low to moderate humidity for many consecutive days — which means that only a few climates are suitable for this method. You also need good air circulation, a minimum of air pollution, and insect control around the food.

If you're willing to deal with the variances in weather conditions and the lengthy drying time, follow these steps:

1. **Wash and prepare your food as specified in your recipe.**

2. **Line your drying trays (or racks) with a double layer of cheesecloth or nylon netting.**

3. **Place your food on the trays.**

    Leave space between your pieces of food so they're not touching another piece or the edge of the tray.

4. **Cover your trays with a single layer of cheesecloth or nylon netting to protect your food from insects and dust.**

    Stretch the cover tightly over the trays, not touching the food.

5. **Place your filled trays on benches or tables in full sunlight.**

    Check your trays at different times of the day, keeping them in full sun at all times. If your nighttime temperature varies more than 20 degrees from the temperature at the hottest part of the day, move your trays to a warmer area (indoors or an enclosed patio area) for the evening, returning them outside when they can be in full sunlight. Relocate the trays if it rains, regardless of the temperature.

    If you use baking sheets or other trays without holes or openings in the bottom, you must turn your fruit to achieve an evenly dried product. After the first side of the fruit has absorbed all the liquid on the top of the food, turn it over and repeat for the other side. After you've done so on both sides, turn the food daily until it's done.

6. **Check your fruit daily for evidence of mold.**

7. **When your fruit appears to be done, completely cool one piece and test it for the level of doneness listed in your recipe.**

8. **Store your cooled food in plastic bags, glass containers, or rigid plastic containers with airtight seals.**

9. **Label your bags or containers.**

Rehydrating your dried fruit

Most dried fruit is used just as it's stored after the drying process. It's great when added to hot or cold cereal or baking batters. It's also perfect if you're always on the go, because it travels well and can be eaten right out of the container.

If you prefer your dried fruit a bit chewier, soften or rehydrate it. *Rehydrating* is the process of adding moisture back to the fruit. Use rehydrated fruit right away because it's not dry enough to go back on the shelf without spoiling.

Your rehydrating options are as follows:

✔ **Boiling water:** Place the desired amount of fruit in a bowl. Cover the fruit with boiling water, allowing it to stand for 5 to 10 minutes to plump, or add moisture, to your fruit. Use this method when adding fruit to jams, chutney, or baked goods. Substitute fruit juice or wine for water.

✔ **Steaming:** Place your fruit in a steamer or a colander over a pot of boiling water (refer to steam blanching earlier in this chapter). Steam your fruit for 3 to 5 minutes, or until the fruit plumps.

✔ **Sprinkling:** Put your fruit in a shallow bowl. Sprinkle the fruit with water or fruit juice. Allow it to soak in the moisture. Repeat the process until the fruit reaches the level of moistness you desire.

Drying recipes, fruit by fruit

Properly dried fruit produces a superior product for use at a later time. After your fruit is dried, properly labeled, and stored, you'll find it hard to believe that 10 pounds of fresh apples produces only 1$\frac{1}{2}$ pounds of dried apples!

Apples

✔ **Varieties:** Apples with tart flavors and firm texture dry best. Some good choices are Pippin, Granny Smith, Jonathan, and Rome Beauty.

✔ **Preparation:** Wash, peel, and core your apples. Slice into rings, $\frac{1}{4}$- to $\frac{1}{2}$-inch thick.

✔ **Pre-treating:** Dipping (refer to "Pre-treating fruit," earlier in this chapter).

✔ **Drying time:** Dehydrator or conventional oven: 130 to 135 degrees for 6 to 8 hours. Sun-drying: 2 to 3 days.

✔ **Testing for doneness:** Soft, pliable, and leathery. Water content: 84 percent.

Apricots

- ✔ **Preparation:** Wash, cut in half, and discard the pits.

- ✔ **Pre-treating:** Dipping (refer to "Pre-treating fruit," earlier in this chapter).

- ✔ **Drying time:** Dehydrator or conventional oven: 130 to 135 degrees for 8 to 12 hours. Sun-drying: 2 to 3 days.

- ✔ **Testing for doneness:** Pliable and leathery, with no moisture pockets. Water content: 85 percent.

Bananas

- ✔ **Preparation:** Use ripe, yellow-skinned fruit with a few brown speckles. Peel and slice to a thickness of $1/4$- to $1/2$-inch.

- ✔ **Pre-treating:** Dipping (refer to "Pre-treating fruit," earlier in this section).

- ✔ **Drying time:** Dehydrator or conventional oven: 130 to 135 degrees for 6 to 8 hours. Sun-drying: 2 days.

- ✔ **Testing for doneness:** Pliable and crisp, almost brittle. Water content: 70 percent.

Blueberries and cranberries

- ✔ **Preparation:** Use plump berries that aren't bruised. Drop into boiling water for 30 seconds. Place the drained berries on paper towels to remove any excess water.

- ✔ **Pre-treating:** None.

- ✔ **Drying time:** Dehydrator or conventional oven: 130 to 135 degrees for 12 to 24 hours. Sun-drying: 2 to 4 days.

- ✔ **Testing for doneness:** Leathery and hard, but shriveled like raisins. Water content: 83 percent.

Cherries

- ✔ **Varieties:** Any sweet or sour cherries work well.

- ✔ **Preparation:** Wash, cut in half, and remove the pits.

- ✔ **Pre-treating:** None.

- ✔ **Drying time:** Dehydrator or conventional oven: 165 degrees for 2 to 3 hours; reduce heat to 135 degrees for 10 to 22 hours. Sun-drying: 2 to 4 days.

- ✔ **Testing for doneness:** Leathery, hard, and slightly sticky. Water content: sweet cherries, 80 percent; sour cherries, 84 percent.

Citrus peel

- ✔ **Varieties:** Grapefruits, lemons, limes, oranges, or tangerines with unblemished skin. Don't use fruit with color added.

- ✔ **Preparation:** Wash and remove a thin layer of peel with a vegetable peeler. Use peel without any of the white, bitter pith attached.

- ✔ **Pre-treating:** None.

- ✔ **Drying time:** Dehydrator or conventional oven: 135 degrees for 1 to 2 hours. Sun-drying: Not recommended.

- ✔ **Testing for doneness:** Crisp, not brittle. Water content: 86 percent.

Grapes

- ✔ **Varieties:** Use seedless varieties.

- ✔ **Preparation:** Dip in boiling water for 30 seconds. Remove stems before or after drying. Drain grapes on paper towels.

- ✔ **Pre-treating:** None.

- ✔ **Drying time:** Dehydrator or conventional oven: 130 to 135 degrees for 24 to 48 hours. Sun-drying: 3 to 6 days.

- ✔ **Testing for doneness:** Shriveled and pliable, with no moisture pockets. Water content: 81 percent.

Nectarines and peaches

- ✔ **Varieties:** Any ripe fruit works well. Clingstone or freestone varieties, where the fruit separates easily from the pit, are easier to work with.

- ✔ **Preparation:** Remove peels and discard the pits. Slice or leave in halves. (*Note:* Peel may be left on nectarines, but place them skin side down, cut side up, on the tray.)

- ✔ **Pre-treating:** Dipping (refer to "Pre-treating fruit," earlier in this section).

- ✔ **Drying time:** Dehydrator or conventional oven: 130 to 135 degrees for 10 to 12 hours. Sun-drying: 2 to 6 days.

- ✔ **Testing for doneness:** Leathery, pliable, and shriveled, with no moisture pockets. Water content: nectarines, 82 percent; peaches, 89 percent.

Pears

- ✔ **Preparation:** Wash, peel, and core. Cut into halves or quarters, or slice to a thickness of ¹/₂-inch.

- ✔ **Pre-treating:** Dipping (refer to "Pre-treating fruit," earlier in this section).

✔ **Drying time:** Dehydrator or conventional oven: 130 to 135 degrees for 12 to 18 hours. Sun-drying: 2 to 3 days.

✔ **Testing for doneness:** Leathery, with no moisture pockets. Water content: 83 percent.

Pineapple

✔ **Preparation:** Use fully ripe fruit. Cut away the peel and the eyes and remove the core. Cut into $^1/_2$-inch-thick rings.

✔ **Pre-treating:** None.

✔ **Drying time:** Dehydrator or conventional oven: 130 to 135 degrees for 12 to 18 hours. Sun-drying: 4 to 5 days.

✔ **Testing for doneness:** Leathery, not sticky. Water content: 86 percent.

Plums

✔ **Preparation:** Wash, cut in half, and discard pits. Leave in half or cut into $^1/_4$- to $^1/_2$-inch-thick slices.

✔ **Pre-treating:** None.

✔ **Drying time:** Dehydrator or conventional oven: 130 to 135 degrees for 12 to 18 hours. Sun-drying: 4 to 5 days. (***Note:*** When drying fruit halves, place them skin side down, cut side up, on the drying tray.)

✔ **Testing for doneness:** Pliable and shriveled. Water content: 87 percent.

Strawberries

✔ **Preparation:** Wash and remove caps. Leave whole, cut in half, or slice to a thickness of $^1/_2$-inch.

✔ **Pre-treating:** None.

✔ **Drying time:** Dehydrator or conventional oven: 130 to 135 degrees for 8 to 12 hours. Sun-drying: 1 to 2 days.

✔ **Testing for doneness:** Pliable, hard, and almost crisp. Water content: 90 percent. (***Note:*** Strawberries don't rehydrate well.)

Recipes to get you started

Dried fruit is a great snack — healthy, tasty, and portable, as the two recipes in this section show. Each recipe uses a variety of dried fruit. If you don't have all the fruits specified, use what you do have. It's all good.

🍑 Dried Fruit Medley

This is a great blend for a quick and nutritious snack. Make up small packages for a grab-and-go snack. **Note:** For this recipe, sun-drying isn't recommended.

Preparation time: 15 minutes

Yield: 4¹/₂ cups

¹/₂ cup toasted almonds	¹/₂ cup dried banana slices
¹/₂ cup sunflower seeds	¹/₂ cup dried pears, cut into ¹/₂-inch pieces
¹/₂ cup dried apples, cut into ¹/₂-inch pieces	¹/₂ cup dried pineapple, cut into ¹/₂-inch pieces
¹/₂ cup dried apricots, cut into ¹/₂-inch pieces	¹/₂ cup raisins

1 Place all the ingredients in a large bowl; stir to combine and distribute the fruit and nuts evenly.

2 Store your mix in home-canning jars or other airtight containers.

Vary It! Substitute your favorite nuts or fruits, or use up small amounts of dried fruit.

⌕ *Fruit Leather*

Fruit leather is dried pureed fruit, rolled up in plastic. The result is a chewy, fruity, taffylike treat. Some good choices for fruit leathers are apples, apricots, berries, cherries, nectarines, peaches, pears, pineapple, and plums.

Preparation time: 20 minutes or longer (determined by the amount of fruit you're pureeing and the preparation involved preparing the fruit for pureeing)

Drying time: Depends on the amount of moisture in your fruit; allow up to 18 hours in a conventional oven.

Yield: 1 cup of fruit puree makes 2 to 3 servings; 2$^1/_2$ cups covers an 18-x-14-inch area, $^1/_4$-inch thick (see ***Tip*** at the end of this recipe)

Fresh fruit of your choice

Water or fruit juice (optional)

Corn syrup or honey (optional)

Ground spices (optional), choose from allspice, cinnamon, cloves, ginger, mace, nutmeg, or

pumpkin pie spice (Use $^1/_8$ to $^1/_4$ teaspoon for 4 cups of puree.)

Pure extract flavors (optional), choose from almond, lemon, orange, or vanilla (Use $^1/_4$ to $^1/_2$ teaspoon for 4 cups of puree.)

1 Cover your drying trays or baking sheets with a heavy-duty, food-grade plastic wrap. If your dehydrator comes with special sheets for your trays, use those.

2 Wash your fruit and remove any blemishes. Prepare your fruit as directed in the guidelines for preparing your fruit in this chapter.

3 Puree the fruit in a blender until smooth. Strain out any small seeds, if desired, with a mesh strainer or a food mill. If your puree is too thick, add water or fruit juice, 1 tablespoon or less at a time. If your puree is too tart, add corn syrup or honey, 1 teaspoon at a time. If you're adding spices or other flavorings, add them now.

4 Spread the puree evenly onto the prepared trays to a thickness of $^1/_8$-inch in the center and $^1/_4$-inch around the edges. If you use cooked fruit, it must be completely cool before spreading it on the trays.

5 Dry your fruit leather at a temperature of 135 degrees in a dehydrator or 140 degrees in a conventional oven. Dry the fruit until it's pliable and leathery, with no stickiness in the center.

6 Roll the warm fruit leather, still attached to the plastic, into a roll. Leave the rolls whole, or cut them into pieces with scissors. Store the rolls in a plastic bag or an airtight container.

Tip: Here's an idea of how much fresh fruit you'll need for one cup of puree: apples, $^1/_2$ to $^3/_4$ pounds (about 2 to 3) for 1 cup; apricots or peaches, $^3/_4$ to 1 pound (about 6 apricots or 2 to 3 peaches) for 1 cup; strawberries, 1 pint of strawberries for 1 cup.

Drying Herbs

If you grow your own herbs or love strolling through local farmers'markets and smelling the lingering aromas of rosemary, basil, parsley, lemon verbena, and whatever else was brought to market, you've probably found yourself having more herbs than you've known what to do with. Air-drying herbs is easy and the perfect solution for saving your fresh herbs.

Presenting your step-by-step guide

If you're harvesting herbs from a garden, do so in the morning after the moisture on the leaves has dried. Also, cut the stems — don't pick them — leaving an extra inch or two for tying them in bunches.

Follow these steps for drying herbs:

1. **Rinse your herbs and pat them dry with a paper towel.**

   Dip them quickly in a bowl of cool water and shake off the excess water. Be sure to get them completely dry to prevent mildew.

2. **Using cotton string or thread, tie the herb stalks near the cut part of the stem in small bunches (no more than five or six stems).**

   Don't mix your herb bunches, because flavors transfer during the drying process.

   If you want to protect the herbs from sunlight and catch loose seeds for planting, put the tied herb bundle in a paper bag with holes or slits cut in it for air circulation. Place the herb bundle upside down in the bag with the stems toward the top opening of the bag. Tie the top of the bag closed.

3. **Hang the herbs (or the herb bag) upside down in a warm room — the kitchen works well — near a south-facing window and out of direct sunlight.**

   Your herbs will dry in two to three weeks with good air circulation. You know your herbs are dry when they crumble easily.

4. **When your herbs are dry, remove the leaves from the stems.**

   Crush soft leaves (like basil, sage, and oregano) by hand. Leave harder leaves (like rosemary, tarragon, and thyme) whole, crushing them with a rolling pin before using them.

5. **Store your dried herbs in small containers.**

   Glass jars with tight-fitting lids work best. For your herbs to maintain the best flavor during storage, keep them away from heat, light, and your refrigerator.

Using your dried herbs

When adding dried herbs to your food, remember that less is best. Dried herbs are stronger than fresh herbs. You can always add flavor, but it's difficult to remove too much of a flavor. Following are two recipes:

- **Herb butter:** Combine your favorite herbs and roll a stick of butter in them to coat the stick, or soften the butter to room temperature and mix the dried herbs directly into the butter. Chill the butter; cut it into slices, or make rounds with a melon baller for serving.

- **Rice mix:** Package ready-to-make mixes with your freshly dried herbs. Combine the following in a bowl: 1 cup of long-grain rice, 2 teaspoons bouillon granules (chicken, beef, or vegetable), 2 to 3 teaspoons of one or more dried herbs, and ¼ teaspoon kosher salt. Transfer the mix to a glass container or clear, food-safe bag. Seal the jar or tie the bag closed. Add a card with the following instructions:

  "Add the rice mix to 2 cups of water in a 2- to 3-quart saucepan. Bring the rice to a boil over high heat, stir, cover, and reduce the heat to medium-low. Cook for about 30 minutes without peeking. Remove the rice from the heat (don't lift that lid to peek) and let it stand for 30 minutes. Fluff the rice with a fork and serve immediately."

Making Jerky

Beef or turkey jerky is a wonderful taste treat. Homemade jerky is superior in quality and flavor to most commercial brands, and it's easy to make. A favorite cut of meat to slice for jerky preparation is flank steak. Whatever your personal preference, figure that 3 pounds of meat yields approximately 1 pound of jerky.

To make your own beef or turkey jerky, follow these steps:

1. **Firm up the cut of meat in the freezer before you begin slicing.**

   Your goal isn't to freeze the meat completely, just enough to help you make the cuts more even.

2. **Remove any excess fat; then slice the meat across the grain to a thickness between ⅛ and ¼ inches.**

3. **Marinate the sliced meat overnight in a refrigerator in a tightly sealed container.**

   Teriyaki marinade tastes yummy, and you can make it easily enough by combining 1 cup of soy sauce, ½ cup of dark brown sugar, 2 teaspoons of ginger, 4 to 6 cloves of crushed garlic, and ½ teaspoon of freshly ground black pepper.

4. **Spray your oven racks with a vegetable spray and then spread the strips of meat across the racks.**

   Be sure to place a sheet of aluminum foil over the bottom of the oven to catch the drippings — unless of course you particularly enjoy creating an awful mess.

5. **Set your oven temperature to 140 degrees, the ideal temperature for drying meat.**

   You'll need an internal oven thermometer because on most ovens, 140 degrees is toward the middle setting of the warm label on the knob — not particularly precise.

6. **Prop the oven door open a few inches so that the moisture can escape easily.**

7. **Let the meat dry for approximately 8 hours.**

   When it's done, the jerky should be dry, but not brittle, to the touch.

Chapter 5

Outdoor Cooking

*P*icture this: a lazy river, a setting sun, a rock to lean against, a slow-rolling campfire, and the sizzle and smell of freshly caught trout being sautéed in a skillet. Or imagine a campsite at twilight with a stew bubbling over a fire.

Although you *can* fix dinner outside using a two-tiered gas grill with an electric side range, in this chapter, outdoor cooking means something a bit different. Namely, it means getting back to basics and enjoying the great outdoors, whether you're cooking in your own backyard or at a campsite.

Anyone can cook in the great outdoors, preparing everything from simple one-dish entrees and desserts to complete multicourse meals. Doing so successfully isn't rocket science. It just takes some hot coals, the right tools, and a few tricks up your sleeve. This chapter tells you what you need to know and includes easy recipes for the beginning camp cook.

Outdoor Cooking Techniques

Cooking outdoors can be as authentic or as convenient as you want it to be. After all, technically speaking, you can place your cookware inside a covered barbecue grill, set the temperature to whatever you want, and call yourself an outdoor cook. Most people, however, use one of the following techniques:

- ✓ **Cooking a single dish over hot embers or coals:** This is the easiest cooking technique for the beginning outdoor cook, because you only have to manage a single dish at a time.

- ✓ **Stacking pans over hot embers or coals to cook more than one dish at a time:** This technique lets you cook plenty of food without taking up any more ground space than single-dish cooking requires (see Figure 5-1). You actually stack your Dutch ovens on top of each other over a heat source. The food that requires the most heat goes on the bottom of the stack, and the food that requires the least goes on top. As you gain more experience with outdoor cooking and want to broaden your repertoire, you may find yourself stacking pans.

Figure 5-1:
Stacked
ovens let
you cook
more than
one item at
a time.

Photograph courtesy of Lodge Manufacturing Co.

This technique works best for foods that require an even distribution of heat rather than foods that require the heat source to come primarily from the top or the bottom of the pan. (Refer to the section "Heat sources and cooking methods," later in this chapter, for information.)

A challenge in stacked cooking is that if you want to check or stir a dish that isn't on the top of the heap, you have to move all the pans above it. Of course, some would argue that this is part of the fun.

✔ **Cooking in a pit:** If you're so inclined, you can actually bury a Dutch oven in a pit of coals. In this method, you build a fire in a hole that you've dug and lined with aluminum foil or stone and, when the coals are ready, place your covered dish inside, cover it with dirt and more coals, and let it cook. This cooking technique is slow. Most dishes cooked by this method take 4 to 6 hours. It's best reserved for dishes that don't need to be tended and that (for obvious reasons) are covered.

Rounding Up the Hardware

When you cook outdoors, chances are you're cooking over an open fire or in coals. If that's the case, use cast iron. Cast-iron cookware travels well, cooks evenly, and cleans up easily — just what you need when you're cooking outdoors. It can also tolerate direct contact with the heat source, which, given the outdoor cooking methods outlined in the preceding section, is a good thing. (***Note:*** If you plan to cook on a camp stove, you can use aluminum pans rather than cast iron, if you prefer.) The following sections outline the cookware and accessories you need for outdoor cooking.

Although you can use any kind of cast-iron cookware you have for cooking outdoors, most people rely on one or two pieces: Dutch ovens (called *camp ovens* when they're designed for outdoor use) and skillets with lids. With either of these pieces, you can cook any dish. (***Note:*** All the recipes in this chapter use a skillet or a Dutch oven.)

A camp oven

Although you can use any Dutch oven outside, the type that has legs and a flanged lid, called a *camp oven,* makes outdoor cooking a little easier. The legs let you keep the Dutch oven itself off the coals (and thus avoid getting the cookware too hot), and the flanged lid lets you put coals on top without worrying about them rolling off onto the ground or, when you lift the lid, into your food. The recipes in this chapter are intended for outdoor cooking, so many of them recommend that you use a camp oven.

If you're shopping for a camp oven, look for one that has a reversible lid. These lids function as both a lid and, when flipped over, a griddle. The griddle side is usually slightly concave, which keeps anything you cook in it — pancakes, eggs, bacon, and so on — from spilling or dripping over into the coals.

A skillet with legs and a lid

Like Dutch ovens, you can also find skillets with flanged lids and legs that keep the bottoms of the pans off the hot coals.

If you don't want to spring for skillets and ovens designed specifically for outdoor use, you can use a *spyder* (essentially a cast-iron trivet) to turn any stovetop cast-iron skillet or Dutch oven into an outdoor cooking machine. See the next section, "Going for convenience and comfort," for more info on spyders.

Going for convenience and comfort

Although the following items aren't absolutely necessary when you cook outside, they can make your task a little easier and safer:

- ✓ **Brush:** You use a brush to remove ashes and coals around your pan and on top of the pan's lid. Any plain old ash brush will do.

- ✓ **Oven gloves:** These gloves are essentially extra-long, extra-thick, fire-resistant oven mitts that are sometimes made of leather.

- ✓ **Long utensils:** You want utensils that are as long as possible but still comfortable and safe to wield. The longer the utensil, the farther from the fire you are. You need the standards — spoon, spatula, meat fork, and anything else you need to stir, turn, or prod your food. You may also want to invest in a pair of tongs or a poker that lets you move charcoal coals around safely.

- ✓ **Heavy-duty aluminum foil or metal trash can lid:** Although not a necessity, using aluminum foil or an upside-down aluminum trash can lid (placed in such a way that it doesn't wobble) can help you control the temperature of the coals, especially if the ground is damp or cool. See the section "Making adjustments for weather conditions" later in this chapter for more information.

- ✓ **Lid hook:** Also called a *lid lifter,* this tool, shown in Figure 5-2, lets you remove the lid from your camp oven or skillet without spilling coals and ashes into your dish. Because it's generally long (around 18 inches), it also keeps you away from the heat (not to mention keeping the hair on your arms intact!). Lid hooks come in a variety of lengths. Choose the longest one you can that still lets you comfortably lift the lid.

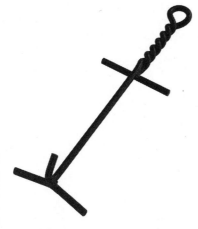

Figure 5-2:
Give that lid
a lift.

Photograph courtesy of Lodge Manufacturing Co.

↳ **Spyder:** Shown in Figure 5-3, a spyder (also known as a *trivet* or *lid stand*) is a three- or four-legged stand that can hold your pans over the fire as the food cooks. A spyder functions as the "legs" for any flat-bottomed cast-iron cookware you may have, essentially turning it into outdoor cookware. Just place the spyder over the coals and your pan on top of the spyder. Instant legs! A spyder can also serve as a place to set a hot lid when you're checking on the food. Spyders come in varying heights.

Figure 5-3: A
spyder with-
out a web.

Photograph courtesy of Lodge Manufacturing Co.

You may want to have two or three spyders of different heights so that you can adjust how close your pan is to the coals.

✔ **Charcoal chimney starter:** A charcoal chimney starter (see Figure 5-4) is beneficial for starting hot coals. It also serves the purpose of keeping extra coals ready and nearby as you cook, because you may need to replenish the hot coals that you use, especially for dishes that cook for a long time.

Figure 5-4:
Gentlemen, start your chimneys.

Photograph courtesy of Lodge Manufacturing Co.

Temperature Control

In principal, outdoor cooking is just like indoor cooking: Using the right cookware and the right temperature, you can make any dish your heart — or your hungry brood — desires. The main difference between the two is how you control the temperature. Your stove has control dials; the rocks or grassy hill that you build your campfire on — even the fire pit in your own backyard — probably doesn't.

When you're cooking outside, your heat source is either wood or charcoal briquettes. Although some people prefer wood embers, most prefer charcoal because it lasts longer and gives you more even heat. For that reason, the recipes in this chapter refer only to charcoal.

Charcoal coals generally give you between 45 minutes and an hour's worth of cooking time, provided that the day isn't windy, which can make the coals burn faster. Avoid charcoal that comes presoaked in lighter fluid: It burns faster.

When you cook outside, you generally don't put your cookware over an open flame. With an open flame, the only way that you can control the cooking temperature is to lift and lower the pan, a task that, although possible, isn't easy. (To make raising and lowering the vessel manageable, you need a tripod or cooking rig.)

The heat source isn't the only added variable when you move from the cozy confines of your kitchen to the great outdoors (or the great backyard). You also have to contend with air temperature, wind, humidity, and the other climactic conditions that Mother Nature doles out. Temperature control in outdoor cooking is as much an art as it is a science. You control cooking temps via the following:

- ✔ The number of coals
- ✔ The location of the heat source
- ✔ Adjustments for weather conditions
- ✔ Your cooking techniques

The following sections go into much greater detail about each of these variables.

The best way to figure out how to control your cooking temperatures is simply to practice and experiment. Before you know it, you'll be cooking up a storm — maybe even *in* a storm.

Number and placement of coals

The number of coals you use and where you put them are key factors in controlling the temperature when you cook in a camp oven. For some cooking techniques (boiling, frying, and sautéing, for example), you put all of your coals under the pan. For these techniques, obviously, you don't need a lid. For other techniques (such as baking and simmering), you arrange some coals on top (hence, you need a lid) and some coals underneath, as shown in Figure 5-5. Simple enough.

Well, almost. Keep reading for explanations of the finer points.

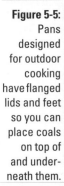

Figure 5-5: Pans designed for outdoor cooking have flanged lids and feet so you can place coals on top of and underneath them.

Photograph courtesy of Lodge Manufacturing Co.

Counting coals

All the recipes in this chapter, and many recipes in other outdoor cooking books, tell you how many coals to place on the lid and how many to place underneath your camp oven or skillet to get the appropriate temperature.

Converting old recipes

Many old recipes don't specify temperature settings. Instead, they offer vague descriptions — to the modern cook's thinking, anyway. If you find old recipes — a common occurrence when you go hunting specifically for cast-iron or outdoor recipes — don't be surprised if the only temperature guide is "Cook (whatever) in a slow oven until done." The following table provides modern equivalents for some of the vague terms you may encounter.

Description	Temperature Equivalent
Slow	250–350 degrees
Moderate	350–400 degrees
Hot	400–450 degrees
Very hot	450–500 degrees

Book I

Country Kitchen Skills

The trick is figuring out how many coals you need when the recipe doesn't specify. Fortunately, cooking temperatures are about the same for indoor conventional ovens as they are for outdoor cooking. So if you'd roast a chicken indoors in a 325-degree oven, you'd use the same temperature when you roast a chicken outdoors. Table 5-1 shows you how many coals you need to attain certain temperatures. The next section, "Heat sources and cooking methods," tells you where to put these coals for different cooking techniques. With this info, you can convert indoor oven recipes (baking, roasting, and so on) for use outdoors.

Table 5-1	Total Number of Coals to Reach Certain Temperatures					
Dutch Oven	*325 Degrees*	*350 Degrees*	*375 Degrees*	*400 Degrees*	*425 Degrees*	*450 Degrees*
8-inch	15	16	17	18	19	20
10-inch	19	21	23	25	27	29
12-inch	23	25	27	29	31	33
14-inch	30	32	34	36	38	40

To increase the temp, you simply add coals; to decrease the temp, you remove them. Although not precise, assume that every coal adds between 10 and 20 degrees of heat. When you just want to keep your food warm, remove all the coals except for a few under and over the dish.

These guidelines are just that — guidelines. If no other factor impacts the actual heat of the coals, the conversions in Table 5-1 are pretty accurate. But add in the factors that often affect cooking temperatures outdoors (wind, air temperature, and so on), and you're going to have to make adjustments. To find out how to do so, see the section "Making adjustments for weather conditions" later in this chapter.

Heat sources and cooking methods

After you know how many coals you need total (see the preceding section, "Counting coals," for tips), you need to figure out where they should go: on the lid of your pan, underneath it, or both. How you divide the coals and where you place them depend on your cooking method. If you're baking, for example, you need the heat to surround your pan; if you're frying, all the heat should come from underneath. Table 5-2 outlines where to place your coals for various cooking methods.

Table 5-2	Location of Heat Source	
Cooking Method	*Where the Heat Should Come From*	*Coal Distribution*
Baking	More from the top than the bottom	For every coal under the bottom, you need three on the lid.
Boiling	Bottom	All coals under the bottom.
Frying	Bottom	All coals under the bottom.
Roasting	Top and bottom equally	Same number of coals on the lid and under the bottom.
Sautéing	Bottom	All coals under the bottom.
Simmering	More from the bottom than the top	For every coal on the lid, you need four under the bottom.
Stewing	More from the bottom than the top	For every coal on the lid, you need four under the bottom.

Spacing out: Oooh, pretty patterns!

When you know how many coals you need and where they should go (as explained in Tables 5-1 and 5-2), you need to arrange them properly. You can't just lump a bunch of coals under the pan and slap another bunch of coals on top. If you do, you create hot spots that can either burn your food or make it cook unevenly. Here's how to arrange your coals:

✔ **For coals under the pan:** Space the coals evenly in a circular pattern, starting at least $1/2$-inch within the outer edge of the pan's bottom.

✔ **For coals on the lid:** Space the coals evenly in a checkerboard pattern.

Making adjustments for weather conditions

In addition to figuring out how many coals to place where (see Tables 5-1 and 5-2), you have to take the weather into account. The air temperature, wind speed, humidity levels, ground temperature, and so on can affect the temperature of your coals. With this information, you can add or subtract coals as necessary to get the temperature that you want.

Your coals will burn hotter if

✔ You have warm breezes or wind.

✔ You're cooking in direct sunlight.

✔ The air temperature is high.

Your coals will be cooler if

✔ The humidity is high.

✔ You're cooking in the shade.

✔ You're cooking at high altitudes.

✔ The ground temperature is cool, or the ground is damp.

To take ground temperature out of the mix, consider not putting your coals directly on the ground. Instead, use heavy-duty aluminum foil, an old charcoal grill pan, or an overturned aluminum trash can lid as a base for your fire. If you find that you cook outdoors a lot, you may want to use a metal table specifically designed for outdoor cooking. The table has a lip around the edge that keeps your coals from falling off and a metal wall on three sides that keeps the wind away. Such a table accomplishes what the other bases do; plus, because you're cooking on a table, you don't have to bend over all the time.

More Tips for the Outdoor Cook

Cooking outdoors isn't rocket science, but it does take a little special know-how. With the basic knowledge outlined in this chapter and the following tips, chances are, your outdoor cooking experience will be a positive one:

✔ When you estimate outdoor cooking times, don't forget to figure in how long it takes to get your coals ready. For charcoal, start your coals 15 to 20 minutes before you need them.

✔ If a dish takes a long time to cook, have hot coals available to replenish the ones you use up. (A charcoal chimney starter is good for this; see the section "Going for convenience and comfort" earlier in this chapter for more on this product.) Add new coals when the old coals start to break up. When you add new coals, increase the amount proportionally on both the top and bottom. Don't add only to the top, for example, or your food will cook unevenly.

✔ To keep the cooking temperature even within the pan or Dutch oven, rotate the lid and the pan in opposite directions regularly. Every 10 to 15 minutes, give the lid a quarter turn in one direction and the pan or Dutch oven a quarter turn in the other direction.

✔ If you have to move coals around (and chances are you will, either to replenish the coals you've used up or to increase or decrease the temperature by adding and removing coals), use long-handled tongs and wear thick oven mitts. After all, you're playing with fire, and what fun is cooking outdoors if you spend all of your time indoors rubbing salve on your burns?

✔ When you rotate the lid or remove it to check on your dish, be careful not to let ashes from the lid drop into your food. When the dish is done, go ahead and brush the ashes away entirely.

When you're first starting out, start simple. Although you can cook anything in a Dutch oven, try your hand at easy dishes (stew, chili, cobbler, and roasted chicken, for example) first. The recipes in this chapter are all great beginner recipes: easy to assemble, easy to make, and delicious.

Experimenting with Some Favorite Recipes

Favorite outdoor recipes share two key characteristics:

✔ They tend to use ordinary ingredients — nothing fancy or hard to find. In fact, most ingredients in typical outdoor fare are those that the majority of cooks already have on hand.

✔ They generally use cooking methods that don't require a lot of attention. It's safe to say you'll never have to stir a sauce over low heat to avoid curdling; typically, in outdoor cooking you dump or layer everything in a skillet or Dutch oven and let it go.

You may suspect that such inauspicious beginnings can only lead to uninspired dishes. Au contraire. Maybe it's the environment: velvety skies, whispering leaves, air filled with the scent of pine, and a fire to warm yourself by. Maybe it's the company: friends and family simply enjoying nature together. But many outdoor cooks swear up and down that *nothing* tastes better than a meal cooked in the great outdoors.

The recipes in this section give you a sampling of some great outdoor dishes — entrees, sides, a couple of desserts, and a breakfast that will get even the pokiest riser up bright and early.

Need help making a campfire? Head to Book IV, Chapter 1. There you'll find out not only how to do it but also how to do it safely.

Pork Chops 'n' Potato Sauce

Pork chops come from the loin portion of a hog, and where they're located on the loin determines both the quality of the meat and its price. So when you go shopping for pork chops, keep in mind these differences: Loin chops have meat on both sides of the bone and are the least fatty and the most expensive. A center cut chop has little to no meat on one side of the bone, but the meat on the other side of the bone is nice and lean. End chops are fattier and don't have the nice, lean meat portion that the other chops offer; they're the least expensive.

Briquettes: 28

Preparation time: 10 minutes

Cooking time: 45 to 60 minutes

Yield: 4 servings

Vegetable oil	2 potatoes, sliced ¼-inch thick
4 pork chops, about ¼-inch thick	1 can (11 ounces) condensed cream of mushroom soup
1 medium yellow onion, chopped	

1 Add the oil to a 14-inch cast-iron camp oven, over 28 hot (gray) coals. Brown the pork chops on both sides. Remove the chops.

2 Sauté the onions. Pull out the onions, lay the chops back in, and spread the onions over the chops. Lay the potato slices evenly over the onions.

3 In a bowl, mix the condensed soup with ¹/₂ can of water and pour the mixture over the ingredients.

4 Reduce the briquettes to about half and simmer until the chops and potatoes are fork tender.

Per serving: *Calories 340 (From Fat 149); Fat 17g (Saturated 4g); Cholesterol 64mg; Sodium 590mg; Carbohydrate 22g (Dietary Fiber 2g); Protein 25g.*

Campsite Beef Stroganoff

When you make traditional beef stroganoff, you prepare everything in stages, cooking the meat first, adding the sauce mixture next, and adding the sour cream last. You cook the noodles separately, and then you combine everything just before serving. In this recipe, after you brown the meat, you cook everything (including the noodles) together. The result is stroganoff that's as yummy and delicious as the original — without the work or attention.

Briquettes: 25

Preparation time: 5 minutes

Cooking time: 50 to 60 minutes

Yield: 4 to 6 servings

2 pounds extra-lean ground beef	*3 cans (8 ounces each) tomato sauce*
1 medium onion, chopped	*1 teaspoon Worcestershire sauce*
¼ teaspoon celery salt	*½ cup sour cream*
¼ teaspoon garlic salt	*1 bag (12 ounces) egg noodles*
Salt and pepper	

1 Brown together the meat, onion, celery salt, garlic salt, salt, and pepper in a 12-inch cast-iron camp oven over 25 hot (gray) coals.

2 While the meat is browning, mix together 1½ cups of water, the tomato sauce, the Worcestershire sauce, and the sour cream in a medium bowl. (The sour cream won't be completely blended, and the mixture will have a few lumps.)

3 When the meat and onion are browned, spread the uncooked noodles evenly over the meat and onion. Pour the liquid mixture evenly over the noodles to moisten all the noodles well.

4 Cover the oven with the lid and place 15 of the briquettes on top, leaving 10 briquettes on the bottom.

5 Cook for approximately 30 to 45 minutes, or until the noodles are fully cooked.

Per serving: *Calories 462 (From Fat 149); Fat 17g (Saturated 7g); Cholesterol 95mg; Sodium 1,032mg; Carbohydrate 46g (Dietary Fiber 4g); Protein 32g.*

Mountain-Man Breakfast

Few pleasures are as delightful as a breakfast cooked outdoors, and this one gives you meat, eggs, and hash browns without the hassle of cleaning separate pans.

Briquettes: 24

Preparation time: 5 minutes

Cooking time: 45 minutes

Yield: 8 servings

2 pounds breakfast sausage	*10 to 12 eggs, beaten with ¼ cup water*
2 pounds frozen hash brown potatoes	*2 cups grated cheddar cheese*

1 Fry and crumble the sausage in a 12-inch cast-iron camp oven over 24 hot (gray) coals. Remove the cooked sausage and drain on paper towels.

2 Using the sausage drippings in the pan, brown the potatoes and spread them evenly in the bottom of the camp oven. Place the cooked sausage over the potatoes.

3 Pour the eggs over the sausage layer. Sprinkle the top with cheese.

4 Cover the oven with the lid and place 16 of the briquettes on top, leaving 8 coals underneath the camp oven. Cook for 20 to 25 minutes, until the eggs are done.

Per serving: *Calories 482 (From Fat 284); Fat 32g (Saturated 11g); Cholesterol 364mg; Sodium 887mg; Carbohydrate 21g (Dietary Fiber 2g); Protein 31g.*

🍅 *Dutch Oven Veggies*

Many people cook their vegetables first and add any seasoning or butter afterward. The result? Bland vegetables that get perked up as an afterthought. This recipe adds the seasoning and butter during the cooking process. Even without the cheese (which is a favorite of grown-ups and kids alike), the vegetables can stand on their own merits. Also, keep in mind that, in a pinch, you can substitute pregrated Parmesan cheese, but if you do, you'll sacrifice flavor. Freshly grated Parmesan beats pregrated Parmesan hands down. Also, you can use virtually any vegetables you want with this recipe; simply make sure that you use 8 cups of veggies total and that you cut them into bite-size pieces.

Briquettes: 24

Preparation time: 20 minutes

Cooking time: 20 to 30 minutes

Yield: 8 servings

1 cup broccoli florets	*1 cup bite-size zucchini pieces*
1 cup cauliflower florets	*1 cup bite-size butternut squash pieces*
1 cup baby carrots	*Salt and pepper*
1 cup mushrooms	*¼ pound butter*
1 cup onions, cut into bite-size pieces	*2 cups shredded sharp cheddar cheese*
1 cup bite-size bell pepper pieces	*2 cups grated fresh Parmesan cheese*

1 Put ¼-inch water into the 12-inch cast-iron camp oven and add the veggies. Season generously with the salt and pepper — more than seems enough. Slice the butter on top of the veggies.

2 Put the camp oven over 24 hot (gray) coals until the vegetable mixture is steaming; then pull out at least half of the coals. Steam the veggies until the carrots are tender.

3 Take the oven off the coals, remove the water with a baster, cover the veggies with the grated cheeses, and put the lid on the oven. Serve when the cheese is melted.

Vary It! To make a lighter version of this recipe, use light butter and cheese that's made with part skim rather than whole milk. To make it lighter yet, take away the cheese entirely.

Per serving: *Calories 344 (From Fat 244); Fat 27g (Saturated 17g); Cholesterol 77mg; Sodium 639mg; Carbohydrate 9g (Dietary Fiber 3g); Protein 17g.*

⟁ *Baked Pears*

Unlike many fruits, pears should ripen off the tree. The only time that you want a tree-ripened pear is if the tree is in your front yard, and you're picking the pear yourself. A tree-ripened pear that has been boxed and shipped across the country will be unpleasantly mushy by the time it hits your grocer's produce section. When you're buying pears, select the ones that feel firm but give slightly at the stem. You can leave them at room temperature to ripen the rest of the way. You'll know they're ready when the skin lightens and the aroma becomes noticeable.

Briquettes: 20 to 24

Preparation time: 15 minutes

Cooking time: 20 to 30 minutes

Yield: 6 servings

3 tablespoons butter	*½ cup pecan pieces*
6 tablespoons light brown sugar	*6 firm Bartlett pears*
1 tablespoon cinnamon	*Ground cloves*
6 crumbled butter cookies	*12 pecan halves*

1 Place 2 tablespoons of the butter in a 12-inch cast-iron camp oven and preheat using 8 to 10 hot (gray) coals under the oven.

2 In a bowl, combine the brown sugar, cinnamon, crumbled cookies, and pecan pieces.

3 Cut the pears in half and gently scoop out the seeds, core, and stem. Sprinkle a pinch of ground cloves onto each pear half, being careful not to use too much (a little goes a long way!). Stuff each pear half with the brown sugar mixture.

4 Place pear halves cut side up in the camp oven. Dot with remaining 1 tablespoon of butter and place a pecan half on each pear.

5 Cover the oven with the lid and place the remaining 12 to 14 briquettes on top of the oven. Cook until hot, about 20 to 30 minutes. Serve while hot.

Per serving: *Calories 291 (From Fat 126); Fat 14g (Saturated 4g); Cholesterol 16mg; Sodium 4mg; Carbohydrate 45g (Dietary Fiber 6g); Protein 2g.*

Apple Crisp

This is a great recipe for fall, when apples are in season and at local produce stands. Of course, it's (almost) equally appetizing any time of year with store-bought apples. The key is the apple. Good cooking apples, which don't turn mushy or gritty, are Rome, Golden Delicious, and Winesap— varieties that are widely available.

Briquettes: 24

Preparation time: 10 minutes

Cooking time: 1 hour

Yield: 8 to 10 servings

10 cups peeled and sliced apples	1½ cups brown sugar
¼ cup lemon juice	1¼ cups all-purpose flour
3 tablespoons lemon zest	1½ cups oats
¾ cup sugar	1 tablespoon cinnamon
½ cup golden raisins	1 teaspoon nutmeg
¾ cup butter	1 teaspoon cardamom

1 Combine the apples, lemon juice, 1 tablespoon lemon zest, sugar, and raisins in a bowl. Spread the apple mixture in the bottom of a 12-inch cast-iron camp oven and place over hot (gray) coals.

2 In a medium bowl, combine the butter and brown sugar. Place the flour in a larger bowl and then cut the butter mixture into the flour. Stir in the oats, cinnamon, nutmeg, cardamom, and the remaining 2 tablespoons lemon zest. Top the apple mixture with this topping mixture.

3 Cover the oven with the lid and place 16 coals on top, leaving 8 coals underneath. Continue cooking until the apples are cooked and the topping is brown, about 1 hour. Serve warm.

Per serving: Calories 500 (From Fat 135); Fat 15g (Saturated 9g); Cholesterol 37mg; Sodium 18mg; Carbohydrate 91g (Dietary Fiber 5g); Protein 4g.

Book II
Traditional Crafts

The 5th Wave   By Rich Tennant

"It was Lieutenant Hooper's idea. He thought it would be nice to add some rustic charm to the unit by stenciling the tanks. This, for instance, is part of our 'Country Cupboard' attack squad."

In this book . . .

"**C**raft" is an interesting word, the meaning of which has, quite frankly, diminished over the centuries. Today it connotes little more than kitschy art made by people who have a little too much time (and construction paper) on their hands. But once it referred to products made by artisans and skilled tradesmen. These people — and the services and products they provided — were so important that during the Middle Ages, craft guilds were established for the sole purpose of protecting them.

And just who belonged to those craft guilds? Candle makers (called chandlers back then), embroiderers (broderers), clothing makers (girdlers), and woolworkers (winders). Other traditional crafts, like knitting and quilting, served not only a utilitarian purpose but also an artistic one. This book reintroduces you to the skills that many earlier craftspeople found both useful and inspiring.

Chapter 1

Making Fabrics from Animal Fibers

*T*he fleeces from fiber animals, such as sheep, goats, and alpacas, can yield some beautiful and unique garments or other knit items. Creating a beautiful sweater to wear is rewarding in and of itself. It's even more satisfying when you can say not only that you knit it yourself, but you can add, "I even made the yarn, and this is from my llama Oggie!"

This chapter takes the fiber-animal owner through the process of getting the fiber off the critter and then getting the fiber into a form you can use in various applications, such as spinning, knitting, or felting. This chapter also includes a section on using the leftover bits to make fun and useful products. After all, one of the main tenets of country living is to avoid the waste of any resource.

Shear Brilliance: Collecting and Processing Fiber

If you have fiber animals (alpacas, some breeds of sheep and goats, llamas, and so on), you're probably in it for the fiber. Of course, you may be raising the critters just because you like them, but why not use that fiber for something unique and truly homegrown? Read on for info on collecting an animal's fleece and getting those fibers in top shape.

After you process the fiber, as explained in this section, you can do a number of things with it. You can spin it into yarn that can then be crocheted or knitted into something yummy, you can weave it into something useful and beautiful, or you can felt it into something wearable or otherwise functional. The later sections of this chapter explore your options.

Shave and a haircut: Getting the fiber off your critters

The first step toward attaining fiber you can use is getting the fleece off your animal, which you do by shearing. Not only does shearing allow you to collect an animal's fleece, but it also makes the animal more comfortable in hot weather. This section runs through the basics of shearing your fleece-producers. *Note:* You harvest the fiber from other, more exotic animals such as the yak or Angora rabbit, by combing the animal, but the focus here is on the more-common practice of shearing.

Choosing the tools

You can use electric or hand shears to shear (or cut) the fleece off your animals. Many people prefer hand shears because the experience is more of a bonding one. You're with your animal for a longer time, and each minute makes the critter more accustomed to your being close. Also, there's no whine of electrical shears to frighten the animal. Of course, using hand shears also makes the job go more slowly. (With electric shears, you can remove the fleece much more quickly, which may be a consideration if you have a large herd — or even if you have more than two or three and can't afford the time hand shearing requires.)

Shearing can be challenging in that you have to subdue the animal, get the fiber off in a useable condition, and avoid cutting the animal's skin. The following sections tell you what you need to know.

If you prefer not to do the shearing yourself, you can hire a professional. Each pro has his or her own unique tricks, and because the shearer does it so often, the shearer can be in and out in no time. Costs vary widely. For instance, a goat shearer may charge $7 per goat, and a llama/alpaca shearer may charge $25 per animal. However, the efficiency may be worth the cost.

Knowing when to shear

To get good quality fiber, you need to shear alpacas, llamas, and sheep once a year, usually in late spring or early summer, depending on your location. Fiber goats (such as the Angora) need to be shorn twice a year, usually in late winter and late summer. Table 1-1 has some notes on fiber collection and also describes the official names of various types of fiber. (Technically, the term *wool* means fiber from a sheep.)

Table 1-1	Fiber Names and Collection Notes	
Animal	*Name of the Fiber*	*Notes*
Alpacas	Alpaca fiber	Shear once a year
Angora rabbits	Angora	Comb the rabbit out at least every other day to prevent matting
Goats	Mohair or cashmere	Shear twice a year
Llamas	Llama fiber	Shear once a year
Musk oxen	Qiviut (undercoat)	Collect the fiber by combing
Sheep	Wool	Shear once a year
Yaks	Down (undercoat)	Collect the fiber in the spring by combing

Book II

Traditional Crafts

Here are some tips on choosing the shearing time:

- **Shear the animal before the weather gets too hot.** Being under all that heavy wool can get really hot in the summertime!

- **Be consistent.** If you decide May is the time to shear, you should shear in May *every* year so the fiber grows to its maximum length. If you schedule a shearing for May after doing it in June the preceding year, the animals' fleeces may not be quite long enough to be top quality because they'll have grown for only 11 months.

- **Shear a pregnant animal just prior to her giving birth.** The birthing process is stressful on the animal, and stress reduces the quality of the fiber. For those animals that are pregnant in the springtime, have them shorn before the birth day.

- **Wait for a dry spell.** Wet fleece is too heavy and unworkable and can clog the shears. (Of course, weather quirks aside, the shearing season is a short one. If you're hiring a professional, you'll most likely need to make an appointment ahead of time.)

Shear on time! If you let the animals go too long without shearing or combing, you're likely to end up with a fleece that's all matted and isn't useable for spinning into yarn.

Tips for raising fiber animals

Depending on where in the country you live, several animals in the fiber category can give you some very fine and fancy fleeces. The wonderful part about raising these animals is that you get to grow old with them (no need to go through the process of slaughtering) and still get something back for all those years of care and feeding. Here are just a few tips on raising fiber animals:

✔ Sicknesses can drastically reduce the quality of the fiber an animal produces. The fiber may not even be usable at the next shearing. Attention to health is of utmost importance, especially with alpacas, which are quite expensive.

✔ A baby's first shearing produces the softest fiber. Males generally produce bigger fleeces than females, and those fleeces take longer to become coarse. Birthing has a lot to do with fiber quality, but that doesn't mean the female fleeces aren't good. Pregnant females should be shorn just prior to giving birth because this blessed event is a big stress-producer and thus a fiber-destroyer.

✔ Stress equals not-so-good fiber, so if you just want the fiber and not babies, castrating the males is best because this procedure makes their coats softer due to reduced stress levels. (Competing for females and fighting with other males is hard work!)

Preparing for shearing day: Getting critters a little cleaner

Animals live outside. They lie in dirt or hay or worse. That means their beautiful coats get dirty. Before you can process the fleece into something you can felt or spin with a spinning wheel, all that dirt and other stuff need to be cleaned out. Cleaning the coat before shearing is easiest (but don't despair; there are ways to do it after the shearing as well). Following are some suggestions:

✔ **Let the animals stay in a clean, grassy pasture.** If you have a pasture with some good grass cover, bring the animals into that pasture and let them hang out in the grass (instead of the dirt) for a few days to a week before shearing day.

✔ **Hand-pick the dirt and debris out of the fleece.** This is an option if you don't have a clean pasture to place your animals in, but this method is a lot of work.

✔ **Blow air through the fleece:** Sheep's fleece is in a tight crimp, but the fleeces of some animals, such as the llama or alpaca, benefit from being gently blown. This air helps get some of the bigger, looser foreign matter out of the fleece. Use something like a leaf blower or Shop-Vac on a low setting.

✔ **Bathe your animals:** Some people bathe their animals before shearing. Bathing critters can definitely help you end up with a cleaner fiber — provided, of course, they don't go and roll in the mud immediately afterwards.

✔ **Coat your animals:** That is, put a little coat or sweater on the critters' backs to protect the fleece.

A good, honest fleecing: Shearing day logistics

On shearing day, everybody has to be rounded up and individually brought into the shearing area. Smaller animals such as sheep and goats are easier to round up, and because they're pretty small, shaving the fleece off doesn't take that long. Larger animals like llamas take a bit longer, due to the surface area to shear as well as their trademark unwillingness to cooperate.

The shearing logistics are easy:

1. **Delay the morning feeding.**

   Don't feed the animal on the morning of shearing day. Wait until the shearing is all over. Shearing is a little uncomfortable anyway, and if the critter has a full stomach, that only adds to the discomfort.

2. **Catch one animal and bring the critter to the shearing area.**

   A flat, clean surface such as a concrete driveway is a good place to shear. This surface easily allows you to pick up the shorn fleeces and clean up the leftovers.

   For llamas that aren't handled regularly, shearing day may be the only time they get haltered and roped, so this can be traumatic for them. Unwilling llamas can spit, so stay out of the line of fire or be resigned to the fact that you're going to get hit.

3. **Shear off the heavy fleece (see Figure 1-1) and bag it.**

   You want to take the *blanket* — the best part of the fleece, which goes over the animal's back. Start at the neck and make cuts close to the skin (to get the longest fiber possible), radiating out across the sides and down to the tail. The idea is to try to take this blanket off in one big piece. Put it in a plastic garbage bag.

   The stuff you shear off the legs and neck may or may not be useable, but you can bag that separately. Label each bag according to its contents (for example, *llama blanket, llama other,* or *alpaca blanket*).

4. **Take the newly shorn critter back to its pasture.**

5. **Sweep out the area after each animal has been shorn so you're ready for the next one.**

6. **Clean and oil your shears so they're ready for the next time you need to use them.**

   If you are shearing the sheep for show or the sheep are very young, clean and sharpen the shears after every shearing. If the sheep are older and you are just shearing them for the product, you can clean and sharpen the shears every other shearing.

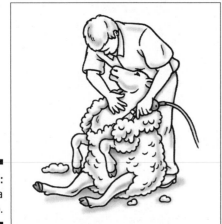

Figure 1-1: Shearing a sheep.

Most raw fleece can be stored forever, provided moths don't chew it up and other animals don't get into it. If you're going to wait awhile before you clean and process the stuff (explained in the next section), you can leave it in the barn. However, the best way to treat fiber is to process it right away and then bring it in the house.

Sheep have a lot of lanolin in their fleece, giving it a greasy feel. Lanolin can affect the color of the fleece and can even show up as staining where different levels of it have collected. It can also harden on shorn fleeces, making them difficult to clean. For these reasons, clean sheep fleeces right away.

Processing the fiber

Now that you have some potentially beautiful fiber materials in bags, what are you going to do with them? Why, get the fiber in useable shape, of course. That means picking through the fleece to select only the best stuff for processing, and then cleaning it and turning it into something you can spin or felt from.

Processing fleeces involves three general tasks: preparing, cleaning, and carding. One option is to let somebody else do the work. Just hand over the bag of freshly shorn fleece and go back later to pick up the finished product. But if you want the sense of satisfaction that comes from doing it on your own, you can do the preliminary cleaning yourself.

Skirting: Separating the best from the not-so-good

After the animal has been shorn, you have to go through the fleece and pick out the not-so-great stuff. *Skirting* is the removal of the undesirable pieces from your raw fleece. Lay the fleece out on a clean surface and hand-pick out the following:

Book II

Traditional Crafts

- ✔ **Contamination:** These particles includes *veg* (vegetable matter — all that dried-up hay stuck in the fleece), dung tags, and bits of wood, wire, and assorted junk that farmers leave lying about the farm that gets caught in the fleece when animals lie in it or rub up against it.

  You can also rig up a *spinner,* which is kind of like a giant salad spinner, to clean off veg.

- ✔ **Kemp:** These are fibers that don't have the barbs that make spinning into yarn possible. They're distinguishable because they're brittle and straight with no crimp — more like stiff hair than soft wool.

- ✔ **Second cuts:** These are fibers that didn't get cut all the way on the first try and are thus shorter, as well as other fibers of inconsistent length. You want the majority of the fibers to be the same length and the same diameter to get the best product. The best yarns are made from fleeces in which most of the individual fibers are the same length. Extra long fibers aren't really an issue, but the short ones are because they can poke out of the yarn, giving it a fuzzy look and a prickly feel. Also, short fibers are often coarser.

  Even if all the fibers have the same length and fineness, they need to be a certain minimum length so the fibers stay together. Longer fibers have more surface area for contact, and thus form a stronger bond.

- ✔ **Anything that's matted or felted or parts that are very coarse:** Part of the skirting process is to remove fiber that's inconsistent with the characteristics of the fleece.

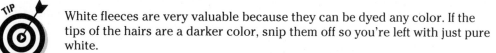

White fleeces are very valuable because they can be dyed any color. If the tips of the hairs are a darker color, snip them off so you're left with just pure white.

Scouring: Washing the fleece

Scouring means washing the fleece to remove dirt, *suint* (natural grease formed from dried perspiration in sheep fleeces), lanolin (a waxy substance), and other substances that may have become embedded in the animal's fleece.

Let the washing machine or your bathtub help with this step:

1. **Fill the washing machine (or bathtub) with hot water and liquid dish soap, about $^1/_2$ cup per full tub.**

   Dawn dishwashing liquid is a good choice because it chemically interacts with the grease but isn't alkaline like soap. (Dawn is what they use to wash birds that have been caught up in an oil slick, so it's presumably gentle enough to use on fleeces.)

   Don't use normal soap for scouring; it causes the fleece to felt.

2. **Put the fleeces in light net bags.**

   Bags that are designed for washing delicate lingerie in the washing machine work well. Fill the bags loosely. If you pack the stuff too tightly, there won't be enough room for the water to circulate.

3. **Lay the net bags in the water and let them soak for 20 minutes.**

   Be sure to push the bags gently into the water until the fleeces are fully wet.

4. **Remove the bags, let them drain, and put them into the sink to drain further.**

   If you're using a washing machine, you can return the fleeces to the machine for the spin cycle. This cycle, although it spins violently, doesn't introduce agitation, so it's a good way to remove a lot of the moisture in a short time.

   Agitation (along with heat) causes the fleece to felt, rendering it unusable for spinning.

5. **Give the fleeces a second bath.**

   I find that one bath isn't quite enough, so repeat the process.

6. **Rinse the fleeces.**

   Repeat Steps 3 through 5 using clear water (do not use soap in this process), for a total of two rinse cycles.

7. **Gently lay the fleeces out to dry.**

   If you have a nice, dry, sunny day, you may attempt to do this outside, but wind or curious animals can introduce some dirt back into the fleece, so indoor drying is recommended. A mesh, sweater-drying rack is ideal for this. Be careful if you have cats, because a fresh fleece may look like a wonderful new bed to them! Drying takes a few hours.

Carding and such: Brushing and combing

Carding means organizing a jumble of fibers so they're more or less parallel. Carding can also remove some, but not all, the veg that thus far has eluded you. You card by hand by using what looks sort of like a pair of big dog brushes (see Figure 1-2). Or, if you have a lot of fiber to process, you can send it off to the pros.

Figure 1-2: Carding by hand aligns individual fibers.

Depending on the quality and length of the fibers, you can get several distinct end products from carding:

- **Clouds:** If the fibers are short and form a weak fiber-to-fiber bond, the structure collapses because it can't support its own weight. The result is a *cloud.* Spinning from a cloud is hard, so the best use for these fibers is probably needle felting (or some of the suggestions in the later section "Using Up All the Fiber Leftovers").

- **Batts:** A carder collects the fiber on a special roller, laying down layer after layer of fibers, to create a *batt.* When the roller is full (or the batt has reached the desired loft), the batt's broken, pulled off the roller, and left flat. People often roll batts in tissue paper to transport them.

  You can spin from batts, but it's not as easy as spinning from rovings. Batts also work as stuffing; they look a lot like the quilt batts you buy in the store. They're also great for wet felting. (See the later section "Locking the Fibers with Felting.")

- **Roving:** A *roving* is a loose, rope-like preparation in which the fibers from the carder are gathered and then lightly *drafted* (pulled apart). You often find roving wound into balls or in center-pull bumps. This preparation requires the least amount of additional work before being spun by a hand spinner.

The primary criterion for roving is that the roving has to be strong enough to survive the rigors of the bump-winder and stay intact when tugged at during the spinning process. Due to texture, the length of sheep's wool that's long enough to make roving may be much shorter than the length needed to make a good alpaca roving.

✔ **Sliver:** A *sliver* is similar to a roving, and the two terms are often used interchangeably. Some camps say that if you add a bit of a twist to a sliver, it becomes roving. Other camps say there isn't a twist to the roving.

✔ **Rolag:** A *rolag* is made by using a pair of hand carders (as opposed to a commercial carder) to organize the fibers. You lay tufts of fiber across the teeth of one of the carders and brush them out with the other. When the fibers are nice and straight, you peel and roll them lengthwise from the bed of the carder. All the fiber comes out of the carder, and you end up with a roll of fiber.

Cuticle fibers are what make fibers cling to each other. Wool has a lot of rather prominent scales. Huacaya alpaca doesn't have as many scales, and the scales aren't as prominent as sheep's wool scales. Suri alpaca and mohair have even fewer scales. The interlocking of these scales — fiber to fiber — is the mechanism that holds roving, batts, and, ultimately, yarn together.

The best way to store processed fiber is to put it in clear plastic garbage bags. Moths like darkness, and the clear bags let in too much light for their taste. Store the bags in an area where mice won't chew through and cats or dogs won't think it's some other animal's territory and thus want to pee on the fiber.

Dyeing in the Wool

Natural fibers such as wool can be easily dyed (well, easily in that the fibers permanently take the dye — it's not always so easy to do procedurally). You can end up with fibers that are any number of colors from the rainbow, especially if you start out with a light color, such as white or light grey.

You can buy one of the tons of dyes available, or you can buy books that are full of recipes for making your own natural dyes from herbs or flowers. Making natural dyes can get complicated because you need a *mordant* (a substance that sets the dye on the wool and makes it permanent), glass pots, rubber gloves, and so on.

One fantastic dye is nontoxic, extremely easy to use, and can be found on the shelves of the local grocery store: Kool-Aid. Yep, wool and Kool-Aid were made for each other. And because Kool-Aid is a food item, you can use your regular kitchen pots and utensils to do the dyeing. *Note:* Kool-Aid works only on animal fibers, so don't try to dye cotton with it.

You can dye unprocessed fleece, processed rovings, spun yarn, or even a finished knitted sweater. In the instructions that follow, the thing you're dyeing is referred to as the *wool:*

1. **Pre-wet your wool by soaking it in a huge pot of warm water for about 20 minutes.**

   Wet wool absorbs the dye more evenly.

   If you're going to dye a skein of yarn that has already been wound into a ball, unwind it and rewind it into a twisted skein (a big loop). If it remains in a ball, the yarn in the center of the ball won't get enough of the dye, and the finished product won't be a uniform color.

2. **Prepare the Kool-Aid dye bath.**

   Fill a 4-quart pot about $2/3$ of the way with water and pour in a package or two of powdered drink mix, depending on how rich you want the color to be (it's hard to determine what the exact outcome will be unless you do the same thing over and over, so have fun playing with different colors). Stir until it's dissolved.

3. **Add the wool, and heat on the stove.**

   Add the wool to the pot, turn on the heat, and heat to a gentle boil for 5 to 10 minutes, keeping the yarn under the water by pressing it down with a big spoon.

4. **Remove, rinse, and dry the wool.**

   Allow the bath to cool before taking the wool out. Rinse until the color runs clear. Squeeze out any extra water, and then wrap the wool in a towel to absorb excess moisture. Let the wool dry on a sweater rack, or, if it's already in yarn form, you can hang it.

If you have a particular use in mind for the dyed wool, dye enough for the entire project at the same time, so the color is uniform.

Spinning and Using Yarn

If you want yarn from your own fiber, the easiest way to get it is to give the fiber to an expert who has a spinning machine. Some of the bigger operations that card fiber can also spin it, giving you a finished product of yarn. However, many people prefer to do their own spinning. In this section, you discover some spinning tools and read about where you can pick up this craft.

Taking the wheel: Spinning implements

Processed fiber can be spun into yarn using a number of styles of spinning implements. The simplest style is a drop spindle. You don't need anything fancy to make one yourself — a dowel, a hook, and a small round disk or wooden wheel will do. A drop spindle works with the same concept as a spinning wheel — making yarn by putting a twist into the fiber — but on a much slower scale. It takes about seven times as long to make the same amount of yarn on a spindle as it does on a wheel. But the spindles are completely portable and can be used where wheels can't, such as in the car, on a plane, or around the campfire. You can even spin while wandering around.

If you opt for a spinning wheel, you can find fold-up styles that you can pack in the car and take to spinning parties or even on camping trips, but they're not as portable and campfire friendly as the drop spindle. Some styles are not only functioning yarn-makers but also beautiful pieces of furniture to grace your living room (see Figure 1-3).

Figure 1-3:
A traditional
spinning
wheel.

You can even get small, consumer-sized electric wheels (see Figure 1-4).

Try out a few different styles of wheels before you decide on one, because you may find you prefer one style over another. If you really get into this craft, you may even find the need for multiple wheels. Find a local store that sells wheels, visit fiber festivals (these typically have people who are showing off and answering questions about all things fiber), or find a spinning group in your area where somebody will let you take a spin.

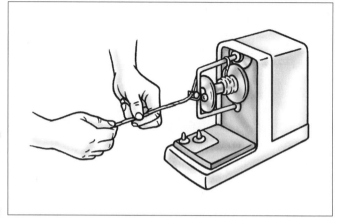

Figure 1-4:
An electric
spinning
wheel.

Book II

**Traditional
Crafts**

Joining classes and clubs to develop your spinning technique

The concept of spinning seems simple enough — one hand holds the fiber as the other hand pulls the fibers out slowly to twist as the wheel turns. But getting all the components of the process to come together to give you what you want takes a little while. Factors that come into play include the amount of twist you put into the fibers, the spinning speed, the blending of fibers, and much more. Take a class, have a friend show you, or at least get a video to see how spinning is done.

A bunch of spinning clubs are around, and chances are good you can find a group near you. Ask at the local yarn shop and join up. Not only is spinning with a group of others a fun get-together, but you can also get tips from people who really know what they're doing.

If you sign up for a spinning class, make sure it actually has to do with fibers. Otherwise, you may be in store for an aerobic workout on a stationary bike!

A good place to start perusing all the intricacies of the craft is at the Joy of Handspinning Web site (www.joyofhandspinning.com).

Getting hooked on knitting and crocheting

Knitting or crocheting is a great way to put all that spun wool to good use. Using knitting needles or a crochet hook, you can make your own fabrics. Knitting and crocheting are great outlets for creativity, because the possibilities for what you end up with are endless. You can play with stitch patterns, colors, and textures and turn out a truly unique garment, purse or fashion accessory, or something else entirely, such as kitchen curtains or teapot covers. Visit your local yarn shop or craft store and sign up for lessons, or check out a book such as *Crocheting For Dummies,* by Susan Brittain and Karen Manthey, or *Knitting For Dummies*, 2nd Edition, by Pam Allen, Tracy Barr, and Shannon Okey (Wiley). For a quick primer on knitting basics, hop to Chapter 2 of this book.

Fruit of the loom: Weaving fabrics

As in knitting and crocheting, weaving lets you make your own fabric. In this case, you pass threads under and over each other in patterns. You decide the patterns, the colors, and the thickness. Using a loom, you make fabric that you can then use in clothing, rugs, tapestries, blankets, baskets, or virtually any other fabric application.

To weave, you need a loom. A loom can be as simple as a couple of two-by-fours and some dowels, or as complex as an electronic floor model that takes up the good part of a small room and needs weeks of lessons to master.

Check at the local yarn store for a group to join, or visit the Handweavers Guild of America (www.weavespindye.org) for a national list of local guilds.

Locking the Fibers with Felting

You can make felt in a couple of ways. One method is to spin the fleece into yarn, knit or crochet it, and then shrink it. Another is to take the unspun fiber and subject it to agitation. Whatever the method, the end product is the same: The agitation causes the individual fibers to hook onto one another, move closer together, and form a dense matt, eliminating any holes that were there before felting. Felting is a very cool thing to watch happen. This section introduces you to a few techniques.

Creating pieces of felt: Wet felting by hand

Wet felting uses hot, soapy water to achieve the effect of felting. For basic felting, gather the following supplies:

- A plastic tablecloth or similar covering to protect your work surface
- The wool to be felted
- A piece of netting that's a little bigger than the surface of the pre-felted wool

✔ Hot, soapy water

✔ A sponge

✔ A ridged washboard

Find a smooth, clean surface to work on, such as a countertop or table, and follow these steps:

1. **Layer the fiber you want to felt on top of the plastic tablecloth.**

   If you're working with a batt, simply pull off the amount you want and lay it down. If working with roving, add the smaller pieces side by side and then add the next row so the sides overlap slightly. You want the surface to be solidly covered with the wool, with no big gaps.

   Lay out another layer on top of and across the first layer, at a 90-degree angle. Continue adding layers (four to six in total) so you provide many opportunities for the fibers to adhere to each other across layers, making a sturdy end product.

2. **Cover the wool with the piece of netting.**

3. **Dip the sponge in hot, soapy water and squeeze out the sponge so it's just damp (no water drips off); starting in the center of the wool, press the sponge into the wool, wetting it and pushing out the air.**

   Move out from the center, pressing and being sure to keep the netting in place, until all the wool is wet and soapy. Remember the following:

   • **Don't sop it.** If water comes up when you press down, it's too wet. With too much water, the fibers just float in the water instead of adhering to each other. Use a towel to soak up the excess.

   • **Keep the wool flat.** If it isn't flat — if bubbles are in the surface — press a little more water into the bubbly spot.

   At this point, you can add strips of another color for accent.

4. **Using your hands, gently rub in a circular motion, covering the entire surface of the wool.**

   Start with the netting still in place. To make sure the fibers don't try to hook to the netting, lift the netting up periodically, keeping a palm on the wool to prevent it from unhooking from its neighboring fibers.

   After you've worked the top side for a while, take the netting off and flip the fabric over. Put the netting back on top of the piece and work on the other side.

5. **When the wool is in soft felt stage, take the fabric in both hands and rub it back and forth.**

   To determine when it's in the *soft felt stage,* pinch a section and lift. If the fibers separate, it needs more rubbing (see Step 4). If it comes up as a solid piece of fabric, it's ready.

Book II

Traditional Crafts

6. **Re-wet the fabric with hot water and rub it across the washboard, turning it every now and then to get it uniform.**

   Rub on all sides and at all angles. The fabric shrinks in the direction in which you rub it. The felt is done when the fabric is firm and doesn't stretch when pulled.

7. **When the fabric is done, rinse out all the soap with warm water and let the felt dry.**

   Rinse the fabric until the water runs clear. Blot out any excess water by rolling the fabric in a towel and letting it sit for a few minutes. Unroll it and lay it out again, shaping if necessary. Let it dry for around 24 hours.

Now you have a piece of fabric that you can use to make something else. For instance, you can lay out a pattern and cut it out to make a jacket or purse, or use the felt as a background for a needle-felting project (see the later section "Entering the art gallery: Needle felting").

Soap's up! Making a felted bar

When made properly, felted bars are like a washcloth and a bar of soap all in one. Because the soap doesn't just wash down the drain (more of it stays inside its casing), the soap lasts as much as three times as long as a regular bar of soap. As you use the felted bar, the wool shrinks around the bar and becomes tighter. When the soap is all gone, you can wash and dry the felt bag and fill it with catnip; pets love to play with it after a good washing.

Here's what you need:

✔ One bar of soap

✔ Enough wool to cover the soap bar completely

✔ A large bowl of hot water

Wrap some unfelted wool around the bar of soap (both lengthwise and widthwise) until it's completely covered. Work near a sink and have a large bowl handy. Working over the bowl, dribble some hot water on the bar while patting it lightly. Don't add too much water at first, or the wool will just fall off. Keep adding a little soapy water and patting and squeezing it lightly, shifting it around in your hands as it starts to lather up.

When the wool is completely wet, squeeze the wool-covered bar in both hands and lightly rub, dribbling on more water periodically to keep the bar nice and soapy wet. It first gets wrinkly and then foams up; then you see it starting to felt, or matt up. Keep squeezing and rubbing (don't forget to get the sides, too) until it looks like a nice, matted fabric. This process takes around 15 to 20 minutes.

Dunk the bar in the bowl of water and see whether the felt casing is snug around the soap. If not, rub a little longer. If it's snug, run some cold water on it to rinse off the suds. (Cold water also serves to temporarily stop the felting process.)

Felting knitted or crocheted projects: Wet felting in the washing machine

The mechanics of wet felting in the washing machine are essentially the same as they are for hand felting (see the preceding section), but you use the washing machine to do the agitation. You also have to start out with a fabric that's already sturdy, such as a knitted piece, because if you just toss some loose fleece into the machine, you'll end up with a matted glob.

The fun thing about felting is you can felt your project just a little or you can felt the snot out of it. Start out with a knitted or crocheted piece that's about one-and-a-half to three times bigger than you want it to be (it will shrink during the felting process). Then follow these steps:

1. **Put the piece you want to felt into some sort of bag, such as a pillow-case or a lingerie washing bag.**

   During the felting process, some of the fibers come off. Keeping everything in a bag makes cleanup easier and is kinder to the machine.

2. **Set your washing machine to the lowest water level and the hottest water temperature, with a cold water rinse.**

3. **Add about $1/2$ teaspoon of detergent, and add the bag with the fabric to the water.**

4. **Let it go through the wash cycle; stop the machine before it goes into the rinse cycle.**

   Take the piece out and check it. Most yarns take 20 to 30 minutes to felt, but your piece may be done earlier or later. If it needs more time, set the machine back to the wash cycle and let it go longer. Repeat until you've achieved the right size and density.

5. **Let the wash finish, allowing the piece to go through the rinse and spin cycles.**

6. **Take the piece out and shape it if necessary; let it dry.**

Entering the art gallery: Needle felting

With *needle felting,* you repeatedly poke a special, barbed needle through the wool to cause the wool's natural barbs to hook together. You can find felting needles at www.mielkesfarm.com or purchase them from other fiber craft retailers.

Besides the barbed needle, you also need a piece of foam to lay your felting material on top of so that, as you poke, poke, poke, the needle doesn't go down into a table (which breaks the needle) or your fingers (which really hurts).

You can use needle felting to do a sort of "painting" on a background. Starting out with an already-felted piece as a background is a good idea. (You can use needle felting to decorate felted hats.) Although the background doesn't have to be a felted piece, it's the easiest background to use because it acts as just another layer of felt for the new dry-felted portion to dig in to. Here's how the process works:

1. **Lay your background fabric over a piece of soft foam padding.**

2. **Pick a thin piece of wool you want to add to the picture and place it on the background.**

3. **Take the needle and poke several times.**

   You see the fibers joining immediately. Keep poking until the new wool piece is attached to the background.

4. **Continue until you're happy with your design.**

Your local yarn store may offer classes on needle felting, or you can see it in pictures in the online tutorial at `http://backtobackknits.com/HowTo/NeedleFelt`. If you don't have your own fiber to use, you can find needle-felting kits online that include a little bit of fiber as well as the needles, felting pad, and instructions.

You can also use needle felting to make some pretty spectacular dolls and 3-D soft sculptures. I've made some felted sheep and goats this way. You start out with a cylindrical shape as the body by rolling a few tufts of fiber and punching them with the needle so the fibers form a solid mass. For the legs, you may want to put some sort of stabilizer inside (like a piece of cording) and felt around that. Place the legs on the body and jab until they're attached. Do the same for the head and a tail.

Using Up All the Fiber Leftovers

Some fiber, after cleaning, is too matted to be processed and spun. You may be tempted to just toss these bits. But you can use them as stuffing for crafts (dolls, teddy bears, and so on), pillows, or even mattresses. You can also use leftover fleece as insulation in outbuildings.

As for the fiber that's still good enough to spin but isn't good enough quality or soft enough to use in garments, you can use it to make animal blankets or household items:

✔ **Pillows and pet mattresses:** Pillows and even mattresses are easy to make, and the end product is light and fluffy compared to its heavier shredded-rubber pillow counterpart. Making a full-sized mattress for your own bed is probably more involved than you want to deal with, but smaller pillows or even animal beds are great candidates for wool stuffing. Simply make a pillow or pet mattress form, decorate it, and then stuff it with wool. A truly, completely done-by-yourself project!

Here are some tips for using fiber to fill pillows or anything else:

Book II

Traditional Crafts

- **Put several layers of fabric around the fiber filler.** Some of the wool fibers can work their way through to the surface, giving the item a bearded look. Alternatively, felt the pillow form — this opens up a whole new avenue of creativity! For example, you could decorate the felted cover using the technique explained in the earlier section "Entering the art gallery: Needle felting."

- **To clean wool pillows and mattresses, wash them gently by hand and don't agitate.** Squeeze out excess water and use a towel to blot the rest of the water. Let them air dry.

Wool is sort of a magic kind of mattress material because it wicks moisture away from the body and helps you sleep a little cooler in the summer and warmer in the winter. It maintains its loft longer than any cotton fiber. Dust mites can't live in it, and it's pretty hypoallergenic. Sounds like a miracle material to me!

✔ **Animal bedding for shorn critters:** After shearing, put the loose, unspinnable fibers in the barn as bedding to help the animals' transition to life without hair. The leftover fiber can come in especially handy when babies arrive and you need extra bedding.

✔ **Household items:** Sometimes the fiber may not be soft enough to use next to the skin. A sweater, scarf, or hat would be too itchy, and all the hard work you'd go to in order to knit it would be in vain because you wouldn't ever wear it. So why not make something out of it that won't irritate the skin? Knitting isn't just for clothing, after all. Make a rug. Or a horse blanket. Or a wall hanging. Or a collection of stuffed animals. The possibilities are endless.

Chapter 2

Knitting Basics

In This Chapter

▶ Knowing what to look for in yarns

▶ Understanding needle size and type

▶ Figuring out how to cast on, bind off, and form basic stitches

▶ Examining a few fun starter projects

••

Knitting is a relatively simple process requiring minimal tools — two needles and some yarn. Its basic structure of interlocking loops couldn't be less complicated. Yet the possibilities for design and pattern innovation are endless. Knitting has more than cozy socks and colorful sweaters to offer; it's also an excellent way to mitigate some of the stresses and frustrations of day-to-day life.

This chapter introduces you to knitting — what it is, what it takes, and how you do it. It also includes a few simple yet attractive and fun projects. Pretty soon you'll be able to explore with confidence the myriad items you can create with two needles and some yarn!

Yarn: The (Quick) Consumer's Guide

Whether you're buying your yarn from a yarn shop, discount retailer, or craft store, or you're using yarn you've spun yourself (flip back to the first chapter in this book for instructions), you need to know a little bit about the different types of yarn and their general characteristics.

Yarn is made from short fibers that are either natural (from animals or plants) or synthetic. The fibers are combed, or *carded,* to align them into a soft untwisted rope (called *roving*). Then they're spun (twisted) into a strand or ply of yarn. This single ply is usually combined with other plies to form the final yarn. The following sections explain the two main factors — fiber and weight — that account for the wide variety of yarns available.

Weighing yarn for project purposes

Yarns come in different *weights,* or thicknesses. The weight of your yarn (among other factors) has a huge impact on the look of your final product and the amount of time it takes to knit it up. A yarn's weight determines how many stitches it takes to knit 1 inch. A medium-weight yarn that knits up 5 stitches and 7 rows to the inch takes 35 stitches to make a square inch of knitted fabric. A bulky yarn at 3 stitches and 5 rows to the inch needs 15 stitches to make a square inch. You can see the difference in Figure 2-1.

Figure 2-1: Different weights create different effects.

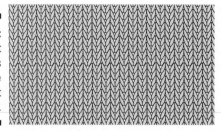 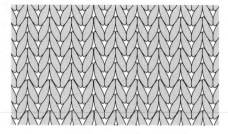

Medium-weight yarn   Bulky yarn

Although there are no official categories for yarn weights, many knitting books and yarn manufacturers use common terms to indicate a yarn's thickness and the size needle the yarn is usually worked on. Table 2-1 lists these categories for you.

Table 2-1		Common Yarn Weights		
Yarn Weight	*Symbol*	*Needle Size*	*Stitches per Inch*	*Common Uses*
Lace	**0** LACE	000–1	8–10	Lace knitting
Superfine, fingering, or baby weight	**1** SUPER FINE	1–3	7–8	Light layettes, socks
Fine or sport weight	**2** FINE	3–6	5–6	Light sweaters, baby things, accessories

DK (double-knitting) or light worsted	**3** LIGHT	5–7	5–5½	Sweaters and other garments, lightweight scarves
Medium, worsted, afghan, or aran	**4** MEDIUM	7–9	4–5	Sweaters, blankets, outdoor wear (hats, scarves, mittens, and so on)
Chunky	**5** BULKY	10–11	3–3½	Rugs, jackets, blankets
Bulky	**6** SUPER BULKY	13–15	2–2½	Heavy blankets, rugs, sweaters (if you favor the trend toward bulky ones)

Book II

Traditional Crafts

The thickness of a given yarn is determined by the individual thickness of the plies, *not* by the number of plies. If the plies are thin, a 4-ply yarn can be finer than a heavy single-ply yarn.

Identifying fiber fundamentals

All yarn is made from natural or synthetic fibers. Different fibers have different qualities — some good, some not so good. Often yarn manufacturers combine different fibers to offset an undesirable characteristic. A *blend* is a yarn made from fibers of different origins — for example, wool/cotton, wool/silk, alpaca/cotton. More than anything else, the combination of fibers in your yarn determines its ultimate look, feel, and wearable comfort. The following sections delve into the various types of yarns out there.

Wool and other fleece yarns

Wool (made from the fleece of sheep) is the queen of yarns, and it remains a popular choice for knitters for a number of excellent reasons. It's a good insulator — warm in winter, cool in summer. Wool can absorb lots of moisture without feeling wet, and it soaks up dye beautifully. It's also resilient — the fibers can stretch and bend repeatedly but always return to their original shape. Wool is soft, relatively lightweight, beautiful to look at, and — key to beginning knitters — easy to knit with because it has just enough give. It also can be pulled out and reknit easily, a bonus when you're just learning the basic stitches.

Following are some of your wool yarn options:

- **Lamb's wool:** This wool comes from a young lamb's first shearing. It's softer and finer than wool from an older sheep's fleece.

- **Merino wool:** Merino wool is considered the finest of the fine wool yarns. Long, lustrous fibers make a soft and exceptionally lovely knitted fabric.

- **Pure new wool/virgin wool:** *Pure new* and *virgin* refer to wool that's made directly from animal fleece and not recycled from existing wool garments.

- **Shetland wool:** Real Shetland wool is a traditional 2-ply heathery yarn made from the small and hardy native sheep of Scotland's Shetland Islands. It's used in traditional Fair Isle sweaters and is typically available in sport or fingering weight (see "Weighing yarn for project purposes" earlier in this chapter for an explanation of weights). This wool originally came in sheep's colors, including all shades of charcoal and deep brown to white. Shetland wool is now also available in an extraordinary range of beautiful, dyed colors.

- **Icelandic wool:** This rustic, soft, single-ply, medium-weight to heavy-weight yarn was traditionally available only in natural sheep's colors (black, charcoal, light gray, and white). Today, you can also find it dyed in bright jewel and heathered colors, as well as in a lighter weight appropriate for thinner, indoor sweaters.

- **Washable or "superwash" wool:** This wool is treated chemically or electronically to destroy the outer fuzzy layer of fibers that would otherwise *felt* or bond with each other and shrink.

Sheep aren't the only animals to provide fibers for yarns. Fuzzy mohair and luxurious cashmere come from Angora and Kashmir goats, respectively. Warm, soft alpaca comes from members of the llama family; *alpacas* are small, South American cousins of the camel. The belly of the musk ox provides the lush and exceptionally warm and light qiviut. Lighter than air and fuzziest of all, angora comes from the hair of Angora rabbits.

Silk, cotton, linen, and rayon yarns

Silk, cotton, linen, and rayon yarns are the slippery yarns. Unlike rough yarns from the hairy fibers of animals, the smooth and often shiny surfaces of these materials cause them to unravel quickly if you drop a stitch. These yarns are inelastic and may stretch lengthwise over time. They're often blended with other fibers (natural and synthetic) to counteract their disadvantages. But silk and cotton, even in their pure state, are so lovely to look at and comfortable to wear that they're well worth knitting.

Synthetic yarns

Originally, synthetics (nylon, acrylic, and polyester) were made to mimic the look and feel of natural materials. Just as wool yarn is spun from short lengths of carded fibers from a sheep's fleece, synthetic yarns begin as a long filament made from artificial (usually petroleum-based) ingredients cut into short lengths and processed to look like wool yarn.

On the plus side, all-synthetic yarns are inexpensive and hold up well in the washing machine. For people who are allergic to wool, synthetics make for a look-alike substitute (at least from a distance). On the downside, all-synthetic yarns don't have the wonderful insulating and moisture-absorbing qualities of natural yarns and therefore can be uncomfortable to wear. They pill more readily than wool or other fibers, and after exposure to heat (a hot iron is deadly), they lose all resilience and become flat.

Because of the problems associated with all-synthetic yarns, manufacturers have come up with new and better applications for synthetics — namely, combining synthetic yarns with other fibers. For example, nylon is extremely strong and light. Blended in small amounts with more fragile fibers such as mohair, nylon adds durability. A little nylon blended with wool makes a superb sock yarn. A bit of acrylic in cotton makes the yarn lighter and promotes memory so that the knitted fabric doesn't stretch out of shape.

Straddling the border between natural and synthetic are soy, bamboo, corn, and other unusual yarns made from plant-based materials. Spun into micro-filaments that are extruded using a process similar to that employed for acrylic and other synthetic yarns, these fibers have become increasingly popular in the past few years, particularly in yarn blends such as soy/wool, bamboo/silk, and even tree-, corn-, and seaweed-derived fibers.

Novelty yarns

Novelty, or specialty, yarns are easy to recognize because their appearance is so different from traditional yarns. Their jewel colors and whimsical textures can be hard to resist. Eyelash yarns, for example, feature tiny spikes of fiber that stick up, resembling eyelashes. Here are some of the more common novelty yarns you may come across:

- **Boucle:** This highly bumpy, textured yarn is comprised of loops.

- **Chenille:** Although tricky to knit with, the attractive appearance and velvety texture of this yarn make your perseverance worthwhile. Chenille is usually available in rayon (for sheen) or cotton.

- **Faux fur:** Fluffy fiber strands on a strong base thread of nylon resemble faux fur when knitted. This novelty yarn is available in many different colors.

Book II

Traditional Crafts

- **Railroad ribbon:** This ribbon-style yarn has tiny "tracks" of fiber strung between two parallel strands of thread.

- **Ribbon:** This is usually a knitted ribbon in rayon or a rayon blend with wonderful drape.

- **Thick-thin:** Often handspun, these yarns alternate between very thick and thin sections, which lends a charmingly bumpy look to knitted fabric.

Some novelty yarns can be tricky to work with. Others — like those with no give, complex textures, or threadlike strands that are easy to lose when you knit from one needle to the other — can be downright difficult. Identifying individual stitches in highly textured yarns is difficult if not impossible, making it hard to fix mistakes or rip out stitches.

Eyeing standard yarn packaging

Yarn is packaged (sometimes called "put up") in different ways — balls, skeins (which rhymes with "canes"), and hanks. Each comes wrapped with a label that you should read carefully because it gives you useful information and lets you know whether the yarn is a good candidate for the project you have in mind. If the yarn begs to be purchased before you know what you want to make with it, the info on the label will guide you as to what kind of project would best suit it.

Label talk

A yarn label offers tons of vital information (Figure 2-2 shows a typical label). Pay particular attention to

- **Gauge (how many stitches and rows per inch) and suggested needle size:** These details give you an idea of what the final knitted fabric will look like. A size 11 needle and a gauge of low numbers (3 stitches and 5 rows to the inch), for example, yield a heavy, chunky fabric. On the other hand, a size 5 needle and a gauge of 5 stitches and 7 rows to the inch yield a finer, more traditional fabric.

- **Fiber content:** This info lets you know whether the yarn is wool, cotton, acrylic, a blend, or something else.

- **Dye lot number and/or color number:** This detail indicates the batch of dye that this yarn comes from. When you buy multiple skeins of yarn, compare these numbers to ensure that they're all the same (meaning all your yarn comes from the same dye batch). Even if you can't detect a difference in color between two balls of different dye lots, chances are the difference will become apparent when you knit them up one after the other.

To avoid unwanted color variations, buy enough yarn from the same dye lot at one time to complete your project. If you have to buy more later, you may not be able to find yarn from the right dye lot.

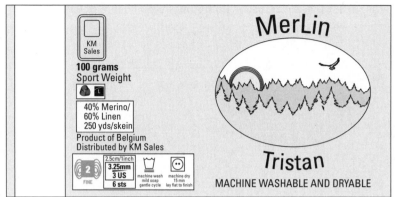

Figure 2-2:
A sample yarn label.

Ball, skein, or hank?

Yarn is packaged in different forms: balls, skeins, and hanks, as shown in Figure 2-3. Balls and skeins come ready to knit. When you find the end, you can cast on and go. Hanks need to be wound into a ball before you can use them. If you try to knit with the yarn in hank form, you'll quickly end up with a tangled mess.

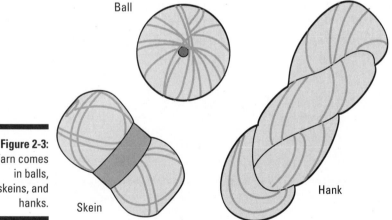

Figure 2-3:
Yarn comes in balls, skeins, and hanks.

To wind a hank into a ball, follow these steps:

1. **Carefully unfold the hank (it's formed into a large circle) and drape it over a chair back, a friend's outstretched arms, or your bent knees (if you're sitting, that is).**

2. **Locate the ends of the yarn, and if they're tied, cut or unknot them.**

3. **With either end, begin by making a butterfly (see Figure 2-4).**

   Wrap the yarn in a figure eight around the thumb and little finger of your hand. Make about 20 passes if you're winding a medium-weight yarn; make more passes for a finer yarn, or less for a thicker yarn.

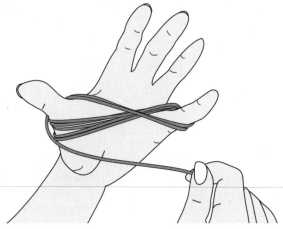

Figure 2-4:
Making a
butterfly.

4. **Take the "wings" off your finger and thumb and fold the butterfly in half, holding it between your thumb and fingers.**

5. **Continue wrapping yarn *loosely* around the folded butterfly (and your fingers), as shown in Figure 2-5.**

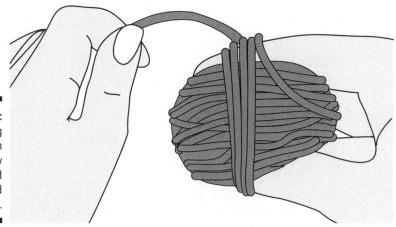

Figure 2-5:
Wrapping
the yarn
loosely
around
thumb and
fingers.

6. **When the package gets bulky, slip it off your fingers, turn it, and continue to wrap the yarn into a ball.**

Neatness isn't important; *looseness* is. Always wrap the yarn around as many fingers as you can, slipping them out when you change position. The space they take up ensures that the yarn isn't stretched as it waits to be knitted. If you knit with stretched yarn, you can guess what happens to your knitted piece when the yarn springs back to size.

Getting to the Point with Knitting Needles

Book II

Traditional Crafts

You have three options when it comes to knitting needles: straight, circular, and double-pointed (see Figure 2-6):

✔ **Straight needles:** Straight needles are generally used for *flat knitting* — knitting on the right side, and then turning and knitting on the wrong side. Straight needles come in many standard lengths ranging from 7-inch "scarf needles" to those that are 10, 13, and 14 inches. The larger your project, the longer the needle you'll need.

✔ **Circular needles:** *Circular needles* are simply a pair of straight knitting needle tips joined by a flexible cable. You can use circular needles to *knit in the round* — knitting in a continuous, spiral-like fashion without turning your work. This technique creates a seamless tube large enough for a sweater body or small enough for a neckband. You can also use circular needles as you would straight needles, to work back and forth — a particularly handy approach for lengthwise-knit scarves, blankets, and other very wide pieces. Circular needles are available in many different sizes and lengths (most frequently 16, 24, 29, and 36 inches, although you can also find them in sizes as long as 60 inches).

✔ **Double-pointed needles:** *Double-pointed needles* (dpns) have a point at each end and are sold in sets of four or five needles. They work the same way as circular needles — in rounds. You use them to make small tubes when there are too few stitches to stretch around the circumference of a circular needle — for items like sleeve cuffs, tops of hats, socks, mittens, and so on. They come in 7- and 10-inch lengths and recently have shown up in 5-inch lengths — a great boon to knitters who enjoy making socks and mittens.

A needle's size is determined by its diameter. The smaller the size, the narrower the needle and the smaller the stitch it makes. Figure 2-7 shows needle sizes and their US and metric equivalents.

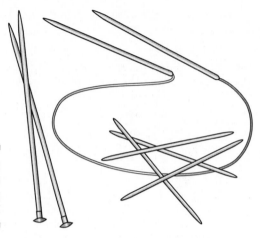

Figure 2-6:
Three kinds
of knitting
needles.

Popular Knitting Needle Sizes

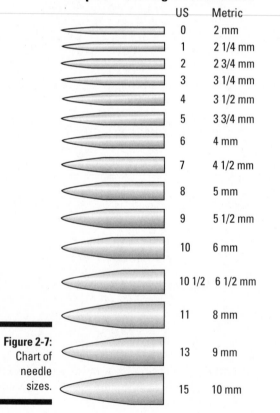

US	Metric
0	2 mm
1	2 1/4 mm
2	2 3/4 mm
3	3 1/4 mm
4	3 1/2 mm
5	3 3/4 mm
6	4 mm
7	4 1/2 mm
8	5 mm
9	5 1/2 mm
10	6 mm
10 1/2	6 1/2 mm
11	8 mm
13	9 mm
15	10 mm

Figure 2-7:
Chart of
needle
sizes.

Casting On

Creating the first row of stitches is called *casting on*. Various ways of casting on exist, and different knitters have their favorites. The following sections outline two common cast-on methods. Whichever you use, be sure to cast on your stitches evenly. They make up the bottom edge of your knitting, and neatness counts.

Here are a couple of tips about casting on:

- ✔ **Don't cast on too tightly.** Doing so makes the first row hard to work because you have to force your needle tip through the loop. If you find yourself doing this, you may want to start over and cast on with a needle one size larger to counteract the tension. Then switch to the requested size for the actual knitting.

- ✔ **When you're casting on a lot of stitches, place a stitch marker at particular intervals — like every 50 stitches.** That way, if you get interrupted or distracted while you're counting (and you will, sometimes multiple times), you don't have to begin counting again at the first stitch. As you work the first row, just drop the markers off the needle.

Book II

Traditional Crafts

Two-strand (or long-tail) cast-on

The two-strand method (sometimes called the *long-tail* method) is a great all-around cast-on. It's elastic, attractive, and easy to knit from. For this cast-on method, you need only one needle: the right-hand (RH) needle.

Here's how to cast on using the two-strand method:

1. **Measure off enough yarn for the bottom part of your piece and make a slipknot on your needle.**

   To figure how long the "tail" should be, you need approximately 1 inch for every stitch you cast on plus a little extra. Alternatively, you can measure the bottom of the knitted piece and multiply this number by 4.

   To make the slipknot, form a pretzel-shaped loop and place your needle into the loop, as shown in Figure 2-8a. Then gently pull on both ends of yarn until the stitch is firmly on the needle but still slides easily back and forth, as shown in Figure 2-8b.

2. **Holding the needle in your right hand with the tip pointing away from your hand, insert your left hand's thumb and index finger into the "tent" formed by the two yarn ends falling from the slipknot on your needle.**

3. **With your left hand's ring and pinkie fingers, catch the yarn ends and hold them to your palm so they don't flap around underneath (see Figure 2-9a).**

Figure 2-8:
Getting the
slipknot (the
first stitch)
on your
needle.

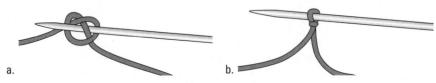

a. b.

4. **With your right hand, pull the needle between your left thumb and index finger so that the "tent" sides aren't droopy.**

5. **With the RH needle tip, go around the yarn on your thumb from the left (see Figure 2-9b), then around the yarn on your index finger from the right (Figure 2-9c), and pull the new loop through (Figure 2-9d).**

Figure 2-9e shows the path your needle takes to catch the loop from your thumb and index finger.

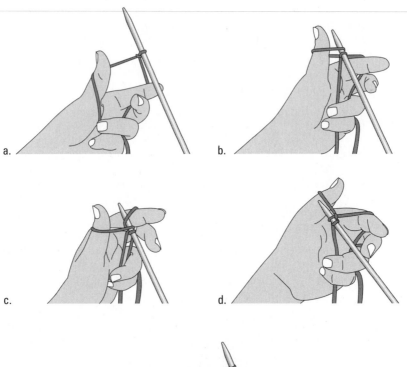

a. b.

c. d.

Figure 2-9:
"Catching"
a loop
from your
left hand.

e.

6. **Tighten this new loop (your first cast-on stitch) onto the needle — but not too tight!**

   You'll quickly find that if you don't let go of the yarn after creating the stitch, you can use your thumb to tighten the stitch onto your needle.

   Although this is your first cast-on stitch, it's also your second stitch on the RH needle, because you also have the initial slipknot.

7. **Repeat Steps 5 and 6 until you have the number of stitches you need.**

   If you need to put your work down, or if you lose your place, you may have to pull the stitches off the needle and start from Step 2 instead.

Although casting on may feel awkward at first and you have to pay attention to each movement, with time and practice, you'll no longer have to think about what your hands are doing. You'll be surprised at how quickly you'll learn the movements and make them smoothly and effortlessly while you think about something entirely unknitterish.

Book II

Traditional Crafts

Cable cast-on (cable co)

The cable cast-on, or *knitting on,* is less elastic than the two-strand cast-on. Use it when you need a sturdy, not-too-stretchy edge. (It's also good for buttonholes). To cast on with this method, follow these steps:

1. **Make a slipknot on your needle, leaving a short tail.**

   Refer to the preceding section for help making a slipknot.

2. **Knit into the first stitch (see Figure 2-10a), but instead of slipping the old loop off the left hand (LH) needle, bring the new loop to the right (see Figure 2-10b) and slip it onto the LH needle (see Figure 2-10c).**

   If you don't know how to make this first stitch, see the later "Knitting know-how" section for instructions.

3. **Insert the RH needle *between* the 2 stitches on the LH needle (see Figure 2-10d and 2-10e).**

4. **Wrap the yarn around the RH needle as you do when you knit and then bring a new loop through to the front (see Figure 2-10f).**

5. **Bring this loop around to the right and place it on the LH needle (see Figure 2-10g).**

6. **Repeat Steps 3 through 5 until you have the number of cast-on stitches you need.**

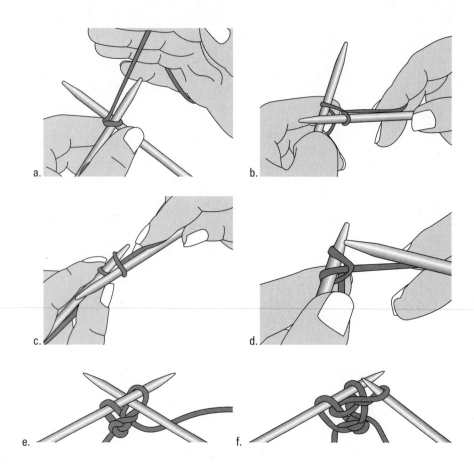

Figure 2-10:
Working
a cable
cast-on.

Now You're Knitting and Purling

Knitted (and purled) stitches are made by using a continuous strand of yarn and two needles to pull new loops through old loops. That's it. The next two sections explain how to create both stitches.

Knitting know-how

To knit, with the yarn in your right hand, hold the needle with the cast-on stitches in your left hand, pointing to the right. Make sure that the first stitch is no more than 1 inch from the tip of the needle. Then follow these steps:

1. **Insert the tip of the empty (RH) needle into the first stitch on the LH needle from left to right and front to back, forming a T with the tips of the needles.**

   The RH needle will be behind the LH needle (see Figure 2-11).

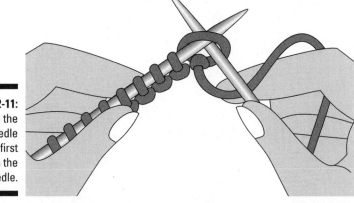

Figure 2-11: Inserting the RH needle into the first stitch on the LH needle.

2. **With your right hand, bring the yarn to the front from the *left side* of the RH needle and then over the RH needle to the right and down between the needles.**

   You can try to maneuver the yarn with your right forefinger, as shown in Figure 2-12a, or just hold it between your thumb and forefinger for now.

3. Keeping a slight tension on the wrapped yarn, bring the tip of the RH needle with its wrap of yarn through the loop on the LH needle to the front.

The RH needle is now in front of the LH needle (see Figure 2-12b). Keep the tip of your left forefinger on the point of the RH needle to help guide the needle through the old stitch and prevent losing the wrap of yarn.

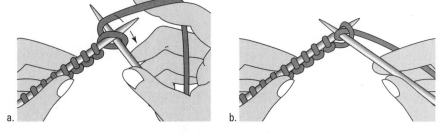

Figure 2-12:
Completing
a knit stitch.

a.   b.

TIP

When you bring the new loop through the old, bring the RH needle up far enough that the new stitch forms on the large part of the needle, not just on the tip. If you work too close to the tips, your new stitches form on the narrowest part of your needles, making them too tight to knit with ease.

Note that when you've finished making a knit stitch, the yarn is behind the needle facing away from you. Be sure that the yarn hasn't ended up in front of your work or over the needle before you start your next stitch.

For left-handed knitters

For better or worse, knitting patterns are written for right-handed knitters (folks who work from the LH [left-hand] needle to the RH [right-hand] needle). If you can master the knitting method instructions presented in this chapter, you won't have to reinterpret patterns in order to work them in reverse. Chances are, like most right-handed knitters, sooner or later you'll work out a series of movements that feels natural and easy, and your stitches will be smooth and even.

What if the initial awkward feeling isn't going away? Try to work in reverse, moving the stitches from the RH needle to the LH one. In the

knitting instructions, substitute the word *right* for *left* and vice versa. To make the illustrations work for you, hold a mirror up to the side of the relevant illustration and mimic the hand and yarn positions visible in the mirror image.

If you find that working in reverse is the most comfortable method, be aware that some directions in knitting patterns, such as decreases, look different when worked in the opposite direction. This quirk will be most problematic for lace patterns, but it's a small price to pay for comfortable knitting. If you decide to work in reverse, *Left-Handed Knitting* by Regina Hurlbert (Van Nostrand Reinhold) may be helpful.

4. **Slide the RH needle to the right until the old loop on the LH needle drops off.**

   You now have a new stitch/loop on the RH needle — the old stitch hangs below it (see Figure 2-13). Congratulations! You've just made your first knitted stitch!

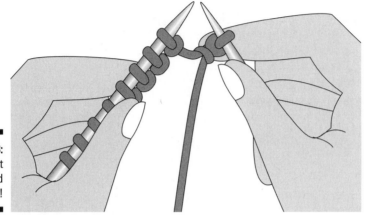

Book II

Traditional Crafts

Figure 2-13:
Your first
knitted
stitch!

5. **Repeat Steps 1 through 4 until you've knitted all the stitches from your LH needle.**

   Your LH needle is now empty, and your RH needle is full of beautiful, new stitches.

6. **Turn your work (that is, switch hands so that the needle with stitches is in your left hand) and knit the new row.**

   When you turn your work, the yarn strand coming out of the first stitch to knit is hanging down in the front. Also notice that the stitch just below the first stitch on your LH needle is larger than the rest and can obscure your view of where your needle should go.

   You may be tempted to pull the yarn strand over the needle to the back to tighten up the stitch. If you do this, it'll look like you have 2 stitches on your needle rather than 1. Keep the strand in front and gently pull down on it, and the big loop if necessary, to better see the opening of the first stitch. Be sure to insert the point of the RH needle in the loop on the LH needle and not into the stitch below.

Repeat these steps for several more rows (or all afternoon) until you're comfortable with the movements. Aim to make these steps one continuous movement, to make even stitches, and to stay relaxed! After you've knitted a few rows, take a look at what you've created: It's the *garter stitch,* one of the most common — and easiest — stitch patterns. You can find it and another common stitch pattern in the later section "Stitches Every Knitter Should Know."

Perfect purling

Purling is working a knit stitch backwards: Instead of going into the stitch from front to back, you enter it from back to front. Combining knit stitches with purl stitches enables you to make a wide variety of textured stitch patterns.

Here's your step-by-step guide on how to purl:

1. **Hold the needle with the cast-on or existing stitches in your left hand, pointing to the right. Insert the tip of the RH needle into the first loop on the LH needle from right to left and back to front, forming a T with the needle tips.**

   The RH needle is in front of the LH needle, and the working yarn is in front of your needles (see Figure 2-14a). This process is the reverse of what you do when you form a knit stitch (described in the preceding section).

2. **With your right hand, wrap the yarn around the back of the RH needle from right to left and down (see Figure 2-14b).**

Figure 2-14: Purling.

a. 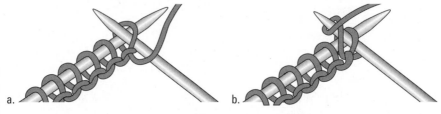 b.

3. **Keeping a slight tension on the wrap of yarn, bring the tip of the RH needle with its wrap of yarn down and through the loop on the LH needle to the *back* side of the LH needle (see Figure 2-15a).**

4. **Slide the old loop off the tip of the LH needle.**

   A new loop/stitch is made on the RH needle. You can see how it should look in Figure 2-15b.

5. **Repeat Steps 1 through 4 until you're comfortable with the movements.**

Figure 2-15: Finishing your purl stitch.

a. 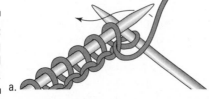 b.

When you purl, the yarn strand comes out of the new stitches on the side of the knitting facing you. When you knit, the yarn comes out of the new stitches on the side facing away from you.

A purled swatch looks just like a knitted swatch. Why? Because purling is simply the reverse of knitting. Whether you knit all the rows or purl all the rows, you're working a garter stitch.

Stitches Every Knitter Should Know

Knitting and purling, covered in the preceding sections, open the door to all sorts of patterns that involve alternating between knit and purl stitches. But as a beginning knitter, you only really need to know two: the *garter stitch*, which you create simply by knitting (or purling) every row, and the *stockinette stitch*, which you create by alternating a knit row with a purl row.

When knitting a stitch, the loose tail of yarn is in *back* of your work. When purling a stitch, the yarn is in *front* of your work. As you switch back and forth between knitting and purling within a row, you need to move your yarn to the front or to the back as appropriate. Unfortunately for novice knitters who often forget to move the yarn accordingly, instructions don't explicitly tell you to bring your yarn to the front or back of your work. They assume that you know where the yarn should be. As you practice the patterns that combine both knit and purl stitches, make sure your yarn is in the proper position for each stitch before you start it and refer to the earlier section "Now You're Knitting and Purling" for a quick review if necessary.

Knits and purls have a quirky but predictable relationship to each other. When lined up horizontally, the purled rows stand out from the knitted rows. Arranged in vertical patterns, like ribbing, the purl stitches recede, and the knit stitches come forward, creating an elastic fabric. When worked in a balanced manner (meaning the same number of knits and purls appear on each side of the fabric), as in seed stitch and its variations, the fabric is stable — it lies flat and doesn't have the tendency to roll in on the edges.

Garter stitch

Garter stitch is the most basic of all knitted fabrics. It's made by knitting every row. (You can create garter stitch by purling every row, too.) You can recognize garter stitch by the horizontal ridges formed by the tops of the knitted loops on every other row (see Figure 2-16). Garter stitch has a lot going for it in addition to being easy to create: It's reversible, lies flat, and has a pleasant rustic look.

Figure 2-16:
Garter
stitch.

Stockinette stitch

When you alternate a knit row with a purl row (knit the first row, purl the second, knit the third, purl the fourth, and so on), you create *stockinette stitch* (abbreviated St st); see Figure 2-17. You see stockinette stitch everywhere: in scarves, socks, sweaters, blankets, hats — you name it. In fact, most beginning and intermediate designs incorporate stockinette stitch.

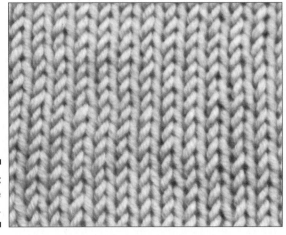

Figure 2-17:
Stockinette
stitch.

In written knitting instructions, stockinette stitch appears like this:

Row 1 (RS): Knit.

Row 2 (WS): Purl.

Repeat Rows 1 and 2 for desired length.

Stockinette fabric looks and behaves in a particular way. To successfully incorporate this stitch into your knitting repertoire, pay attention to the following:

✔ **Stockinette stitch has a right and a wrong side** (though, of course, either side may be the "right" side depending on the intended design). The right side is typically the smooth side, called *stockinette* or *knit*. On this side, the stitches look like small Vs (refer to Figure 2-17). The bumpy side of stockinette-stitch fabric, shown in Figure 2-18, is called *reverse stockinette* or *purl*.

✔ **Stockinette fabric curls on the edges.** The top and bottom (horizontal) edges curl toward the front or smooth side. The side (vertical) edges roll toward the bumpy side. Sweater designers frequently use this rolling feature deliberately to create rolled hems or cuffs, and you can create easy cords or straps simply by knitting a very narrow (say, 4 or 6 stitches across) band in stockinette stitch. But when you want the piece to lie flat, you need to counteract this tendency by working the 3 or 4 stitches on the edge in some stitch that lies flat (like garter stitch, described in the preceding section).

Book II

Traditional Crafts

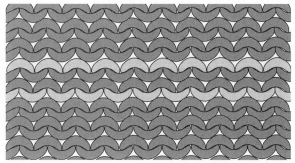

Figure 2-18: Reverse stockinette showing the purl (or bumpy) side.

Binding (Or Casting) Off

To finish your knitted piece, you have to *bind off,* meaning you need to secure the stitches in the last row worked so that they don't unravel. Binding off is easy to do if you follow these basic steps:

1. **Knit the first 2 stitches from the LH needle. These become the first 2 stitches on your RH needle (see Figure 2-19a).**

2. **With your LH needle in front of your RH needle, insert the LH needle into the first stitch worked on the RH needle (the one on the right, as shown in Figure 2-19b).**

3. **Bring this loop over the second stitch and off the tip of the RH needle, as shown in Figure 2-19c.**

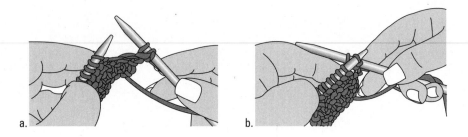

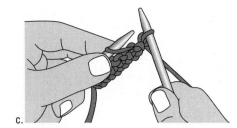

Figure 2-19:
Binding off
a stitch.

At this point, you have 1 stitch bound off and 1 stitch remaining on your RH needle.

4. **Knit the next stitch on the LH needle so that you again have 2 stitches on your RH needle.**

5. **Repeat Steps 2 through 4 until you have 1 stitch remaining on your RH needle.**

   Don't bind off too tightly (which, unfortunately, is easy to do). Knitting should be elastic, especially around neck edges if you want to be able to get a sweater on and off comfortably (and who doesn't want that?). To avoid a tight and inelastic bound-off edge, try working the bind-off row on a needle one or more sizes larger than what you've been using.

6. **Cut the yarn a few inches from the needle and pull the tail through the last stitch to lock it.**

   If the piece you've just bound off is to be sewn to another piece, leave a tail that's 12 inches long or longer for a built-in strand to sew up a seam.

Practice Projects

The projects in this section give you practice on working the basic knit stitches and reading and understanding patterns for knitted garments. As a bonus, you end up with a scarf, a bag, or a hat that you can wear yourself or give to friends and family.

Everywhere Bag in Garter Stitch

This basic bag is handy for carrying your wallet, keys, and some lip balm. Make it larger and throw in your glasses case and a notebook. Make it even bigger, add a pocket, and use it for a knitting bag. So cast on and get started!

Materials and vital statistics

- **Measurements:** 8 inches x 9 inches, with a 4-inch flap

- **Yarn:** Tahki Donegal Tweed (100% wool); 3.5 ounces; 1 skein; any color

- **Needles:** One pair of size US 7 (4^1/$_2$ mm) needles

- **Other materials:** One button, any size

- **Gauge:** 18 stitches per 4 inches in garter stitch (4^1/$_2$ stitches per 1 inch)

Directions

All you need to do to make this versatile bag is knit a rectangle, sew up the sides, make and attach a cord for the strap, make a button loop, and attach a button. Voilà!

Knitting the bag

Cast on 38 stitches (abbreviated sts) and work in garter stitch until the piece measures 22 inches in length.

Bind off and steam lightly.

Sewing the side seams

Measure down 9 inches from one edge and fold your piece with wrong sides together. Sew the sides closed. You should have 4 inches left over for the flap. How you sew the sides closed doesn't really matter, but to make a neat seam, use a tapestry needle and a strand of the same yarn.

Making and attaching the cord strap

You can make cords in a variety of ways. Here's a good method to get you started:

Cast on 189 sts (about 42 inches of stitches).

Work in garter stitch for 3 rows.

Bind off.

Using the same yarn you used for the bag, sew the ends of the strap to either side of the top of the bag.

Forming the button loop and attaching the button

You can make a small button loop just as you would make the cord strap — just make it shorter.

Cast on 8 sts.

Knit 1 row.

Bind off.

To attach the button loop to the bag, center the loop on the bag flap with the ends 1 inch or so apart and attach it with yarn. Using embroidery floss or sewing thread, sew your button on the bag, making sure it's opposite the loop on the flap.

Garter Ridge Scarf

This scarf is quick to knit up and cozy when finished — and you don't have to worry about sewing any seams! Make it in a soft yarn in a color of your choice, and you'll end up with a subtly textured striped scarf.

Materials and vital statistics

✔ **Measurements:** 12 inches x 60 inches

✔ **Yarn:** Heavy worsted-weight yarn; approximately 300 yards

✔ **Needles:** One pair of size US 10 (6 mm) needles; tapestry needle for weaving in the ends

✔ **Gauge:** Not crucial to this project

Directions

Note: Because this scarf takes more than one skein of yarn, you must know how to join a new skein when the first one runs out. For instructions, see the sidebar "Joining yarn.")

Cast on 38 sts.

Rows 1, 3, 5–11, 13, 15, and 16: Knit.

Rows 2, 4, 12, and 14: Purl.

To discourage the edges from rolling in, work a selvedge stitch on the edges by knitting the first and last stitch of every row.

Repeat these 16 rows until your scarf reaches the desired length. End the scarf by working Rows 1–5.

With the WS facing, bind off by *knitting* every stitch for the final garter stitch ridge.

Weave in the loose ends.

Joining yarn

When you run out of yarn as you're knitting, you need to join a new ball of yarn to the end of the old ball. When possible, start a new ball of yarn on an edge that will be enclosed in a seam (try *not* to start a new ball of yarn on an edge that will be exposed). To join yarn at an edge, knit the first stitch of the next row with both ends held together, drop the old strand, and carry on. Or knit the first few stitches with the new yarn only, stop, and tie the two ends together temporarily in a bow to secure them. Either way, leave the ends at least 4 or 5 inches long so you can weave them in later.

If you run out of yarn in the middle of a row, your options are the same: Tie a temporary knot with both yarns, leaving 4- or 5-inch ends; or knit the next stitch with both strands, drop the old one, and continue knitting from the new ball.

Finishing

Gently steam or *wet block* the scarf (that is, get it wet, gently press out the excess moisture, and then lay it out to dry).

Variations

You can express your creativity — and practice new skills at the same time — by altering the basic Garter Ridge Scarf in either of the following ways:

- ✔ Work the scarf in a yarn of a different weight and with the appropriate needles.
- ✔ Make the scarf multicolored by using different colors of yarns.

Two-Way Hat

The hats in this section are based on the same basic principle: Adult human heads are about the same size (give or take a little), and these hats will fit no matter what yarn you use so long as they're knitted in the round with some decreases at the top. A good way to make sure a hat will fit is to try it on after you've knit 1 or 2 inches; rip out the existing stitches and move up or down a needle size if the hat's a little too small or too big.

Plain Hat with Rolled Brim

This most basic of hats is nicely shaped for just about every head size. Add any stitch pattern you like after knitting the first 5 rounds. If you stop the stitch pattern just before the decreases, you don't have to worry about adjusting the decreases to the pattern.

Materials and vital statistics

- ✔ **Measurements:** 21 inches in diameter x $7^1/_2$ inches
- ✔ **Yarn:** Worsted-weight wool; 100 yards
- ✔ **Needles:** One 16-inch size US 7 ($4^1/_2$ mm) and size US 8 (5 mm) circular needle; four or five size US 8 (5 mm) dpns; yarn needle to weave in ends
- ✔ **Other materials:** Stitch marker
- ✔ **Gauge:** 4 stitches and 6 rows per 1 inch

Directions

Using a size US 7 circular needle, cast on 80 sts. Join round, being careful not to twist the stitches, and place marker to denote beginning of round.

Knit 5 rounds.

Switch to size US 8 needles and knit 5 inches.

Begin decreases:

Note: Decreases (and increases) are essential in patterns that require shaping. The notation k2tog means "knit two stitches together." To perform this maneuver, you knit the next two stitches at the same time (instead of inserting the RH needle into one stitch on the LH needle, you insert it into two stitches and then knit as you normally would by wrapping your yarn around the needle and pulling the loop through both stitches at the same time). In this pattern, the decreases create the hat's shaped crown.

Round 1: * K8, k2tog; rep from * to end of round.

Round 2 and all even rounds: Knit without decreasing.

Round 3: * K7, k2tog; rep from * to end of round.

Round 5: * K6, k2tog; rep from * to end of round.

Round 7: * K5, k2tog; rep from * to end of round.

Note: At this point, you may want to switch to double-pointed needles (dpns) because the diameter of the round is much smaller than the circular needle's length. Simply distribute the remaining stitches evenly over three or four dpns and knit with the remaining needle (the fourth or fifth, depending on how many you're using).

Round 9: * K4, k2tog; rep from * to end of round.

Round 11: * K3, k2tog; rep from * to end of round.

Round 13: * K2, k2tog; rep from * to end of round.

Round 15 to end: Continue knitting (* k2, k2tog *) until fewer than 10 stitches remain.

Cut yarn, leaving at least a 12-inch tail.

Finishing

Thread tail onto yarn needle and slip remaining stitches onto yarn needle. Pull opening closed, push yarn tail to reverse side of fabric, and weave in ends.

Ribbed Watchman's Cap

This classically masculine hat looks great on women, too — just choose a bright color. Patterned yarn such as a handpainted, multishade colorway will be broken up by the 3-stitch rib, which is an interesting visual effect.

Materials and vital statistics

- ✔ **Measurements:** 21 inches in diameter x 7$\frac{1}{2}$ inches

- ✔ **Yarn:** Worsted-weight wool; 125 yards

- ✔ **Needles:** One 16-inch size US 9 (5$\frac{1}{2}$ mm) circular needle; four or five size US 9 dpns; yarn or tapestry needle

- ✔ **Gauge:** 4 stitches and 6 rows per 1 inch

Directions

Cast on 84 sts.

* K3, p3; rep from * until piece measures 6 inches.

Begin decreases (*Note:* if you don't know how to decrease, refer to the directions for the Plain Hat with Rolled Brim):

Round 1: * P1, p2tog, k3; rep from * to end of round (70 sts).

Round 2: * P2, k3; rep from * to end of round.

Round 3: * P2, k1, k2tog; rep from * to end of round (56 sts).

Round 4: * P2, k2; rep from * to end of round.

Round 5: * P2tog, k2; rep from * to end of round (42 sts).

Round 6: * P1, k2; rep from * to end of round.

Round 7: * P1, k2tog; rep from * to end of round (28 sts). Switch to dpns, dividing stitches evenly.

Round 8: * P1, k1; rep from * to end of round.

Round 9: * K2tog; rep from * to end of round (14 sts).

Round 10: * K2tog; rep from * to end of round (7 sts).

Cut yarn, leaving at least a 12-inch tail.

Finishing

Thread tail onto yarn needle and slip remaining stitches onto yarn needle. Pull opening closed, push yarn tail to reverse side of fabric, and weave in ends.

Chapter 3

Hand-Sewing Basics

. . . .

In This Chapter

▶ Getting your sewing supplies together

▶ Finding out about fabric

▶ Becoming familiar with basic hand-sewing stitches

▶ Trying out practice projects

. . . .

Getting to admire a project you've completed using beautiful fabrics and hand-stitching is very gratifying, and you're likely to hear praise from friends and family, too. On top of that, you can save money sewing. Wow, what a hobby!

This chapter lists the tools you need to hand-sew and explains basic hand-sewing techniques and how to read a sewing pattern — info that can come in handy if you extend your repertoire into more complex sewing projects. It also includes basic hand-sewing tasks, like hemming, and a few simple but great-looking projects. After you have a couple of projects under your belt, chances are you'll love to sew.

This chapter focuses on hand-sewing. Machine-sewing is the preferred method for garment construction and complex projects. For the details on everything you need to know about machine-sewing, check out *Sewing For Dummies,* 2nd Edition, by Janice Saunders Maresh (Wiley).

Assembling Your Sewing Kit

Like most hobbies, successful sewing projects begin with a few good tools, a few basic supplies, and a little know-how. The first section details hand-sewing tools that any hand-sewer needs. The second section explains notions that you're likely to need or encounter in the patterns you buy. The rest of the chapter is dedicated to know-how.

Common hand-sewing tools

Sure, you can collect some of these tools from your household — those old scissors from the garage, the ruler from your desk drawer, and pins scavenged from freshly opened dress shirts — but you'll have a better sewing experience if you use tools intended for the job.

On pins and needles

Needles come in many shapes, sizes, and types. The needle you select depends on the fabric you use and the project you want to sew. Generally, the finer the fabric you work with, the finer the needle, and the heavier the fabric, the heavier the needle. When selecting needles for hand-sewing, choose a variety pack, which gives you from five to ten needles of various lengths and thicknesses. Some even have different-sized eyes. In a pinch, you can use any hand needle as long as the point can easily penetrate the fabric and the eye doesn't shred the thread.

You need pins to sew. I recommend using long, fine, glass-head pins. The glass head fits comfortably in your fingers when you pin through multiple layers of fabric, and the extra length makes pinning more secure. Plus, if you accidentally press or iron over the glass heads, they don't melt like the plastic ones may.

Thimbles

Thimbles are essential for hand-sewing. Although your fingers are fabulous tools, they leave a little to be desired when it comes to pushing a needle through heavy thicknesses of fabric. Thimbles, which are like little hard hats for fingers, protect the soft pads of your fingers from potential pain. They come in a variety of sizes; choose one that comfortably fits the middle finger on your dominant hand.

Scissors and seam rippers

Although you can buy a variety of sewing scissors, I recommend 8-inch bent dressmaker's shears and 5-inch trimming shears. The bent dressmaker's shears are the best tool for cutting fabric. The bent-angle blade gives your index finger a place to rest when you have a long cutting job, and it prevents you from lifting the fabric off the table, ensuring a more accurate cut. The trimming scissors come in handy for trimming smaller areas on a project and for clipping threads.

When shopping for shears or scissors, make sure you test them on a variety of fabrics. They should cut all the way to the tips of the blades.

When you make mistakes (which you will), you need a seam ripper to rip out (or unsew) the stitches. A *seam ripper* is a little tool with a point that lifts the stitch off the fabric as the blade cuts the thread. ***Note:*** You can't sharpen seam rippers; so when one becomes dull, buy another.

Keeping your shears and scissors sharp

Dull scissors can make cutting a real drag: You have to work twice as hard to use them, and the results aren't nearly as good. Keep your shears and scissors sharp so they're a pleasure to use.

If you want to keep your scissors sharp, the first rule is to not use them to cut anything you don't normally cut when sewing: that means no cutting plastic, cardboard, wire, and the like. The blades become rough and dull and not only will they chew or snag your fabric, but they'll also wear out your hand when you try to use them. The second rule? Have them sharpened periodically. Most sewing machine dealers sharpen scissors and shears. In addition, many fabric stores have a scissors-sharpener who visits the store periodically. After the pro finishes sharpening your shears or scissors, check to see that they cut to the point.

Tape measure

All kinds of tape measures are available. A plastic-coated fabric tape measure is a good choice. This tape doesn't stretch, so you always get accurate measurements. Most tapes are $5/8$-inch wide, the width of a standard seam allowance, and 60 inches long. Many tapes come with both metric and U.S. measurements and are two-toned, so you can readily see when the tape is twisted.

Keep your tape measure handy by draping it around your neck, but remember to take if off when you leave the house — no one is likely to see it as a fashion statement.

Fabric markers

To help you match up your fabric pattern pieces exactly the right way, the pattern for a project includes *match points,* called notches and dots, which are printed right on the pattern tissue. To use these match points, you have to transfer them from the pattern to the fabric, using fabric markers. You can choose from a variety: disappearing dressmaker's chalk, wash-out pencil, vanishing marker, and so on. The one you choose depends primarily on the fabric you want to mark. Some are better for light-colored fabrics; others are better for dark-colored fabrics. If you're not sure which to select, the clerk at the fabric store can guide you.

Irons

When you sew, you need a good iron. Choose one that has a variety of heat settings and can make steam. Also, choose an iron that has a smooth, non-stick *soleplate* (the part that heats up); these are easy to clean.

You also need a press cloth to place between the iron and the fabric to prevent shine and over-pressing. Use a clean, white or off-white, 100-percent cotton or linen tea towel or napkin, or purchase a press cloth.

Threads and notions

Obviously, you can't sew without thread. All-purpose sewing thread is the type and weight of thread that works well for most fabrics. You can find several all-purpose brands at your local fabric store. When choosing a thread, unwrap a strand and place it on your fabric. You want the thread color to be slightly darker than your fabric for a good match.

But you often need other things too: tapes, trimmings, ribbons, piping, laces, elastics, zippers, and so on, all of which are lumped together under the category of *sewing notions* or *findings*. If you're using a pattern, the back of the pattern envelope tells you exactly which notions you need for a particular project. Common notions include

- **Bias tape:** Bias tape is a long, continuous strip of woven cotton/polyester-blend fabric. Bias tape conforms to a straight edge, such as a seam allowance, and can be easily shaped to fit a curve or hem edge. Bias tape comes in several configurations, including single-fold, extra-wide, double-fold, hem facing, and hem tape.

- **Elastic:** Elastic comes in many different configurations and widths to accommodate various uses. For example, *drawstring elastic* has a drawstring running through the center of it — perfect for use in drawstring shorts and sweat pants — and elastic *braid* is used in waist or wrist casings.

- **Ribbons:** Ribbons come in hundreds, if not thousands, of configurations, fiber contents, widths, colors, finishes, and textures. Grosgrain ribbon, for example, has a ribbed texture and is very easy to sew. You can use ribbons for everything from trimming apparel to decorating floral arrangements.

- **Zippers:** Zippers come in a variety of types and configurations, such as conventional nylon coil zippers, invisible zippers (those that, when sewn in properly, end up looking like a seam), and molded-tooth zippers (which have zipper teeth made either of metal or nylon).

- **Fasteners:** This category includes things like buttons, snaps, hooks and eyes, and so on — basically, the things that keep your blouse from popping open and your pants from falling down. These come in a variety of sizes, shapes, and colors.

Choosing the Right Fabric

You can often find a list of recommended fabrics on the back of your pattern envelope. If you're new to sewing, don't stray from the advice on the envelope concerning the choice of fabric, or the final product may not look as good or fit as well as you intended, even if you achieve the color you want. When you make something from a pattern you create yourself, it helps to know the characteristics and advantages and disadvantages of common fabric types. This information not only comes in handy when selecting fabric but also when buying clothes off the rack.

Becoming familiar with fabric types

Although you can sew any fabric by hand with the right needle and thread, doing so can be very challenging. Heavier and thicker fabrics are more difficult to hand-sew, as are very sheer, slippery fabrics. In addition, the resulting seam may not be strong enough to tolerate much wear and tear. For that reason, the following list sticks with fabrics that are practically guaranteed to give you hand-sewing success and nice, strong seams. These fabrics are available by the yard:

- **Broadcloth:** A light- to mid-weight, evenly woven cotton or silk fabric used in men's shirts. Broadcloth is also made in wool for fine wool suiting.

- **Chambray:** A light- to mid-weight, evenly woven cotton or cotton blend you find in work clothes, shirts, and pajamas. Chambray is usually made with a colored warp yarn and a white filler yarn. This fabric resembles denim but is lighter in weight.

- **Denim:** A strong, mid- to heavy-weight, twill weave fabric in which the warp yarn is a color (usually blue) and the filler yarn is white. Denim is available in many weights, depending on the end use, and is great for jeans, jackets, skirts, and home decor projects.

- **Flannel:** A light- to mid-weight, plain or twill weave cotton or wool fabric. Cotton flannel that's brushed has a soft, fluffy surface and is used for work shirts and pajamas. Wool flannel isn't usually brushed and is used as a suiting.

- **Fleece:** A light- to heavy-weight, *hydrophobic* (water-hating), double-sided, polyester knit used in pullovers, jackets, mittens, booties, blankets, slippers, and scarves. A common trade name for this type of fleece is Polarfleece. You can also find sweatshirts in fleece made with cotton and cotton/polyester blends.

Reading fabric labels

In the fabric store, you see the fabric wrapped around *bolts* — cardboard flats or round tubes. Flat bolts of fabric stand at attention on tables, and tube-type bolts are stored upright in a rack or threaded with a wooden dowel and hung horizontally for easy viewing. At the end of flat bolts, you find a label that tells you many important things about the fabric, including the fiber content, care instructions, price per yard, and, often, the manufacturer. Tube bolts often have a hangtag that contains the same information as the bolt-end label.

The fabric's width determines how much fabric to purchase for a particular project. Reading the back of your project's pattern envelope helps determine how much fabric to buy based on the fabric width. (See the section "Understanding the pattern and its parts" for more information on reading pattern envelopes.) The most common fabric widths are as follows:

- ✔ **42 to 48 inches wide:** Most woven cotton, cotton blend, novelty print, dressmaking, and quilting fabrics come in this width.

- ✔ **54 to 60 inches wide:** Many knits, woolens, and home decor fabrics come in this width.

Occasionally, you find a fabric that is 72 inches wide, and sheer fabrics, such as bridal tulle, come up to 120 inches wide.

Getting to know your fabric

Before you do any sewing with any piece of fabric, you need to understand some basic fabric terminology. Why? Understanding the parts of the fabric and cutting your pattern pieces on-grain means that seams stay pressed and straight, pant legs and sleeves don't twist when you wear them, and the creases in your pants stay perpendicular to the ground. Take a look at Figure 3-1 to get acquainted with fabric's four key facets:

- ✔ **Selvages:** The finished edges where the fabric comes off the looms; the selvages are parallel to the lengthwise grain.

- ✔ **Lengthwise grain or grainline:** The grainline runs the length of the fabric, parallel to the selvages. On knit fabrics, the lengthwise grain is usually more stable and less stretchy than the crosswise grain.

- ✔ **Crosswise grain:** This grain runs across the width of the fabric, from selvage to selvage, perpendicular to the lengthwise grain. On knit fabrics, most of the stretch is usually across this grain.

- ✔ **Bias:** 45 degrees between the lengthwise and crosswise grains.

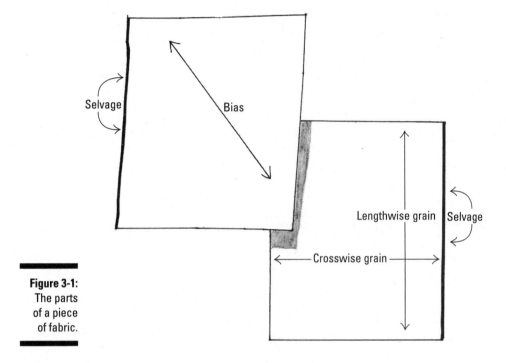

Figure 3-1:
The parts
of a piece
of fabric.

Fundamentals of Hand-Sewing

Used to be most people (yes, men too) knew how to thread a needle and perform basic stitches. Then along came the sewing machine and manufactured clothing, and hand-sewing (except for the occasional mending job) and the skills that went with it fell by the wayside. Well, this section reintroduces you to these fundamental skills.

Threading a needle

To begin threading a hand needle, reel off a strand of thread about 18 to 24 inches long. Longer threads tend to tangle and wear out before you use them up. Starting with the end of the thread that comes off the spool first, cut the thread cleanly and at an angle with a sharp pair of scissors. Cutting at an angle puts a little point on the thread so that it slips easily through the eye. Here's a little pointer: The cheapest sewing notion you can find is your own saliva. Moisten the thread end to help it glide right through the needle's eye.

Some needles have very small eyes; some people have very poor eyesight. A *needle threader,* which you can find at your local sewing supply store, can help with tight threading situations. To use a needle threader, poke the fine wire through the eye of the needle, push the thread end through the wire loop, and then pull. The wire grabs the thread and pulls it through the needle's eye, as shown in Figure 3-2.

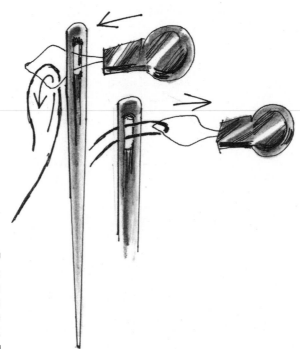

Figure 3-2:
Threading a
needle with
a needle
threader.

Self-threading hand needles make threading even easier. To use a self-threading needle, hold the needle and a length of thread in one hand. Pull the thread end across the self-threading eye so that the thread lies in the notch. Snap the thread into the notch until it clips into place, as shown in Figure 3-3. If the thread keeps coming unthreaded after many uses, you've worn out the self-threading eye, so throw away the needle and use a new one.

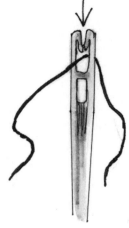

Figure 3-3:
Threading
a self-
threading
needle.

Tying the knot

To stop the thread from pulling completely through the fabric when you sew, you need a knot at the thread's end. The following steps tell both lefties and righties how to tie a sewing knot:

1. **Hold the thread between your thumb and index fingers and wrap a loop of thread around the tip of your opposite index finger, as shown in Figure 3-4.**

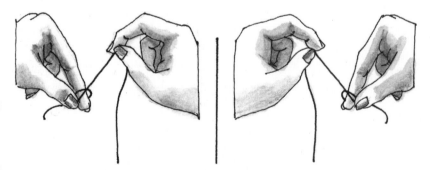

Figure 3-4:
Make
a loop.

2. **Roll the loop between your finger and against your thumb so that the loop twists, as shown in Figure 3-5.**

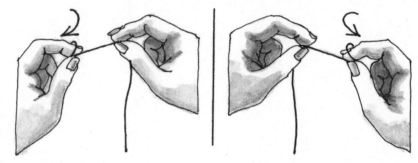

Figure 3-5:
Twist
the loop.

3. **Slide your index finger back while rolling the thread until the loop is almost off your finger, as shown in Figure 3-6.**

4. **Bring your middle finger to the twisted end of the loop, remove your index finger, and firmly place the middle finger in front of the twisted thread against the thumb, as shown in Figure 3-7.**

5. **Pull on the thread with the opposite hand to close the loop and form the knot.**

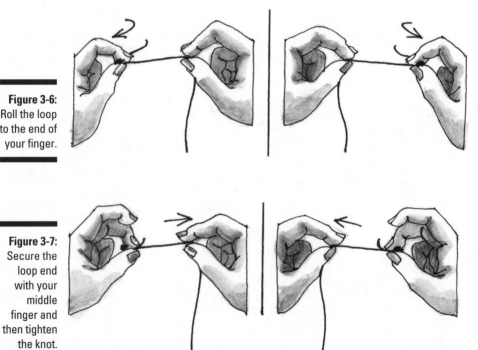

Figure 3-6:
Roll the loop
to the end of
your finger.

Figure 3-7:
Secure the
loop end
with your
middle
finger and
then tighten
the knot.

Common hand-sewn stitches

Any given sewing job may entail one of several types of stitches, and you definitely need the right stitch for the job. For example, you shouldn't use a hand-basting stitch to permanently sew together a pair of overalls; the stitches are too far apart, and your overalls fall apart the first time you attempt to lift that bale or tote that barge. In this section, I familiarize you with the basic hand stitches and their uses.

The securing stitch

In hand-sewing, you secure the end of a stitch by sewing a knot — regardless of the type of stitch. To sew a knot, take a small backstitch and form a loop over the point of the needle. When you pull the thread through the loop, it cinches the thread and secures a knot at the base of the fabric (see Figure 3-8). When securing a high-stress area, sew two knots.

The hand-basting stitch

You use hand-basting stitches to temporarily hold two or more layers of fabric together. Each basting stitch should be about $1/4$-inch long with less than $1/4$ inch between stitches.

For hand-basting, choose a color of thread that contrasts with the fabric. This makes the stitches easier to find and pull out after you sew in the permanent stitches.

Working from right to left (for right-handers) or from left to right (for left-handers), weave the point of the needle in and out of the fabric, working it through the fabric (see Figure 3-9).

The running stitch

You use this very short, even stitch for fine seaming, mending, and gathering. The stitch is short and tight and, as a result, is usually permanent. Use it for quickly closing a torn seam. To make a running stitch, weave the point of the needle in and out of the fabric making very short ($1/16$-inch), even stitches before pulling the needle through the fabric (see Figure 3-10).

Figure 3-8: Use this technique to securely fasten a hand-sewn stitch.

Figure 3-9:
You baste
by simply
weaving the
needle in
and out of
the fabric.

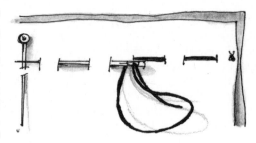

Figure 3-10:
Use short,
even
stitches
when
fashioning
running
stitches.

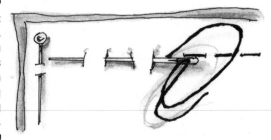

The even backstitch

The even backstitch is the strongest hand stitch. Because of its durability, this stitch is useful for repairing seams on fabrics that are denser or heavier than those you would repair with the running stitch. To create the even backstitch, pull the needle up through the fabric and poke the needle back into the fabric half a stitch behind where the thread first emerged. Bring the needle up half a stitch in front of where the thread first emerged (see Figure 3-11). Repeat for the length of the seam.

Figure 3-11:
The even
backstitch
is extremely
strong.

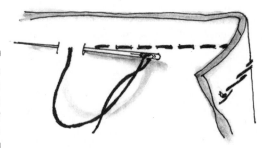

The blind hemming stitch

You take these stitches inside the hem allowance between the hem and the garment. With a little practice, a fine needle, and fine thread, good blind hemming stitches don't show on the right side — hence the name *blind*.

You need to turn up the hem allowance and press it into place before you use the blind hemming stitch. You should also finish the edge of the hem by pinking the edge (cutting it with pinking shears).

Fold the hem allowance back ³/₈ inch and take the first short stitch ¹/₄ inch from the hem edge. Take the next short stitch by catching only a thread of the fabric. Continue with stitches spaced about ¹/₂ inch apart, catching the hem allowance in a stitch and taking as fine a stitch as possible into the garment. Stitch back and forth between the hem allowance and the garment around the hemline until you complete the blind hemming (see Figure 3-12).

Figure 3-12: Blind hems require fine stitches about ¹/₂ inch apart.

The slant hemming stitch

This stitch is the fastest — but least durable — of the hemming stitches because so much thread is on the surface of the hem edge. (If you've ever caught your heel in your hem and pulled it out, you may be the victim of a slant hemming stitch.) So use the slant hemming stitch only if you're in a hurry and you're hemming the bottom of a blouse that you tuck in. Take a stitch around the hem edge and then up through the garment, catching only a thread of the garment fabric (see Figure 3-13).

The hemming slipstitch

You use the hemming slipstitch when working with (guess what?) a folded hem edge. This stitch is very durable and almost invisible. Fasten the thread to the hem allowance by poking the needle through the fold of the hem edge and bringing it up through the fabric. With the point of the needle, pick up one thread from the garment and work the needle back into the fold of the hem edge (see Figure 3-14). Then repeat the process.

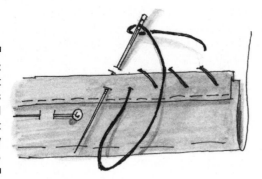

Figure 3-13:
The slant stitch is quick and easy but not very durable.

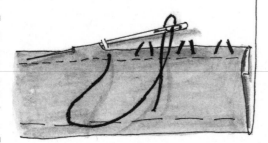

Figure 3-14:
The hemming slipstitch is very durable and nearly invisible.

The even slipstitch

You can join two folded edges by using the even slipstitch. Most often, this stitch comes into play when you want to repair a seam from the right side because the seam is difficult to reach from the wrong side of the project.

Fasten the thread and bring it out at the edge of the fold. Taking fine stitches, work the needle, slipping it through the fold on one edge and drawing the thread taut. Take another stitch, slipping the needle through the opposite, folded edge (see Figure 3-15).

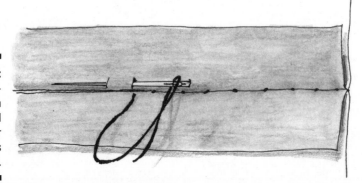

Figure 3-15:
Use the slip-stitch to join two folded edges or seam lines together.

Working with Patterns

Most hand-sewing projects, like those included in this chapter, don't require sewing patterns. But if the project you're working on is particularly complex, or if you've decided to hand-sew (or machine-sew) a garment, you'll need to know how to decipher a standard sewing pattern.

Patterns are marketed in several ways:

- **Through pattern magazines:** Most bookstores and grocery stores carry a selection of these on their newsstands.

- **In pattern catalogs at fabric stores:** These catalogs are organized into categories ranging from dresses and children's clothing to crafts and home decor projects. Within these sections, you often find patterns categorized by degree of difficulty, with emphasis placed on projects that are easy to sew.

- **On display or spinner racks at fabric stores:** Specially priced and promotional patterns are often featured this way.

- **Through online pattern vendors:** You can check out Simplicity patterns at www.simplicity.com and Butterick, McCall's, and Vogue patterns at www.mccall.com. Or for more options, enter the type of pattern you're looking for into your search engine's browser.

Regional and national fabric chain stores often carry fabrics and patterns for both clothing and home decorating, plus everything else you need to complete clothing, home decor, crafting, and quilting projects, and more. Stores that specialize in home decorating fabrics usually don't carry clothing patterns.

Even a pattern labeled *easy* or *quick* may be difficult and time-consuming for a rookie. Many pattern instruction writers assume that you have a certain amount of general sewing knowledge. If you're a real beginner, look for patterns with few seams and simple lines.

The *Sewing For Dummies* patterns, published by Simplicity Pattern Company, are a perfect choice. They have the latest projects and the easiest-to-follow sewing directions you can find. If you're in a quandary about a particular pattern, have a sales associate at the fabric store help you.

Understanding the pattern and its parts

Few things are more intimidating than trying to figure out all the hieroglyphics on the various parts of a pattern, as shown in Figure 3-16.

Book II

Traditional Crafts

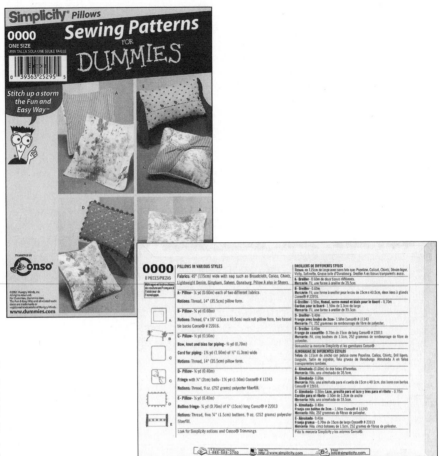

Figure 3-16:
Front and
back of
a pattern
envelope.

Info on the outside of the pattern

On the front of the pattern envelope, you often see several style variations of the same project. In the world of sewing, people call these style variations *views*. One view may have a collar, long sleeves, and cuffs. Another view may have a V-neck and short sleeves. In home decor patterns, you may have several views in one pattern for a basic window treatment. Another pattern may have several pillow views. Views simply give you style options for creating the same basic project.

The back of a pattern envelope contains the following information about your project:

- ✔ **The back of the project in detail:** The front of the pattern usually just shows the front of your project. The back of the pattern shows you the back of the project. You see details like kick pleats or a back zipper — information you may want to know before buying the pattern.

- ✔ **A description of the project by view:** Always read the description of a project on the back of the pattern envelope. Drawings and photographs can deceive, but this written description tells you exactly what you're getting.

- ✔ **How much fabric to buy:** This information is based on the width of the fabric you choose, the view you make, your size, and whether your fabric has nap or not. If your fabric has nap, the pattern requires you to buy a little more fabric.

- ✔ **A list of notions needed for specific views:** These notions include items such as the number and size of buttons, the zipper length and type, elastic width and length, shoulder pad style and size, hooks and eyes, and so on.

Book II

Traditional Crafts

Info on the inside of the pattern

Inside your pattern envelope, you find the following items necessary for your project:

- ✔ **Pattern pieces:** Some pattern pieces are printed on large pieces of tissue paper. Others are printed on sturdy pieces of white paper and are called *master patterns.*

- ✔ **Key and glossary:** These references help you decipher the markings on the pattern pieces.

- ✔ **Pattern layout:** This guide shows you how to lay out the pattern pieces on the fabric for each view.

- ✔ **Step-by-step instructions for putting the project together:** The project instructions may run more than one page. If so, staple the pages together in the upper-left corner and post them in front of you as you sew. You can easily check off each step as you finish it.

Some home decor projects, such as pillow patterns, include tissue or paper pattern pieces. Others, such as sofa slipcovers and some window treatments, don't include a paper pattern because there's no standard size or style of sofa or window. In these patterns, you find printed, step-by-step instructions that look like the pattern guide sheet that comes with a typical pattern.

Decoding the pattern pieces

Look at your pattern pieces. You have only one sleeve, half of a front top, half of a back top, half of a facing, half of a collar, and so on. Did the company forget to print the whole pattern? No. You fold the fabric in half the long way (usually with the right side of the fabric to the inside), and then you lay the pattern pieces out and cut them on a double fabric layer. So most of the time, you need only half of the pattern to make a complete garment.

In addition to identifying information (the pattern number, name of the pattern piece, and letter or number of the pattern piece), all pattern pieces have the following information (Figure 3-17 shows the full gambit of markings you may find on a pattern piece):

- **Grainline:** The most important pattern marking, the grainline symbol is a straight line that usually has arrowheads at each end. The grainline parallels the *selvages* (finished edges) of the fabric.

- **Size:** Many pattern pieces show several sizes. Each size is marked clearly, so you shouldn't have too much trouble keeping them straight.

- **Number of pieces you need to cut:** Often, you need to cut more than one of each pattern piece.

- **Cutting line:** This heavy, outer line on the pattern piece lets you know where to cut. Sometimes you see scissors symbols on this line.

- **Seam line or stitching line:** You usually find this broken line $1/4$ to $5/8$ inch inside the cutting line. Multiple-sized patterns may not have a seam line printed on the pattern. Read the pattern guide sheet to determine the width of the seam allowance.

- **Notches:** You use these diamond-shaped match points on the cutting line for accurately joining pattern pieces together. You may find single notches, double notches, and triple notches all on one pattern.

- **Circles, dots, triangles, or squares:** These shapes indicate additional match points that aid in the construction, fit, and ease in putting the project together. For example, large dots on the pattern may indicate where you gather a waistline.

- **Place-on-fold brackets or symbols:** Use these symbols to lay out the pattern piece exactly on the fold, which is also the lengthwise grain of the fabric. When you cut out the pattern piece and remove the paper pattern, the fabric opens into a full piece.

- **Directional stitching symbols:** These symbols, which often look like small arrows or presser feet symbols, indicate the direction you sew when sewing the seam.

- **The hemline:** This direction on the pattern shows the recommended finished length of the project, which varies from person to person. But, even though the hemline may vary, the *hem allowance* (the recommended distance from the hemline to the cut edge) doesn't.

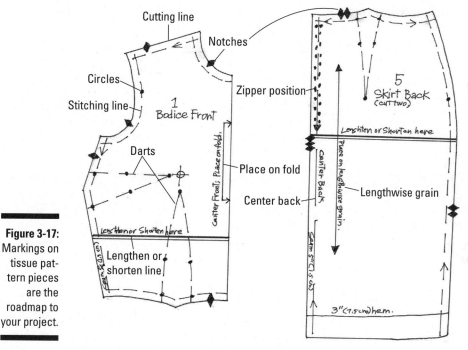

Figure 3-17: Markings on tissue pattern pieces are the roadmap to your project.

Preparing your fabric

Using fabric straight off the bolt is a little like eating an unbaked apple pie: You can do it, but the results aren't going to be good. Before laying and cutting out your project and before sewing a stitch, do the following:

1. **Preshrink your fabric to see how it behaves (how much it shrinks, whether the colors run, and so on).**

   For washable fabrics, preshrink your fabric as you would the finished project. For example, if you plan to wash your finished garment in the washing machine with regular-strength detergent and then dry it in the dryer, wash and dry your fabric in the same way to preshrink it.

2. **Press your fabric smooth and flat, and refold it to the original bolt fold so that the selvages are even.**

3. **Examine the refolded fabric and, if necessary, pull the fabric back on grain.**

   When you fold it in half so the selvages are together, are the raw edges perpendicular to the selvages and the selvages parallel to one another? If so, the fabric is ready for the layout and cutting process. If not, the fabric may have been cut off the bolt unevenly, or the fabric needs to be pulled back on grain. To do so, unfold the fabric again, pull it on the bias (refer to Figure 3-1 for the bias), and straighten it. If you have a large piece of fabric, get a helper to pull the yardage from one corner while you pull on the yardage from the opposite corner.

You also want to preshrink any trims, tapes, and piping you plan to use with your project: Wrap them around your hand and remove your hand from the trim, creating a *hank*. Put a rubber band around the hank and wash it along with the project's fabric. Note that upholstery fabrics, which are often dry clean only, do not need to be preshrunk.

Laying out the pattern

Once your fabric is preshrunk and pressed (explained in the preceding section), you're ready to lay out your pattern. Follow these steps to lay the pattern pieces on the fabric:

1. **Find and cut apart the paper pattern pieces you need to make your project view; set them aside.**

   When you cut the paper pattern pieces apart, don't cut them out right on the cutting line; leave a little of the paper past the cutting line. Leaving the extra paper makes cutting out the paper pieces faster and easier.

2. **Locate the lengthwise grain or place-on-fold symbols on the paper pattern pieces.**

   Before laying the pattern on the fabric, mark these symbols with a highlighter for easy reference.

3. **Fold and lay the fabric on a table or cutting board, as shown in the pattern guide sheet instructions.**

   The *right side* of the fabric is the pretty side that everyone sees. The *wrong side* of the fabric is the inside that nobody sees when you wear the project. When you lay out the pattern for cutting, be sure that you lay out all the pattern pieces as shown in your pattern guide sheet instructions. The pattern guide sheet shows the right side of the fabric shaded in a darker color than the wrong side of the fabric, so you can see what's going on in the step-by-step illustrations.

   If the fabric is longer than your table or cutting board, prevent the excess fabric weight from stretching and pulling on your fabric by folding it and laying it on the end of the table.

Book II

Traditional Crafts

4. **Following the layout the pattern guide sheet suggests, lay out the pattern on-grain, making sure that the grainline is parallel to the selvages as shown in Figure 3-18.**

Figure 3-18: The grainline of your pattern should be parallel to the selvages when you lay out a pattern.

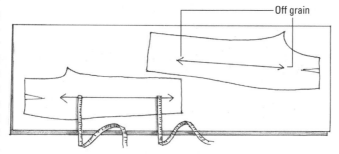
Off grain

Check that each pattern piece is placed precisely on-grain by poking a pin straight down into one end of the grainline, measuring the distance from the grainline to the selvage, and then pivoting the paper pattern until the opposite end of the grainline measures exactly the same distance from the selvage. However, use this technique only if a cutting board or table pad protects your tabletop.

Now you're ready for pinning and cutting, explained in the next section.

Pinning and cutting out your pieces

Pin the pattern piece to the doubled layer of fabric so that the pins go through both fabric layers and are perpendicular to and on the inside of the cutting line. This prevents the fabric from shifting during the cutting process.

(You don't need to pin every inch. Just pin at the notches and everywhere the pattern changes direction. On long, straight edges, such as pant legs and sleeve seams, place pins every 4 inches or so.)

Cut out your pattern pieces using a pair of sharp dressmaker's shears. For accuracy, cut in the middle of the solid cutting line marked on the pattern tissue, trying not to lift the fabric off the table too much when cutting.

Rather than cutting around each individual notch, save time by cutting straight across the notches on the cutting line. After you completely cut out the pattern piece, go back and, with the tip of your sharp scissors, snip into the notch about $1/4$ inch. A single notch gets one snip in the center of the notch; a double notch gets two snips, one in the center of each notch; a triple notch gets three snips. When you go to match up the pattern pieces at the notches, just match up the snips — a fast and accurate task.

Making marks that matter

After you cut out the pattern pieces, you're ready for marking. Marking is important because you don't want to get halfway through a project, notice that the pattern guide sheet tells you to sew from this mark to that mark, and realize that you forgot to mark something (or thought it wasn't important). So dutifully mark all dots, circles, triangles, squares, darts, pleats, and tucks.

Projects You Can Sew by Hand

If you consider that folks have been sewing since humankind moved out of draped animal skins, you realize that anything you can sew by machine today — garments, home decor, and more — you can sew by hand as well. The projects in this section are designed to give you practice mastering the small, even stitches that are the hallmark of all skillful hand-sewing.

One-piece fringed envelope pillow

Make this really easy pillow using a fabric that complements your decor and a sensational decorator trim called *bullion fringe,* a long fringe with twisted, looped ends that's often used on pillows, upholstery, and slipcovers. (It even makes nice doll hair.) After making this easy pillow, you may amaze even yourself with your newfound creativity and sewing skills.

To make this project, you need the following materials in addition to the usual sewing implements (see the earlier section "Common hand-sewing tools"):

✔ One 18-inch pillow form

✔ ½ yard of 48- or 54-inch-wide home decor fabric

✔ Thread that matches the fabric

✔ One-yard bullion fringe to coordinate with the fabric

Follow these steps to create the pillow:

Book II

Traditional Crafts

1. **Cut the fabric into an 18-x-46-inch rectangle, as shown in Figure 3-19.**

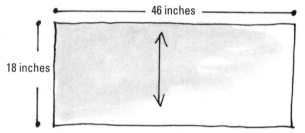

Figure 3-19: Cut your pillow fabric into an 18-x-46-inch rectangle.

46 inches

18 inches

2. **Press and stitch a ½-inch hem on both short ends of the fabric. Use the securing stitch at the beginning of the seam, the even backstitch for the entire seam, and the securing stitch again at the end of the seam.**

3. **Cut the bullion fringe in half and place the two 18-inch lengths on the pillow cover, as shown in Figure 3-20.**

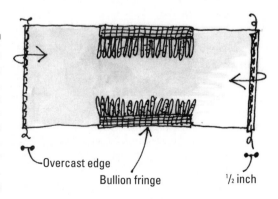

Figure 3-20: Hem both short ends, and then center the two lengths of fringe on the pillow cover fabric.

Overcast edge

Bullion fringe

½ inch

4. **Place the trim on the right side of the fabric, centering it on the sides of the fabric so that the lip edge of the fringe is even with the raw edges.**

5. **Fold the short ends toward the center, right sides together, so that the pillow cover measures 18 inches square, as shown in Figure 3-21.**

   The short ends overlap each other about $4^1/_2$ inches and sandwich the bullion fringe in the seam line.

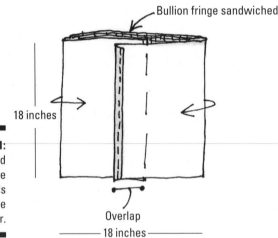

Bullion fringe sandwiched

18 inches

Overlap

18 inches

Figure 3-21:
Fold and overlap the short ends toward the center.

6. **On both sides of the pillow cover, sew a $^1/_2$-inch seam, using the even backstitch for the entire seam and the securing stitch at both ends of each seam.**

7. **Press the seams flat and together.**

8. **Turn the pillow cover right side out, and pop the pillow form into the cover through the opening in the back.**

Trimming sheets and towels

Want to get the most bang for your sewing buck? Buy towels and sheets on sale and add your own trim. It takes just minutes and about 4 yards of lace to turn the ordinary into *Wow!* You can use a similar technique to coordinate your towels and shower curtain. You can even personalize towels for your family members by using a different trim for each person. It just takes a little know-how.

Decorating sheets

Mail-order catalogs are a great source of decorating ideas. Catalogs like these have been known to feature lace-trimmed sheet and pillowcase sets that retail for hundreds of dollars. You can knock off these linens for a fraction of that price by adding a little lace trim to the hems of plain sheets you buy on sale. In this section, you find out how to add lace to your linens.

To make this project, you need the following materials in addition to the usual sewing implements (see the earlier section "Common hand-sewing tools"):

Book II

Traditional Crafts

- ✔ One flat sheet
- ✔ Two pillowcases
- ✔ Four yards of lace or trim for a full or queen sheet and pillowcases; five yards of lace for a king sheet and pillowcases
- ✔ Thread to match the lace or trim

Follow these steps to add new life to your sheets:

1. **Preshrink the sheets and lace the way you plan to care for the sheets (refer to the earlier section "Preparing your fabric" for info on preshrinking).**

   If you're using polyester lace on cotton/poly-blend sheets, preshrink only the sheets. Polyester doesn't shrink, but cotton does.

2. **Cut a length of lace long enough to go around the hem of one pillowcase plus 1 inch for seam allowances. Repeat for the second pillowcase.**

3. **Using a ¹/₂-inch seam allowance, sew the short ends of the pillowcase lace together using the even backstitch for the entire seam. Make one lace circle for each pillowcase.**

4. **Press the seams open and then turn the lace circles right side out.**

5. **Pin the lace onto each pillowcase, on the right side, so that the straight edge of the trim is just below the ready-made stitching on the pillowcase hem edge, as shown in Figure 3-22.**

6. **Stitch the lace to the pillowcase using the running stitch, sewing it on just below the ready-made stitching at the hem.**

7. **Cut the lace the length needed to span across the hem of the flat sheet plus 1 inch for seam allowance.**

8. **Turn back the two short ends of the lace ¹/₂ inch and press.**

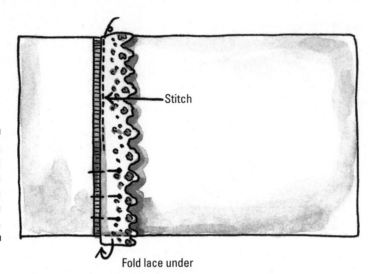

Stitch

Figure 3-22:
Pin and
stitch the
lace to the
pillowcase
hem edge.

Fold lace under

9. **On the right side of the sheet, pin the lace so that the straight edge is just below the ready-made stitching on the hem edge, and the short ends of the lace are turned under and pinned to the sheet.**

10. **Stitch the lace to the sheet using the running stitch.**

    Stitch up one short edge of the lace (where you turned in and pinned the edge), across the long straight edge and down the other short edge on the other side.

11. **Press your creation.**

    Show off your new, fancy sheets by making the bed so that the decorated side of the sheet shows as a cuff over the blanket or duvet cover.

Trimming towels

Want to add a custom look to your bathroom? Trim your towels to match your shower curtain. This project is easy, looks great, and costs a fraction of the price you'd pay for a similar designer towel.

Because only one side of a towel shows when you hang it from a towel rack, you may as well save yourself some trouble and decorate just one side. The instructions in this section show you how to decorate one side of two towels, but you can also decorate both sides of one towel or double the materials and repeat the steps to have two super-fancy, fully decorated towels.

To make this project, you need the following materials in addition to the usual sewing implements (see the earlier section "Common hand-sewing tools"):

- ✔ Two bath towels
- ✔ ¼ yard of fabric of a width that's at least 2 inches more than twice the width of your towels (If you make a shower curtain, use the leftover fabric to trim towels to match.)
- ✔ 2½ yards of ⅝-inch-wide grosgrain ribbon (the kind with ribs).
- ✔ All-purpose thread to match the ribbon

Follow these steps to trim a towel at both ends:

Book II

Traditional Crafts

1. **Preshrink the towels, ribbon, and fabric (used for banding the towel) the way you plan to care for the towels.**

   Preshrinking makes your towels last longer and wear better, and the decorative bands don't shrink as much when you dry them on the permanent-press setting of your dryer.

2. **Cutting on the crosswise grain (see "Getting to know your fabric" earlier in this chapter), cut a fabric band 3 inches wide and twice as long as your towel is wide, plus 2 inches for seam allowances.**

   For example, if your towel is 24 inches wide, your fabric band should be 50 inches long.

3. **Cut two lengths of the grosgrain ribbon the same length as the fabric band.**

4. **Pin one length of ribbon along the top edge, and one length of ribbon along the bottom edge of the fabric band, overlapping the fabric with the ribbon by ½ inch, as shown in Figure 3-23.**

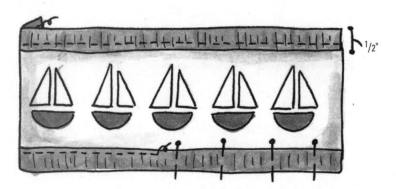

Figure 3-23:
Pin the ribbon to the fabric.

5. **Stitch both lengths of ribbon to the fabric band using the running stitch, sewing just inside and right next to the straight edge of the ribbon (refer to Figure 3-23).**

6. **Press the band smooth and flat.**

7. **Cut the long band in half so that you have two shorter strips the same length.**

8. **Center one fabric band over the woven decorative part of the towel and pin it in place.**

9. **Turn under the short ends of the fabric band ¹/₂ inch, making them even with the edges of the towel, and then press and pin them.**

10. **Stitch the fabric band in place using the even backstitch or the running stitch, sewing around all four edges of the band.**

11. **Repeat Steps 8 through 10 with the other fabric band, placing it on another towel or on the opposite end of the towel you've already decorated.**

Now hang up your newly decorated towels, stand back, and admire your work. Pretty easy, huh?

Reversible table runner

Try your hand at sewing tassels by making this easy table runner. You can create this pretty runner to run either the width or the length of a table — use it in place of placemats or a tablecloth.

To make the runner, you need the following supplies in addition to the usual sewing implements (see the earlier section "Common hand-sewing tools"):

- ¹/₂ yard of 60-inch-wide home decor fabric
- ¹/₂ yard of 60-inch-wide complementary home decor fabric
- Thread that matches the fabric
- Two decorator tassels (optional)
- One yardstick

Follow these steps to make your runner:

1. **Take one piece of the 18-x-60-inch fabric and, using your dressmaker's chalk, mark the midpoint of the short ends.**

2. **At the marks, fold the fabric toward the center as though you were making a paper airplane, as shown in Figure 3-24.**

   You should have a point at each end. Press each fold.

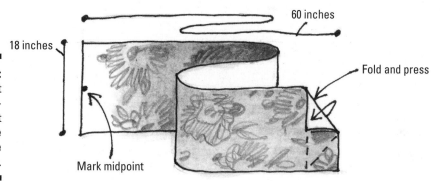

Figure 3-24:
You don't need a pattern to cut and shape your table runner.

Book II

Traditional Crafts

3. **Cut your table runner along each of the fold lines on both ends of the fabric.**

4. **Repeat Steps 1 through 3 for the other piece of fabric to create the reversible side of the runner.**

5. **If you want to use tassels, pin them to the right side of the tapestry fabric so that the loop is in the seam allowance and the top of the tassel is as close to the seam line as possible.**

6. **Pin the contrasting fabric to the tapestry fabric, right sides together (see Figure 3-25).**

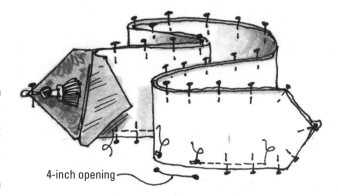

Figure 13-25:
Pin the right sides of the fabric together.

7. **Starting on one long side and leaving about a 4-inch opening, sew all the way around the table runner $1/2$ inch from the raw edges, using an even backstitch (see Figure 3-26 for a complete illustration).**

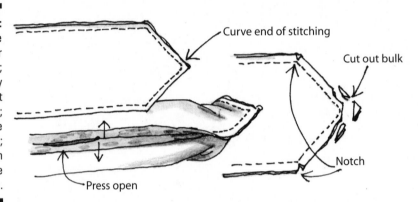

Figure 3-26:
Sew the runner together; trim away the bulk at the point; notch the corners; and then press the seams open.

Curve end of stitching

Cut out bulk

Notch

Press open

8. **Trim excess fabric and tassel cord from around the points of the runner. Don't trim closer than $1/8$ inch.**

9. **Press the seam flat and together.**

At the opening, press the seam back toward the center of the runner on both edges (as if it were turned right side out). This technique makes the opening almost invisible and easier to close by hand.

10. **From the wrong side, press the seam allowance open over a seam roll or seam stick (if you have one), pressing as close to the points as possible.**

If you don't have a seam roll, press the seam open as well as possible by using your iron and ironing board.

11. **Turn the runner right side out and press the edges.**

12. **Close the opening using the even slipstitch.**

Chapter 4

Patchwork and Quilting Basics

· ·

In This Chapter

▶ Getting familiar with basic patchwork and quilting terms

▶ Gathering the necessary supplies

▶ Reviewing basic patchwork and quilting techniques

▶ Making simple projects

· ·

*J*oining pieces of fabric together to form a larger unit of fabric is the
basic technique of *patchwork*. Most patchwork projects involve stitching
together square, triangular, or rectangular pieces of fabric. In this chapter,
you gain exposure to the wide world of fabrics, and you gather quick and
easy techniques for making patchwork projects to enhance your home with
warmth and personality — and to give as treasured gifts.

Quilting refers to sewing lines or patterns through layers of cloth, sometimes
with padding between them. Put the two together, and you have more than
patchwork quilts; you have a singularly unique craft that more than almost
any other harkens back to simpler days.

Making the patchwork potholder, patchwork pillow, and patchwork quilt
from the patterns and steps in this chapter gives you the experience you
need to make many patchwork projects, including many kinds of quilts. The
same principles for creating a potholder apply to creating a quilt — the only
difference between the two is size.

Patchwork and Quilting Lingo

Knowing what's involved before you begin patchwork helps you decide
which projects you want to make. With that in mind, get ready to familiarize
yourself with several key terms. (***Note:*** Some of the following terms relate
only to quilting, a project that most fabric crafters make after they master the
basics of patchwork.)

- **Backing:** The piece of fabric used on the underside of the patchwork (front) piece of fabric.

- **Basting:** Long, loose stitches used to hold the top, batting, and backing of a quilt together before quilting. You remove these stitches after you quilt each section.

- **Batting:** Soft lining used between two layers of fabric that you quilt. Batting makes quilts puffy and gives them warmth. You can also use batting for potholder padding.

  Most quilts are made with a thin layer of cotton or synthetic batting, but you can purchase batting in varying degrees of thickness, each appropriate for different kinds of projects. Batting also comes in small, fluffy pieces that you can use for stuffing projects, such as sachets, pin cushions, pillows, and ornaments.

- **Binding:** A method of finishing the raw edges of fabric. You can use strips of contrasting fabric or packaged bias binding.

  Instead of using separate binding, many quilters cut the project's backing slightly larger than the top piece so they can bring the extra fabric forward to finish the edges of the top piece of fabric. Alternately, you can cut the backing the same size as the front and turn the front (patchwork top) to the back.

- **Blocks:** Small pieces of fabric sewn together in a specified design to create a square or rectangular block. Use an individual block to make a patchwork pillow, or sew several blocks together to create a quilt top.

- **Borders:** Fabric strips that frame a pieced design. A border is usually narrow or wide and can be made from one of your patchwork fabrics or from a contrasting fabric. Use borders to frame quilt blocks or to enlarge a quilt top so that it extends over the sides of a mattress. You can also use more than one border around a patchwork project.

- **Piecing:** The act of joining fabric patchwork pieces together in a design or pattern to form a block.

- **Quilting patterns:** Lines or markings on fabric that make up a design for quilting. A quilting pattern can be straight, curved, elaborately curlicued, gridlike, or diamond-shaped. You can also follow the seam lines where pieces of fabric are joined with small quilting stitches. When quilting, you make small hand or machine stitches along these lines.

- **Sashes or strips:** Narrow pieces of fabric used to frame individual blocks and join them together. Sashes or strips often appear in contrasting colors.

✔ **Seam allowance:** The specified measurement of fabric found between the stitch or seam line and the fabric edge. When directions state that you must sew two pieces of fabric together, begin stitching $1/4$ inch in from the fabric's raw edge, unless otherwise indicated.

✔ **Setting:** The act of sewing together quilt blocks to form a finished quilt top.

✔ **Top:** The front layer of a quilting project that shows the right side of the fabric. Patchwork or appliquéd pieces create the project's top fabric.

Fabric (And Other Stuff) You Need

If you're interested in doing patchwork, the material you're probably most interested in (and inspired — or intimidated — by) is the fabric. Fabric is the main concern of any patchwork project; what kind, how much to buy, and what colors or prints work together.

✔ **Fabric type:** Most fabric crafters prefer 100-percent cotton fabric. Whatever your preference, make sure all the fabric used in your patchwork project is of the same weight.

✔ **Fabric quantity:** You can never have too many different fabric patterns to choose from when you design a patchwork project. Chances are you'll often need ten times more variety to choose from than what you originally think you will.

✔ **Fabric colors and prints:** Gathering a varied selection of both light and dark prints for your patchwork projects is always a good idea, because the colors and patterns of your chosen fabric greatly affect a project's design.

Calico, a printed cotton fabric with a small, all-over pattern, often floral, works well with patchwork projects because you can use the small prints effectively together, and it comes in a wide variety of colors to choose from. Pretty floral prints work well with alternating solid colors that match the calico print colors.

You also need to decide on your backing material. You can use a sheet, muslin, or one of the fabrics that you used for the patchwork on the top of your project. (Unlike fabric that you buy in a store, which is generally only 45 inches wide, a bed sheet can cover the back of any size quilt without piecing.) Most crafters prefer 100-percent-cotton backing. Regardless of your preference, a light backing color is usually better than a dark backing color because the latter may show through projects with thin batting and light fabric.

In addition to fabric, you also need the following items to make patchwork projects:

- **Cutting board:** Use this handy tool for quick measuring and cutting when making patchworks. You can obtain cutting boards from fabric stores or mail-order sources.

- **Iron:** Working on any patchwork project without having an iron on a padded stool or chair next to the sewing machine isn't practical. Why? Because after each stitching step, you need to press the fabric and seams using the steam setting.

- **Marking pen:** If you need to trace a pattern or design from a book and transfer it to your fabric, use a marking pen. You can find water-soluble marking pens, made specifically for marking quilting lines on fabric, in fabric shops. After you finish quilting, you can remove the pen marks by spraying them with a plant mister or by patting over the lines with a damp sponge.

- **Needles:** Crafters sew most patchwork piecing with a sewing machine but do most of the quilting by hand. To hand quilt, you need #7 and #8 sharp needles (often called *betweens*).

- **Rotary cutter:** This tool, which resembles a pizza cutter, allows you to cut several layers of fabric at once, more accurately than you could with scissors.

- **Ruler and yardstick:** You can't work without these two tools. Use a metal ruler as a straightedge to accurately cut fabric. Use a yardstick to cut lengths of fabric on which you must mark and cut at least 36 inches at one time.

- **Shears and scissors:** You need a good pair of shears to cut your fabric. Shears have one straight and one bent-angle blade to make accurate cutting easier. Also, invest in a pair of small, pointed scissors (known as *snipping scissors*) to snip threads as you stitch and quilt. (See Book II, Chapter 3 for tips on keeping your shears and scissors sharp.)

- **Straight pins:** Use special quilting pins — extra-long $1^3/_4$-inch sharp pins — if you can. Regular straight pins are fine, but the extra-long steel pins made especially for quilting work best for holding three layers of material together.

- **Template:** A template is a rigid, full-size pattern that you use to trace design elements. You can cut templates out of cardboard, manila paper, plastic, acetate, or sandpaper. When your project requires a repeat design, use acetate because it's transparent and produces clean, crisp edges. Sandpaper's main advantage is that it doesn't slip when you place it facedown on fabric. If you cut one paper design, pin the pattern to the fabric to use as a cutting guide for more efficiency.

✔ **Thimble:** If you quilt by hand, use a thimble. Without one, you run the risk of bleeding on your fabric if you poke yourself with your needle.

✔ **Thread:** Cotton-blend thread works best for all piecing and quilting projects.

Basic Know-How for Patchwork and Quilting

Although quilting projects vary in their specific instructions, you generally do things in the following order:

1. **Gauge how much fabric you need and select the fabrics you want to use.**
2. **Cut your fabrics.**
3. **Piece the patchwork together, following the pattern, and then attach any fabrics to frame the quilt.**
4. **Piece your backing together.**
5. **Layer your patchwork top, batting, and backing together, and then baste the layers together.**
6. **Trace your quilt pattern, and then quilt the project.**
7. **Finish the outer edges by adding binding.**

Sounds simple enough, but how do you calculate the amount of fabric to buy for your project? If the back of a patchwork pillow isn't patchwork, what is it? How do you enlarge or reduce a pattern that isn't the right size for your project? How do you make a template? Check out the following sections for an easy-to-understand breakdown of these technical basics.

Estimating fabric yardage

If you follow project directions, the amount of each kind of fabric that you need is listed. However, when you make projects without directions, such as quilts, determining the amount of fabric that you need can be tricky. To estimate yardage for a bed quilt, for example, follow these steps:

1. **Measure your bed when it's fully made, noting the length, width, and depth of your bed, including the box spring.**

   A fully made bed means with the bed pad, sheets, and blankets over the mattress.

2. **Decide how low you want the quilt to hang.**

   That is, decide whether you want your quilt to overhang slightly, over-hang to the top of the dust ruffle, or drop to the floor, and whether you want your quilt to extend up and over the pillows.

3. **Add the number of inches determined in Step 2 to the measurements you took in Step 1 to make the quilt large enough to hang where you want it to.**

Have a quilt pattern that you like but the quilt size doesn't fit your bed? You can add or subtract from the border measurements to make it fit. Changing the pattern's measurements usually doesn't change the quilt's basic design.

Making and assembling your patchwork pieces

Patchwork quilts are constructed of blocks of fabrics sewn together. The blocks themselves are pieced together with patches, and the overall look of the quilt is determined by how many — four, five, nine, and so on — are used to create each block and how the patches are put together. Although you can get as creative as you want with piecing together the patches and the blocks, there are many popular patterns to choose from: log cabin, flying geese, piano keys, and so on. How the specific piecing is done depends on the pattern you choose.

There's nothing illicit about strip piecing

Strip piecing consists of sewing strips of different fabrics together and then cutting them into units that you arrange to create a patchwork top. The strip-piecing method works well when you make a quilt with a pattern that requires many fabric pieces. Instead of repeatedly cutting and sewing individual squares together, you can sew two or more strips of fabric together and then cut those strips into equal pieces called *units* by using the strip-piecing method. You can then arrange the equal pieces (units) and stitch them together in different positions (as in the project directions) to form your patchwork pattern.

Follow these instructions (and keep an eye on Figure 4-1) to get in on the strip-piecing act:

Row 1: With right sides facing together and long edges aligned, sew equal-width strips of fabric together and mark off units (with a light pencil and ruler) equal to the width of the strips.

Row 2: Cut out each unit along the marked lines.

Row 3: Sew another group of strips (with three different fabrics) together in the same manner as Row 1 and cut out the units as in Row 2.

Row 4: By joining a unit from Row 2 to each side edge of a unit from Row 3, you can create a multicolored quilt block quickly and easily.

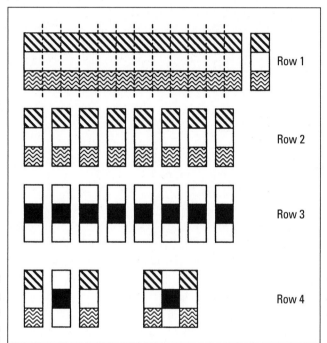

Row 1

Row 2

Row 3

Row 4

Figure 4-1:
The steps to strip piecing.

Now you're joining triangles to create squares

Follow these steps (illustrated in Figure 4-2) for a quick and easy way to join light and dark triangles to create squares of any size.

1. **Determine the size of the patchwork squares that you want.**

2. **Add 1 inch to your determined patchwork-square size and then mark that size off on the wrong side of the light fabric.**

   For example, if you want to create 2-inch squares, mark off 3-inch squares.

3. **Draw diagonal lines through each square, as shown in Figure 4-2a.**

4. **With the light and dark fabrics' right sides facing and raw edges aligned, pin the marked light fabric to the dark fabric of the same size.**

5. **Stitch $1/4$ inch away from the diagonal lines, on each side of the lines, as shown in Figure 4-2b.**

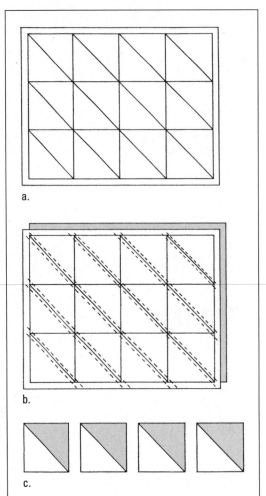

Figure 4-2:
Using two
triangles
to create a
square.

a.

b.

c.

6. **Cut all the solid lines of the squares to make individual squares of light and dark triangles.**

7. **Open the seams of the squares you cut out and press.**

8. **Repeat these steps 11 more times.**

    You now have 24 squares, each made up of a dark and a light triangle patch, as shown in Figure 4-2c.

So you want to sew small squares together

When you need to make patchwork pieces from small squares of fabric (approximately 1 to 1¹/₂ inches), use the easy method shown in Figure 4-3 to stitch them together.

1. **With their right sides facing, pin together individual sets of two small fabric squares each.**

2. **With your sewing machine, stitch along one side of the pinned fabric edges of one set, but don't cut the thread when you finish stitching.**

3. **Run the sewing machine for two or three more stitches and then feed the next set of squares through.**

4. **Continue to stitch all the square sets with this method so that you end up with a string of patches connected by threads.**

5. **After you make enough pieces of patchwork for your project, cut the threads between the squares and separate them.**

6. **Open each set of squares and press with your iron.**

Figure 4-3:
Sew small
squares in
multiples to
save time.

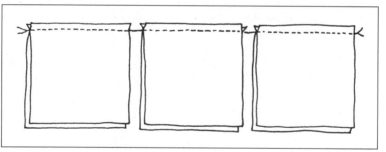

Piecing the backing

If you make a quilt, tablecloth, wall hanging, or other large patchwork project, you may have to piece panels together to make the correct backing size. Use the following steps to piece your project's backing:

1. **Cut two pieces of fabric to the appropriate length for your project.**

   Most fabric is 45 inches wide, so you now have two 45-inch-wide lengths of fabric.

2. **Cut one of the pieces of fabric in half lengthwise to produce two narrow strips of the same size.**

3. **Stitch one of these two matching panels to each long-sided edge of the second piece of fabric.**

   Now you have a piece of fabric wide enough for your backing that doesn't have a seam down the middle. Two seams make the back of a quilt look neater than a seam down the middle of the back of the quilt; a tablecloth lays flatter on a tabletop with two seams than with one down the middle. Also, working with three smaller pieces of fabric is more manageable than working with two larger pieces of fabric.

4. **Press the seams open.**

If you use a bed sheet the same size as the patchwork top, good news! You have a solid backing that doesn't require piecing.

Transferring designs

You can find many interesting designs in quilting magazines, in-store booklets, quilting books, and so on. Once you find a design you like, you need to transfer it to your fabric. Keep these things in mind:

✔ If the design is already the right size, great. Otherwise, use a copy machine to make it larger or smaller for your purposes.

✔ You can combine designs — putting a smaller design within a larger one, for example. When you do, transfer the larger design first; then fill in with the smaller one. (Here's a little tip: If the small design doesn't quite fit into the space, you can easily leave off part of it or adapt it to fit.)

To transfer a design to your fabric, follow these steps:

1. **Trace the pattern pieces or a quilting design onto tracing paper.**

2. **Pin together a piece of dressmaker's (carbon) paper, the tracing paper with the pattern, and the fabric.**

   Place the dressmaker's paper on the right side of the fabric with the carbon side down. Lay the tracing paper on top and pin the tracing, the carbon, and the fabric together.

3. **Trace all the pattern lines.**

   Use an erasable fabric marker, erasable pen, or a fine-line disappearing marking pen to transfer the design to the fabric.

4. **Remove the dressmaker's paper and tracing paper.**

   The transfer lines appear on the fabric so you can use these lines as a guide for cutting out the pattern from the fabric.

Making a template

Templates enable you to trace design elements onto your fabric. You can buy ready-made quilt templates or just make your own. If you use cardboard, manila paper, or acetate as template material, you need to first trace your design so you can transfer the pattern to the template.

Use these steps to make a cardboard or manila paper template:

1. **Trace the design onto carbon paper.**

2. **Place the tracing facedown on the template material and use a pen or pencil to rub over each traced line.**

   The outline transfers to the cardboard.

3. **Remove the tracing paper and go over the lines again with a ballpoint pen to make them more legible, if needed.**

4. **Cut the design outline from the cardboard.**

   Retractable craft knives work well for cutting templates.

If you prefer to use acetate rather than cardboard or manila paper, trace the design onto tracing paper (as in Step 1), but then place the acetate over the tracing and cut out the design shape.

Using acetate for template material has several advantages. You can use it many times without it losing its sharp edges, and because it's clear, you can trace a pattern directly onto it. Further, you can see through acetate, which allows you to position it exactly where you want it when you place it on the fabric. For example, if you're using a floral print, you may want to center a flower in the middle of the template.

Quilting your patchwork: Hand quilting 101

Quilting consists of sewing layers of fabric and batting together to produce a padded structure held together by straight, even, small stitches. Generally the final step in a patchwork project, the quilting process makes the project interesting and gives it a textured look.

When you need to fill large areas of a background (such as a border or large plain blocks between patchwork blocks) with quilting, choose a simple design. Background quilting should never interfere with patchwork or appliqué elements.

Follow these steps to hand quilt:

1. **Using a workable length of thread, thread your needle and knot one end.**

   Cut a piece of thread approximately 18 to 20 inches long. Thread the needle so that roughly 8 inches of thread goes through it. Make a small knot in the long end of the thread, leaving a 1-inch tail below the knot. Make the knot in only one end of the thread so that you quilt with a single strand of thread.

2. **Bring the needle up through the back of the patchwork to the top front (where you start the first line of quilting), give the knotted end a good tug, and pull it through the backing fabric into the batting.**

   You make all subsequent quilting stitches through all three layers of fabric. Each time you rethread the needle though, be sure to pull the first stitch into the batting to avoid knots on the underside of your quilted project.

3. **Make small running stitches (refer to Book II, Chapter 3), following your premarked quilting pattern.**

   Alternatively, make a line of stitches ¹/₄ inch on each side of all the patchwork seam lines.

   Make sure you don't stitch into the ¹/₄-inch seam allowance that resides around the outside edge of the patchwork top.

4. **When you come to the last 3 inches of thread, take one last stitch into the patchwork fabric, but not out through the backing. Instead, push the needle up again an inch from where you put it in; then pull it through the patchwork top and away from the remaining thread. Snip the end of the thread (if a tiny end shows) close to the top of the fabric.**

   The thread is now secure inside the batting.

5. **Repeat Steps 1 through 4.**

How do you keep your pattern lines straight? That's easy! Just make grids that you can follow as you sew along. For a simple way to make quilting grid patterns of squares or diamond shapes, use a yardstick or masking tape.

To make a square grid, follow these instructions:

1. **Place a yardstick across the top edge of your fabric and use a marking pen to mark the material along the edge of the yardstick.**

   Don't worry about using the marking pen; it washes out of fabric easily.

2. **Without lifting the edge of the yardstick from the fabric, turn it over sideways and, once again, mark along its edge.**

3. **Continue across the fabric to the bottom edge.**

   This method creates perfect, 1-inch spaces between each yardstick line.

4. **Lay the yardstick along one side edge of the fabric and repeat the line-marking process to create a 1-inch grid across the fabric.**

5. **Quilt stitch along the marked lines.**

You can use various sizes of masking tape rather than a yardstick to increase or decrease line spacing.

Follow these steps to make a diamond grid:

1. **Place the yardstick diagonally across one corner of the patchwork fabric and mark the material with a marking pen.**

2. **Without lifting the yardstick from the material, turn the yardstick over and mark the new line. Continue to turn the yardstick over and mark each line until you reach the opposite corner.**

3. **Repeat this process in the opposite direction.**

Book II

Traditional Crafts

Country Potholders

Potholders make excellent patchwork projects for beginners because they teach you the basic fundamentals of patchwork and quilting and because making a potholder produces a useful kitchen tool. You can stitch these small patchwork projects by hand or with a sewing machine.

Tools and materials

$\frac{1}{4}$ yard of green plaid homespun fabric

$\frac{1}{4}$ yard of dark solid coral homespun fabric

$\frac{1}{4}$ yard of light coral plaid homespun fabric

16-x-16-inch piece of quilt batting for each potholder

Note: All measurements for each project include $\frac{1}{4}$-inch seam allowances.

Crafting the potholders

The potholders in this project consist of pink and green plaid homespun fabric. Homespun fabric is heavy woven cotton that looks and feels like linen. You can find this fabric in any fabric store. Homespun comes in many colors, so you can make these projects in colors that match your kitchen. Whatever colors you choose, you can piece together each of these 8-x-8-inch potholders in a different patchwork pattern. You can make one pattern or all four patterns (see Figure 4-4).

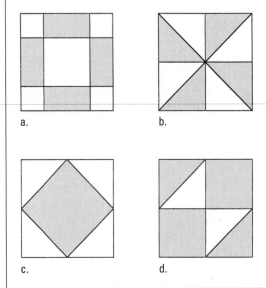

a.

b.

c.

d.

Figure 4-4:
Four patchwork potholder patterns.

Big square/little square potholder

1. **Cut the following shapes from your fabric:**

   - 4 rectangles from the green plaid, each $2^1/_2$ x $4^1/_2$ inches

   - 1 square of the dark solid coral, $4^1/_2$ x $4^1/_2$ inches

   - 4 squares of the light coral plaid, each $2^1/_2$ x $2^1/_2$ inches

2. **With the fabrics' right sides facing and raw edges aligned, stitch a small coral square to each short end of a green rectangle. Open the seams and press seam allowances towards the dark color with an iron.**

3. Repeat with the other three green rectangles and small coral squares.

4. Along the long edge, stitch a green rectangle to each side of the 4½-inch coral square. Open the seams and press with an iron.

5. With the right sides facing and raw edges aligned, join the fabric rows together, placing the wide row between the two narrow rows, as shown in Figure 4-4a.

To finish your potholder, see "Finishing the potholders" later in this section.

Pinwheel potholder

1. Cut the following shapes from your fabric:

   - 2 squares of green plaid, each 5 x 5 inches, cut into two equal triangles

   - 2 squares of light coral plaid, each 5 x 5 inches, cut into two equal triangles

2. With the fabric pieces' right sides facing and raw edges aligned, stitch a green triangle to a coral triangle along the long edges of each.

3. Repeat Step 2 to make four green and coral squares. Open the seams and press with an iron.

4. Stitch the green and coral squares together, alternating green and coral, as shown in Figure 4-4b. Open the seams and press with your iron.

Head to the later "Finishing the potholders" section for guidance on completing your potholder.

Square-in-a-square potholder

1. Cut the following shapes from your fabric:

   - 1 square of green plaid, 6⅛ x 6⅛ inches

   - 2 squares of dark solid coral, each 5 x 5 inches, cut into two equal triangles

2. With the fabrics' right sides facing and raw edges aligned, stitch each coral triangle, along the diagonal, to each side of the green plaid square to make a larger square (see Figure 4-4c).

3. Open the seams and press with an iron.

To finish your potholder, see "Finishing the potholders" later in this section.

Hourglass potholder

1. **Cut the following shapes out of your fabric:**

   - 1 square of green plaid, 5 x 5 inches, cut into two equal triangles
   - 2 squares, each of green plaid, 5 x 5 inches
   - 1 square of light coral plaid, 5 x 5 inches, cut into two equal triangles

2. **With the fabric pieces' right sides facing and raw edges aligned, stitch a green triangle to a coral plaid triangle along the diagonal. Open the seams and press with an iron.**

3. **With the right sides facing and raw edges aligned, stitch a green and coral plaid square to a plain green square on the coral side, as shown in Figure 4-4d. Open the seams and press with an iron. Repeat this step with the remaining squares.**

Head to the following "Finishing the potholders" section for guidance on completing your potholder.

Finishing the potholders

To finish your potholder, follow these steps:

1. **Cut a 1½-x-6-inch strip from any piece of remaining fabric to make a hanging loop for your potholder.**

2. **With wrong sides facing, fold the strip in half lengthwise and press with the iron. Turn the raw edges in ¼ inch, press with your iron, and stitch along the long edge of the fabric.**

3. **Fold the strip into a loop and overlap the raw ends. Pin the raw ends of the loop to one corner of the top of the potholder.**

   The loop should be lying on the front of the patchwork top.

4. **Cut the batting in half so you have two 8-inch square pieces.**

5. **Cut an 8½-x-8½-inch backing piece from either the green or the coral fabric.**

6. **Pin one piece of batting to the back of the potholder top and quilt along all the seam lines of the potholder's design.**

7. **Pin the second piece of batting to the wrong side of the backing fabric.**

8. **With the fabric's right sides facing and all the edges aligned, stitch around three sides and four corners of the potholder, leaving about a 3-inch opening on one side for turning.**

   Make sure the hanging loop is between the two fabric sides and that you catch the raw ends of the loop as you stitch.

9. **Turn the potholder right-side out and push the corners out with a pencil eraser or a crochet needle. Press the potholder with your iron.**

10. **Turn the potholder's raw edges to the inside and stitch the opening closed.**

Patchwork Pillow

Making an oversized pillow requires patchwork and quilting techniques. The generous 24-inch-square size of this pillow project makes it ideal for your sofa, bed, or for lounging on the floor. The pillow's patchwork border frames a center panel of fabric that you quilt in a pattern of circles.

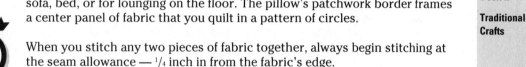

When you stitch any two pieces of fabric together, always begin stitching at the seam allowance — $\frac{1}{4}$ inch in from the fabric's edge.

Book II

Traditional Crafts

Tools and materials

$\frac{1}{2}$ yard of 45-inch-wide blue calico (or color of your choice)

$\frac{3}{4}$ yard of 45-inch-wide muslin

Needle and white thread

24-inch-square piece of quilt batting

Compass

24-inch-square pillow form (sold in fabric shops) or stuffing, such as Poly-Fil

Crafting the pillow

The steps for this project are divided into distinct tasks to help you keep track of your progress: creating the patchwork top, marking and quilting your top, and assembling your pillow.

Creating the patchwork top

1. **Cut the following shapes from the printed blue fabric:**

    - 1 square, $12\frac{1}{2}$ x $12\frac{1}{2}$ inches

    - 20 squares, $2\frac{1}{2}$ x $2\frac{1}{2}$ inches each

    - 4 strips, $2\frac{1}{2}$ x $12\frac{1}{2}$ inches each

2. **Cut the following pieces of muslin:**
   - 8 strips, $2^1/_2$ x 12 inches each
   - 16 squares, $2^1/_2$ x $2^1/_2$ inches each

3. **Cut 1 backing piece of fabric (either muslin or printed), $24^1/_2$-inches square.**

4. **With the fabrics' right sides together and raw edges aligned, pin one $2^1/_2$-inch muslin square to one $2^1/_2$-inch blue calico square.**

5. **Stitch along one side edge of the fabric. Open the seams and press with your iron from the wrong side.**

6. **Join the two squares you've already stitched with another blue calico square on the opposite side of the muslin square in the same way as in Step 5. Open the seams and press with your iron.**

   Stitching these three squares of fabric together creates a row of two printed blue square patches with a muslin square in between (see Row 1 in Figure 4-5).

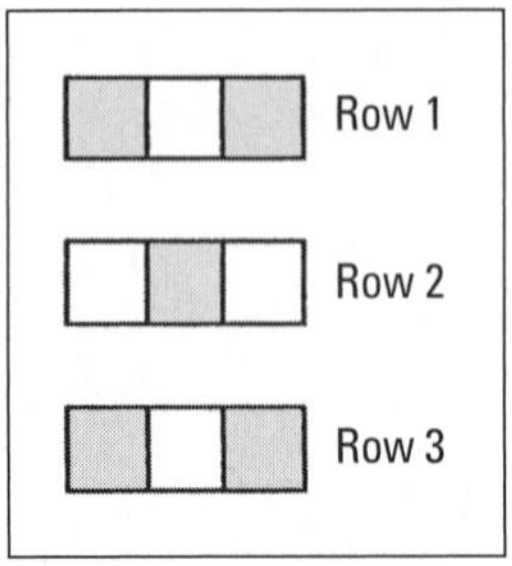

Figure 4-5:
Joining squares to make rows.

7. **Repeat Steps 4 through 6 to make a row of one muslin square, one printed blue square, and a muslin square (see Row 2 in Figure 4-5).**

8. **Repeat Steps 4 through 6 to make a row of one printed blue square, one muslin square, and one printed blue square (see Row 3 in Figure 4-5).**

9. **Repeat Steps 4 through 8 until you have 12 rows of fabric — 8 rows like Row 1 and 4 rows like Row 2.**

10. **With the fabrics' right sides together and raw edges aligned, pin Rows 1 and 2 together and stitch across the long edge on top. Open the seams and press the fabric's wrong side with your iron.**

11. **With the right sides together and the bottom raw edge of Row 2 aligned with the long edge of Row 3, pin Rows 2 and 3 together. Stitch along the long edges of the fabric to join Rows 2 and 3. Open the seams and press with your iron.**

   Congratulations! You've just created a patchwork block. (See Figure 4-6.)

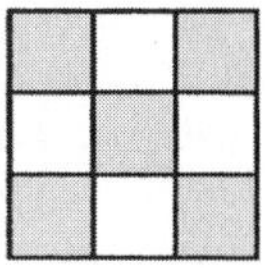

Figure 4-6:
Joining
three rows
to make a
block.

Book II

Traditional
Crafts

12. **Repeat Steps 10 and 11 to make three more patchwork blocks. The patchwork blocks make up each corner piece of the pillow.**

13. **With the fabrics' right sides facing and raw edges aligned, pin one of the 12-inch-long muslin strips to one of the 12-inch-long blue strips and then stitch along one long edge of the fabric. Open the seams and press with your iron.**

14. **Pin another 12-inch-long muslin strip to the long edge of the blue strip (right sides facing) and stitch together. Open the seams and press with your iron.**

15. **Repeat Steps 13 and 14 to make three more borders.**

16. **With the fabrics' right sides facing, pin one border to one edge of the printed blue 12½-inch center fabric square and then stitch the edges together (see Figure 4-7). Open the seams on the fabric's wrong side and press with your iron.**

17. **Repeat Step 16 on the opposite edge of the center square.**

18. **With the fabrics' right sides facing and raw edges aligned, pin and then stitch one patchwork block to each short edge of the two remaining borders (see Figure 4-8). Open the seams and press with your iron.**

Figure 4-7:
Joining
borders to
the center
piece.

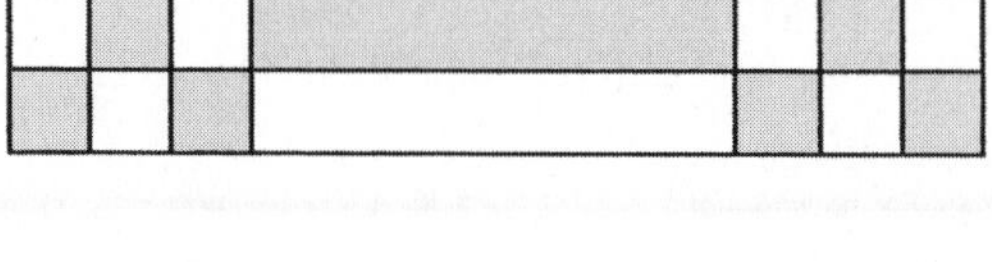

Figure 4-8:
Joining cor-
ner pieces
to borders.

19. With the fabrics' right sides facing and raw edges aligned, pin and then stitch the pieces that you made in Step 18 to the top and bottom edges of the central square to complete the pillow top assembly, as shown in Figure 4-9. Open the seams and press with your iron.

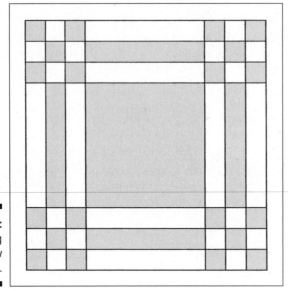

Figure 4-9:
Assembling
the pillow
top.

Marking the pattern and quilting the top

When your patchwork top is complete, it's time to mark and stitch your quilt pattern. Follow these steps and refer to Figure 4-10 to see what the finished product should look like:

1. Place the pillow top on a hard surface. Use a compass and a light pencil to draw overlapping, 5-inch circles in the center square on the right side of the fabric (see Figure 4-10).

2. Use a ruler to make diagonal lines across the borders with $1/2$-inch spaces between the lines.

3. With the front of the fabric facing up, pin the pillow top to a piece of quilt batting and a piece of muslin.

4. Sew running stitches (see Book II, Chapter 3) along the lines you drew in Steps 19 and 20 to quilt the pillow.

Figure 4-10:
Arrange
your circles
like this.

Assembling the pillow

With your pillow top quilted, you're ready to put everything together:

1. **With right sides together, pin the quilted pillow top and backing together.**

2. **Stitch around three sides and four corners of the pillow, leaving a $^1/_4$-inch seam allowance.**

3. **Turn the fabric right-side out and press with your iron. Turn in the open edges $^1/_4$ inch and press with your iron.**

4. **Insert the pillow form, or stuff with the stuffing until the pillow is full to your satisfaction.**

5. **Slip stitch the opening closed, as shown in Figure 4-11.**

   See Book II, Chapter 3 for instructions on slipstitching.

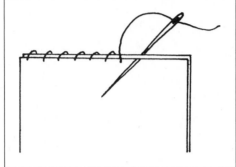

Figure 4-11:
Slip stitch-
ing the
opening
closed.

Stuffed Patchwork Cat

You can use this stuffed patchwork cat, shown in Figure 4-12, as a pillow, a child's toy, or a doorstop. (To use it as a doorstop, fill the finished cat with sand or weigh down the bottom with a brick.) You make this 13-inch-high cat from 1-inch squares of light and dark and solid and printed fabrics that you stitch together. The patchwork cat's backing fabric is a solid piece of fabric that you cut from one of the fabrics you use on the front of the cat. You quilt the grid pattern of this cat by hand.

You can make this project to use up scraps from other projects.

Tools and materials

52 1¹/₂-x-1¹/₂-inch squares, made of assorted calico scraps

52 muslin squares, each 1¹/₂-x-1¹/₂ inches

Calico fabric, 8 x 13¹/₂ inches (for the project's backing)

Stuffing, such as Poly-Fil

Tracing paper

Note: All measurements include ¹/₄-inch seam allowance.

Book II

Traditional Crafts

Figure 4-12:
A stuffed patchwork cat.

Crafting the cat

1. **With the fabrics' right sides facing and raw edges aligned, stitch a calico square to a muslin square along one edge. Open the seams and press with your iron.**

2. **Continue to join squares in this way, alternating a calico square with a muslin square, until you have 13 rows with 8 squares each. Press all the seams to the same side.**

3. **With the fabrics' right sides facing and raw edges aligned, join all the rows so that the light and dark squares lie above and below each other.**

   This step creates a patchwork piece of fabric that's approximately 8$\frac{1}{2}$ x 13$\frac{1}{2}$ inches.

4. **Enlarge the cat pattern shown in Figure 4-13 by 210 percent (to 13$\frac{1}{2}$ inches high) and transfer the enlargement to tracing paper. Make a separate enlargement of the cat's tail.**

   To enlarge your design, use a copy machine. See the earlier section "Transferring designs" for more info on transferring patterns.

5. **Pin the enlarged pattern to the right side of the patchwork fabric and cut out the pattern of the cat only.**

6. **Pin the pattern of the tail to the remaining piece of patchwork fabric and then cut it out.**

7. **Cut the cat and tail pattern pieces from the 8-x-13$\frac{1}{2}$-inch calico backing fabric.**

8. **With the right sides facing and raw edges aligned, stitch the tail pieces together, but leave the straight edge open so you can fill it with stuffing.**

9. **Turn the tail fabric right-side out and use a pencil eraser or crochet hook to stuff the tail tightly with stuffing.**

10. **Pin the raw edges of the tail in position on the wrong side of the patchwork cat's front.**

11. **With the fabric's right sides facing and raw edges aligned, pin the backing to the front of the cat, with the tail between the two pieces of fabric. Stitch all around, leaving the bottom end open.**

12. **Use snipping scissors to make small, evenly spaced snips into the excess fabric of the seam allowance (but not into your stitches) around all the cat's curves, including all the corners.**

13. **Turn the cat right-side out. Press with your iron.**

14. **Stuff the cat tightly with stuffing. Turn the raw edges of the fabric's opening to the inside and slip stitch the opening closed (refer to Figure 4-11).**

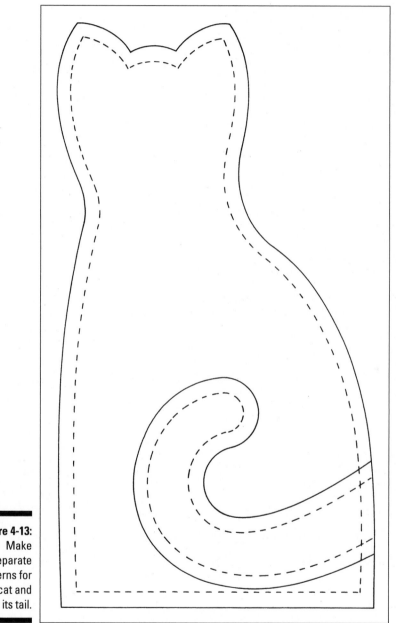

Figure 4-13:
Make
separate
patterns for
the cat and
its tail.

Pinwheel Baby Quilt

Quilts make great gifts for newborn babies and are easy to take care of. The more you wash a quilt, the softer it gets and the better it looks. The 24-x-32-inch baby quilt (shown in Figure 4-14) is the perfect size for a bassinet, carriage, or stroller and is an easy sewing-machine project. Finish the edge of the quilt with eyelet trim, satin binding, or bias binding, which are available by the yard in fabric shops.

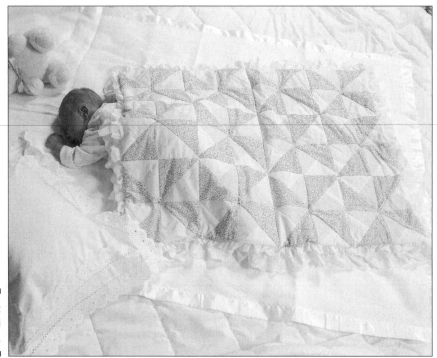

Figure 4-14: A pinwheel baby quilt.

Tools and materials

Basic sewing craft kit

Tracing paper

Cardboard

$1/4$ yard of white fabric (cotton or polyester/cotton blend)

$1/4$ yard of pink fabric (cotton or polyester/cotton blend)

1 yard of blue calico (includes backing)

1 yard of quilt batting

3¹/₄ yards of 2-inch-wide eyelet (optional)

3¹/₄ yards of 1-inch-wide eyelet (optional)

1 skein pink embroidery floss

Note: All fabric is 45 inches wide. All measurements include a ¹/₄-inch seam allowance.

Crafting the quilt

To make following these instructions easier, the various tasks are broken into three separate sections.

Book II

Traditional Crafts

Making the patchwork top

1. **Trace Patterns A and B in Figure 4-15, enlarge them by 125 percent, and transfer them to your desired template material (see the earlier section "Making a template") to make templates.**

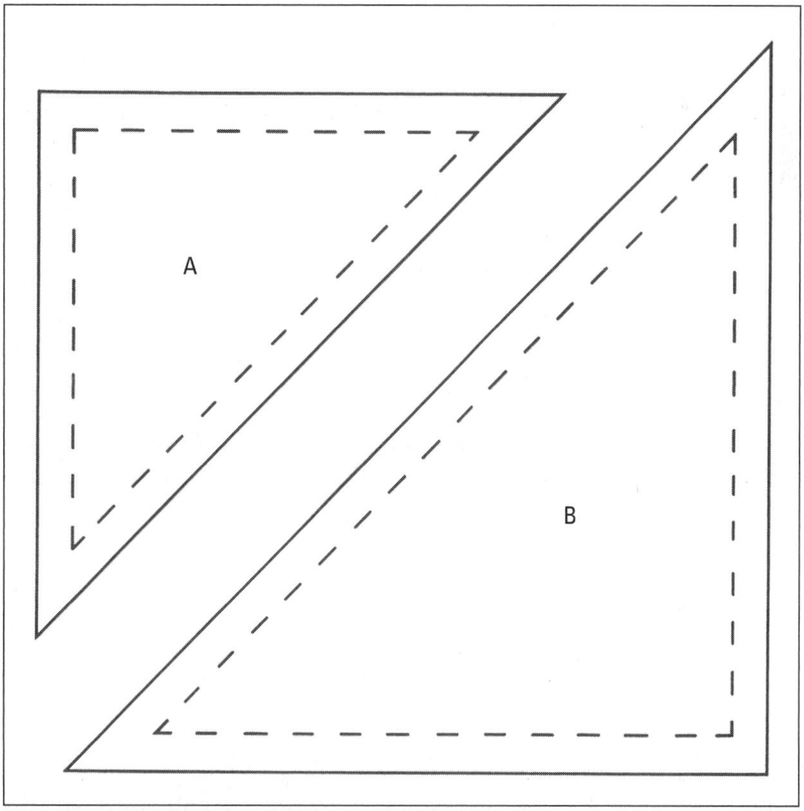

Figure 4-15:
Pattern
pieces
for the
pinwheel
quilt.

2. **Cut the following shapes from the fabrics:**

   - 48 white Pattern A triangles

   - 48 pink Pattern A triangles

   - 48 blue calico Pattern B triangles

   - 24$^1/_2$-x-32$^1/_2$-inch backing piece

   See Figure 4-16 for diagrams to help you assemble the pinwheel baby quilt as you follow the steps.

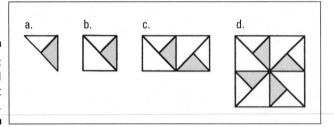

Figure 4-16: Pinwheel baby quilt diagrams.

3. **With the fabrics' right sides together and raw edges aligned, pin a white Pattern A piece to a pink Pattern A piece and then stitch along one of the triangle's short edges to make a larger triangle, as shown in Figure 4-16a. Open the seams and press with your iron on the wrong side.**

4. **Repeat Step 3 to make 48 larger pieced triangles.**

5. **With the fabrics' right sides together and raw edges aligned, pin a pieced triangle to a blue calico Pattern B triangle and then stitch along the triangle's diagonal to make a square. (See Figure 4-16b.) Press open the seams on the wrong side.**

6. **Repeat Step 5 to make 48 patchwork squares.**

7. **With the fabrics' right sides together and raw edges aligned, pin two of the 48 squares together, as shown in Figure 4-16c, to make half of the pinwheel block. Press open the seams on the fabric's wrong side.**

8. **Repeat Step 7 to make 24 pinwheel block halves.**

9. **With the fabrics' right sides together and raw edges aligned, pin two pinwheel block halves together to form a block, as shown in Figure 4-16d. Stitch along the fabric's bottom edge. Press open the seams on the fabric's wrong side.**

10. Repeat Step 9 to make 12 blocks.

11. With the fabric of the patchwork blocks' right sides together and raw edges aligned, stitch two blocks together along a side edge. Press open the seams on the wrong side.

12. Repeat Step 11 to make a row of three blocks, as shown in Figure 4-17. Press open the seams on the wrong side.

Figure 4-17:
Stitch three
blocks in
a row.

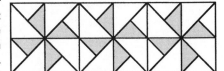

Book II

**Traditional
Crafts**

13. Repeat Steps 11 and 12 to make three more patchwork-block rows.

14. With the fabrics' right sides facing and raw edges aligned, pin two patchwork-block rows together and stitch across their bottom edges. Open the seams and press with your iron on the fabric's wrong side.

15. Repeat Step 14 to join all four rows to make the quilt's top, shown in Figure 4-18.

Figure 4-18:
The
pinwheel
baby
quilt top.

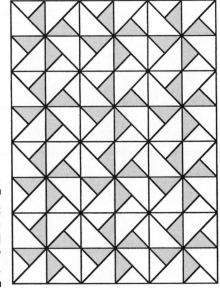

Adding the eyelet

The quilt's eyelet trim is optional. If you prefer not to trim your quilt, skip to the section "Assembling and quilting the pieces."

1. **With the raw edges matching, pin the 1-inch-wide eyelet to the front of the 2-inch-wide eyelet and stitch across the bottom edge to join the two eyelet fabrics.**

2. **With the right sides of the eyelet facing the front of the quilt, pin the raw edges of the eyelet all around the quilt top. Overlap the eyelet ends where they meet.**

3. **Stitch the eyelet all around the quilt top, $1/4$ inch from the edge of the patchwork top.**

Assembling and quilting the pieces

1. **With right sides facing, pin the backing fabric and the quilt top together.**

2. **Center the pinned fabric over the quilt batting and re-pin all three layers together.**

3. **Use fabric shears to trim the excess batting to the quilt's size.**

4. **Stitch around three sides and four corners of the quilt, leaving one edge of the quilt open. Turn the quilt right-side out.**

5. **Turn the raw edges of the fabric's opening to the inside $1/4$ inch and press the quilt with your iron.**

6. **Slip stitch the quilt's open edge closed.**

7. **Using approximately 6 inches of embroidery floss for each bow, tie the center of each block.**

   Cut a 12-inch piece of embroidery floss and thread your needle with it. (Don't make a knot at the end of the floss.) Insert the needle through the top of the quilt in the center of the first block (the intersection of the four triangles), without pulling the thread all the way through, and then bring the needle back up through the quilt in the same spot so that both ends of floss are on the front side of the quilt. Pull the needle off the thread. Make a knot and then a bow, and cut the ends of the floss. (You need approximately 6 inches of floss for each bow.)

Chapter 5

Making Candles

Creating candles can be a relaxing and rewarding hobby. Because today's supplies and materials make fashioning attractive candles easy, you don't need to purchase them. And because candle-making isn't an expensive hobby, you can decorate your home with candles and even give them as gifts.

Nothing quite compares to the feelings of pride and pleasure that come from looking at a beautiful, burning candle and knowing that you created it with your own two hands. Like any hobby, candle-making requires a few supplies, a little know-how, and a bit of practice — all of which you can find here.

This chapter explains how to make candles using paraffin and beeswax. Important differences exist if you use other waxes, such as gel wax and vegetable-based waxes. Before you make candles with these substances, make sure you understand their requirements and know how to do so safely. To find out more about how to use these waxes, or to take your candle-making skills to new heights, check out *Making Candles and Soaps For Dummies* by Kelly Ewing (Wiley).

Equipment and Supplies

To get started on the right foot with candle-making, you need some standard equipment and a few basic supplies. Fortunately, many of the items you need (with the exception of wax and wicks) are items you likely already own. What you don't have, you can probably find at reasonable prices.

Basic equipment

Making candles doesn't have to be expensive. You can use many items that you already have at home, or you can buy them cheaply at garage sales. If you do need to buy necessary equipment at a store, you can almost always find coupons for it in your Sunday newspaper. If you don't have what you need on hand and don't want to drive to stores, you can also order what you need via the Internet.

So now that you know how to get your supplies, you need to be familiar with them and what they do when it comes to candle-making. The following list walks you through the basic equipment required to make candles:

- ✔ **Heat source:** What you're basically doing in candle-making is melting solid wax over a heat source. Your stove, of course, is perfect for this function, but some people like to use a small camping stove. Regardless, it doesn't matter whether your stove is gas or electric. What you don't want to use is a microwave oven: The temperature is too hard to control, and you can easily overheat the wax.

- ✔ **A double-boiler-type pot for melting your wax:** A *double boiler,* shown in Figure 5-1, is basically a large pot with a smaller pot inside. If you don't own a double boiler, you can use a small pot placed inside a larger pot to get the same effect. Use a trivet or small tin cans to prop the small pot up so that it doesn't rest on the bottom of the larger pot and make sure the top of the smaller pot is at least $^1/_2$ inch above the rim of the larger pot. (No matter what kind of melting vessel you choose, remember that you're going to pour the wax from the container directly into your mold. Consequently, a melting pot with a spout is helpful.)

    Wax heats up quickly and can explode if it gets too hot, which is why you almost always must use an indirect method of melting it. Do *not* melt your wax in a pot directly on your burner.

- ✔ **Thermometer:** You can either purchase a specialized wax thermometer or use a candy or cooking thermometer, as long as it can register temperatures ranging from 100 degrees Fahrenheit to 300 degrees Fahrenheit. You can find thermometers that attach to the side of your melting pot by checking your local craft store, cooking store, or online candle-making resource.

- ✔ **Mold(s):** Your first candles will probably be made in a *mold,* a hollow object into which you pour your melted wax. As the wax cools, it hardens and takes on the shape of the mold. The type of material your mold is made of doesn't matter. In fact, you have many mold options, from store-bought ones, to molds you recycle from household items, to molds you make yourself.

Figure 5-1:
You need
a double
boiler (or
some varia-
tion thereof)
to melt
your wax.

A thermometer is one of the absolute most important pieces of candle-making equipment. Don't even try to make candles without one because it's too dangerous! Wax gets hot quickly, and unlike items you cook, you can't eyeball it and know by sight that you've overdone it. The only way to properly guarantee the temperature of your wax is with a thermometer.

✔ **Dipping can:** If you're going to be dipping taper candles (see the section "The basic taper candle" for the technique), then you want some type of metal container that's wide enough and tall enough to dip your wicks into (like the one shown in Figure 5-2). Of course, you can purchase these cans, but you can also use something from home. If you're lucky and your melting pot is at least 12 inches wide, save some cash and searching and just use it to dip your candles in.

✔ **Ladle or large metal spoon:** As the wax melts, you need to stir it occa-sionally. A ladle or large metal spoon works well for this purpose. As long as you don't leave the spoon in the wax mixture, you can even get by with a long-handled plastic spoon, which is easy to clean and doesn't absorb wax or scent.

✔ **Mold sealer and releasing agent:** *Mold sealer* (also called *wick sealer*) is a special putty that you use to close up the hole where you thread in your wick so that the wax doesn't leak out. A *releasing agent* (also referred to as *mold release*), which you spray inside your mold, makes your finished candle less likely to stick to its mold.

Vegetable oil works just as well as any releasing agent out there. Just apply a thin amount of oil to the inside of your mold and *voilà!*

✔ **Wick tabs:** Thin metal bases that attach to the bottom of untabbed wicks are called *wick tabs.* (Some wicks come with the tabs already attached.) You often use wick tabs for votives and container candles, because they help your wick stand up straight. If you use molds that don't have a hole in the bottom for your wick, you can also use these tabs to help your wick stay at the bottom of your candle when you pour the wax.

✔ **Objects that let you color, scent, and otherwise decorate your candles:** Wax dye, which you use to color your wax, comes in a variety of forms, including powder, liquid, and solid chips. You can also add fragrance by using essential oils, synthetic scents specially formulated for candles, and herbs.

Figure 5-2:
For dipping tapers, you need some type of a dipping can that's at least 12 inches wide.

Wax

Wax is the wick's fuel. Without it, your candle won't burn. When making candles, you can choose from several different types of waxes. As mentioned previously, this chapter focuses on paraffin and beeswax — the waxes that most candles are made out of and that are easiest to find.

Paraffin wax: The winner and still champion!

Paraffin, an inexpensive, petroleum-based wax, is the most popular wax for making candles. If you're new to candle-making, paraffin wax makes a great starting point. Because of its colorless and odorless nature, it's also a good choice if you want to add color and scent.

Paraffin wax comes in different melting points, ranging from 104 degrees Fahrenheit to 160 degrees Fahrenheit. The melting point you choose depends on the type of candle you want to make. When you're buying paraffin, check the wax's label for both its melting point and the type of candle it's best used to create.

Don't be tempted to do one-stop shopping and buy your paraffin wax at the grocery store. This wax isn't the type for candle-making. Instead, it's used for sealing food that you've jarred.

Book II

Traditional Crafts

Beeswax: The benefits of honey, with no stings attached

Beeswax is an all-natural product that, when burned, gives off a pleasant honey aroma. In addition to its natural golden shade, beeswax is available in white and other colors. You can buy beeswax in honeycomb sheets, blocks, or beads. Beeswax's low melting point (approximately 140 degrees Fahrenheit) and strength (if you drop it, it dents, but doesn't shatter) make beeswax a great wax to use when you're making container candles with children. On the downside, beeswax can be a little bit pricier than paraffin.

Wicks

Although you can use almost any wick to make a candle, the best wick allows your candle to burn longer and cleaner. In general, wicks come in three main types:

- ✔ **Flat-braided wicks** vary in the number of plies used. In general, the more plies in the wick, the thicker it is, which makes it more suitable for larger candles. Flat-braided wicks are best for tapers.

- ✔ **Square-braided wicks** are (as you can imagine) square. Unlike flat-braided wicks, the number of plies used isn't indicated in the wick's thickness, so knowing the right size to use is a little more difficult. The solution? Follow the manufacturer's recommendation or eyeball the size. Square-braided wicks are best for beeswax candles, pillars, and other large candles.

✔ **Cored wicks** consist of plies braided around a metal, cotton, or paper core. The core helps the wick stand up straight when the candle is poured and while it burns. Cored wicks are usually attached to a *wick tab,* or flat metal piece at the bottom of a candle. Metal cored wicks can be used for any type of candle, but they're especially good for container candles, votives, and tealights. Paper cored wicks are best for votives, tealights, and container candles.

Some cored wicks contain lead. Make sure that the candles you have burning in your home aren't releasing this dangerous toxin. To test for lead, simply rub the tip of an unburned wick on a piece of plain white paper. If you see a light gray mark on the paper, the wick contains a lead core. *Note:* Lead cored wicks haven't been available in the United States for many years; that's not necessarily true of candles or wicks manufactured elsewhere. So carry a bit of paper in your purse or wallet when you go candle shopping so that you can perform the same quick lead test before you buy.

Additives

Wax additives change the crystalline structure of wax, which then affects attributes such as the candle's appearance or burning time. If you're having problems with your candles (particularly mottling, cracking, or burning issues), wax additives may be just what you need to fine-tune them. The most common additives are

✔ **Stearin:** Almost always added to paraffin candles, *stearin* lengthens a candle's burning time, shrinks the wax so that you can remove it easily from molds, gives your candle a glossy finish, hardens your candle so that it's less likely to bend or tilt, and more. To add stearin to wax, you simply add it to the wax while the wax is melting.

Don't use stearin when you're pouring your wax into a flexible rubber mold (it rots the mold; use vybar instead) or when you're making container candles (you don't want the wax to shrink; use microcrystalline instead).

✔ **Vybar:** A great replacement for stearin when you're pouring your wax into flexible molds, *vybar* comes in two types. Simply choose the one that best matches your wax's melting point. Vybar helps eliminate bubbles, increases the strength of your candles, gives you a smooth surface, and enables you to add more fragrance. As with stearin, you can simply melt it along with your candle wax.

✔ **Microcrystalline:** Used to help candles stay softer longer and prolong their burning time, *microcrystalline* is found in two basic types:

  • **Hard microcrystalline:** This type lengthens a candle's burning time, improves its finish, and makes it stronger. Hard microcrystalline has a high melting point, and you use it only in minute quantities — 1 teaspoon of melted microcrystalline per 1 pound of wax. Be sure to melt the hard microcrystalline first and then add it directly to your wax.

  • **Soft microcrystalline:** This type has a low melting point and is what you use when you make container candles because it enables the wax to stick to the sides of containers better. Use approximately 10 percent soft microcrystalline for your container candles.

Most of the time, microcrystalline is already included in your wax, so you don't need to add it. Always read your package's label. If the wax already includes microcrystalline, don't add any more of this additive.

Use an additive only after you've determined that other factors — type of wax, wick, and temperature — aren't the problem.

Book II

Traditional Crafts

Candle-Making Know-How

Not sure what type of candle you want to create? Well, you have a variety of options, as the following list and Figure 5-3 show:

✔ **Container:** *Container candles* burn in the actual container that you pour them into. In essence, the container is your mold. (The later section "The container candle" shows you how to make a container candle.) One perk of container candles is that the container keeps the wax from dripping onto your carpet, counters, or tables.

✔ **Floating:** *Floating candles* do just as they're named and float in water. They're often used in centerpieces.

✔ **Pillar:** *Pillar candles* are sturdy and thick. They can be short or tall and square or round. Some pillar candles are huge and contain multiple wicks. These candles are usually referred to by their diameter and height, as in a 3-x-5-inch pillar candle.

✔ **Taper:** *Taper candles* are long and slim and look elegant as centerpieces on your dining room table or on your fireplace mantel. Although taper molds are available, if you want to make these elegant creations, you can simply dip your wicks into melted wax. Go to "The basic taper candle" for instructions on creating taper candles.

✔ **Tealights:** *Tealight candles* are the same diameter as votives, but are just 1 inch high. You can place them in a tealight holder or place them under something, such as a pot of simmering potpourri or a lampshade.

✔ **Votives:** *Votive candles* are short, small candles that are only 2 to 3 inches high and ½ inch in diameter. Unlike pillar candles, votive candles are classified according to how long they burn. Most votives are 10-hour or 15-hour candles.

Figure 5-3: You first need to decide what type of candle you want to make. Clockwise from top left: pillar, taper, container, floating, tealight, and votive candles.

No matter what type of candle you make, you perform the same general tasks: You get yourself and your workspace ready; you prepare your molds and/or wicks; you heat and pour your wax; and so on. The following sections explain all the key components essential to candle-making, including how to stay safe while you do it.

Prepping your workspace and yourself

If you've ever had a burning candle drip on your carpet, then you know how difficult removing wax can be. That's why you need to take time to prepare your workspace — unless, of course, you enjoy scraping wax off your countertops and removing stains from your clothes.

The kitchen's the best place to make your candles simply because that's the most likely place for your heat source, the stove. Follow these steps to get your workspace ready:

1. **Choose an area near the stove where you have enough counter space to work.**

   You need to be able to arrange all your supplies nearby, as well as have enough room to work. The closer you are to your heat source, the better off you are.

2. **Line your countertop with aluminum foil, wax paper, or even an old dropcloth or sheet.**

   Someone may have suggested that you use newspaper to line your countertop when making candles. Don't! Although newspaper is indeed an inexpensive alternative — especially if you subscribe to a daily one and you're going to toss it or recycle it anyway — the heat from the wax may cause the newsprint to get on your countertop.

   If you're using aluminum foil or wax paper, turn up the edges at least an inch to prevent runoffs from leaky wax.

3. **Tear off a few extra sheets of foil or paper.**

   You can always use extra foil or paper, so have it ready now, before you need it. For example, after you pour your wax into the mold, you can use these extra sheets to place your mold on for extra coverage.

4. **Get out anything else you may need, based on the project you're making.**

   Just as you would when making a recipe, make sure that you read through the project you're making and get those supplies ready now as well. Good all-purpose items to have on hand include potholders and paper towels.

   Having a fire extinguisher on hand is a good idea, too. After all, it can never hurt to be overly prepared!

5. **Shoo kids and pets from the room.**

   When you're making candles, your kitchen is no place for your kids or pets. Find a sitter, have your partner entertain your children, or make candles while the kids nap. Let your dog outside for a potty break or move your cat to a different room.

Believe it or not, you also want to dress for the occasion. (Didn't know candle-making had a dress code, did you?) Although you don't have to wear a specific candle-making uniform, you do need to put a little thought into what you're wearing. Put on something that you don't mind getting a little wax on and avoid wearing clothes that shed — unless you *want* your candles to have some fur.

Book II

Traditional Crafts

Don't overlook eye protection. Safety goggles can go a long way in protecting your eyes from splashes. And if you find yourself making lots of splashes, you may even want to consider wearing long sleeves and pants the next time.

Getting your wick ready

When you light a candle, the wick allows heat to travel down to the wax, melting it along the way. The wick then sucks up the melted wax to keep the candle burning. If the melted wax isn't being used up at the right pace, the problem centers on the wick. So in order for a wick to do its job efficiently, it needs a little care from you during the candle-making process.

Choosing the right wick size

For your candle to burn nicely, you need the right-sized wick. The size of wick you require depends mainly on your candle's diameter. Table 5-1 gives you a general guide for choosing your wicks.

Table 5-1	Sizing Your Wick
If Your Diameter Is . . .	*You Probably Want a Wick That's . . .*
0–1 inch	Extra small, 20 ply
1–2 inches	Small, 24 ply
2–3 inches	Medium, 30 ply
3–4 inches	Large, 36 ply
4 inches or more	Extra large, 40-plus ply

If your candle is large — say, more than 5 inches — use multiple wicks. Simply divide your diameter by three to come up with how many wicks you need for candles larger than 5 inches. For example, if your candle has a diameter of 9 inches, you want to use three medium or large wicks. Never use more than five wicks in a candle, however.

Figuring out the right wick length for your candle is a lot more cut and dried than sizing your wick: Just take your candle's height and add 4 to 6 inches extra for a pillar candle or $1/2$ to 1 inch extra for a votive candle. The extra length gives you ample room to knot the wick on the bottom and secure it at the top of the mold.

Priming your wick

A *primed wick* is a wick soaked thoroughly with wax (something that's usually done by you or the wick manufacturer). Priming does several things for your wick. It

- ✔ Jump-starts the combustion process by getting wax into the wick before you even light the candle
- ✔ Helps keep water droplets or additives from clogging the wick
- ✔ Makes the wick stronger so that you have an easier time threading it inside the candle
- ✔ Eliminates air inside the wick so you don't have unsightly bubbles
- ✔ Makes the wick more likely to stand on its own so that, when you thread it through the top of the candle, it actually protrudes upright and not all drooped over

To prime your wicks, follow these steps:

1. **Place your wax for priming in your double boiler and melt it until it reaches 190 degrees Fahrenheit.**

2. **Dip your wick into the melted wax for approximately 5 minutes (see Figure 5-4).**

   You may see bubbles escaping from the wick. Don't remove the wick from the wax until the bubbles have disappeared.

3. **Place the wick somewhere (on aluminum foil, wax paper, or a candle rack) to dry.**

   The wick will stiffen as it cools.

   Running the wick between your thumb and index finger as it cools makes it smoother and easier to thread into your mold. This optional step also makes the wick look better in your container or votive candle.

Most of the time, you use a primed wick in candle-making, but when you're making tapers by dipping them in wax, you use an unprimed wick. The dipping process itself primes the wick for you.

Attaching a tab to your wick

A *tabbed* wick is a wick that has a metal base (or *wick tab*) attached at the bottom of it, as shown in Figure 5-5. Tabs help your wicks stand upright and remain on the bottom of your container candles when you're pouring wax. Just as you can prime your wicks (described in the preceding section), you can also tab them.

Figure 5-4:
To prime
your wick,
just melt
your wax,
dip your
wick, and let
it cool.

Figure 5-5:
A wick tab
provides
support for
your wick so
it stands up
straight and
remains at
the bottom
of your
containers.

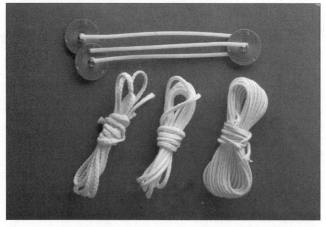

To tab your wick, you need only a pair of pliers: Simply thread your wick into
the open part of the tab (see Figure 5-6a) and then use the pliers to close the
tab around the wick (see Figure 5-6b).

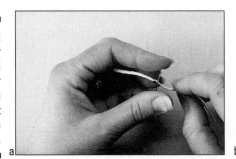

Figure 5-6:
To tab your wick, thread it into your tab and then squeeze it closed with your pliers.

a   b

Getting your mold ready and adding the wick

Before you can pour wax into a mold, you need to get it ready. That means spraying it with a releasing agent or wiping it with a thin film of vegetable oil before adding the wick. Most one-piece molds have a hole at the bottom that allows you to thread your wick into your candle. To add the wick, follow these steps:

1. **Thread your wick through the bottom of the mold (as shown in Figure 5-7a).**

2. **Pull the wick to the top of the mold and tie it to a wick rod.**

   The rod lies across the top of your mold, as you can see in Figure 5-7b.

3. **From the bottom of the mold, pull the wick taut (see Figure 5-7c).**

4. **Place mold sealer around the wick hole so that your wax doesn't leak out of your mold (as shown in Figure 5-7d).**

   If you're finished product looks like Figure 5-7e, you're now ready to add your wax. See the next section for instructions on how to heat and pour your wax.

Working with wax

Making candles isn't as simple as heading to your local craft store to buy "candle wax" and then returning home to melt and mold it into a candle. Not only do you have to know what kind of wax you need but you also need to know how to handle it. In the following sections, you discover the ins and outs of working with wax.

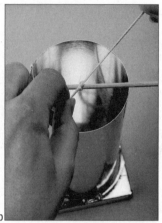

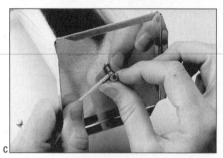

Figure 5-7:
Adding your
wick to
your mold.

Figuring out how much wax you need

The easiest way to come up with your magic wax number is to simply fill your mold with water and measure how much liquid you used. (Be sure to block the mold's wick hole first.) Then do a quick calculation: For every 3.5 fluid ounces of water, you need 3 ounces of unmelted wax.

Don't forget to melt a little extra wax so you have enough to repour into the mold to make up for the wax shrinking as it cools.

Melting wax

Follow these steps to melt your wax:

1. **Determine the amount of wax you need.**

   If you're unsure about the amount, see the preceding section.

2. **Place your wax in the top part of your double boiler.**

   If you're using a slab of wax, break it into smaller pieces so that it melts more quickly and evenly. Forget your hands; use stronger tools, such as a screwdriver.

   Choose your burner carefully. You don't want to heat your wax too close to the wall, or you may run into smoke damage if you overheat it. Also, make sure that your double boiler is centered over the burner.

3. **Add water to the bottom section of the double boiler.**

   If you're using two pots rather than an actual double boiler, the water should reach about two-thirds up the smaller pot's sides.

4. **Over medium heat, bring the water to a rolling boil.**

   High heat will cause the water to boil too hard, and it may splash into your wax.

5. **Heat your wax until it's melted.**

   Boil your water for a while (the candle projects in this chapter give you approximate times), but don't forget to recheck the bottom pot occasionally to make sure that it still has enough water to cover at least two-thirds of the sides of the smaller pot.

   If wax gets on your burner, clean it up after the wax cools.

6. **Check your wax's temperature with your thermometer; when it reaches the correct temp, you're done.**

   You need to constantly check your wax's temperature. Place your thermometer directly in the wax and then immediately wipe off the wax after reading the temp. If your thermometer has a clip on it, you can actually attach it to the side of the pot and leave it there. That way you don't have to keep inserting and cleaning it to monitor the wax's temperature.

Pouring — and repouring — melted wax

If you're like the majority of candle makers, you pour your melted wax into a prepared mold (refer to the earlier section "Getting your mold ready and adding the wick" for details). To pour your wax, be sure to do the following:

1. **Carefully grab your melting container and begin pouring your wax smoothly into your mold.**

   Stop about ¹/₂ inch before you reach the top of the mold. If you drip any wax down the side of the container, simply use a towel to wipe it up. Likewise, if water drips down the container's side, wipe it off. (You don't want to get water into your wax.)

   Don't forget that you're working with hot items: Obviously your pots and wax are hot, but so are the molds you just poured hot wax into. Aluminum molds in particular heat up more than others. Be careful and use potholders!

2. **Very gently tap the side of your mold to remove any air bubbles.**

   The type of wax you're using determines what you do after you pour your wax. For example, if you're making a paraffin mold candle and want a smooth, shiny finish, or simply want the candle to cool faster, you may want to place your mold into a cold water bath for a while. For details on making a paraffin mold candle, see the later section "The basic molded candle."

3. **Let the wax inside the mold cool for a while before pouring your extra wax (you'll have to reheat it) to fill in any holes that have occurred as the wax cools.**

   Wax shrinks as it cools. The act of adding more hot wax to a nearly cooled candle is called a *repour*.

4. **Let your wax cool again, and then do a second repour.**

5. **Allow the wax to cool completely before removing your candle from the mold.**

   Don't forget to admire your handiwork!

Dealing with leftover wax

If you have any leftover wax, you can either store it for later use or discard it. To discard the leftover wax, just put it into a half-gallon, cardboard milk container and let it cool. After the wax hardens, take it out and throw it away.

 Never throw melted wax down the drain. After wax returns to a cool, hardened state, it clogs up your drain. Along those same lines, don't throw your boiling water down the drain, either. More than likely, it contains wax pieces as well. Pour the boiling water outside or let it cool so that you can remove the wax first.

If you want to reuse the wax, place it in a flexible container. After it hardens, remove the wax and place it in plastic bags for later use. Be sure to label the bags with the types of waxes you used.

Book II

Traditional Crafts

 Don't think that you can save time by leaving the wax in your melting vessel and then remelting it later. Some candle makers out there remelt this way regularly, but doing so involves a huge potential risk: The top wax layer doesn't melt as quickly as the bottom, and the liquid wax underneath causes an unexpected explosion of hot wax.

Playing it safe

Working with hot substances means you need to take the proper precautions. Wear thick potholders whenever you're removing your double boiler from the stove, as well as when you're pouring or repouring your wax. The following sections provide additional, valuable safety information for when you're heating wax, treating spills, or putting out a fire.

Heating wax

Unless you're rolling beeswax candles, you must melt your solid wax into liquid wax. You don't want to get your wax too hot, though, or it may combust, causing a fire. Here are the key points to melting wax safely:

- ✔ **Never leave your wax unattended as it melts.** If you see smoke, you know you're in danger of a fire. Immediately turn off the heat.

- ✔ **Don't melt your wax over direct heat or in a microwave.** Using a double boiler slows the heating process and helps ensure your safety.

- ✔ **Make sure you have enough water in your double boiler.** Use enough to cover about two-thirds of the sides of the top pot.

Treating spills and burns

Alas, despite your best intentions, wax is bound to appear somewhere you don't want it to — either while you're making your candles or while you're burning them. Perhaps the wax is on your floor, your carpet, your clothes, or yourself. Regardless, the next two sections show you how to handle such situations.

Hot wax on you

No matter what type of hot wax you spill on yourself, the basic treatment is the same.

1. **Immediately place your injured body part in cool water.**

   Don't use cold water because extreme temperature shocks your skin.

2. **When the wax cools and hardens, gently peel it off.**

3. **Treat your wax burn like any other burn.**

   If your skin isn't blistered, use calamine lotion or aloe vera (*not* butter). If your skin *is* blistered, definitely call your doctor or visit your local immediate care center.

Hot wax on something other than you

If the hot wax gets on something other than your body, follow these steps:

1. **Wait until it hardens before you try to clean it up.**

   Otherwise, you're just spreading the goo and making a bigger mess. If you want to speed along the hardening process, try rubbing an ice cube on the wax to help cool it. If the item is movable, such as clothing, you can even place it in the freezer.

2. **After the wax hardens, try to scrape up what you can.**

   A wooden spatula works particularly well for scraping up hardened wax. Watch out if the wax is on something hard though, such as flooring or countertops, because you can scratch the object's surface if you're not careful.

3. **If your spill is on your carpet or clothing, and scraping didn't get all the wax off, cover the area with paper towels or newspaper and iron over it.**

   Keep replacing the paper towels or newspapers and ironing the spot until the wax disappears.

   If this method doesn't remove the wax from your clothes, try taking them to a dry cleaner because dry cleaning chemicals can often remove wax from fabric. Just let the shop know what it's dealing with when you drop off the garments.

You may not be able to remove wax from porous material, such as unfinished wood, unglazed tile, or concrete.

Extinguishing a fire

Unfortunately, mishaps occur. Although a fire shouldn't be in your future if you're checking your temperature regularly during the melting process, you need to be prepared to deal with one just in case.

Turn off your heat source immediately if any of the following occurs:

- ✔ You check your wax's temperature, and it's dangerously high (anything over boiling point, which is 212 degrees Fahrenheit).
- ✔ Your wax begins to smoke.
- ✔ You smell something burning.
- ✔ Your wax ignites and catches fire.

Be aware that you may have no signs of an impending fire. Unlike water, wax doesn't bubble when it reaches 212 degrees Fahrenheit.

If you think you're in danger of a fire, don't try to move your pan. A fire may occur at any minute, and you don't want to take the chance of spreading it or spilling dangerously hot wax everywhere.

Wax is actually oil, so never pour water on it in an attempt to put it out if it's on fire. If a fire occurs, smother the flames instead by using a metal lid, a damp cloth, a fire blanket, some baking soda, or an extinguisher — just not water!

After you've eliminated the fire, don't touch the pan right away because it's hot. When it's cooled down, you can clean up just as you would any other fire — air out the area, throw away the pan after it cools, and call a fire repair company if the damage is severe.

Candle Projects

Whether you're digging through the trash can in search of your empty yogurt cup from lunch (wash it, please!) or holding a freshly purchased pillar mold, this chapter is for you. Here, you get to try your hand at some basic projects: a molded candle, two dipped tapers, a rolled beeswax candle, and a container candle.

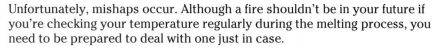

Book II

Traditional Crafts

Always read through a project before you begin so that you can properly prepare your workspace and make sure that you have the necessary supplies. (For more on preparing your workspace and gathering the appropriate equipment, see the earlier section "Prepping your workspace and yourself.")

The basic molded candle

The type of candle you'll probably make the most is a basic molded candle. You can use the technique described in this section to make many different types of candles. The type of mold you use doesn't matter; the steps are still pretty much the same. And if you're using a store-bought mold, professional-looking results are almost guaranteed.

After you choose your mold, determine the amount and type of wax you need, and pick your wick (refer to the earlier "Choosing the right wick size" section for details), follow these steps:

1. **Melt your wax to the package's specified temperature.**

   Aim for 190 degrees Fahrenheit — the temperature at which you pour the wax — if you're recycling wax or you're unsure of the right temperature. Maintain that temperature for half an hour.

   If you're not certain how to melt wax, see the detailed steps in the earlier section, "Melting wax."

2. **Spray your mold with a mold release, such as silicone or vegetable spray.**

   Using a releasing agent helps you remove your candle from the mold.

3. **Cut your primed wick so that it's 2 inches longer than your finished candle's height and then insert it into your mold.**

   For instructions on inserting your wick, see the earlier section "Getting your mold ready and adding the wick."

   You can do Steps 2 and 3 prior to melting your wax if you're worried about time or if you prefer not to multitask.

4. **When your wax reaches the required temperature, add any additives, color, or scent.**

   Unless you're using a flexible mold, add stearin in proportion to 10 percent of your wax; if you're using a flexible mold, use vybar. (Refer to the section titled "Additives" for info about these products.)

After you add these ingredients, your wax's temperature will probably drop, so continue heating your wax a little longer until it reaches the proper temperature again.

5. **Remove your wax from the heat and slowly and smoothly pour it into your mold.**

   Be careful not to get any water into your wax. The section "Pouring — and repouring — melted wax" offers tips on pouring your wax.

6. **Wait a few minutes and then gently tap the side of your mold to remove any air bubbles.**

7. **As your wax cools, poke holes in the wax around the wick to release tension.**

   If you don't, the wax pulls the wick off-center and may create a concave section on the outside of the candle.

8. **After your wax has cooled quite a while, reheat the extra wax you saved and pour it into any holes that have occurred as the wax cools.**

9. **Let your wax cool almost completely and then do a second repour.**

   Don't rush this step. If you repour the wax while the candle is still hot and liquid, you're just adding more hot wax that has to shrink.

10. **After your candle has cooled completely, remove it from the mold by taking away any mold sealer that you used.**

    The bottom of the mold now becomes the top of your candle.

    If your candle isn't coming out of your mold, you may not have let it cool long enough. Wait a few hours and try again later.

11. **Clean up the candle.**

    Use a craft knife or other sharp object to level off the bottom of the candle and trim the wick. Use a paper towel or cloth to wipe around your candle and remove any extra wax.

    Congratulations! Your candle is now ready to burn.

The basic taper candle

You can make basic taper candles (refer to Figure 5-8) in two ways: You can dip them (the ways pioneers did), or you can buy a taper mold and follow the steps in the preceding section. This section focuses solely on how to dip a candle.

The dipping process is pretty straightforward: You basically melt the wax, dip both ends of a wick in it, let it cool, and repeat 20 to 30 times or more until your candle is the desired width. You don't have to do anything special to create the tapered look — it just happens naturally. Here's how the process works:

1. **Figure out how tall you want each taper to be, add a couple extra inches so that your wick protrudes, double that amount, and then add 4 inches for space.**

   When you make tapers, you usually dip in pairs, but you use only one wick. If you want to create 6-inch tapers, for example, then you take 6 inches plus 2 inches to get 8 inches. You multiply that number by 2 to get 16 inches (enough wick for two candles) and then add 4 inches to the total so that you have space in between the candles. (You don't want the ends of your wick to touch each other when you dip.) So to make two 6-inch tapers, you need to cut your wick to 20 inches.

2. **Tie a weight to each end of the wick so that it stays submerged and straight while you dip.**

   Rocks work just fine as weights. You remove these weights later when the wick is strong enough to stay straight.

3. **Melt twice the wax (plus 10-percent stearin) you think you need at 170 degrees Fahrenheit, the temperature at which dipping works best.**

   When you dip candles, you usually use paraffin wax or a mixture of beeswax and paraffin. Either way, you probably need to add the usual 10-percent stearin. (For more on stearin, see the earlier section "Additives.") You need to have plenty left over so that you have enough wax to dip in.

4. **Fill your dipping can with wax.**

   Make sure that your dipping can is tall enough to accommodate the size of the candle you want to make. Also, fill the dipping can fairly full so that you can dip almost all the way up the wick. You have to keep adding wax to the dipping can throughout the process to keep it full.

5. **Dip your wick into your melted wax.**

   You want to dip your wick deep enough so that you have only a couple inches of undipped wick remaining. Don't linger too long on this dip, though. You want your wick in the wax for only a second. Plunge it in and then remove it smoothly so that the wax doesn't blob. Meanwhile, keep these tidbits in mind:

   • If your taper looks bumpy, your wax isn't warm enough.

   • If your wax isn't building up on your wick, your wax is too hot.

WARNING!

• If the wax isn't firming up enough between dips, you need to let it cool longer in between dips.

Make sure that the ends of your wick don't touch each other, or you end up with a wax glob. You can use your hands to keep the ends apart, or you may want to use a straw, dowel rod, or piece of cardboard (refer to Figures 5-8a and 5-8b).

6. **Place your wicks over a rack or dowel rod until they cool.**

   The cooling process takes approximately 3 minutes. Basically, the wax should feel cool to the touch.

7. **Repeat Steps 5 and 6 until your candle is the diameter you want.**

   You may have to dip your candles 20 or 30 times, or even more. Every time you dip, more wax builds up on your wick. Eventually, your wick becomes two tapers.

Figure 5-8: To dip a taper, dip your trimmed wick into melted wax, allow it to cool, and then redip your wick repeatedly until you reach your desired diameter.

TIP

If you want your taper surfaces to be glossy, dip your tapers immediately into cool water after your last dip into the wax.

8. **Let your tapers cool a few hours before handling them and trimming your wick to $1/4$ inch.**

9. **Size the base, if necessary.**

   In general, taper candles are ⁷/₈ inch in diameter at the bottom so that they can fit into most candleholders. If you're not using a mold, you probably need to cut the base of the candle down to that size. To cut the taper's base to the size of the candleholder you plan to use, use a craft knife and score around the base of your cooled candle. Then remove the strips of wax until your taper fits perfectly into the desired holder.

As you can see, dipping candles is a fairly easy process. The most difficult part is often simply waiting for the wax to cool between each dip. If you're impatient, you may want to create several tapers at once so that you're constantly dipping in rotation and don't have to wait.

The rolled beeswax candle

A simple beeswax candle can create quite a buzz and may just be the perfect first candle for beginners. In fact, this project is particularly ideal for young children. Why? Because you don't need to melt any wax or use a lot of fancy equipment. You simply roll sheets of beeswax into a round candle. (You can easily make other shapes as well.)

The only downside is that beeswax is sticky at any temperature, and it gets even stickier when it's warm. (So don't let your child touch her hair when messing with this stuff!) But it's not so sticky that you and your youngster can't work with it. (In fact, that stickiness can actually work in your favor because the beeswax sheets adhere to each other as you roll them.) You just need to make sure that you don't pick up any extra fuzz.

When you roll your candle, you want your beeswax sheet to be at room temperature. Ideally, it has been at this temp for at least a few days.

To roll a beeswax candle, you need two sheets of beeswax and a primed wick. Here's what you want to do:

1. **Cut your primed wick so that it's ³/₄ inch longer than the height of your finished candle.**

   If you're using a normal beeswax sheet, which measures 8 inches x 16 inches, your candle will be about 8 inches tall, so you want your wick to be approximately 8³/₄ inches. If you want to make two 8-inch tapers instead, just cut the sheet in half long ways and roll two candles.

   When working with beeswax, use a wick that's one size larger than you'd normally use. See the earlier sections "Wicks" and "Getting your wick ready" for details on choosing the correct wick type and size and for info about what to do if your wick isn't already primed.

2. **Lay your beeswax sheet on a hard surface and place your wick along the edge, as shown in Figure 5-9a.**

3. **Apply pressure, smoothly but firmly rolling the edge of the sheet around the wick, and continue rolling the beeswax into a cylindrical shape.**

   As shown in Figure 5-9b, you want to make sure you're rolling straight. Otherwise, your edges won't align. You also want to roll tightly enough so that you don't trap air between the layers, which can affect how well your candle burns.

   If you want to make a square candle, just flatten each side with a hard object as you roll. If you want to make a shorter candle, cut the short side of the beeswax sheet in half prior to rolling it.

Figure 5-9:
Making a beeswax candle is as simple as adding a wick and gently, but tightly, rolling it into a candle.

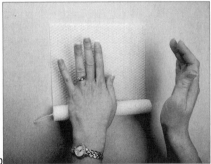

4. **When you reach the end of the first sheet, attach your second sheet of beeswax by firmly pinching the edges of each sheet together and then continue rolling.**

   For a larger candle, you can use as many sheets of beeswax consecutively as you need to reach your desired diameter.

5. **Trim your wick.**

   Wait at least a day, preferably longer, before lighting your new masterpiece.

You want your beeswax to be at least room temperature or warmer, or it will break. If you're having trouble, try using a hairdryer to heat the sheets. But don't go too warm, or the wax may begin to melt and become a sticky mess.

The container candle

If you're the creative type, you may find yourself gravitating toward container candles. The technique for making a container candle is very similar to making a molded candle. The container, in essence, acts as your mold. The only difference is that you don't use the additive stearin because you want the wax to adhere to the sides of your container. Instead, you may want to opt for 2-percent soft microcrystalline, which has the opposite effect of stearin. (See the earlier section "Additives" for details.)

After you choose your container, determine the amount of wax you need, and select the best wick, follow these steps:

1. **Melt your wax to the package's specified pouring temperature.**

   If you're recycling wax, or you're unsure about the temperature you want, heat the wax to 190 degrees Fahrenheit. (See the earlier section "Melting wax" for directions if you're not sure how to melt wax.)

2. **Cut your primed, tabbed wick so that it's 1 inch longer than your container.**

   You want your wick primed so that it's strong enough to stand up when you pour the wax. The wick tab helps your wick stay in place at the bottom of your container.

3. **When your wax reaches the required temperature, add any additives, color, or scent you want.**

   If you add anything to your wax, your wax's temperature will probably drop, so heat it a little longer until it reaches the proper temperature again.

4. **Remove your wax from the heat and slowly and smoothly add a ¹/₂-inch layer of wax to your container.**

5. **Rest your tabbed wick in the center of your candle.**

   You want the wick to rest on the bottom of the container, so it needs to be tabbed. If your wick isn't tabbed, you can easily tab it yourself, as long as you have the supplies. (See the earlier section "Attaching a tab to your wick" for a quick how-to.)

6. **After the wax cools, add another ¹/₂-inch layer of wax.**

   You want only about an inch at the top of your container that's uncovered by wax.

7. **As the wax begins to harden, poke holes around the wick.**

8. **Pour another ¹/₂-inch layer of wax to fill in the holes you pricked.**

   This step reduces the temperature of the wax so that your candle doesn't shrink as much. It also helps you avoid the nasty center hole that sometimes develops as the wax burns.

9. **Repeat Steps 7 and 8 until the container is full and the surface remains level.**

10. **Allow the candle to cool completely.**

11. **Trim your wick to ¹/₄ inch.**

Glass tends to break if it comes into contact with a flame for a long time, so trimming your wick is especially important when working with this type of container. If you're using glass and you think that the length of the wick may cause the wick to touch the sides of your container or candleholder, by all means, shorten the wick's length. Other ways to help avoid this problem include making sure that your wick is centered when you pour your wax and that you're using a good-quality glass container that can withstand heat.

Book III
Edible Gardening

In this book . . .

Thomas Jefferson loved farmers. He considered them the most virtuous of Americans, and he considered farming the "most tranquil, healthy, and independent" of occupations. (And just for the record, he wasn't talking about agribusiness, or farmers/investors who only see their crops as up or down on the commodities market.)

Growing your own food is rewarding. How many other jobs produce a reward as tangible and pleasant? It's healthy: The labor and the product both enhance your health. And it's fun: Try not to smile when you harvest your first crop. This book tells you everything you need to know to begin.

Your mission now? Go forth and cultivate.

Chapter 1

Planning Your Edible Garden

In This Chapter

▶ Saying good-bye to run-of-the-mill gardens

▶ Drawing up a plan for your edible garden

▶ Knowing your growing season

*F*or many gardeners, growing food is the real reason for gardening. There really isn't anything quite like the feeling of satisfaction a gardener gets from nurturing and encouraging a tomato plant to put forth the most gorgeous and delicious tomatoes imaginable, or harvesting a healthy and tasty bunch of berries from a tree planted right in your front yard.

While the other chapters in Book III tell you everything you need to know about growing vegetables (Chapter 2), herbs (Chapter 3), and fruits, nuts, and berries (Chapter 4) — as well as how to maintain your garden so that you can produce the produce you want — this chapter is devoted to getting you started. And that means helping you put together a plan that details not only what you want to grow, but where and how you want to grow it.

Planting Plots with Personality

A lot of planning goes into your edible garden, but that doesn't mean it has to resemble a miniature farm, with perfectly-spaced rows of typical vegetables or fruit trees lined up like soldiers. Here are some suggestions for distinctive gardens to get your mouth watering and your creative juices flowing.

Ornamental edible gardens

Just because you plan to use the produce from the plants you grow doesn't mean your garden has to look utilitarian. If you treat your edible plants like ornamental plants — and arrange them for looks as well as for growing characteristics — you can end up with a garden that not only produces delicious, healthful food but also looks darn good while doing it.

Figure 1-1 shows a plan for a summer vegetable-flower garden that could be tucked into any sunny corner of a front or back yard. The garden in Figure 1-1 includes a variety of vegetables, herbs, and flowers, arranged along a central path.

To make this kind of planting work, consider these suggestions:

- **Match the bloom seasons of flowers with the growth cycles of vegetables and other edible plants.** In other words, mix flowers that grow in cool weather with vegetables that like similar conditions. Chapter 2 gives you all the information about vegetable planting times. (You can find out more about planting flowers in *Gardening Basics For Dummies,* by Steven A. Frowine and the editors of the National Gardening Association [Wiley].)

- **Mix in herbs — like parsley, chives, and thyme (described in Chapter 3).** Most of these are great ornamentals in their own right.

- **Match cultural needs of the plants.** Most vegetables need a constant supply of water. Don't combine these with flowers that like it on the dry side.

- **Give your plants enough room to grow; don't crowd them.** If the flowers have a spreading habit, you may even plant things farther apart.

- **Put short plants in front, tall plants in back.** The idea is to create a smooth transition in sizes from the front of the bed to the back. That way, you'll be able to see everything — smaller plants won't be blocked or shaded by taller ones.

- **Leave room to harvest.** Use stepping stones or paths so that you can harvest vegetables, herbs, and fruits without damaging your flowers.

- **Have a color theme.** Cluster colors that blend well: pink pansies planted at the base of ruby-colored rhubarb, white alyssum planted with green chard, red leaf lettuce planted with purple Johnny-jump ups, or red petunias planted at the base of pepper plants.

- **Plant foliage vegetables and herbs.** Vegetables and herbs with colorful or bold textures combine well with flowers. Use a lot of basil, chard, kale, lettuce, cabbage, chives, parsley, and other leafy vegetables.

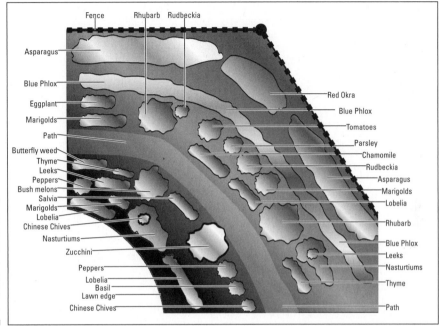

Figure 1-1:
Sample ornamental edible garden using flowers and vegetables.

Fence   Rhubarb   Rudbeckia

Asparagus
Blue Phlox
Eggplant
Marigolds
Path
Butterfly weed
Thyme
Leeks
Peppers
Bush melons
Salvia
Marigolds
Lobelia
Chinese Chives
Nasturtiums
Zucchini
Peppers
Lobelia
Basil
Lawn edge
Chinese Chives

Red Okra
Blue Phlox
Tomatoes
Parsley
Chamomile
Rudbeckia
Asparagus
Marigolds
Lobelia
Rhubarb
Blue Phlox
Leeks
Nasturtiums
Thyme
Path

Themed edible gardens

Why limit yourself to growing only carrots, corn, and beans — the staples of many vegetable plots and home gardens? Get creative! Group vegetables by their special uses. Grow a historic garden. Grow a garden based on food themes. This is where gardening gets really fun, and you're limited only by your imagination (and the length of your growing season). The following list describes several popular garden themes:

- ✔ **Greens Garden:** Do you love lettuce and other salad greens? Grow a colorful greens garden filled with different colors and textures of lettuce, endive, corn salad, radicchio, spinach, Swiss chard, and parsley.

- ✔ **Mexican Salsa Garden:** Are you addicted to salsa? Create a special nook for your own salsa garden, complete with different varieties of tomatoes, tomatillos, cilantro, peppers, and onions.

- ✔ **Oriental Stir Fry Garden:** Do you love to wok it up? Grow all the ingredients you need for a stir fry by planting pac choi, Chinese cabbage, snow peas, garlic, and scallions.

Book III

Edible Gardening

✓ **Pizza Garden:** This one's for the kids. Design a circular garden and, in triangular sections (like pizza slices), grow favorite pizza toppings such as peppers, onions, and tomatoes.

✓ **Three Sisters Garden:** Add a historic flair to your vegetable garden by growing corn, pole beans, and squash in a traditional Native American garden.

Theme gardens don't have to take over your entire garden. All that's required is a corner or one raised bed. Just remember the spacing requirements for your plants.

You can also create a small-space block garden. Often called the "square-foot garden," this square bed is only 3 feet wide but still packs a lot of punch for a petite plot: The bed is divided into nine 1-foot squares, each planted with a different vegetable. Containerized vegetable gardens are a good idea if all you have is a small patio or rooftop.

Growing up — on a trellis or a teepee — saves space, too. Consider training pole beans, peas, Malabar spinach, cucumber vines, small melons like Charentais, and mini pumpkins to grow skyward.

Mapping Out Your Garden

Designing an edible garden is both a practical and a creative process. Practically speaking, you have to arrange your plants so that they have room to grow and so that taller vegetables don't shade lower-growing ones. Different planting techniques fit the growth habits of different kinds of vegetables. And you should also think about access: How will you get to your plants to harvest, weed, or water them? Despite these practical considerations, creativity is also important to the design process. After all, vegetables can be good-looking as well as practical, as the preceding sections suggest.

In the following sections, I give you the basics so that you can start to sketch out a garden plan of what to plant and where to put it. I also provide a sample garden design to get your juices flowing. Before you know it, you'll be a gardening wizard!

Deciding on rows, hills, or raised beds

Before you sketch a garden plan, you need to decide how to arrange the plants in your garden and how you'll water them. You can use three basic planting arrangements: rows, hills, or raised beds.

Planting in rows for roominess

Any vegetable can be planted in rows, but this arrangement works best with types that need quite a bit of room, such as tomatoes, beans, cabbages, corn, potatoes, peppers, and summer squash.

Growing vining plants in hills

Hills are best for vining crops such as cucumbers, melons, and winter squash. You can create a 1-foot-wide, flat-topped mound for heavy soil, or you can create a circle at ground level for sandy soil. You then surround the soil with a moat-like ring for watering. Two or three evenly spaced plants are grown on each hill. Space the hills the recommended distance between rows of the vegetable you're planting.

Planting small veggies in raised beds

Raised beds are kind of like wide, flat-topped rows. They're usually at least 2 feet wide and raised at least 6 inches high. Raised beds are best for smaller vegetables that can be planted close together, such as lettuce, carrots, onions, spinach, radishes, and turnips. Vegetables in raised beds can be planted in random patterns or in closely spaced rows.

Any planting area that's raised above the surrounding ground level is a *raised bed*. It can simply be a normal bed with the soil piled 5 or 6 inches high, or it can be a bed located in a large container with wood, stone, or masonry sides.

Raised beds have several advantages:

- ✔ **They rise above soil problems.** If you have bad soil or poor drainage, raised beds are for you. You can amend the garden soil in the raised bed with the same sterile potting soil you use for containers. And because you don't step on the beds as you work, the soil is more likely to stay light and fluffy — providing the perfect conditions for root growth.

- ✔ **They warm up early.** Because more of the soil in raised beds is exposed to the sun, the soil warms early, allowing for early planting and extended harvest seasons.

- ✔ **They consolidate your work.** By growing your vegetables in raised beds, you can maximize your fertilizing and watering so that more nutrients and water are actually used by the plants rather than being wasted in the pathways.

- ✔ **They're easy on your back.** If you design the beds properly (about 24 to 36 inches high and no wider than 4 feet), raised beds can make vegetable gardening a lot more comfortable. You can sit on the edge (cap the edge to make it more bench-like) and easily reach into the bed to weed or harvest.

Book III

Edible Gardening

✔ **They're attractive.** Raised beds add a wonderful organized formality to the vegetable garden. They can be made from materials that match your house, patio, or deck. A series of raised beds can create an attractive focal point in your yard.

The one downside of permanent raised beds is that it's difficult to get a tiller inside the bed to work the soil. However, with some of the newer lightweight tillers, maneuvering a tiller inside a raised bed is getting easier. You can also turn the soil by hand with an iron fork; it's more work than using a tiller, but it's effective.

In dry areas such as the desert Southwest, the traditional bed is not raised — it's sunken. Dig into the soil about 6 inches and make a small wall of soil around the outside of the bed. This design allows the bed to catch any summer rains, protects young plants from drying winds, and concentrates water where the vegetables grow.

Planning your planting

As you plan your garden, you need to know how far apart to space your plants, how many plants you need to purchase for a particular size plot, and how much yield to expect.

Vegetable spacings are just guidelines, derived from agricultural recommendations for maximum yield per acre. With close attention to soil preparation, watering, and fertilizing, you can plant closer and still get a good harvest. You can also find compact, space-saving varieties of many vegetables, fruits, and herbs.

Although closer planting is possible, if you plant so close that plants have to compete with each other for food, water, and light, you'll eventually get smaller harvests or lower-quality vegetables.

Penciling it in

Drawing a garden plan doesn't require any landscaping expertise. Once you determine the location and dimensions of your garden, you just need a piece of graph paper and a pencil, a list of vegetables, fruits, and herbs you want to grow, and maybe a seed catalog or two. With these things in hand, you can start drawing. Fill in spaces for your favorite crops, taking into account the space requirements of the crops you want to grow; whether you want to plant in rows, beds, or hills; and how much of each vegetable you want to harvest. Garden design has any number of possibilities. Just keep in mind a few things:

✔ **You can't plant everything.** Choose your crops carefully.

✔ **Not all plants have it made in the shade.** Tall crops, such as corn and tomatoes, should be placed where they won't shade other vegetables. The north end of the garden is usually best.

✔ **These roots aren't made for walking.** Plan your garden with walkways (at least 2- to 3-feet wide, wider if you need to use a wheelbarrow or garden cart) so you can get to plants easily without damaging roots.

Planning on paper helps you purchase the right amount of seeds or transplants and use space more efficiently. It's a good way to see the possibilities for *succession planting* (following one crop with another) and *interplanting* (planting a quick-maturing crop next to a slower-maturing one and harvesting the former before it competes for space). For example, you may see that you can follow your late peas with a crop of late broccoli, and you can be ready with transplants in July. Or you may see that you have room to tuck a few lettuce plants among your tomatoes while the vines are still small. Figure 1-2 shows a sample of what your garden plan might look like.

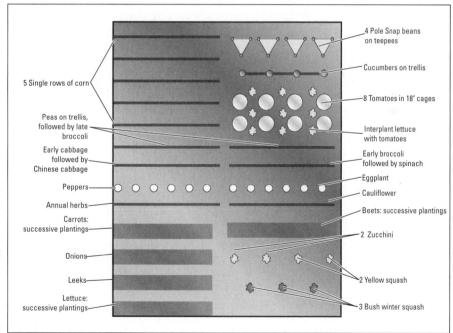

Book III

Edible Gardening

Figure 1-2: Sample vegetable garden plan.

Frost Dates and the Length of the Growing Season

You should know two very important dates for your area if you want to grow anything successfully: the average date of the last frost in spring and the average date of the first frost in fall. The number of days between the average date of the last frost in spring and the average date of the first frost in fall tells you the length of your *growing season*, which can range from less than 100 days in northern or cold winter climates to 365 days in frost-free southern climates. This info is important because it tells you

- ✔ **What to plant:** Many warm-season vegetables need long, warm growing seasons to properly mature and are difficult, if not impossible, to grow where growing seasons are short. So how do you know whether your growing season is long enough? Just check the mail-order seed catalogs or individual seed packets. Each variety has the number of days to harvest or days to maturity (usually posted in parentheses next to the variety name). This is the number of days it takes for that vegetable to grow from seed (or transplant) to harvest. If your growing season is only 100 days long and you want to grow a melon or other warm-season vegetable that takes 120 frost-free days to mature, you have a problem. The plant will probably be killed by frost before the fruit is mature.

  In areas with short growing seasons, it's usually best to go with early ripening varieties (those with the shortest number of days to harvest). You can also find many effective ways to extend your growing season, such as starting seeds indoors or planting under floating row covers (blanket-like materials that drape over plants, creating warm, greenhouse-like conditions underneath).

- ✔ **When to plant:** Cool-season vegetables are generally planted 4 to 6 weeks before the last spring frost. (Fall planting of cool-season vegetables is less dependent on frost dates, but is usually done 8 to 12 weeks before the first fall frost.) Warm-season vegetables are planted after the last spring frost or in late summer in warm areas for a fall harvest.

- ✔ **When to protect warm-season vegetables:** Frosts kill warm-season vegetables. The closer you plant to the last frost of spring, the more important it is to protect plants. And as the fall frost gets closer, so does the end of your summer vegetable season — unless, of course, you protect your plants.

To find out frost dates for your area, ask at your local nursery or contact your local cooperative extension office (look in the phone book under "county government").

Frost dates are averages, meaning that half the time the frost will actually come earlier than the average date and half the time it will occur later. They're also usually given for large areas. If you live in a cold spot in the bottom of a valley, frosts may come days earlier in fall and days later in spring. If you live in a warm spot, your frost may come later in fall and stop earlier in spring. Listening to your evening weather forecast is one of the best ways to find out whether frosts are expected in your area.

 Don't trust the weathercasters? Do a little prognosticating yourself: Go outside late in the evening and check conditions. If the fall or early spring sky is clear and full of stars, and the wind is still, conditions are right for a frost. If you need to protect plants, do so at that time.

Book III

Edible Gardening

Chapter 2

Vegetables, Glorious Vegetables

* *

* *

For the cost of a packet of seeds, you can have your own, homegrown produce. The requirements are simple: good soil, moisture, and full sun. This type of gardening is usually called vegetable gardening, even though it also involves growing items that are technically fruit, such as tomatoes and melons (Chapter 4 can fill you in on growing traditional fruits and berries). Growing your own produce — or vegetables, as it were — can be fun and fairly easy for the beginning gardener. This chapter gives you the basics. If you want even more information, check out *Gardening Basics For Dummies* by Steven A. Frowine and The National Gardening Association (Wiley).

Growing your own veggies really isn't and shouldn't be about saving money — though you may, even after factoring in your labor. It's about freshness (and thus nutrition; freshly harvested vegetables are always nutritionally superior to anything you buy at a supermarket — even at your local farmers' market). It's about flavor — oh boy, is it about flavor! And it's about reconnecting with the land.

Vegetable Basics: Hybrids, Heirlooms, and Growing Seasons

Lots of wonderful and worthwhile types of vegetables are available — too many to list, in fact. You could garden all your life and still not get around to growing all the tempting choices that would prosper in your particular region! But that's what makes vegetable gardening possible for everyone and keeps it so interesting.

What this section does share is information about hybrids and heirlooms so that you can decide whether one type or another suits your needs. It also explains the growing season and days to maturity: two factors you need to consider before you pick *any* vegetable to grow in your garden.

Because of the wide variety of vegetables available, don't limit yourself to the same old, same old. Instead, favor vegetables that are too expensive at the store or never available locally, or treat yourself to new foods or enticing variations on old standbys.

Factoring in growing season and days to maturity

To figure out whether the growing season in your area is conducive to the type of vegetable you want to grow, you need to know two things: the growing season in your area (obviously) and the number of days it takes a vegetable variety to mature (called days to maturity).

First, get an idea of the growing season that you have to contend with. Typically, the vegetable-gardening season is summer, bookended by late spring and early fall. Gardeners mark the start by the last spring frost date and the finish by the first fall frost date (although some crops, like parsnips and kale, can stay out in the cold a bit longer and even gain improved flavor). Then determine the days to maturity of the vegetable variety you're interested in planting. The preceding chapter explains how.

With this info, you can match your vegetables to the length of your growing season. If your growing season is approximately 90 days, growing anything billed as maturing in that amount of time or less ought to be easy. If you push the envelope, be prepared to help that variety with an early start indoors or some extra coddling in the fall. With experience, you'll find out what you can and are willing to do.

Table 2-1 gives an overview of which vegetables tend to do better during which seasons.

Table 2-1	Ideal Seasons for Growing Vegetables	
Type	*Description*	*Examples*
Cool-season vegetables	These plants tolerate some frost and temperatures between 55 and 70°F. As such, they're fine choices for gardeners in northern areas or, in milder climates, for growing in a cool spring or fall.	Asparagus, beets, broccoli, Brussels sprouts, cabbage, carrots, cauliflower, collard, endive, kale, kohlrabi, lettuce, onion, Oriental greens, parsnip, peas, potato, radish, spinach, Swiss chard, turnip, and turnip greens
Warm-season vegetables	These plants are readily harmed by frost; they also fare poorly in cold soil. Grow these plants in temperatures ranging from 65 to 80°F. They're good in the South and West year-round and elsewhere during the height of summer.	Beans, corn, cucumber, eggplant, melons (muskmelon/cantaloupe, watermelon), pepper, sweet potato, pumpkin, squash, sweet corn, and tomato
Perennials	These edible plants live from one year to the next, typically producing good crops their second or third seasons and thereafter. You can grow them in most climates, providing a protective winter mulch if warranted.	Asparagus and rhubarb

Book III

Edible Gardening

The following sections offer advice on how to get the most of your growing season, whether it's long or short — or even in the winter!

Long growing seasons

If your growing season is long and warm, you can get started earlier and maybe even plant two or three rounds of crops. You may, however, have to contend with hot, dry weather at the height of summer, which is stressful for some vegetable crops (so mulch them and supply extra water).

Short growing seasons

You can have a very bountiful vegetable garden. Choose vegetables that mature faster, and try some season-extending tricks. Here are two favorites:

✔ **Start seeds early indoors or in a cold frame.** A *cold frame* is basically a box made of such materials as wood or concrete blocks covered with a glass or plastic sash that protects smaller plants from extreme cold and wind. Raise your plants to seedling-size until putting them out in the ground is safe. (See the upcoming section "Starting your own seeds indoors.")

✔ **Use plastic coverings to keep a plant and its immediate soil nice and warm.** You can get plastic from row-cover sheeting or tunnels, cones, recycled milk jugs, or water-wall wraps, shown in Figure 2-1.

Figure 2-1:
A water wall, consisting of plastic sleeves filled with water, offers protection in cold weather.

Growing vegetables in winter

You can grow some vegetables during the winter. Really! In mild climates, you can enjoy kale, carrots, leeks, and root vegetables all winter long. You may have to mulch them and then poke underneath the mulch to harvest, but, hey, it's worth it! You can even sow salad greens in October and harvest extra-early in spring. Mmm.

Defining hybrids

You may see the term *hybrid* on seed packets and in seed catalogs. All it means is that the vegetable variety in question is a result of a cross (through pollination) between two parent plants of the same species but different subspecies or varieties.

Uniformity, predictability, and disease resistance are the results of combining the genetic traits of two good parents. In fact, hybrid offspring are often more robust and productive than either parent. Something called *hybrid vigor* often appears, a healthy exuberance that seems to result from the good qualities of one parent canceling out the bad of the other. It takes quite a bit to produce a hybrid — at least one that has the desirable traits you want. But don't fret. Seed companies do all the work, winnowing out the duds and making sure the plants can replicate desirable results with precision. All you have to do is buy the good seeds.

Favorite hybrid vegetables include "Big Boy" beefsteak tomatoes, "Blushing Beauty" bell peppers, "Nantes" carrots, "Salad Bowl" leaf lettuce, "Silver Queen" sweet corn, and "Crenshaw" cantaloupe melon.

What's the catch? Actually, there are two.

- **Hybrids are more expensive.** Producing hybrid seed requires the seed company to maintain the two parent lines and often to laboriously hand-pollinate, so hybrid seeds are more expensive than the alternative.

- **You can't save and replant the seeds.** The resulting plant won't "come true" — that is, it won't be the same, and, indeed, it may exhibit various mongrel qualities from either of its parents. So you're bound to purchase fresh, new hybrid seeds each year if you want to grow a hybrid variety that you like.

Book III

Edible Gardening

Appreciating heirlooms

Heirloom vegetables are vegetable varieties that people save and pass on for such home-gardening virtues as excellent flavor and a prolonged harvest period. Commercial seed companies, on the other hand, breed for uniformity, the ability to withstand shipping (thicker, tougher skins on tomatoes and squash, for instance), and all-at-once ripening (for harvesting convenience). You may prefer heirlooms. The older ones that are still in circulation have obviously stood the test of time and should be worthwhile.

Saving your own seeds

Whether it's a nice tradition, a survival skill, or a way to honor gardeners of the past, saving seeds from your favorite vegetable varieties is a fun and rewarding skill. At season's end, you have to harvest ripe seed, extract it from its fruit, dry it, and store it in a cool, dry place until you need it next year. If you'd like to give seed-saving a try, try starting with squash or pumpkins — they're easy.

If you plan to save seeds, keep this little caveat in mind: Depending on what else you grow in your garden, cross-pollination can interfere and must be prevented, either by covering flowering crops (to keep insects and bees from tampering with them or the wind from contaminating them) or staggering planting dates.

Favorite heirloom vegetable varieties include "Moon and Stars" watermelons, "Tom Thumb" baby butterhead lettuce, "Gold Nugget" winter squash, "Ragged Jack" kale, "Super Italian Paste" tomatoes, "Henderson's Bush" lima beans, and "French Breakfast" spring radishes.

What's the catch with heirlooms? Well, they're not as perfect or uniform-looking. Because heirlooms aren't commercially bred, they may be more colorful and more variable in size and shape than their hybrid counter-parts. Also, their skins may be thinner, so you get great flavor, but they don't travel well and may be vulnerable to bruising — or they may have lots of seeds inside (as in certain squashes and pumpkins), causing you a bit of extra work to separate out the edible parts.

For details on techniques, as well as much more fascinating and useful information on heirloom vegetables, check out Seed Savers Exchange (www.seedsavers.org).

Getting Your Vegetable Garden Ready

Most produce is, of course, grown in a vegetable garden, and it's always best to get your garden started before acquiring your plants. Before you even begin to dig into the soil, the first step is to design your garden.

Sketching out your plan

The best planning advice is simple: Start small. Just be sure you locate your garden in a spot where expansion is possible, in case you want to make your garden bigger in the coming years. As for the actual size of your garden, that depends on what you want to grow. Just to give you a general idea, here's what you can put in the following standard-size gardens:

- A 6-x-8-foot plot can support a couple tomato plants, maybe some bush beans, and some lettuce.

- A 10-x-18-foot plot can hold all that, plus a couple space-consuming squash plants and cucumbers, and maybe some carrots or beets.

- A 20-x-24-foot plot can hold all that, plus peppers, leeks, broccoli, turnips, and maybe some herbs as well.

- A 40-x-60-foot plot allows you more of everything, plus some bigger items, such as asparagus, rhubarb, or corn. (Corn isn't worth growing unless you can have a dozen or more plants. Otherwise, they don't pollinate or pollinate completely, and you end up harvesting gap-toothed ears.)

Sketch out your vegetable garden plan on paper ahead of time. Figure out how much space to allot to individual plants — and don't forget to allow for space between the rows, or paths, so you can tend the plants. (Mature sizes of various vegetable varieties are noted on seed packets and often in catalog descriptions.) The following sections give you a couple ideas about how to arrange your plants.

Book III

Edible Gardening

Succession planting

Allow for succession planting: If something is harvested early in the summer — lettuce, say, or peas — you can then free up that space for another crop, such as carrots. Succession planting is a good trick, but to pull it off, you may need to do some research and be willing to invest some time and effort. See Figure 2-2 for a succession planting plan that may work for you.

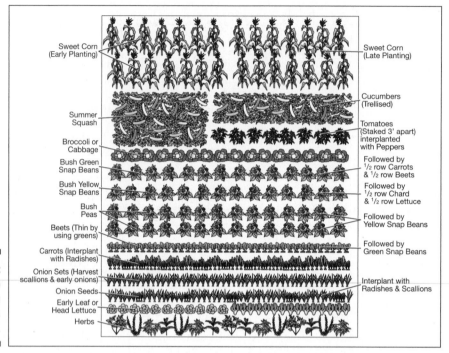

Sweet Corn (Early Planting)

Summer Squash

Broccoli or Cabbage

Bush Green Snap Beans

Bush Yellow Snap Beans

Bush Peas

Beets (Thin by using greens)

Carrots (Interplant with Radishes)

Onion Sets (Harvest scallions & early onions)

Onion Seeds

Early Leaf or Head Lettuce

Herbs

Sweet Corn (Late Planting)

Cucumbers (Trellised)

Tomatoes (Staked 3' apart) interplanted with Peppers

Followed by ½ row Carrots & ½ row Beets

Followed by ½ row Chard & ½ row Lettuce

Followed by Yellow Snap Beans

Followed by Green Snap Beans

Interplant with Radishes & Scallions

Figure 2-2:
Garden plan
showing
succession
plantings.

Interplanting

Intercropping, also called *interplanting,* is really very simple. It means having
two different plants share the same part of the garden in an alternating or
checkerboard pattern. This setup can look rather nifty, and it has practical
advantages too. Smaller, faster-maturing plants can grow with larger, slower-
growing ones, so you always have something to harvest. And plants that
appreciate a little shade can grow in the shelter of taller ones (grow pole
beans next to lettuce or spinach, for example). See Figure 2-3 for an example.

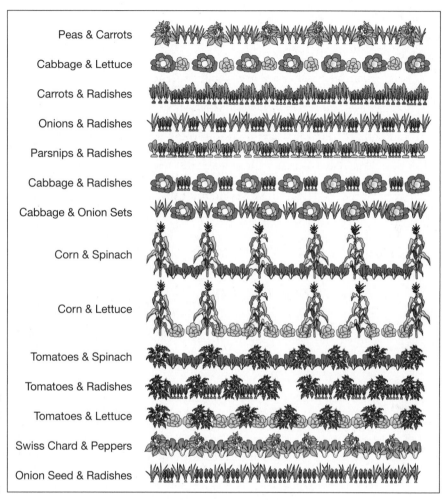

Peas & Carrots

Cabbage & Lettuce

Carrots & Radishes

Onions & Radishes

Parsnips & Radishes

Cabbage & Radishes

Cabbage & Onion Sets

Corn & Spinach

Corn & Lettuce

Tomatoes & Spinach

Tomatoes & Radishes

Tomatoes & Lettuce

Swiss Chard & Peppers

Onion Seed & Radishes

Figure 2-3:
Garden plan
showing
inter-
planting.

Book III

Edible
Gardening

Working with the sun: Where to plant vegetables

Most fruiting vegetables like the environment sunny and open — the soil is warm, and light is plentiful. Examples of sun-loving vegetables include tomatoes, peppers, squash, beans, okra, eggplant, and corn. If your veggies get the sunlight they need, they grow easily, developing and ripening their fruit with minimal stress or impediments. If conditions are not ideal, they make less fruit and take longer to ripen. They may also lean or grow toward the light source in a bid to get as much as they can.

To maximize needed sun, site your vegetable garden in a south-facing spot; plant taller plants to the north end so they don't cast shade over their shorter fellows.

Some vegetables are less dependent on full sun, which can fade or dry out their foliage or slow their growth. Some just like cooler temperatures. Vegetables that gardeners grow for their leaves fall into this group, as do ones with edible roots. Examples include lettuce, mixed greens (mesclun), chard, potatoes, carrots, and turnips.

To maximize sheltering shade, grow these vegetables in an east- or west-facing garden; site taller plants and objects (including trellises, teepees, and caged or staked tomatoes) in front of and to the south of these shade-lovers. Or grow these plants earlier in spring or in the fall. when the sun is lower in the sky — assuming you have enough time to ripen them before winter comes, that is.

Making your bed

As much as you may be tempted to toss a packet of seeds into a pile of dirt and let the plants grow where they fall, you're likely to be better off working with some kind of system. The following sections provide info on how you can design around a natural garden, raised beds, or existing landscaping.

More ambitious vegetable gardens need plenty of paths and rows to allow access — for you, for a hose, for a wheelbarrow. Ideally, you want access from all four sides of a particular bed. Build pathways into your master plan when you're first sketching out the layout (refer to the earlier section "Sketching out your plan" for instructions). Then, to clarify where the paths are and also to prevent weeds from seizing the open space, "pave" the paths with a layer of straw (not hay), dried grass clippings, or gravel.

Natural garden beds

Natural garden beds can be in-ground or mounded up, with no need for wooden edges. Either way, work the soil between 8 and 12 inches deep to accommodate the roots of most vegetables. To prepare a natural garden bed, you need to first remove as many weeds as you can and then rototill the area. When new weeds sprout, remove them as soon as possible — while they're young and before they go to seed (and produce more weeds!)

If you're turning part of the lawn into a garden, you first need to remove the sod. Use a sod knife (a special tool that can be rented) or a spade. For larger jobs, you can rent a sod cutter, which is a machine that penetrates the soil about three inches deep and cuts off the roots of the sod so that it can then be rolled up and removed. Once the sod's gone, rototill.

Don't try to rototill over the grass. First of all, only larger rototillers are capable of doing this, and secondly, if you till in the grass, it will be impossible to completely remove the grass and it will constantly re-sprout — a real pain!

Raised garden beds

Using raised garden beds is a very practical way to construct a good vegetable garden. Raised beds have good drainage, the soil warms up quickly in the spring, they're easy to weed (high off the ground), and you're less likely to step on and compact the soil, enabling roots to grow better (roots like looser, well-aerated ground). You can create raised garden beds in two ways:

- **Building a box and filling it in:** You can make bottomless wooden boxes between 8 and 12 inches deep; set them in a sunny, flat area; fill with good soil; and away you go. You can establish the walls of the box using wood, plastic, cinder blocks, or even bales of hay. Just be sure the walls are securely in place before adding soil to the interior. You can use native soil if its quality is good; otherwise, use a mixture of half native soil and half purchased soil.

- **Building up the earth and boxing it in:** You can build up the earth for planting, plant your garden, and then put up wood walls to support the raised soil, as shown in Figure 2-4. (Construction tip: Brace each corner with a corner post for extra stability.) If you use more than one raised bed, space them so you can walk between them or bring a wheelbarrow down the row.

If you're using wood for the walls of your raised bed, use untreated lumber. Treated wood may leach harmful preservatives, which is not a risk you want to take when raising edibles. Rot-resistant redwood or cedar is great; other softwoods, including pine, tamarack, and cypress, can also do but tend to rot away and need replacing after a few years.

If tunneling rodents are an issue where you garden, keep them out of your raised bed by lining the bottom with a layer of chicken wire. Use a slightly-too-big piece so you can pull it partway up the sides and tack or staple it in place.

Book III

Edible Gardening

a

b

Figure 2-4:
Making a
raised bed.
First, build
up the earth
for planting
(a). Then
plant your
garden
(b). Finally,
put up the
wooden
walls to
contain
everything
(c).

c

Prepping your soil

The biggest mistake beginning vegetable gardeners make is using lousy or too-thin soil. Gardening is not rocket science, folks (even if NASA *is* working on growing vegetables in space). Please, before a single vegetable begins its potential-filled life in your yard, prepare a good home for it! This prep work can save you untold disappointment and, perhaps more than any other factor, assure a bountiful and delicious harvest.

If you're working with a brand-new vegetable garden (or bringing back to life one that fell fallow), I suggest you stake it out and get it ready the autumn before you plan to plant. This act gives the soil and the things you've added time to settle and meld. It also means you have less work to do next spring.

If a fall start isn't possible or practical, go ahead and prepare the ground in spring — but don't start too early. If the ground is still semi-frozen or soggy, digging in the soil can compact it and harm its structure. How do you tell whether it's ready to be worked in? Grab a handful and squeeze — it should fall apart, not form a mud ball.

Follow these steps when preparing your soil:

1. **Dig deep — 6 to 8 inches minimum.**

   Most vegetables are content with 6 to 8 inches of good ground for their roots to grow in. If you're planning to grow substantial root crops (potatoes, say, or carrots), go deeper still — up to a foot or more (yes, you can use a technique called *hilling,* where you mound up good soil around crops like potatoes, but this method doesn't excuse your making a shallow vegetable garden).

2. **Fill 'er up with organic matter.**

   Add lots and lots of organic matter! Try compost (make your own — see "Composting for Vegetable Gardens" later on), dehydrated cow manure, shredded leaves, well-rotted horse manure (call nearby stables), or a mixture thereof. If your yard happens to be blessed with fertile soil, adding organic matter is less crucial, but most soils can stand the improvement. Mix it 50-50 with the native soil.

Whether your area's soil is notoriously acidic, very sandy, or quite obviously lousy for plant growth, adding organic matter can improve whatever you've got. Just remember to replenish the organic matter at the start of every growing season or maybe even more often. (If the soil stubbornly resists improvement, resort to setting raised beds atop it and filling these bottomless boxes with excellent, organically rich soil.)

Choosing among Seeds, Seedlings, and Transplants

Generally, most gardeners buy their vegetables as seed packets or as young transplants or container plants. People often purchase plants and seeds in the spring from a variety of places, including markets, home stores, and nurseries. Racks of veggies sprout up everywhere in the springtime! You'll notice different brands and companies but, quite frankly, not huge differences in price.

Whether you choose to grow plants from seed or buy started plants may depend on cost, the kind of selection you want, when you want to begin, and the type of plant. Read on for the basics of how these beginnings vary. You can even combine the options and grow your own transplants from seeds.

Buying seeds

Seed packets are popular because they help save money and provide a broader, more interesting selection. When you open a new seed packet, you quickly notice an awful lot of little seeds in there! Why so many? For a couple reasons: The company wants to make you feel as though you're getting something substantial for your money. Plus, you'll sow more than you'll actually end up growing, because some won't sprout or will be thinned out later. The packet includes enough seeds for successive sowings or to save for next year.

Little seeds, like lettuce seeds, tend to dry out if stored for a year, whereas big seeds like beans can keep for several years.

The packet will give you guidance on when (and where) to start your seeds. Certain seeds, for example, should be started indoors, well before the garden outside is awake yet. So read the labels to see whether indoor starting or *direct-sowing* (sowing outside, when the soil and weather are warm enough) is recommended for the area where you live. (See "Getting Your Veggies into Your Garden: Planting and Sowing" for more information.)

Make sure you keep your seeds in a dry, cool (non-freezing) place until you're ready to sow them.

Buying nursery transplants

You can purchase transplants, container plants, or seedlings locally — at a garden center, home store, farmers' market, spring fair, or from roadside entrepreneurs — or from mail-order companies. Someone else has done the seed-starting work for you; all you have to do is choose, take 'em home, and care for them. Transplants are the way to go if you can't or don't want to bother with seed-starting, or if you wait till the last minute to decide what you're growing this year. They cost more, but they're more convenient.

If you buy transplants and can't get them into the ground right away, set them in a sheltered spot out of the hot sun and the wind, and water them often (small pots dry out alarmingly fast, and young plants can't tolerate neglect).

You can shop for different varieties (buy three different kinds of tomatoes, for example), but the selection may not be too exciting, comparatively speaking.

Vegetables to buy pre-started include tomatoes, peppers, and eggplants. Other vegetables, like corn, carrots, and potatoes, don't transplant well from a wee pot to the garden. Direct-sow these plants.

Starting your own seeds indoors

A sure way to banish the winter blues, as well as get a jumpstart on your vegetable garden, is to start some seeds indoors early. To find out how early, consult the back of the seed packet; you want to time it so you have several-inch-high seedlings in late spring, after the danger of frost in your area has passed.

Here's a general list to get you started; you can tinker as you get more experience raising various sorts of seeds. Yep, get out your calendar — some counting backwards is in order:

- **Onions:** Start seedlings 12 to 14 weeks before the safe planting-out day (which, in the case of onions, is 4 to 6 weeks before the last frost)

- **Broccoli, collards, and cabbage:** Start seedlings 5 to 6 weeks before the safe planting-out date (which is after the danger of snow and ice is past but while nights are still chilly)

- **Lettuce:** Start seedlings 5 to 6 weeks before the safe planting-out day (which is 4 to 5 weeks before the last frost)

- **Peppers:** Start seedlings 8 to 12 weeks before the last frost

- **Tomatoes and eggplant:** Start seedlings 6 to 8 weeks before the last frost

- **Cucumbers and melons:** Start seedlings 2 to 4 weeks before the last frost

If you start too early, your seedlings may be too big too early, making them a little hard to accommodate and care for — you may even have to start over.

Getting your seeds started

Once you know when to begin, you're ready to get your seedlings started. Follow these steps, and refer to Figure 2-5:

1. **Select a good spot.**

    In milder climates, gardeners can sow seeds early in a cold frame or greenhouse, if they have one. Everyone else has to make do indoors. The best spot is an area out of the path of household traffic. You don't want people bumping into your tender sprouts or curious pets coming around. The spot should also be warm and out of drafts. A basement, sun porch, or spare room are all good options. Some people even raise seeds on the tops of dressers, cabinets, or refrigerators!

2. **Provide light.**

    Some seeds germinate under a thin layer of soil mix and some are pressed lightly on top, but in all cases, the seedlings that sprout need between 12 and 16 hours of light per day — that's a lot.

    Sunlight from a window is not at all ideal. It's pale and limited in late winter and early spring. To make your seedlings grow, you need artificial light. Fluorescent is best, and a timer at the outlet can help you regulate the hours it shines on your baby plants. Figure 2-6 shows a good light setup.

3. **Prepare pots or flats (which need drainage holes).**

    Begin with sterile seed-starting mix. (This mix is available in bags wherever gardening supplies are sold. It looks like very fine potting mix.) Fill the containers about three-quarters full with dampened, not drenched, mix (Figure 2-5a). Tamp the surface flat and level with the flat of your hand or a small piece of wood before sowing.

4. **Sow the seeds.**

    The back of the seed packet can tell you how deep to sow the seeds and whether you should cover them with mix. The packet can also tell you how far apart to place the seeds. Sow carefully by hand — a pencil tip is a useful tool when placing small seeds (Figure 2-5b).

    Don't sow too many seeds! Overplanting can lead to a forest of seedlings, growing too thickly for you to thin them without damaging some.

    If you're sowing into a flat, make little furrows with the pencil tip or a finger and space the seeds up to an inch apart (Figure 2-5c).

5. **Cover the container with plastic.**

    Cover the container the very day you plant. Plastic wrap is great, but depending on the size of your starting containers, you can also use a plastic bag (Figure 2-5d). This covering holds in warmth and humidity, giving the seeds the best chance to absorb moisture and get going. Don't seal too tightly, though. A tight seal causes condensed water to drip back down into the mix, making things too soggy.

6. Check back daily to add water and let the plants breathe.

Don't let the planting mix dry out, or the seeds' growth will come to a halt. The best way to keep developing seedlings evenly, consistently moist is with bottom watering. Just set the container into a few inches of water (in the sink or a tray) and let it wick up the water it needs before returning the container to its spot. Also be sure to open the bag a couple hours every few days to let the soil breathe some fresh air. Then close it back up.

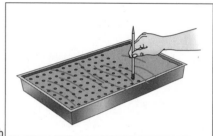

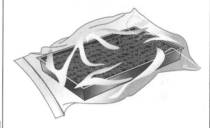

Figure 2-5:
Seed-
starting
trays.

Book III

**Edible
Gardening**

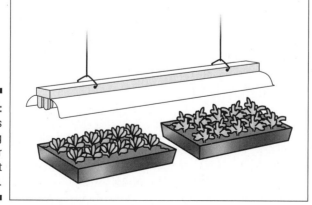

Figure 2-6:
Seedlings
growing
under
fluorescent
lights.

Taking care of the seedlings when they sprout

The first little seeds usually take a week or two to poke up their heads. But what a thrill! Here's what to do now to ensure that they survive and thrive:

- ✔ **Snip away extras.** Use tiny scissors (fingernail or beard-clipping ones work well) to gently cut weaker seedlings away at soil level. Pulling, rather than cutting off, can damage the roots of the surrounding seedlings. The properly spaced survivors gain better air circulation, which is important for their health, and their developing roots don't have to compete for precious resources.

- ✔ **Water from above with a fine spray.** As the seedlings grow bigger, bottom watering may no longer be practical.

- ✔ **Shift the flat's plastic covering on and off for ventilation.** When the young plants become too tall, remove the plastic covering completely.

- ✔ **Start fertilizing.** A diluted, half-strength flowering-houseplant fertilizer delivered with a regular watering is just fine. Fertilize about every two weeks.

- ✔ **Check that the seedlings are well-rooted when they're several inches high.** Never tug on the stem! Gently tug on the true leaves (not the first, or *cotyledon,* leaves that come up). If the seedlings hang on and otherwise look husky, they're ready to get hardened off (see the next section).

Hardening off your seedlings

The hardening-off process is the interim step between life in a pot (or seedling container) and life in the ground. Its purpose is to ease the seedlings from their plush life indoors to the realities of life in the real world — outdoors in your garden.

To harden off your seedlings, take these measures (the process takes about two weeks):

- ✔ After the threat of frost has passed, move your seedlings outside to a place that's sheltered from sun and wind. Start with an hour a day, and gradually work up to 24 hours over a two-week period. (Bring the seedlings indoors or cover them on chilly nights or if frost threatens.)

- ✔ Stop fertilizing them.

You need to harden off any plant that you're transplanting, whether it's one you started or bought at a nursery. If you bought your transplants from somewhere else, you may be able to shorten the hardening-off time by asking the seller whether the plants have been hardened off. (If they were displayed for sale outdoors, you can pretty well assume that they were.)

Once your seedling has been hardened off, it's ready to be planted in your garden. Head to the next section.

Getting Your Veggies into Your Garden: Planting and Sowing

How you plant vegetables really depends on the form in which you've acquired them. Are you direct-sowing seeds? Or are you planting transplants that you've either purchased or grown on your own indoors? The following sections tell you what to do in either case.

 Before you put anything in the ground, make sure you know when your growing season begins as well as whether your veggies are cool-season or warm-season (see the earlier section "Factoring in growing season and days to maturity"). Cool-season vegetables are more tolerant of cooler temperatures (some can even go outdoors before the last frost), so you can start these and put them in the ground earlier. Warm-season vegetables, however, should be put out or sown only after all danger of frost is past.

Planting transplants and seedlings

You can plant your seedlings and transplants after they've been hardened off (refer to the earlier section "Hardening off your seedlings") and the soil is ready and sufficiently warmed up. When all of these conditions are met, you're ready to go.

Ideally, work on an overcast day (or plant late in the day), when the hot sun won't stress them or you. Here's what to do:

1. **Water the seedlings well the morning you plan to plant.**

2. **Dig individual holes.**

   Make the holes at least as deep and wide as the pot the seedling comes in. How far apart to dig depends on the plant. The tag that came with the seedling or the seed packet should have this information, but when in doubt, allow more elbow room rather than less. Seedlings may look puny, but if you give them a good home, they'll soon take off like gangbusters.

3. **Pop each plant out of its pot carefully, handling the seedlings by gently gripping the leaves.**

   Tease apart the roots on the sides and bottom so they'll be more inclined to enter the surrounding soil in their new home. Place the roots gently in their hole and tamp the soil in around them firmly to eliminate air pockets.

You can plant tomato seedlings deeper than they were growing in their pots. In other words, you can bury much of the stem with no harm done; just keep one or two sets of leaves above ground and gently remove the lower ones. Not only does this planting depth lead to better stability in the hole, but the stem also responds by making more roots along the buried part.

4. **Water; then mulch.**

   Gently soak each seedling, using a wand attachment on your hose or a watering can. Then lay down an inch or two of mulch an inch out from the base of each seedling and outward to conserve soil moisture as well as to thwart sprouting weeds. Don't let the mulch touch the stem, or you risk insect and pest problems later on.

Offer a little protection. Sudden exposure to sun and wind can stress out little plants. Get them through the first few days by setting some boxes or boards nearby to create a barrier — or set a few lawn chairs out in the garden over the seedlings. It helps.

Sowing seeds directly

Gardeners generally sow seeds directly in the garden after the last frost, when the soil has warmed up and the weather seems to have settled into an early-summer groove. Vegetables that you can direct-sow include lettuce, onions, peas, radishes, turnips, beets, cabbage, carrots, beans, corn, parsnips, cucumbers, lettuce, and tomatoes (in warm climates).

Don't sow seeds too early! Direct-sowing in cold and/or soggy soil is a bad idea — it's muddy work for you, and the seeds usually sprout poorly or rot; then you have to start over. Best to wait for the right time.

Assuming that the garden area is prepared and ready to go, head outdoors one fine day with seed packets, a trowel, a planting dibble or hoe (depending on the size of the project), and something to sit on. Be prepared to get a bit dirty and sweaty and to feel the warm sun beam down on your head and shoulders as you work. Don't rush — putting seeds in this good Earth is a wonderful, soothing, productive feeling!

Follow these steps:

1. **Make planting holes or furrows.**

   Recommended planting distances are noted on the seed packets.

2. **Follow the "three friends" rule — plant three seeds per hole.**

At least one will likely sprout well. If all three do, you can thin out two of them later to favor the most robust one.

3. **Cover each hole as you go, tamping down the soil to eliminate air pockets.**

4. **Label.**

   The now-empty seed packet, stapled to a small stick, is a long-time labeling favorite, but you can simply use a marker to write the name of the vegetable (and variety if you're growing more than one of the same kind) as well as the date on a stick and plunge it in at the head of the row.

5. **Water well with a soft spray so you don't dislodge the seeds.**

   A wand hose attachment is good, as is a watering can with a rose head. If your vegetable garden is fairly big, use a sprinkler.

6. **Mulch.**

   Lay down an inch or two of mulch after watering the entire bed; keep the mulch an inch away from your new planting so that the seeds don't have to try to get through the barrier. Mulching conserves soil moisture and discourages sprouting weeds.

Caring for Your Growing Veggie Garden

Book III

Edible Gardening

Your job isn't done after you plant or sow your seeds. A growing garden needs quite a bit of tender, loving — and ongoing — care. Your prime duties now are to make sure that your vegetables are properly fed, have the necessary support, and are protected from pests. Sounds a lot like raising a teen, without the attitude or drama.

For more detailed information on how to keep your garden healthy, turn to Chapter 5.

Watering your vegetable plants

In general, most vegetables use about 1 inch of water per week (1 to 2 inches in hot, dry climates). If you don't get water from rainfall, you have to supply it. With that info in mind, be aware that each vegetable has a critical period when you need to be especially careful about watering or your crop may be ruined. Table 2-2 shows the important watering periods for different types of vegetables.

Table 2-2	Critical Watering Periods for Vegetables
Vegetable	*Important Watering Stage*
Bean, lima	When flowering and forming pods
Bean, snap	When flowering and forming pods
Broccoli	When forming a head
Cabbage	When forming a head
Carrot	When forming roots
Cauliflower	When forming a head
Corn, sweet	When silking, tasseling, and forming ears
Cucumber	When flowering and developing fruit
Eggplant	Give uniform supply of water from flowering through harvest
Melon	During fruit set and early development
Onion, dry	During bulb enlargement
Peas	When flowering and during seed enlargement
Pepper	Give uniform supply of water from flowering through harvest
Potato	When tubers set and enlarge
Radish	When forming roots
Squash, summer	When forming buds and flowering
Tomato	Give uniform supply of water from flowering through harvest
Turnip	When forming roots

Fertilizing your vegetable garden

Fertilizer is anything, organic or inorganic, that provides nutrients for growing vegetable plants. If your vegetable garden has fertile soil enhanced by compost and other organic materials, fertilizing may not be urgently necessary. Still, vegetables are a hungry group, and feeding them can certainly speed growth and improve your harvest.

The main nutrients are nitrogen (N), phosphorus (P), and potassium (K). They offer the following benefits:

- **Nitrogen:** Enhances the growth of leaves and stems
- **Phosphorus:** Helps flower, fruit, seed, and root production
- **Potassium:** Ensures general vigor and increases your plants' resistance to disease

The three numbers that appear on the labels of general-purpose fertilizers represent these three main nutrients. A fertilizer such as 10-10-10 is a *balanced* fertilizer because it contains equal proportions of all three nutrients, whereas a 15-0-0 is obviously nitrogen-heavy. For most vegetable crops, your best bet is a balanced fertilizer.

Other elements are necessary for plant growth in addition to the big three, but plants need them in much smaller amounts, and they're often already present in the soil. Also, many commercial fertilizers include them.

There are three different ways to fertilize your crops:

✔ **Side-dressing:** This term means sprinkling some fertilizer beside the plant, rather than on the plant itself, or scratching dry fertilizer into the soil with your fingers or a trowel or fork. See Figure 2-7.

Dry fertilizer that remains dry never does any plant any good. Dampen the garden before and after fertilizing so the fertilizer can get into the soil and down to the roots, where it's needed.

✔ **Foliar feeding:** You add foliar fertilizer to water (diluted according to label directions, of course) and then spray it right onto the leaves — the plant *foliage*.

Liquid fertilizers are concentrated, so you have to dilute them with water according to label directions; you're allowed to do two half-strength doses rather than one full-strength, if you like.

✔ **Top-dressing:** Top-dressing is applying fertilizer over the surface of the garden.

Book III

Edible Gardening

Figure 2-7: Side-dressing fertilizers.

Always follow label directions regarding how much fertilizer to apply. Too much is not good — you can overdose or burn your plants. Good timing is also important. Usually, you're advised to feed the plants at planting time to get them off to an early and vigorous start. A second, midseason application is worthwhile if you're growing a succession of crops in the same row or intercropping (see "Sketching out your plan," earlier in this chapter, for info on these growing methods).

Using frames and supports for veggies

Oh, those little seedlings — how fast and tall some of them grow! Midway through the summer, they're big; by August, they're out of control. You compromise the health as well as the manageability of certain crops, not to mention their productivity, if you don't step in with some kind of support. (Support is also important if your vegetable garden is out in the open and is occasionally subject to blustery winds.) Vegetables that need or benefit from support include peas, pole beans, tomatoes, cucumbers, small squash and zucchini, mini pumpkins, and melons.

Add support well before the plant becomes unwieldy. The time to get started is when a plant is a few inches high. You can position the support much more easily then, and, more importantly, when you plunge a support into the ground near a seedling, you don't harm it or its root system. Procrastinate, and you may.

Your support options include:

- **A wooden, metal, or plastic stake:** Plunge this support deep (a foot or more) into the ground near the plant so the support will be stable when it's weighted down with foliage and fruit. Site the stake near the main stem (not right on top of it! — a few inches away) and secure the plant loosely with soft ties as it grows; as the plant fills out, it'll eventually hide these ties from view.

- **A trellis:** Don't use the sort of trellis you train a climbing rose or clematis on but rather something broader and less decorative, something with plentiful horizontal wires or slats for tying onto.

- **A teepee:** A teepee is a good choice for climbing plants that can get rather tall, such as pole beans or miniature pumpkins and squash. You can buy a wooden, plastic, or metal teepee, or rig one out of branches and twigs pruned from your yard.

- **The fence:** A climber or tall-growing veggie can lean on the fence if you site the plant nearby, but you may have to help guide it and anchor it with string and/or the occasional tie.

✔ **Cages:** Wire cages are sold specifically for supporting tomatoes, but they're useful for other vegetable crops as well, such as sugar-snap peas, cucumbers, and smaller melons. Get the tallest cages you can or put one atop another, because many tomatoes easily grow 6 feet or taller, easily toppling shorter cages. See Figure 2-8.

To secure the veggies to the support, don't use material that abrades or cuts into a plant, such as wire or twist ties. Instead, use something soft, like lengths of cloth (rip up old T-shirts or pillowcases) or plastic tape. Also, when you tie, loop one end around the support first, and then pull the tie over to the plant and make a loop there as well — like a figure eight (see Figure 2-9). Do this tying loosely. This way, the plant won't be harmed, and it can also move a bit, safely, in a breeze.

Adding covers

Row covers (see Figure 2-10) are usually made of plastic or spun synthetic fabric. They serve as miniature greenhouses. They hold in heat, protect the plants against wind, and, in some cases, shade the plants and reduce their exposure to insects.

Figure 2-8: Two different types of tomato cages.

Figure 2-9:
Supporting
a melon.

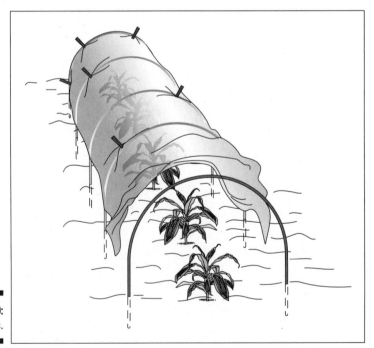

Figure 2-10:
Row covers.

Dealing with vegetable pests

If you build it, they will come, sorry to say. Because you're growing edible
plants, you should be very reluctant to throw chemical remedies at pest

problems in your vegetable garden. Fortunately, you can choose from plenty of proactive, less-risky strategies and deterrents.

Of course, as with so much of gardening, a plot with good soil, ample fertilizer and water, and elbow room for good air circulation resists such problems better than an unkempt or crowded one. Also, always

- ✔ Select disease-resistant varieties.
- ✔ Clean up garden debris promptly.
- ✔ Keep after and yank out all weeds, which harbor and feed various pests.
- ✔ Rotate crops.

If you find that your crop is under attack, figure out who or what the culprit is. Watch at odd hours, such as in the morning or evening, set a trap, or creep in close to the affected plants and look under leaves and in nodes (where leaf stalks meet the stem). Telltale signs of an invader include nibbled leaves and collapsing stems — here again, a little poking around should reveal the culprit. If it's an icky bug, capture a few, stick 'em in a small plastic storage bag, and show them to someone who can help you identify them. If you can't find the pest, a sample of typical damage should help your expert identify the culprit.

Fungal diseases

If you're battling a fungal disease, you can try using a garden duster (shown in Figure 2-11) to apply a very fine coat of powdered fungicide to the surfaces of leaves. This is most effective when done early in the morning — there's no breeze, and the leaves have dew on them so the dust adheres better to the plants.

Keep in mind, though, that there's not much that home gardeners can safely do if the vegetables have fungal disease. If disease is suspected, your best bet is to uproot the plant and discard it in the trash, not the compost pile.

Rodents, rabbits, and other miscreants

Mice, shrews, moles, voles, gophers, and other little rodents often burrow in mulch, either to nest or to root around for seeds to eat. Replace the mulch with gravel. Or reduce it, or at least scrape it away from the bases of your plants. A cage or barrier of chicken wire or poultry netting under or around the perimeter of the garden can also discourage the rodents, provided the holes are too small for them to squeeze through. You can also try trapping them or flooding their holes/tunnels with the hose. A cat that's a good mouser is the best bet.

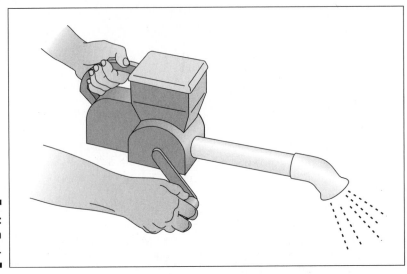

Figure 2-11:
Garden
duster.

Rabbits, woodchucks, raccoons? These brazen marauders may make you homicidal enough to reach for a gun, hand grenade, or poison-baited trap, but you can choose from some less drastic (and more humane) tacks. The best defense, quite honestly, is a good garden fence (include a gate, of course, so *you* can get in and out). Select one that's tall enough to discourage climbing over, but also sink it several inches into the ground to discourage digging under. Other remedies that are said to work include hot sauce, commercial repellents, bags of human hair (collected from a salon), a noisy radio, water-gun repellents, and leaving an alert dog nearby.

Deer

First of all, let's be completely frank here: Gardening in deer country is a challenge. The combined effects of fewer natural predators and shrinking habitats mean that the deer population is exploding while its natural food supplies are falling. And when deer are hungry, they'll eat almost anything, including the contents of your vegetable garden.

The best defense is a good garden fence. But because deer are good leapers, it needs to be quite tall — 8 feet or so. A lower fence may work if you set it at a 45-degree angle or even lay it on the ground on the theory that deer don't like to get their hooves snagged. For extra insurance or if the deer are really hungry and persistent, you need an electric fence (hardware, home, and farm-supply stores sell this) or a double fence — two 10-foot fences, 6 feet apart.

Birds

Birds are mainly a threat to newly planted seeds and ripening fruit (especially berries — see Chapter 4). Cover the seeds with soil and/or netting to discourage them; cover plants with netting until the fruit is ripe and you're able to pick the harvest.

Bugs

Identifying the invading insect is key. Capture a few and show them to someone who knows (a garden-center staffer; a landscaper; or another, more experienced vegetable gardener) or look the bugs up. If you can't find the bug itself, take in the damaged part of the plant. Once you know what you're dealing with, you can devise a plan of attack.

- **Aphids:** These tiny insects are usually green but may be red, brown, gray, or black. They stunt and distort plant growth and spread disease.

  - **Favorite targets:** Broccoli, cauliflower, kale, cabbage, and Brussels sprouts.

  - **First control:** Knock them off with a stiff blast from the hose.

- **Beetles:** Identification is important because some beetles are perfectly harmless. The main vegetable-garden villains are cucumber beetles, Colorado potato beetles, and little flea beetles.

  - **Favorite targets:** Cucumbers, squash, pumpkins, melons, and potatoes (aboveground growth).

  - **First control:** Either hand-pick them off or use row covers or other physical barriers to keep them away from their favorite plants.

- **"Worms" (moth larvae):** Cabbage loopers and corn earworms are the worst vegetable-garden pests.

  - **Favorite targets:** The fruit of cabbage-family crops, corn ears, and ripening tomatoes.

  - **First control:** Protect your plants with row covers. And because the worms can overwinter in garden soil, turn over the soil in late fall to expose them to freezing temperatures. Also, rotate your crops.

- **Caterpillars:** Not all caterpillars are harmful, so be careful when identifying them.

  - **Favorite targets:** The leaves of any vegetable plant.

  - **First control:** Hand-pick them off.

- **Cutworms:** These little larval fellows relish young seedlings, which they neatly chop off at the soil line.

  - **Favorite targets:** Beans, corn, peppers, tomatoes, and cabbage.

Book III

Edible Gardening

- **First control:** Because they don't like to climb, a collar around the vulnerable plant should keep them out (make it from a can or stiff cardboard).

✔ **Leaf miners:** Tiny insect larvae that travel within leaf tissue, leaving meandering trails and weakening the plant, thereby reducing its harvest.

- **Favorite targets:** Cucumbers, peppers, squash, melons, and tomatoes.

- **First control:** Pick off and dispose of affected leaves.

✔ **Leafhoppers:** Very small flying pests that pierce and suck the life out of plant parts, especially foliage (though they love bean blossoms).

- **Favorite targets:** Beans, lettuce, potatoes, tomatoes, and squash.

- **First control:** A collar of aluminum foil around the base of a plant can deter them.

✔ **Root maggots:** These critters are most active in spring as little egg-laying flies.

- **Favorite targets:** Cabbage, broccoli, cauliflower, Brussels sprouts, kale, radishes, and onions.

- **First control:** Sprinkle coffee grounds or fireplace (wood) ashes around vulnerable plants. Fine-mesh screen cages may also deter these maggots.

✔ **Snails and slugs:** Crowded, damp conditions prove irresistible to these slimy nibblers. They're most active at night.

- **Favorite targets:** Any vegetable plant!

- **First control:** Erect copper barriers around vulnerable plants (these give them an unpleasant "electric shock"), trap them with pie tins of beer, or spread diatomaceous earth on the ground (it feels like flour but is full of sharp particles that irritate their skin). Cocoa hull mulch deters them, whereas some bark or wood mulches have pieces that are large enough for these slimy critters to sleep under during the day. Put out a single board in the garden, and the snails and slugs will use it for shelter during the day. Lift it up and scrape them off.

Notice that I'm not rushing to recommend spraying chemicals in a vegetable garden. Try other tactics first (some suggestions are outlined in the preceding list) and spray with pesticides only as a last resort. Examples of sprays that you can use include insecticidal soap, neem oil, horticultural oils, and garlic or pepper spray.

If you do use a pesticide, be sure to get the right product for the targeted pest (most sprays are most effective when used in the early stages of a pest's development), follow the directions on the label to the letter, and thoroughly wash your harvest before eating or cooking.

Composting for Vegetable Gardens

Perhaps you've been wondering why so many vegetable gardeners have compost piles. The short answer is that it's downright sensible. Compost is a bountiful and free source of organic matter, which vegetables adore and consume like crazy. Compost adds humus to your garden and acts as a natural, slow-release fertilizer. Plus, composting lets you feel virtuous and efficient because you're not sending perfectly useful materials away with the household garbage.

Although you can buy compost from a gardening center, a better solution is to make your own. It's less expensive (even though bag for bag, store-bought compost may not strike you as terribly expensive, it really starts to add up when you're caring for a vegetable garden), and it's easy.

Following is the short course on creating compost for your vegetable garden; if you need mountains of compost or get really into composting, you can try some more-sophisticated methods and rigs:

1. **Pick a good spot — one that's level and sunny.**

   The location should be level and out of the way of foot traffic but not far from your vegetable garden. A sunny spot is better than a shady one, because warm sunshine helps the pile warm up so the contents break down faster.

2. **Erect a square or circular cage (at least 3 feet x 3 feet) on the spot you've chosen.**

   A 3-x-3-foot cage is the minimum size you need to be effective. You can buy commercially available bins of tough black plastic with a lid on top and a hatch in the bottom ("Darth Vader" bins), or you can make your own out of chicken wire, concrete blocks, wooden pallets, lumber, or even piled-up hay bales.

3. **Create a base in the bottom of your compost bin.**

   Set or scoop in a layer (several inches to a foot thick) of thin branches, chopped-up corn stalks, or something along those lines.

4. **Add material to compost (grass clippings, wood bark, and so on), arranging it in layers and adding water if necessary.**

   A proper compost pile, if viewed in cutaway, resembles a layer cake. Each layer should be a few inches thick. Alternate green (grass clippings, young pulled weeds) and brown (ground dried leaves, shredded bark) layers. See Table 2-3 for lists of acceptable and unacceptable composting materials.

   If you're adding dry material, soak the pile with the hose or a watering can right after adding the material to moisten it.

5. **Check on your pile and turn it every few days or whenever you add more material.**

A good mix heats up to between 100 and 120 degrees — on warm summer days, you may see the pile steaming. Turn it (with a stick, shovel, or pitchfork, whatever works) to keep it working. Your compost is ready to use when it fails to heat up again after turning.

If your compost pile seems to be breaking down too slowly, you can add these jumpstart materials in moderation to boost things a bit: commercially available compost booster (beneficial microorganisms), bloodmeal, bonemeal, cottonseed meal, or dried manure (from vegetarian animals only).

Table 2-3	Do's and Don'ts for Vegetable Garden Compost
Include These Things	**Leave These Things Out**
Coffee grounds and tea leaves (even tea bags; just remove the staple)	Big chunks of yard debris
Crushed eggshells	Plants that are diseased or full of insect pests
Corncobs (chop or grind them up first)	Weeds
Vegetable and fruit peelings and leftovers	Plant debris that has been treated with weed killer or pesticides
Shredded leaves	Any meat product (bones, grease, and fat included)
Shredded newspaper (just the black-and-white pages)	Fruit pits and seeds (they don't break down well and attract rodents)
Straw (not hay — it contains weed seeds)	Cat, dog, or other pet waste (which may contain meat products or parasites)
Prunings from your yard (chopped small)	
Lawn clippings	

Veggie plants soak up the materials that come out of the compost. When in doubt as to what should and shouldn't go into your compost pile for your vegetable garden, follow this general guideline: If you wouldn't put it or part of it in your mouth, then don't put it on your compost pile! This rule isn't foolproof, but it can definitely give you peace of mind.

Chapter 3

Spicing Things Up with Herbs

- -

In This Chapter

▶ Knowing when, where, and how to plant herbs

▶ Giving your herbs the care they need

- -

*I*f you suspect that the definition of *herb* is a bit loose, you're right. It includes not only rosemary but also nasturtiums, and fast-growing annuals as well as long-lived perennials. Defining an herb is easier said than done, but the important thing to keep in mind is that herbs are plants that not only have ornamental merits but are also useful in some way. Gardeners grow many herbs for their foliage, which is often deliciously scented; others value herbs for their edible flowers, seeds, or roots. A lot of herbs are a boon in the kitchen, adding exciting new dimensions to all sorts of recipes. Still others are reputed to have healthful or healing properties (Book VI details the many ways you can use the medicinal quality of herbs).

Even with that broad definition, the majority of herbs have common growing conditions and harvesting techniques. Herbs are usually very easy to find — look for them where you buy your annuals and perennials. Or perhaps you have some friends, relatives, or neighbors who won't mind you taking some herbs from their yards and planting them in your own. And here's some really good news: Herbs are among the easiest and most rewarding of all plants to raise. This chapter fills you in on what you need to know to grow and care for herbs.

Planting Herbs: A Lesson in Adaptation

No hard and fast rules govern the planting of herbs. Herbs are wonderfully versatile and flexible, and they come in a huge variety of annual and perennial types of plants.

The main thing to do is to pay attention to the type of herb you're trying to plant: Is it an annual? A perennial? Fast-growing? Slow-growing? Is it an invasive plant, like mint, or does it get along well with other plants? These considerations are important before you start adding herbs to your garden — and probably even before you acquire the herbs themselves! Do your research beforehand: To find out more about the growing habits of certain herbs, ask your gardening friends or the staff at the local nursery.

Getting the timing right

When you plant your herbs really depends on the plant, but you can't go wrong planting herbs the same way you plant vegetable seedlings: Plant them in the garden after all danger of frost is past (see Book III, Chapter 2 for info on vegetable gardening). The reason this strategy works for most herbs is that a lot of them aren't especially tolerant of the cold. This technique also gets them in the ground under encouraging conditions — warm soil, warm air, and a good summer stretching out ahead of them. They should surge right into robust growth.

Obviously, if your climate is fairly mild (as in the South and Southwest, the Gulf Coast, and most of California), you can plant herbs earlier in the year than, say, someone in New England or the upper Midwest, who's better off waiting until Memorial Day or so.

Avoid planting herbs — even if you spot plants for sale somewhere at a bargain price — in the heat of summer. Planting then stresses out even dryland natives such as oregano and lavender. And, obviously, don't put out herbs just as a cold winter is coming on. If you want to enjoy some herbs during the winter months, you're better off growing them in pots that you bring indoors to a sunny windowsill. See the upcoming section titled "Potting your herbs."

Determining the best place to plant

When you're deciding where to plant your herbs, just remember that most herbs like plentiful sunshine and appreciate well-drained ground (as opposed to very dry or very soggy sites). Read on for your placement options.

Inviting herbs into your current garden

If you're considering planting your herbs in a preexisting garden, here are two options:

✔ **Herbs growing by vegetables:** Adding edible herbs to your vegetable garden is a good idea. They like the same growing conditions of fertile soil and full sun, and when you're in the mood for a spontaneous summer meal, everything you need is right at hand. Some of popular choices include basil, dill, parsley, cilantro, fennel, thyme, and chives.

✔ **Herbs mingling with flowers:** This type of planting works best for herbs with pretty flowers of their own, as well as ones that can contribute attractive foliage. Imagine not just how pretty the flower bed will be but also the intriguing homegrown bouquets you can assemble if you widen your palette to include some herbs. Favorite choices include sage (especially the kinds with colorful leaves), dill, mint, basil (especially the purple-leaved kind), artemisia, and borage.

Creating an herb garden

For many gardeners, the best solution for growing herbs is just to put them all in their own garden. Follow these simple rules:

✔ **Place taller herbs at the back or in the middle of a bed, with shorter ones at their feet.** This type of arrangement lets you see, appreciate, and access everything for care and harvesting.

✔ **Allow every plant ample room to spread.** If some herbs emerge as thugs over time, stealing the stage from less aggressive growers, just chop them back or take them out of the display altogether. (Check for square stems on plants — these can indicate that you're dealing with thugs.)

Herbs that are meant to be alone are tall or tend to hog horizontal space. They also monopolize resources of soil nutrients and water, or have a tendency to grow rampantly. If you really want them, why not just segregate them in their own area, bed, or pot (as explained in the next section)? Plants that do better solo include mint, oregano, and marjoram.

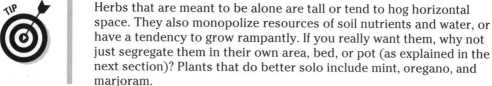

Book III

Edible
Gardening

You can choose from many types of herb gardens, but generally they're either formal or informal. You'd be wise to plan a formal garden ahead on paper, making a geometric design that's to your liking, whether it's composed of squares or composed to look like slices of a pie. Then, when you decide to put your plan into action, install the edgings and pathways first, using bricks, rocks, gravel, or even grass. Edging plants such as small boxwood plants, germander, or a sheared low hedge of lavender or dusty miller also work but require more care.

If you prefer informal herb gardens, take note: A casual bed devoted to all herbs can have the delightful look of a cottage garden, or it can look like a jumble. A jumble is bad. It's hard to care for and harvest from, and crowded plants become more vulnerable to pests and diseases. So make a plan on paper for this sort of herb garden too — set it up like your vegetable garden or your favorite flower garden — and then see what happens, making alterations as you see fit. Aim for a harmonious mix of foliage colors and types, with the occasional exclamation point of a flowering herb.

Potting your herbs

A lot of people like to grow herbs in pots, an approach that contains their growth and makes them handy for cooking. Container gardening is also a terrific way to raise edible herbs that you use often in your kitchen. And it's a great way to corral invasive herbs (like mint, lemon balm, and lemon verbena) and keep them from wandering and taking over.

The most important thing to do for potted herbs is keep them watered; potted plants dry out notoriously fast, and cycles of soaking and drying out aren't good for a plant's health, even a tough little herb plant. ***Note:*** The Mediterranean herbs — such as thyme, rosemary, lavender, sage, and oregano — prefer poor, almost sandy soil; they'll rot if they get too wet. Use a sand or pebble mulch around them.

Site potted herbs where you won't forget about them, such as right outside the back door or on the patio in full sight of the kitchen window. A window box is a particularly effective and practical way to grow herbs in a container.

Mixed displays can look great. Fill larger pots with several different herbs or assemble a gathering of individual pots and array them on a deck or patio. You can even tuck a potted herb into your garden proper as an accent, shifting it around as you see fit. If color or interest seems to be lacking, just choose especially decorative or colorful pots — they make a dramatic difference and add to the fun.

Frequently harvesting potted herbs has an important benefit, by the way. When you snip off the tips, the remaining plant is inspired to grow more thickly and compactly — which looks better in a pot.

Putting herbs in their place: How to plant

Planting herbs is as easy as 1-2-3 and really isn't much different from planting flowers or vegetables.

Make sure you water your herbs thoroughly on planting day. Then water the plants often in the following days and weeks until they become well-established. Well-established herbs may be fairly tolerant of droughts, but that doesn't excuse you from getting them off to a good start while they're young.

Planting herbs in a garden

When planting a new herb in a garden, just follow these basic steps:

1. **Using a trowel, dig a hole in a sunny spot with well-drained soil.**

   The hole should be slightly deeper and wider than the pot the herb is currently in. Add a little compost or other organic material to the bottom of the hole for the roots to grow into. Then scrape the sides of the hole to loosen the roots, which encourages the herb's root system to grow beyond its current size.

2. **Pop the plant out of its pot.**

   If tugging is necessary, handle the plant by its stem, never by its leaves. Using your fingers, gently tease the roots on the bottom loose and loosen some on the sides as well.

3. **Plant the herb at the same depth it was growing in the pot (if you're not sure, look closely on the stem for a soil line).**

   Backfill soil in and around the hole and firm everything into place with your hands to eliminate air pockets. Soak thoroughly.

When choosing a planting spot, be sure to take into account your herb's expected mature size. You don't want it to be crowded or cramped because then it won't be as healthy or productive.

Planting herbs in a container

Planting herbs in a container is a bit different from planting in a garden. Follow these steps:

1. **First, choose an ample-sized pot and be sure it has a drainage hole in the bottom.**

   Most herbs can't tolerate wet feet.

2. **Fill the pot with damp potting soil mix.**

   Moistening the mix ahead of time makes the job soooo much easier!

3. **Pop the herb seedling out of the pot you bought it in, place it in its new pot, and water it.**

Book III

Edible Gardening

Containers, particularly clay pots, tend to dry out quickly, especially when placed in the sunny spots that herbs like. Although many herbs are tough customers and can tolerate drought, subjecting them to extreme cycles of drought and drenching causes stress.

Raising herbs from seed

The majority of herbs are easy to grow from seed. Also, some types of herbs — interesting, offbeat, or rare varieties — are often for sale only in seed form. Here's the good news: Unlike some flower and vegetable seeds, you don't have a long wait from sowing to productive plant.

To plant your herb seeds, follow these steps:

1. **Place sterile soil mix into the flat or pot in which you plan to keep the herb(s).**

   Be sure the flat or pot contains drainage holes to prevent the possibility of rot.

2. **Sow the seeds on top of the mix or under a thin layer of mix, whichever the seed packet recommends.**

   The packet should also advise you how far apart to sow the seeds.

   The biggest mistake beginning herb gardeners make when sowing seeds is sowing too thickly. Many herb seeds are quite small, and seed companies give you much more than you need in a single packet (for example, a typical packet of basil seeds can have 250 individual seeds in it!). Don't use them all at once.

3. **Care for the seeds for a few weeks, or until the seedlings are several inches high and ready to be transplanted.**

   During this period, you'll need to make sure they get the proper light (the seed packet has details). Water them and thin the plants, especially if you sowed the seeds too thickly and now have a forest of small plants.

   • **To water:** Bottom watering is advisable. Simply place the container in a tub or sink and gradually add warm water (which penetrates the soil quicker than cold water) until it reaches a depth of about half the height of the container in which the seeds are sown. Let the container sit in this warm water until the surface of the soil in the container is wet (look for a darker color). You may have to wait an hour or so. Then either remove the seed container from the tub or let the water out of the sink and allow the excess water to drain from the container.

• **To thin:** Wait until the seedlings have at least a second set of leaves before thinning. When they do, carefully, carefully cut out the weaker plants with tiny scissors.

Taking Care of Your Herbs

Caring for herbs isn't much different than attending to other annuals and perennials, but herbs may have a few special requests. The following sections tell you how to make sure your herbs have what they need to succeed, including protection from the baddies of the insect (and mite, snail, and slug) world.

Providing an herb's basic needs

Although each type of herb has its own growing requirements, it's pretty safe to say that most herbs are unfussy plants. Most prefer full sun and prosper in good, moderately fertile soil. And most require that the soil be well-drained so that they get the moisture they need to grow but don't suffer from wet feet. If your chosen site is lacking in any of these requirements, take steps to improve it. Clip back overhanging trees and shrubs. Add organic matter, such as compost and/or dampened peat moss, as well as some sand to poor soil to improve its texture.

Herbs rarely need fertilizer. In fact, excess fertilizer may lead to lax, floppy growth that's unattractive and vulnerable to diseases and pests. It may also inhibit flowering.

Some herbs like "sweeter" soil (soil with a higher pH, or *alkaline soil*). If your garden's soil is toward the acidic side, a sprinkling of lime powder or chips at the herb's base at planting time may be in order. Examples of herbs that prefer this sweeter soil include chia, lavender, and echinacea.

Some herbs prefer soggy ground. The drawback is that if you put them in such a spot, they may grow too rampantly; be willing to let them do as they will. If that's not practical, simply raise them in a pot and keep the pot well-watered and/or set in a saucer of water so the growing mix is perpetually damp. Examples of herbs that go for soggy ground include mint, bee balm, cardamom, chervil, goldenseal, and sorrel.

Book III

Edible Gardening

Caring for potted herbs indoors

Herbs are easy and fun to grow inside, which may also extend the harvest for you if you have cold winters. They're best on a kitchen windowsill, provided it gets plenty of sun. That way, they're handy when you need them for a recipe; plus the sight of them certainly adds character and a pleasant fragrance to your kitchen. Here are a couple other tips:

✔ **Turn herbs occasionally so they're healthier and look fuller and/or balanced.** Potted herb plants naturally grow toward the source of sunlight, and they may start to lean or look one-sided unless you give them a quarter-turn every few days.

✔ **Trim or harvest often.** Life in a pot is pretty confining for most herbs, and you don't want them to outgrow their space or start getting floppy or lanky. Cut off tips frequently. This trimming inspires the plant to branch and grow more densely and compactly.

After a while, your herbs may naturally peter out and need to be replaced. So enjoy them to the fullest while they're in their prime!

Dealing with herb pests

Believe it or not, many herbs are pest-free, which is one of the many reasons gardeners find these plants so easy and fun to grow. Some herbs even *repel* pests from themselves as well as adjacent plants. However, you may meet a handful of pests in your herb-growing ventures. If you do, act quickly to rescue your harvest, either by treating the plant or by tearing it out and getting rid of it before the problem can spread. Check out Table 3-1 for a rap sheet of the major troublemakers.

Table 3-1	Pests and the Herbs They Dine On		
Pest	*Appearance*	*Effect on Plant*	*Food Preference*
Aphids	Tiny sucking insects that congregate in groups; they may be white, greenish, or black.	A severely infested plant turns yellow and dies.	Caraway, lovage, nasturtium, and oregano
Carrot weevils	Tiny, hard-shelled brownish bugs.	Carrot weevils attack the roots as well as the top of the plant.	Parsley

Pest	Appearance	Effect on Plant	Food Preference
Japanese beetles	Green- and copper-colored bugs that are about ½" long.	These bugs are voracious foliage eaters.	Basil and echinacea
Leaf miners	Bugs that start as tiny, yellowish larvae and turn into small, black flies with yellow stripes.	Affected leaves have meandering tunnels and blotches.	Lovage, oregano, and sorrel
Scales	Bugs that look like small waxy or cottony bumps.	Scales feed by sucking sap, and they leave behind telltale honeydew (which, in turn, attracts ants and sooty mold).	Bay, myrtle, and rosemary
Slugs and snails	You know these slimy characters! But you may not always see them — they're most active at night.	Slugs and snails devour foliage.	Basil, calendula, and sorrel
Spider mites	A wee relative of the spider.	Spider mites suck plant juices, leaving telltale pinprick spots and puckering.	Angelica, germander, lemon verbena, mint, oregano, rosemary, sage, and thyme

Book III

Edible Gardening

The pests that go after herbs may seem as varied as the herbs themselves, but here are a few defensive strategies you can take to protect your herbs:

- Make sure your herbs are in good health, well-watered, and, in particular, have sufficient elbow room.

- Remove affected leaves. Also, pull out severely infested plants and throw them away before the problem spreads.

- Dislodge small infestations with a spray from the hose. Larger insect pests may be hand-picked and destroyed.

- ✔ If you have to spray, try insecticidal soap, which is nontoxic. Make sure the pest you're targeting is listed on the label and then carefully follow the directions regarding how and when to apply.

- ✔ You can combat certain pests with beneficial insects (such as ladybugs or lacewings). Look for more info — as well as assistance in attracting or acquiring the right helper — from a good garden center or from your cooperative extension agent, or do an online search.

- ✔ Get a little help from some friends. Some herbs may help each other out by keeping pests at bay.

If you succeed in beating back a pest and later want to use the herb for fresh eating or cooking, be sure to wash it thoroughly first!

Chapter 4

Adding Fruits, Berries, and Nuts

In This Chapter

▶ Deciding what kind of fruit to grow

▶ Purchasing fruit-producing plants

▶ Planting and caring for fruitful trees, shrubs, berry patches, and vines

*H*omegrown fruits, berries, and nuts take more time and care than some other kinds of gardening. Although soft fruits like strawberries, grapes, and raspberries yield delicious results within a few months or less, tree fruits and nuts require more patience and can take several years to be productive. Fruits and nuts also require a different sort of preparation than non-fruit-or-nut-bearing trees and bushes. But at harvest time, the work is all worth it! In almost every region of North America, you can find a type or variety of fruit or nut that's well-adapted and fairly easy to grow.

Note: Many gardeners group fruits, berries, and nuts together because the cultivating methods are similar for all of them. For the sake of making the descriptions in this chapter simple, references to "fruit" include fruit, berries, and nuts, unless otherwise stated. Also, all the fruits in this chapter are perennial (they come up every year and are winter hardy) and all, except strawberries (which die back to the ground), are woody.

For now, though, let your imagination savor the aroma of sun-warmed fruit, picked fresh in your own yard. Then read on as I help you make that vision a reality.

Fruit Basics: Choosing the Right Fruits for Your Garden

Choosing the type of fruit you can support and grow is important and makes the difference between easy success and frustration or failure. Before you get your heart set on a certain kind of fruit you want to grow, do a little research. Not all types of fruit are suitable for home gardens, owing to their size or growth and maintenance requirements. Date palms and pineapple, for instance, are tough to grow. However, home gardeners do have a wide range of choices available. Here are some examples:

- **Tree fruits:** Apple, apricot, cherry, citrus fruits, crabapple, pear, peach, nectarine, plum, avocado, loquat, kumquat, pineapple guava, pomegranate, persimmon, banana, and fig
- **Vine fruits:** Grape and kiwi
- **Shrub fruits:** Blackberry, raspberry, gooseberry, currant, and blueberry
- **Ground-covering fruits:** Strawberry and melon (for info on growing melons, see Chapter 2 of this Book, on vegetable gardening)

The following sections explain what factors you should consider as you decide what kind of fruit to grow.

Figuring the wait time from planting to harvest

Fruits come later in a plant's seasonal cycle. First the flowers bloom, and then the petals fall as the fruit starts to swell (pollination from the same or an adjacent plant may be necessary — bees often help out). Small, hard, and green at first, a fruit expands in size and changes color on the way to becoming juicy and ripe, with the seeds or pits nestled within (except in the odd case of strawberries).

So when can you start picking bushel loads of fruit? The answer to that depends on the type of fruit you're growing. Some produce delicious results within a few months or less; others can take years. Before you run to the nursery, consider how long you'll have to wait before getting a yield. Ground-covering fruits are annuals (at least in a climate that has frost), while strawberries are perennials, but both produce fruit the first year. Most shrub fruits take two or three years to yield substantial amounts of fruit. Fruit trees take a few to several years to bear fruit, depending on the variety and the type of rootstock they're on. Dwarf fruit trees tend to bear sooner, within 3 years, while trees on standard rootstocks can take 4 or more years.

When is a veggie a fruit?

Here's a bit of garden trivia. A *fruit* is defined as a ripened ovary. You can think of it as a "pregnant flower." Using this definition, many plants that are known as veggies, like melons, cucumbers, tomatoes, and peppers, are literally fruits. But while they may be fruits technically, they're still considered veggies by gardeners.

Getting the lowdown on chill factors

You can find many named *cultivars* (cultivated varieties) within each type of fruit. You need to choose one suitable to your climate and growing conditions. Some fruit plants are obviously better-adapted to certain climates than others. Avocados don't work as a crop in cold regions; some pears and raspberries are better in mild areas, while others are adapted to northern climes; most apples (but not all) thrive in cold, northern areas. Although you may be able to push your boundaries or cheat a bit in your garden with smaller plants, coddling a more substantial resident such as a big bush, vine, or tree isn't always practical.

Book III

Edible Gardening

Take your cue from what sorts of fruits appear to be prospering in your area or what's for sale at your local nursery. Call your nearest Cooperative Extension Service office and get recommendations not only for the types of fruits but also for the most suitable and cold-hardiest cultivars within each kind. In the meantime, here's what you need to know about high-chill and low-chill fruits:

- ✔ **High-chill:** High-chill trees require more hours with temperatures below 44 degrees Fahrenheit (7 degrees Celsius) to break dormancy and grow in the spring. High-chill trees don't perform well in mild climates. Many apple, pear, cherry, and deciduous fruit and nut trees are rated by the number of hours of chill they require.

- ✔ **Low-chill:** Low-chill deciduous fruit trees require fewer hours of temperatures below 44 degrees Fahrenheit (7 degrees Celsius) in order to break dormancy. These types of deciduous fruit and nut trees do best where winters are mild.

Review Table 4-1 for further details on popular trees. ***Note:*** *Chill hours* means the total cold-season hours below 44 degrees Fahrenheit (7 degrees Celsius).

Table 4-1	Chill Requirements of Fruit and Nut Plants		
Fruit	*Chill Hours*	*Fruit*	*Chill Hours*
Almond	400–700	Japanese plum*	500–1,600
Apple*	400–1,800	Kiwi*	400–800
Apricot*	350–1,000	Kiwi "Twei" (female)	0–200
Asian pear (Chinese)	400–600	Kiwi "Vincent" (female)	0–200
Asian pear (Japanese)	300–750	Mulberry	400
Avocado	0	Nectarine*	200–1,200
Blackberry	200–700	Peach*	200–1,200
Blueberry (Florida)	0–200	Pecan	300–1,600
Blueberry (northern)	700–1,200	Persimmon	100–500
Chestnut	400–750	Pistachio	800–1,000
Citrus	0	Plumcot (apricot-plum cross)	400
Crabapple	300–500	Pomegranate	100–200
Currant	800–1,500	Quince	100–500
European pear	600–1,500	Raspberry*	100–1,800
European plum	700–1,800	Sour cherry	700–1,300
Fig	100–500	Strawberry	200–300
Filbert (hazelnut)	800–1,600	Sweet cherry (most)	600–1,400
Gooseberry	800–1,500	Walnut*	400–1,500
Grape	100–500		

*Low-chill varieties that need less chilling are also available.

Studying your size accommodations

Adding fruit plants of some kind to your home landscape is not just about harvesting delicious fruit. The size of the plant is important, as is the relative beauty of its flowers and foliage. Ideally, the plant fits in and enhances the attractiveness of your yard even when it's not producing fruit.

Pick a plant that fits into its allotted space in your home landscape. Be realistic, because fruit-bearing plants already require consistent maintenance without you also having to constantly cut them back in an effort to get them to fit in a too-small area.

To find out predicted mature size of a specific cultivar, look on the label, ask a nursery staffer, or look up the plant in a reference book, in a nursery catalog, or on the Internet. If your space is limited, go looking for a *dwarf cultivar* or one explicitly billed as having a *compact growth habit.* For instance, check out the "Colonnade" apple tree, which has a single main trunk that only grows to 10 feet tall with short branches. Don't consign yourself to a career of constant shaping and pruning to keep an eager plant small unless you have the time and inclination! (Constant chopping back also runs the risk, of course, of reducing your potential harvest, not to mention making the plant look awkward or unattractive.)

Generally, two kinds of fruit trees are suitable for a home garden: regular and dwarf or semi-dwarf. The latter are best if your space is limited, of course. Caring for and harvesting from fruit trees often requires a longer reach, namely the use of a ladder and pole saws or long-reach pruners. Examples of favorite taller or larger fruit plants include apple, pear, peach, apricot, plum, and citrus (lemon, orange, and grapefruit) trees, and kiwi vines.

Book III

Edible Gardening

Easy access, baby

Access may also be a consideration for you. If you dream of simply strolling out with a basket and gathering up fresh fruit, choose a fruit that doesn't require you to use a ladder to harvest it. Examples of favorite, more-compact growers include currant, gooseberry, blueberry (both high-bush and low-bush), strawberry, and some blackberry, raspberry, and grape cultivars. Figure 4-1 shows a typical strawberry garden plan that allows easy harvesting.

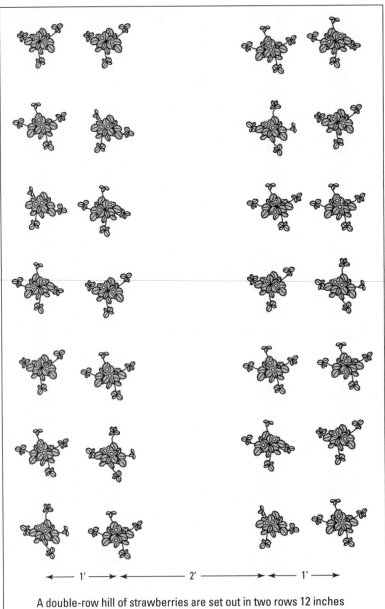

Figure 4-1:
Strawberry
garden plan
aligned
for easy
harvesting.

1′   2′   1′

A double-row hill of strawberries are set out in two rows 12 inches
apart; between the double rows is a 2-foot path for walking.

Here are a few more ideas to consider as you explore how to fit fruits into your garden:

- ✔ Use a line of berry plants as a property boundary.

- ✔ Put single berry plants at the corners of your vegetable garden.

- ✔ Use a shrub or small fruit tree in your foundation planting.

- ✔ Plant a fruit tree in your entryway garden (so long as it gets enough sun).

- ✔ Create a small orchard in your back forty.

- ✔ Expand your vegetable garden to include a strawberry or melon patch.

- ✔ Add a berry bush or two to an informal shrub border.

- ✔ Plant berry bushes at the base of a gazebo (not blocking, of course, the way in).

- ✔ Site one or more fruit trees in an informal lawn, on a slight slope, or in another open area.

- ✔ Plant fruit trees in your street-side curb strip (after some soil improvement, no doubt).

- ✔ Plant a fruiting vine so it grows over a pergola or archway, creating shade below.

- ✔ Grow a dwarf fruit tree in a large container on a sunny patio or deck.

If you have the room, you can install a full-blown fruit garden, like the one in Figure 4-2.

Because some plants can't pollinate themselves, you may have to allow room for two or more plants. See the following section for details.

Book III

Edible Gardening

Going solo or in pairs: Looking at pollination

Certain fruits require cross pollination to set their fruits. Sometimes, planting more than one of the same variety is sufficient, but other times, you must plant a different variety of the same type of fruit to get the best results. It is very difficult to generalize which fruits this pertains to. The best approach is to carefully read the catalog or ask the salesperson you are buying from whether the plant is self-fruitful or requires a different or additional pollinator. If your supplier can't answer this question, buy from someone else. You need a supplier who knows for sure.

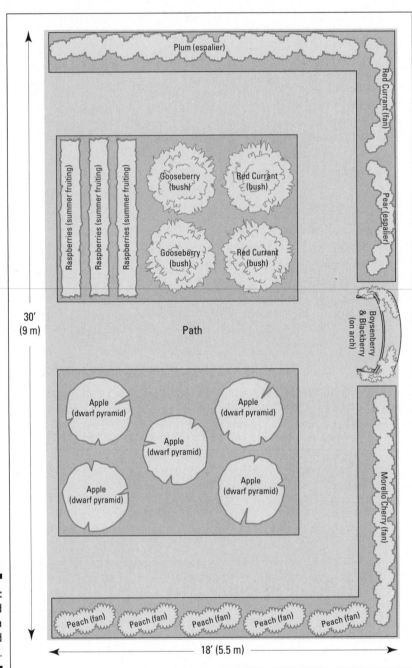

Figure 4-2:
A suggested plan for a good-sized fruit garden.

Getting Your Soil Ready for Fruits

Before you acquire your plants, take time to prepare the soil. It is far better to deal with the soil before you plant than after — a berry bush, fruit tree, or strawberry patch is a major landscape investment, so there's no sense in cutting corners from the get-go. A good time to start prepping your soil is during the year *before* you plan to plant your fruit bearers.

Attending to soil quality

Good-quality soil is especially important when raising edibles. You want your crop to be both safe and tasty. The following suggestions can help you achieve your goals:

✔ **Do a soil test on the intended spot.** Buy a kit, follow the directions, mail the sample into a lab, and await recommendations.

On the test form, be sure to put the name of the fruit you intend to raise. That way the recommendations for soil improvement that come back from the lab will be tailored to that crop. For example, blueberry bushes prefer a lower pH, so the lab may suggest that you add some sulfur to make your ground more acidic; peach trees and certain European grape cultivars like conditions a bit more alkaline, and some supplemental lime may be in order. Note that these amendments take time to move through the soil, so try to add them the fall prior to spring planting.

✔ **Add organic matter.** Organically rich soil, not surprisingly, is ideal. It offers a slow-release reservoir of nutrients your fruit-bearing plants need and relish. Dig some in ahead of time, and replenish it at least annually. It lightens heavy clay soil and improves sandy soil, making the entire area more hospitable to plant roots. Good choices include compost, well-rotted manure, rotted sawdust, chopped up leaves, and spent mushroom soil. Adding periodic doses of fertilizer can also help your crop along, but you need this initial foundation.

Book III

Edible Gardening

Digging the right-sized hole

As with so many other plants in your garden, fruit-bearing plants need ample space for their roots to develop. Sufficient soil both nourishes and anchors plants. Take measure of how extensive the root system is on planting day, and then go farther to allow for future growth.

For example, because strawberry plants generally send their roots 6 to 12 inches down, you should provide them with prepared soil that's at least that deep, with several more inches to spare. An apple or plum tree, on the other hand, may send roots many feet deep into the ground over the course of its life; you're not likely to be willing or able to excavate a major hole and have to count on the chosen spot having decent soil. Just give a young root-ball ample space. A hole 12 to 18 inches deep and wide usually does the trick. Remember to scrape the sides of the hole with your shovel or trowel to loosen the soil and thus make it easier for the roots to expand.

As for width, accommodate the root-ball and then some. For a fruit tree, although you may not dig a hole that extends as far as the branches and roots may someday extend, you can spread amendments out that direction, mix them in, and leave them to work their way down gradually.

Buying Your Fruit Bearers

Unlike some annual and perennial flowers and veggies, fruit-bearers are not plants you want to try raising from seed — it takes forever! Not only that, but many fruit bearers do not *come true* (have the traits of their parent plants) from seed. For the fastest and most gratifying results, buy plants. You can buy them in containers, balled-and-burlapped, or bare-root.

If you shop at a local nursery, buy the largest plants you can find and afford so you can get off to a faster start. Confirm that the plant's well rooted by poking into the soil mix and/or tipping the pot and sliding it out to see for yourself. Favor plants with buds over ones that are already flowering, because the trip home or the transition from pot to garden soil is likely to make them jettison blooms early in favor of establishing their roots in their new home. New buds, flowers, and eventually fruit will come along in due course!

If you choose bare-root plants — which may look like nothing more than a slender branch (a *whip*) with some roots — you need to be concerned particularly with the quality of the root system. Many broken or dried-out roots are not a good sign. You may end up trimming either the top growth or the roots prior to planting (see "Bare-root plants," in the upcoming planting section), but you want to head into the project with a good plant.

If you're going the mail-order route, shop with a specialist. Avoid nurseries where the plants aren't clearly or fully identified as well as those that offer fruit plants only as a sideline. You want people who propagate and ship the plants themselves; they know what they're doing, and this streamlined system also keeps the quality higher and the costs down. Find such companies in the ads in gardening magazines (particularly in the classified ads in the back) or online.

To make sure you get a healthy plant, follow this general advice:

- ✔ **Always buy from a reputable source.** Ask around, nose around, and examine the source's guarantee and refund policy. Your local Cooperative Extension Service office may be able to point you toward good nearby sources.

- ✔ **Don't bother with bargain-hunting.** You get what you pay for.

- ✔ **Require a label and/or accurate identification.** This label includes not only the type of plant (for example, apple or Northern highbush blueberry) but also the cultivar ("McIntosh" or "Bluecrop," respectively).

- ✔ **Ask or look for some assurance that your choice is "certified" or "virus-tested."** Virus-infected plants don't always look diseased, at least not at first. If you skip this step and bring home an infected plant, it'll decline over time, and you may never know why or think you did something wrong.

- ✔ **Check visually for plant health.** Both top growth and the root system should be intact and in good condition, showing no signs of damage, rot, galls, or pests.

Planting Fruits

Book III

Edible Gardening

The key to a bountiful fruit harvest is in the planting: when you plant, where you plant, and how you get the plants in the ground. In determining the right planting time, climate is important, as is the specific planting location. And of course, planting a balled-and-burlapped tree requires a different technique than does a container plant or a bare-root one. This section walks you through everything you need to know. You also get the basics on planting a berry patch.

Choosing the best time to plant fruits

Here's the basic principle about timing, folks: Plant to allow maximum time for the fruit plant to get growing before the most stressful conditions of the year occur. In colder climates, get the plants in the ground in the springtime so they can enjoy a nice, long summer before cold weather arrives in the fall. Wait until the danger of frost has passed so young buds aren't harmed or killed. Plant bare-root plants as soon as you can work the ground in spring.

In mild climates, the stressful time is the height of the hot summer, so you're often better off planting fruits in the fall or early winter. This timing allows young stock to establish their root systems before being called upon to produce new spring growth. Still-warm soil and, hopefully, drenching fall rains can welcome the new arrivals and hasten this process along.

Deciding where to plant your fruits

Gardeners talk about three main factors to consider when finding a home in your landscape for fruit, nut, and berry plants. Ideally, you want to satisfy all these conditions so your crop doesn't struggle:

- ✔ **Sun:** Plentiful sun is a requirement — I'm talking at least six to eight hours a day, or even more. Fruit simply doesn't develop or prosper in shady conditions (even plant foliage may suffer or be sparse). So choose a south-facing spot, or, in a pinch, one that faces east or west. (Morning sun — an east-facing exposure — is better than west because it dries morning dew; morning dew that hangs around too long can cause fruit to rot.)

- ✔ **Elbow room:** Pick a site out in the open, well away from the shade cast by a house, other building, fence, or other obstruction. Prune back any nearby shrub or tree branches that may be encroaching. Planting distances vary depending on the type of fruit and the rootstock it's on. Read the planting distance guidelines in the catalog or on the plant label.

- ✔ **Drainage:** Look for a spot with decent soil and good drainage. Avoid naturally damp spots or those that hold rainwater for more than 12 hours. No berry-producing plants or fruit trees like wet feet. Being waterlogged deprives the roots of needed oxygen and may actually inhibit the uptake of some soil nutrients.

If drainage is iffy in your yard, favor an upland spot or slope. In any event, planting fruits in the lowest part of your landscape is never advisable. Heavy clay soil is a problem — though improving drainage by digging in lots of organic matter is possible. Alternatively, you can go to the trouble of creating a broad and deep (up to a foot, depending on what you plan to grow) raised bed. See Chapter 1 of this Book for more info on raised beds.

So, you know to plant your fruit plants in a place where the sun is ample, the drainage is good, and the soil is well-nourished. Here are some places you *don't* want to plant:

- ✔ **On steep slopes:** Slopes are hard to plant, and the plants are hard to care for.

- ✔ **In the middle of a pampered lawn:** Lawn fertilizer is too nitrogen-heavy for fruit plants to tolerate, and mowers and string trimmers can be a hazard.

- ✔ **Against a wall or fence:** Barriers crowd a plant, and poor air circulation is not good for its health (the exception is an espaliered fruit tree — see the upcoming section titled "Supporting and training your fruit").

Getting your fruit in the ground

How to plant fruit depends very much on the type of fruit you want to plant and what form it comes in. In the following sections, you first get some pointers on planting according to whether the fruit you purchase is initially in a container, a bare-root plant, or a balled-and-burlapped tree. Then I tell you how to plant a berry patch, which entails a slightly different approach.

Container plants

Berry bushes and some small fruit trees often come in containers. Assuming you have an appropriate spot ready, the planting process is simple and logical if you follow these steps:

1. **Choose a good day.**

   On the best of days, all danger of frost is past, but the weather is overcast or drizzly. A hot, sunny day is too stressful. If the weather is clear, at least plant later in the day.

2. **Prepare the plant first.**

   Water it well and let excess water drain away. Groom it lightly, trimming away any damaged branches and leaves. Pinch off most (but not all) of the buds, if any exist; this act encourages the plant to redirect its energies toward root development. After the plant establishes itself, it'll surely generate new buds, anyway.

3. **Pop the root system out of the pot.**

   If the root system is thick and dense, sliding a butter knife or stick around the perimeter should dislodge it, or perhaps you can cut the container away with tin snips. Tease the roots loose on the bottom and a bit on the sides — this encourages the plant to venture out into its new home in your garden soil. If the plant is root-bound, score the sides at four or so even intervals with a sharp knife, slicing only about an inch in — this scoring severs girdling roots and inspires new feeder roots to start growing.

4. **Plant it at the same level it was growing in the pot, and water.**

   Backfill soil into the hole and firm it into place to eliminate air pockets. Water well, let the ground settle, and add more soil as needed.

Bare-root plants

Most fruit trees, and sometimes berry-producing shrubs, are sold as bare-root plants; strawberry plants are commonly sold in small bare-root bundles. These plants are dormant, which means you can buy and plant them earlier in the gardening year — as soon as the soil is dry enough to crumble easily in your hand. If you can't plant right away, store bare-root plants in a cool, shaded spot and keep them moist.

Book III

Edible Gardening

On planting day, here are the steps to follow:

1. **Prep the plant.**

   Unwrap the plant, and if the roots are more than a foot long or look damaged or frayed, trim them back with clean, sharp clippers. Then soak the roots and stem in a bucket of tepid, muddy water (add a handful of soil) for a few hours or overnight to rehydrate them. As for the top growth, if the plant has branches, shorten them to a few inches (cutting to just above an outward-facing bud). This trim inspires vigorous, spreading growth. If the tree or shrub is a mere whip (single stem), cut it back to 2 or 3 feet tall if the grower hasn't already done so.

2. **Make a mound inside the hole.**

   Use the excavated soil (or a mixture of it and some organic matter) to make a mound in the hole. You'll set the plant here and array the roots on it, so make the mound tall. To allow for some settling, adjust the height of the mound so the plant will stand about 2 inches higher than it stood at the nursery (How do you know? Look for the telltale, old soil line low on the trunk).

3. **Add the plant and position it.**

   Place the tree or shrub atop the mound and spread the roots out evenly on all sides. Be careful not to bend or break them, and don't crowd them either. If the tree is branched, orient it with the lowest branch facing southwest — this positioning will eventually help shade the trunk and lessen the chance of sunscald. If the site is out in the open and windy, lean the tree ever so slightly into the direction of the prevailing winds.

4. **Backfill.**

   Hold the plant steady (or get a helper to do so) and scoop soil back into the hole. You may have to bounce the plant up and down slightly as you work to settle the soil among the roots. When it stands on its own, add more soil, tamping it down gently with your hands as you work to prevent air pockets.

5. **Create a basin.**

   Make the basin about a foot or two out from the trunk, mounding up soil to several inches high. Fill it partway with compost or other organic material, which will nourish the new young feeder roots that are developing. Top off with some weed-inhibiting mulch.

6. **Water.**

   Finally, soak slowly and thoroughly today and at least once a week for the rest of the season, unless you get good rainfall. A young fruit tree or berry bush is a thirsty plant.

Balled-and-burlapped plants

Fruit trees and larger berry-producing shrubs may be available in balled-and-burlapped form. This indicates that the plant was recently field-dug, and the purpose of the burlap or other cloth and trusses is to hold the soil protectively in place around the root-ball. Here are the steps to follow to return the plant to the ground in your own yard:

1. **Get the hole ready.**

   The size of the root-ball in this case is perfectly obvious, which is nice. Make the hole slightly bigger, both for maneuverability and also to encourage the roots to move outward in their new home. Assuming the plant is not too big, you can check your work by temporarily holding the trussed plant in the hole.

2. **Double-check depth.**

   Set the trussed root-ball in the hole, and then place a piece of lumber or a rod of some kind across the top of the hole. The top of the root mass should meet it. If not, you know what to do — take it out and dig more, or backfill a bit.

3. **Unwrap the plant.**

   Do this unwrapping outside the hole but right nearby. Cut off or unwind all rope, twine, string, or whatever is holding the burlap or cloth in place. Be especially careful to get off any material binding the trunk. Modern burlap may contain synthetic (plastic) material that practically never decays, so don't leave the burlap on. Some root-balls are also enveloped in a planting bag or wire basket — whatever you have, remove it.

4. **Plant.**

   Set or wiggle the root-ball into the prepared hole and backfill thoroughly to eliminate air pockets. If the tree is branched, orient it with the lowest branch facing southwest to eventually help shade the trunk and lessen the chance of sunscald. If the site is windy, lean the tree slightly into the direction of the prevailing winds.

5. **Create a basin and water.**

   Make the basin about a foot or two out from the trunk, mounding up soil to several inches high. Fill it partway with compost or other organic material, and top off with some weed-inhibiting mulch. Soak slowly and thoroughly at planting and at least weekly till the end of the season (unless you get good rainfall). Watering is particularly critical because the root-ball may have dried out while it was out of the ground, despite its protective wrapping.

Book III

Edible Gardening

A berry patch

Want to grow raspberries, blackberries, or marionberries? When you plant a berry patch, you have to prepare an entire area and install future support. I advise starting with a single row. The reason for the trellis is that it keeps your plants upright (rather than in a slumping tangle); this method keeps the plants drier and thus less prone to disease, and they're much easier to harvest from.

Don't grow cultivated berries anywhere near wild brambles or near an area where you grow or have recently grown eggplants, peppers, tomatoes, potatoes, or strawberries — all these plants can host diseases that are harmful to cultivated berries.

Here are the steps to follow when creating your berry patch:

1. **Make the row.**

   Clear an area of all weeds, grass, and physical obstructions. The row should be about 2 feet wide and as long as you want.

2. **Create a planting trench.**

   The roots of berry bushes are likely to grow down to about a foot deep, so excavate to at least that depth. Improve the soil with organic matter and with amendments that adjust the pH, if recommended by a soil test.

3. **Erect support.**

   The object is to keep the canes off the ground and not to crowd them. You want good air circulation, which lessens the chance of disease. Use posts made of rot-resistant wood (like cedar) or metal posts. Plunge the posts deeply into the ground, add braces if warranted, and then run strong wire between them to support and confine the plants. Your support setup options include

   - A patch with posts at four corners

   - Single posts at each end of your row

   - Single posts with crosspieces

   The standard advice is to rig the wires at 2- to 3-foot intervals.

4. **Plant.**

   Space the bushes at even intervals, 2 or 3 feet apart down the row and right under the lowest wire. Follow the previous planting directions in "Container plants," including giving each plant a good soaking.

5. **Cut back.**

After planting and watering are complete, tiptoe into the patch with your clippers and cut the plants off at ground level. I know, this shearing sounds drastic, but you may be eliminating canes that harbor diseases; plus, you don't want the plants to charge into early growth and fruiting. Instead, this step forces your new berry plants to focus on establishing and expanding their root systems. New canes will appear soon enough.

Taking Care of Fruit-Producing Plants

Modern fruit cultivars are bred to be productive and deliver a bountiful harvest. This trend is all well and good, but there are downsides. The sheer volume and weight of lots of fruit can cause a plant to slump, slouch, bow down, or trail fruiting branches on the ground. Also, humans aren't the only critters who like to eat fruits and nuts, and keeping these crops protected well enough so that you have something to show for all your hard work can be challenging. In this section, I give you the pointers you need to keep your fruit healthy, happy, and plentiful enough to enjoy!

Watering

Although too much water or poor drainage can drown a plant or encourage disease, fruit plants still need moisture. Shallow-rooted crops, like blueberries and strawberries, especially need ample water. Even if your climate provides natural rainfall, you may still have to supplement it. The most critical periods are at planting time and during fruit swell.

I recommend trickle irrigation for watering berry-producing plants, either with a soaker hose, a regular hose set quite low, or an in-ground system with emitters especially designed for this purpose. These methods allow the water to reach the roots evenly and gradually and yet avoid wetting the fruit (wet fruit is susceptible to rot, a particular concern for raspberries, blueberries, and strawberries).

Fertilizing

Unlike, say, vegetable crops, the majority of fruit-bearing plants are not heavy feeders. If your soil is fertile or you've improved soil fertility prior to planting, feeding is not a big part of maintenance. (Sure, commercial orchards dose their trees and bushes on a regular basis, but they're aiming for maximum yields; home growers can afford to be less indulgent.)

Book III

Edible Gardening

In any event, apply fertilizer to soil that's neither excessively acidic nor alkaline (address soil acidity prior to planting by having a soil test done and taking any corrective measures needed).

When you do feed your fruit trees or berry plants, use a complete, balanced, all-purpose fertilizer applied at the rates described on the label. More is not better! A dose in spring as the growing season begins is a good idea, and you may want to fertilize once again when the fruit is starting to form. (Don't feed later in the season, which can inspire fresh new growth that may not have time to harden before cold weather sets in and potentially damages tender shoots.)

Some fertilizers can be top-dressed. Top dressing is the surface application of fertilizer that is scratched into the top inch or two of the soil. You poke others into the ground at intervals above the root system. The nutrients get to the plant roots only when watered in. In fact, you're best off watering before and after feeding the plants. Refer to Chapter 1 of this Book for more on fertilizing.

No particular type of fertilizer can compel your fruit to bear at an earlier age. The age of bearing is mainly influenced by the variety, how and when you prune, and by some rootstocks in the case of grafted fruit trees.

Cutting back on mulch

I know, I know, you're always being told to mulch garden plants to keep weeds at bay and conserve soil moisture. But mulching is not as critical with many fruit plants because the trees tend to cast shade over their bases, which helps with such matters. Mulch can even be a detriment in a berry patch or small orchard because it can harbor pests — hungry little rodents or voracious slugs.

Supporting and training your fruit

To keep your harvest off the dirt and in the air where it's able to develop freely and enjoy good air circulation and plentiful sunshine, supports may be in order. A wide variety is available, depending on the fruit you want to grow. Figure 4-3 shows two of the many ways — a Kniffen trellis and a Pendelbogen — to train grapes with supports.

Supports help keep a developing harvest visible and serve to train the fruit so as to make it easily accessible. They also ensure a larger harvest. This support may involve anything from bracing boards under a heavy branch to a sturdy trellis to rigs of posts and wire. Figure this need into your plans when selecting both a spot and a cultivar.

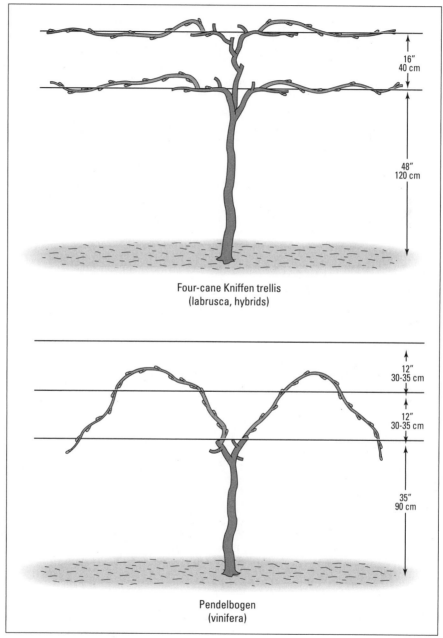

16"
40 cm

48"
120 cm

Four-cane Kniffen trellis
(labrusca, hybrids)

12"
30-35 cm

12"
30-35 cm

35"
90 cm

Pendelbogen
(vinifera)

Book III

**Edible
Gardening**

Figure 4-3:
Two
common
grape-
training
systems.

All the systems have one thing in common: They are designed to keep the vines off the ground so the fruit has good air circulation and exposure to sunlight, and is easier to harvest. If your vines don't end up looking just like a book drawing, don't worry. It's not critical.

Fruit-tree training systems, on the other hand, are designed to not only expose the fruit to good air flow (to reduce disease) and to bright sunlight (to ripen the fruit), but to encourage a tree structure that is strong and will encourage more fruit production. The ones in Figure 4-4 are fairly easy to follow, but others may be equally successful.

Espalier trees are trained to grow in one dimension or plane (see Figure 4-4). They are commonly used against fences or buildings. Their shapes can be quite artistic and ornamental. In addition to being aesthetically pleasing, they also result in high-quality fruit that is easy to tend and harvest.

Pruning

Fruit-bearing plants need regular pruning. It keeps the plants in bounds, attractive-looking, healthy, and — perhaps most importantly — helps them be more productive.

Here's the general rule: Prune fruit plants when they're dormant. You're better able to see what you're doing without a lot of foliage and so forth in the way, both in terms of shaping the plant and making sure you cut right above a bud. You also get little or no sap bleeding. And when growth starts up, the plant should grow as you plan and direct.

Always use clean, sharp tools when you prune. *Clean,* because you don't want to spread disease, and *sharp,* because blunt cutters mash and crush stems and branches. And always use the right tool for the job; applying a hand-held clipper to a thick branch is frustrating and foolish.

If any of this sort of maintenance is too difficult, too dangerous, or too time-consuming, consider scaling back your plans or hiring qualified help. Whatever you do, don't let the problem go. A neglected fruit tree or berry patch is a sorry sight, not to mention hard work to reclaim.

Tree fruits

A crop of tree fruits can be heavy, so a fruit tree needs to be shaped from an early age so that its framework is strong enough to bear the weight. That said, do no more pruning on a young tree than is totally necessary, or you risk delaying its first crop.

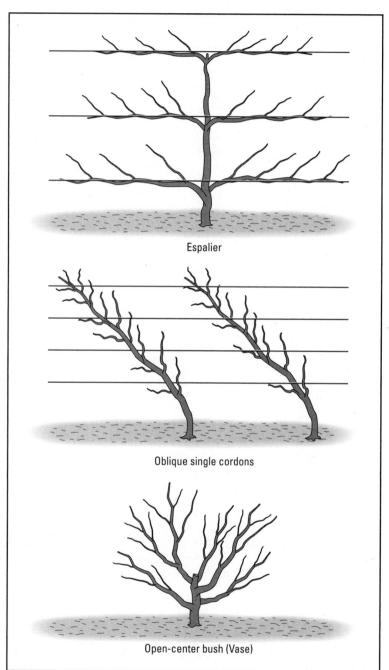

Espalier

Oblique single cordons

Open-center bush (Vase)

Figure 4-4:
Three common fruit-tree training methods.

Scaffold limbs are evenly spaced, come out from the main trunk at wide angles, and over time have a spiral arrangement around the trunk. Take out branches that crowd, cross, or shade others, right at the trunk (leave no stubs, in other words).

In later years, do an annual pruning to maintain this early form. Cut to reduce the fruit load and stimulate new shoot growth. How much should you cut? It depends on the size and heft of the particular fruit and the bearing habit of the tree. So read up in more detail on your particular tree or get the advice of a more experienced fruit grower.

Apple, pear, and other fruit trees often have *June drop,* a time when immature fruits fall from the tree. This natural fruit loss is a reminder to thin the fruit. Too many fruits clustered too closely together don't ripen well, nor do they reach their ideal size. Thin so you have 6 inches between fruits. Remember that pruning and thinning are harder on you than on the plant.

Shrub fruits

Fruits that grow on bushes need to be prevented from becoming crowded; a tangle is difficult to prune, tricky to harvest from, and more prone to diseases and pests. You don't have to do much the first season or two, but in subsequent years, you have to make an annual habit of thinning out the older wood (branches and canes). This pruning makes way for the new shoots, which, believe me, are *always* coming on. If you see a lot of new shoots, you may even have to thin out some of them. Figure 4-5 shows how to prune raspberry bushes; you can apply this method to most other shrub fruits.

Some berry plants produce fruit on first-year canes, some on second-year canes, so be careful that you don't cut out all the productive canes in your zeal to control the patch. You can find out which kind your berry bushes are either by simply observing or by asking when you purchase the plants.

The normal bramble life cycle of many shrub fruits is to produce a vegetative cane *(primocane)* in the first year; it overwinters, becomes a fruit-producing cane *(floricane)* the following year, and then dies. So your training becomes a cyclical matter of supporting these stems, encouraging them to stand up and trail outward along the wire, and removing them at ground level when they're through at the end of their second year. You can use cloth ties or just guide the fast-growing, lax, thorny stems.

Vine fruits

How you prune grapes, hardy kiwi, and other vining fruits depends on the sort of support you've chosen for them and how much space you allow them to fill. At the outset (the year you plant), cut back rather drastically to a few buds. This trim channels energy into growth of one or two main stems or "trunks."

Figure 4-5:
Raspberries
should be
pruned so
that they
don't grow
together
too densely.
Dense
bushes
produce
less fruit.

Prune old shoots to 6 in (15 cm)

Book III

Edible
Gardening

Subsequent side branches, evenly spaced off the main trunk, are called *cordons* and are considered more or less permanent. Often, the more of these, the better — they make for a fuller and more productive vine in the long run. So give the plant good care (regular water, fertilizer, and so on) in its first season or two to encourage plenty of cordons. Off of these come the third tier of branches, known as *fruiting arms.* These structures get a season to produce and then should be cut back somewhat or all the way back to the originating cordon in order to stimulate new ones and a fresh crop. That's it. Not as hard or complex as you thought, eh?

If you don't prune a vine fruit each year, it can soon grow longer and higher until the fruit you want is far out of reach. To bring it back down into range, all you need to do is cut it back until all that remains are the main trunk and some evenly spaced cordons; cut back while the plant is dormant.

Dealing with fruit pests

Homegrown fruits are so delicious that we aren't the only ones who like to eat 'em. If a certain kind of pest or disease is a common problem in your area, choose a fruit plant variety that's billed as resistant. Your local cooperative extension agent should be able to help you with this selection. Naturally, a healthy plant is a more resistant one. So take good care of your fruit plants, making sure they have the sun, space, air circulation, water, and food they need to thrive. In particular, water at the base of the plants so the foliage and fruit don't become wet; this method heads off all sorts of fungal problems at the pass.

In case these preventive measures fail, the following sections outline some tactics for warding off the competition.

Targeting birds, bugs, and beasties

No matter how healthy your plant is, you may still end up doing battle with the animal kingdom:

- ✔ **Birds:** These flying scavengers adore berries and strike with precise timing, at the peak of ripe perfection. Don't allow this pilfering! Cover the plants after flowering is over (so you don't thwart pollination) but before green fruit begins to ripen. Use plastic netting, cheesecloth, or anything that covers the plants but still lets in light, air, and water (see Figure 4-6). For larger berry patches, some gardeners rig a wooden framework over them and drape the protective cloth over this; then they can just lift one end to harvest, like raising a flap to enter a tent.

  If covering the trees with netting isn't practical, try draping netting over the lower branches and letting the birds have the higher-up fruit, which is harder for you to harvest, anyway. Hanging bright and noisy objects from the branches, such as pie tins, sometimes works.

- ✔ **Rodents:** Gnawing critters can do extensive damage to fruit trees. Wrapping the trees with a protective covering sometimes helps. Also, be sure not to pile mulch up against the trunk of the trees over winter. Doing so can provide a cozy hiding place for these creatures that may make a meal of the tree bark during the freezing weather.

- ✔ **Bugs and other creepy crawlers:** Sorry to say, you're up against all sorts of buggy threats, from ravenous caterpillars on apple trees to aphids, mealybugs, and spider mites that infest citrus trees. If you're already growing an allegedly resistant variety and you're genuinely giving your plants good growing conditions and good care, the situation seems so unjust! What can you do? You're not out of the fight yet:

Figure 4-6:
A fruit tree
or shrub
covered
with netting
keeps birds
at bay.

- **Practice good sanitation.** Remove all plant debris at the base of the plants and groom the plants often to get rid of any growth or fruits in poor condition or already affected. Get rid of all of this material — send it away with the household garbage!

- **Identify the culprit.** You can't truly fight back until you know thy enemy. If you need help with identification, take an affected plant part and/or the suspect to your local nursery or a knowledgeable landscaper.

- **Try nontoxic weapons first.** If practical, knock off pests with a blast from the hose or hand-pick the offenders. Spray with insecticidal soap (or a fungicide, if the problem is a disease and not a pest). Introduce beneficial insects that target this pest.

- **Spray pesticides only as a last resort and with an appropriate product for the problem.** Always follow label instructions to the letter regarding dose and timing, and protect yourself with full-body clothing and goggles.

- **Inspect and wash off all fruit before eating or cooking it.** You may decide to tolerate small imperfections rather than declare an all-out war.

The blanket effect: Spraying fruit trees

It's a cold, hard fact: Unless you don't mind finding tunnels in your ripe fruit, biting into a fat worm, or having to discard the crop you worked so hard to grow, you have to do at least some spraying. The spraying is preventive. It controls both bugs and diseases that can harm your crop.

Organic or synthetic, the product you want for this job is either a dormant oil or an all-purpose mixture of fungicide and insecticide labeled for orchard use. You can buy these products at any nursery or garden center in the springtime. Follow the label instructions regarding application and timing to the letter, and be sure to wear protective clothing and use a good, clean sprayer.

Halt spraying two or more weeks before harvest, and always wash your fruit before eating or cooking it.

Following are times that are typically good for spraying:

- **Early spring, when tips of buds are swelling and showing green:** This spraying combats late scab, brown rot, and other common woes. The first spray of the season is the most important and should head off at the pass numerous potential pest problems. It controls scab (an early-spring problem, technically a fungus) and early flying insects, such as coddling moths.

- **A few weeks later, when leaf buds (not flower buds — leaf buds are thin and pointed) are just unfurling:** Like the first spraying, round two fights late scab and brown rot.

- **At blossoming, when the fat, colored blossom buds (usually white or pink) are almost ready to burst open:** This prevents diseases that attack these young flowers and will eventually infect the developing fruit.

- **At petal fall, when nearly all petals are off the tree:** Insects are beginning to hatch just now, so this spray is especially critical.

- **Later sprays — every week or two, as needed:** These sprays control mites, sawflies, curculios, and apple maggots, as well as summer diseases like scab and brown rot.

Chapter 5

Maintaining Your Edible Garden

In This Chapter

▶ Watering, mulching, and fertilizing for optimal results

▶ Getting rid of weeds

▶ Helping your plants breathe

After planting your edible garden, you want to keep it growing vigorously until harvest. To do that, you need to keep your plants healthy and well-nourished throughout the growing season. If you let up just a bit on water or fertilizer, your harvest will be small or of poor quality. If you've ever tasted a cucumber harvested from a plant that has dried out, you know how bitter a poor harvest can be. But don't worry. In this chapter, you find out everything you need to know to keep your garden happy.

Watering Basics

Although Mother Nature is often very generous with rain, there are times when she leaves gardens with a dry spell. Flooding isn't good for your garden, but neither is drought. If your plants don't have adequate water at the right time, they can easily die. But not all plants have the same watering needs, so you have to be discriminating.

Different plants need different amounts of water. Some vegetables, like celery, are real water lovers and prefer to have moist soil around their roots at all times.

The depth of a plant's roots also makes a difference. Shallow-rooted plants (like onions and cabbage) need more careful watering during dry spells than deeper-rooted plants (like tomatoes), which can pull water from greater depths.

Why water matters: A short science lesson

Sure, without moisture, plants die. Everyone knows that. But you may not know why water is so incredibly vital. The answer is threefold, actually:

✔ Sufficient water pressure within plant tissues creates *turgor,* or rigidity, so the plant can stand up. A plant without turgor pressure collapses.

✔ Water keeps nutrients flowing from the soil, into the roots, and through the plant parts; it keeps the show going.

✔ The show is the chemical process of photosynthesis, which you no doubt remember from biology class in high school. The plant uses light, carbon dioxide, and water to make sugar (a pretty impressive trick). Without photosynthesis, plants can't grow or develop flowers or fruit. And the byproduct, which is so beneficial to the Earth, is oxygen.

The plant's growth stage — where it is in its life cycle — is also a factor. Here are some general watering guidelines for different growth stages:

✔ **Seedlings and germinating seeds:** Seedlings with small root systems near the soil surface and germinating seeds benefit from frequent, gentle watering, which enables them to sprout and emerge quickly. Water once or twice a day to keep the soil lightly and evenly moist to a depth of 2 inches if it doesn't rain.

✔ **Transplants:** After you plant transplants in your garden, water them frequently (daily if hot and dry) to help the roots recover from transplant shock.

✔ **Established plants:** Once plants have been in your garden for a few weeks and are beyond transplant shock, water deeply (to a depth of about 6 inches). Dig into the soil with a trowel to see how far the water has penetrated. Watering to this depth encourages roots to penetrate deeply, where they're less susceptible to drought. Give the soil a chance to dry out slightly before watering thoroughly again.

Keeping a close eye on your plants is easier said than done, of course, but the following sections tell you what you need to know, to keep in mind, and to watch out for when evaluating just how much moisture your garden needs.

The tell-tale signs of water woes

How do you make sure your garden has the right amount of moisture? Relying on natural rainfall would be nice, but natural rainfall is hard to count on as the natural rain cycles are not necessarily in synch with the gardening seasons in many parts of the country. You need to keep an eye on things and pay attention to your plants.

A plant that doesn't get enough water displays warning signs, in this order (***Note:*** The earlier you notice the signs, the better for the plant and your harvest):

1. Flower petals and buds droop, or fruit if it has developed.

2. Leaves droop and then shrivel.

3. Stems flop.

4. Roots go limp.

Obviously, if your plants are in this condition, they need water ASAP. However, these symptoms can be misleading at times. Some plants, like tomatoes, peppers, and eggplants, tend to droop slightly during the heat of the day, even if the soil has enough moisture.

Your index finger is the best indicator of when the soil is dry enough to warrant watering. Dig down several inches into the soil; if the soil is dry to the touch 3 to 4 inches down, it's time to water.

Too much water is also a problem. It starves the plant roots of oxygen. In addition, some plant diseases (like mildew and blight) travel via water and can easily develop and spread in soaked conditions. Unfortunately, an over-watered plant looks the same as one that's underwatered: It wilts. Its roots are too damaged by lack of oxygen to draw in water. It's a classic case of water, water, everywhere, but not a drop to drink! The obvious solution is to reduce watering (and resolve the drainage problems).

Book III

Edible Gardening

Determining which watering system to use

For many gardeners, getting enough water to their gardens is the biggest gardening challenge. The following sections outline your options.

However you water, keep these things in mind:

✔ Water your garden early in the day, before the sun is fully overhead. Watering late in the day can make plants susceptible to diseases that cause them to rot.

✔ Water at soil level to avoid water lost to wind. Watering the entire plant can cause fungal problems. (On a very hot day, however, watering the leaves can lower leaf temperatures.)

✔ No matter what kind of garden you have or which watering system you use, infrequent deep soakings are better than frequent shallow waterings, which cause roots to develop in the upper few inches of the soil, where they're likely to dry out.

Hoses

Watering with a hose is probably the most common way that gardeners water. It's simple, and some might say therapeutic. Who hasn't seen a gardener after a long day at work come home and take some time to hose down the garden with a cup of coffee or drink in hand? However, watering with a hose is wasteful and doesn't saturate the ground evenly. And honestly, for a large garden, who enjoys hauling hoses around? A hose is great, however, for watering containers, individual, large plants, such as tomatoes, and in conjunction with the basin method.

If you don't have an outdoor spigot close to your garden for convenient hose hookup and watering, divert the rainwater from your roof to a rain barrel. In areas with plenty of rain, consider several barrels hooked up together to take the benefit of overflow. Various mail-order suppliers sell rain barrels.

To reduce drowning risks to pets and children, make sure you either get a barrel that's tall enough to keep them out, or put a cover on the barrel. To keep mosquitoes, leaves, and debris out, cover with a screen. Most commercial rain barrels only have a small opening at the top. Raise the barrel (concrete blocks work well) so that the spigot is high enough for a watering can to fit under, and to make hose attachment easy.

Sprinklers

A sprinkler is an effective way to water plants in sandy soil, which absorbs water quickly. However, if you have heavy clay soil that absorbs water slowly or if your garden is on a slope, the water may run off and not sink into the soil where the plants need it. Keep in mind that as taller plants such as corn and tomatoes grow, sprinklers tend to be less effective because the water hits and damages the foliage, while not thoroughly watering the soil. Also, a lot of water is lost to evaporation, especially on a windy day.

Soaker-hose irrigation

A soaker-hose system consists of a rubber hose perforated with tiny pores that leak water, as shown in Figure 5-1. You can lay the hose between rows or curve it around plants. Water leaks out of the hose and onto the soil, leaving your plants dry and reducing evaporation. Its primary limitation is that it delivers water unevenly on sloped or uneven ground.

Figure 5-1:
A soaker
hose.

Furrows

Furrows are shallow trenches between raised beds that channel water. The beds can be 1 to 3 feet apart — the wider apart they are, the more water you need. You use a hoe to dig a furrow at planting time and then plant the seeds or transplants on top of the raised beds, in between furrows. When you're ready to water, fill the furrows completely with water and then wait a while, or fill them more than once so that the water penetrates down as well as sideways into the raised soil. Poke around with your finger to make sure that the water has penetrated the bed. Furrows work best in arid areas with clay soil, such as the Southwest, where streams or groundwater can be used in the garden, but little natural rain falls during the growing season. Furrows don't work well in sandy soil because the water soaks in before it can reach the end of the furrow.

Drip irrigation

Drip irrigation systems are more efficient than furrow or standard overhead watering because they supply water exactly where it's needed. They use small spray heads or spaghetti-like emitter tubes to drip water right onto the root zone of each plant. Drip irrigation works best for permanent plantings because it takes time to install the emitters for each plant.

Delivering water slowly and at ground level is good for many reasons:

- ✔ It encourages deep rooting.
- ✔ It eliminates many disease problems.
- ✔ It results in fewer weeds.
- ✔ It discourages runoff.
- ✔ It saves on the amount of water used.

Install drip irrigation after you've planted seeds or transplants. Drip irrigation systems are available from garden or irrigation suppliers, or you can go to a plumbing supply store where they can help you lay out a system custom-made for your garden.

Basins

A basin is a donut-like depression around a plant that you fill with water. You make a basin in a 2-foot diameter circle around the base of the plant. Basins work particularly well for watering sprawling plants like melons and squash early in the season. After the plants mature, however, their roots will grow out of the diameter of the basin, and this method won't be effective any longer. For tomatoes and other vertical plants, they work well throughout the gardening season.

Automatic irrigation systems

Automatic irrigation systems take the work out of watering your garden by letting you program how often and how long you want the system on. Once you have one, you'll never go back to hand watering and dragging hoses. Although more affordable today than ever before, the cost of materials and installation is pricey compared to the other options. Still, if you're looking for convenience and consistency, the benefits outweigh the cost:

- ✔ Your plants get watered regardless of whether you remember to water or have the time. You can even program the system to water in early hours of the morning while you are asleep!

- ✔ By watering regularly, your plants won't go through the dry spells that happen when you forget to water (or when the neighbor kid you hired to water while you were on vacation forgets to water). In addition, in times of drought, you are likely not to lose plants.

    ✔ Preprogramming your system gives you quite a bit of control over how much water your plants get. Because you can individually program each station, you can ensure that the plants in different areas get the amount of water they need.

Automatic systems aren't "set and forget." You need to adjust them with the changing seasons, turning them off or cutting down watering time during wet seasons and increasing the time during dry seasons. Most importantly, install a rain sensor so that the irrigation is not on when it is raining.

Mulching Magic

Mulch is any material, organic or inorganic, that you place on the surface of soil, usually right over the root zone of growing plants. Mulch is a good gardening habit but not mandatory. But, ooh boy, do the benefits make it worth the effort! Mulching your garden

    ✔ Inhibits weed germination and growth (and not only are weeds unsightly, but they also steal resources from your plants).

    ✔ Holds in soil moisture, protecting your plants from quickly drying out.

    ✔ In cold-winter areas, prevents *frost-heaving,* in which plants are literally pushed out of the ground by the natural expansion and contraction of the soil as it alternately thaws and freezes. (Do not apply winter mulch until the ground is frozen.)

    ✔ In hot-summer areas, helps keep plant roots cooler.

    ✔ Can provide much of the nutrition a plant needs if you use an organic mulch.

    ✔ Lessens the chances of certain diseases attacking your plants.

    ✔ Adds an attractive look to your garden.

Sound like good enough reasons to use mulch? Assuming you're convinced, read on for the lowdown on mulches.

Knowing your mulches

First of all, there really isn't any "right" or "best" mulch. Benefits vary in different climates and parts of the country. Some mulches are free, right in your own backyard; you can purchase others locally. When buying bagged mulch, look for the seal of the Mulch and Soil Council. It guarantees that mulch is what the label claims, and that it does not contain any toxic CCA from recycled pressure-treated lumber. Table 5-1 provides the basic information you need to know about some of the more popular options.

Book III

Edible Gardening

Table 5-1	Comparing Mulching Options	
Type of Mulch	**Advantages**	**Concerns**
Grass clippings	Free, readily available, and easy to apply	Decays quickly, so you have to replenish it often; if you use weed killers on your lawn it may kill mulched plants; can turn slimy if you apply more than 3/4 inch at a time; if the grass went to seed before you cut it, the grass seeds can germinate in your garden beds (yikes!)
Bark	Looks neat and attractive; stays where you put it; slow to decay; available in a variety of sizes — small-, medium-, and large-sized chips, and shredded	Best on large plants; most types too big to use with vegetables; pine bark mulch is fairly acidic, which you may or may not want for your garden; if you apply up against tree and shrub trunks, you may create a hiding spot for bark-damaging rodents or insects, especially during winter; avoid artificially colored products
Shredded leaves	Free (in autumn, run fallen leaves over with a lawn mower or put them through a leaf shredder); smothers weeds very well; helps hold in soil moisture; feeds the soil as they decompose	Oak leaves can lower your garden soil's pH; decompose and need to be replenished at least once a year
Cocoa hulls	Attractive; smells like chocolate; feeds the soil as it breaks down	Breaks down fairly quickly; replenish once or twice a year
Compost	Is free if you have your own compost pile; attractive; adds nutrients to the soil as it breaks down; great for fruits and vegetables	Makes a good place for airborne weed seeds to germinate; most folks don't produce enough compost to mulch their gardens
Nut hulls	Peanuts, hazelnuts, pecans, and other nut hulls; free from your or neighbors' trees, or low cost from local processing plants; best around trees or shrubs	Depend on local availability; do not use walnut hulls as they contain juglone, which suppresses plant growth

Type of Mulch	Advantages	Concerns
Pine needles	Attractive; free; great in woodland plantings and under strawberry plants; slow to break down	Acidify the soil
Straw	Is cheap and easy to apply	Is so light it can blow or drift away; may harbor rodents, especially over the winter months; isn't very attractive for ornamental plantings
Newspaper	Free (if you get the paper daily); creates a great weed barrier (wet 4 to 6 pages and lay on soil); terrific way to recycle	Unattractive (just cover with a thin layer of ornamental mulch)
Hay	Is cheap and easy to apply	May harbor rodents, especially over the winter months; isn't very attractive for ornamental plantings; probably contains weed seeds
Gravel, pebbles, or stone	Has a nice, neat look (though not "natural"); is easy to apply; won't wash away easily and will last a long time; doesn't need to be replenished	Can allow weeds to sneak through; provides no benefits to the soil; can warm the soil underneath too much; a challenge to rake if leaves fall on it
Plastic (garden plastic, black plastic)	Keeps weeds at bay; holds soil moisture and warmth in	Watering and feeding is hard (you need to cut openings for plants); can be difficult to apply unless you're doing an entire area at one time; isn't very attractive; can overheat soil and sterilize it

Book III

Edible Gardening

How to apply mulch — and how much

Here's what you need to know to ensure you get the most from your mulch year-round:

  ✔ **When you plant:** Applying mulch right after planting something is easy. Use a shovel or scoop with a trowel. Spread the mulch over the root-zone area but not flush up against a plant's base or main stem (which can smother it or invite pests or disease).

Depth depends on the sort of plant. Annuals and perennials are fine with an inch or so of mulch; shrubs, roses, and trees need 3 or 4 inches or more. Vegetables in general need a 2- to 4-inch layer of mulch.

✔ **During the growing season:** Add more mulch midway through the growing season or whenever you notice the mulch appears depleted. You may have to get down on your knees or wriggle around a bit as you try to deliver it where it's needed without harming the plant or its neighbors. Again, use less for smaller plants, more for bigger ones.

✔ **In the fall or for winter protection:** Depending on the severity of your winters and the amount of snow cover you expect (a blanket of snow acts as a protective mulch, actually), you want to cover an overwintering plant well after the ground has frozen (otherwise you keep the soil warm and the roots keep everything growing).You can cut down perennials first and then practically bury them under several inches of mulch. You shouldn't trim back shrubs and rosebushes at this time, but you don't have to be as careful as you were with midsummer mulching because the plant is no longer growing actively. For freezing winters, 6 or more inches around the base of these is a good amount.

These amounts are guidelines only. You have to tailor them to your climate, growing season, and specific plants.

Using Fertilizer in Your Edible Garden

Even if you have the healthiest soil around, growing fruits and vegetables is an intensive process that takes many important nutrients from the soil. So you need to add some fertilizer to your soil to keep it in optimum shape to feed your plants. How much fertilizer you add depends on the soil and the plants you're growing.

Determining your soil's nutrient needs

Sixteen elements are essential for healthy plant growth, along with energy from sunlight for photosynthesis, the process by which plants use carbon dioxide from the air and water from the soil to produce sugars that enable them to grow. Plants require nitrogen, phosphorus, and potassium in relatively large quantities. Plants take up these three nutrients — often called macronutrients or primary nutrients — from the soil. If your soil doesn't contain enough of these nutrients, you can supply them by fertilizing. However, if the soil pH isn't right, these and other elements get locked up in the soil.

The following sections explain how to tell whether your soil has too much or too little of these particular nutrients.

Get your soil tested. Do-it-yourself kits are readily available, but a professional testing is best. Check with your local cooperative extension service; it may perform one at little or no cost. A good soil test will give you the soil pH and a nutrient analysis, including suggestions for amending the soil. Taking samples from each garden area is a good idea because the pH can vary greatly around your property. For instance, concrete foundations leach calcium, which makes the soil alkaline.

Nitrogen

Nitrogen (N) is responsible for the healthy green color of your plants. It easily moves around in the soil and can leach away from plant roots as a result of rain or watering. Therefore, you need to be sure that your plants receive a steady supply of nitrogen all season long.

Plants with a nitrogen deficiency show yellowing (in older leaves first) and slowed growth. With plants like tomatoes, a nitrogen deficiency may first appear as a reddening of the stems and the undersides of the leaves. A plant with too much nitrogen has soft-textured, succulent growth that attracts aphids and other insects. Because nitrogen leaches out of the soil quickly, if you have too much, stop fertilizing, wait, and eventually the problem will solve itself.

You can supplement soil nitrogen by adding compost; decomposing organic matter (leaf mold or well-rotted manure); organic fertilizers, such as blood meal and cottonseed meal; or chemical fertilizers.

Phosphorus

Phosphorus (P) helps promote good root growth, increased disease resistance, and fruit and seed formation. Plants lacking in phosphorus are stunted and sport dark green foliage and purplish stems and leaves (on the older leaves first). Phosphorus is not available to plants in soils with a high pH; lime to lower it to a pH of 6 to 7.5 to make it available.

Sources of phosphorus include minerals, organic matter, inorganic fertilizers (such as rock phosphate), and organic fertilizers (such as bone meal). Unlike nitrogen, phosphorus doesn't move quickly through soil, so add a fertilizer containing phosphorus to the root zone before planting, instead of sprinkling it on the soil surface. Side-dressing is a waste of money and resources.

Potassium

Potassium (K), also called potash, promotes vigorous growth and resistance to disease and cold. A deficiency is hard to diagnose; often once it's recognized, it's too late to save the plant. Soil minerals provide potassium, as do organic matter (wood ash) and inorganic fertilizers, such as potassium sulfate and granite dust.

Book III

Edible Gardening

Calcium, magnesium, and sulfur

Calcium, magnesium, and sulfur are known as *secondary nutrients*. Plants need them, but not to the same extent that they need nitrogen, phosphorus, and potassium. Most alkaline soils contain these elements naturally, and few soils are deficient in sulfur. Most home garden soils contain these nutrients, but you can do specific tests on the leaves to detect any deficiencies.

In regions where the soil is acidic, liming to keep your soil's pH in a good growth range provides adequate calcium and magnesium. Epsom salts provide magnesium, which makes long stems (like roses and tomatoes) strong.

Micronutrients

Micronutrients (iron, manganese, copper, boron, molybdenum, chlorine, and zinc) are elements that plants need in tiny amounts. Too much of one of these elements is often as harmful as too little.

A micronutrient deficiency or excess may mean that your soil is too acidic or too alkaline, so you can correct the problem by changing the pH rather than by adding more nutrients. Sometimes, changing the pH sufficiently to increase micronutrient levels isn't practical, or you may need to give a plant a micronutrient quickly while you try to change the soil pH. In such cases, micronutrients are applied as chelates (from the Latin word for claw). *Chelates* are added to other chemicals, in this case micronutrients, to keep them available to plants when soil conditions are unfavorable. Apply chelated micronutrients to your soil, or, better yet, spray them on plant foliage.

Choosing a fertilizer: Chemical or organic

You have to weigh the advantages and disadvantages of chemical and organic fertilizers to decide which products are best suited to your needs and preferences.

Chemical fertilizers

Chemical fertilizers are synthetically manufactured. They include elements such as sodium nitrate, potassium chloride, and superphosphate. Chemical fertilizers come in liquid, granular, powder, or pellet form, and choosing a form is a matter of personal preference. If you want to fertilize when you water with a watering can, use a liquid fertilizer. If you want to sprinkle some fertilizer around each plant, use a granular fertilizer or pellets.

Here are the advantages of chemical fertilizers:

✔ Chemical fertilizers are widely available, relatively inexpensive, and easy to store, and vary widely in formulations and forms, so you can tailor a fertilizer program to your soil and plants.

✔ Most chemical fertilizers are rapidly available to plants. The exception is fertilizer that has been manufactured in slow-release form, in which case the fertilizer pellets break down and release the fertilizer slowly.

✔ A liquid or a dry powder chemical fertilizer that you mix with water is completely soluble, and its nutrients are quickly available to plants — an advantage when plants need a quick boost, such as right after transplanting.

Here are the disadvantages of using chemical fertilizers:

✔ Chemical fertilizers add no organic matter to your soil and contribute nothing to improving soil structure.

✔ Because chemical fertilizers are more concentrated than natural fertilizers, they can have a greater effect on soil pH, which can damage soil microorganisms.

✔ Manufacturing chemical fertilizers requires large amounts of energy, usually supplied by nonrenewable resources. Though not directly impacting your garden, producing chemical fertilizers does place a strain on the overall environment.

✔ Most chemical fertilizers are a quick fix for plants.

✔ Adding chemical fertilizers to lawns in early spring causes them to green up earlier, requiring earlier and more frequent mowing.

Organic fertilizers

Natural fertilizers — animal and green manure, compost, blood meal, kelp, fish emulsion (hydrolyzed fish is even better), cottonseed meal, granite dust, and rock phosphate — have several advantages:

✔ Many natural fertilizers contribute organic matter to your soil, improving its structure, and they can contribute micronutrients.

✔ Most natural fertilizers supply a slow but steady diet for plants.

✔ Some natural fertilizers, such as manure, may be inexpensive.

Here are some disadvantages to using organic fertilizers:

✔ Some organic fertilizers are bulky and hard to store and transport.

✔ Their slow release of nutrients, in some cases dependent on the action of soil microorganisms, may not provide plants with an adequate nutrient supply when it's needed.

✔ Complete organic fertilizers are available; as with complete chemical fertilizers, the three major nutrients are present, but usually in a lower concentration, such as 1-2-1. Don't let the low numbers fool you; in the long run, they provide plenty of nutrients.

Book III

Edible Gardening

Using wood ashes to provide nutrients

Wood ashes are a source of potash and phosphate, although the exact amounts of these nutrients depend on the type of wood burned (hardwoods generally contain more nutrients than softwoods), the degree of combustion, and where the wood was stored (for example, dry storage prevents nutrient leaching). A general analysis is usually in the range of 0 percent nitrogen, 1 to 2 percent phosphate, and 4 to 10 percent potash. But the major benefit of wood ashes is as a liming agent to raise the pH of the soil. Naturally, if you live in an area where soils are alkaline, don't use wood ashes as a soil amendment; they raise the pH even higher.

Apply wood ashes to your soil in moderation (no more than 10 to 20 pounds per 1,000 square feet of garden) because they may contain small amounts of heavy metals, such as cadmium and copper. These metals build up in plants if you add too much wood ash to the soil and can kill the plants — or harm *you*, if you eat lots of those plants.

Understanding a fertilizer label

Commercial fertilizers are labeled with three numbers, which indicate the fertilizer's nutrient content. The first number indicates the percentage of nitrogen, the second number shows the percentage of phosphorus, and the third number represents the percentage of potassium. For example, a 5-10-10 fertilizer contains 5 percent nitrogen, 10 percent phosphorus, and 10 percent potassium. It's called a complete fertilizer because it contains some of each type of nutrient. In contrast, bone meal has an analysis of 4-12-0. It's a good source of phosphorus but doesn't provide any potassium. The other materials in a commercial fertilizer that the analysis numbers don't account for are generally filler — unimportant materials that add bulk to the bag so that the fertilizer is easier to spread.

How much to use? Soil tests are the best way to correct deficiencies, but fertilizer bags also give general dosage recommendations for gardens. Most fertilizer recommendations for maintenance fertilization (rather than to correct a deficiency) are made according to how much nitrogen a crop needs. If you have a recommendation for 3 pounds of 5-10-10 fertilizer per 100 square feet, but the fertilizer you have on hand is 5-10-5 fertilizer, apply 3 pounds of 5-10-5. Even though the 5-10-5 fertilizer's percentage of potassium is less than that of the 5-10-10, it offers the recommended amount of nitrogen.

Side-dressing

Depending on the type of fertilizer you use, the crops you grow, and the type of soil you have, you may need to add repeat doses of fertilizer throughout the growing season — a practice called *side-dressing*. For example, because sandy soils don't hold nutrients well, giving plants small, regular fertilizer applications ensures a steady supply of nutrients. If you use a slow-release fertilizer, you may not need to side-dress until late in the season (if at all); check the label on the fertilizer package for details.

Both chemical and natural fertilizers can be used for side-dressing. A 5-10-10 fertilizer is a good choice for many crops. Use 1 to 2 tablespoons per plant, or 1 to 2 pounds for every 25 feet in a row, depending on the size of your plants.

Too much fertilizer can be more harmful than too little. Excess fertilizer accumulates in the soil in the form of salts and damages plant roots. Be sure that growing conditions enable plants to use the fertilizer that you apply. For example, don't add fertilizer during a dry spell if you can't irrigate your garden, because without adequate soil moisture, roots can't take up nutrients. And if cool weather causes your plants to grow slowly, go easy on the fertilizer until the temperature warms up.

The kind of plants that you grow makes a difference in how much you side-dress. Plants that take a long time to mature (such as tomatoes and eggplants) and heavy feeders (like corn) generally benefit more from side-dressing than quick-maturing crops, such as lettuce, or legumes like peas and beans, that fix their own nitrogen. See Table 5-2 for some general side-dressing guidelines.

Book III

Edible Gardening

Table 5-2	Deciding When to Side-Dress
Edible	*When to Side-Dress*
Beans, green	No need to side-dress.
Beet greens	Two weeks after leaves appear.
Beets	When tops are 4 to 5 inches high. Go light on nitrogen, which encourages leaf growth.
Blackberries	Renew organic mulch in spring.
Broccoli	Three weeks after transplant. Go light on nitrogen.
Brussels sprouts	Three weeks after transplant; again when sprouts begin to appear.
Cabbage	Four to six weeks after planting.
Carrots	Three weeks after plants are well established and no longer seedlings.
Cauliflower	Four to six weeks after planting.
Celery	Three weeks after setting out; again six weeks later.
Corn, sweet	Three weeks after planting; again when plants are 8 to 10 inches high; again when tassels appear.

(Continued)

Table 5-2	Deciding When to Side-Dress
Edible	**When to Side-Dress**
Cucumbers	When they first begin to run (form vines and sprawl); again when blossoms set.
Currant	Annually in spring.
Eggplant	Three weeks after planting.
Figs	Annually in spring.
Gooseberry	Annually in spring.
Kale	When plants are 6 to 8 inches tall.
Lettuce, head	Three weeks after transplant; again when heads form.
Lettuce, leaf	Three weeks after transplant.
Melons	When they begin to run; again a week after blossom set; again three weeks later.
Onions	Three weeks after planting; again when tops are 6 to 8 inches tall; again when bulbs start to swell.
Peas	No need to side-dress.
Peppers, sweet	Three weeks after transplant; again after first fruit set.
Potatoes	When plants bloom.
Pumpkins	When plants start to run; again at blossom set.
Radishes	No need to side-dress.
Raspberries	Renew organic mulch in spring.
Spinach	When plants are about 3 to 4 inches tall.
Squash, summer	When plants are about 6 inches tall; again when they bloom.
Squash, winter	When plants start to run; again at blossom set.
Strawberries	For day-neutrals, after the blossoms set; monthly for the next two months (four months in warm climates).
Tomatoes	Two to three weeks after transplant; again before first picking; again two weeks after first picking. Go light on nitrogen.

Waging War on Weeds

A weed is any plant that's growing where you don't want it to. Some weeds are worse than others, but in general, you don't want any weeds in your garden because they compete with your plants for light, water, and nutrients. If you have a lot of weeds, you'll have weaker plants and a less substantial harvest. Besides, weeds look terrible.

The key to battling weeds is to get to them early before they're firmly established. When they're young, weeds are easier to pull and less likely to produce seeds that cause problems down the road.

Battling weeds before planting

You can reduce weeds in your vegetable beds many different ways. The following sections explain some things that you can do before planting your garden.

Planning for easy weeding

This is an I-know-I'll-never-be-rid-of-them-so-I-might-as-well-make-my-life-easier ploy. Simply leave enough room between rows so that you can weed the soil easily.

Solarizing the soil

When you solarize the soil, you use the power of the sun to kill weeds. This technique works best in the middle of summer. The only downside to solarizing is that it takes a while and it kills all the living organisms in the soil. Follow these steps to solarize your soil:

1. **Prepare your bed for planting (or cut existing weeds down to ground level) and water it well.**

2. **Dig a 6-to-12-inch-deep trench around the perimeter of the bed.**

3. **Cover the entire bed with thick clear plastic (4 mil) and place the edges of the plastic in the trenches. Fill the trenches with soil, and then wait.**

   The temperature gets so hot underneath the plastic that it kills insects, disease organisms, and weeds. It usually takes a few months of solarizing to get a beneficial effect.

Book III

Edible Gardening

Battling weeds after planting

After planting, you have several choices for reducing weeds:

- ✔ **Mulch.** Applying a good thick organic mulch is one of the best ways to battle weeds. Even if mulch doesn't smother the weeds and their seeds, the weeds that do come up are easy to pull. Planting through black plastic is also a very effective way to keep weeds from becoming a problem. See "Mulching Magic," earlier in this chapter, for more on mulch.

- ✔ **Pull the weeds by hand.** While they're young, weeds come out of the ground easily. Get 'em, roots and all, whenever you see them.

✔ **Cultivate.** Simply hoeing or lightly turning the soil between vegetables exposes the weeds' roots and kills many of them. Cultivating is most effective when it's done often (a few times a week in the first month or so of gardening) and when the weeds are small. You can find cultivating tools designed especially for this purpose.

✔ **Keep garden paths clean.** Try to keep your garden paths as weed-free as possible; otherwise, weeds will creep into your planting beds. Try covering the paths with a thick mulch to keep weeds from becoming established.

Air! Air! Plants Need Air!

A sometimes overlooked necessity for plant life is air (and not just carbon dioxide). Without air, plants struggle and perish. Yes, the free oxygen in the air is part of the photosynthesis recipe, produced by the plants themselves, but another practicality is even more visible here. Air movement around your plants prevents disease, especially fungal diseases that gain a foothold when the air is too "close" and humid and when wet leaves can't dry or don't dry quickly.

Underground, oxygen between the particles of soil is important. Plant roots or, more accurately, their little root hairs, are busy. They take in that oxygen, absorb water, and then release carbon dioxide. If this process is thwarted, as it is in waterlogged soil, the roots can't function properly. They begin to rot, and the plant surely suffers.

Short of setting up a fan in your garden, here's what you can do to make sure your plants are getting plenty of air:

✔ **Don't let soil get compacted.** If it's quite wet, don't walk on it or dig in it. Loose soil is airy soil.

✔ **Add organic matter.** You've heard it before, but it bears repeating. The addition of organic matter, especially in dense clay soil, helps keep it aerated.

✔ **Never kill an earthworm.** Earthworms help break up and aerate your soil. Rejoice in their presence! Welcome them!

✔ **Make sure your garden is well-drained.** If you have standing water or find an area that's always damp, figure out what the drainage problem is and fix it.

✔ **Don't crowd your plants together in the garden bed if they're susceptible to mildew or black spot.** Give everyone a little elbow room!

Book IV
Getting Outdoors

In this Book . . .

You can't get more back-to-basics than being out-doors. Not just outdoors as in not inside, but truly outdoors. Go fishing, take a camping trip, round up the kids and go creek stomping — whatever gets you observing, enjoying, and interacting with nature.

The natural world is a remarkable thing, full of beauty and adventure and, if you're not prepared, potential danger. That's why this book also explains everything you need to know to stay safe when you're out and about in the wild.

Chapter 1

Basic Camp Skills

. . . .

In This Chapter

▶ Tying knots

▶ Keeping your knife in tiptop slicing-and-dicing shape

▶ Constructing a campfire responsibly

▶ Sharpening your survival skills

. . . .

You can buy all the gear in the world to make you look good outdoors, but you just can't buy skill or experience. In the outdoors, skills derived from experience can mean the difference between a successful adventure and one that you'd just as soon forget. When you foray into the great outdoors, you need to have a few basic skills under your belt: how to tie knots, sharpen a knife, and build a fire — simple skills that make you a more confident and safer person outdoors. And because the allure of the outdoors is its combination of beauty and unpredictability, this chapter includes some general survival skills, too.

Tying Basic Knots

Ropes and knots are as much a part of any skilled outdoor adventurer's arsenal as a knife, a compass, and some waterproof matches. With just a little rope-tying know-how, you can modify and even secure your world. You can attach a boat to your car rack, take up the slack in a sagging tent line, secure a person to a rope in a rescue situation — the list is endless.

Which knots are best? Well, literally thousands of different knots exist (some obsessed knot-tiers with entirely too much time on their hands claim that there are more than 4,000), each with its own purpose and use. Be thankful that this chapter limits your skill-set requirements to a few basic knots that (if tied properly) should see you through almost any situation you may encounter outdoors.

The accompanying illustrations are the best means for figuring out how to tie the knots. Study them along with the descriptions and then practice, practice, practice.

To make matters easier, this chapter uses a few simple terms:

- **Running end:** The shorter or active end of the rope that you weave in and out of the knot.

- **Standing end:** The longest and least active end of the rope. It's the opposite end of the rope from the running end.

- **Bight:** Simply, a bend in the rope.

- **Stopper knot:** A knot designed to stop a rope from sliding through a loop, hole, or, in the case of climbing, a descending device. (Rappelling off the end of a rope isn't impossible and is no laughing matter.) The basic overhand knot is most typically used as a stopper.

Bowline

The *bowline,* shown in Figure 1-1, is best known to sailors and climbers. As a climber's knot, the bowline has its roots in the days when a climber tied directly into a rope with a loop around his waist. As such, the bowline is still a very useful knot to know for rescue situations — or any time you need to tie a *secure loop* in the end of a rope (meaning a tight knot that won't come undone). To tie a bowline, do the following:

1. **Form a small loop by crossing one end of the rope over the other.**

2. **Bring the running end of the rope up through the bottom of the loop, around the stopper end of the rope, and then back down through the loop.**

3. **Pull taut.**

"The rabbit comes out of the hole, around the tree, and back down the hole again" is the chant often used by folks remembering how to tie this knot. The hole is the small loop you form by crossing one end of the rope over the other. The rabbit is the rope's running end.

Clove hitch

Used most often to secure tent lines to poles or stakes (and sometimes as a temporary mooring line for a canoe or kayak), the *clove hitch* is a classic outdoor knot (see Figure 1-2). Here's how to make a clove hitch:

1. **Take the running end of the rope and wrap it once around the pole, fence post, or stake, passing it under the standing end before completing the wrap.**

2. **Continue around the post, pole, or stake once more — this time going above the standing end with the running end.**

3. **After completing the second wrap, feed the running end back through itself and above the standing end wrapped around the pole and then pull tight.**

   You can add security to the line by adding a stopper knot at the end of the rope's running end so that it can't pull through on itself.

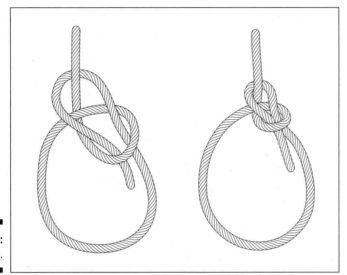

Figure 1-1:
Bowline.

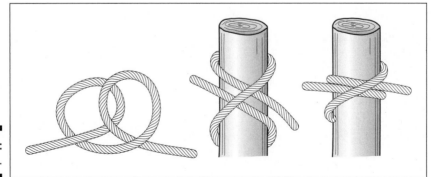

Figure 1-2:
Clove hitch.

Fisherman's knot

The *fisherman's knot,* which has been called many names over the centuries, including a waterman's knot, is designed to attach two lengths of rope of equal diameters securely together to form a longer length of rope (see Figure 1-3). To tie a fisherman's knot, follow these instructions:

1. **Begin by placing the two ends of two ropes next to each other.**

2. **Pass the running end of Rope 1 under the running end of Rope 2, pass it back over the top of both ropes, push it up through the loop you just formed, and pull tight.**

3. **Take the running end of Rope 2 and pass it under the running end of Rope 1 (behind the knot you just formed) and over the top of both ropes before pushing it up through the loop you just formed.**

4. **Pull the two knots together by pulling in opposite directions on the standing ends of each rope.**

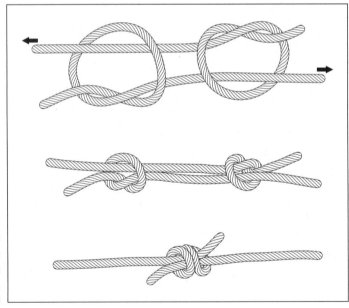

Figure 1-3:
Fisherman's
knot.

Figure eight

Like its name implies, the *figure eight* knot forms a figure eight in the rope (see Figure 1-4). This knot is used as a stopper knot at the end of a rope or as a means to prevent a rope from unraveling. Here's how to tie a figure eight:

1. **Cross the running end of the rope over the standing end.**

2. **Wrap the running end around the standing end.**

3. **Feed that end back through the loop you just formed.**

Figure 1-4:
Figure eight.

Figure eight threaded

Like its cousin, the *figure eight threaded* knot forms a figure eight in the rope with a loop below the knot (see Figure 1-5). You can use this knot to tie into a climbing harness or to create a secure loop for pulling or hauling items. The figure eight threaded also forms part of the trucker's hitch described later in this chapter. Follow these steps to construct the figure eight threaded:

1. **Cross the running end of the rope over the standing end.**

2. **Wrap the running end around the standing end and then feed that end back through the loop you just formed.**

3. **Form a bight in the running end below the eight and begin threading the running end back through the loop, retracing the rope as it winds and twists through the original eight.**

    Be careful to follow the path exactly so that the running end parallels and pairs up with itself on the original knot, exiting back toward the standing end.

4. **Add a stopper knot to prevent the running end from slipping.**

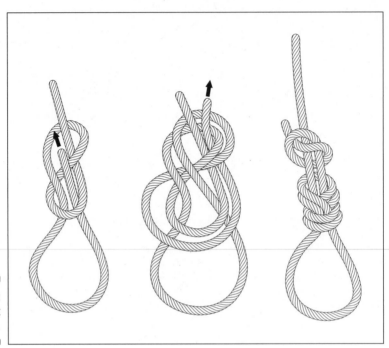

Figure 1-5:
Figure eight
threaded.

Two half hitches and two half hitches slipped

One of the most widely used knots for hanging objects from branches, posts, poles, and so on, the *half hitch* is easy to tie. Here's how:

1. **Wrap the running end of the rope around the object you're securing it to.**

2. **Feed the running end around the standing end and then back up, or through the loop you formed between the pole, post, or branch and the rope.**

    Congratulations! You've just completed one half hitch.

3. **Wrap another loop around the standing end of the rope below the first hitch to create two half hitches (a more secure knot, as shown in Figure 1-6).**

To create a quick-to-untie knot, slip the knot. To do this, create a bight in the running end of the rope and feed the bight through the loop, leaving the last inch or so of the running end sticking out (see Figure 1-7). A quick tug on the running end releases the knot.

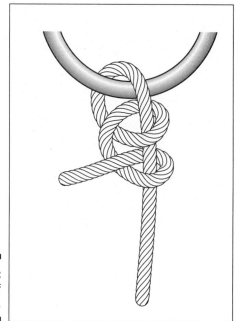

Figure 1-6:
Two half
hitches.

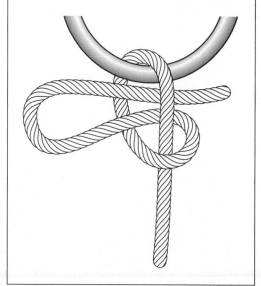

Figure 1-7:
Two half
hitches
slipped.

Round turn and two half hitches

This knot is best used to fasten large items to a roof rack (you can also use the trucker's hitch, described later in this chapter, for that purpose, although that knot isn't as versatile); to secure a boat to a mooring overnight; or to fasten a line to a beam, post, or branch when you want the line to be able to support a heavy load. To form this knot, follow these instructions:

1. **Wrap the running end of the rope around the beam, post, or branch twice.**

2. **Secure the running end to the standing end with two half hitches (see Figure 1-8).**

   Refer to the preceding section for guidance on forming two half hitches.

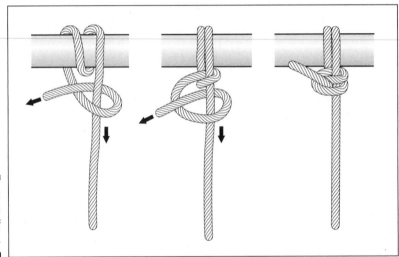

Figure 1-8:
Round turn and two half hitches.

Constrictor knot

People often use the *constrictor knot* (see Figure 1-9) to close sacks and bags whose drawcords have worn out or disappeared. The constrictor knot also works great on the end of a rope to prevent it from unraveling, or as a rope clamp to hold two items firmly together. Here's how to form this handy knot:

1. **Wrap the running end around your desired object once, passing it under the standing end to form one wrap.**

   Be sure to leave this first wrap loose enough to form a slight loop.

2. **Complete a second wrap, this time above the first wrap so that the running end crosses over the standing end.**

   Feed the running end back under itself as you complete this wrap.

3. **Pass the running end up through the loop formed by the first loose wrap and then pull both ends of the rope snug.**

   If you want to be able to easily untie the knot, slip it by putting a bight in the running end. Then pass this bight through the loop formed by your first wrap.

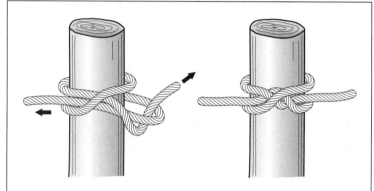

Figure 1-9: Constrictor knot.

Taut line hitch

Probably the most important knot to know for securing lines that tend to loosen or sag over time, such as tent guy lines and clotheslines, the *taut line hitch* (see Figure 1-10) can hold securely in one direction but be easily slid in the other. Consider it a sort of rope ratchet. Follow these instructions to create the taut line hitch:

1. **Wrap the running end of the rope around a tent stake, post, pole, or branch.**

2. **Wrap the running end around the standing end twice (toward the stake, post, pole, or branch) and then make a second wrap.**

3. **Feed the running end of the rope under the standing end above the wraps, around the standing end, and then back through the loop you just formed.**

   The running end should now point away from the stake, post, pole, or branch and toward the standing end.

4. **Pull tightly to secure.**

Book IV

Getting Outdoors

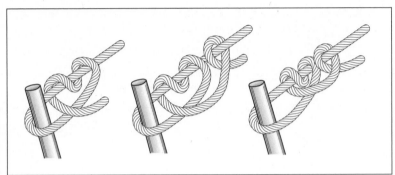

Figure 1-10:
Taut line
hitch.

Trucker's hitch

What person hasn't tied the nightmare knot on a luggage rack or truck bed? You know the one — all twists, tucks, bends, and overlaps with no logic or hope of ever actually untying the thing when you need to release the load. Well, help is at hand. Here's how to tie the *trucker's hitch,* which is really three knots in one (see Figure 1-11).

1. **Start with a bowline or figure eight and tighten, leaving about a loop about 5 inches in diameter below the knot.**

   Refer to earlier sections for guidance on tying a bowline or figure eight knot.

2. **Toss the end of the rope without the bowline or figure eight in it over the item you want to secure and bring it back around.**

3. **Pull the slack out of the rope by holding onto the bowline or figure eight loop.**

4. **Twist the free end of the rope as illustrated, forming a loop.**

5. **Bend the free end of the rope above the loop to form a bight, push the bight through, and give it a quick tug.**

   The quick tug tightens the first loop around the bend, forming a new loop.

6. **Pass the free end through the bowline or figure eight loop and back down through the loop; then pull.**

   As you pull the rope through and it tightens, the loop binds on the rope, securing it under tension. You can secure any load under extreme tension this way.

7. **Tie off the end of the rope (as a final precaution) by using two half hitches slipped.**

See the earlier section for guidance on forming two half hitches slipped.

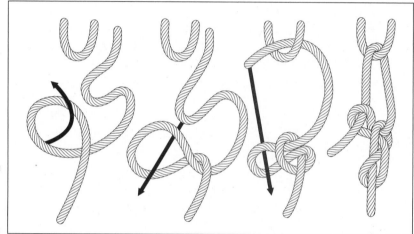

Figure 1-11:
The trucker's
hitch.

Knife Sharpening 101

Numerous guidebooks, articles, and how-to instruction manuals address the importance of knives as tools for outdoorsy folks, yet few also speak about knife sharpening. Why? Doesn't anyone use knives anymore? It's a fact that as a knife blade gets used, it grows dull and less efficient. Perhaps people use their knives until they dull and then buy new ones, although that's doubtful. It stands to reason, then, that if you own a knife, you should also own a sharpening tool, such as a simple Arkansas stone.

Using a sharpening stone

An *Arkansas stone,* a type of sharpening stone, is a relatively thin, 3-inch-long rectangular block of stone that's typically coarse to the touch on one side and fine on the other. A stone is perfectly flat on each side and rough enough — like sandpaper — that you can work out the burrs, knicks, and dull areas of a knife's blade quite easily. The fine side of the Arkansas stone is for finishing your work and putting a nice, smooth edge on your knife.

To sharpen a blade, follow these steps:

1. **Choose the angle you want to achieve.**

   Most pocket knives should be sharpened at a 20- to 25-degree angle. See the next section "Getting a good angle" for help in determining what angle you need.

2. **Smoothly and with even pressure, begin moving the blade in an even, circular motion without lifting it from the stone. Complete several full rotations in a counterclockwise direction first.**

   A circular motion produces the most consistent edge. The closer you maintain a consistent angle throughout the sharpening process, the better the edge you'll achieve. With a little practice, you'll find it's easy to do.

   Count the number of rotations you make! You'll do the other side the same number of times but in the opposite direction.

3. **Turn the blade over and make the same number of smooth, circular motions in a clockwise direction.**

4. **Repeat Steps 2 and 3 until you have the edge you want.**

Some people douse hand stones with oil or water before and during sharpening. The idea is to keep the metal shavings and bits of stone in suspension so they don't clog the sharpening stone and affect its honing efficiency. Yet an increasing number of knife experts recommend that you don't use oil or water on your hand stone. Sharpen your blades dry, and you achieve maximum performance from both the stone and the knife.

A sharpening stone should be flat in order to do its job effectively. However, the grinding process wears a noticeable belly or curvature in sharpening stones over time. You can tune your stones periodically by rubbing them back and forth on 100-grit silicon carbide sandpaper placed on an absolutely flat surface. If after performing this first aid to your stone you still notice a curvature, say good-bye to it and purchase a new one.

Getting a good angle

Contrary to myth, the angle of a blade's cutting edge has nothing to do with sharpness — larger- and smaller-angled cutting edges are equally sharp. The angle at which you choose to sharpen a blade (see Figure 1-12), and consequently the angle to which the cutting edge gets ground, affects the durability and drag of the cutting edge. In other words, the smaller the angle, the less drag, but the more delicate the cutting edge will be. A larger angle means more blade drag but also more durability — less frequent sharpening is required.

Easier sharpening

Is it possible to maintain an exact angle with only a sharpening stone? Yes, but only with lots of practice. A far better solution is to outfit yourself with a knife-sharpening system. With a specially engineered clamp and angle guide, anyone — even a youngster — can precisely sharpen a knife blade to a desired angle. GATCO and Lansky Sharpeners are two of a number of companies offering specialty knife-sharpening systems. Suggested retail prices range from about $40 to $100.

Knife experts recommend the following sharpening angles as a guide:

- ✔ **11 to 15 degrees:** Highly delicate edge for hobby knives, woodcarving tools, and specialty blades. This type of blade requires frequent sharpening.

- ✔ **15 to 17 degrees:** A moderately delicate edge used in fillet, boning, and other thin specialty blades. This type of blade requires frequent sharpening.

- ✔ **17 to 20 degrees:** Common angle for kitchen knives. The frequency of sharpening depends on what you're cutting.

- ✔ **20 to 25 degrees:** Wider bevel and more durable edge intended for pocket knives, folding hunting knives, fixed-blade field knives, and serrated knife blades. These types have a durable and long-lasting cutting edge.

- ✔ **25 to 30 degrees:** Widest bevel and longest lasting of the edges. These types are only intended for heavy-duty use (think utility knives for cutting cardboard, carpet, wire, and linoleum).

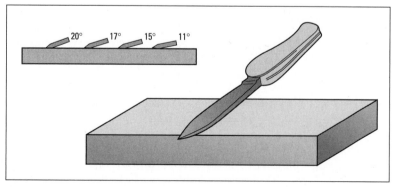

Figure 1-12: Choose a sharpening angle based on how you'll use the blade and how often you want to sharpen it.

Book IV

Getting Outdoors

Building a Campfire Safely and Responsibly

Fires were once necessary for survival, but for the most part, this fact is no longer true. In today's world, people cook with stoves, shed light with lanterns, and provide warmth through shelter and clothing. However, mankind may never shake the romantic appeal of a crackling fire deep in the woods under a star-flecked sky. For those intoxicated with the thrills of adventure, the campfire serves as an after-dark elixir — warmly coaxing forward camaraderie, tall tales, and quiet reflections. The following sections explain how to build a safe, efficient campfire — and how to clean it up when you're ready to move on.

Choosing a site for the fire

When selecting the site for your campfire, pick an area that's free from ground debris, roots, and other vegetation that may catch fire and spread the flame to surrounding trees. Don't build a fire under overhanging tree limbs or within 10 to 15 feet of any shelter. Building a fire in a cave or next to wet or damp rocks is also dangerous because water or moisture in the rocks can be brought to the boiling point, causing steam to expand and explode the rock, much like a bomb.

Try to find an area that has natural wind breaks and clear it of all loose debris. If your campsite has a preexisting fire ring or pit, then use that. Don't build a fire in a new site where a fire ring already exists, even if it isn't in the most ideal location aesthetically.

Selecting firewood

Pick the right kind of firewood, and your campfire will not only burn brightly and warmly but also with less smoke and greater cooking efficiency. Remember that every fire starts with patience and kindling — not necessarily in that order. Your kindling should be made up of very small, dry twigs that, when lit using a firestarter, will catch fire quickly and help to start the flame eating into the larger wood.

Each type of wood has its own special characteristics that lend themselves to particular types of fires. If you know how to identify various trees and the deadwood lying around them, you'll soon be building fires that are the envy of everyone.

Following are some important characteristics to remember when choosing your firewood:

- **Aspen** is moderately difficult to ignite, has fair cooking characteristics, throws off a moderate number of sparks, produces very little smoke, and adds nice flavor to fish and meat.

- **Birch** is very easy to ignite, has fair cooking characteristics, throws off a moderate number of sparks, produces moderate amounts of smoke, and adds nice flavor to fish and meat.

- **Fir** is very easy to ignite, has poor cooking characteristics, throws off large quantities of sparks, produces heavy smoke, and isn't advised for cooking.

- **Maple** is difficult to ignite, has excellent cooking characteristics, throws off very few sparks, produces very little smoke, and adds a very nice flavor to fish and meat.

- **Oak** is difficult to ignite, has excellent cooking characteristics, throws off very few sparks, produces very little smoke, and adds a nice, subtle flavor to fish and meat.

- **Pine** is very easy to ignite, has poor cooking characteristics, throws off large quantities of sparks, produces heavy smoke, and isn't advised for cooking.

- **Spruce** is very easy to ignite, has poor cooking characteristics, throws off large quantities of sparks, produces heavy smoke, and isn't advised for cooking.

Gathering firewood responsibly

Let the following tips guide you as you choose firewood:

- **Never cut down trees or branches, living or apparently dead.** To do so can cause irreparable harm to the tree and disrupt an available habitat for animals. And it's illegal in most regions anyway.

- **Select only wood that's 1 to 2 inches in diameter and lying broken on the ground.** (Figure 1-13 gives you an idea of sizes.) This wood is more readily consumed by the flames, resulting in hotter coals and a better fire for cooking and heating.

- **Always gather your wood away from camp.** Doing so helps to prevent immediate depletion of vital wood resources lying around the camp area.

Book IV

Getting Outdoors

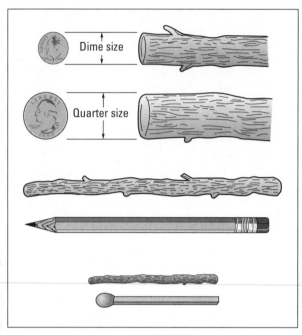

Figure 1-13:
Twig size
guide.

Constructing the fire

Every campfire must be constructed in some way. In the case of both drive-in and backcountry campgrounds, where *fire rings* (circles of rocks that enclose fire sites to prevent embers and coals from scattering) or designated fire pits already exist, your fire-building tasks are limited to constructing a fire that provides hot coals for cooking or flames for warming.

If a fire site or location doesn't exist and the area you're camping in permits the building of fires, then you need to construct a place to start your fire. You can see descriptions for building mound fires or pit fires, and also using a fire pan, later in this chapter. In all cases, be sure to build a fire that's small enough to be easily scattered after the coals are cool and then covered over or removed before you leave. Why? So that the next person who follows in your steps can experience the joy of discovering a wild place without finding evidence of your passing.

Because you have to clean up the campfire when you're done, stop adding wood to the flames approximately one hour before finishing the fire. Keep pushing the partially burned pieces of larger wood into the center or hottest coals of the fire. You may find that you need to add very small pieces of

---

Creative fire-starting materials

Sure, you can light a fire with one match, but pack along some home-remedy kindling and some waterproof matches anyway. Why? Because they'll light the fire when things don't go exactly according to plan — like when Mother Nature opens the fire hose on your camp and douses your fire-building plans. Try carrying a lighter and an old plastic film canister filled with wooden strike-anywhere matches. As for starting materials, here are a few ideas to get the flames roaring in no time:

✔ Commercial firestarters such as fire ribbon or petroleum-based tablets (Esbit by MPI Outdoors, for example) work very well.

✔ Fill each hole of an old egg carton with shredded newspaper and several spoonfuls of sawdust. Pour in melted *paraffin* (wax) to bind the sawdust and newspaper into a solid lump. After the wax hardens, you have one dozen wax-based firestarters.

✔ Fill a film canister with lint from your drier. (Make sure that the lint comes from wool, cotton, and fleece and not fire-retardant fabrics.)

✔ Look to nature. Even in the worst storm, you can find dry tinder around the base of tree trunks, under rock ledges, in tree hollows, and next to downed logs.

✔ Make your own kindling from a larger log that's soaked on the outside but dry on the inside by whittling down to the dry center. Whittle dry shavings from this piece.

---

wood, twigs, and the like, to keep the fire hot enough to consume any larger sections of wood. Also, because cleaning up a fire immediately after you've doused the flames is infinitely more difficult, don't build a campfire in the morning. For info on cleaning up your campfire, head to the later section "Cleaning up your fire."

Teepee fire

The teepee fire, shown in Figure 1-14, is the very best fire for quick lighting, even in severe weather. It puts out a tremendous amount of heat, even with a relatively small fire, and is quite easy to maintain.

Follow these steps to build a teepee fire:

1. **Bunch up a ball of frayed bark, dried grasses, and tiny twigs from a pine tree, evergreen, or other available tree, along with your fire-starting materials (if you have them).**

2. **Lay very small twigs and sticks — not much larger than the kindling — against one another and over the ball to form a teepee shape.**

   Leave a small opening through which you can place a match to ignite the fire.

Book IV

Getting Outdoors

3. **Continue adding more wood, gradually longer and thicker (up to the width of two fingers).**

   Maintain the shape of a teepee at all times.

4. **After the teepee is built to your satisfaction, carefully strike a match, shield it from the wind, and place it next to the waiting ball of kindling to ignite it.**

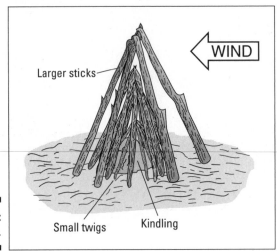

Figure 1-14: Teepee fire.

When adding wood, lay each piece carefully into the flame and always keep the shape of the teepee intact. Don't toss or arbitrarily throw wood on a fire because at best doing so sends up a shower of sparks, creating a fire and safety hazard, and at worst it can destroy the fire.

Pit fire

Use a pit fire (see Figure 1-15) only where ground vegetation won't be damaged or where there are only a few inches of underlying *duff* (the dead layer of leaves, plants, and needles covering the forest floor). You make a pit fire by digging a shallow hole where the mineral soil is exposed and the duff is cleared away, making cleanup easier and dramatically reducing the chance of starting a forest fire.

To build a pit fire, simply follow these instructions:

1. **Scrape away all the duff, exposing the mineral soil underneath.**

   Clear an area larger than the fire you intend to build.

2. **Create a shallow pit that's wider than your fire and several inches deep.**

   Use a small backpacking trowel or your hands to create the pit and be sure to save the earth you've removed because when the fire is out, you want to return the earth to cover up the evidence of your passing.

3. **Build your fire in the pit, keeping it small and efficient and never allowing it to grow larger than the pit you've constructed.**

   To build your fire, follow the directions for the teepee fire in the preceding section.

Figure 1-15:
Pit fire.

Mound fire

Mound fires are ideal when you can find suitable mineral soil that can be dug without disturbing the natural area (see Figure 1-16). Streambeds and sandy areas around boulders are great mineral soil sources.

Figure 1-16:
Mound fire.

Follow these steps to build a mound fire:

1. **Choose a large flat rock that's either portable or immobile, or create a rock base by placing two or more relatively flat rocks side by side.**

2. **Spread soil at least 3 inches deep on top of the rock base, creating a wide platform that's larger than the area the fire will use — 2 to $2^1/_2$ feet wide is usually sufficient.**

   You can use a trowel and one of your cook pots to gather and spread the soil. Just be sure to wash out the cook pot before using it for its intended purpose.

3. **Build a small and efficient fire directly on top of the mineral soil, making sure that it never grows larger than the base of soil on top of the rocks.**

   To build the fire, follow the directions for the teepee fire earlier in this chapter.

Fire pan

Although common with river runners, fire pans are gaining popularity with other wilderness adventurers (see Figure 1-17). Certainly, the prospect of lugging an iron fire pan in a backpack isn't an inviting thought; however, many lighter alternatives are out there.

Figure 1-17:
Fire pan.

The following steps explain how to build a fire in a fire pan:

1. **Place the fire pan on a layer of small rocks or line it with mineral soil so the heat won't scorch the earth.**

   Your fire pan can be a pie-sized aluminum pan or a store-bought, manufactured pan.

   Instead of using mineral soil, you can lay several 3-foot-long strips of heavy-gauge aluminum foil side by side with a 1-inch overlap. You can also retire an old aluminum space blanket and fold it into a 3-foot-by-3-foot square.

2. **Cover the aluminum with several inches of mineral soil.**

   This step stops the heat from damaging the fire pan or scorching the earth beneath it.

3. **Build a small and efficient fire directly on top of the soil, never allowing it to grow beyond the boundaries of the fire pan or foil barrier.**

   To build your fire, follow the directions for the teepee fire earlier in the chapter.

Cleaning up your fire

Nothing should be left in the fire ring but ashes. No trash. No unburned wood. No bits of the dinner you didn't eat. In addition, you need to make sure that the fire is truly out —meaning no hot embers are left — and that the site looks like it did (or better) when you leave.

Dousing embers

If you need to add water to douse any embers, do so slowly and sprinkle it on instead of soaking the fire and surrounding soil. Speed up the process by stirring the coals while sprinkling additional water until the embers are out and the fire is cold.

When you think all the embers are out, check the fire for live embers by carefully placing your palm near, then on, the fire site. (If the fire is still smoking, don't touch it. Sizzling flesh isn't a good indicator of an extinguished fire.) If, as you place your hand near and then on the ashes, you don't sense heat, stir the ashes carefully and look for hot embers again. If you still see none, then carefully sift through the ashes with your fingers. Again, if you don't feel any warmth, the fire may be declared dead.

Spreading the ashes

After the fire is cold, crush any large lumps of charcoal. Spread the ashes and crushed charcoal away from the site, leaving no sign of your campfire. Also, pick out any food or other trash remnants. Burying or scattering fire-blackened or charred trash with your fire's ashes isn't appropriate.

Returning the site to its original condition

If you had to build the fire site, be sure to fill in the pit, scatter the mound, or fold up and carry out the fire pan. Rinse off the rock from the mound fire before placing it back in its natural setting. Camouflage evidence of your campfire with duff. If the fire ring already existed when you arrived, leave it assembled after cleaning up the ashes and trash.

When you discover multiple fire rings at a single campsite, do the land a favor and dismantle all but one — pick the one in the safest location and in a spot that appears to have the least impact upon the ground or surrounding area. When dismantling fire rings, place any fire-blackened rocks blackened side down and camouflage them. Take the time to carefully scatter the ashes from the dismantled rings, pick out the trash, and camouflage the sites.

Basic Survival Skills

Fear and panic are by far the greatest dangers to any human being in the outdoors. Although natural acts and other unforeseeable circumstances claim injuries and lives each year, most deaths and injuries can be prevented by staying calm and thinking a situation through. Staying calm isn't so easy to do, however, if you have only limited knowledge or information upon which to draw to help you in times of crisis. That's why developing basic wilderness skills that can help you in the event of an emergency is so important. The key is to know how to stay oriented, how to find shelter, and how to find water — all covered in the following sections.

Examining the art of staying found

When Daniel Boone was asked whether he was ever lost, his reply was, "Disoriented for a couple of days, maybe. Lost, never." The major difference between Mr. Boone and the majority of weekend wilderness explorers is skill. Mr. Boone could always hunt, trap, find water, build a shelter, make a boat, and gradually find his way out of most predicaments. The average family, however, has neither the acquired wilderness skills to survive off the land nor the time to spend wandering aimlessly.

Before venturing into the great outdoors, you must realize that anyone can get lost. All it takes to disorient most people outdoors is a dense mist, a few unplanned turns in the woods, nightfall, or a storm. The so-called instinctive "sense of direction" is only as good as the information used to create that sense.

Staying aware of your surroundings

A good sense of direction comes from keeping your senses wide open to all sources of information — sights, sounds, smells, and even feelings. Teach yourself to be aware of significant landmarks such as a tall tree, a prominent rock, or a large meadow. Practice looking in 360-degree sweeps — check out the route you're traveling from the front, side, and back. Quite often, a tree that looked so unique and significant in one direction looks completely different when viewed from another.

Sounds like a rushing river, cars on a road, and a lighthouse's foghorn are also important bits of info. Don't overlook the smell and feel of an area, either. A valley may feel damp and smell a certain way. Water can quite often be smelled from a distance. Individually, each of the senses contains a fragment of information to help you stay found. Combine all these fragments into careful and complete observations, and you begin to create a good sense of direction.

Teach your children about the area you're going into as well. Because most children find topographic maps confusing and impossible to understand, try drawing a special map for them instead. Show them where major landmarks, roads, and water sources are; how the trail looks; where you plan to camp; and where some of the nearby towns are.

Knowing what to do if you become lost

I'm lost! That initial moment of panic surges through the human mind and body like a runaway train. If not controlled, the body soon follows the urge to act like a runaway train and very often takes off plowing through bushes, trees — anything — in a desperate effort to be found. This type of panic is all too common and can lead to further disorientation, complete exhaustion, dehydration, injury, and even death. So instead of going off in a panic, take these actions:

> ✔ **Sit and think.** Lost people usually wind up in deeper trouble when they panic and begin frantically attempting to find their way back to home or camp. If you take the time to sit down and think carefully, a solution usually becomes evident. Look around painstakingly, retracing your steps in your mind. Very often, after some calm thinking, you can discover the trail or route home.

Book IV

Getting Outdoors

REMEMBER

It's critical for your children to understand the importance of staying in one place if they have no idea where they are. Wandering children make for extremely difficult rescues.

✔ **Explore methodically.** Sometimes the route home isn't clearly evident, and you may feel a need to get up and explore the surrounding area in search of a trail. This approach is okay if you can accurately mark the area you're now standing in so that you can return to it after the initial search. From that original sit-down point, you can begin working your way outward in a circular pattern until you discover a familiar piece of ground or terrain. While working your way out in this circular fashion, always keep your original starting position in sight.

From each familiar point that you discover, establish another landmark that now identifies this area and repeat the process. Essentially, you move from familiar point to familiar point and mark your progress along the way. After you discover a trail or road that's recognizable, you can then head out in a straight line toward home or help.

Seeking shelter

If you're really lost and have no clue in which direction home or camp lies, then finding shelter should be your priority. Although small caves, *deadfalls* (fallen dead trees), hollow logs, and eroded overhangs appear to be good shelters in warm and sunny weather, these natural shelters often aren't ideal. At best, natural enclosures usually can provide only temporary refuge, and at worst, they can become death traps.

Sheltering naturally

With any shelter you look for or build, your primary considerations should be wind protection, rain or snow protection, and heat retention.

✔ **Wind protection:** Protecting yourself from the wind is extremely important because a strong wind coupled with rain can cause your body to lose heat rapidly — you can die of hypothermia even if the air temperatures is 50 degrees. Wind also rapidly increases the body's rate of dehydration. Protection from wind is the easiest kind of protection to find, because almost anything — a fallen log, a dense bush, or a large rock — can protect you from the sides and break the wind.

✔ **Rain or snow protection:** Rain or snow protection is more difficult to find because your shelter must provide protection from above as well as from the sides. Dense bushes, thick brush piles from logging road construction, downed trees, natural caves, and large rock piles are all candidates for a natural shelter that will protect you from rain and snow.

> ✔ **Heat retention:** Most natural shelters can't provide the third important criterion for shelter selection — heat retention. To add that, you need to gather dead leaves, twigs, and grasses to line and stuff the natural shelter you select to help you stay warm.

Natural shelters can be dangerous, and you must know how to identify the dangers. Deadfalls, rock piles, and caves are all potential homes to a variety of animals and insects. You must take care not to suddenly disturb a nest of bees, a poisonous snake, or a bear. Perhaps even more dangerous is the possibility that the natural shelter could collapse at any moment, trapping you inside or underneath something heavy. Be very cautious around deadfalls. Where one tree has fallen, more may be ready to tumble, given a strong enough wind.

Another possible hazard of a natural shelter is that it camouflages whatever is in it very well. If you use a natural shelter, leave some sign outside the shelter that you're there. This sign should be somewhat obvious and visible enough so that snow or debris falling on the ground won't obscure it.

Building your shelter

Building a shelter is perhaps the best way to stay warm, dry, and secure, and a constructed shelter stands out from the surrounding environment unlike the natural shelters described in the preceding section. Although many survival books teach you to a build lean-to, A-frame, igloo, and even cabin, the quickest and most efficient shelter to create is one that uses only available material lying on the forest floor and requires no tools to build. Anyone, even a child, can construct this shelter in about 90 minutes by following these steps:

1. **Pick an area that has good drainage, isn't going to get washed away, and won't get buried under a falling tree or avalanche of rocks.**

   Make absolutely certain that the area you've selected isn't over an animal hole, an ant's nest, or a thicket of poison oak, ivy, or sumac.

2. **At the shelter site, find a large rock, stump, log, or other support.**

   Logs or downed trees can work as one wall, but downed trees with large enough trunks aren't always present. Ideally, the log or rock support should be about 3 feet high.

3. **Find a large stick several inches across and approximately 5 feet long — or longer if the person using the shelter is taller.**

4. **Lean one end of the stick on the rock, log, or stump so that the other end rests on the ground, forming a ridgepole for your shelter.**

Book IV

Getting Outdoors

5. **Collect a large number of smaller sticks to lean along each side of the ridgepole, creating a frame for your shelter.**

   Remember to leave the opening or door to the front and one side, facing away from the wind.

6. **Crawl inside the shelter, making sure you have enough room to lie down comfortably so that you don't kick or otherwise disturb the sides when moving about.**

7. **Pile twigs, dried leaves, and small branches on top of the framework you've built.**

   Create a generous layer of leaves and twigs — approximately 2 to 3 feet thick is appropriate.

8. **On top of that layer, add a snug layer of small branches and twigs that's heavy enough to help hold the inner layer in place, even in a strong wind.**

   Don't make this additional layer so heavy that it crushes or compresses the leaves and twigs making up the inner lining.

9. **Stuff the inside of the shelter full of dried leaves, pine needles, ferns, and so on, so that the interior is loosely filled from top to bottom.**

10. **With the shelter now complete, squirm and snuggle inside, feet first.**

    This type of shelter will keep an adult or child warm and dry for days, even in the worst conditions.

Finding water

Dehydration is a killer. Therefore, finding water is second only to finding shelter in the scale of importance for survival situations. With a good shelter and a water supply, a person can survive for a very long time, even without food. That said, be wary of any water you come across. Most water on Earth today is polluted to some degree. Chemical or biological pollutants can turn a very basic survival situation into a critical emergency. For this reason, water must be treated or purified to be considered safe.

Treating the water

Water can be treated in several ways. The boiling method is the best guarantee of purification because it destroys all biological pollutants. If you have a pot or cup with you, build a fire and bring the water to a rolling boil to purify it.

Another water-treatment method is filtering, but filtering in a survival situation doesn't remove most dangerous pollutants. Also, most folks aren't usually carrying a commercial filter with them when they find themselves in a survival situation. To filter very muddy or debris-filled water, pour the water through a bandanna or other piece of cotton clothing so that particles are filtered out.

Chemical purification works very well in removing biological but not chemical impurities. Products made of iodine such as Potable Aqua or Polar Pure are easy to use and very effective chemical treatments for water. If you camp with children, teach them how to use these products properly and safely. If your child carries a compact survival kit with him or her, include a bottle of Potable Aqua in it.

Discovering water

You can either find water or create it. The easiest way to get water is to discover a stream or moving water source. Moving water is the least likely to be polluted. Tree stumps, potholes, and stagnant ponds are other water sources, but they're typically the most likely to be dangerously polluted. Sometimes, digging down into a damp streambed uncovers a water source that will regularly fill the hole. You can even obtain water from dew-soaked leaves and grasses. Instead of crawling around licking the leaves, soak up moisture with a cotton cloth and then squeeze out the water into your mouth. As a last resort, you can opt to create water using the solar-still method explained in the next section.

Making a solar still

Water distillation using a solar still is a method of creating water where none is evident. This method requires a large plastic sheet, a cup, and a length of plastic tubing (see Figure 1-18). Knowing how to create a water-distillation system is very useful, and the water is pure.

Follow these steps to set up a solar still:

1. **Find an area that's damp or located in a dry streambed or at the bottom of a gully, and dig a hole about 2 feet deep and 3 feet across.**

   The earth you're digging in should be damp near the bottom. However, if the dirt is dry, drop in green leaves, urinate in the hole, or add a small amount of water to provide moisture for condensation.

2. **Place a cup in the center of the hole and rest one end of the plastic tubing in the bottom of the cup.**

3. **Cover the hole with the clear plastic sheet, leaving the other end of the plastic tube protruding out to one side.**

4. **Seal the edges with dirt so that no moisture can escape and no air can get in the hole.**

Book IV

Getting Outdoors

5. **Weight down the center of the plastic sheet with a rock so that the point of the inverted cone is directly above the cup.**

The sun, even on a hazy or partly cloudy day, will warm the earth and cause moisture from the soil in the hole to evaporate and condense on the underside of the plastic. The condensation rolls down the plastic and drips off the weighted end into the cup. You'll be able to drink out of the cup by using the plastic tube sticking out of one side of the plastic sheet. This method works well, and the condensation or distilled water is pure, even if the moisture source is not (for example, if the moisture source is urine or badly polluted water).

Figure 1-18:
The water from a solar still is pure. (Drinking tube not shown.)

Chapter 2

Map and Navigation Basics

*W*hy do people get lost? For many reasons, and the majority are completely avoidable. The most common mistake is not packing a map and compass because you're "just going out for a quick hike on a clearly marked trail." All you have to do is be daydreaming or chatting with your hiking partners to walk off one trail and onto another, completely unaware. Another mistake is lack of preparation. You can imagine the routine — the trip is on so you grab a map, toss the compass in the pack, and go, with no forethought or map homework. Yet another reason for getting lost is trusting your partner, who may be just as hopelessly lost as you are.

Everyone who wants to safely enjoy the great outdoors should master basic navigational skills and be able to use them. An amazing number of people dutifully carry a map and shiny new compass, yet have absolutely no idea where they are, where they're heading, or where they came from. Sure, packing a topographic map and a compass fulfill the "be prepared" mandate, but what good are they if you don't know how to use them? You may as well bring a world atlas or road map — they'll be as much help as a topographic map in the backcountry if you don't have basic map and compass skills.

The art of staying found involves not only using your head and remaining observant (topics covered in Book IV, Chapter 1) but also applying map and compass skills properly. This chapter delves into those skills in detail.

Reading a Map

A *topographic map* is a one-dimensional representation of a three-dimensional environment. Cartographers create the three dimensions by using contour lines to show where hills, mountains, valleys, and canyons are located (see

Figure 2-1). A trained eye can look at a flat map with all the contour lines and see valleys, mountains, ridges, and more. The following sections give you the skills you need to unlock a map's hidden treasures and, yes, even to fold one like a pro.

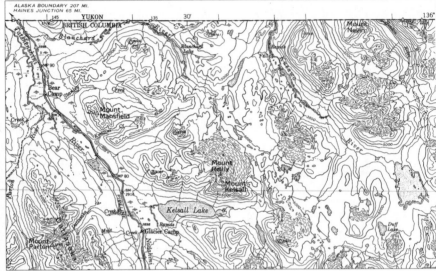

Figure 2-1:
Portion of a topographic map with contour lines at 500-foot intervals.

Because a map can provide only so much info, a complete picture of how easy or difficult a particular terrain is to negotiate may not be evident until you're actually attempting to navigate it. Never forget that a map is but a tool — not the gospel on what you may or may not encounter.

Familiarizing yourself with standard map colors and symbols

Topographic maps are printed in color, with different colors indicating different objects.

- **Green:** Forested or vegetated areas
- **White:** Open terrain
- **Brown:** Contour or elevation lines
- **Blue:** Water, as a lake, river, or stream
- **Black:** Man-made features such as trails, roads, and buildings

Man-made features on topographic maps should always be suspect, even on privately printed maps that claim to be up-to-date. Why? Because a building that existed when the map was printed may have vanished due to fire, weather, flood, or other reasons. Or the sole building that was there when the map was printed may have grown into a suburb of many buildings.

Many other symbols are used to depict such things as mines, ghost towns, marshes, swamps, waterfalls, and caves. The key to these symbols doesn't appear on the map but on a separate sheet that you can obtain for free from the United States Geological Survey (USGS). Phone 888-ASK-USGS (888-275-8747) or go online (`ask.usgs.gov`) for information.

Seeing in 3-D when looking at a map

Translating the one-dimensional image printed on a map into a three-dimensional representation of the world takes practice. Fortunately, topographic maps are designed to add height and depth to a flat picture. Figure 2-2, for example, shows a topographic map of a twin-peaked mountain, plus four two-dimensional views.

Have patience and take heart — seeing 3-D on a flat map isn't as difficult as it may appear at first. Think about it this way:

✔ Widely spaced contour lines indicate a gradual slope.

✔ The more packed the contour lines are together, the steeper and more severe the terrain. Closely spaced contour lines may mean a cliff.

✔ Contour lines that roughly form circles, each getting smaller in size with each gain in elevation, indicate hills or mountain peaks. A summit is often marked with an *X*, with a number printed next to it indicating the exact elevation of that peak.

✔ Contour lines that bend into a V (the V may look more like a U if the terrain is sloping very gently) represent a canyon, valley, or sloping ridge. If the V is pointing uphill, toward a point of higher elevation, then it's forming a canyon. If the V is pointing downhill, toward a point of lower elevation, then it forms a ridge. It stands to reason then that a stream in a V would indicate that the V is a canyon and points toward higher points of elevation.

✔ V-shaped valleys on a map are typically steep and more difficult to navigate. On extremely pronounced V shapes, expect the sidewalls of the canyon to be steep and almost impossible to scramble up or down. If you're on the canyon floor, you'll probably be there to stay until you exit either upstream or downstream. U-shaped valleys, on the other hand, are far more gentle and easier to navigate through.

Book IV

Getting Outdoors

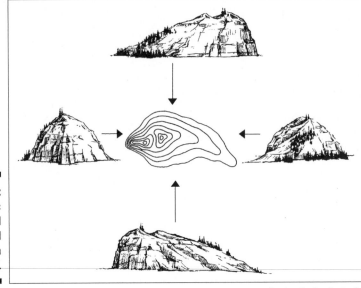

Courtesy Jon Cox, Brunton Co.

Figure 2-2:
Topographic
maps add
height and
depth to a
flat picture.

Aside from telling you how steep the terrain is, the interval between contour lines alerts you to something else. Consider a map with a contour interval of 50 feet. This interval means the cartographer drew a contour line on the map for every 50 feet of elevation change up or down. But what this also means is that the map may not include some pretty impressive stuff — like that 30-foot-high chunk of rock you see ahead, or a 35-foot cliff or 25-foot-deep wash. The reason these objects don't show up is simply that they're all smaller in scale than 50-foot up/down intervals.

Ensuring you have the right map

Obviously, you want to make sure you're using the right map for the area you're in. Fortunately, every map features info about what area it covers. On a USGS map, this area info appears in two places: in the lower-left corner and in the upper-right corner along the white border that surrounds the map. The United States is divided into quadrants based on lines of latitude and longitude, and each quadrant most often carries the name of a significant geographical feature or municipality falling within the quadrant's boundaries.

USGS maps print adjoining map information along their borders so that you can effectively link maps of the same series and scale. Typically, the names of corresponding and adjoining maps are printed at each corner, one at each side, and one at both the top and bottom of the map. You can also find a silhouette picture of the region the map series covers, divided into equal quadrants — the map you're using will be the shaded one. This way you can see where the map fits into the entire region's mapping picture and how many adjoining maps you may require to navigate across it.

Grasping a map's scale

The USGS prints its maps in what are known as *series* (7.5-minute, 15-minute, and so on). Although you can still find 15-minute series maps, the USGS publishes mostly 7.5-minute series maps these days.

The Earth is divided into 180 degrees of latitude, displayed as horizontal lines running east-to-west on map and 360 degrees of longitude displayed as vertical lines connecting the poles running around the globe. Degrees of latitude are measured from 0 degrees at the equator to 90 degrees the poles – 90 degrees north for the north pole or 90 degrees south for the south pole. Degrees of longitude are measured 180 degrees to the east and 180 degrees to the west of the prime meridian.

In navigational terms, minutes and seconds have absolutely nothing to do with time and everything to do with a unit of distance measurement. A 7.5-minute series map represents an area of the Earth's surface that is 7.5 minutes (one eighth of a degree) of longitude wide by 7.5 minutes (one eighth of a degree) of latitude high.

Waterproofing a map

Making a see-through, waterproof cover for your maps is an easy way to prevent your much-needed navigational tools from turning into shredded piles of unreadable mush when the weather turns damp — and you know it will at some point. All you need is a large, freezer-weight, zip-top bag and a few sections of sturdy, waterproof tape, such as duct or packing tape.

Simply cut the tape into a strip long enough to completely adhere to one sealed edge of the bag from top to bottom. Press one half of the tape, lengthwise, onto the side edge of the bag, leaving the other half of the tape hanging over the edge. Now flip the bag over and fold the tape down on the other side of the bag. Repeat each step twice more, once for the bottom and

once for the remaining side. You now have a wonderful waterproof map container that's reinforced on three edges.

Some other ways to protect a map from water include

✔ Painting on a product called Stormproof, or other map-waterproofing treatments by Aquaseal or Nikwax, available at most map and outdoor specialty stores. The clear chemical coating renders maps waterproof, flexible, and able to be written on.

✔ Using a coating of Thompson Water Seal or another brick and masonry sealant to make a map water-repellent, but not waterproof.

Book IV

Getting Outdoors

In a typical 7.5-minute map, the scale is 1:24,000, which means that one unit of measurement on the map equals 24,000 units of the same measurement full-sized. In a 1:24,000 scale map, 1 inch equals about $^1/_8$ of a mile, or nearly 2,000 feet. At the bottom of most maps is a bar scale that allows you to make to-scale measurements that correspond to foot, mile, or kilometer distances.

Although the bar scale printed at the bottom of your map is a straight line, most trails never remain straight for more than several hundred yards. And trails have a nasty habit of gaining and losing elevation, so although a trail line on a map may look like 1 mile, you may clock several miles as you hike it. Still, measuring your route somewhat accurately does allow you to plan your trip with some idea of how long it will take.

Using either red or white narrow-gauge electrical wire is a great way to measure distance on a map because electrical wire (the kind used in model building, that is) is very flexible, holds its shape, doesn't stretch, and can be marked with an indelible ink marker. Follow these steps:

1. **Cut a 12-inch section of the wire, and mark $^1/_4$ and 1-mile increments on it with a fine-tipped, indelible black ink marker.**

    Using dots for the $^1/_4$-mile marks and a complete band around the wire for the 1-mile marks works best. Be sure to meticulously match your marks to those on the map's bar scale.

2. **Place one end of the wire at your starting point and then gradually bend and contour the wire to match the twists and bends of your trail or route of travel (see Figure 2-3).**

    After you're done bending and contouring, you can count up the miles and determine just how far your planned route is, how far it may be to your estimated rest points, and how far it is to points of scenic interest, water, and so on.

Determining latitude and longitude

Degrees of latitude and longitude are indicated in the corners of most maps. Reading up from the bottom-left or bottom-right corner of a map, black ticks and/or fine black lines indicate changes in minutes and seconds of latitude (explained in the preceding section). Latitude in the Northern Hemisphere (north of the equator) increases as you move north and toward the top of the map. Black ticks and/or fine black lines indicate changes in minutes and seconds of longitude when reading from the bottom-right or top-right corner of a map. Longitude in North America increases as you go west.

Photo by Brian Drumm

Figure 2-3:
Measuring
trail dis-
tance with
a piece of
electrical
wire.

Folding a map

A properly folded map — yes, there is such a thing (see Figure 2-4) — makes opening and closing your map a simple matter, even in windy weather. Further, the accordion configuration collapses to pocket size with ease. After you establish the creases, any map folds up and down almost without effort.

1. **Lay the map flat, printed side up.**

2. **Fold it in half vertically, with the printing inside the first fold, and establish the first crease.**

   Make this and every subsequent crease clean and sharp.

3. **Open the map back up, and working with only the right half of the map, fold the right side in half toward the center, resulting in quarter-folds.**

4. **Fold the outside quarter-fold back to the edge, producing an eighth-fold. Use this fold as a guide and fold the other quarter the same way.**

   Half the map should now have four accordion-style folds.

Book IV

**Getting
Outdoors**

5. **Repeat Steps 2 through 4 on the map's other half.**

   You should end up with a full accordion of eight folds in a long shape like a ruler.

6. **Fold the map in the shape of a Z so it's in thirds.**

   Voilá! Now you can look at any section without having to completely unfold the map, and it snaps into place almost by itself.

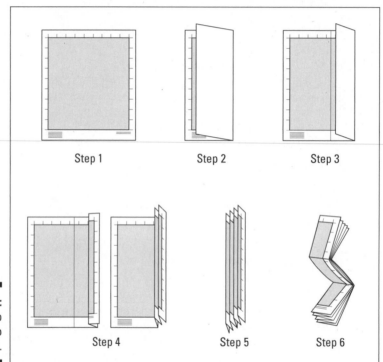

Figure 2-4:
How to
fold a map
properly.

Step 1   Step 2   Step 3

Step 4   Step 5   Step 6

Compasses: A Primer

A compass is a mechanical device that uses the Earth's magnetic field as a directional aid. The idea is that, by knowing where north is, you can figure out the other directions and find your way to wherever you want to go. With a compass, you can plot a course, stay on course, determine the location of a landmark or destination point, or follow a course outline by a guidebook or a friend.

Buying a compass

When you're considering buying a compass, look for the following basic features (at minimum):

- ✔ Rotating bezel or azimuth ring with a 360-degree dial in 2-degree graduations (see the later section "Understanding compass parts" for descriptions of these parts)
- ✔ A clear baseplate with inch and millimeter scales
- ✔ A direction-of-travel arrow engraved into the baseplate
- ✔ A rotating magnetic needle mounted in a clear capsule filled with liquid to reduce shake and movement
- ✔ Orienting lines engraved or printed onto the bottom of the rotating capsule

Figure 2-5 shows the basic features of a compass. Additional features, such as a sighting mirror (making it a *prismatic* compass), built-in adjustable declination, clinometers, and a magnifying glass add to a compass's cost but are very useful if you plan to become serious about your navigational skills.

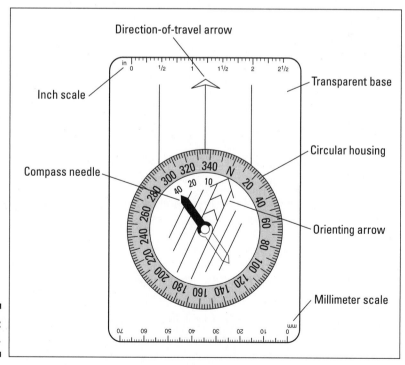

Figure 2-5: Compass.

If you can, purchase a compass that has a declination-adjustment feature built in — it costs $20 or so but is well worth it.

Defining declination

Declination is simply the difference between true north, which is what all maps are based on, and magnetic north, which is what all magnetic needles point toward. In a perfect world, they'd be the same, but in reality, magnetic north and true north are often very different. For example, using a compass as your guide, if you ignore declination on a simple 2-mile hike from your car to a nice lakeside campsite, you could end up in a valley several thousand yards away!

Declination is either west or east depending on which side of true north the compass needle points. On USGS topographic maps, arrows printed on the bottom margin of the map indicate declination. The arrow with a star above it indicates true north. The shorter arrow with "MN" above it indicates magnetic north. If the MN arrow is on the left side of the true north arrow, declination is west, and you need to add the indicated degree amount to correct your bearing. If the MN arrow is on the right side of the true north arrow, declination is east, and you need to subtract the indicated degree amount to correct your bearing.

If you have a compass with the declination adjustment feature built in, the compass makes these adjustments for you automatically. You just have to turn a screw or adjust the housing once for the compass to read true. Of course, you also have to remember that each time declination changes, often from map to map, you need to manually adjust the compass to the new setting.

Understanding compass parts

Besides a needle and a big N, how complicated can a compass be? Oh, not very, but some parts, including features that come into play every time you take a bearing and set a course, warrant further explanation.

- ✔ **Azimuth ring (housing):** The circular housing with textured edges, often liquid-filled, that rotates within the compass base for taking or setting bearings. Degree markings, from 0 to 360, are typically etched into its surface, making up the azimuth ring or graduated dial.

- ✔ **Gun-type sights:** Most often found on *prismatic* (sighting) compasses and used like the sights on a gun for sighting and taking bearings with maximum accuracy.

- ✔ **Index line:** The mark on the front of the sight or compass baseplate where you read the indicated bearing.

✔ **Line of travel or direction of travel:** A line or arrow engraved on the compass's baseplate that points you in the direction you need to go to reach your desired destination.

✔ **Liquid damping:** Liquid damping allows the needle to come to rest rapidly and helps to hold the needle steady, allowing for faster and more accurate readings. Compasses without liquid damping leave the user waiting for what seems a lifetime for the needle to stop spinning — and squinting to determine which point the bouncy needle is actually pointing to. The better compasses use a kerosene-based fluid or some other additive to ensure the liquid doesn't freeze or boil from –40 degrees to 120 degrees.

✔ **Mirror:** Incorporated into a hard-case lid that folds down over the top of the compass housing, the mirror is used to make prismatic in-line sightings, the most accurate method of using a hand-held compass. A prismatic compass allows you to hold the compass at eye level, sighting both the distant object through the gun-type sight and the compass face at the same time.

✔ **Orienting arrow:** The outlined arrow engraved into the base of a compass housing and often lined with red paint. The arrow is made to exactly outline the outside of the magnetic needle. By centering or *boxing* the magnetic needle within the orienting arrow's outline, both pointing in the same direction (unless back-sighting), you can determine your bearing or direction of travel.

✔ **Protractor:** A feature that allows you to more easily plot a bearing on a map.

✔ **Sighting line:** The line you sight along on a hand-held compass in order to take a bearing.

Caring for your compass

Compasses are designed to work even when you subject them to rough handling like banging 'em against rocks, dropping 'em onto hard surfaces, and using 'em in the dirt. However, if you want your compass to work when you need it, a little TLC is in order.

Always practice the following:

✔ **Protect your compass as much as you can.** Try tucking your compass inside your shirt to protect it when it's hanging around your neck and not in use. If you have a sighting compass with a cover, keep it closed when not in use.

✔ **Never leave your compass sitting in an extremely hot environment.** Places such as on a rock under intense desert sun or on the dashboard or in the glove compartment of your car are horrible places to leave your compass. Extreme temperatures can cause the damping fluid in your compass to rupture the housing and leak out, rendering your compass useless.

Book IV

Getting Outdoors

✔ **After applying insect repellents, be sure to clean your hands thoroughly before touching your compass.** The chemicals in repellents (most typically DEET) can eat the ink off your compass's housing. Worse, DEET has been known to affect the plastic housing of a compass, causing it to cloud up and even crack.

✔ **Be prepared to eliminate a static charge that builds up on your compass from time to time.** Over time, the needle on your compass may begin to act sluggishly, even appearing to stick to the bottom of its liquid-filled housing. Most often, this slowdown is due to a buildup of static electricity within the housing, and you can easily correct it by rubbing a small amount of water directly over the housing to disperse the static charge.

It isn't uncommon for a small bubble to appear in your compass's liquid-filled housing when you're using the tool in high elevations or below-freezing temperatures. The bubble forms because the fluid within the housing contracts or expands at a faster rate than the housing, resulting in a vacuum-type bubble. This bubble doesn't affect the performance of your compass because the liquid's sole purpose is to dampen or slow down the movement of the magnetic needle. Typically, a bubble disappears when the compass is returned to room temperature or to a lower elevation. If the bubble remains, you can correct the situation by placing the compass in a warm (not hot) spot, such as a sunny windowsill. Should the bubble grow in size, you may have a small, almost imperceptible leak in the liquid-filled compass housing, and that means you need a new compass.

Navigation Basics: Using Your Tools

By using the natural means of navigation described in this chapter, combined with your basic tools — the map and compass, explained in the previous sections — you have the means to travel anywhere you want without fear of getting lost. That doesn't mean you'll never be disoriented, but disoriented and lost are two different conditions. When you're disoriented, you're confused about your location but have confidence in your navigational abilities. When you're lost, you're confused about your location and have no idea which way to turn to get found. The next several sections offer some basic tips that can get you into the navigational mood. Consider them the first steps in developing your navigational skills.

By no means should you consider these sections the complete and final word on navigation. To become really proficient, you need to read, study, and practice, practice, practice — perhaps even by joining an orienteering club (almost every major city throughout North America has one). By going out on a regular basis with the club, your skills will become sharper and sharper, and before long, you'll be far less likely to get lost.

Orienting your map

To find where you are on a map, you must first orient it so that it represents a two-dimensional image that comes as close as possible to exactly paralleling the three-dimensional world you're standing in. You can do that with or without a compass, as explained in the following sections.

Orienting a map without a compass

The quickest way to orient a map is by using easily identifiable landmarks. If you can identify a nearby peak, for example, or a rock outcropping, lake, or point where two trails intersect, or a point that's unique enough to have a map symbol or designation, then placing yourself on your map is easy.

After you know your exact position on the map, spin it until other points of reference on the map line up with the same points of reference that you see on the surrounding landscape. Good navigators keep their maps in constant orientation to the surrounding landscape as they travel.

Orienting a map with a compass

No matter how good you are, eyeballing your map to the lay of the land is only roughly accurate. For complete accuracy, you need to use your compass to correctly orient your map to your surroundings. Because your map is printed with the edges lined up with true north, and because your compass needle always points toward magnetic north, you must account for declination in order to correctly align your map. Here's how:

1. **Correctly set your compass declination adjustment.**

   Refer to the earlier section "Defining declination."

2. **Place the edge of the compass baseplate along the printed edge of the map and hold it there.**

3. **Carefully rotate the map until the red end of the magnetic needle is centered (boxed) in the orienting arrow.**

Your map is now oriented to magnetic north and the surrounding landscape.

Establishing a bearing in the field to stay on course

Imagine that you're hiking toward a distant landmark that you can see from where you are now but that will soon disappear when you enter the woods or descend into a valley. How can you be sure you'll stay on course? Figure 2-6 shows you how to hold your compass as you follow these steps:

1. **Hold your compass level at waist height and point the direction-of-travel arrow at the landmark.**

   If you have a prismatic compass, you need to hold it at eye level, sight through the gun-type sight, and view the housing in the mirror.

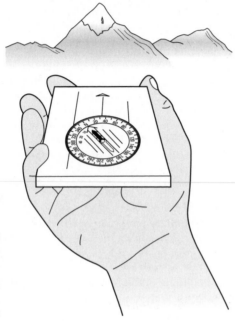

Figure 2-6:
Taking a bearing in the field.

2. **Rotate the compass housing until the red end of the magnetic compass needle is centered (boxed) within the orienting arrow.**

3. **Read your bearing in degrees at the center index point.**

   The *center index point* is where the compass housing meets the direction-of-travel arrow on the compass baseplate.

4. **To follow the bearing you get from Step 3, pick a point of reference in front of you and then look over your shoulder and pick a landmark directly behind you (called your back bearing) that you won't lose sight of.**

   Make sure the first significant point of reference you pick — a rock or a large tree, for example — is in line with the direction-of-travel arrow and is one that you won't lose sight of until you reach it.

5. **Walk directly toward the point of reference without touching your compass dial.**

Don't worry that you can no longer see the original landmark you're hiking to because your compass reading has already been set at the index.

6. **When you reach the reference point, hold the compass level once again, turn your body until the north end of the compass needle centers itself exactly inside the orienting arrow, and find another point of reference in line with the direction-of-travel arrow.**

Before you move toward the new point of reference, you need to verify that the landmark you chose in Step 4 is in the right place (that is, it's in line with the direction-of-travel arrow).

7. **With the compass still held level, turn toward your back bearing until the white end of the compass needle is now centered inside the orienting arrow.**

If the landmark is in line with the direction-of-travel arrow, you're on course for the original landmark as planned. Turn around and head directly to your next selected point of reference.

8. **Repeat the procedure until you arrive at your selected destination.**

Taking a map bearing

You have your map out and you know where you want to go, but you can't see it — kind of like not being able to see the forest for the trees. No worries! A couple quick procedures with your map and compass can help you get your bearing and get on your way.

1. **First, orient your map using your compass.**

Refer to the earlier section "Orienting a map with a compass."

2. **Place the edge of the compass baseplate with the direction-of-travel arrow pointing from your current location on the map toward your intended destination.**

The edge of the baseplate should exactly connect your current location and your intended destination.

3. **Being careful not to move either the map or the compass, rotate the compass housing until the north end (red end) of the compass needle centers itself exactly inside the orienting arrow.**

The index point indicates your degree bearing.

4. **Without moving the compass housing, stand up, holding the compass level at your waist, and rotate your body until the north end of the compass needle centers itself exactly inside the orienting arrow.**

The direction-of-travel arrow indicates your course.

You see your destination on the map but not in person

You can see where you are on the map, that much is certain. Perhaps you've even picked out an interesting-looking summit on the map, not too far from where you are now, and you want to explore it. But in scanning the terrain, you're having a hard time picking the desired summit out of the several others clustered nearby. What do you do?

Follow the steps in the preceding "Taking a map bearing" section to establish a bearing and rotate your body. Then you can determine which summit is the one you want to explore by holding the compass at waist level until the magnetic needle is centered (boxed) within the orienting arrow. The correct summit is the one that the direction-of-travel arrow is pointing toward.

If you're using a prismatic compass, hold the compass at eye level, sight through the gun-type sight, and view the housing in the mirror. The summit will be the one your gun-type sight is lined up on.

You see a landmark but can't place it on the map

You can see your desired destination (a distant summit), and you know where you are on the map, but you have no idea which summit on the map is the one you're looking at in the field (Figure 2-7). Here's what to do:

1. **Orient your map.**

2. **Hold your compass level at waist height and point the direction-of-travel arrow at the mountain's summit.**

   For a prismatic compass, hold the compass at eye level, sight through the gun-type sight, and view the housing in the mirror.

3. **Rotate the compass housing until the red end of the magnetic compass needle is centered within the orienting arrow.**

   Your bearing may be read in degrees at the center index point — where the compass housing meets the direction-of-travel arrow on the compass baseplate.

4. **Taking care not to move the map, place one edge of the compass baseplate directly on your current location on the map.**

5. **Without moving the compass housing or the map in any way, pivot the compass around your known location point until the red end of the magnetic compass needle is centered within the orienting arrow.**

6. **Draw a line, either in pencil or with your imagination, along the edge of the baseplate toward the summit indicated on the map.**

   The summit you're looking at in the field is the one intersected by the line drawn from your location.

Figure 2-7: Finding on the map what you can see on the horizon.

Working your way around obstacles

What happens if you come to a natural obstacle you hadn't counted on — an obstacle that stands directly in your path and established compass bearing, like the one shown in Figure 2-8? No problem!

1. **Take as close to a 90-degree bearing (hard right or left turn) as possible and begin walking beside the obstacle, counting your steps.**

2. **After you reach a point where you can resume hiking in the direction of your original compass bearing, stop counting and remember how many steps you took.**

3. **Turn 90 degrees back so that you're walking on the same heading you were on when you encountered the obstacle; walk until you're clear of the obstacle again.**

4. **Turn 90 degrees in the opposite direction you originally took in Step 1 and retrace your steps, counting until you walk the exact number of paces you noted in Step 2.**

   You're now back on your original course, this time on the other side of the obstacle you encountered.

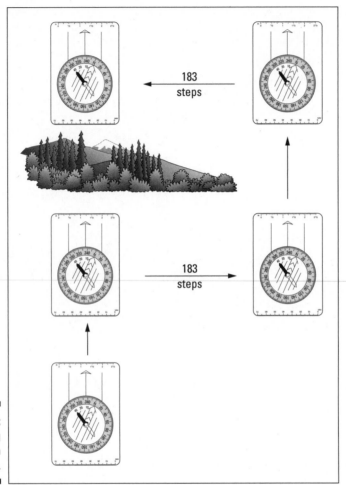

Figure 2-8:
Working
around an
obstacle.

Making sense of trail markers

How do you know whether you're on the right trail or not? Trails are marked
in many different ways throughout North America. Blazes — a *blaze* is a diamond, circle, or dotted "i" carved into a tree about 6 to 8 feet off the ground —
are common. Painted blazes or metal plates nailed to a tree are also common.
These identifiable trail markers are placed on both sides of the tree and at
regular intervals so that you can spot the next blaze within a few feet of leaving the last one.

Sometimes finding the next blaze involves a little search-and-find mission. Don't panic and, above all, don't head out blindly along a route just because it supposedly looks like a trail. Thousands of trails exist in the woods simply because animals use them and not because humans created them.

When the trail heads above the treeline or through open, treeless areas (deserts, vast plains, and the like), trails are often marked with *cairns* — piles of rocks. Sometimes, in challenging terrain where route-finding is a matter of life and death, cairns have been replaced by 5-foot-high wands with reflective tape or paint. Mount Washington in New Hampshire and Mount Katahdin in Maine are two such areas.

Don't add to trail markers that already exist — for example by flagging or building new cairns. Just because you think the trail needs a marker doesn't mean you're right. For instance, you could be off-route, and adding a marking may only confuse those who follow you.

Book IV

Getting Outdoors

Chapter 3

Weathering the Outdoors

- -

In This Chapter

▶ Reading clouds clearly

▶ Understanding how terrain impacts wind and weather

▶ Recognizing signs from Mother Nature

▶ Staying safe in dangerous weather

- -

*A*lthough you can't do much about the weather, you can figure out how to read and understand changes in weather patterns and to know what those changes mean. Without this know-how, the best you can do is react blindly to the circumstances that Mother Nature may throw your way. But with it, you can face your outdoor excursion with reliable preparedness. Often, that difference alone may determine the margin of comfort and safety that separates disaster from adventure.

In this chapter, you discover some basic tips for predicting changes in weather patterns and some safety precautions for riding out the inevitable storms. If you'd like to learn more about meteorological concepts, check out another book I wrote, *Basic Essentials Weather Forecasting* (published by the Globe Pequot Press).

To hone your weather-predicting skills, keep a weather eye on the sky. The more aware you are and the more you know about what causes weather, the more perceptive your observations will be and the more accurate your guesses as to the weather's outcome. But never forget: Weather forecasts are only educated guesses, never statements of fact. Always be prepared for the worst.

Predicting Weather Changes by Reading Clouds

Cloud watching is more than simply picking out shapes that look like pirates or giraffes. By observing clouds and identifying them, you can gain a fairly good insight into what the next 12 to 24 hours of weather may bring.

Clouds form whenever vapor from the earth condenses and is lifted skyward. In simple terms, a cloud is visible because the moisture has cooled below the dew point and condensed into particles that reflect light. The hotter and more humid the air that's rising, the more dense the clouds that form — think of thunderheads in the Midwest on hot, humid afternoons.

Types of cloud formations

The main types of cloud formations you need to concern yourself with when letting your eyes surf across the sky are cirrus, cumulus, cumulonimbus, and stratus, shown in Figure 3-1.

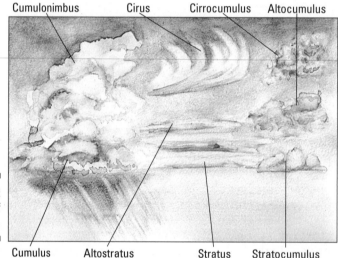

Figure 3-1:
Types of
clouds.

Cumulonimbus   Cirus   Cirrocumulus   Altocumulus

Cumulus   Altostratus   Stratus   Stratocumulus

Cirrus

Made up predominantly of ice crystals, cirrus clouds are arguably some of the most beautiful of the cloud formations, leaving milky white swirls and curls etched across the sky (see Figure 3-1). Cirrus clouds, with the exception of cirrostratus (thicker, sheetlike clouds that can mean snow or rain is coming), indicate fair weather will hold for a while.

Cumulus and cumulonimbus

Often referred to as *heap clouds,* cumulus formations are typified by their heaped or fluffy shapes (refer to Figure 3-1). Small, lumpy cumulus clouds are considered "fair weather" clouds. Grayish and puffy, these clouds form in masses early in the day and are often precursors to an afternoon thunderstorm. As cumulus clouds stack vertically and begin to form a flat base with a towering center and an anvil-shaped upper, they become cumulonimbus clouds ("nimbus" means rain producing), creating the classic thunderhead, which can mean heavy precipitation, thunder, lightning, and hail.

Stratus

"Stratus" means layered, essentially formless with no real defining base or top. Fog is a type of stratus cloud that lies close to the ground and is caused when the Earth's surface cools. This cooling effectively lowers the air temperature, resulting in condensation. A variety of stratus clouds exist:

- **Cirrostratus:** High-level (usually around 20,000 feet), veil-like cloud formations composed of ice crystals and often spreading out over a very large surface area. Halos are frequently observed in cirrostratus clouds, indicating a lowering of the cloud ceiling and possible precipitation within 48 hours.

- **Altostratus:** Medium-level clouds (usually hovering around 8,000 feet) that are flat or striated and dark gray in color. A darkening of the cloud cover indicates possible precipitation within 48 hours.

- **Nimbostratus:** Low-level, dark, and thick clouds, often without any real defining shape. Their ragged edges, known as *scud,* produce steady precipitation.

- **Lenticular clouds:** Well known in the Sierra Nevada, lenticular clouds, known formally as *altocumulus lenticularis,* are lens-shaped clouds that form at or around mountain peaks due to a cresting or wave in the airstream passing over the peak. As air is forced up the mountain ridge, it cools, condenses, and forms as a cloud near the peak. As the air passes over the peak and heads back down the ridge, it warms, and moisture evaporates. Because condensation is occurring only at the peak, the cloud forms only at the peak, and even though winds are whipping through it, the cloud remains stationary.

Book IV

Getting Outdoors

Messages in cloud movements

You can make some general predictions about the weather without being able to tell a cirrus cloud from a stratus cloud.

If clouds are massing and generally increasing in size and density, the weather is possibly changing for the worse. Clouds moving more quickly across the sky indicate a change in wind velocity and also a change in pressure, indicating an approaching storm.

Because the various cloud formations take on different appearances and altitudes, it's possible, although sometimes difficult, to observe the movements of two or more different cloud formations across the sky. Cloud formations that are moving in separate directions and at different altitudes often announce an impending storm.

Finally, observe cloud movements and wind direction together. If both the cloud movements and wind direction are the same, any weather will come from the direction the wind is blowing.

Geographic Weather Variations

Although the weather may be warm and sunny on a mountain ridge, temperatures may be downright cold in the valley below it. How so? The answer is microclimate influences. Differences in temperature and humidity in various microclimates are created by different degrees of solar warming, radiation, and evaporative cooling. Knowing what these are and how they work can make the difference between a chilly night huddled in your sleeping bag under a cold air-sink, or basking comfortably several hundred feet away under moonbeams. Of course, if the weather is foul, microclimatology is a moot point — foul weather is a constant with no microclimate sanctuaries.

Mountains and valleys

Hike anywhere in any mountain range and you'll note one constant feature: Wind blows up the mountain during the day (as shown in Figure 3-2) and down the mountain at night (see Figure 3-3). Why? Two forces are at work, both caused by radiation as the Earth's surface loses more heat than it absorbs during a clear night. As the ground gives off heat, that heat rises, and the Earth cools. The air close to the ground becomes colder more quickly and, because it's denser than warm air, begins to flow, rather like water, downhill — toward valley bottoms and desert floors. As the cool air rushes down the mountain (this is the breeze you feel), it displaces the warm air, forcing it upward and keeping a cycle of air going. As the warm air gets forced out, the cool air pools and collects in the lower reaches, creating places often referred to as *cold sinks*.

In broad valleys covered with dense meadow grasses, frost pockets may form, even though the temperature just 500 to 1,000 feet higher is a comfortable 50 degrees. The broader the valley and the more vertical the surrounding mountainous ridges, the more marked the temperature contrasts will be. The narrower the valley, the less dramatic the temperature differences between top and bottom will be, because the walls tend to radiate heat from one to another, trapping potential heat loss from the valley bottom.

As the early morning sun begins to warm the valley, the winds reverse themselves and begin rushing up the mountain as the warm air begins to rise. Remember, however, that the air can only be warmed if the sun hits it, which explains why the side of the valley that's getting the sun first experiences upslope winds, whereas the side of the valley still in the shade experiences cool downslope winds.

Cloudy conditions or a presence of strong winds in the area will alter the topographical variations in the wind and temperature pattern. Cloudy conditions act as an insulator, reducing radiant heat loss and holding a thermal layer of air closer to the Earth's surface. Windy conditions may overpower the gentle nature of upslope or downslope winds and also alter the potential temperature variances.

Winds that flow up and down a valley or canyon floor operate in a similar manner to winds that flow up and down a valley's walls. As temperatures fluctuate between the higher elevations (mountains, ridges, or foothills) at one end of the canyon or valley and the lower elevations (deserts or plains), winds also fluctuate in intensity and direction. Canoeists and rafters know this fact well — many an afternoon wind blowing upstream from the heated elevations below has thwarted their efforts to paddle successfully. It's important to note, however, that canyons and valleys channel wind, too, and it's entirely possible — probable in fact — that winds will roar up or down the canyon or valley no matter what time of day it is.

The ups and downs of adiabatic temperature fluctuations

Here's a word to drop into your next weather conversation: *adiabatic*. Sounds like "diabetic," but it's not related. Adiabatic is the term explaining why air cools as it rises and warms when it falls. To get just a little more technical, air cools approximately 5.5 degrees for each 1,000 feet of elevation gain. It warms at about the same rate during elevation loss. As air meets a mountain and is forced over it, the air pressure falls, and the temperature also falls as the air expands. When the air pours over the peak and begins to descend, air pressure and temperature both rise again.

Condensation throws a monkey wrench into the entire process, however. Just as adiabatic cooling lowers the temperature of air, any condensation that may occur warms it. The net effect on humid air being pushed up over a mountain peak is an average temperature cooling of 3.2 degrees per 1,000 feet. Once at the peak, the air begins to warm as it descends, and no further condensation occurs. Adiabatic warming of this air happens at the normal 5.5 degrees for each 1,000 feet of elevation loss.

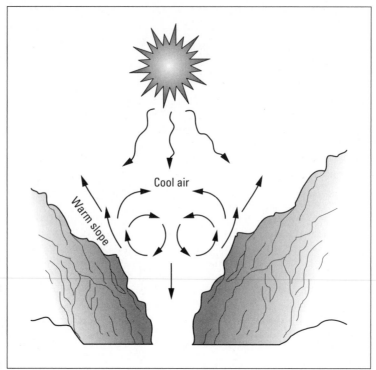

Figure 3-2:
Day wind
blowing up
a mountain.

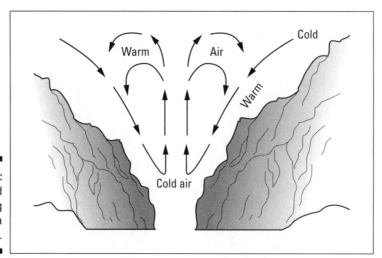

Figure 3-3:
Night wind
blowing
down a
mountain.

Estimating wind speed

Devised by Sir Francis Beaufort in 1805, the wind speed chart, now known as the Beaufort Scale of Wind Force, is an excellent and extremely accurate method of estimating wind velocity.

Wind Speed in Miles Per Hour	Effects on Land
0–1	Smoke rises straight up; calm.
1–3	Smoke drifts.
4–7	Wind felt on face; leaves rustle.
8–12	Leaves and twigs constantly rustle; wind extends small flag.
13–18	Dust and small papers raised; small branches moved.
19–24	Crested wavelets form on inland waters; small trees sway.
25–31	Large branches move in trees.
32–38	Large trees sway; must lean to walk.
39–46	Twigs broken from trees; difficult to walk.
47–54	Limbs break from trees; extremely difficult to walk.
55–63	Tree limbs and branches break.
64+	Widespread damage with trees uprooted.

Snowfields, glaciers, and wintry environments

In many mountain environments, the presence of year-round snowfields and glaciers creates localized wind conditions in the valleys directly below. These winds are caused by the cool air that flows off the glacier or snowfield, displacing the surrounding warmer air that hugs the valley floor. Fairly gentle and warm, these winds dissipate quite quickly.

Winds originating from glaciers or snowfields will occur as long as the surface temperature of the snow is sufficiently different from the surface temperature of the ground below the lip of the glacier or snowfield.

The cold wind that emanates from ice caves underneath a glacier also has a significant effect on the growing season of plants. For example, in the Cascade range near the Canadian border, several ice caves are located adjacent to areas where the growing season of the plants and flowers consistently begins several weeks after that of plants only several hundred feet away. This situation occurs because the colder air near the ice makes the plants think the growing season has not yet begun. This knowledge works well if you're trying to get a photograph of various flowering alpine plants and miss the first bloom due to miserable photography weather.

Oceans and lakes

Anyone who has spent anytime at all hiking, boating, or camping near the shore of a large body of water, such as the ocean or any one of the Great Lakes, is probably familiar with the daytime onshore winds and the nighttime offshore breezes. As with snowfields and glaciers (see the preceding section), temperature differences between the land and the ocean or lake must be sufficient for winds to occur. Unlike snowfields and glaciers, clouds reduce the temperature contrasts. Winds typically are most common when the days are sunny and warm and the nights are clear.

Wind chill index

The wind chill equivalency index demonstrates the actual cooling effect on bare skin when exposed to air under the following temperatures and wind speeds. Although understanding wind chill has very little to do with being able to predict weather patterns, you should realize the impact wind and temperature have on the body so that you can make safe decisions about dress and travel. In the table, for example, if the temperature is 20 degrees above zero and the wind is blowing 15 mph, the wind chill equivalent is 6 degrees below zero.

		Temperature							
		+40	**+30**	**+20**	**+10**	**0**	**−10**	**−20**	**−30**
Wind (in mph)	**5**	37	27	16	6	−5	−15	−26	−36
	10	28	16	2	−9	−22	−31	−45	−58
	15	22	11	−6	−18	−33	−45	−60	−70
	20	18	3	−9	−24	−40	−52	−68	−81
	25	16	0	−15	−29	−45	−58	−75	−89
	30	13	−2	−18	−33	−49	−63	−78	−94
	35	11	−4	−20	−35	−52	−67	−83	−98
	40	10	−4	−22	−36	−54	−69	−87	−101

Generally, onshore breezes begin around mid morning and continue until early to mid afternoon. The wind is typically steady and can result in a dramatic drop of onshore temperature, sometimes as much as 10 to 15 degrees. Evenings and early mornings are usually calm. Offshore breezes often begin shortly after dusk and continue until early morning.

Deserts

Thermally created low-pressure systems often develop in desert areas. As superheated air rises skyward, it creates a *void,* a low-pressure area that must be filled. The resulting effect is strong horizontal winds that rush in as the pressure attempts to equalize, creating dust devils and sandstorms.

Portents and Omens from Mother Nature Herself

Mother Nature provides a lot of weather clues, some in the form of rhymes but all fairly simple and easy to remember. This section presents just a sample of them — including a few you may already know.

Morning or evening sky

"Red sky at night, sailor's delight. Red sky in morning, sailors take warning." This weather proverb means that if the clouds take on a reddish hue in the morning, you can expect rain by the end of the day. If the evening sky is red, the weather will probably remain clear the following day.

Geese and seagulls

Geese and seagulls have a reputation for not flying before a storm. Biologists theorize that this behavior is because geese and seagulls have a harder time getting airborne in low-pressure (thin-air) conditions. Or maybe they're just a lot smarter than people give them credit for and don't want to get stuck out in a storm.

Book IV

Getting Outdoors

Mosquitoes and black flies

If you've camped beside a body of fresh water prior to a storm's arrival, you know that mosquitoes and black flies inevitably swarm and feast heavily up to 12 hours before the storm hits. You can bet the storm is almost upon you when the feasting frenzy subsides and the little buggers fly away to hide — about an hour before the weather turns.

Frogs

Frogs of all shapes and colors have an uncanny tendency to increase their serenading several hours before a storm arrives. The reason they do this isn't so much that they're reliable weather forecasters. Rather, the increased humidity in the air from an incoming storm allows them to stay comfortably out of the water for longer periods (given that their skin must be kept moist at all times).

Halo around the sun and moon

In the summer, the sight of a hazy halo around the sun or moon is a good indication that a change in the present weather pattern is in the forecast — most often rain.

Frost and dew

The presence of heavy frost or dew early in the morning or late in the evening is a fairly reliable indicator that you can expect up to 12 hours of continued good weather.

Wind

"Wind from the south brings rain in its mouth." Low-pressure systems create cyclonic winds that rotate in a counterclockwise direction. Because low-pressure systems are frequently associated with rainstorms, the rhyme proves quite accurate. Counterclockwise wind rotations create wind that blows from the south — wind that brings in the rain.

High-pressure systems are often associated with clear or clearing weather, with clockwise rotating winds. Keep aware of wind directions, and you'll keep your finger on the weather's pulse: Is it beating fair or foul?

Campfire smoke

By observing the smoke from your campfire, you can tell what type of pressure system is in the area, low or high. If the smoke from the fire hangs low to the ground and dissipates into the branches, a low-pressure system is present and rain is possible. If the smoke rises in a straight, vertical column, high pressure rules and you can anticipate fair weather (see Figure 3-4).

Figure 3-4:
Low-hanging campfire smoke indicates rain, but smoke rising in a vertical column indicates fair weather.

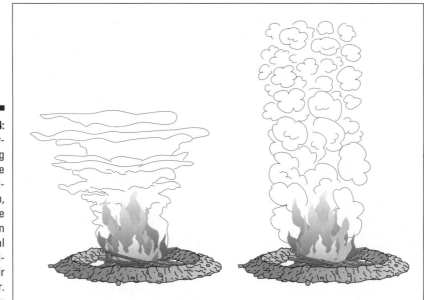

Crickets

Believe it or not, you can estimate the air temperature (in degrees Fahrenheit) by counting the number of chirps a cricket emits over a 14-second period and adding 40 to the number. So, if a cricket chirps 25 times over 14 seconds, you add 25 to 40 and arrive at 65 degrees. Scientific studies have proven that crickets are correct within a degree or two more than 75 percent of the time.

Keep in mind, though, that air temperatures closer to the ground where the cricket resides will differ from the temperatures a few feet higher by as much as several degrees.

Deer, bighorn sheep, and elk

Animals such as deer, bighorn sheep, and elk, which are common in mountainous areas, commonly move down a mountain and into sheltered valleys as a storm approaches. They then move back up the mountain as a storm gets pushed out. The trouble with this weather indicator is that by the time you see the animals moving, the storm is already bearing down.

Surviving Weather Emergencies in the Great Outdoors

Lightning, tornadoes, snowstorms, and wildfires — all are powerful, natural events that result directly or indirectly from weather phenomena. And all can be safely avoided in most cases by following a few precautions.

Thunderstorms and lightning

Lightning is caused by the attraction of unlike electrical charges within a storm cloud or the earth. The friction caused by rapidly moving air particles, churning from the violent updrafts and downdrafts of air, leads to a building up of strong electrical charges. As the electrical pressure builds, charges between parts of the cloud or from the cloud to the earth are released, taking the form of lightning. Up to 30 million volts can be discharged by one lightning bolt. This power or explosive heating of the air is what causes the compressions of thunder.

Thunderstorms are a dangerous companion to have when traveling exposed on a mountain peak. If a thunderstorm approaches when you and your hiking party are on an exposed peak or ridge, take the following precautions:

- ✔ **Get off the ridge or peak if at all possible.** Even moving to a few feet below the highest point is better than not moving at all.

- ✔ **Get away from your pack.** The metal in your pack conducts electricity, making you a prime target for a lightning strike.

- ✔ **Position yourself on a dry surface.** Ideally this dry surface is an insulated one, such as a sleeping pad. If the sleeping pad gets soaked with rain, however, it's useless and even dangerous because water conducts electricity.

- **Don't lie down or sit.** Instead, crouch with your feet close together. The idea is to minimize the available surface area through which possible ground currents from nearby lightning strikes may move.

- **Don't huddle next to a lone tree.** Doing so is rather like hugging a lightning rod and expecting to be safe. Choose a cluster of trees instead and place yourself in the middle, preferably in an open area.

- **Spread out the people in your group so theyíre at least 25 to 30 feet apart.** The idea behind this tactic is to minimize the potential damage and injury if lightning does strike. With the group spread out, chances are only one person will be injured (if at all), leaving the rest of the party able to provide lifesaving assistance after the storm moves on.

- **Avoid any depressions or caves.** Such areas usually have moisture in them, making them more susceptible to conducting electricity.

- **If you're caught on a lake in a thunderstorm, assume a crouching position toward the middle of the boat.** Try to minimize your contact with wet objects.

Tornadoes

Tornadoes are perhaps the most violent and intense of all known storms, with winds in excess of 300 mph recorded in the vortex. Man-made structures seem to literally explode as the extremely low pressure within the vortex of a tornado causes the normal pressure trapped within structures to expand rapidly, ripping buildings to shreds from the inside out.

Violent updrafts recorded between 100 to 200 mph within the center of the funnel cloud have been known to suck anything within the tornado's path hundreds of feet in the air before hurling the objects some distance away. Over bodies of water, funnel clouds lift water into the air, creating what's known as a *waterspout*.

Book IV

Getting Outdoors

How far away is that thunderstorm?

You can roughly judge the distance of an approaching storm by observing the lightning's flash followed by the resounding boom of thunder. For this method, count slowly, "one one-thousand, two one-thousand, three one-thousand" and so forth to approximate one second elapsed for each thousand counted.

After the lightning has flashed, begin to count. When you hear the thunder, stop counting. Every five seconds of elapsed time indicates one mile of distance. In other words, if the count reaches "seven-one thousand," you can safely assume that the approaching thunderstorm is approximately 1.5 miles away.

Most tornado-related injuries and deaths are caused by debris flying through the air and objects falling over. If a tornado approaches, take these precautions:

- ✔ **If you're outside:** Curl up in a tight ball in a drainage ditch, a culvert, or any other depression that will protect you, and cover your head.

- ✔ **If you're driving:** Get out of your car and seek shelter in a sturdy building if one is nearby. If you're out in the open, lie flat and face-down on low ground, and cover your head. Don't attempt to wait out the passing tornado inside your car.

- ✔ **If you're indoors:** Leave the windows closed and seek shelter in a basement, if you have one, or in a room located in the center of the home with no windows or the fewest number of windows possible. Curl up against a wall, and cover your head.

- ✔ **If you're in a mobile home, RV, barn, or small building that you know isn't sturdy or firmly anchored to the ground:** Get out. The tornado will toss the structure about like a house of straw, and you're in more danger inside it than you are outside of it.

Chapter 4

Field Guide to Freshwater Fish (And How to Clean Them)

In This Chapter

▶ Getting the scoop on a variety of freshwater fish

▶ Scaling, gutting, and filleting fish

▶ Cleaning fish — without a ton of mess

*W*here you live and the common fish in your local waters have a great deal to do with your catch options when fishing. Through the 50 or so generations that people have fished for sport (rather than necessity), they've sought out fish that offer a bit of a challenge to hook. How well the fish fight is another big consideration. Whether or not they taste good also counts. And personal preference plays a role as well — some people find that one type of fish is more fun to catch than another.

Of course, before you can enjoy the fish you hook and land, you have to clean them. No, cleaning fish isn't the most fun part of fishing. In fact, on a cold night, standing at the dock and filleting a mess of bluefish is a miserable, smelly job. But if you want to eat fish, you have to clean fish, unless of course you're a parent, in which case, you can have your kids clean them.

Trout

If the number of words written about a fish is any indication of popularity, then the trout is the runaway winner. A great deal of what has been written about trout is just a bunch of hot air, but separating the fish from a bunch of gasbag fishing writers, trout is a supreme game fish that is at least the equal of any other sport fish.

In the old days, an angler was judged by how many trout he or she brought home. These days, thanks largely to the influence of American anglers, catch-and-release is more the rule. If you kill the occasional trout, however, don't let anyone make you feel guilty about it. After all, it's a delicious fish. On the other hand, if you kill every trout that you catch, you're being more greedy than wise.

Trout are the top predator in their environment: They stand at the top of the food chain in many rivers and streams. Top predators are, of necessity, rarer than animals lower down the chain. A little bit of pressure can alter the quality of angling in a stream very quickly. So enjoy yourself and enjoy your meal, but remember that the fish you return to the stream will grow larger and have babies, giving you more fishing fun in the long run.

The champ: Brown trout

The brown trout is a fish designed for the angler in the following ways:

- ✔ It often feeds on the surface.
- ✔ It rises to a properly presented fly.
- ✔ It fights like the dickens.
- ✔ It's one of the wiliest and most rewarding fish taken on rod and reel.
- ✔ Its instinct to dash for cover when hooked adds up to a great fight for the angler.

A cold-water fish, the brown trout lives in lakes and streams and is most active when the water temperature is in the 60s. A temperature much above 80 degrees is liable to kill brown trout. This fish, shown in Figure 4-1, is covered with spots everywhere but its tail. The majority of these spots are deep brown (like coffee beans, but with a light yellow halo), but you can also find a few red and yellow spots sprinkled around its body. Brown trout are long-lived animals and can weigh up to 40 pounds, but most stream-bred browns average less than 1 pound each.

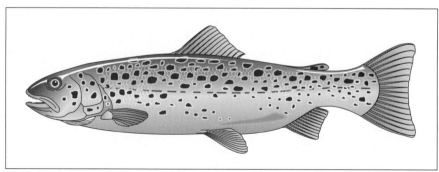

Figure 4-1:
The brown
trout.

The brown didn't acquire a reputation as a "gentleman's fish" because it had particularly good manners and went to the right school. The simple fact of the matter is that rich English gentlemen with time on their hands embraced the sport of angling and popularized it everywhere. Because their local fish was the brown trout, it became the fish of choice for sportsmen there and in the New World. If the English sportsmen had started out in Georgia rather than England, the largemouth bass would probably have a lot of flowery literature devoted to it. If those same anglers had lived in Mississippi, people may well have written about the simple virtues and great sporting qualities of the catfish.

High jumpers: Rainbow trout

Rainbow trout have many of the same characteristics of brown trout; they eat like them, feed like them, behave like them, and so on. In fact, rainbow trout coexist nicely with brown trout in many streams. But whereas the brown prefers the slower water and calmer pools, you can count on finding the rainbow in the more oxygen-rich and swift-running riffles. Of course, this scenario is what you'd expect from a fish that dominates the streams of the Rocky Mountains.

If you ask a hundred anglers to name the most memorable aspect about the fight of a rainbow, you may well have a hundred answers singling out the rainbow's leaping ability. Although the brown, when hooked, usually *sounds* (dives to the bottom) and makes for cover, the rainbow's instinct is to leap and run and leap some more. These acrobatics are thrilling and, on light tackle, demand a sensitive touch.

As Figure 4-2 shows, the rainbow may have spots over its whole body (although in many rivers and lakes, the larger rainbows are more often silver overall). A much more reliable sign of "rainbowness" is the pink band or line that runs along the flank of the fish from shoulder to tail. But even this indicator isn't always 100-percent foolproof, because some stream-borne rainbows have a faded, almost invisible band and many spots, as do the brown and brook trout.

Book IV

Getting Outdoors

Figure 4-2:
The rainbow trout is the leapingest trout — and also one of the hardiest fish.

Guess what? More than a decade ago, scientists decided that the rainbow trout isn't a trout after all. The same Englishmen who provided the lore of the brown trout decided to call the rainbow a trout, probably because of the rainbow's troutlike characteristics. (Whenever the English arrived in a new country, they gave the local fish and game the names of similar animals back in Merrie Olde England.) Now the rainbow trout is officially recognized as a smaller cousin of the Pacific salmon family.

Colorful favorites: Brookies

Like the rainbow, the brook trout, or *brookie,* isn't really a trout. It *is,* however, the fish that fills the trout niche in the cooler streams of the northeastern United States, east of the Allegheny Mountains. The brook trout is actually a char, which makes it a relative of the lake trout (also not a real trout, as explained in the later section "Big macks: Lakers"), the Dolly Varden, and the Arctic char.

That the brookie is found only in wilderness areas explains part of anglers' fondness for it: This fish is a sign of pure water and a healthy ecology. Brookies like cooler water and can't stand the higher temperatures that the brown and the rainbow can tolerate.

Before Europeans cleared the great hardwood forests of the northeastern United States, most streams had the shade and pure water that brook trout need. But with the clearing of the forests and the coming of brown trout and rainbow trout, the brookie often retreated to the less-accessible headwaters of many streams. As explained by the principle of "smaller fish in smaller water," many people whose only brook trout experience is on these smaller waters assume that the brookie is typically smaller than the rainbow or the brown. Wrong. In the old days on Long Island, for example, many brookies ranged from 4 to 10 pounds.

Although much praised for its great beauty, many anglers regard the brookie as an empty-headed glamour-puss. This isn't to say that very wary, hard-to-catch brookies aren't out there, but by and large, most of them are prettier than they are smart.

The brook trout features many red spots that are surrounded by a blue halo. Its fins end in telltale black-and-white tips, and both its belly and fins have an orange cast that can be quite brilliant (and appear almost crimson during spawning season). The tail of the brook trout is more squared off than that of the brown or rainbow (see Figure 4-3), hence the nickname "squaretail."

Figure 4-3:
The brook trout, originally a native of the east coast of North America, is universally admired for its gorgeous coloring.

A native cousin: Cutthroats

You can think of the cutthroat — which is really a cousin to the rainbow trout — as the Rocky Mountain version of the brook trout (described in the preceding section) because in many undisturbed waters, the cutthroat is the native fish. But because of ranching, logging, and the introduction of other game fish, the cutthroat has generally retreated to unpressured headwaters. It's hard to tell in Figure 4-4, but cutthroats get their name from the slash of red or orange on their jaws and gills.

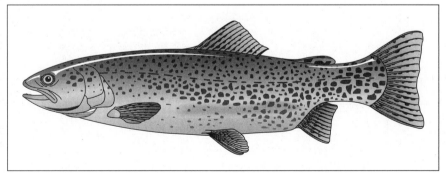

Figure 4-4:
The cutthroat trout is most easily identified by the red and orange slashes around its lower jaw and gills.

Book IV

Getting Outdoors

Steelhead: A salty rainbow

Almost all species of trout, if given the chance, drop downstream to the ocean where they usually grow to much greater size than trout confined to streams and lakes. Sea-run brookies and browns (meaning those that forage in the ocean and return to spawn in fresh water) also appear in North America, but the main target for anglers of sea-run trout is the *steelhead,* which is nothing more than a rainbow trout that has gone to sea. Steelhead have usually lost the distinctive coloration of the freshwater rainbow (although they still have the pink lateral line). As their name suggests, steelhead have a bright, metallic color.

Although supposedly not as intelligent as the brown trout, cutthroats (sometimes called *cuts*) can be extremely selective. They don't have the head-shaking determination of the brown or the leaping instinct of the rainbow, but in all of Troutdom, there's nothing like the surface take of the cutthroat: It comes up, sips the fly, and shows you its whole body before descending with the fly. All you need to do is come tight to the fish, and you're on.

The cutthroat is the native trout in the drainage of the Yellowstone River, where it's protected by a complete no-kill policy in all the flowing water in Yellowstone Park. To fish cutthroats at the outlet of Yellowstone Lake, however, is one of the great angling experiences in North America.

Big macks: Lakers

Widely known as Mackinaws or gray trout, the lake trout (or *laker*) is the largest char. It requires colder water than any other freshwater game fish, optimally about 50 degrees, and will die at 65 degrees.

Right after ice-out in the spring, and right before spawning in the autumn, lakers may be taken in shallow water. But during the rest of the season, you have to fish deeper, often trolling with wire line or lead core.

Unlike all the other trout (meaning true trout as well as rainbows and chars), the laker spawns in lakes, not streams. As shown in Figure 4-5, the laker, like the brookie, is heavily spotted. It has a forked tail (in contrast to the square tail of the brookie). The largest one ever taken on rod and reel weighed 66 pounds, 8 ounces, and was caught in Canada's Great Bear Lake on July 10, 1991. A 102-pound laker was netted in Lake Athabasca in Saskatchewan.

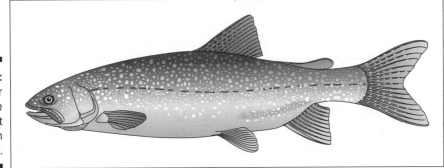

Figure 4-5:
The laker looks like a giant brookie with a forked tail.

Some lamebrains dumped a few lakers in Yellowstone Lake a few years ago. Prior to that, this lake had held the last pure strain of cutthroats in the Rockies. Unfortunately, the lakers began to prey on young cutthroat fry. Even worse, because lakers don't run up rivers like cutthroats do, about 20 percent of the food supply of the grizzly bear, osprey, and eagle is now gone from the local Yellowstone ecosystem — a prime case of messing with Mother Nature.

The Basses

Trout may win the number-of-pages-written-about-them contest, but if the number of anglers counts for anything, then the basses (largemouth and smallmouth) are certainly the most popular game fish in America. The largemouth and smallmouth are not, however, true basses. That distinction belongs to the basses of Europe, who had first dibs on the name. The American basses actually belong to the sunfish family. When you stop to consider this situation, though, the largemouth and smallmouth don't know or care what they're called; and the American basses, also known as the *black basses,* are pretty amazing game fish.

Trying to pick up a bass by grabbing its body is about as easy as trying to diaper an angry baby. The little suckers can really squirm. Even worse than babies, bass have spiny fins that can deliver nasty pricks. With a bass (and with many other soft-mouthed fish), however, you can nearly immobilize it if you grab it by the lower lip, holding it between thumb and forefinger. Be very careful of hooks though, especially lures that have multiple treble hooks.

Book IV

Getting Outdoors

Largemouth: A real catch

The largemouth bass, originally a native of the Mississippi drainage and the southeastern United States, was recognized early on as a prime game fish and has since been transplanted all over. Lakes, rivers, streams, and brackish coastal water all have populations of largemouth bass. These fish take lures, plugs, flies, plastic worms, real worms, crayfish, and crickets. In short, they're opportunistic feeders and are most catchable when the water is in the range of 65 to 75 degrees.

As shown in Figure 4-6, the jaw of the largemouth bass extends farther back than the eye (which isn't true of the smallmouth bass described in the next section). The largemouth is usually dark gray to dark green in color with a dark band along the lateral line. Its dorsal fin is divided into two distinct portions: hard spines in front and softer ones in the rear. The largemouth is also known as the *bucketmouth* because of its large mouth, which appears even larger when it attacks your lure, fly, or bait.

Truly, no experience in angling is as thrilling as the moment that a largemouth bass takes a topwater plug. There you are, on a still summer day, a few dragonflies buzzing around a lily pad, a frog or two basking in the heat. You cast a topwater plug to the lily pad and let it rest for a few seconds. Then you twitch it a couple times. A fierce ripple knocks into your plug, followed by the cause of the onrushing water — a ferocious largemouth bass that engulfs the plug. The instant it feels the hook, the largemouth shakes its head and jumps or dives, or both. It's quite the impressive sight.

Smallmouth: The gamest fish

Like its largemouth cousin, the smallmouth bass is a native of the Mississippi drainage, which makes it a true heartland fish. Whereas the largemouth likes slow or still water with lots of food-holding weeds, the smallmouth prefers clean, rocky bottoms and swifter water, ideally in the range of 65 to 68 degrees. Any warmer than 73 degrees and you can forget about finding one. Lake-dwelling smallmouth often school up, which means that if you catch one, you can catch a bunch. In rivers and streams, they're more solitary. The smallmouth is a pretty opportunistic feeder in general, but if you give it a choice, both crayfish and hellgrammites score well.

As shown in Figure 4-7, the smallmouth has a series of dark vertical bands along its flanks. The dorsal fin is one continuous fin (as opposed to the separate spiny and soft parts on a largemouth's fin). Another difference is that the smallmouth's upper jaw doesn't extend backward beyond its eye.

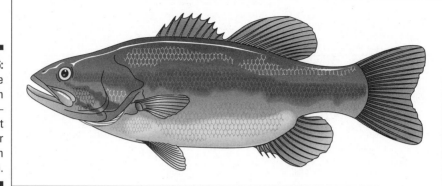

Figure 4-6:
The largemouth bass — the most sought-after game fish in America.

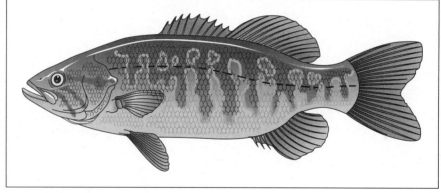

Figure 4-7:
The mouth of the smallmouth isn't that small, but its upper jaw is shorter than the large-mouth's.

Good Eats: Walleye

On a number of trips to the state of Minnesota, more than one angler has been known to say, "You can have your bass, and you can have your trout, but the walleye is the best eatin' fish there is, bar none!" This largest member of the perch family does indeed rank right up there with the best in terms of taste. In fact, its excellent flavor may explain why walleye are often the preferred fish when they're available. In addition to being delicious, they're found in schools, hang out around underwater structures, and usually locate themselves near a drop-off. In other words, they behave just as a textbook game fish should — not a pushover, but not impossible to catch either.

Note: In many places, you can hear people talk about a walleyed pike, which is a local name for walleye but not an accurate one. The pike is a completely different animal, as explained in the next section.

Book IV

Getting Outdoors

As you can see in Figure 4-8, the walleye is a torpedo-shaped fish with big eyes, a brownish-greenish color, and a white tip on its tail and dorsal fin. The walleye requires a great deal of water and is rarely found in smaller lakes or ponds. Clear water and a rocky bottom are also high on its list of environmental preferences, as is a water temperature in the mid-60s (and certainly never higher than the mid-70s). The walleye eats any bait fish that's available; both leeches and worms are terrific bait if you can't find any bait fish.

The take of the walleye is subtle, not unlike the way a bass plays with a worm and then swims away with it before finally deciding to eat. Be sure to give the walleye time to accomplish this maneuver before striking.

The walleye is a very light-sensitive fish, so although you may take one in shallow water, chances are you'll do so only in low-light conditions.

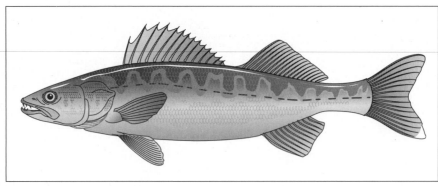

Figure 4-8: You can always tell a walleye by the white tip on its tail.

Pike and Its Cousins

For flat-out mean looks, nothing in freshwater rivals the looks of a pike, muskellunge, or pickerel. A long fish with big eyes, a pointed snout, and rows of stiletto teeth, the average pike looks like what you might get if you crossed a snake, a bird, and a shark.

When landing a pike, muskie, or pickerel, be extremely careful of its sharp teeth. These fish are about the nastiest creatures in freshwater fishing. As shown in Figure 4-9, the safest way to land any of 'em is to grab 'em by the eye sockets (not the eye!).

Northern pike

The most popular member of the pike family is usually known simply as the pike but is also sometimes called a *northern*. By either name, it's a native of the Great Lakes and its cooler tributaries.

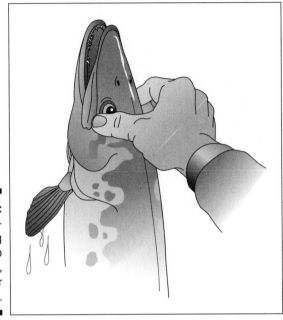

Figure 4-9:
The finger-preserving way to land a pike, muskie, or pickerel.

You're liable to find pike in weedy shallows where they wait for prey to ambush. As stealthy as a lion in wait and as swift as a springing panther, pike stalk and pursue their prey most actively at water temperatures in the mid-60s.

As shown in Figure 4-10, the pike is a sleek and ferocious-looking predator that's clearly designed to attack and devour. All forms of bait fish, game fish, birds, muskrats, frogs, snakes, snails, leeches, and anything else the pike finds within striking distance can eventually find its way into a pike's belly.

Depending on the type of bait you use, follow this advice when striving to snare a pike:

- ✔ **When fishing with live bait:** Give the pike time. Sometimes it'll snare a bait fish crosswise and take some time to maneuver it into swallowing position. Usually, a pike pauses right before it swallows any bait. When the pike pauses, strike.

- ✔ **When fishing with artificials:** Strike when the pike does. You'll be rewarded by the sight of the writhing form of the pike rocketing from the water. Don't be fooled when the pike seems to surrender after a fierce, but short, initial run. As soon as it sees you or your boat, you usually get a very satisfying second (and even third) run. The Daredevle is an amazingly effective pike lure.

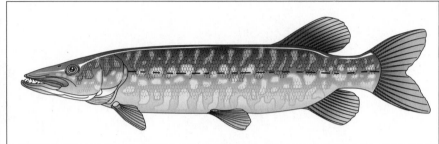

Figure 4-10:
The northern pike is a well-designed killing machine.

Muskellunge

If you're the kind of person who likes the odds in the state lottery, you should enjoy fishing for muskellunge, or *muskie*. The old-timers say that fishing for muskie takes 10,000 casts for every strike. And then when you do get a muskie on, its teeth are so sharp, it can be so big, and its fight can be so dogged, that it takes brawn and skill to land one. If you do though, you have a real trophy.

Like the pike featured in the preceding section, the muskie hangs out in likely ambush spots: weed beds, deep holes, drop-offs, and over sunken islands. Although it spends most of its time in the depths, the muskie appears to do most of its feeding in shallower water (at less than 15 feet). Optimum water temperature for muskies is in the low 60-degree range.

The muskie is a northern fish, found in the upper parts of the Mississippi drainage, the St. Lawrence River, all over New England, and throughout most of Canada. It's an opportunistic predator that strikes any number of baits or lures in any number of ways. Sometimes a muskie strikes far from your boat; other times it follows a lure right up to the gunwales. Because the muskie is so completely unpredictable, a beginning muskie fisherman should hire a guide or a local expert for help until getting the hang of snaring this beast.

Figure 4-11 shows a muskie. Note that its appearance is quite similar to that of a pike. You can't always be sure which is which unless you get pretty close to the fish, in which case you can see that the muskie, in contrast to the pike, has no scales on its lower cheek and gill covers. Its markings tend to look like dark bars or spots, whereas northern pike usually have lighter-colored spots that are shaped like beans.

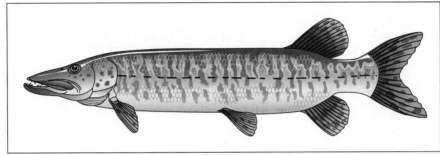

Pickerel

Though smaller than the pike and the muskie, the pickerel is in every other way as pugnacious and predatory as its larger cousins. The pickerel is to angling what the toy is to a box of Cracker Jack — the toy isn't the reason you buy the snack, but it's a nice surprise when you get a good one. Likewise, many a bassless day has been saved by the voracious appetite of the pickerel. Figure 4-12 shows a chain pickerel, whose dark green side markings appear to line up like the links of a chain.

If you're working a spoon or spinner, you have a better chance if you retrieve your lure parallel to a weed bed, because you never know where a pickerel may be hanging out. Fishing for pickerel in water in the upper 60s usually garners the best results.

Figure 4-12: The chain pickerel looks like a miniature pike, but these two predators don't commonly coexist in the same waters.

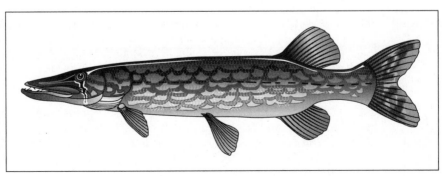

Book IV

Getting Outdoors

Pacific Salmon

Few fish are as delicious as the Pacific salmon (which is one of the reasons they're so heavily harvested by commercial fishermen). Pacific salmon come upstream to spawn and have pink flesh, just like Atlantic salmon do. The two types of fish even taste the same. But the six species of Pacific salmon (including the coho and chinook) are completely different animals than the Atlantic salmon, which is the only true salmon. The Pacifics are the much larger, mostly ocean-going cousins of the rainbow trout.

Some years ago, Pacific salmon were introduced into the Great Lakes to help control the spread of the alewife herring. The alewives were so plentiful and the salmon fed so well on them that the Great Lakes now hold the greatest fishery for both the coho and chinook sport-fisherman. In their natural range, however, overfishing has dangerously depleted them, as has the construction of dams.

Pacific salmon prefer cold water, about 55 degrees. They move with currents and tides to maintain themselves in that *thermocline,* which is a fancy way of saying "a region in a body of water with a specific temperature." As for where they're located, a cold front may bring Pacific salmon close to shore, but a wind also may drive the cold water and the fish farther offshore. When looking for them in a lake, using a thermometer to check water temperature is absolutely necessary.

Shallow-water and stream anglers have the most luck when Pacific salmon gather at stream mouths just before spawning. Fishing when the salmon are still bright, or fresh from the ocean or lake, can be great sport with these brawny, athletic fish. After they've been in the stream for any length of time, landing even a 30-pound fish is about as much fun as lugging a duffel bag full of books up a steep staircase.

As with many saltwater fish, or fish that spend a good amount of time in saltwater (the term for fish that live in both fresh and saltwater is *anadromous*), the chinook and coho like flashy, bright-colored lures. For bait, you may be hard-pressed to find better than smelt or alewives. Salmon eggs are a fine choice as well. (Which always begs this question: Why would a fish want to eat its next generation?)

Figure 4-13 shows the coho and chinook salmon. The usually smaller coho has black spots only on the upper part of its tail, whereas the chinook's tail is spotted on both top and bottom. The chinook's dorsal fin is spotted; the coho's isn't. The gum in the lower jaw of the coho is grayish, but the same gum in the chinook is black.

In many areas, particularly in the Great Lakes, fish can pick up toxic pollutants. The presence of pollutants doesn't make Pacific salmon less fun to catch, but eating fish from these waters isn't a good idea. Always check the local health advisories before you take a fish for a meal.

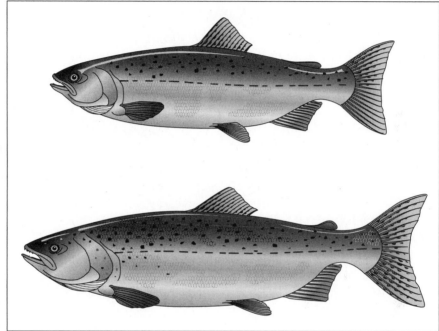

Figure 4-13:
For many freshwater anglers, the coho (top) and chinook (bottom) salmon are by far their largest quarry.

Panfish

Panfish is really a catchall category that includes a whole range of fish, including most of the sunfish (except the largemouth and smallmouth bass) as well as crappie. Panfish are called panfish because they fit in a frying pan. This fact tells you something — namely, that panfish are good to eat.

In addition to edibility, another good feature of panfish is their catchability. Whether caught with a cane pole, fly rod, or light spinning rig, panfish are extremely sporty. Worms, grubs, crickets, little spinners, popping bugs, dry flies, small jigs, bread balls, and corn are all effective panfish catchers. Because they're often the runts of the pond or stream, panfish pretty much attack anything that looks remotely edible.

Some of the more popular panfish include the following, all shown in Figure 4-14:

Book IV

Getting Outdoors

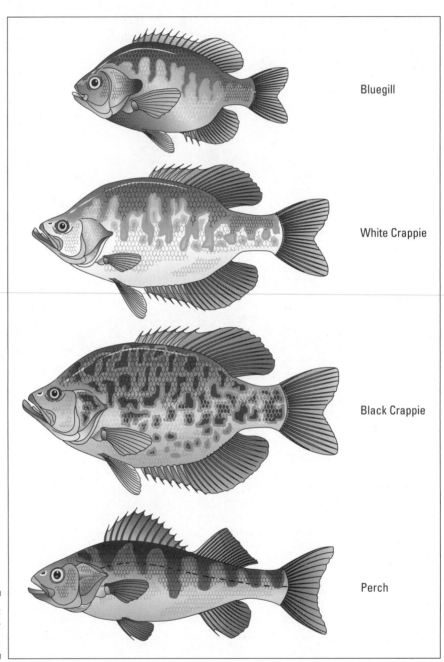

Bluegill

White Crappie

Black Crappie

Perch

Figure 4-14:
Four popular
panfish.

- **Bluegill:** Sometimes known as the *bream,* the bluegill has a blue edge to the breast area and a dark ear flap. It's probably the most-caught sport fish in America.

- **White crappie:** Very widespread all over North America, this fish takes all kinds of bait and small lures. It thrives in silty and slow-moving water and flourishes in the South. The white crappie is the only sunfish with six spines on its dorsal fin.

- **Black crappie:** This fish prefers somewhat clearer water than the white crappie. Because of its mottled skin (the white crappie is more barred), a local name for the black crappie is *calico bass.*

- **Perch:** Both white and yellow perch are utterly delicious fish. French chefs steam them in parchment and call the process *en papillote.* In Door County, Wisconsin, the old-time commercial fishermen would get the same effect by wrapping their perch in wet newspapers along with some onions, salt, and pepper and throwing them on the housing of their overworked diesel engines. Because these fishermen cooked on the domes of their engines, their meals were called "domers."

Catfish

The United States is home to more than 20 species of catfish (including bullheads). They're very popular because of their catchability, accessibility, affordability (due to the relatively low cost of the tackle required to catch them), and delicious taste. People usually eat crispy fried catfish the way they eat potato chips — until the last one is gone. Figure 4-15 clearly shows the difference between proper catfish and bullheads. Notice, however, that both have long whiskers, or *barbels.*

Because catfish are nocturnal feeders, they rely on touch, taste, and smell to identify food. Some of the most nose plug-requiring baits — called, appropriately, *stinkbaits* — attract catfish even though they smell as ripe as a marathoner's sweat socks.

 When bait fishing, keep your bait on the bottom. That's where the catfish are. Lures aren't that productive except with the channel cat, which is found in somewhat clearer moving water and often takes a deep-running plug, spoon, or jig.

Catfish are active in warm water and may be taken with water temperatures in the high 80s.

Book IV

Getting Outdoors

When you handle a catfish, it will "lock" together its pectoral and dorsal fins. The projecting spines are very sharp and carry a toxin. Though not fatal, a wound from these spines can be nasty and painful. If you're pricked while handling a catfish, treat the wound immediately with a disinfectant because swift action often nullifies the poison. Then apply a bandage. Your revenge on the catfish is that you get to eat it.

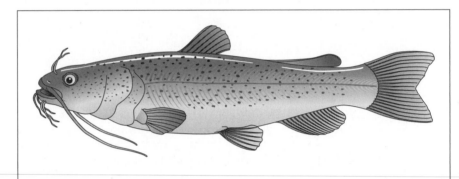

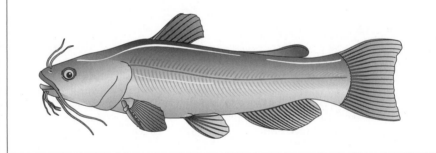

Figure 4-15:
The channel cat (top), a true catfish; a bullhead (bottom).

Shad

The shad, which is a large member of the herring family, lives most of its life at sea and returns to the river of its birth to spawn and die. The shad doesn't feed after it enters a river, but it can be induced to strike a brightly colored fly or lure. Because most shad lures, called *darts,* look like really cheesy costume jewelry, you have to wonder about what shads are thinking.

When hickory shad are in the rivers, thousands of white pelicans come in from the Atlantic to feast on their carcasses. In the northern part of the United States, the main river systems for shad anglers are the Delaware, Susquehanna, and Connecticut, where you can take them from a boat or while wading.

When playing a shad, remember that its mouth is very soft. Give it room to run. If you try to *horse* the fish (meaning muscle it in), you'll surely pull your lure or fly out. If you let it run, it'll reward you with a number of beautiful leaps, just like a salmon.

Both the American and the hickory shad have the large scales and deeply forked tails characteristic of the herring family, as shown in Figure 4-16. The hickory shad is generally smaller though, and its lower lip extends out past its upper lip.

Figure 4-16:
American shad (top) and hickory shad (bottom).

Atlantic Salmon

The Atlantic salmon is regarded by many as the aristocrat of fishes. Perhaps it has this reputation because you have to be an aristocrat to be able to afford a few days on one of the choice salmon rivers. Not surprisingly with something that has become the sporting property of upper-class gentlemen, you must fish for Atlantic salmon with a fly rod. On many rivers, you also have to rent a guide. Don't hold any of this against the Atlantic salmon — it had very little to do with all the tradition surrounding it.

The Atlantic salmon is a cousin to the brown trout but spends most of its time at sea (although a salmon's infancy is passed in a river, and it's to that river that it returns to spawn). Shown in Figure 4-17, this fish doesn't die after spawning once, so you may return a salmon to the stream after catching it and be confident that it may well return to create even more fish the following year.

This practice is good because the Atlantic salmon is a pressured animal. Despite the efforts of fishery biologists, transplanting this magnificent game fish to the Pacific has proved impossible. Perhaps if the current Atlantic salmon population is preserved, its numbers will return to what they were back in George Washington's day, when these fish were so plentiful that farmers used them for fertilizer!

If plenty of action is what you crave, salmon fishing isn't for you: Just one fish a day is a very good average on most streams.

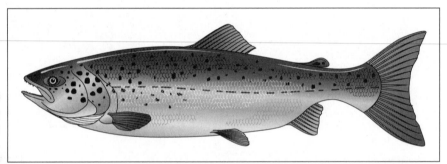

Figure 4-17:
The Atlantic salmon.

Cleaning and Storing Your Catch

For the sake of good eating, as well as being a nice person, you really should kill a fish right away (the exception is if you have a live well on your boat that's big enough to hold fish and keep them alive). Leaving a fish to flop, squirm, and suffocate — whether it's in your creel, in an ice chest, or lying on the sand at the beach — is never good form. If you want to eat your catch, killing it quickly provides two great advantages:

- A quick kill allows you to dress the fish at the peak of freshness. All those guts can affect the flavor of the fish if you leave them in there all day.

- As with tomatoes or peaches, bruised tissue is mealy. A dead fish doesn't flop around and bruise its flesh trying to escape.

Invest in a small club called a *fish priest*. When you have a fish you want to eat, just whack it over the head a couple times to kill it quickly.

Of course, after you kill your fish, you have to store it and clean it. The following sections offer techniques for doing both.

Storing fish for transport

Part of the reason that fish can turn so quickly is that they're so delicate. When handled with proper tender loving care, a well-cooked fish is one of the freshest-tasting meals you can eat. A.J. McClane, a revered angler and fishing journalist, once explained the smell of fresh fish by saying that all fish, when kept properly fresh, will smell a little bit like a cucumber that you just sliced open.

Following are the basics on the various schools of thought on properly storing fish. Take your pick:

- **Willow creel:** The *willow creel,* a basketlike cage for storing fish that's made out of willow branches, is a freshwater-angler classic for a reason: The weave of the willow branches allows air to circulate, which is what you want. If you use a willow creel, the accepted old-timey way to keep fish is to line the bottom of the creel with green grass and then to put layers of grass between the layers of fish. This method is good for a few hours (no more) in hot weather.

- **Canvas creel:** Less pricey than a willow creel, a canvas creel usually has a washable plastic liner inside a canvas outer bag. If you dip the creel in water and get it good and soaked, evaporation helps cool the fish. As with the willow creel, the canvas creel is for the freshwater angler.

- **Ice chest:** Open the chest; put the dead fish in; and close the chest. It's that simple.

- **Live well:** You can find *live wells,* compartments through which water passes, on many boats. In most cases, you can keep fish alive in them for hours.

- **A stringer:** A *stringer* is a piece of string, rope, or a specially designed set of metal clips passed through one gill of the fish. You can keep a mess of fish alive this way by tying one end of the string to your boat and putting the other end (with all the fish on it) back in the water.

Cleaning, or Why God made day-old newspapers

Fish cleaning can be a kitchen-destroying operation, what with scales flying everywhere, drying and sticking to everything, and guts sliding off the counter and clogging up the sink. (Honestly, part of the reason many wives secretly hope their husbands come home fishless is that they don't want to deal with the mess!) Guess what — it doesn't have to be that messy. Whenever possible, clean your fish before bringing it into the kitchen.

You need only one tool to dress most fish: a good knife. The Dexter, an American-made, carbon steel knife that retails for less than $20, is a good one; it sharpens easily, holds an edge fairly well, and performs double duty for vegetable slicing, cheese slicing, and any other general chopping or slicing chore. The Martini, which is a very thin Finnish fillet knife that also works well as an all-rounder, is good, too — but in the end, the Dexter works the best. Its blade is thin and has a slight curve that works well for filleting tasks, and it has enough oomph to cut through the backbone of a larger fish when you're making steaks. The downside is that it doesn't come with a sheath or holder. Instead, most anglers fashion a case for it out of two pieces of cardboard taped together.

Scaling

Although every fish has scales, not every fish needs to be scaled. The scales on a trout, for example, are so small that you don't have to worry about them. In fact, you wouldn't know there were any scales on a trout if someone hadn't told you.

Note: If you're going to fillet your fish and remove its skin, you don't need to scale it. Otherwise, here's what you do:

1. **Lay out about four spreads of newspaper.**

2. **Run your knife against the grain of the scale.**

   Your motion should be firm enough to remove the scales, but not so strong that they go flying all over the place.

3. **When you've finished scaling, lift the fish and peel back the top sheet of paper.**

4. **Lay the fish down on the next (clean) sheet of newspaper and throw out the top sheet with the scales.**

5. **Rinse the fish.**

Gutting

You gut a fish to get rid of the organs in the body cavity. These organs are filled with all kinds of gunk, including digestive juices. For this reason, you want to exercise care when slitting open the fish's belly. You'll have less mess and keep the flesh fresher if you don't pierce the organs while gutting.

To gut a fish the right way, follow these instructions:

1. **Lay out about four spreads of newspaper.**

2. **With your knife blade pointed toward the fish's head, pierce the stomach cavity and make a slit toward the head.**

   Try not to make too deep a cut, just enough to get through the top layer of skin and flesh.

3. **Pointing the knife toward the tail, completely open the stomach cavity.**

4. **Reach in and pull out the guts.**

5. **Detach the gills with the knife, or simply pull away.**

6. **Wrap the guts and gills in the top sheet of paper and discard.**

Filleting

Filleting a fish requires a certain amount of touch, but expending a little more effort at the cleaning and filleting stage is worth it, because it means no bones at the eating stage. When you get the hang of filleting, you can zip through a pile of fish pretty quickly, and it gives you a sense of accomplishment that you can do something as well as the old-timers.

Don't worry too much if you don't get absolutely all the meat off the fish when you first start filleting. The idea at the beginning is just to get some meat. If you skin the fish, as recommended, you don't have to scale it first. Obviously, if you're going to use the skin, scale it — unless you really enjoy eating scales.

Following are the basics of filleting a small fish (up to about 5 pounds), as shown in Figure 4-18:

1. **Cut off the head just behind the gills.**

2. **Hold the fish by the tail, and with the knife blade pointing away from you and across the body of the fish, begin to cut toward where the head used to be.**

   Use the backbone to guide your knife.

3. **To take the skin off, begin by holding the fillet by the tail, skin side down.**

4. **Hold the knife crosswise across the fillet and insert the knife between the skin and the flesh.**

   Don't worry if you don't get this move perfect at first.

5. **While holding the skin, cut in the direction of the former head.**

Book IV

Getting Outdoors

When you have a larger fish, the tail-to-head method of filleting can be a little awkward. In this case, opening the fish like a book is an effective approach, as shown in Figure 4-19. Follow these steps:

1. **Make a deep cut just behind the gills (about halfway through the thickness of the fish).**

2. **Cut a slit a few inches in length along the top of the fish (the dorsal side).**

3. **Using the tip of your knife, separate the flesh from the bones, as illustrated.**

   If you do this step properly, the fish opens up just like a book.

4. **When completely open, finish cutting away the fillet by moving the knife along the "spine of the book."**

Cutting steaks

Fish steak is a time-honored dish, but many people don't go in for cooking fish steaks because they're too dry. Here's some advice: Just make thinner steaks, about an inch or less.

You can use a Dexter knife for making steaks, or a wide-bladed chef's knife (the kind chefs use on TV to chop vegetables).

Follow these steps to cut fish steaks (referring to Figure 4-20 as you go):

1. **Scale the fish.**

   Refer to the instructions in the earlier "Scaling" section for guidance.

2. **Make a row of cuts crosswise along the fish.**

   Space the cuts so that they're the thickness of the steaks.

3. **Cut down to the backbone.**

4. **With a mallet, a rolling pin, or a thick branch, strike the back of the knife blade so that it goes through the backbone.**

   This isn't the place to perfect a big swing for your rock-breaking technique in case you ever end up on a chain gang. A short chop should do it.

5. **If your stroke doesn't completely detach the steak, continue to cut through the flesh and skin until the steak falls away from the rest of the fish.**

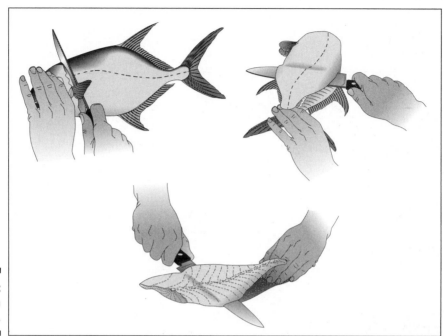

Figure 4-18:
Filleting a
small fish.

Figure 4-19:
Try this
technique
for filleting
larger fish.

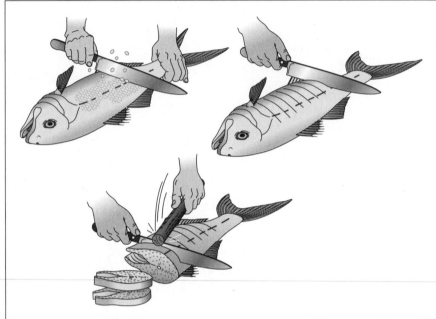

Figure 4-20:
Cutting a
fish into
steaks.

Freezing for freshest taste

Frozen fish doesn't have the consistency of flesh that has never been
frozen. The physics behind this fact are simple: Living cells are filled with
water; water expands when frozen, and this expansion breaks down tissue.
However, if you aren't going to eat fish right away — like within a day — then
you really should freeze it to keep the fish tasting fresh.

For example, many people often express that they don't like the taste of
bluefish. It's too oily, they say, or too fishy. What they're really referring to is
the taste of fish oil that has come in contact with the air and turned rancid.
Bluefish has a lot of oil, so unless you cook it on the day you catch it, it will
have that oily, fishy taste. Freezing stops this process short and preserves
the fish's fresh taste.

Freeze fish that you've filleted first. Wrap each fillet in wax paper and store
them all in a sealable plastic bag, keeping the fillets flat.

Chapter 5

Outdoor Fun for Adults and Kids

In This Chapter

▶ Checking out several activities to do outdoors when imagination fades

▶ Watching wildlife and gathering specimens

▶ Making great photographs of your adventures

▶ Stargazing through the seasons

You can do an infinite number of activities to entertain everyone in your camping party, whether they're adults or children — or adults acting like children.

As with any activity you choose, be sure that it always adheres to these guidelines: It must be safe; it must not disturb the wildlife; it must not damage the environment in any way; it must not disturb other campers; and it should be fun.

That said, turn your campers loose! Youngsters (of all ages) are limited only by their imaginations when it comes to having fun on a camping trip. Choices include such all-time favorites as tree climbing, crawfish hunting, firefly chasing, cloud watching, meadow crawling, and playing hide-and-seek, among many tantalizing alternatives.

Fun and Games

When your campers finally run out of their own great ideas for fun, you can be ready with a long list of suggestions. The following sections present some favorite games and other fun activities to enjoy with children or an adventurous group of adults.

Fox and hare

Fox and hare is a fun game that teaches anyone to become aware of his surroundings to such an extent that he's able to follow the trail of something because of the signs it leaves. Begin by designating the hare (usually an adult) and the foxes (usually children and another adult for supervision). Initially, give the hare a two- to five-minute head start — enough that the foxes lose sight of him. During this time, the hare leaves signs for the foxes to follow, such as bits of colored paper on the ground or in branches, that aren't too obvious yet are distinct enough to be followed with minimal effort. As the foxes gain more and more experience, give the hare a longer head start; the hare in turn begins leaving bits of paper that more closely match the color of the terrain. As a variation, the hare can drag a branch behind him, leaving a more subtle trail for the foxes to follow.

The goal of the game is for the foxes to successfully follow the trail of the hare and catch the hare. So feel free to use your imagination to adapt the hare's role and the trail he leaves any way you want.

Blind trust

Blind trust teaches participants to listen carefully to directions and to use their other senses of awareness. It also teaches important communication and leadership skills.

Play this game in a fairly wooded area with some small hills and narrow gullies or other obstacles. Blindfold all in the group except the designated leader. For the first time around, the designated leader should be an adult. The idea is for the leader to guide his group through the woods, going over, around, and under obstacles using only voice commands to give directions. At no time is the leader allowed to move obstacles or touch the players.

Have a parent or other adult keep a watchful eye on the group at all times to maintain a margin of safety. Otherwise you could wind up with a child trying to lead her group over a gully using a narrow log as a bridge.

Snapshot

Snapshot is great fun, and you can play it anywhere. It teaches children to use their observation skills efficiently and accurately. One person plays the role of the camera or lens, and the other person works the shutter or picture-taking button. The person guiding the camera searches for beautiful, interesting, or creative images that the camera can photograph. He sets up the camera, who must keep her eyes closed until told to open them, so that a picture can be taken. The camera guide snaps the photo by tapping the camera on the shoulder or hand. The camera opens her eyes without moving or twisting about and stares at the image in front of her. After about five seconds, the camera guide taps the camera's shoulder or hand, and the camera closes her eyes.

Allow your child to be the photographer, using you as the camera, and you'll be afforded a unique and quite possibly very moving look at how your child views what's fascinating and beautiful.

Stalking

In the game of stalking, one person, the prey, sits with his eyes closed at one end of a roughly 25-feet-wide clearing. Everyone else tries to stalk the person without being heard. If the prey hears a sound, he points to the direction it came from and opens his eyes. If the stalker is able to freeze and not move while the prey is watching, then the game continues. If, however, the prey opens his eyes after pointing and the stalker moves at all — even a flinch — the stalker becomes the prey.

Sledding

All it takes is one wild, snow-spraying ride on a sled to bring out the youth that's hibernating in many adults. Winter play is all about snow and getting around on it. But you don't have to shell out big bucks to experience the thrill of sledding. Look around for the following free or inexpensive sled substitutes:

- ✔ **Garbage bags:** Get a box of 20 or more 36-gallon-size, heavyweight, garden-variety garbage bags. Double up the bags, slide your legs inside (if you can fit) or sit on top (although this method isn't nearly as secure), and rip off a run or two before the bags shred into oblivion.

- ✔ **Discarded inner tubes:** Find these objects at a local truck stop or truck repair center. If they're available, you can often get them for the price of a few patches to seal the holes.

- ✔ **Cafeteria tray:** If you went to high school or college in any state that had snow on the outdoor menu, you're probably familiar with a favorite pastime: racing downhill perched on a serving tray pinched from the school cafeteria. The ride is wild, fast, uncontrolled, and monumentally unforgettable. Find a tray for about $1.50 at a restaurant-supply store.

Book IV

Getting Outdoors

- **Air mattresses:** For a cushy ride at high speeds, opt for a cheap plastic air mattress available for about $10 at any camping or sporting goods store. If the mattress survives the day, you can sleep on it that night.

- **Snow shovel:** Yes, there's even a school in New Mexico that teaches you the finer points of shovel racing. Suffice it to say that all you really need is a large snow shovel, a steep hill, and a smidgen of insanity. Sit on the shovel, holding the handle in front of you, lift your feet, and hang on! You can buy a snow shovel for about $15 at any hardware store, or simply borrow your neighbor's — tell him you'll shovel his driveway when you return.

Campfire songs

Singing around the campfire is a time-honored tradition. If you're completely inept at remembering songs, pick up a copy of *Campfire Songs* by Irene Maddox. This book features 192 pages of rounds, songs, and ballads — many with guitar chords, should you happen to be musically inclined.

Nature Activities

Encouraging folks to tune in to the world around them is important. For many, the sights and sounds of the night air in the mountains or desert are sources of discomfort and anxiety simply because they don't know what they are. Yet everywhere you look, nature is there. To see nature, all you have to do is open your eyes and ears, whether you're hiking down a trail or sitting quietly by a campfire. The following sections offer ideas to help you enjoy all the not-so-hidden gems that nature has to offer.

When you go traipsing off into the wild, remember to respect private property (always get permission before venturing out) and keep in mind some simple tips:

- **Don't pick plants or disturb nature in any way when on public property.** "Look but don't touch" is the creed here. Touching and picking disturbs the beauty for others who may want to experience in the future what you're enjoying in the present.

- **Respect nature by treating habitats with care.** No turning over rocks, breaking apart downed logs, or poking sticks into holes. After all, animals live in these places.

- **Pick wildflowers or plants on private land only when you have permission and only if you don't decimate the habitat in the process.** Pick selectively and conservatively — and only if there are many plants to choose from.

✔ **Never pick an endangered plant or wildflower, no matter where it may grow or how many you see in the meadow or forest.** This meadow or forest may be the last one in which these plants are growing! How do you tell what's endangered and what's not? Ask a ranger or other informed person. When in doubt, don't touch.

If you're out experiencing nature, having the right gear can enhance the experience. The naturalist gear you need varies depending on your level of expertise. Junior naturalists (beginners) should choose only from those items listed in the "Junior naturalist" list. Casual naturalists (avid novices) should choose from everything in both the "Junior naturalist" and "Casual naturalist" lists. Hard-core naturalists (experienced, even a little) may choose their gear from all three lists.

✔ **Junior naturalist (beginner)**

- Aquarium net for viewing aquatic life
- Bug viewer
- Crayons in various shades
- Envelopes for collecting leaves and seeds
- Mini field guides, such as *Peterson First Guides*
- Notebook and pencil
- Plastic hand lens
- Plastic minibinoculars
- 6-inch ruler

✔ **Casual naturalist (avid novice)**

- *Audubon Pocket Guides*
- Binoculars (7 x 35 is an adequate and versatile choice)
- Magnifier (5x to 10x magnification is best)
- Microcassette recorder
- *Peterson Field Guides*
- Plastic containers for specimens

✔ **Hard-core naturalist (experienced, even a little)**

- Butterfly net for collecting insect life
- Camera (a waterproof point-and-shoot is best for all-around use)
- Compass
- Plaster of Paris mix to make impressions of animal tracks

Book IV

Getting Outdoors

- Pocket knife
- Reference books
- Small plastic vials for collecting specimens
- Small trowel
- Small waterproof paper notebook
- Tape measure
- Thermometer
- Tweezers
- Yardstick

Hanging out in a hammock

There's an art to doing nothing, which is, frankly, one of the things you should specialize in when outdoors. For that very reason, you should tote along a couple of hammocks whenever you car-camp. No, there aren't always places to hang them in camp, but when there are, a hammock's presence announces to the world: "Mellow dude in camp — do not disturb."

Swinging gently in the late afternoon sun while the breezes tease the leaves in the trees above is perhaps one of the most relaxing moments imaginable. However, don't just flop into a hammock, because relaxation will be the farthest thing from your mind.

Folks who lie end-to-end in a hammock find little rest and relaxation — their hindquarters drag the dust while their heads and feet point skyward. The secret is in proper positioning. If you lie diagonally in a hammock, forces that you learned about in high school physics come into play and — presto — your body gains support, and your mind finds peace. Consider keeping a stuff sack filled with a soft parka (for under your head), a water bottle, and a favorite book handy for ultimate relaxation. If mosquitoes or biting flies are a problem, keep a head net handy, too.

Playing world above/world below

A quiet, observational activity, world above/world below only works if your children are feeling calm and not overly agitated. To study the world above, have everyone lie still on their backs, looking up. (This game is best played under a dense canopy of leaves or swirling clouds, or in dense, tall grass.)

World below is, as you'd expect, the opposite of world above. All the players lie on their stomachs and watch the world as it passes by underneath their faces. World below works outstandingly well at a stream or lake edge, above a tide pool, or in a dense patch of grasses or fallen leaves. If the ground is cold or hard, bring *ensolite* (sleeping) pads for everyone to lie on.

Practicing a night-world vigil

Going on a night walk with your children in the wilderness is a wonderful experience you shouldn't miss. It can, however, be somewhat unsettling for first-timers and is best enjoyed if a little forethought and preparation go into the adventure. If you can rehearse a night-world vigil at home, so much the better. Here's how:

Pick a night that's going to be clear with no moon. Turn out all the lights in the house so there's a minimum of artificial light illuminating the backyard. With a flashlight, walk out into the backyard and sit down under a tree or somewhere that's comfortable. Bring a blanket along if desired.

With the flashlight on, show your child that although it seems lighter with the flashlight, your vision is really limited to the beam of the light. Now, turn off the light, sit quietly, and notice the following:

- **Sights:** How does the backyard seem different in the dark? Why? When the time seems right, walk back to the house without the flashlight. Point out to your child how much better his vision is without the light.

- **Sounds:** Explain and talk about each sound as you hear it: a dog barking, a bat flitting through the air, a siren, or a mouse rustling in the compost pile. Begin to help your child distinguish between those sounds that are heard in the day and those heard at night. Ask him why some animals only come out at night and what makes them different from daytime animals.

Hugging a tree

Hugging a tree is an excellent exercise that teaches children to tap into their perceptual skills. Blindfold your child and lead her to a nearby tree. Ask her to get to know the tree by hugging it, touching it, smelling it, and listening to it. Ask her to describe the tree to you — its size, its age, and its shape. After your child feels that she really knows the tree, lead her away, spin her around, and remove the blindfold. Then ask your child to find her tree. Children discover that accomplishing this task requires all their senses and that it's possible to "see" and "know" an object without eyes. After your child finds her tree, let her blindfold you and lead you through the exercise so you can be a participant too.

Going for a stream walk

A stream walk is a terrific nature activity, but it requires you to take some safety precautions. Be sure that everyone wears old tennis shoes and that the day is warm. Beware of slippery rocks, sharp sticks and other objects, poisonous snakes, and hypothermia. Don't stay in the cold water too long. Bring along magnifying glasses, aquarium nets, several face masks, and clear plastic dishes about 6 inches across, or your homemade underwater viewing can. (See "Checking out tide pools," later in this chapter, to find out how to assemble your own viewing can.)

Choose a section of stream that's not too difficult to navigate through, not too long (and with easy exit points), and not too deep. The idea is to wade down the middle of the stream slowly and methodically. Look for minnows, frogs, tadpoles, and crawfish. Use the aquarium net to scoop up animals and look at them in the dishes. Use your masks or place the dishes in the water for a glass-window view of the stream below the surface. Romp, play, and get dirty. Wallow in mud holes and explore every nook and cranny. If you come upon a still pool, have your children stand quietly, observing the world below them through masks or the glass dishes floating on the surface. If they're able to stand quietly enough for longer than a minute, they'll get a peek at another world swimming around their legs and feet.

Mucking around in a swamp

Swamp mucking is a variation on the stream walk (covered in the preceding section) with one major exception: You get really muddy. The idea is to actually crawl through the swamp, following open waterways and animal paths. Talk about immersing yourself in nature!

Use obvious caution before diving into a swamp that may be home to alligators, water moccasins, leeches, or snapping turtles.

Walking barefoot

Walking barefoot is a most natural and yet rarely enjoyed experience that encourages you to slow down, feel the ground underfoot, and relive an almost primal instinct. Be sure that the ground you're going to walk over is relatively free from sharp rocks, thorns, and yes, even glass. Lead your youngsters through the woods single file. Teach them to walk as if they're hunting by taking a very small and very careful step forward to the outside ball of their descending foot. Very slowly, and without putting any weight on it, roll the foot to the inside of the ball. If nothing that may break with a loud snap or pop is felt underfoot, carefully lower the heel and then put full weight on the foot. If your child becomes adept at this way of walking barefoot, he'll be able to sneak up closely to birds and animals without spooking them.

Buying and using binoculars

Binoculars are an important addition to any outdoor adventurer's equipment list. They bring the distant world close enough to view, allowing you to visually leapfrog up a mountain, capture the intricate detail of a hawk's feathers high overhead, or scan the surface of a lake — all without moving a step. Choosing the right binoculars, however, can be confusing, especially because hundreds of models are available with prices ranging from $10 cereal-box sport glasses to $700 autofocus binoculars that use the latest in microchip technology.

Before you shop, do your homework and make a list of your needs. Are you going to use your binoculars primarily for viewing wildlife, sports, stars, or a combination of these subjects? Will you use them in normal lighting, in the shadows of late evening, or in the deep forest? Will they be routinely exposed to elements or relatively protected? Is durability a factor?

Then decide how much you're willing to spend. If you're only going to use the binoculars once or twice a year, you can probably get away with a lower-priced model. But don't settle on the cheapest pair you can find. You may regret your choice later. Generally, the higher the price, the better the optical quality and the more durable the housing — to a point. Beyond $250 to $300, you probably won't notice the difference.

Binoculars fill virtually any indoor and outdoor need imaginable, from opera to football to wilderness exploration. However, no binoculars meet every need. The following is a recommended application for a select sampling of magnification powers:

- **6 x 30:** Stadium sports, indoor sports, theater, bird-watching at a home feeder

- **7 x 25:** Stadium sports, hiking, bike touring, nature observation

- **7 x 35:** General purpose, stadium sports, bird-watching, boating, wildlife observation

- **7 x 50:** General purpose, bird-watching, boating, stargazing, hunting

- **8 x 40:** Wildlife observation, stargazing, long-distance bird-watching

After buying your binoculars, keep them in good condition by following these tips:

- **Never touch binocular lenses with your fingers.** Instead, remove grit and grime with a few puffs of a blower brush (found in most photo stores) and then brush away any remaining particles. Remove haze and fingerprints by gently wiping with a lens tissue dampened with a drop of lens cleaner.

- **Don't leave your binoculars in the hot sun, the trunk of your car, or anywhere else where heat may warp the casing.**

- **Keep your binoculars stored in a padded nylon or leather case.** Add a packet of silica gel to help absorb any moisture.

- **Clean the exterior of your binoculars only with a lint-free cotton cloth or a silicon-impregnated cloth that some manufacturers supply with your purchase.**

Book IV

Getting
Outdoors

Checking out tide pools

Tide-pooling, especially with a young child or an older adult who's young at heart, is an absolute hoot. Poking and peering into pools searching for crabs, sea urchins, seashells, sea cucumbers, octopi, starfish, and the like can keep an explorer occupied and entertained for hours.

To make the trip more enjoyable, bring an underwater viewing "eye." You can easily make your own by cutting the end off an old #10 coffee can, covering it tightly with clear plastic wrap, and securing the wrap in place with a rubber band. When you get to a deep tide pool that you want to look into, just place the underwater viewing can in the water, plastic end down, and look through the can like a viewing window. You'll be amazed by how clearly you can see.

Sometimes, you may want to turn over a rock or log to see what lives under it. Do so carefully and gently, taking care not to crush what lives underneath. Replace the rock, with equal care, when you're finished looking.

Don't collect anything from the beach that's alive — in most cases, doing so is illegal. Besides, marine animals are much better cared for in a wild environment. As you wander, also remember that most beachfronts are considered public property right along the waterline, but after you head up the beach, above the high-tide limit, you enter a zone that may or may not be private. It's your responsibility to know whether you're treading on public or private beachfront property. If in doubt, ask at the public access point before venturing out. And one more thing: Never turn your back on the ocean — you risk getting drenched by a sneaky wave.

Gazing at the stars

The lights of a city mask the stars, leaving no chance to see the world beyond Earth unless you step away from the city and gaze skyward from a mountaintop or an open field. For most city-trapped folk, seeing a million pinpricks of light twinkling against the inky-black backdrop of a night sky is a new experience. Stargazing takes practice and patience, but with a star wheel (available at most nature, outdoor specialty, or hobby stores) and a star guide, you'll open up a new world for yourself and your family or friends.

The following are some favorite and easily found stars and constellations:

- ✔ **North Star:** The beauty of the North Star is that it stays in one place in the sky and always to the north of you. You can locate this star, also known as Polaris, if you can find the Big Dipper. To pick the North Star out of the mass of other twinkling stars, find the Big Dipper and then look to the two stars that make up the lip of the dipper's ladle. The North Star lies above the two stars, known as pointer stars, in a relatively straight line, approximately four to six times the distance between the two stars.

- ✔ **Cassiopeia:** This star was named for the wife of King Cepheus, an Ethiopian king. According to mythology, she was turned into a constellation as punishment for her vanity. Look for a five-star cluster shaped like a W or an M on the north/northeast horizon just before midnight in a summer sky.

✔ **Ursa Major:** You can find this constellation (also known as the Great Bear) near the Big Dipper, which actually makes up a part of the bear. The dipper makes up the bear's back, with the handle standing in for the bear's nose. Three pairs of stars make up the bear's paws.

✔ **Bootes:** Also known as the Herdsman, this constellation resembles a large kite and is located below the Big Dipper. At the constellation's base lies Arcturus, the fourth-brightest star in the sky (look for its distinct orange color).

✔ **Leo:** You can find the lion just below the bear's paws between the Great Bear and the western horizon. The bluish-white star Regulus sits near the lion's chest and behind its front leg.

The section "Star Maps" at the end of this chapter features a series of star maps you can use when stargazing.

Taking a sunrise hike

Getting up before the sun rises probably isn't high on your agenda unless you're a mountaineer seeking to reach a summit before the sun softens the snow. However, many campers miss out on a very special and spiritual time outdoors by experiencing sunrise only from the protected confines of a tent and sleeping bag.

Though the groans can be loud and clear when you wake folks an hour before dawn, the grins, oohs, and ahs following a sunrise breakfast experience are usually unanimous. Select a safe route up to a suitable lookout point that's no more than a 30-minute hike from camp. Headlamps and flashlights are a must. After safely nestling into the lookout area, quiet the group and watch the thin sliver of light appear on the eastern horizon. Colors often dance in the sky as the sun pushes fingers of light through the velvet curtain of dawn before exploding onto the scene as a warm, golden orb.

After the initial show is over, it's time to fire up a camp stove, whip up hot cocoa and coffee, and hand out bagels, cream cheese, dried fruit, or whatever your breakfast dreams desire — within reason of course. After you've experienced one sunrise, you'll want to see hundreds more.

Book IV

Getting Outdoors

Capturing Moments in Freeze Frame

A picture is worth a thousand words, provided the picture is a keeper. Many aren't. You know the kind: snapshots that are too light, too dark, too far from the subject, or full of distracting stuff. The next few sections show you how to avoid the fate of such flawed photos when enjoying the outdoors with family and friends.

Making shots worth showing

The following tips can help you ensure that your shots are worth showing to friends (see *Photography For Dummies,* 2nd Edition, by Russell Hart [Wiley] for more tips on capturing the perfect image):

- ✔ **Don't center the subject.** Centered subjects in a photo look stiff, posed, and downright amateur-ish. Place the subject of your photo off to one side and let the light or surrounding landscape add to the story you're trying to tell.

- ✔ **Use a sense of scale in your photos.** A giant sequoia or a distant mountain that looks huge to you appears as nothing more than a tiny image in print unless you place an object of known size in the picture to establish a relationship of scale. For example, try slipping a penny into the picture next to tiny flowers to show just how small they really are.

- ✔ **Block the glare.** A flare across your favorite shot can be prevented if you use a lens hood or cup your hand just above or to the side of the lens to block out stray light.

The essence of most amateur wildlife photography is defined by animal butts — way off in the distance. Anticipate the shot, move in front of the action, and then set up the photograph so your image fills as much of the frame as possible.

Keeping the camera handy

A camera doesn't do you much good if you can't get to it. Often a well-intentioned photographer spends an entire day hiking without taking one shot because the camera sits safely secure inside a backpack. The key to taking photographs during the day is to make your camera accessible. SunDog, LowePro, Tamrac, and PhotoFlex are some of the better known manufacturers of padded camera cases that can be carried as a chest pouch or attached to a waist belt. Some people prefer a chest pouch, although it does limit your "at the feet" visibility, which is a drawback if you're negotiating difficult terrain. Others prefer an ordinary fanny pack, which they spin around so the pack carries in front — a move that can make the pack a nuisance on steep climbs because it's always in the way of your thighs and knees.

Star Maps

The following pages contain eight star maps — four each of the Northern and Southern Hemispheres — to help start you on your starry way.

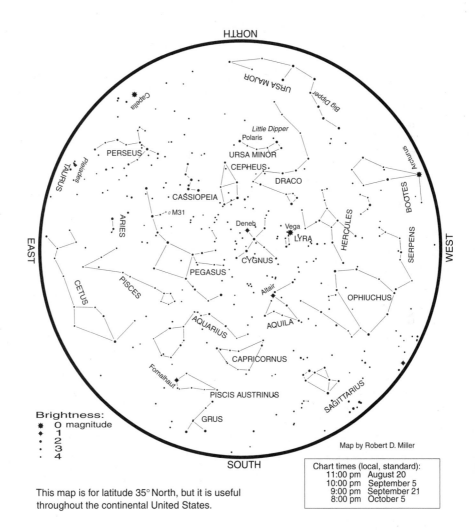

Brightness:

✷ 0 magnitude
✦ 1
• 2
· 3
· 4

Map by Robert D. Miller

Chart times (local, standard):
11:00 pm   August 20
10:00 pm   September 5
9:00 pm   September 21
8:00 pm   October 5

This map is for latitude 35° North, but it is useful throughout the continental United States.

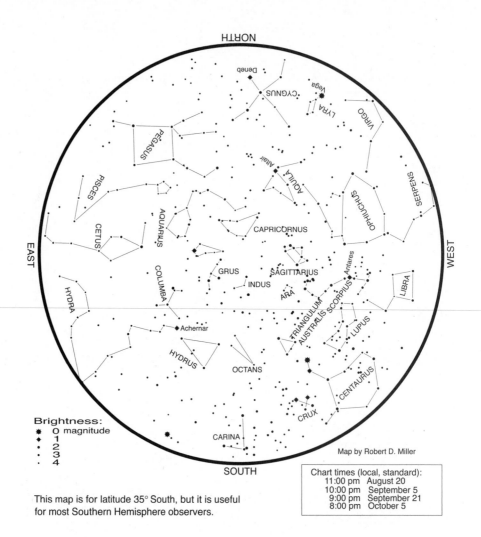

Brightness:
* 0 magnitude
* 1
* 2
* 3
* 4

Map by Robert D. Miller

Chart times (local, standard):
11:00 pm   August 20
10:00 pm   September 5
9:00 pm   September 21
8:00 pm   October 5

This map is for latitude 35° South, but it is useful for most Southern Hemisphere observers.

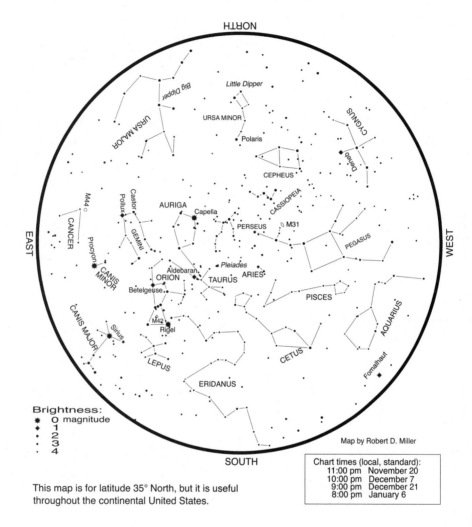

NORTH

Big Dipper

Little Dipper

URSA MINOR

URSA MAJOR

Polaris

CYGNUS

Deneb

CEPHEUS

M44

CANCER

Castor

Pollux

GEMINI

AURIGA

Capella

PERSEUS

M31

CASSIOPEIA

PEGASUS

EAST

Procyon

CANIS
MINOR

Pleiades

Aldebaran

ORION

Betelgeuse

TAURUS

ARIES

PISCES

WEST

CANIS MAJOR

Sirius

M42

Rigel

AQUARIUS

CETUS

LEPUS

ERIDANUS

Fomalhaut

Brightness:
* 0 magnitude
* 1
* 2
* 3
* 4

Map by Robert D. Miller

SOUTH

Chart times (local, standard):
11:00 pm   November 20
10:00 pm   December 7
9:00 pm   December 21
8:00 pm   January 6

This map is for latitude 35° North, but it is useful
throughout the continental United States.

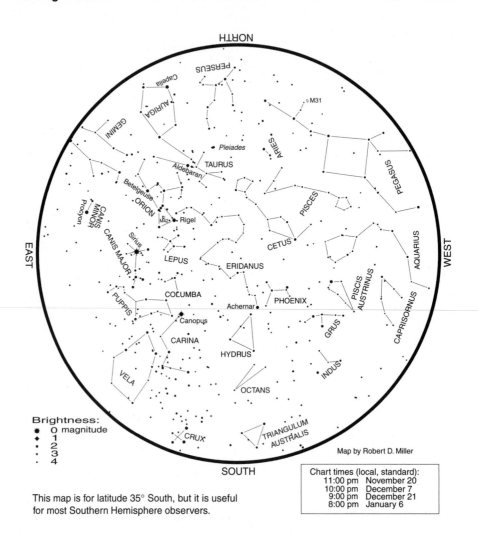

Map by Robert D. Miller

Brightness:
- 0 magnitude
- 1
- 2
- 3
- 4

Chart times (local, standard):	
11:00 pm	November 20
10:00 pm	December 7
9:00 pm	December 21
8:00 pm	January 6

This map is for latitude 35° South, but it is useful for most Southern Hemisphere observers.

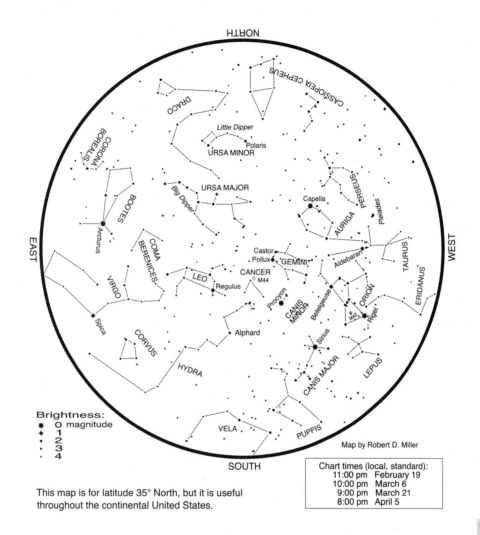

Map by Robert D. Miller

Brightness:
* 0 magnitude
* 1
* 2
* 3
* 4

This map is for latitude 35° North, but it is useful throughout the continental United States.

Chart times (local, standard):
11:00 pm   February 19
10:00 pm   March 6
9:00 pm   March 21
8:00 pm   April 5

Book IV

Getting Outdoors

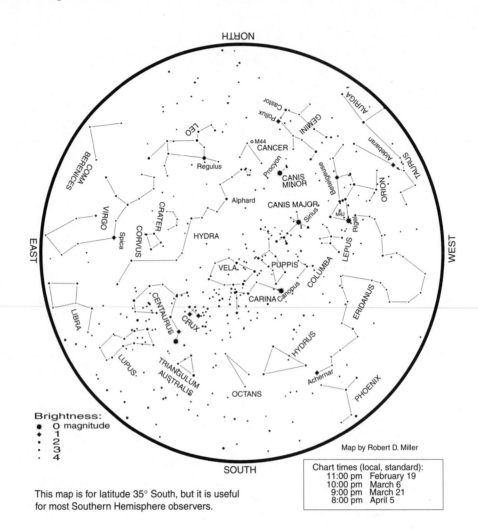

Brightness:
* 0 magnitude
* 1
* 2
* 3
* 4

Map by Robert D. Miller

Chart times (local, standard):
11:00 pm February 19
10:00 pm March 6
9:00 pm March 21
8:00 pm April 5

This map is for latitude 35° South, but it is useful for most Southern Hemisphere observers.

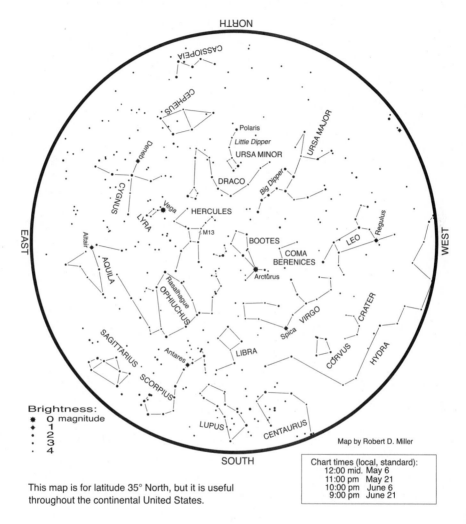

Brightness:
* 0 magnitude
* 1
* 2
* 3
* 4

Map by Robert D. Miller

This map is for latitude 35° North, but it is useful throughout the continental United States.

Chart times (local, standard):
12:00 mid. May 6
11:00 pm May 21
10:00 pm June 6
9:00 pm June 21

Book IV

Getting Outdoors

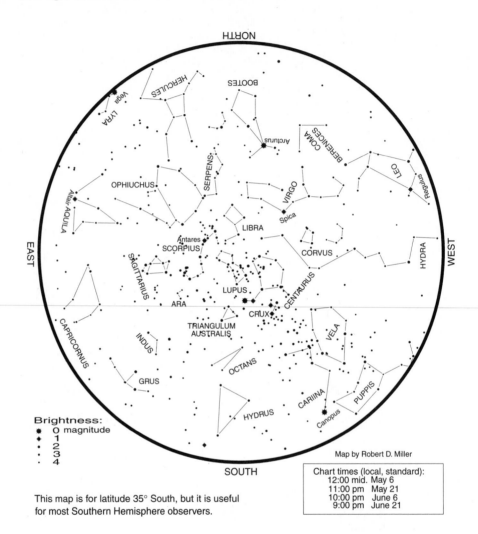

Map by Robert D. Miller

Brightness:
* 0 magnitude
* 1
* 2
* 3
* 4

Chart times (local, standard):
12:00 mid. May 6
11:00 pm May 21
10:00 pm June 6
9:00 pm June 21

This map is for latitude 35° South, but it is useful for most Southern Hemisphere observers.

Book V
Raising Farm Animals

The 5th Wave   By Rich Tennant

"I try to see to it that it's not all work for my bees."

In this book . . .

*I*f the only animals you've had in your life thus far are a dog, a cat, a caged parakeet, or a fish (or any combination thereof), you're in for a real treat. Your version of living a country lifestyle can include farm animals, too!

If you've already been thinking about expanding your menagerie and know just what you want, this book is just for you. It tells you how to go about picking, finding, and caring for your latest additions. If the idea has never crossed your mind and you don't know where to begin, this book helps you decide which kind of farm animal is right for you. (And don't count yourself out if you live in the city or on a relatively small piece of land. Not all farm animals take up a lot of space. Think bees!)

Chapter 1

Selecting Farm Animals

*Y*ou've probably already shared your home with a dog or cat or two. But living on a farm or in a home with a large tract of land opens up opportunities for sharing your life with other types of animals that you may not have dealt with in the past. A farm just isn't a farm without some animals, and with all that acreage, it'd seem empty without hooves or at least some paws trotting around the grounds.

Although raising animals requires some work (a *lot* of it with some animals), work isn't the only thing farm animals bring you. Animals can enrich your life — whether they're pets, workhorses, or beings that give you something back (meat, eggs, fiber, and so on). With the proper care and attention to their needs and feelings, you and your animals can become a great team.

This chapter gives you plenty of critter options to consider, but by no means does it present an exhaustive list of what you can do on your farm. Take these ideas as a starting point and use your imagination to come up with something unique that works for you. Check with local 4-H groups, your veterinarian, and local farms for ideas on the kinds of animals that thrive in your area, and get started.

Meeting the Common Farm Animals

Although the types of animals you can share your farm with are numerous, most people think of the ones in this section first. Indeed, these creatures are the usual suspects (but don't let this list limit your imagination — check out the later sections in this chapter for some other ideas). For info on individual breeds of cattle, goats, horses, sheep, and the like, check out `www.ansi.okstate.edu/breeds`.

You may want to start out with something that won't take up a lot of your time and money while you decide whether you like raising animals. Here's how costs compare:

- ✔ Animals requiring little initial output and maintenance are the smaller ones, such as fowl (chickens, ducks, geese, and turkeys), rabbits, goats, and sheep.

- ✔ Medium- to high-cost animals are the larger ones: camelids, cattle, and pigs. Some can have a pretty high initial cost. For example, female alpacas can cost as much as a quality horse, and a good cow can be more expensive than a poor horse. On the other hand, maintenance costs are relatively low.

- ✔ The highest-cost animals in terms of initial outlay and maintenance are horses. Even though you can get horses cheaply (see Book V, Chapter 2 for more on how to acquire your animals), they require a lot of maintenance.

Cattle

"Cattle" is a collective term referring to a group of cows, probably the number one creature people think of when they think of farm animals. ("Cow" technically refers to adult females, but calling the group of them cows is okay, even if calves and bulls are in the group as well.)

Cattle come in several varieties, each with its own characteristics, but generally they're raised for meat, milk, or help with chores. And you can't forget one more function of a cow or any other farm animal — simply having them around because you like them! Here are the major functions of cattle:

- ✔ **Dairy cattle:** Making the commitment to having dairy cattle means you have to be pretty much married to your farm (or at least you need workers who are). Dairy cattle must be milked twice a day during the time they produce milk (usually for six to nine months after giving birth), either by hand or machine, or they go dry. The milk is then processed into milk, cheese, butter, or yogurt. Common breeds of dairy cattle include Ayrshire, Brown Swiss, Guernsey, Holstein, Jersey, and Milking Shorthorn.

- ✔ **Beef cattle:** These types of cows are chosen and raised to be slaughtered. Unless you want to sell the tender meat of the calf (veal), it takes about two years before one of these guys is old enough and beefy enough to sell for food. Besides the meat you can get from your cattle, you also can tan the hide and use it for leather or suede clothing, furnishings, or even art. Common breeds of beef cattle include Angus, Herford, and Kobe.

✔ **Draft cattle:** Although the draft jobs have gone mostly to horses or machinery in modern times, a small operation can still use these beasts to help with various farming chores, such as hauling or plowing.

Another option in the cattle category is to get a mini cow. The claim is that due to their smaller size (and thus less feed consumption and less space needed per animal), beef production per acre on a small farm can be greater with mini cows than with larger animals.

Horses, ponies, donkeys, and mules

Every little kid's dream is to own a horse or a pony. Of course, kids know nothing about what's involved in caring for them; they just love the idea of galloping through the countryside on their very own friend Flicka. For many people, that dream doesn't die as they grow older. Horses, after all, can be a ton of fun. You can go backpacking with them, have them participate in rodeos or other shows, or simply entertain that childhood dream and go for a gallop through the countryside.

And don't forget their donkey and mule cousins. Donkeys, although a little smaller and probably not great for carrying adults, can be hitched up to carts. Both donkeys and mules are fun for kids' rides or for helping you around the farm.

Caring for horses is where the work part comes in, but if you love your animals, this work is a labor of love. Following are a few basics, and you can check out *Horses For Dummies,* 2nd Edition, by Audrey Pavia and Janice Posnikoff (Wiley), for more detailed help in caring for your horse.

✔ Horses need attention — and a lot of it. They need shelter from the weather; nutrient-rich food; a constant supply of clean water; clean, mucked out stalls every day; daily grooming and exercise; and good bedding (standing on a hard surface all day isn't good for them).

✔ Horses need quite a bit of room to thrive. Although horses have no set space requirements, you generally want at least 1 acre per horse.

✔ Horses are social animals that get bored, depressed, or surly if they don't have regular contact with humans and other animals. If you keep them in a barn, someone needs to ride them daily.

Horses love treats, and bringing some into the pen or pasture means you're about to get mobbed. But don't worry — they're not carnivores, so you're safe!

Swine

A pig farm isn't something to go into lightly. Yes, you can get some very tasty meat from a pig, but the work required is probably more than is desirable for the scope of a small farm. Pork prices tend to be low (although prices vary widely, pork tends to be about 40 to 50 percent less per pound than, say, a nice steak), so small farms often have trouble recovering their investments. Following are some facts to consider about raising pigs:

✔ If you're going for the meat angle, pigs generally need to be about 260 pounds (that takes roughly six months) before they're considered meaty enough to butcher. Translation: You're going to have a lot of food to feed and a lot of waste to clean up after!

You can find inexpensive sources of food for pigs by going to local restaurants or grocery stores and asking for their unusable food, such as the outer leaves of lettuce.

✔ Baby male pigs need to have their eyeteeth cut by a veterinarian so that they don't chew each other up. Fighting is in pigs' nature when they get to a certain age, and if left unchecked, the fights can be deadly.

✔ Pigs should be kept in a pen, and that pen must be cleaned out regularly. (Not doing so is what leads to the stereotype that pigs stink.) Pigs have a reputation for smelling bad, and many people find pig odor particularly offensive. However, proper waste disposal and hygiene can keep odors down.

✔ If allowed to roam in a larger fenced-in area, pigs clear the land by rooting with their powerful snouts. They also scratch their backs on trees and destroy the bark.

Pigs can be fun pets if you want to keep them on a smaller scale (just one or two animals). Consider getting a Vietnamese Potbelly pig (visit www.pigs4ever.com for more info about these guys). This breed is pretty clean (some people even keep them in the house), and individuals can have endearing personalities. A pot-bellied pig can seem like a dog sometimes as it follows you around and cuddles up to you, and it loves to be scratched behind the ears.

If you have guard dogs running around, make sure the pigpen is secure (meaning no dogs can slip under the fence) to keep both the dogs and the pigs safe from each other. Until you know how your particular animals will interact, don't let them do so unsupervised.

Sheep

Sheep are pretty easy to care for. Some people continually question their intelligence (mostly because of their strong herd mentality — where one goes, all others follow), but their reputation for feeble-mindedness isn't entirely true. They can recognize you, and each one has a personality.

Your sheep can provide you with more than wool. For instance, you can make their milk into cheeses or yogurt, and sheep's waste makes for good fertilizer that doesn't smell badly the way cow manure does. Although most sheep breeds are multipurpose, some sheep are bred for specific qualities — meat, milk, or wool. For instance, Dorset sheep are good milk producers, Suffolks produce good meat, and Rambouillet sheep produce fine wool. Because literally hundreds of breeds exist, your best bet is to check into what's appropriate for and available in the area where you live.

The process of preparing sheep fibers for spinning is the same as for other fiber animals, but sheep fleeces tend to contain a lot of lanolin, which creates a greasier feel and makes them a little harder to clean. Different breeds have different characteristics (like the lanolin-less Icelandic or the Shetland, whose fleece is the finest of the sheep breeds), but all fiber sheep produce a warm wool that you can make into clothing or lots of other products. (Check out Book II, Chapter 1 for some ideas.)

Some factors to consider when looking at whether you want to raise sheep include the following:

✔ Sheep eat grass. If you live in an area where grass is plentiful, your job of feeding them is easy, and you don't need a lawnmower; in a dry, desert area, you must supply all the feed.

If you own a very large area and only a few animals, you may be able to get by with just turning your sheep loose in the pasture and letting them have at it. However, some pasture management is far preferable. Try rotating your pasture: Give the critters an area to graze on and block off another area to give the soil a break from their trampling and to plant a cover crop to put nutrients back into the soil.

Grazing sheep can ruin your lawn if left unchecked, because they tend to chew it down to the ground. (This behavior was one of the main causes of the sheep-versus-cattle rancher wars in the early days of the American West.) Keep feed on hand to counteract this tendency.

✔ Sheep must be sheared once a year, usually in midspring. Not shearing them causes their wool to get long and matted, making it difficult for them to get around. Also, you can't process matted wool at all.

✔ Although sheep roam freely across the countryside in some areas, it's best to fence them in (away from coyotes and mountain lions, for example) and put a guard animal in with them. Dogs are good for guarding sheep.

✔ In the United States, most of the meat that comes from sheep comes from the babies — the lambs — making this type of animal one of the hardest ones to let go. Lamb meat (from sheep less than a year old) is the most tender, but mutton (meat from an older sheep) can be tastier, albeit a bit tough. The sweetest lamb meat (as well as from any animal for that matter) comes from the day the lamb is weaned.

Goats

Goats are some of the most domesticated animals and have been raised for thousands of years for their meat, milk, and fiber. The babies also have pretty darn cute faces, making sending one to the butcher a not-so-easy decision.

Depending on the condition and age of the slaughtered goat, the meat (sometimes called *chevon*) is similar to lamb, veal, or venison but is lower in fat and cholesterol. Goat milk makes wonderful cheeses, yogurt, and even ice cream. The milk is lower in lactose than that of other animals, and people who are lactose intolerant can ingest it favorably.

Goats raised for their fiber have similar characteristics to meat goats in terms of their care and behavior, but their coats are vastly different. They're soft and curly, and the fiber you can get from them is wonderful. The Angora, Cashmere, and a number of crosses are the most popular breeds that fit into this category. Despite what the Angora goat's name implies, you don't get angora fiber from it. Angora goats actually produce *mohair,* which ranges from very fine and soft to coarse and scratchy (angora comes from rabbits — see the next section). Goat fleeces have little oil in them, so they're easy to clean in preparation for processing into yarn.

Cashmere is a relative term. Some say *any* fiber goat can produce this fiber and that cashmere refers to a characteristic of the fiber itself (it must be 0.5 micrometers in diameter and be at least 3.175 centimeters long). Others say the goat that originated in the region of Kashmir is the only one whose fiber you can accurately call cashmere. People agree, however, that the fiber comes from the soft undercoat of the fiber goat. The fleece from the Kashmir-turned-cashmere is also known as *pashmina.*

Following are some pointers on goat care:

- ✔ You have to treat fiber goats as fiber goats. That means not using them as pack goats or putting them on a leash and taking them for a walk. Packs and collars cause their prized fiber to mat, and matted fiber isn't usable.

- ✔ Goats tend to be escape artists, so fences need to be strong and sturdy. Chicken wire and a couple of metal posts aren't enough — you need something stronger, such as chain link or metal fence panels.

- ✔ Goats can eat almost anything because their digestive systems can break down and glean nutrients from nearly any organic material. However, although they may *like* to eat shirts off your clothesline, doing so doesn't keep goats healthy. They also like to eat shrubs and weeds and can even digest some plants that are toxic to cattle and horses, making them great weed clearers.

Rabbits

You've probably heard the phrase "tastes like chicken" when someone is describing an unusual meat. Well, that description holds true for the meat of the rabbit, which is low in cholesterol. Rabbits, which eat grass and leafy weeds, are more productive and cheaper to feed than chickens. A rabbit can produce up to 1,000 percent of its body weight in food per year, which brings new meaning to the phrase "multiplying like a rabbit." Additionally, you can skin and butcher about five rabbits in the same amount of time it'd take to do a chicken.

Rabbits also produce a fine, soft fiber. Rabbit fur is very soft, and people have used rabbit pelts for years as fur accents on coats or hats, among many other uses.

The fiber of the Angora rabbit can also be spun into a super-soft yarn known simply as *angora*. Rabbits such as the Angora shed their coats a few times a year. (Yes, that means you can get the fiber and still keep the critter.) Brush them regularly to keep their coats free of knots and add the stuff you brush off to your to-be-spun pile. For rabbits that don't shed their coats, you can shear them or you can brush or hand-pull the loose fibers out. (You know it's time to harvest the rabbit's fur when you notice clumps of wool sticking to its cage.)

Here are a few rabbit-related tidbits to consider:

✔ Rabbits don't need much space to be happy, which is fortunate because they should be kept confined to reduce the threat of predators.

✔ Take care when building their enclosures to ensure their safety. Hutches should be well above the ground and out of the way of curious dogs and other smaller critters, like skunks.

✔ Because Angora hair is so long and soft, it has a tendency to mat and shed. (Remember, matted fiber is no good.) Not only does shedding mean you lose potential spinning fodder but it can also make a mess of the cage and cling to your clothes. Regular brushing is crucial.

Small and Medium Birds: Fancying Fine, Feathered Farm Friends

The most popular type of farm poultry is the chicken, but you may want to think about others such as turkeys, ducks, geese, quail, or peacocks — these birds also produce delicious meat or eggs and can be fun to have on your farm.

Chickens

The following sections focus on keeping chickens for eggs or meat. In meat birds, the meat builds up quickly, whereas egg-layers put their energy into egg production. A bird that performs dual duties is heavier than an egg-layer and produces fewer eggs than a standard layer, but it also produces more eggs than a meat bird.

Once a year, chickens *molt* (lose all their feathers), but don't worry about seeing bald birds running around — the feathers are lost a few at a time. Chickens' feathery coats take a couple of months to refurbish, but the birds don't go bald while this is happening. They do, however, get rather ratty-looking. Just take a deep breath and remember that seasonal molting is normal.

Keeping hens for eggs

Chickens kept primarily for laying eggs are called *layers.* The job of these birds is, of course, to lay eggs, and on average, they do that about once every 25 hours — or a little less than once per day — optimally speaking. They produce fewer eggs if something stresses them, such as not being fed enough or having a predator in the pen. Their bodies are smaller than the meat-producing birds and thus require less feed because they don't need to maintain muscle mass.

Some factors that affect their laying include

- **Daylight:** If the chicken house is set up with lighting and you give the birds 12 or more hours of daylight, you can keep the egg production up.

- **Temperature:** The optimal temperature for chickens is between 70 and 75 degrees Fahrenheit. As the temperature rises, the eggs produced get smaller and have thinner shells.

  Chickens actually self-regulate their temperatures and can survive harsh conditions, such as winter temps that are below freezing and summer temps that can rise to triple digits.

- **Molting:** In the fall, most hens start molting and stop laying eggs for a while.

- **Age:** Laying hens start laying eggs at about 6 months of age. Their egg production peaks at about 2 years of age, after which they lay fewer but larger eggs. If they get old enough, they eventually stop laying. ***Note:*** When laying chickens get past their productive years, they're often sold as stewing chickens. The meat is very tough, and stewing is the best way to make it edible.

Laying hens produce eggs regardless of whether a rooster is around, because egg production is part of the female chicken's bodily functions. If eggs are your goal, you don't need a rooster (except, of course, to give you that feeling of *really* being on a farm when the bird starts crowing in the wee hours of the morning). Some vegetarians are more interested in unfertilized eggs (those that are produced on rooster-free farms) because the eggs never have the potential of becoming a baby chicken.

Keeping chickens for meat

A chicken egg takes 21 days to hatch, and most meat chickens are bought as day-old chicks. Birds grow very fast, and the best meat is available when they're still pretty young. The idea is to get a meat chicken big as fast as possible. After all, the longer you have to feed a chicken, the less money you make. Most meat chickens have a life span of 6 to 8 weeks; thus, they don't produce eggs (which happens at about 6 months of age.)

Meat birds are bred to have large breasts, so if they live beyond 6 to 8 weeks, their bodies get too big, and they may start to break legs or have other problems. Meat birds shouldn't be encouraged to roost, because jumping off of those roosts puts strain on their legs.

Turkeys

Turkeys, of course, are the most popular Thanksgiving meal. They need to be a bit older than chickens do at slaughter — *hens* (females) should be 14 to 16 weeks old, and *toms* (males) should be 19 to 20 weeks old. Most commercial turkeys are bred to have a lot of meat on them, meaning they're unable to fly. Consequently, you need to provide them with protection not only from the elements but also from predators, because they can't fly up to the top of the barn if something gets too close.

Turkeys eat grain with a little higher protein content that what you'd give a chicken, and they have a life expectancy of about 10 years.

Did you know that turkey feathers are ground up and used commercially as filler for certain animal feeds? Also, studies on the fibers in yarn have shown that a little bit of the fiber from turkey feathers can make very good insulation material.

Ducks and geese

Ducks are typically raised for their meat, eggs, and down. Their meat is often used in gourmet foods in pricey restaurants (*foie gras* is one example). Their eggs are larger and richer than those of chickens and thus are prized among chefs. Ducks are popular animals to have on the farm because they're easy to care for (they're happy with kitchen scraps), they eat bugs, and they're just fun to watch. They can also act as alarms and fend off small predators.

Geese are hardy birds and aren't as susceptible to diseases as some of their poultry cousins. They're easy to care for because they're foragers — by eating their favorite food, they help control your weeds (and clean up your grass clippings!). Also, their eggs are a delicacy, and their feathers (particularly their down) make for soft and warm insulation material.

Game birds

Game birds come in several varieties, including peacocks, partridges, quail, pheasants, grouse, pigeons, doves, and guineas. Raising them on your farm can be lucrative if you find the right markets. Besides producing meat and eggs, they can also be used in hunting. People may use them for training hunting dogs or birds of prey in falconry. Or you can sell game birds to a commercial hunting operation. Such operations set the birds loose and charge hunters to come on their land and hunt them.

Some states require a license to raise game birds because they're considered protected. Check with your state to see what the rules say you can do with them.

Llamas and Alpacas: Spinning Out Info on Camelids

Camelids are popular on farms these days. The more common camelids are the llama and the alpaca, but two more critters — the guanaco and the vicuña — also fit into this family, and a few of these not-so-common family members are popping up across the U.S.

Camelids are *ruminants* (cud-chewers) like cattle, but they have three stomach compartments like their cousins the camels. They don't have hooves but rather walk on two toes, making them kinder to the environment when backpacking. Just looking at these guys brings joy to your spirit. They're like funny-looking horses with darling faces and curious personalities.

If you're interested in breeding these critters, you obviously need both a male and a female (although you can always rent a male for a night out with your girl). Careful attention to the expectant mother's health and welfare can result in a lucrative money-making opportunity: After a gestation period of about $11\frac{1}{2}$ months, you may be rewarded with a baby girl that can fetch you more than $15,000.

Most people raise alpacas and llamas for their fleece. The following sections note the differences between the two major camelids and zero in on managing their behavior.

Deciding between llamas and alpacas

Which camelid is right for you? Llamas and alpacas are both good for fiber, but if you're after very high-quality fiber, go for the alpaca. If you want a dual-duty animal — not only a fiber-producer but also a beast of burden that's a lot of fun to hike with — go for the llama. Price may also come into play for you. Alpacas are more expensive than llamas, and females are more expensive than males. The next couple of sections describe both animal types in detail.

The various breeds of camelids are alike enough that they can interbreed. However, doing so is frowned upon, so discourage interbreeding by keeping any intact males away from females.

Llamas

Llamas (see Figure 1-1) are the biggest of the camelids, and they can live as long as 29 years. They grow to about 4 feet high and up to 450 pounds, and they can carry approximately 80 pounds (or a little less or more, depending on the individual), so they're not built to carry an adult. However, they don't mind toting small children around.

As pack animals, llamas fare better than horses because

- They eat anything along the trail, so you don't have to pack much in the way of food for them.
- They don't spook as easily as horses.
- Their feet, being made of a soft material, are kinder to the environment.
- They can last for as many miles as you can.

Figure 1-1:
A llama is a great pack animal.

Llamas are pretty easy to find inexpensively. (You may be able to find them at auctions for as little as $25.) The market for these guys just isn't what it used to be. However, some llamas bred for specific traits (such as a finer-quality fiber or very strong legs and backs) or those that are already trained (for carrying packs or following on a lead) can still bring in a decent price.

Llama fiber isn't the softest around, so it's not as desirable for knitwear that goes close to the skin. However, it's very warm and is thus a great fiber for several other projects, such as outerwear (heavy coat-sweaters), horse blankets, rugs, or stuffings. You can also use it for felting (check out Book II, Chapter 1 for this technique) or blend it with other fibers.

Alpacas

Alpacas are the queens of the camelids. Their fiber is very soft (one of the world's most luxurious in fact) and is sought after in the knitwear market for next-to-the-skin garments. It comes in many colors — from pure white to several shades of browns, grays, and black — and is grease-less, making it nearly hypoallergenic and easy to clean and spin.

Alpacas have a life span of about 25 years. Their cute faces and small bodies (they stand about 3 feet tall and weigh from 100 to 200 pounds) make them endearing to young and old alike.

There are two types of alpaca, each with its own fiber characteristics:

- ✔ **Huacaya:** The more popular Huacaya (pronounced wah-*kie*-ya) produces a sheep's wool-like fiber that's dense and soft. The Huacaya alpaca looks like a smaller, fluffier llama (see Figure 1-2).

- ✔ **Suri:** The Suri, which comprises about 20 percent of the total alpaca population, produces a longer, silkier fiber. The Suri looks like it's wearing dreadlocks (see Figure 1-3).

If you're interested only in the fiber, you can get by with just males. Educate yourself on the properties to look for and be sure to find a reputable dealer. You can check out the dealer with the Alpaca Owners and Breeders Association (www.alpacainfo.com) before making an investment.

Figure 1-2: The fleece of Huacaya alpacas is dense and fluffy, similar to sheep's wool.

Figure 1-3:
Suri alpacas
have fine,
lustrous
fleece.

Although the alpaca industry has been around since the 1980s (when the enjoyable creatures were first imported from South America), alpacas are very expensive to acquire, so the market is still somewhat limited. How much dough do you need to get started in the alpaca business? Here's an idea:

- ✔ High-quality, proven females — meaning those that have given birth successfully — can go for as much as $30,000 dollars.

- ✔ Unproven females, including new *crias* (babies), can cost as little as $10,000 because there's no guarantee they'll be able to get pregnant or take the pregnancy to full term. You pay less and take the chance.

- ✔ Breeding-quality males go for $2,500 and up.

- ✔ Fiber-quality males (but nonbreeders) typically go for $500 to $1,500.

Working around camelid temperament

A common misconception about camelids is that they spit at people. In reality, camelids spit at *other* camelids. (If you're caught in the crossfire, however, prepare to be hit.) Only a few reasons can make you the actual target:

- ✔ If you're trying to halter a particularly uncooperative llama, you'll likely get hit with spit.

- ✔ If you're shearing a camelid that hasn't been sufficiently halter-trained, it may show its displeasure of the process by nailing you.

- ✔ If you become an implied threat to a new *cria* (baby), Momma Camelid may put you back in your place with a well-aimed glob of goo.

You can check out a few other camelid behavior issues in the following sections.

Making friends

Camelids are herd animals, so having only one isn't a good idea because camelids get lonely. Also, unless someone works with them from their birth (through cuddling, petting, brushing, and so on), they won't be as cuddly as they look. You may be tempted to pet them or even hug their necks. They hate that! "Just feed me and dispense with the touching" is a normal attitude.

Be careful when training a newborn. If you teach it that people are just big camelids and there's no need to run away, you'll end up with behavior problems down the road. With too much human interaction, males start to think that you're really just a big llama or alpaca. That's bad when they get old enough to breed because they may see you as competition and pick a fight with you if you get too close to their females.

Camelids (specifically llamas) need to be trained for serving as pack animals because their normal instinct is not to let you touch them. Several good books and workshops are available to help you in that arena, such as TTEAM (Tellington Touch Every Animal Method; www.camelidynamics.com). The training takes a little time and love, but the results are very rewarding.

Dealing with fights

Intact (unneutered) males fight. This fighting isn't a constant occurrence, but it's an inevitable one nonetheless. The males make loud screechy noises, which can be disconcerting, especially to your neighbors. But the sound is normal, and you can't stop it short of separating them — which is a bad idea because they'll get lonely. (Think of it as an "I hate you sometimes, but I still want you near" sort of relationship.) You may notice that very shortly after the fight, the males bed down next to each other or eat side by side from the food trough.

A rogue intact animal faced with females in the next pen may not settle down and may continue to attack the other males in its enclosure. Castration is your best bet for dealing with this aberration of the camelids' getting-along rule.

Raising Creatures that Buzz, Swim, and Squirm

Not all farm animals are cuddly, nor do they all have feet! A few more ideas for your menagerie come in the form of some not-so-cute (yet still functional!) critters. The ones featured in the following sections all give back to their environment. They work wonderfully in conjunction with other animals and crops and thus make great supplements or side businesses if you're already raising cows or goats or whatever.

Integrated agriculture is a concept in which each piece in an operation cooperates somehow with the other pieces. The result is a waste-free system — everything is reduced, reused, and recycled. On a small scale, you can use worms and fish to prepare manure for use on plants.

Getting the buzz on honeybees

Bees on a farm are generally bigger than those found in nature. Unlike other animals you raise for food, honeybees don't have to give up their lives in order for you to reap their benefits. Honeybees are pretty much the only insects that produce food for humans, and they play a major role in pollinating plants. In addition, an average hive yields about 4 gallons of honey (after you leave some for the bees). *Note:* Your results may be a lot more or less, depending on your particular conditions. Here are some other considerations:

- ✔ You must manage the hive, or the bees will die, and even careful management isn't a guarantee of success.

- ✔ A bee's life span is about 2 to 3 years, but that number can be cut way short for several reasons, like disease and changes in temperature.

- ✔ A beekeeper is required by law to use standard equipment consisting of removable frames so that diseased bees can be easily taken out of the hive.

For lots more info about beekeeping, head to Book V, Chapter 5.

Testing the waters with fish

Fish can be fun to raise because they're rather easy to care for, but what types to raise and even whether you *can* raise fish depend on your state's laws. The most common types of farm-raised fish are catfish, followed by trout.

If the fish are for your own enjoyment, you have little to do in the way of caring for them. For instance, if you have a natural pond on your property, you don't have to do much besides catch the fish. With man-made ponds, you need to take care of feeding the fish and keeping their homes free of pests.

If you're raising fish for food, you have more health-related issues to consider, such as being careful about the herbicides you use for controlling aquatic plants and keeping the fish disease-free. Fish raised in captivity have some problems their wild counterparts do not. First of all, their diet is different, so they can have a different taste or color. They also have less room to swim and can be prone to diseases, so you have to consider using antibiotics.

Breaking ground with earthworms

Worms may be the easiest to care for of any animal on your farm. All you need to do is provide a place for them to proliferate and prosper (perhaps a pile of the organic matter that comes out of your other critters) and keep them moist. They turn that organic matter into worm *castings,* some of the best stuff you can use to add nutrients to the soil in your garden. If you live near a good fishing locale, build your kid a roadside stand and sell some of the worms to local fishermen.

Don't throw worms into your compost pile, despite their digestive magic. A properly maintained compost pile reaches temperatures of 140 degrees, and subjecting worms to that heat means fried worms.

Provide your worms with their own enclosure. A simple box will do, but make sure you add air vents. Add a bit of shredded newspaper for bedding, toss in some dirt, and add organic matter or table scraps. Put the worms on top of the pile and let them worm their way into the mix. Add more food scraps periodically so the worms always have plenty of nourishment for their own bodies and thus more stuff to make their castings out of.

Clarifying What You Want

After you have an idea which type of animal you want, ask yourself just what you want this animal to do on your farm. Are you interested in just a few companion animals? Do you want to provide meat for your family? Do you want to raise and sell or show animals? Or are you a fiber person who wants to spin yarn and knit something up from materials that came from your own animals?

The next step is to weigh your options. For instance, say you're interested in raising animals for their fiber. Here are a few to consider:

- **Shetland sheep:** These critters are small and easy to handle and have a fine fiber.

- **Angora goats:** Goat fiber is a step up from sheep's (though goats are a little harder to raise).

- **Suri alpacas:** Alpaca fiber is a step up from goat's; however, the alpaca is way more expensive to acquire and feed.

If you're after good-quality fiber, you may not care if an individual animal isn't particularly friendly to you or if its legs are less than show quality. However, if you want the animal to show, then every aspect of it has to be perfect.

Some other issues that matter when you're looking for animals are age, gender, pregnancy possibilities, and what kind of shape they're in. The next few sections highlight how these factors fit into your animal-buying decision.

Make sure you have an idea of what you're getting into before embarking on any animal-buying venture. Some animals require a great deal of attention (horses are one), and some require extra-sturdy facilities (rabbits need protected from predators). Some need special care (for instance, fiber goats must be shorn twice a year). Do some research — peruse the Web, ask your neighbors, or chat with someone at the cooperative extension office to get ideas on what you can do. Find out the animal's food and shelter needs, expected life span, adult size, common problems, and so on.

Choosing a breed

Before you plunk down the money or the time investment in an animal, research the breeds and their common qualities. For instance, if you're interested in dairy cows, the Ayrshire is known for its easy births, strong calves, and longevity. The Jersey cow is a little smaller breed known for its high milk-fat content and its good-tempered disposition.

After deciding on a breed, educate yourself. Look up an association (you can find tons, such as the Alpaca Owners and Breeders Association, the Quarterhorse Association, and so on) and see what the official breed standards are and what to expect from a certain breed. If you're looking to show and breed an animal, then you need to invest in the highest-quality animal you can afford. You may not be able to resell a lower-quality animal.

Considering age

The age of an animal always matters. You may want to get an adult so you can see what the critter has grown into, or you may want to get a baby so you have a better chance of molding it behaviorally into what you want for your farm. Either way, you need to consider these facts:

- ✔ **An older animal can have problems that may or may not be fixable.** Some nutritional problems can be fixed, but that depends on how far along they are. For instance, severe malnutrition can reach a point where the animal can't recover. White muscle disease can be fatal in sheep and goats, but even if it isn't, these animals still have a permanent weakness. (See Book V, Chapter 4 for the scoop on white muscle disease.)

- ✔ **Babies can have special problems.** If they're taken from their mothers too soon, babies can have nutritional or behavioral problems; they may *imprint* on you — meaning they see you as a parent — and not know how to act as animals when it comes to breeding and the like. (See Book V, Chapter 3 for more info on behavioral considerations.) Most reputable breeders don't sell a baby until it's weaned, but you may have occasional opportunities to raise a really young animal if it's orphaned or rejected by its mother. An exception may be baby goats, which are purposely bottle-fed so they'll make friendlier pets.

Buying a trained critter may save you loads of time and headaches and be a better bargain in the long run. If you've never owned a horse before, you may be tempted to acquire a young, untrained animal that has a reasonably low price tag. (Hey, training the horse yourself is part of the experience, no?) However, training an animal is something *you* need to be trained on, so you may have to hire someone else to train the animal and show you what to do. A beginning rider and an improperly trained horse are a dangerous combination. Sometimes an older animal is better.

Looking at gender and fertility

Keeping males, females, or both means a few differences in care. For instance, males tend to fight, especially if they're reproductively intact. If you don't care about breeding, have the males fixed. They'll be calmer, and in the case of fiber animals, you'll get better fleeces. (Stress affects the quality of fleeces — if the males are always fighting, you may see a loss of fiber quality.) And naturally, male birds can't lay eggs.

Females, of course, can get pregnant, which requires extra care during birth (even if that means being in the barn at 3 a.m.; see Book V, Chapter 4 for more details on medical care for animals). Females may also be smaller, have a different quality of feathers or fleece, or have behavioral differences.

If you want to breed your animals, you can keep both males and females (in separate pens so you can control who gets to date whom), or you can hire out your males for studs or take your girls to the neighbors' for a night on the town.

Sometimes you can buy a pregnant animal and end up with a two-for-one deal. Although this prospect may sound great, make sure you're prepared to deal with complications that can come with pregnancy (and the possibility that you may lose both mother and baby). Also, make sure you're willing to do the extra work that goes along with having newborns.

Determining how many you desire

The number of animals you should get depends on how much land you have and how much labor you can devote to care. Whatever you decide, ask the person you're getting an animal from, or somebody who has animals, about how many critters he or she recommends in your situation.

Some animals are herd animals and should never be isolated. Owning at least two animals is always a good idea so they can keep each other company. But that doesn't always mean two of the same breed — you can start out with one cow in the same pen with a few sheep, for example.

Chapter 2

Acquiring Animals

- -

In This Chapter

▶ Knowing when and where to purchase an animal

▶ Judging animals and sellers

- -

*W*hen you go to acquire an animal, you need to match what a particular seller has to offer against your specific needs. Some sellers provide better support than others. If this is a new venture for you, you may want the current owner to help you pick just the right animal for your needs and be available for consultation after the sale, in case you run into something you don't know how to handle. If you already have some experience with a particular type of animal, you may simply be looking to make a quick and economical transaction, with no support necessary.

Some animals are very easy and affordable to acquire. Others are much more expensive and take some legwork and education in order to know just what you're getting into. In this chapter, you find advice on evaluating animals and breeders and finding the right seller for you.

Factoring in Time and Distance

Perhaps you've decided to acquire a cow for your farm. Before you grab your credit card and rush out to the 24-hour cattle store, take some time to consider whether now is really the best time to get that cow — or horse, or chicken, or whatever animal you have a hankering for.

When and where you get your new animal family members are important factors to consider first.

Knowing when to buy

Sometimes, timing your acquisitions just right can save you a lot of money or trouble (or both). The time of year can make a difference in the amount of work you'll have to do, as well as in the odds that you'll raise your animals successfully.

A very young animal taken on in the middle of the winter or a baby without its mother is tougher to raise. You have to make sure these animals are kept warm, both day and night.

Summertime can be bad in some parts of the country, too. If temperatures get really high, you need to be able to provide shelter so the animal can get out of the scorching sun. A nice, big tree can help provide shade.

During going-out-of-business and moving sales, you may be able to get some good-quality animals for a relatively low cost, but be careful. Many breeders use going-out-of-business sales as an excuse to dump their poor-quality or nonproducing animals on the unsuspecting public. Don't buy anything without doing some research first.

You can often get good prices on chicks and ducks right after Easter. Check shelters, country stores, or even pet shops. People get them for their seasonally inspired cuteness and then realize the cuteness is going to wear off.

The forces of nature can also play a role in timing. For example, in one case, extensive brush fires led to a hay shortage, which led to a dramatic increase in the price of hay. Farmers who were unable to afford the high prices were forced to sell off some of their stock at rock-bottom prices. Watch for opportunities like these, and you may be able to get a little (or a lot) more animal for your money than you would otherwise. (Just make sure *you* can afford to feed your new critters!)

Going local or out of state

Whereas 20 years ago getting an animal from another state or even country was only for the rich and famous, now the average person can arrange the sale and transport of anything from parakeets to prize racehorses. Going the distance can be worthwhile if you find something that isn't easily attainable locally, but getting something a little closer to home is almost always a better idea.

One advantage to purchasing closer to home is that it means the animal is accustomed to the climate you live in. Another plus is that you don't have to deal with the logistics of transportation.

If you find something in a different state — or even in a faraway part of your own state — you have to come up with a way to get the animal from there to you. Larger animals are typically shipped in trailers, but smaller ones, like dogs, can go by air.

Before you put down the big bucks for an out-of-state animal, be sure to check with your state to see whether you have to adhere to any regulations in order for the critter to come into the state. Some states have laws about transporting animals across their borders. In that case, be sure you negotiate with the current owner to decide who's going to take care of any necessary shots and exams and make sure you factor that into the total cost of the animal. You may also have to deal with a *quarantine,* a requirement that certain animals stay in a state shelter for a specified time before being allowed out into the general population.

Evaluating Sellers and Animals

Most animal sales go off without a hitch, but some less-than-honest people are out there. Unless you dream of playing plaintiff on a daytime TV court show, be savvy about the buying process so you don't end up buying a dud — or fail to get anything at all.

Looking for credible sellers

Watch out for scams, whether perpetrated by individuals or auctioneers. If you're dealing with a private party (as opposed to a business), getting into trouble may be a little easier because the seller can disappear after the sale and leave you with no support.

Online transactions can also be risky because you may not actually meet the seller. In such a case, you wind up doing your business over the phone and having your purchase shipped to you. Because a not-so-honest person can hide behind anonymity, you can find plenty of horror stories of online transactions gone bad. Always, always be careful!

To make a long-distance transaction as safely as possible, heed the following advice:

- **Check references.** A good way to get information on distant sellers and animals is to check for references with other buyers or with an animal association. Another place to check is with the Better Business Bureau.

- **Browse online rating systems.** Some online sites have a rating system where buyers and sellers rate their transactions. A seller with close to 100-percent positive feedback is likely to be good to you as well.

- ✔ **Investigate whether the seller has a Web site.** Most scammers don't spend the money for a Web site.

- ✔ **Keep your credit card in check.** You may want to withhold credit card information until you're sure the deal is legitimate.

Judging individual animals

Judging individual animals comes down to doing research beforehand so you have an idea of what to look for. Consider trying one or more of these research tactics:

- ✔ **Attend an animal show.** You can find local shows for all sorts of animals, including dogs, horses, llamas, and alpacas.

- ✔ **Surf the Internet.** Gobs of information are available online.

- ✔ **Read farming magazines.** Numerous magazines targeted to the farmer may help you recognize what constitutes a quality animal.

- ✔ **Get help from those in the know.** Friends, neighbors, and even the local vet are good people to ask for help with deciding on an animal. Maybe your neighbor has a particularly good animal that has siblings just waiting for you to take home. Ask the local vet about a particular animal or seller to see whether he or she has an opinion.

When you're considering the purchase of a specific animal, arrange an actual meeting if possible. Doing so allows you to see for yourself how the animal looks and acts. Especially with big-ticket animals (those you'll be spending several thousands of dollars for), you may want to make multiple visits to the farm where the animal currently lives to see how the critter and all its buddies are doing. Watch to see how they interact with each other and with humans.

Sometimes, as in the case of an auction, you have only a short time to evaluate the animal, so make the most of it. Go with your gut. Occasionally, an animal just speaks to you — you see something in the animal that makes the decision for you.

If you have to evaluate an animal long-distance, your task is more challenging, but you can take some steps to protect yourself. Get online and take a look at the available animals. Call and talk to the seller and have him or her send more photos — pictures from the front, back, and side, as well as close-ups of the teeth and legs. Videos are nice, too. However, remember that pictures aren't foolproof — dishonest sellers can send you pictures of a different animal or touch up the photos. If the seller shows the animals and has awards, then chances are you're purchasing a decent animal.

Ask for papers that show the animal's family history. In some cases, family history can tell you whether the parents or grandparents are known for producing good-quality offspring. Jot down their names and look them up online.

Finding the Best Source of Animals

You can find farm animals for purchase through a variety of sources: breed associations, classified ads, even friends and family. This section introduces these and other places you can look to find animals.

Before you start searching for an animal to bring into your family, be sure you're ready for the critter to join you. If you start looking and find the perfect deal on the perfect animal but you don't have a fence or shelter, you'll be frantic trying to get the place in order and still get in on the deal. If you already have some animals and are bringing a new one into the fold, have a holding pen ready to put the new one in while everybody gets used to the changes.

Consulting your friends and neighbors

What better place to get an animal than from a neighbor? You may know the animal personally, or at least you know how the owners treat their animals. Besides, your neighbor is just across the fence if you have a question that comes up.

If your friends and neighbors don't have animals to sell, they're likely to be able to connect you with trustworthy sources.

Seeking out reputable breeders

Some people find their purpose in life is to breed animals and sell them to discriminating buyers. Reputable animal breeders know everything there is to know about the breeds they raise and are very discriminating about which animals they allow to mate. The resulting offspring thus have characteristics that should be allowed to proliferate. You can find breeders

 ✔ Through lists in your local chapters of animal organizations (such as the Alpaca Owners and Breeders Association)

 ✔ By word of mouth

 ✔ Via an Internet search

Even those breeders in far corners of the country can be well-known as good, conscientious breeders whom anyone, anywhere can buy from with confidence.

Some uneducated breeders think their poor-quality animals are the best and try to sell them as such. So educate yourself before buying. If you want a second opinion, ask the vet or other breeders what they think of a particular breeder. Request papers and references, and check out the breeder before you buy.

Finding animals in the classifieds

Classifieds — in a newspaper, on a Web site, or even just in a note tacked to the board at the local grocery or farm store — are ways to get the word out that an animal is in need of a new home. Hence, they're good spots for you to look when you're in the market for an animal. Peruse these places:

- **Neighborhood bulletin boards:** Some feed and tack stores (and even grocery stores in rural communities) have good old-fashioned corkboards right inside their doors where you can post a note with a push pin. These are good places to find some great treasures.

- **Your local newspaper:** Check the classifieds in the local paper. Most newspapers have a section for pets and/or livestock. One benefit of going this route is that the sale is personal. You can meet the animal and the current owners before the sale, and you may be able to call on those owners if you have questions after the purchase. Another benefit is that the sale is local — the animal usually doesn't have to be transported very long distances or across state lines.

- **Online classifieds:** Lots of Web sites have want-ad sections where you can get all sorts of things, even animals. These days, even your local newspaper likely has an online counterpart where you can peruse the classifieds online. For starters, check out the following:

  - **AgriSeek:** www.agriseek.com is a national site geared toward livestock, tools, farm services, and other agricultural categories.

  - **craigslist:** www.craigslist.org is a national site with local subsites that sometimes offer animals for adoption.

Visiting county and state fairs

County and state fairs are good places to find animals. During the show, the animals are available for viewing or meeting. These animals have been well taken care of and are highly trained. The cattle and pigs are sold to slaughter, but you can join in the bidding to get a great pet. You can also find ducks, chickens, rabbits, goats, and sheep. Farmers come to fairs from all over, so fairs can be a really great place to buy your animals if you don't mind competing with other buyers.

Adopting from a rescue group

Sometimes animals end up in a rescue shelter for one reason or another. Perhaps the previous owners got in over their heads and realized they just couldn't manage caring for the critters. Or perhaps the animals became displaced due to a death in the owner's family.

Checking with an animal rescue group can turn out to be a great idea, especially if you're looking for a companion animal. You can find some gems at a low cost. However, some rescued animals may have health problems or special training needs, so make sure you know what you're getting into.

Bidding on animals at auctions

Rural areas sometimes hold regular animal auctions, which are quick and easy ways for people to get rid of animals that are unwanted for whatever reason. Maybe they have too many, they don't want to raise a certain type of animal anymore, or they're getting out of the farm business altogether. Here are some tips for buying at an auction:

✔ **Get there early and take a look at what's on the table that week.** It always helps to go look with somebody who knows more than you. Perhaps a neighbor who has been through the auctions (maybe on both sides of the sale) can give you pointers on what constitutes a good animal and a good price.

✔ **Talk to people while you're there.** You can sometimes pick up some tidbits just by chatting with fellow auction-goers. A casual remark by, say, one of the assistants at the auction can give you some amazing insight. You may discover the history of an animal, what others think is a fair price, or even a secret fact about an animal's health.

✔ **Know what you want to spend and stick to that limit.** Getting caught up in the bidding is far too easy, so keep a level head. Yes, this may be an awesome animal, but animals come and go in auctions every week. Of course, there are always exceptions. If you know an animal's history and you really want that one, maybe you're prepared to go a bit higher than what you think is a decent price. Splurging is okay, but don't let this attitude be the norm.

✔ **Dress for the occasion.** Attending an auction means you may be out in the elements for a few hours, so you'll be walking around an area that's not conducive to wearing nice shoes or pants.

Animals put up for auction vary in terms of quality, so find out about certain breeds before you go. Have an idea of what to look for in the animal. Go a few times before you do any bidding so you can get a feel for what happens at an animal auction — what other people bid on, how much the animals go for, and so on. You may want to visit the auction several times to see how it works before participating.

If you go to an animal auction, beware of two things:

✔ **Often, animals that go to auction are of poor quality, have injuries, or are unhealthy.** Some big breeding farms may be getting out of the business or reducing their stock, but often they're simply getting rid of the animals they can't sell. For example, some breeding farms buy mares, breed them to their stallions, and then have a going-out-of-business or reducing-my-herd auction, when in reality the animals they're selling were never a part of their normal breeding program in the first place. Buyer beware!

✔ **Some auctions have some not-so-honest auctioneers.** If the auctioneer sees that you're not a regular (a greenhorn who may not know the business of auctions), he may invent an opponent to get you to keep bidding and bringing the price up. You may, in fact, be the only person bidding on a particular animal, but he nods to a nonexistent bidder behind you (whom you can't see) to make you think you're *not* alone in the bidding. It may be a good idea to have a friend or two stand behind the crowd to make sure you don't fall for this trick.

Chapter 3

Caring for and Feeding Your Animals

. . . .

In This Chapter

▶ Keeping your animals clean

▶ Feeding and watering your animals

▶ Dealing with behavior issues

. . . .

*W*hen you have critters, you're responsible for their care. Throwing a bale of hay into the pen just isn't enough. Like humans, animals need daily nourishment and protection from the elements, at least to some degree. To give your animals the best chance of having happy, healthy lives, you need to provide them with good nutrition, sufficient exercise, dry bedding, good air circulation, and safety from predators. You can avert a lot of health problems by paying attention to basic hygiene and care. This chapter covers animals' basic needs and addresses a few of their behavioral issues.

Taking Care of Basic Hygiene

The maxim "Cleanliness is next to godliness" applies to animals as well as to humans. Keeping your animals clean is the best way to ward off diseases. In the following sections, you find out how to keep your critters in good, clean shape.

Keep records of actions that don't take place every day and note when they happen — especially those that occur annually, such as shearing — so you know when the next treatment should be. As you take care of daily hygiene, use the contact to make sure everything is okay and to bond with your animals so you become familiar with their individual personalities. More thorough monthly checks are a good idea because animals can hide their illnesses, and changes in their conditions can be subtle. Book V, Chapter 4 presents some standard signs of illness or injury, as well as possible treatments.

Because animals need to be restrained or corralled at times, such as when they need grooming or shots, you should find out how to properly restrain them. Doing so makes some of the daily tasks involved in their care a lot more enjoyable for both of you. See "Training animals for human interaction," at the end of this chapter, for details.

Cleaning house: Maintaining the living area

One basic way to keep animals happy and healthy is to give them a nice place to stay. Here are three cardinal rules for keeping your animals' shelter in good condition:

 ✓ **Keep it fresh and dry.** Change the bedding regularly and make sure the pen has ample drainage — no big puddles or large piles of doo-doo allowed. Not only is wet and soiled bedding uncomfortable to lie down in but it's also a health hazard. It promotes bacterial growth both in the bedding and on the animal, which can lead to infections.

 Dispose of manure and soiled bedding in a conscientious way. When mucking out a stall (yep, that's the official term, and you only have to clean out a stall once to know why it's called this), you can add the soiled bedding to your compost pile. If your animals are producing way more manure than you can reuse yourself (for composting or for direct application), put a sign out advertising that you have some for free or for sale, or donate the extra to organizations such as local parks or landscaping companies.

 ✓ **Keep it well-ventilated.** In the summer, you don't want hot, stuffy air to build up inside and make the animals uncomfortable. In the winter, humidity from urine, manure, and body moisture can accumulate and lead to respiratory infections, including pneumonia. Being continually subjected to the smell from ammonia in urine is bad for the immune system, especially for pigs. Thus, pigpens are typically equipped with fans to regulate air turnover.

 ✓ **Keep it warm.** During the winter months, you need to provide extra straw.

The beastly barber shop: Bathing and grooming

Most farm animals don't get actual baths, but you may notice that they frequently take dirt baths. They roll in the dirt to fend off bugs, placing a dirt barrier on the skin. Rolling around also serves as a great back scratcher. However, you don't need to squirt critters with a hose unless they get really icky and dirty or you're getting them ready for a show.

Grooming and shearing are sufficient means of keeping your animals' coats beautiful and keeping the animals comfortable and smelling their best. Hair, hooves, and nails also require attention.

Brushing and cleaning coats

Grooming isn't just done to make animals look pretty. Grooming makes critters more comfortable by freeing their coats of caked-on mud and feces, mats, stickers, and burrs.

Part of the daily care for some animals, especially horses, involves brushing the coat. For others, such as cows, proper bedding is enough to keep them clean. Whatever the grooming method, a clean animal is a happy and healthy animal.

Shearing hair

Shearing, which takes place in late spring or early summer, allows a good, clean, unmatted coat to grow in. It keeps the animal comfortable through the hottest part of the year; by the time winter hits, the coat is long enough to keep the animal warm again.

Fiber animals, such as sheep, Angora goats, and llamas, require shearing once or twice a year. You may also want to consider shearing other long-haired animals as needed to help them feel more comfortable, even if their hair isn't usable for yarn or fiber. See Book II, Chapter 1 for information on shearing your animals.

Trimming toes and checking hooves

Animals that roam on soft ground — grass or mud — need extra work on their feet. Nails and hooves grow just like human fingernails and need to be trimmed periodically. Hooves and pads can also collect debris and need to be cleaned out.

Failure to care for hooves can lead to serious problems and can even render an animal lame.

Animals whose pastures contain a lot of rocks have a better opportunity for their nails and hooves to wear down naturally — the rocks act as natural files — so in those cases, you may not have to trim their hooves at all, or at least not very frequently. However, if the animals live or frequently stand on very rocky ground or pavement, their hooves can chip and crack. Animals need their hooves to walk, so *hoof crack* needs immediate attention from a veterinarian or a farrier.

Having your animal shod

Horse hooves are made of keratin (the same substance that hair and fingernails are made of), which is a relatively soft material. Improper hoof care can lead to infection and lameness, so find a reputable *farrier* in your area to take care of the shoeing and trimming.

Heavy loads on hard surfaces are a recipe for hoof problems, so if you're going to have your horse carry heavy loads (like a full-grown man) or plan to have the critter spend a lot of time on hard surfaces, you need to have it shod. Oxen that you use to pull heavy loads may also benefit from shoes.

However, not all horses need shoes. With proper hoof trimming, horses that don't carry loads or walk on hard surfaces usually do okay without shoes. For information about natural hoof trims, ask your farrier about the *barefoot method*.

Feeding Your Animals Right

You can't typically find food for your animals in the grocery store (although the pet aisle *may* have some products, such as Purina Rabbit Chow). Your best bet is to seek out a farm or country store. Local independents and national chains — such as IFA (Intermountain Farmers Association) Country Stores, Mills Fleet Farm, Tractor Supply Company, Blain's Farm & Fleet, and others — can undoubtedly help you with a good part of the supplies you need, especially bagged feed, supplements, and salt licks. Or you can find some supplies on the Internet and have them shipped anywhere in the world.

Hay, however, you have to find locally. Look in the classified ads in the local newspaper (under "hay and alfalfa" or "livestock"), find sources through word of mouth from your neighbors, or check message boards at the country stores.

After you find a hay source, try to work with the same people every time. You'll be considered a good customer, and they'll be more apt to work with you during emergencies (like when you run out of hay, even though you were meaning to call to order more).

Storing feed properly

Buying small quantities of animal feed isn't very efficient, so buying in bulk is the way to go. And bulk purchases mean you need good storage facilities to keep weather from destroying the feed and local wildlife from eating it up.

Hay should be stored inside a barn or, at the very least, covered with a tarp to protect it from weather and wildlife. You can store other feeds, such as minerals or treats, in plastic tubs.

If the moisture content of hay is more than 22 percent, bacteria can cause a chemical reaction that produces a lot of heat. The haystack can spontaneously combust, causing a fire. Avoid packing the bales closely together, and leave some air pockets in your haystack. Good circulation greatly reduces the possibility of fire. Keep an eye on the hay for the first six weeks after baling — temperatures above 150 degrees are dangerous.

Finding the right diet

The right diet is important for a healthy life, and each animal has individual dietary needs. Table 3-1 gives you the basics, but within a category, you may have animals that need more or less than the average or that may require supplements. Your vet, cooperative extension service, and neighbors can give you more specific advice.

Table 3-1		Typical Foods for Livestock		
Animal Type	**Main Food**	**Daily Amount**	**Treats**	**Extra Needs**
Camelids	Pasture, browsing materials (twigs and prunings), and grass hay	2% of body weight	Grain, apples (no core), vegetables (lettuce and carrots), fruit scraps	Trace mineral mix formulated for llamas; you may need llama supplements
Cattle	Dry matter or grass hay; alfalfa is too high in protein, so use it for sick animals only	2% of body weight	Commercially made beet pellets, maybe mixed with a little molasses; avoid grain (too high in calories)	Salt licks

(continued)

Table 3-1	Typical Foods for Livestock			
Animal Type	**Main Food**	**Daily Amount**	**Treats**	**Extra Needs**
Chickens	Feed purchased at farm stores	Chickens tend to self-regulate food intake, so fill a bucket and refill when it's empty	Greens such as fresh pasture, alfalfa, cabbage, lettuce, grain sprouts, and Swiss chard	For laying hens, opt for a feed with a higher protein mix to promote egg production
Goats	Grass hay (no alfalfa) and pasture grass	2–4 pounds of hay per day	Some browsing materials (prunings and wild grape vines); avoid grain (it's too high in calories)	Salt and copper mixture
Horses	High-nutrition feed, such as grass, clover, or alfalfa hay	Varies, depending on what they're used for (work, pet, or show); an adult doing light work generally gets 2% of its body weight	Grain, apples (no core), and carrots	On average, 50–60 grams of salt per day; lactating females or high-performance horses need a higher-protein diet
Pigs	Grazing materials (grass, roots, or other vegetable matter); commercially bought pig feed supplemented with alfalfa or grass hay	5–6% of body weight until they reach 100 pounds; 5% of body weight from 100–150 pounds; 4% of body weight after 150 pounds	Treats, especially leftovers (be careful not to give them anything they can choke on, such as corn cobs or whole potatoes)	Salt and trace minerals

Animal Type	Main Food	Daily Amount	Treats	Extra Needs
Rabbits	Unlimited fresh grass or Timothy hay (or hay pellets) and a variety of fresh vegetables	A minimum of 1 cup packed green foods per 2 pounds of body weight, once daily	Carrots and limited amounts of lettuce (too much causes diarrhea); no corn, cabbage, crackers, beans, breakfast cereals, bread, nuts, pasta, peas, popcorn, or other human treats	Salt licks
Sheep	Grass hay (no alfalfa) and pasture grass	2–4 pounds of hay per day	Carrots or weeds from the garden; no grain (it's too high in fat)	Copper-free salt licks

Improper feeding can introduce health problems such as weight loss, listlessness, and hair loss. Hoofed animals sometimes develop *laminitis,* an inflammation of the *lamina propia* (the internal structure of the hoof). This condition can develop when the feed doesn't contain enough protein, contains too much freshly cut grass, or contains too much grain. Keeping a good eye on the hooves can help you spot problems like this before they get out of hand.

Supplementing with salt licks and mineral sources

Most animals need some sort of mineral supplement, depending on the breed, the area, and the quality of feed. Most animals benefit by having a salt lick nearby (country stores have salt blocks and specially designed holders for them), but some also need other minerals that aren't in their primary feed. For example, goats need a small amount of copper in their diets, which you can provide with a supplement found at the farm store.

Sheep's livers can't handle much copper, so be careful not to leave copper mixture around if you have sheep and goats in the same pasture. If a sheep gets too much copper, that copper breaks down its blood cells, clogging up vital organs and leading to kidney or liver failure.

Trace mineral blocks or grains are also available and, depending on the animal and the soil in your region, you may need to get some. Certain areas of the United States have soil that's deficient in selenium, so the hay that grows there lacks sufficient quantities of this mineral, which aids in muscle health. This deficiency can be rectified by purchasing a salt block with selenium. Check with your local country store, neighbor, or cooperative extension service to see what — if any — trace minerals your animals may need. Soil tests can also reveal deficiencies.

Indulging your animals with treats

Who doesn't love treats? Animals are no different from humans in that respect. However, just as chocolate probably shouldn't be one of your major food groups, animal treats are something critters should eat in moderation.

Handing out treats is more for social bonding than for nutrition. Treats come in many forms. The most common are grains or fruit and veggie scraps. Read on for details and see Table 3-1 for some specific suggestions and restrictions.

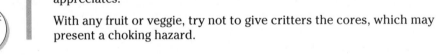

- **Grains:** Grain comes in so many mixtures! Barley or oats are the most common, but you can also mix in corn, molasses, and all sorts of other things. Your local country store has some basics, and you can ask the workers there or your neighbors for mixture recipes.

  Grain is high in carbohydrates and can pack on the pounds — a pro or con depending on an animal's individual needs.

- **Fruits and vegetables:** Some fruits are good treats, and some aren't. Apples, for example, are a big favorite with horses. Animals also love certain veggies — lettuce is popular, as are carrots. Cows and other animals love crushed corn. Try various veggies to see what your crew appreciates.

  With any fruit or veggie, try not to give critters the cores, which may present a choking hazard.

Providing a Continuous Source of Clean Water

A good, reliable source of clean, fresh water is essential to any animal's well-being. Just putting out a bowl or bucket of water isn't always enough. Many farm animals step, sit, or roll in their water bowls, or even throw them in the air. Thus, getting a water bowl, bucket, or system that's designed especially for livestock or poultry is a good idea. Automatic, heated waterers are particularly helpful during the winter (see "Preventing freezes" later in this chapter).

Estimating water needs

Book V

Raising
Farm
Animals

In hot, dry conditions, a mature cow needs between 10 and 20 gallons of water a day! Other animals may not need that much, but they still need a lot. So a reliable water source is absolutely necessary. If you don't have an automatic system on your property, you need to regularly fill buckets or troughs to keep your animals hydrated.

Water access points should be located where they're most convenient to you, because you're the one who tends to their maintenance.

Of course, each pen needs its own water source. The size of the buckets or troughs depends on the number and type of animals you have in each pen. Water needs vary by season, conditioning, and life stages. An average horse needs 10 to 12 gallons per day, but nursing mares in the summer can require up to 25 gallons per day. Monitor water intake to see what your animals need and then provide a bucket or trough that accommodates at least two days' worth of water.

Considering common water sources

Some properties are fortunate enough to include natural water sources, but many people need to bring water to their animals. You can get pretty creative with how you keep your animals hydrated.

Streams and stock ponds

A natural stream or stock pond on your property can eliminate the need to bring water to your animals (unless of course you're in an area where the winter season means frozen water).

However, not all stream and pond water is suitable for drinking. With all the chemicals used in today's farming and salt on the roads in the wintertime, let alone animal feces (not knowing anything about *E. coli* and *Giardia,* animals aren't careful about leaving the stream to urinate or defecate), contaminants get into the water supply.

A fast-moving stream can reduce contamination problems. Ponds, on the other hand, are relatively static water supplies. Dirt, leaves, and feces can accumulate, creating a breeding ground for bugs and germs.

You may not be able to tell how good water is simply by looking at it — a nice, clear pond or stream with no muddy residue or algae may still be contaminated. If you want to use a stream or pond for stock watering, get it tested.

If the water gets your stamp of approval, here are some options for getting it to your critters:

✔ Set up corrals (fences) so that each separate pen has access to the water but animals can't go between pens. Use fencing or gates that go down to the bottom and prohibit any animal from sneaking under and entering another (forbidden) pen.

✔ Let the animals wander down to drink at will. With this option, limit access points so the critters don't trample the entire bank, speeding up erosion and dirt accumulation.

✔ Use an automatic waterer to pump water into a trough (and maybe even a small swimming hole) and prevent the animals from actually walking into the water. See the later section "Automatic waterers" for information on how this device works.

✔ Allow gravity to pull water down into your troughs.

Wells

Wells are a great source of water for your animals. Use a well to supply water to an automatic waterer the same way you use it to supply water to your house. You can simply use hoses or install underground lines directly out to the animals. Some well water is incredibly nice — fresh and pure. However, other water contains unwanted minerals that you may need to filter out.

Manually filled buckets and troughs

The old-fashioned way of supplying water involves manually filling some sort of container, such as a bucket, trough, or large drum (see Figure 3-1). An old bathtub actually works really well as a waterer. You can also use plastic barrels with the tops cut off, or you can make a trough out of a 50-gallon drum that has been cut in half. Every week, water troughs need to be emptied and cleaned, and the water replaced. In the winter, troughs must be heated to prevent freezing.

Automatic waterers

If your waterer is set up to automatically refill (a pretty cool concept, by the way), a float in the system detects when the water goes below a certain level, triggering the valves to open and fill the waterer back up.

You can automate underground pipes or use temporary lines, such as above-ground drip irrigation hoses. You can even install temperature regulators to prevent the water from freezing by turning on heat.

These systems can be electric, solar powered, or even energy-free. They may be commercially made or do-it-yourself. The station where you configure the system should be in a location that's easy to get to, so you can easily make modifications, change batteries (if using solar power), or just check on it.

Figure 3-1:
A cow
drinks from
a water
trough.

Preventing freezes

In many parts of the U.S., winter equals cold temperatures, and that means the water in outside water buckets is going to ice up. But the small farmer has a couple options for keeping fresh water from freezing: a heated water bucket, usually a plastic one with an embedded heating coil and plug, or a submersible tank de-icer that's placed directly in the bucket. Both are shown in Figure 3-2.

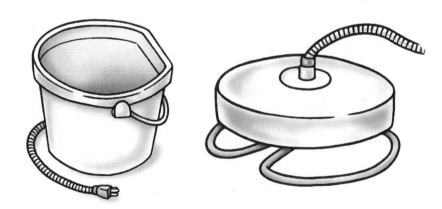

Figure 3-2:
A water
bucket with
a built-in
heating
element
(left) and a
submersible
tank de-icer
(right).

If the animals drink directly from the trough (meaning it's not a holding tank that you draw water from), consider using a heater design that screws into the plug in the bottom of the trough rather than one that has a cord that drapes over the top. Animals can pull out cords draped over the top, allowing the water to freeze and possibly burning out the unit.

If you run an electrical cord outside to plug in your heating elements, protect the connection from moisture. Plug the heating element into the plug and then wrap the entire connection with lots of electrical tape. That way, no water can get in and cause a short.

Letting Your Animals Romp

Animals don't like to be cooped up, and subjecting them to this treatment can affect their health and temperament. Being in the fresh air, stretching their legs, and chasing their friends around the pasture aren't just enjoyable activities — they're therapeutic!

Busting loose is a year-round activity. Don't assume your animals don't want to go outdoors just because it's cold or snowing outside. Although animals seek the shelter of their enclosure at times (during sideways-blowing snow comes to mind!), most animals really like and even prefer to be in the fresh air, and they generally go outdoors (at least for a little while) in even the harshest weather.

Proper exercise depends on the animal.

- ✔ Horses that live in stables need the most attention. Riding them regularly is best. Otherwise, you can consider getting a circular motorized walker that looks sort of like a merry-go-round. You hook the horse up to it and turn it on, and it walks the horse.

- ✔ Llamas tend to run around at times and don't really need anything further, unless you want them in hiking shape. Then you need to regularly take them for a spin around the neighborhood.

- ✔ Cows, especially those you're raising for meat, don't need a lot of exercise because that means weight loss.

Protecting Your Precious Critters

Animals can't always fend for themselves, so it's up to you to act as their caretaker, providing reliable shelter for protection from predators and the weather. The specific type of shelter needed depends on which animals you have. Rabbits need separate hutches; chickens and other small birds need housing; and sheep and goats need a guard animal.

Animals should have inside shelter when the weather gets really nasty. Some, like llamas, don't seem to notice when the weather is bad, but most run for cover and need a comforting place to go.

Besides separate shelters and guards, fencing is a must. Not only does fencing keep your animals from straying away, but it also serves to keep larger predators out of the pens.

Dogs are one of the worst predators of many farm animals, so your fencing should be dog-proof (which also makes it coyote- and fox-proof). Introduce dogs to your farm animals slowly and don't leave them without a chaperone until you're sure they get along. Dogs can attack and be attacked. Cats usually get along well with other farm animals, except for baby birds and rabbits.

Never tether an animal to a fence post and leave it there. A tied animal is vulnerable to predators, and the restraints prevent it from getting exercise. The poor critter can also get rope burns or even severe injuries from the rope.

Handling Disconcerting Behavior

Each animal has an innate personality, and sometimes personalities clash. Additionally, some of the things you do (or don't do) directly affect the way your animals behave. The next few sections present some of the behavioral problems you may encounter.

Keeping your critters from thinking you're one of them

Animals aren't four-legged humans, so don't treat them as such — even if you have to take special care of a young one. Doing so can cause problems down the road. If you have to bottle-feed an animal, get the little one back with a herd or flock as soon as you can. The adults in the group can show the newbie the ropes.

Bottle-feeding has its benefits: It typically produces tamer animals, making them easier to catch when the time comes to shear them or trim their hooves. But there are trade-offs. The following sections cover some of the hazards of blurring the boundaries between animal-human relationships.

For both nutritional and behavioral reasons, babies should stay with their mothers until they know how to eat on their own. If you're going to give an animal to another farm that doesn't have other animals of its kind or age, you may want to leave the baby with its mother for a couple more months. Also, keep in mind that herd animals don't do well if you take them out of the herd altogether. Llamas, for instance, should always go in pairs (at minimum) because they need social interaction with another of their kind.

Aggression

If you teach a male animal that it's just another person, the critter may treat people as competition for the females during breeding season, making it very aggressive toward people. Aggression carries over into other aspects of the animal's life as well. Competition for food can cause a friendly little cow to turn on you if it thinks you want to deprive it of some of the food in the trough.

Aggressive behavior manifests differently for different animals. For example, llamas typically don't spit at people, but if your llama thinks it's the same as you, you're a prime target.

Having billy goats think you're one of them can have an unwanted and down-right gross consequence. During the *rut* (mating season), they get stinky with urine. Apparently in the goat world, stinky is attractive, and the stinkiest guy always gets the girl. If you happen to go out into the pen with grain, your old pal Mr. Goat may come running to rub up against you. Like llama spit, a stinky goat is right up there with things you don't want to smell like.

Regardless of the amount of (over)bonding you've had with your goats or sheep, you should never turn your back on the males. If they see you as a threat, they may charge and can easily knock you down. Some people have been killed this way — by hitting their heads in a fall or being trampled. That's not a good way to go.

Improper socialization

A female that gets a lot of attention as a youngster doesn't typically turn aggressive on you. The main concern is that the animal won't be properly socialized. If a female bonds too closely with humans, it may not fit as well in the herd because it wants attention from you, not its peers.

When a young animal leaves its mother too early, the little one may not have had enough time to figure out how to *be* that animal and how to interact with others of the breed. Without the proper socialization, the critter may not know how to get along because nobody put it in its place when it got out of hand as a youngster. Or it may not pick up the things a mom teaches in those early days, such as what to eat or even how to play.

Managing social problems

If too many animals are occupying a small space, or if you have trouble suppressing the aggressive actions of a dominant animal, you'll see some fighting and general meanness. Animals compete for food, water, attention from you, and sometimes even the prime resting spots. Here's how to deal with these issues:

- **Handling overcrowding:** To get around overcrowding, either thin the herd or make a new pen so the living quarters are a more spacious. Establishing a few separate feeding places is also helpful.

- **Removing weapons:** Goats typically use their horns to fight and to establish the pecking order, but these horns can cause injury to other goats (and humans). A common practice is to *disbud* them (remove the bud or beginning of the horn) when a goat is 3 to 7 days old. You can also dehorn an older animal, but that process is more involved, requiring a sedative and a veterinarian.

- **Castrating aggressive males:** Testosterone may increase aggression, so having males castrated may be helpful. Although larger animals have to be taken to the vet, smaller animals, such as goats, can be castrated by placing bands around the testicles at an early age. The blood supply is slowly cut off, and the testicles shrivel up and fall off.

   Never use old, brittle bands that can break, because if the castration process has started and the band breaks before the process is complete, you can lose the animal to gangrene. Make sure you get some training before you try this method or you do it under the supervision of a professional.

- **Separating aggressors:** Separating aggressive animals is better than subjecting animals to injury. You may have an animal that's simply mean or just doesn't get along with the rest of the herd. You can either experiment with different roommates until you find a good combination or house the aggressive animal by itself.

Training animals for human interaction

Unless you plan to take your farm animals to shows or turn them into movie stars, most can do without training. You need to be able to control your animals somewhat to get them to go into holding pens, for instance, but most animals are either small enough for you to get them where you want them or they naturally follow the herd.

A couple of exceptions are horses and llamas that you intend to use as pack animals. Training is essential with these creatures because they're large, and you need to get very close to ride them or to put a pack on their backs. At the very least, you need to halter-train them so you can lead them around. Untrained, they may panic and hurt you.

The earlier you start training animals, the better. As they get older and stuck in their ways, training them becomes increasingly difficult. Starting training early is also a good way to ensure better handling for maintenance tasks, such as grooming or medical attention.

Chapter 4

Providing Medical Attention

- -

In This Chapter

▶ Covering the animal first aid basics

▶ Understanding the importance of properly administered vaccinations

▶ Knowing when to call the vet

▶ Preparing for the pitter-patter of little hooves

- -

*Y*ou can head off a lot of trouble with your animals simply by keeping their living conditions clean and taking care of their basic food, water, and shelter needs (all of which are covered in Book V, Chapter 3). However, you still have to provide medical attention from time to time. Doing so keeps your animals healthy and stops any potential problems from getting beyond the point of fixing.

Sad but true, animals become sick, get into fights, or have difficult births — situations that can require medical attention and know-how. You can provide some of this care yourself if the problem is minor, which is good because calling on a vet can be pricey, especially if he or she has to come out to your property.

For other procedures, you want to call for backup. This chapter helps you determine what you can do yourself, points out some of the common ailments that are most likely to crop up, and explains a few animal-specific problems. ***Remember:*** These tips are only guidelines — consult your vet for specific advice.

Unless you've had plenty of training, don't try to self-diagnose. If you misdiagnose a problem, you could end up with an even bigger medical issue on your hands. A simple eye infection, for example, can look like a scratch, but treatment for a scratch when the problem is actually an infection can lead to loss of the eye. You can check out the *Merck Veterinary Manual* (www.merckvet manual.com) if you want to read more about animal ailments.

Putting Together Your Animal First-Aid Kit

Minor problems and emergencies are facts of life, even with animals, so having a first-aid kit for your farm friends is a must. The next couple sections give you an idea of what to include. Keep your kit wherever's most convenient for you, possibly inside the house to ensure it's free from nosy critters.

The best place to acquire animal first-aid supplies is your local veterinarian, because vets know all the ins and outs of animal care. But you can always try these other options, too:

- ✔ **A farm or country store:** In the Southwest, a chain called Intermountain Farmers Association (www.ifacountrystore.com) has just about everything you need. Mills Fleet Farm stores (www.fleetfarm.com) in the Midwest are similar.

- ✔ **The Internet:** With just a click of a mouse, you can now easily find products that once weren't so easy to get. Country stores may sell products online, or you can check out a medical supplier such as United Vet Equine (www.unitedvetequine.com).

Including creams, antiseptics, sprays, and meds

You can easily take care of minor accidents and injuries yourself if you have the necessary supplies. A basic animal first-aid kit should have at least these items:

- ✔ **Antibiotic cream:** You use antibiotic cream for minor wounds to remove bacteria and prevent more from growing.

- ✔ **Bag Balm:** Its intended use is to keep cows' udders soft (thus its name), but it's also really good on anything that's dry and cracked, such as noses, calluses, or foot pads.

- ✔ **Fly repellent spray:** Face it, animals attract flies. In many cases, the fly problem can be worse than whatever smells the animals make. Dealing with flies is a big job in the hot summer months.

Fly prevention is particularly necessary around sick or injured animals. Flies get into wounds and lay eggs, which hatch into really disgusting creatures — maggots.

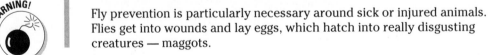

✔ **Gentle antiseptic solution:** Some people prefer to use antiseptic solutions such as chlorhexidine diacetate (Nolvasan) on wounds and cut umbilical cords because these solutions aren't as irritating as iodine or hydrogen peroxide.

✔ **Hydrogen peroxide:** Because of how it foams up, hydrogen peroxide does a good job of getting dirt out of wounds. You can also use it as a *disinfectant* (to sterilize inanimate objects) or as an *emetic* (to make animals vomit) if they get into rat poison.

✔ **Iodine:** An iodine solution is a good topical antibacterial solution.

Tincture of iodine, a stronger solution that's 7 percent iodine, isn't recommended because it can be very irritating to the skin. You don't want to get any in the eyes for sure.

✔ **Miscellaneous medications:** Deworming meds or vitamins can help. For allergies, maybe include some diphenhydramine hydrochloride (Benadryl), which is used mostly in small animals — such as dogs — that get stung by wasps or bees.

✔ **Scarlet oil:** Used primarily in horses or mules, scarlet oil is a nondrying topical antiseptic used to promote healing in the treatment of cuts, wounds, abrasions, or burns. You can find it at your local farm store.

Do what the vets do: Use scarlet oil for anything above the knees and a light iodine solution for anything below the knees.

Gathering basic equipment

In addition to the topical solutions listed in the preceding section, your first-aid kit also needs some basic equipment for monitoring temperatures, cleaning and covering wounds, and otherwise taking care of your farm friends' hygiene. Here are some tools of the trade:

✔ **Basic bandaging material:** You typically use bandages on extremities — after all, you'd go through an awful lot of bandages if you were to wrap them around the animal's chest! Wrapping up a wound on a leg, neck, or tail can help speed recovery and keep flies off.

✔ **Bulb syringe:** A bulb syringe is great for sucking fluid out of a newborn's nose and mouth to help it breathe on its own.

✔ **Clean cloths:** Use clean cloths to create hot packs for treating injuries around larger body parts, such as an animal's torso. See the later section "Treating minor scrapes and cuts" for details.

✔ **Flytrap:** The more flies you can trap, the fewer you have buzzing around your animals and breeding more little pests. Stick with a heavy duty flytrap, such as the Ridmax one shown in Figure 4-1, or order some fly parasites — tiny, wasplike insects that eat fly pupae.

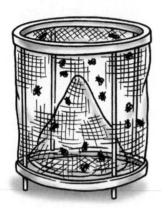

Figure 4-1:
This type
of flytrap,
which is
very useful
in barns,
traps more
flies than
flypaper.

✔ **Gauze pads:** These pads come in a variety of sizes (typically 2 inches, 3 inches, and 4 inches square) and with different plies (the more layers, the more they soak up). Have a supply of several different sizes and plies on hand for whatever comes up.

✔ **Long cotton swabs:** Useful for cleaning tight spaces such as little puncture wounds, abscesses, and the occasional ear (you may even be able to remove ticks this way), cotton swabs are handy to keep around. But use them with care — if you don't have a good hold on the animal, you can cause further injury.

✔ **Syringes:** Keep a few syringes of different sizes on hand. Use them to flush solutions (like hydrogen peroxide) into a wound, feed newborns, or give oral liquid medications.

✔ **Thermometer:** Thermometers are, obviously, for taking temperatures. Make sure you label it *rectal* (once a rectal, always a rectal). Choose from the old-fashioned glass kind that usually takes about a minute to register the temperature or the newfangled digital kind that gives a reading in a few seconds.

For those times when your animal has to go to the vet, you also need some sort of transport. Smaller animals such as goats or sheep can ride in the cab of a pickup truck or inside a large dog kennel in the truck bed. For larger animals, you really need a trailer.

An Ounce of Prevention: Scheduling Vaccinations

Every species has different preventive vaccination needs, with emphasis on the word *needs*. If you don't get regular vaccinations for your animals, sickness and even death can be just around the corner. Although you can't possibly vaccinate against all diseases an animal can get, each animal you own should receive at least a few basic vaccines. Find a vet with farm animal experience and schedule regular visits. In rural areas, you may be able to find a mobile vet who comes to you.

Good hygiene, up-to-date vaccinations, and all that preventive stuff pay dividends in money and time down the road. Routine maintenance and attention to minor problems can help keep your animals comfy and happy.

Knowing the basic vaccines

Just as humans receive childhood vaccinations, animals should be given vaccinations against some diseases as a matter of course. Which diseases you have to watch out for depends on what's prevalent in your area, the history of your herd, and whether a disease is likely to be contracted. But as a general rule, consider the following vaccinations:

- ✔ **Tetanus:** All animals can get tetanus, but horses are particularly prone to it. The tetanus bacteria is in soil and is usually introduced into animals via a puncture wound — from nails, barbed wire, or any kind of deep cut. Tetanus causes *lockjaw* (where the animal's jaws actually lock up so it can't eat), convulsions, and sensitivity to light.

- ✔ **Clostridial diseases:** Animals can catch all sorts of diseases from *Clostridium* bacteria, including foot root, botulism, and intestinal diseases. (Tetanus is actually a clostridial disease.)

- ✔ **Rabies:** All animals are susceptible to rabies, a nasty virus that's transmitted by bite wounds and often causes death. There are two types of rabies:

    - *Dumb rabies* causes an animal to become dull and lethargic and not want to eat anything.

    - *Furious rabies* causes aggressive behavioral changes and foaming at the mouth.

✔ **Brucellosis:** This disease causes stillbirths and miscarriages in cattle and is also transmittable to people. The human form of this disease, called *undulant fever,* is a flulike disease with symptoms that never go away. It's incredibly hard to cure, and the infected human usually has a chronic flu, exhibiting symptoms every couple of weeks.

✔ **Mastitis:** Animals that produce milk (cattle or goats) can get *mastitis,* an infection of the mammary gland (the udder) that causes clotted milk or a hard or tender udder.

✔ **Nasal infections and pneumonia:** Pigs should be vaccinated against these conditions.

Young animals are often more susceptible to infection and are thus more likely to benefit from certain vaccinations that may be unnecessary when they get older. For instance, young animals may need to be vaccinated against respiratory diseases.

Consulting your vet for immunizations

Not all vaccines are alike. Some may not induce a good enough response; others may generate unforeseen reactions. So in terms of the health of your animals, your local vet is usually the best-qualified person to evaluate vaccines and choose one that's likely to have the best results. How often your animals need vaccinations will vary — your vet can help you set up a schedule.

Still need convincing? Following are some other reasons the vet is likely the best one to be administering these (and really any) meds:

✔ In very rare cases, animals have bad reactions to vaccines. If you give the vaccine yourself, you may not pick up on the reaction, or you may not get your animal to the vet in time to treat it. One such reaction is severe anaphylactic shock, which causes difficulty breathing and a sudden drop in blood pressure — the animal can just collapse. Death can occur within a very short time, so getting help fast is critical.

✔ Vaccines require proper handling. They should be refrigerated, diluted correctly, not exposed to heat or freezing temperatures, and administered with a sterile syringe.

✔ Some vaccines go under the skin *(subcutaneous),* and some go in the muscle *(intramuscular).* Neither type should go into the vein. If given the wrong way, these vaccines may not be effective at all, or they may cause death or other serious health consequences.

✔ Manufacturers don't (and can't) guarantee that all animals given their vaccine will be able to produce the required antibodies to fight off the disease the vaccine was formulated against. The best way to ensure that your vaccine is effective is to have a vet select and administer it.

> ✔ Syringes and needles are considered hazardous waste and must be disposed of in specific ways. You can't just toss a used needle into your wastebasket.
>
> ✔ Only a licensed veterinarian can administer the rabies vaccine. If you give it yourself, the state considers your animal to be unvaccinated.

 Believe it or not, you can have an expert administer your animals' vaccinations affordably. Try arranging it so that all your animals are being vaccinated at the same time. You pay a base fee for the vet to come out to the farm and then a charge per animal. Better yet, there may even be a financial break when you get to a certain number of animals.

Administering the vaccinations yourself

Although most vets don't recommend that you do vaccinations yourself (see the preceding section for several reasons why), many farmers do vaccinate their own animals — and this decision mostly has to do with money. If you have 40 sheep, paying a vet to vaccinate them all can cost a pretty penny. And some animals that aren't very expensive themselves may not warrant spending so much on vaccinations — the house call for the vaccination may cost more than the animal is worth. This isn't a good mindset, but it's one that some farmers get into.

 Most vets are willing to show farm animal owners how to administer shots, so consult with yours before undertaking the task yourself. Remember, though, that only a licensed vet can administer a rabies vaccine for it to be considered valid by the state.

Caring for Sick or Hurt Animals

Despite all your attention to their health, animals sometimes get sick or hurt. They may have encounters with wildlife and end up losing. Sometimes a minor medical problem balloons into a bigger one. The following sections offer help recognizing signs of sickness, understanding treatments you can use, and knowing when to call in the veterinary cavalry.

 You can't know what's *abnormal* until you know what *normal* is. When you go out to feed your animals, give them a once-over to check for health problems. Keep a close eye on them so you can catch the minor scrapes and take care of them before they become major infections. Daily observation tells you the animals' habits, what they like, and how they react to different situations.

Watching for signs of sickness

Determining whether your animal is just having a bad day or really is sick and in need of attention isn't always easy, but a few red flags always demand action.

- ✓ **Limited activity:** If you notice an animal is down, that doesn't necessarily mean there's a problem. It may just be resting or basking in the sun. But if an animal is down for a while, try to get the critter up and see what it does.

- ✓ **Loss of appetite:** Sometimes animals just don't want to eat. Maybe the day's too hot, or perhaps they're wiped out and need rest first. Or maybe the food is actually bad, and they just refuse to eat it. All these scenarios are possible, but if one of your animals continually sniffs its food without eating, something's wrong.

  A good way to test an animal's appetite is to give it oats or other favorite treats. If an animal that usually becomes putty in your hands when oats are offered suddenly isn't interested, it's probably ill.

- ✓ **Weight loss:** Animals may become thin because they simply aren't getting sufficient food, which may be the result of an infection that's draining them of nutrients and energy. Weight loss may also be due to parasites, poor nutrition, or a case of bad teeth that need dental care.

- ✓ **Reduction in milk production:** Milk production is an even more sensitive gauge than appetite for some animals. Lactating females produce plenty of milk. If their milk production is off, you know something's up.

- ✓ **Other obvious signs of disease:** Many other symptoms can indicate that your animal isn't feeling up to snuff. Excessive coughing, a runny nose, diarrhea, or anything else that's just not normal for the animal probably means medical attention is necessary.

If you're concerned, call your vet and ask whether he or she thinks you should bring the animal in (or whether a house call is in order).

Wearing the doctor's cap: What you can do

You can take care of a few basic tasks yourself when you see that your animals aren't in the best of health. The next several sections cover ways you can treat and monitor a sick or injured animal.

Taking temperatures

Temperatures outside the normal range can indicate many problems. If you see a difference in temperature, it's probably time to call a vet. Here are some possible causes of low or high temperatures:

Low Temperature	*High Temperature*
Shock (from blood loss, trauma, heart problems, or allergic reactions)	Infections (bacterial and viral)
Hypothermia (prolonged exposure to subnormal temps)	Heat stroke (hyperthermia)
	Seizures
	Drug reactions

Animal temperatures must be taken rectally. To do so, follow these steps:

1. **Secure the animal.**

   You have to secure the animal because taking its temperature isn't going to be met with cooperation. Plus, if the animal balks (maybe violently), you can get hurt, or the thermometer may break. Not good.

2. **Tie a piece of rubber tubing or twine around one end of the thermometer, secure an alligator clip to the other end of the tubing, and clip that to the animal's hair.**

   Animals can suck the instrument up into the rectum or push it out with quite a bit of force. If it gets sucked in, you can pull it out, and if the animal tries to push it out, the alligator clamp prevents it from going flying across the room.

3. **Lubricate the thermometer with something such as Vaseline or K-Y Jelly.**

4. **For a glass thermometer, put it about halfway in the animal's rectum and leave it in about one minute (or follow the instructions for your particular thermometer).**

5. **Clean the thermometer after use.**

   Get rid of any residue with soap and water first. Then dip the thermometer in alcohol for a few minutes to sterilize it.

Different animals have different normal temperatures. Use Table 4-1 as a guide when you're checking temperatures, normal or otherwise.

Table 4-1	Normal Temperatures for Common Farm Animals
Animal	*Normal Temperature (° F)*
Camelids	Around 101
Cattle	101–102
Dogs or cats	100.5–102.5
Goats	101.5–103.5
Horses	100–101
Pigs	102–103
Sheep	100.9–103.8

Treating minor scrapes and cuts

Scrapes and cuts happen. An animal may get caught up in the fencing, or get a little too aggressive at the grain bucket. A minor scratch isn't a matter of life or death, but taking care of it can mean making the animal more comfortable and preventing the minor problem from turning into a major one.

Determining what's minor is kind of a judgment call. Check the size of the injury (the surface area) as well as how deep it goes. Then follow these guidelines:

- ✔ If the cut goes *full thickness* — in other words, it goes all the way through the skin and into the tissue below it so that you can move the two sides of the cut in opposing directions — then the wound is serious, and you should call your vet.

- ✔ Regardless of whether the cut is full thickness, if it's at or near a joint, the eyes, or a vital organ, it's a concern. You don't want to mess with that injury yourself.

- ✔ A surface cut or one that's only 1 inch or so long is probably going to be okay and should respond favorably to minor treatments.

To treat minor cuts, clean them with hydrogen peroxide or an antiseptic solution and then bathe them in some sort of antibiotic ointment or Bag Balm to protect them (ask your vet for product recommendations). Then cover the wound with a sterile bandage. Keep bandages dry and clean and change them every day, or at least every other day.

Don't wrap bandages too tightly! No bandage at all is better than one that cuts off circulation.

When you can't wrap a bandage around the injured body part (such as a torso), wash out the wound with an antiseptic solution or a half-strength hydrogen peroxide solution (one part hydrogen peroxide and one part water). To reduce swelling and decrease blood flow, put a cold pack on the affected area for 10 to 15 minutes (or however long the animal sits still for it).

If the wound becomes infected, soak a clean cloth in hot water and place it on the wound for a few minutes (or as long as the animal lets you). This hot pack stimulates blood flow and promotes local immunity. Finally, put some antibiotic ointment or Bag Balm on the wound to protect it from other bacteria. With horses, you may want to consider an antiseptic spray such as Wound-Kote, which medicates and dries.

As long as the cut continues to heal, you're okay. If it gets worse, a visit to or from the vet is in order.

Deworming

In veterinary terms, *worms* aren't the squishy creatures you use when you go fishing. They're parasites that get into an animal's gastrointestinal (GI) tract from a variety of sources. Mostly, animals ingest them from eating grass or other foodstuffs off the ground, but animals can also be born with them.

Worms in the GI tract rob an animal of necessary nutrients. Getting rid of them, or *deworming,* is a routine act that decreases the worm load that's stealing nutrition from the animal. Some deworming medications are injected, whereas others are given orally. Either way, they usually have to be administered more than once within a short period of time so you can be sure all worms are cleaned out.

You can obtain deworming meds from a farm supply store and administer them yourself, but check with your vet for specifics.

Giving vitamin supplements

Whether your animals need vitamin supplements depends on their health and the conditions in their environment. Check with your vet, the local cooperative extension service, or the country store for information about what your animals' diets may be lacking.

Here are some common vitamin shots:

- **Vitamins A, D, E, and K:** Mostly, animals obtain these vitamins from dietary sources, but in some cases, an animal may need an extra boost because its food sources don't contain enough. Vitamin supplement shots can alleviate many symptoms of deficiency, such as lethargy, a poor coat, or an inability to gain weight.

- **Vitamin B:** This vitamin is an appetite stimulant that can be given to an animal at any point in its life (including while it's a newborn) if it isn't eating and needs a little push.

- **Vitamin E or selenium:** Some goats and sheep receive these shots subcutaneously at birth to ward off white muscle disease. After the initial shot, the animal may need a booster.

  White muscle disease is a degenerative disease that causes anything from mild stiffness to obvious pain upon walking, or even an inability to stand if it attacks the skeletal muscles. It can also cause difficulty breathing, a frothy nasal discharge, and fever if it affects the heart muscles.

Before administering vitamin shots yourself, have your vet show you how. Vitamin or mineral blocks, which are similar to a salt lick, are also a good way to get these nutrients into your animals. You can purchase these meds from a local farm supply store.

Determining when you need a vet

Some situations are just too much for the average farmer to deal with, so you need an expert to come to the rescue. Typically, you can find a mobile vet in your area, but sometimes you may have to load your animal into a trailer and take it to the vet.

No matter where you live, you can usually find a 24-hour emergency clinic for smaller animals; rural communities often have a 24-hour number to call for large animals. In some places, the local large-animal vets form a cooperative where each vet does a stint of on-call duty and then has time off. You can obtain this phone number from your vet or local farm store.

You absolutely must call a vet when you notice that an animal

- **Has obvious external injuries:** Such injuries include profuse bleeding, a huge gash or lump, and/or an obvious broken bone.

- **Is extremely depressed, lethargic, or thin:** Consider any of these conditions a cause for alarm. (Of course, your animals will never reach this point because you're watching them daily, right?)

- **Is completely uninterested in food:** You should be concerned if an animal hasn't touched its food after 24 hours and isn't interested in treats. Horses shouldn't even go this long. If they're not eating, watch them continually. If they go down, that could be a sign of colic.

- **Lays down and doesn't get back up:** An animal that can't get up has usually crossed into the serious category. If you can't get your animal to stand, something is drastically wrong.

If a horse goes down and starts to roll, get it up immediately and walk it. You now face two potential problems — *colic,* which means the horse can't defecate or vomit due to abdominal problems, and the rolling, which can cause the intestine to twist. Call the vet and continue to walk the horse until he or she arrives. If your vet has given you some flunixin meglumine (Banamine, an anti-inflammatory prescription drug), he or she may instruct you to give the horse a shot to relieve its pain. But beware — a Banamine shot can mask signs the vet needs to diagnose the kind of colic.

Provided you have access to a 24-hour emergency clinic, your vet is only a phone call away. You can call and ask whether the symptoms you're seeing are serious, or whether you can do some treatment yourself. Bottom line: If you need a vet, call right away. Waiting can mean your animal won't pull through.

As a courtesy to your vet's private life, try to take care of potential emergencies as soon as they arise instead of waiting until you can't put them off anymore. Yes, emergencies do happen — sometimes in the middle of the night — and your vet will do what he or she can to help save your animal. But maintaining a good rapport with your vet is always a good idea, and part of that relationship means not having to call in the middle of the night because you didn't handle a situation during regular hours.

Book V

Raising Farm Animals

Bracing Yourself for Birthing Season

Yes, animal babies have been born throughout the ages — usually without any help from humans. But matters can and do go wrong, and if you're there to assist in the birth (or the immediate aftermath) and deal with any problems, then animals that wouldn't otherwise make it on their own can have a chance at life. You want to be sure you have all of your bases covered at birthing time — especially if your animals are prize racehorses or alpacas that you hope to sell for big bucks!

Predicting due dates

If you know the time of conception, you can consult Table 4-2 and have a pretty good idea of when the baby will arrive. Sometimes knowing precisely when the deed happened is easy because you've put two critters into a separate pen and let them get to know each other better.

Table 4-2	Gestation Periods for Common Farm Animals
Animal	*Gestation Period*
Camelids	11½ months
Cattle	9 months
Chickens	21 days
Dogs and cats	58–63 days
Goats	150 days
Horses	340 days
Pigs	114 days
Rabbits	33 days
Sheep	148 days

When a couple of critters share love behind your back, you can still do tests to determine whether a pregnancy has occurred. Animal pregnancy tests skip straight to the ultrasound, which works the same as with humans in that it sends out a sound wave that bounces through the body and shows up as a picture. You don't need to anesthetize animals — they don't seem to mind the noninvasive procedure. You do, however, have to shave the belly and rub some jelly on it to aid in the transmission. (***Note:*** Horses are the exception. Their ultrasound tests are done through the anus — a procedure most mares aren't too happy about.)

Preparing for a birth

A lot of animal births go off without a hitch — hence the reason you may come home from a day out and find a baby llama or horse on the ground. However, with a few precautions to keep the mother comfortable, you can aid your farm friend in the birthing process and increase the chances of a successful birth.

✔ **If you have an idea of the due date, put the mother into an isolated area beforehand.** Opt for a place under some sort of shelter where she can stay warm, dry, stress-free, and away from outside interference. That means no screaming children or barking dogs. Stress causes more adrenaline production, which can actually stop females from pushing. Wind and other weather nuisances should also be lessened or eliminated.

✔ **Keep a good watch on the mother during this close-to-the-big-moment time, and adjust feed as needed.** Watch momma closely, a few times every day. Installing a video camera can allow you to do your watching while still getting your chores done. You may want to get a halter alarm, which goes off when the animal lies down; this device, along with the camera system, can allow you to be in the house (even asleep) right up until the blessed event.

As the time draws nigh, the mother gets restless and obviously uncomfortable — she stands up, lies down, and then does it all again. When she starts doing this, she may want or need to go off her feed for about 24 hours. Watch for contractions and for the mother to start bearing down and pushing. If all goes well, a little bubble will come out, followed by a nose or foot.

You usually don't need to step in at all, unless of course there's a birthing problem. See the later section "Birthing problems: Dystocia" for guidance in this situation.

✔ **Have an indoor space and plenty of dry straw or bedding available.** If the birth occurs in the colder months, you want to bring mother and babe inside for awhile. And if your farm facility isn't ready to house them, be prepared to improvise. For example, if your newborn farm friend arrives in winter, it may need to spend the first month of its life with its mother in your garage with a space heater.

Following up on a normal birth

Most of the time, you don't need to do anything after the mother gives birth except fawn over the new baby. But even after a perfect birth, you can take some steps to ensure the baby's and mother's safety and comfort.

✔ Dip the umbilical cord in a bit of Nolvasan or other nonirritating antiseptic solution. Maybe even clamp off the cord and permanently tie it off with some string.

✔ Make sure the baby gets dried off. The mom usually does this, but sometimes you need to help. Use some clean straw to rub the baby and get it good and free of the birth goo.

✔ Ensure mother and babe are both warm and dry.

✔ Watch to be certain the baby takes its first milk within the first half hour or so. This first milk is known as *colostrum,* a nutrient- and antibody-rich substance that's vital to the newborn's health.

✔ Consider weighing the baby periodically to be sure it's putting on weight.

✔ If you own several animals that are having babies at the same time, you may want to tag 'em so you can keep track of them.

Handling difficulties during and after birth

Despite your precautions, sometimes animal births just don't go by the book. A baby can be stillborn or breech. The birth can take a lot longer than you expect. Or an umbilical cord can get wrapped around the little one. The following sections delve into some problems that can occur during or after the birth of your new farm friend.

Birthing problems: Dystocia

Dystocia is a fancy name meaning "difficult birth," and that can mean anything from a birth that's taking too long to one where the mother is in excessive discomfort to one where the baby is coming out backward or even stillborn.

Watch for signs something is amiss. For instance, perhaps the mother's water has broken and she's in labor, but nothing is coming out. If a mother goes through this scenario for more than a couple of hours, call the vet immediately. In horses, you don't even want to wait that long. Horses have been known to rupture the uterus pushing a foal that won't come out. Call the vet if the mare is pushing for ten minutes and nothing is coming out, or if the baby is *breech* (you're seeing the baby's rear end rather than its head).

You may also want to elicit the help of a neighbor who has gone through difficult births in the past and knows what to do.

If the baby isn't breathing at birth, clear the airway so the little one can begin breathing easily on its own. A bulb syringe — or a turkey baster — is great for sucking fluid out of babies' mouths and noses so they can breathe. Tear any remaining sac off from around the nose. If that doesn't do it, rub the baby vigorously. Ideally, the mom instinctively knows what to do, but you may have to help, especially on a first birth if she's particularly nervous. You may even have to do mouth-to-mouth resuscitation.

Mothers rejecting their babies, or vice versa

A mother occasionally rejects her baby for not-so-obvious reasons. Sometimes you can figure them out, but sometimes you just don't know why. One speculation is that Charles Darwin's "survival of the fittest" theory applies here. Perhaps the mother knows that a particular baby isn't strong enough to make it, and she wants to give her energy and attention to the others that she has more hope for.

Perhaps the mother has *mastitis* (an infection of the mammary glands) and nursing is very painful for her, so she turns away from her babies. Or the mother may be sick herself — perhaps wiped out from a difficult birth or something more serious that you don't know about. Or maybe she's just a nervous first-timer and doesn't want to or doesn't know how to take on a newborn.

Sometimes the baby is the one that doesn't take to the mother. The little one may be too weak or too cold to get up and nurse. Or the baby may have a cleft palate or other abnormality that prevents it from nursing. Sometimes, the baby simply doesn't learn the suckle reflex and thus isn't taking to the usual form of nursing. (In horses, this baby is called a *dummy foal.*)

Whatever the reason, rejection does happen, and you're left with a baby that isn't going to make it on its own and isn't going to get any help from the mother. The next section explains how to raise the little one yourself.

The future of orphans or rejected babies

Mothers can die in childbirth or shortly afterward from non-birth-related accidents, leaving you with a newborn that needs constant attention if it's to have a chance in life. Or you may have an infant that for some reason isn't able to nurse from its mother.

Either way, if you plan on raising this newborn, you have to have the right facilities and the time to devote to a very needy creature that must be kept warm and fed at regular intervals throughout the day and night. Although raising an orphan requires a huge commitment of time and patience, it can be very rewarding and the only reasonable choice for those who reject the alternative — letting the baby die.

The bad news is that animals without a mother of the same species can be robbed of natural immunities and thus grow up to be less hardy. The first 12 to 24 hours of an animal's life are critical for several reasons. Besides the obvious reasons of feeding and protection, this time is when the mother produces *colostrum* — a thickened, antibody-rich milk that's important for giving the baby a natural immunity. The mother actually can produce colostrum for a couple of days after birth, but the baby can absorb it only during these first hours.

If babies *do* get colostrum from their mothers during the critical first hours of their lives, they're blessed with a passive immunity, meaning they're more apt to fend off minor and common illnesses. This immunity from their mother's milk tides them over until their bodies can produce their own immunities. After the important absorption of colostrum, a baby can be successfully raised by a member of another species — like you! Without it, the little one's immune system is compromised, and the baby is susceptible to all manner of infections.

Birth defects

Animals can be born with any number of birth defects. Some mean the critter can't possibly survive; some mean it's handicapped but still able to live a decent life; and some mean the baby just needs a little help. Common birth defects include

✔ **Cleft palates:** An animal with this condition can't successfully nurse and instead inhales milk when it tries to suckle, causing a condition called *inhalation pneumonia*. Only surgery can fix a cleft palate.

✔ **Umbilical hernias:** An animal with an umbilical hernia has a hole in its abdominal wall because its skin didn't close correctly over the umbilical cord. Some smaller openings can close up on their own, but if they're bigger than the size of a quarter, they need veterinary attention.

Some less-common birth defects include two heads, multiple limbs, or a missing anus. Many other defects are possible, and if you experience one, you must consult a vet to determine whether the animal has a chance of survival.

Deciding to give a newborn up

Sometimes on a farm, you're forced to make tough decisions that you wouldn't have to make if the animal were your only cherished pet. If you want a successful farm, however, you have to let some of your animals go. Here are some reasons you may not be able to keep your little ones:

✔ You simply own too many animals. If you allow animals to breed, your flock or herd is going to grow, and there may come a time when you reach the limit of what your acreage can handle. Thus, you simply can't feed or accommodate all the new babies.

✔ Animals can grow up to be too aggressive. Keeping an aggressive animal on your farm may negatively affect your other critters and your financial and time investments in them.

✔ A baby just isn't responding to all the help and love you're lavishing upon it.

Ideally, you can find a good home for the young ones that are placeable. But in many instances, an animal that didn't do anything wrong may have to face a less favorable fate. Making the decision to send an animal to the butcher or to adopt it out to another farm is especially hard when it's one you nurtured from birth.

Chapter 5

Beginning Beekeeping

In This Chapter

▶ Deciding what equipment and tools to get

▶ Getting your bees and setting up house

▶ Caring for your bees throughout the year

Since becoming a backyard beekeeper, I've grown to deeply admire the remarkable qualities of bees. As a gardener, I've witnessed firsthand the dramatic contribution they make to plants of all kinds. With honeybees in my garden, its bounty has increased by leaps and bounds. And then there's that wonderful bonus that the honeybees generously give me: a yearly harvest of sweet liquid gold.

Bees are simply wonderful little creatures. Interacting with them is an honor and a privilege. People who love nature in its purest form will love bees and beekeeping. In this chapter, you find out everything you need to know to begin your adventure keeping bees.

Evaluating Your Beekeeping Potential

Why has mankind been so interested in beekeeping over the centuries? I'm sure the first motivator was *honey*. After all, for many years and long before cane sugar, honey was the primary sweetener in use. But the sweet reward is by no means the only reason folks are attracted to beekeeping. For a long time, agriculture has recognized the value of pollination by bees. Without the bees' help, many commercial crops would suffer serious consequences. Even backyard beekeepers witness dramatic improvements in their gardens' yields: more and larger fruits, flowers, and vegetables. A hive or two in the garden makes a big difference in your success as a gardener.

Being part of the bigger picture: Save the bees!

The facts that keeping a hive in the backyard dramatically improves pollination and rewards you with a delicious honey harvest are, by themselves, good enough reasons to keep bees. But today, the value of keeping bees goes beyond the obvious. In many areas, millions of colonies of wild (or *feral*) honeybees have been wiped out by urbanization, pesticides, and parasitic mites, devastating the wild honeybee population. This is why gardeners report seeing fewer and fewer honeybees in their gardens. Backyard beekeeping has become vital in our efforts to reestablish lost colonies of bees and offset the natural decrease in pollination by wild bees.

But not everyone is cut out to be a beekeeper. The question you need to ask yourself is, "Are *you* someone who'd make a good beekeeper?" Here are some things to consider in your answer:

- ✔ **Climate:** Unless you live on a glacier or on the frozen tundra of Siberia, your climate is probably suitable for beekeeping. Bees are remarkable creatures that do just fine in a wide range of climates.

- ✔ **Space requirements:** You don't need much space to keep bees. Although bees travel miles from the hive to gather pollen and nectar, foraging an area as large as 6,000 acres, you need only enough space to accommodate the hive itself.

- ✔ **Zoning and legal restrictions:** Most communities are quite tolerant of beekeepers, but some have local ordinances that prohibit beekeeping or restrict the number of hives that you can have. Check with your town hall, local zoning board, or state agricultural experiment station to find out what's allowed in your neighborhood.

- ✔ **Costs and equipment:** Figure on investing about $200 to $400 for the hive, equipment, tools, and medication. In addition, you'll spend $50 to $70 for a package of bees and a queen.

- ✔ **Time and commitment:** Beekeeping isn't labor intensive. Other than your first year (when it's a good idea to inspect the hive frequently to find out more about your bees), you need to make only five or six visits to your hives every year. Add to that the time you spend harvesting honey, repairing equipment, and putting things away for the season, and you'll probably devote 19 to 28 hours a year to your hobby (more if you make a business out of it).

- ✔ **Allergies:** A fact of life as a beekeeper is that you're going to get stung once in a while. If you're uncertain about whether you're allergic or not, or whether your allergy to bees is severe, check with an allergist, who can determine whether you're among the relatively few who should steer clear of beekeeping.

Bee Basics

Beekeepers really love their bees. That may sound weird to you if you aren't a beekeeper (yet!), but virtually everyone who keeps bees will tell you the same thing and speak with deep warmth about "their girls" (the majority of the bees in a hive are female — see the next section). Backyard beekeepers grow to deeply admire the remarkable qualities of these endearing creatures. Once you get to know more about bees' value and remarkable social skills, you'll fall in love with them too.

The three bee castes

Although you may think that all bees look exactly alike, actually three different castes make up the total population in any hive: worker, drone, and queen. Shown in Figure 5-1, each has its own characteristics, roles, and responsibilities. Upon closer examination, the three types even look a little different, and being able to distinguish one from another is important.

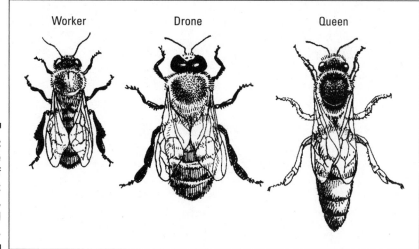

Figure 5-1:
The three castes of honeybees: worker, drone, and queen.

Her majesty, the queen

The queen bee, shown in the center of Figure 5-2, is the heart and soul of the colony. Only one queen lives in a given hive. She is the largest bee in the colony, and she is the only female with fully developed ovaries. The queen's two primary purposes are to produce chemical scents that help regulate the unity of the colony and to lay eggs — lots of them. She is, in fact, an egg-laying machine, capable of producing more than 1,500 eggs a day at 30-second intervals.

The queen is the reason for nearly everything the rest of the colony does. She's the only bee without which the rest of the colony cannot survive. A good quality queen means a strong and productive hive.

Figure 5-2:
A queen and her attendants.

Courtesy of John Clayton

The industrious little worker bee

The majority of the hive's population consists of worker bees. Although females, worker bees lack fully developed ovaries. Worker bees do a considerable amount of work. In fact, during the busy season, they literally work themselves to death. The specific jobs and duties they perform during their short lives vary as they age. Initially, a worker's responsibilities include various tasks within the hive. At this stage of development, worker bees are referred to as *house bees,* and they perform tasks associated with the health and upkeep of the hive itself. As they get older, their duties involve work outside of the hive as *field bees.* During this period, the worker leaves the hive to forage for pollen, nectar, and water.

The woeful drone

Drones, the only male bees in the colony, make up a relatively small percentage of the hive's total population. Drones have no other responsibility than to hang around because they may be needed to mate with a new virgin queen.

Book V

Raising Farm Animals

They don't forage for food from flowers — they have no pollen baskets. They don't help with the building of comb — they have no wax-producing glands. Nor can they help defend the hive — they have no stingers and can be handled by the beekeeper with absolute confidence.

When the weather gets cooler and the mating season comes to a close, the worker bees systematically expel the drones from the hive. This is your signal that the beekeeping season is over for the year.

The honeybee life cycle

Honeybees develop in four distinct phases: egg, larva, pupa, and adult. The total development time varies a bit among the three castes of bees — 16 days for queens, 21 days for worker bees, and 24 days for drones — but the basic, miraculous process is the same.

1. **Egg:** The queen lays a single egg in each cell that has been cleaned and prepared by the workers to raise new brood. Spotting these eggs is one of the most basic and important skills you need to develop as a beekeeper. It isn't an easy task, because the eggs are mighty tiny (only about 1.7 millemeters long), as you can see in Figure 5-3. But finding eggs is one of the surest ways to confirm that your queen is alive and well. It's a skill you'll use just about every time you visit your hive.

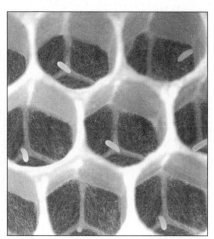

Figure 5-3: Note the rice-like shape of the eggs and how the queen has positioned them standing up in the cells.

Courtesy of Stephen McDaniel

2. **Larva:** Three days after the queen lays the egg, it hatches into a *larva* (the plural is *larvae*). Healthy larvae are snowy white and resemble small grubs curled up in the cells. Tiny at first, the larvae grow quickly, shedding their skin five times. Within just five days, they're 1,570 times

larger than their original size. At this time, the worker bees seal the larvae in the cell with a porous capping of tan beeswax. Once sealed in, the larvae spin a cocoon around their bodies.

3. **Pupa:** When it's enclosed in the spun cocoon, the larva is officially a *pupa* (the plural is *pupae*). The transformations that take place now are hidden from sight under the wax cappings. But if you could, you'd see that this little creature is beginning to take on the familiar features of an adult bee. After 12 days, the now-adult bee chews her way through the wax capping to join her sisters and brothers.

Basic Equipment for Beekeepers

To become a beekeeper, you need some supplies — namely, a hive and a few essential pieces of equipment. You can buy these pieces separately, but I recommend buying a basic start-up kit. Many suppliers offer them, and they're priced to save a few bucks. Make certain that your kit contains these basic items:

- Bottom board
- Lower and upper deep
- Honey super
- Inner and outer covers
- Frames and foundation for both deeps and the honey super
- Hardware to assemble stuff (various size nails, foundation pins, and so on)
- Veil and gloves
- Smoker
- Hive tool

The following sections explain these and other beekeeping paraphernalia you may find helpful.

The hive and its parts

Woodenware refers to the various components that collectively result in the beehive. Traditionally these components are made of wood — thus the term — but some manufacturers offer synthetic versions of these same components (plastic, polystyrene, and so on). My advice: Get the wood. The bees accept it far more readily than synthetic versions. And the smell and feel of wood are much more pleasurable to work with.

Many different kinds and sizes of beehives are available, but worldwide, the most common is the 10-frame *Langstroth hive.* Invented in 1851, its design hasn't changed much in the last 150 years, which is a testament to its practicality. I strongly recommend that you choose a Langstroth hive. The hive parts are completely interchangeable, and they're readily available from any beekeeping supply vendor.

This section discusses, bottom to top, the various components of a modern Langstroth beehive. As you read this section, refer to Figure 5-4 to see what the various parts look like and where they're located within the structure of the hive. The assembly instructions that come with the hive explain how to put the whole thing together.

- ✔ **Hive stand:** The entire hive sits on a hive stand, which elevates the hive off the ground, improving circulation and minimizing dampness. The best ones are made of cypress wood, which is highly resistant to rot.

- ✔ **Bottom board:** The *bottom board* is the thick bottom floor of the beehive. Like the hive stand, the best bottom boards are made of cypress wood.

- ✔ **Entrance reducer:** When you order a bottom board, it comes with a notched wooden cleat. The cleat serves as your *entrance reducer,* which limits bee access to the hive and controls ventilation and temperature during cooler months.

  Beekeepers use the entrance reducer only for newly established hives or during cold weather. This is the reason the entrance reducer isn't shown in Figure 5-4. For established hives in warm weather, the entrance reducer isn't used at all.

- ✔ **Deep-hive body:** The deep-hive body contains ten frames of honeycomb. The best quality ones are made of clear pine or cypress and have crisply cut dovetail joints for added strength. You'll need two deep-hive bodies to stack one on top of the other, like a two-story condo. The bees use the *lower deep* as the nursery, or *brood chamber,* to raise thousands of baby bees. The bees use the *upper deep* as the pantry or *food chamber,* where they store most of the honey and pollen for their use.

- ✔ **Queen excluder:** If you plan to collect honey, you should use a queen excluder, which you place between the deep food chamber and the shallow honey supers. The queen excluder consists of either a wooden frame holding a grid of metal wire or a perforated sheet of plastic. As the name implies, this gizmo prevents the queen from spoiling the clarity of the honey by entering the honey super and laying eggs. (When you're not collecting honey, it should not be used.)

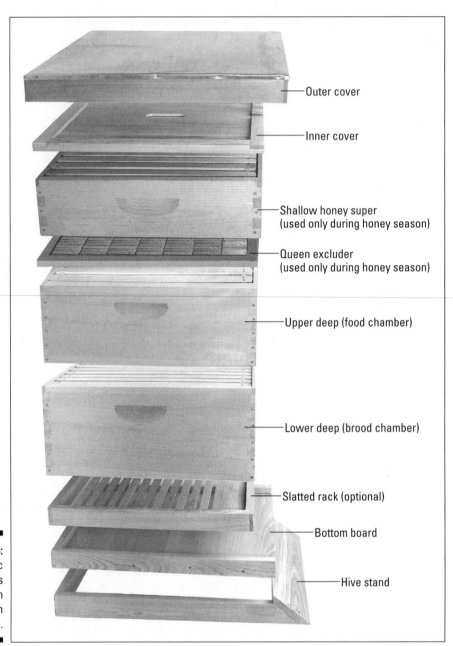

Outer cover

Inner cover

Shallow honey super
(used only during honey season)

Queen excluder
(used only during honey season)

Upper deep (food chamber)

Lower deep (brood chamber)

Slatted rack (optional)

Bottom board

Hive stand

Figure 5-4:
The basic
components
of a modern
Langstroth
hive.

✔ **Shallow honey super:** You use shallow honey supers to collect surplus honey — your honey. The honey that's in the deep-hive body you need to leave for the bees. Supers are identical in design to the deep-hive bodies — and assemble in a similar manner — but supers are shallower and therefore weigh less, making them easy to handle during the honey harvest.

✔ **Frames:** Ten deep frames are used in each deep-hive body, and nine shallow frames usually are used in each shallow honey super. Each wooden frame contains a single sheet of beeswax foundation (described in the next bullet). The frame firmly holds the wax and enables you to remove these panels of honeycomb for inspection or honey extraction.

✔ **Foundation:** Foundation comes in two forms: plastic and beeswax. Although plastic foundation has some advantages, bees are slow to accept plastic, and I don't recommend it for the new beekeeper. Instead, purchase foundation made from pure beeswax. Beeswax foundation is vertically wired for strength, and imprinted with a hexagonal cell pattern that guides the bees as they draw out uniform, even combs. Your bees find the sweet smell of beeswax foundation irresistible and quickly draw out each sheet into 7,000 beautiful, uniform cells (3,500 cells on each side) where they can store their food, raise brood, and collect honey for you! Like frames, foundation comes in deep and shallow sizes — deep for the deep-hive bodies and shallow for the shallow supers.

✔ **Inner cover:** The best quality inner covers are made entirely of cypress wood. Budget models made from pressboard or Masonite also are available, but they don't seem to last as long. The basic design consists of a wooden frame that houses flat planks of wood. In the center is a precut oval hole. When assembled, the inner cover resembles a shallow tray (with a hole in the center). A notch is cut out of one of the lengths of frame. This ventilation notch is positioned to the front of the hive. The inner cover is placed on the hive with the "tray" side facing up.

✔ **Outer cover:** Look for cypress wood when buying an outer cover. Cypress resists rot and lasts the longest. Outer covers assemble in a manner similar to the inner cover: a frame containing flat planks of wood. But the outer cover has a galvanized steel tray that fits on the top, protecting it from the elements.

You must have a means for feeding your bees once they're in the hive. I strongly recommend using a good quality hive-top feeder. Alternatively, you can use a feeding pail.

An assortment of beekeeping tools

As a beekeeper, you'll find that you use a variety of tools. Two tools — the smoker and the hive tool — are a must for the beekeeper. You'll use them every time you visit the hive. In addition to these two items, you'll also need protective clothing when visiting the hive: a long-sleeved, light-colored shirt (bees don't like dark colors) and long pants tucked into slip-on boots, a veil, and, when necessary, gloves. Other gadgets, gizmos, and doodads are also available to the beekeeper. This section describes my favorites.

Smoker

The smoker will become your best friend. Smoke calms the bees and enables you to safely inspect your hive. Quite simply, the smoker is a fire chamber with bellows designed to produce lots of cool smoke. Smokers come in all shapes, sizes, and price ranges. The style that you choose doesn't really matter. Learn how to light it so that it stays lit, and never overdo the smoking process. A little smoke goes a long way.

Hive tool

The versatility of the simple hive tool is impressive. Don't visit your hives without it! Use it to scrape wax and propolis off woodenware, loosen hive parts, open the hive, and manipulate frames. You can choose from various models (see Figure 5-5).

Figure 5-5:
Two
varieties of
hive tools.

Veils and gloves

Don't ever visit your hive without wearing a veil. Although your bees are likely to be gentle (especially during your first season), it defies common sense to put yourself at risk. Veils come in many different models and price ranges. Some are simple veils that slip over your head; others are integral to a pullover blouse or even a full jumpsuit. Pick the style that appeals most to you. If your colony tends to be more aggressive, more protection is advised. But remember, the more you wear, the hotter you'll be during summer inspections.

While a veil is necessary, gloves are less critical. New beekeepers like the idea of using gloves, but I urge you not to use them for installing your bees or for routine inspections. You don't really need them at those times — especially with a new colony or early in the season — and they just make you clumsier. The only times that you need gloves are

- ✔ Late in the season (when your colony is at its strongest).
- ✔ During honey harvest season (when your bees are protective of their honey).
- ✔ When moving hive bodies (when you have a great deal of heavy work to do in a short period of time).

Elevated hive stand

Elevated stands eliminate the need for bending (good for you) and deter skunks from snacking on your bees (good for the bees). The simplest elevated stands are made from four 14-inch lengths of two-by-four (use these for the legs) and a single plank of plywood that is large enough to hold the hive (see Figure 5-6). Put the entire hive on top of the elevated stand, raising it a little more than 14 inches off the ground. Alternatively, fashion an elevated stand from a few cinderblocks or use posts of various sorts.

Figure 5-6: You can build a simple table stand to elevate your hive.

Bee brush

The long, super-soft bristles of a bee brush enable you to remove bees from frames and clothing without hurting them. Some beekeepers use a goose feather for this purpose. Keep that in mind in the event you have an extra goose around the house.

Getting Your Initial Bee Colony

You'll need some bees if you're going to be a beekeeper. But what kind do you get when you can choose from many different races and hybrids of honeybees, each with its own advantages and disadvantages? As a beginning beekeeper, your best bet is to start with the Italian honeybee. It's the number-one choice in the world for good reasons: The Italian honeybee is gentle, productive, and does well in many different climates. Look no further in your first year.

When it comes to obtaining your bees, you have a couple of options: You can order a package of bees, which will come to you via the mail; or you can get a colony already started by a local beekeeper. The following sections describe these options in more detail.

Ordering package bees

One of your best options and by far the most popular way to start a new hive is to order package bees. You can order bees by the pound from a reputable supplier. Bee breeders are found mostly in the southern states and will ship just about anywhere in the continental United States.

A package of bees and a single queen are shipped in a small wooden box with two screened sides (see Figure 5-7). The bee package is about the size of a large shoebox and includes a small screened cage for the queen (about the size of a matchbook) and a tin can of sugar syrup that feeds the bees during their journey. A 3-pound package of bees contains about 11,000 bees, the ideal size for you to order. Order one package of bees for each hive you plan to start.

Be sure to order a marked queen with the package. *Marked* means that a small colored dot has been painted on her thorax. This dot helps you spot the queen in your hive during inspections. It also confirms that the queen you see is the one that you installed (versus discovering an unmarked one, which means your queen is gone and another has taken her place).

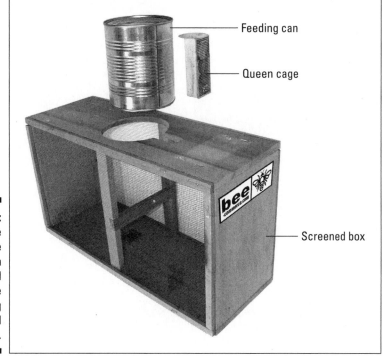

Feeding can

Queen cage

Screened box

Figure 5-7:
Package
bees are
shipped in
screened
boxes. Note
the feeding
can and
queen cage.

 When ordering package bees, time your order so that you receive your bees as early in the spring as the weather allows. This gives your colony time to build its numbers for the summer "honey flow" and means your bees are available for early pollination.

Buying a "nuc" colony

Another good option for the new beekeeper is to find a local beekeeper who can sell you a *nucleus* (or *nuc*) colony of bees. A nuc consists of four to five frames of brood and bees, plus an actively laying queen. All you do is transfer the frames (bees and all) from the nuc box into your own hive. To find a supplier in your neck of the woods, check your yellow pages under "beekeeping," call your state's bee inspector, or ask members of a local beekeeping club or association.

 Look for a reputable dealer with a good track record for providing healthy, disease-free bees. Ask whether the state bee inspector inspects the establishment annually. Request a copy of a certificate of health from the state. If you can find a reputable beekeeper with nucs, this is a convenient way to start a hive and quickly build up a strong colony.

Capturing a wild swarm of bees

Here's an option where the price is right: Swarms are free. But I don't recommend capturing a swarm of wild bees for the first-year beekeeper. Capturing a wild swarm is a bit tricky for someone who has never handled bees. And you can't be sure of the health, genetics, and temperament of a wild swarm. In some areas (mostly the southern United States)

you face the possibility that the swarm you attempt to capture may be *Africanized* bees, a very aggressive and easily agitated bee hybrid that resulted from attempts in the mid-twentieth century to improve honey production by crossing African bees with honeybees. My advice? Save this adventure for year two.

Welcoming Your Bees to Their New Home

Before your bees arrive, you need to order and assemble the components that will become their new home. Get together all your hive parts (woodenware) and the instruction sheets that come with them, and then assemble the equipment from the ground up. When you have the hive built, you can turn your attention to the arrival of your girls.

You may not know the exact day that your bees will arrive, but many suppliers at least let you know the approximate day they plan to *ship* your package bees. About a week before the anticipated date of arrival, alert your local post office that you're expecting bees. Make sure that you provide the post office with your telephone number so you can be reached the moment your bees come in. In most communities, the post office asks that you pick up your bees at the post office. Seldom are bees delivered live right to your door. Instruct the post office that the package needs to be kept in a cool, dark place until you arrive.

Bringing home your bees

When the bees finally arrive, head to the post office to pick them up and then follow these steps:

1. **Inspect the package closely.**

   Finding some dead bees on the bottom of the package is normal. If you find an inch or more of dead bees on the bottom of the package, however, fill out a form at the post office and call your vendor, who should replace your bees.

2. **Take your bees home right away (but don't put them in the hot, stuffy trunk of your car).**

3. When you get home, spray the package liberally with cool water using a clean mister or spray bottle.

4. Place the package of bees in a cool place, such as your basement or garage, for an hour.

5. After the hour has passed, spray the package of bees with basic sugar syrup (see the section "Recipes for Sugar Syrups").

   Don't *brush* syrup on the screen; doing so literally brushes off many little bee feet in the process.

Putting your bees into the hive

Putting your bees into their new home is the fun stuff. Take your time and enjoy the experience. You'll find that the bees are docile and cooperative. Read the instructions in this section several times until you become familiar and comfortable with the steps.

If at all possible, hive your bees either in the late afternoon on the day that you pick them up or the next afternoon. Pick a clear, mild day with little or no wind. If it's raining or cold, wait a day. If you absolutely must, you can wait several days to put them in the hive, but make certain that you spray them two or three times a day with sugar syrup.

To hive your bees, follow these steps:

1. Thirty minutes before hiving, spray your bees rather heavily with basic medicated sugar syrup (see the later section for the recipe).

   Don't go so far as to drown them with syrup. Use common sense, and they'll be fine.

2. Using your hive tool, pry the wood cover off the package.

   Pull the nails or staples out of the cover, and keep the wood cover handy.

3. Jar the package down sharply on its bottom so that your bees fall to the bottom of the package.

   This jarring doesn't hurt them!

4. Remove the can of syrup and the queen cage from the package, and loosely replace the wood cover (without the staples); examine the queen in the queen cage.

   She's in there with a few attendants. Is she okay? In rare cases, she may have died in transit. If that's the case, go ahead with the installation as if everything were okay, but call your supplier to order a replacement queen (there should be no charge). Your colony will be fine while you wait for your replacement queen.

5. **Slide the metal disc on the queen cage to the side slowly.**

   Remove the cork at one end of the cage so that you can see the white candy in the hole. If the candy is present, remove the disc completely. If the candy is missing, you can plug the hole with a small piece of marshmallow. If your package comes with a strip of Apistan (designed to control mites during shipment), remove it from the back of the queen cage.

6. **Out of two small frame nails bent at right angles, fashion a hanging bracket for the queen cage (see Figure 5-8).**

7. **Spray your bees again, and jar the package down so the bees drop to the bottom.**

8. **Prepare the hive by removing five of the frames, but keep them nearby.**

   At this point you're using only the lower deep-hive body for your bees.

9. **Hang the queen cage (candy side up) between the center-most frame and the next frame facing toward the center (see Figure 5-9).**

   The screen side of the cage needs to face toward the center of the hive.

10. **Spray your bees liberally with syrup one last time; then jar the package down.**

11. **Toss away the wood cover and then pour (and shake) approximately half of the bees directly above the hanging queen cage. Pour (and shake) the remaining bees into the open area created by the missing five frames.**

12. **When the bees disperse a bit, gently replace four of the five frames.**

   Do this gingerly so you don't crush any bees. If the pile of bees is too deep, use your hand (with gloves on) to disperse the bees.

13. **If you're using a jar or pail for feeding (and not a hive-top feeder), place the inner cover on the hive; then, invert a one-gallon feeding pail above the oval hole in the inner cover, add a second deep super on top of the inner cover, and fill the cavity around the jar with crumpled newspaper for insulation.**

   The inner cover is used only when a jar or pail is used for feeding. If you're using a hive-top feeder, you place it in direct contact with the bees without the inner cover in between, so skip this step and go to Step 14.

14. **If you're using a hive-top feeder, place it on top of the hive; otherwise, go to Step 15.**

15. **Plug the inner cover's half-moon ventilation hole with a clump of grass.**

   You want to close off this entrance until the bees become established in their new home.

16. **Now place the outer cover on top of the hive. You're almost done.**

17. **Insert your entrance reducer, leaving a one-finger opening for the bees to defend.**

Leave the opening in this manner until the bees build up their numbers and can defend a larger hive entrance against intruders, which takes about four weeks. If you don't have an entrance reducer, use grass to close up all but an inch or two of the entrance.

Figure 5-8:
A hanging bracket for the queen cage.

Figure 5-9:
Hang the
queen
cage from
the center
frames.

Place the entrance reducer so that the openings face up. Doing so allows the bees to climb up over any dead bees that may otherwise clog the small entrance.

Your new colony's first eight weeks

For the newly hived colony, some specific beekeeping tasks are unique to the first few weeks. The following sections outline what specific things to look for during the initial eight weeks. As you perform these inspections, remember to

- ✔ **Choose the right time for the inspection.** Choose a mild, sunny day (55 degrees Fahrenheit or more) with little or no wind. Always visit your hive sometime between 10 a.m. and 5 p.m.

- ✔ **Use the proper inspection procedure.** Smoke, open the hive, and remove frames one by one for inspection, working your way toward the center of the hive.

  For more information on this procedure, see the section "Smoker," earlier in this chapter, and the upcoming section "Inspecting Your Hive."

- ✔ **Check to make sure your hive-top feeder has enough sugar syrup, and replenish it as needed.** You can find the recipe for sugar syrup in the later section, "Recipes for Sugar Syrups." Just pour it into the feeder.

After putting your package of bees in the hive, you'll be impatient to look inside to see what's happening. Resist the temptation! You must wait one full week before opening the hive. The colony needs this first uninterrupted week to accept its new queen. Any premature disturbance to the hive can result in the colony rejecting her. The colony may even kill her, thinking the disturbance is somehow her fault.

Looking in: A week after hiving your bees

After the first week, you can conduct your first inspection. What are you looking for? The queen. You want to know that she's been released and is laying eggs.

- ✔ **To inspect the frames:** Smoke and open your hive, and remove the first frame. Place it vertically on the ground, leaning it against the hive. Other than a few occasional bees, not much will be happening on this frame because, in all likelihood, the bees haven't moved much beyond the center of the hive and therefore haven't had time to draw the outer part of the foundation into honeycomb yet. As you continue your inspection of each subsequent frame, though, you should begin to see more and more going on. Toward the center of the hive you should see that the girls have been busily drawing out the wax foundation into honeycomb.

- ✔ **To verify that the queen was released:** When you reach the two frames sandwiching the queen cage, look down in the hole where the candy plug was. If the candy is gone, that's wonderful! It means worker bees have opened the cage and released the queen. Remove the cage and peek inside to confirm that the queen has been released. Place the cage near the entrance so that any worker bees you find exploring in the cage can find their way back into the hive.

✔ **To remove any burr comb:** You're likely to find that industrious bees have built lots of *burr comb* (sometimes called *natural comb, wild comb,* or *brace comb*) in the gap created by the queen cage. To remove this bright white comb of perfectly symmetrical cells, use your hive tool: Sever the burr comb where it's connected to the frames and then slowly lift it straight up and out of the hive. You'll probably find it covered with bees. If the queen is on the comb, gently remove her from the comb and place her back into the hive. To remove the other bees, shake them loose with sharp downward motions that you halt abruptly just above the frames.

✔ **To look for eggs:** Take a close look at the frames that were near the queen cage for evidence that the queen has laid eggs. If you see some, you know the queen is already at work.

If you don't find the queen or any eggs, you may have a problem. Wait another few days and check again. If you still find no evidence of the queen, you need to order a new queen from your bee supplier.

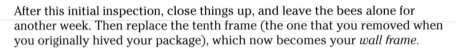

After this initial inspection, close things up, and leave the bees alone for another week. Then replace the tenth frame (the one that you removed when you originally hived your package), which now becomes your *wall frame.*

The second week

During this inspection, you want to determine how well the queen is performing. As always, look for eggs, your ongoing assurance that the queen is in residence. Note that the bees have drawn more of the foundation into honeycomb. They work from the center outward, so the outer five to six frames probably haven't been drawn out yet. That's normal.

By the second week, you can easily see larvae in various stages of development (see Figure 5-10). They should be bright white and glistening like snowy white shrimp!

To evaluate your queen, estimate how many eggs her majesty is laying. If you have one or two frames with both sides ³/₄-filled with eggs and larvae, your queen is doing a fantastic job. Congratulations! If you have one or two frames with only one side filled, she's doing moderately well. If you find fewer than that, she's doing poorly, and you need to consider replacing her as soon as possible.

The third week

Again, you're evaluating the queen's performance, so look for eggs. By now, you'll also begin seeing capped brood — the final stage of the bees' metamorphosis. *Capped brood* are tan in color, with brood cappings on older comb being darker. The capped brood are located on frames that are closest to the center of the hive. Cells with eggs and larvae are on the adjacent frames. Above each, you'll notice a crescent of pollen and, above the crescent of pollen, a crescent of nectar or capped honey. This is a picture-perfect situation.

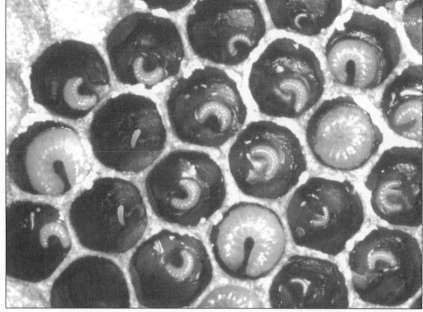

Figure 5-10:
Larvae go
through
various
stages of
develop-
ment. Note
the eggs in
this photo
as well.

Courtesy of Dr. Edward Ross, California Academy of Sciences

A spotty and loose brood pattern may be evidence of a problem. You may have a poor queen, in which case she should be replaced as soon as possible. Sunken or perforated brood cappings may be evidence of disease, in which case you must diagnose the cause and take steps to medicate.

The third week also is when you need to start looking for *queen cells.* Queen cells can appear in two places: on the upper two-thirds of the frame or on the lower third of the frame (see Figure 5-11). When they're on the upper two-thirds of the frame, they're *supersedure* cells. Bees create supersedure cells if they believe their queen isn't performing up-to-par and needs to be replaced. The bees create *swarm cells* on the lower third of the frame to raise a new queen in preparation for the act of *swarming,* which usually happens when the hive becomes too crowded and the colony decides to split in half — with half the population leaving the hive (swarming) with the old queen and the remaining half staying behind with the makings for a new queen (one of those developing in a swarm cell). ***Note:*** Swarming seldom is a problem with a new hive this early in the season.

If you spot more than three to four supersedure cells, you need to order a new queen because giving the bees a new queen is far better than letting them create their own. Furthermore, you'll lose less time and guarantee a desirable lineage.

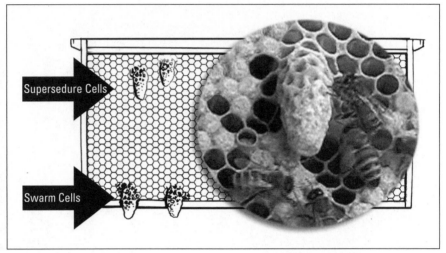

Figure 5-11: Super-sedure cells are located in the upper two-thirds of the frame; swarm cells are located along the bottom third.

The fourth week

Perform your inspection as always, looking for evidence of the queen (eggs) and a good pattern of capped brood, pollen, and capped honey.

If all's well, by the end of the fourth week the bees have drawn nearly all the foundation into comb. They've added wax to the foundation, creating the comb cells in which they store pollen, honey, and brood. When seven of the ten frames are drawn into comb, you want to add your second deep-hive body. To do so, smoke your hive as usual and then follow these steps:

1. **Remove the outer cover and the hive-top feeder (or the inner cover, if one is being used).**

2. **Place the second deep directly on top of the original hive body and fill the new second story with ten frames and foundation.**

3. **Put the hive-top feeder directly on top of the new upper deep and below the outer cover, replenishing sugar syrup if needed.**

4. **Replace the outer cover.**

The upper deep will be used during the early summer for raising brood. But later on it serves as the food chamber for storing honey and pollen for the upcoming winter season.

Timing is important. If you wait too long, the colony may grow too fast (with up to 2,000 new bees emerging every day!), become overcrowded, and eventually swarm. If you add the second deep-hive body too early, the colony below loses heat, and the brood may become chilled and die.

The fifth through eighth weeks

By the fifth week the frames should be jam-packed with eggs, larvae, capped brood, pollen, and honey. Watch for movement under the capping. New bees will chew their way out of the cell and crawl out.

Following are the other tasks you'll perform during these weeks:

- ✔ **Improve ventilation:** At week five or six, when the weather is milder and the colony is robust enough to protect itself, you need to improve hive ventilation by opening the hive entrance. Turn the entrance reducer so that the larger of its two openings (the one that's about 4 inches wide) is in position. You can remove the entrance reducer completely in the eighth week following the installation of your bees.

- ✔ **Watch for swarm cells:** During weeks six through eight, be on the lookout for swarm cells in the lower third of the frames. When you find eight or more of these swarm cells, you can be fairly certain the colony intends to swarm. (***Note:*** Continue to look for supersedure cells as well.) Refer to the section, "The third week," for an explanation of supersedure and swarm cells.

- ✔ **Manipulate the frames of foundation:** By week seven or eight, manipulate the order of frames to encourage the bees to draw out more foundation into comb cells. To do this, place any frames of foundation that haven't been drawn between frames of newly drawn comb. Don't place these frames smack in the middle of the brood nest, though, because doing so splits (or breaks) the nest apart, making it difficult for bees to regulate the environment of the temperature-sensitive brood.

Inspecting Your Hive

Virtually all inspections are to determine the health and productivity of the colony. The specifics of what you're looking for vary somewhat, depending upon the time of year. But some universal rules-of-the-road apply to every hive visit.

- ✔ **Check for your queen.** Look for indications that the queen is alive and well and laying eggs. If you actually see her, that's great and reassuring! But finding the queen becomes increasingly difficult as the colony becomes larger and more crowded. When that happens, look for *eggs*. Although they're tiny, finding the eggs is much easier than locating a single queen in a hive of 60,000 bees. Refer to Figures 5-3 and 5-10 to see what eggs look like.

✔ **Look for food and brood.** Each deep frame of comb contains about 7,000 cells (3,500 on each side). Honeybees use these cells for storing food and raising brood. When you inspect your colony, note what's going on in those cells to help you judge the performance and health of your bees. Do you see ample pollen and nectar? Are there lots of eggs and brood? Does the condition of the wax cappings over the brood look normal — or are the cappings perforated and sunken in?

✔ **Inspect the brood pattern and brood cappings.** A tight, compact brood pattern is indicative of a good, healthy queen; a spotty brood pattern (many empty cells with only occasional cells of eggs, larvae, or capped brood) is an indication that you have an old or sick queen and may need to replace her. How does the capped brood look? These are cells that the bees have capped with a tan wax. The tan cappings are porous and enable the developing larvae within to breathe. The cappings should be smooth and slightly convex. Sunken-in (concave) or perforated cappings indicate a problem.

So how do you look for all these things? By opening up the hive and taking a look. The approach for inspecting your hive doesn't vary much from one visit to another. You always follow certain procedures, as the following sections explain. After a few visits to the hive, the mechanics of all this become second nature, and you can concentrate on enjoying the miraculous discoveries that await you.

Removing the first frame

Always begin your inspection of the hive by removing the *first frame* or *wall frame*. That's the frame closest to the outer wall. Which wall? It doesn't matter. Pick a side of the hive to work from, and that determines your first frame.

Removal of the wall frame is a basic and important first step every time you inspect a colony. The removal of this frame gives you a wide-open empty space in the hive for better manipulating the remaining frames without squashing any bees. Always be sure to remove the wall frame from the hive before attempting to remove any other frames. Here's how to proceed:

1. **Insert the curved end of your hive tool between the first and second frames, near one end of the frame's top bar (see Figure 5-12).**

2. **Twist the tool to separate the frames from each other.**

   Your hand moves toward the center of the hive — not the end.

3. **Repeat this motion at the opposite end of the top bar.**

   The first frame should now be separated from the second frame.

Book V

Raising
Farm
Animals

4. Using both hands, pick up the first frame by the end bars (see Figure 5-13).

Gently push any bees out of the way as you get ahold of the end bars. With the frame in both hands, *slowly* lift it straight up and out of the hive. Be careful not to roll or crush bees as you lift the frame. Easy does it!

Figure 5-12: Use your hive tool to pry the wall frame loose before removing it.

Figure 5-13: Carefully lift out the first frame and set it aside. Now you have room to manipulate the other frames.

Never put your fingers on a frame without first noting where the bees are, because you don't want to crush any bees, nor do you want to get stung. Bees can be easily and safely coaxed away by gently pushing them aside with your fingers.

Now that you've removed the first frame, gently rest it on the ground, leaning it vertically against the hive. It's okay if bees are on it. They'll be fine. Alternatively, use a frame rest if you have one.

Working your way through the hive

Using your hive tool, loosen frame two and move it into the open slot where frame one used to be. That gives you enough room to remove *this* frame without injuring any bees. When you're done looking at this frame, return it to the hive, close to (but not touching) the wall. Do *not* put this frame on the ground.

Work your way through all ten frames in this manner — moving the next frame to be inspected into the open slot. When you're done looking at a frame, always return it snugly against the frame previously inspected. Use your eyes to monitor progress as the frames are slowly nudged together.

Be careful not to crush any bees when pushing the frames together. One of those bees may be the queen! Look down between the frames to make sure the coast is clear before slowly pushing the frames together. If bees are on the end bars and at risk of being crushed, you can use the flat end of your hive tool to gently coax them to move along. A single puff of smoke also urges them to move out of the way.

Holding up frames for inspection

To properly hold and inspect each frame, stand with your back to the sun and the light shining over your shoulder and onto the frame so that the sun can illuminate details deep in the cells and help you to better see eggs and small larvae. Here's an easy way to inspect both sides of the frame (Figure 5-14 illustrates the following steps):

1. **Hold the frame firmly by the tabs at either end of the top bar.**

   Get a good grip. The last thing you want to do is drop a frame covered with bees. Their retaliation for your clumsiness will be swift and, no doubt, memorable.

2. **Turn the frame vertically; then turn it like a page of a book, then return it to the horizontal position.**

   Now you're viewing the opposite side of the frame.

When inspecting frames, all your movements must be slow and deliberate. Change hand positions sparingly. Sliding your fingers across the frames as you reposition your hands is better than lifting your fingers and setting them down again, because you may land on a bee. As you turn the frame, you want to avoid any sudden and unnecessary centrifugal force that may disturb the bees.

A few minutes into your inspection, you may notice that all the bees have lined up between the top bars like racehorses at the starting gate. Their little heads are all in a row between the frames. Kind of cute, aren't they? They're watching you. That's your signal to give the girls a few more puffs of smoke to disperse them again so that you can continue with your inspection.

Replacing frames

After you've inspected your last frame, nine frames should be in the hive and one (the first frame you removed) leaning against it or hanging on the frame rest. To put the first frame back in the hive:

1. **Slowly push the nine frames that are in the hive as a single unit toward the opposite wall of the hive.**

   That puts them back where they were when you started your inspection. Pushing them as a single unit keeps them snugly together and avoids crushing bees. You're now left with the open slot from which the first frame was removed.

2. **Smoke the bees one last time to drive them down into the hive.**

3. **Pick up the frame that's outside the hive, remove the bees on it if necessary, and ease it back into the empty slot.**

   If bees are still on it, with a downward thrust, sharply knock one corner of the frame on the bottom board at the hive's entrance. The bees fall off the frame and begin walking through the entrance to the hive. With no bees remaining on your first frame, you can easily return it to the hive without the risk of crushing them.

4. **Make certain that all ten frames fit snugly together.**

   Using your hive tool as a wedge, adjust the ten-frame unit so that the space between the frames and the two outer walls is equal.

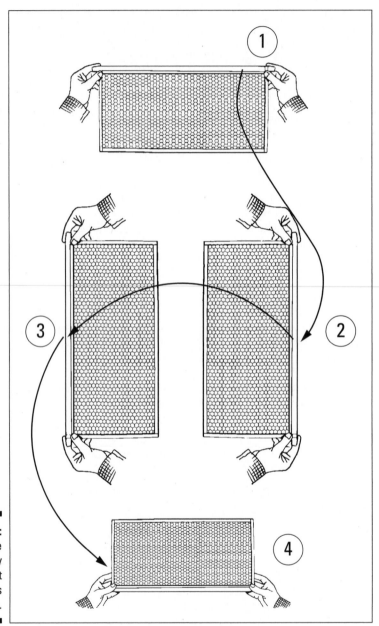

Figure 5-14:
The correct way to inspect both sides of a frame.

Closing the hive

You're almost finished. Now it's time to close the hive.

- ✔ **If you're using a hive-top feeder,** put the feeder back in place immediately on top of the hive body and, if the pantry is getting low, add more sugar syrup. Then replace the outer cover, first making sure it's free of any bees. From the rear of the hive, slide it along the inner cover, again, gently pushing any bees out of the way (the bulldozer technique). Ease it into place, and adjust it so that it sits firmly and level on the inner cover.

- ✔ **If you're not using a hive-top feeder,** remove any bees from the inner cover using a downward thrust and sharply knocking one corner of the inner cover on the bottom board at the hive's entrance. Then slide the inner cover in position from the rear of the hive so that you don't crush any bees. (Note that the notched ventilation hole is positioned upward and toward the front of the hive. This notched opening allows air to circulate and gives bees a top-floor entrance to the hive.) Now replace the outer cover.

Make sure that the ventilation notch on the outer cover isn't blocked. From the rear of the hive, shove the outer cover toward the front of the hive. Doing so opens the notched ventilation hole in the inner cover and gives the bees airflow and an alternate entrance.

Chores throughout the Year

This section contains a suggested schedule of seasonal hive activities and important tasks for the beekeeper. Note, however, that geography, weather, climate, neighborhood, and even the type of bees influence the timing of these activities.

Those lazy, hazy, crazy days of summer

Nectar flow usually reaches its peak during summer. That's also when the population of the colony usually reaches its peak. When that's the case, your colony is quite self-sufficient, boiling with worker bees tirelessly collecting pollen, gathering nectar, and making honey. Note, however, that the queen's rate of egg-laying drops a bit during the late summer.

Late in summer the colony's growth begins to diminish. Drones are still around, but outside activity begins slowing down when the nectar flow slows. Bees seem to be restless and become protective of their honey.

Here are some activities you can expect to schedule between trips to the beach and backyard barbecues:

- ✔ Inspect the hive every other week, making sure it's healthy and that the queen is present.

- ✔ Add honey supers as needed.

- ✔ Keep up swarm control through mid-summer; late in the summer there's little chance of swarming.

- ✔ Harvest your honey crop at the end of the nectar flow. Remember that the colony requires at least 60 pounds of honey for use during winter.

Falling leaves point to autumn chores

Most nectar and pollen sources become scarce as days become shorter and weather cools in autumn. All in all, as the season slows down, so do the activities within your hive: The queen's egg-laying is dramatically reduced, drones begin to disappear from the hive, and hive population drops significantly. Your bees begin bringing in propolis (resin), using it to chink up cracks in the hive that may leak the winter's cold wind. The colony is hunkering down for the winter, so you must help your bees get ready. When helping your bees prepare for the upcoming hardships of winter months, you must

- ✔ **Inspect your bees (look inside the hive) and make certain that the queen is present.** If you don't see the queen herself, be sure to look for eggs, *not* larvae. Larvae can be three to eight days old, so just finding larvae is no guarantee that you have a queen.

- ✔ **Determine whether the bees have enough honey.** Your bees need plenty of food (capped honey) for the winter. Make certain that the upper deep-hive body is full of honey. Honey is essential for your bees' survival, because it's the fuel that stokes their stoves. Without it, they're certain to perish.

  In cooler, northern climates, hives need about 60 to 70 pounds of honey heading into winter. If your winters are short (or nonexistent), a honey reserve of 30 to 40 pounds is sufficient.

- ✔ **Feed and medicate your colony.** They'll accept a two-to-one sugar-syrup feeding until colder weather contracts them into a tight cluster (this is the winter syrup recipe in the later section, "Recipes for Sugar Syrups"). At that point, temperatures are too cold for them to leave the cluster, so feeding them is useless.

✓ **Provide adequate ventilation.** During winter, the temperature at the center of the cluster is maintained at 90 to 93 degrees. Without adequate ventilation, the warm air from the cluster rises, hits the cold inner cover, and causes condensation to drip down onto the bees as ice-cold water. That's a big problem! The bees will become chilled and die. To keep your colony dry, permanently glue four pieces of wood the size of postage stamps to the four corners of the inner cover's flat underside. (You can use the thin end of a wood shingle or pieces of a popsicle stick.) This neat ventilation trick makes an air space of ¹⁄₁₆ inch or less between the top edge of the upper deep-hive body and the inner cover.

✓ **Wrap the hive in black tar paper (the kind used by roofers, see Figure 5-15) if you're in a climate where the temperature gets below freezing for more than several weeks.** Make sure that you don't cover the entrance or any upper ventilation holes. The black tar paper absorbs heat from the winter sun and helps the colony better regulate temperatures during cold spells. It also acts as a windbreak.

Figure 5-15: Wrap your hive in tar paper and place a rock on top to help keep your colony warm in winter temperatures.

Put a double thickness of tar paper over the top of the hive, and place a rock on top to prevent cold winds from lifting the tar paper off. Cut a hole in the wrapping to accommodate the ventilation hole in the upper deep-hive body.

✓ **Provide a windbreak if your winter weather is harsh.** If you didn't place your hives where they're protected by a natural windbreak of shrubbery, you can erect a temporary windbreak of fence posts and burlap. Position it to block prevailing winter winds.

Clustering in a winter wonderland

Winter is the slowest season of your beekeeping cycle. Your bees are in their winter cluster, toasty and warm inside the hive. Now is the time to do the following:

- ✔ Clean, repair, and store your equipment for the winter.

- ✔ Monitor the hive entrance. Brush off any dead bees or snow that block the entrance.

- ✔ Make sure the bees have enough food! The late winter and early spring is when colonies can die of starvation. Late in the winter, on a nice, mild day when there's no wind or bees flying, take a quick peek inside your hive. It's best not to remove any frames. Just have a look-see under the cover. Do you see bees? They still should be in a cluster in the upper deep. Are they okay?

  If you don't notice any sealed honey in the top frames, you may need to begin some emergency feeding. But remember that once you start feeding, you *cannot* stop until the bees are bringing in their own pollen and nectar.

Spring is in the air: Starting your second season

Spring is one of the busiest times of year for bees (and beekeepers). It's the season when new colonies are started and established colonies come back to life.

As the days get longer and milder, the established hive comes alive, exploding in population. The queen steadily lays more and more eggs, ultimately reaching her greatest rate of egg-laying. The drones begin reappearing, and hive activity starts hopping. The nectar and pollen begin coming into the hive thick and fast. The hive boils with activity, and you face many chores in the springtime.

The first thing you need to do is conduct an early inspection. The exact timing of this inspection depends upon your location (earlier in warmer zones, later in colder zones). Do your first spring inspection on a sunny, mild day with *no wind* and a temperature close to 50 degrees. (A rule of thumb: If the weather is cold enough that you need a heavy overcoat, it's too cold to inspect the bees.) During this inspection, do the following:

✔ **Determine whether your bees made it through the winter.** The clustered bees should be fairly high in the upper deep-hive body. If you don't see them, can you hear them? Tapping the side of the hive and putting your ear against it, listen for a hum or buzzing. If it appears that you've lost your bees, take the hive apart and clean out any dead bees. Reassemble it and order a package of bees as soon as possible. Don't give up. All beekeepers lose their bees at one time or another.

✔ **Make sure that you have a queen.** Look down between some of the frames. Do you see any brood? If so, that's a good sign that the queen is present. To get a better look, you may need to carefully remove a frame from the center of the top deep. If you don't see any brood or eggs, your hive may be without a queen, and you should order a new queen as soon as possible, assuming, that is, the hive population is sufficient to incubate brood when the new queen arrives. What's sufficient? The cluster of bees needs to be *at least* the size of a large grapefruit (hopefully larger). If you have fewer bees than that, you should plan to order a new package of bees (with a queen).

✔ **Ensure the bees still have food.** Looking down between the frames, see if you spot any honey. Honey is capped with white cappings (tan cappings are the brood). If you see honey, that's great. If not, you must begin emergency feeding your bees.

This inspection must be done quickly, because you don't want to leave the frame open to chilly air.

The following sections explain your other springtime tasks.

Feeding the colony

A few weeks before the first blossoms appear, begin feeding your bees (regardless of whether they still have honey). Feed the colony sugar syrup to stimulate the queen and encourage her to start laying eggs at a brisk rate. The first gallon needs to be medicated with Fumidil-B, but subsequent gallons aren't medicated. Continue feeding until you notice that the bees are bringing in their own food. You'll know when you see pollen on their legs.

Feed the colony pollen substitute, which helps strengthen your hive and stimulates egg-laying in the queen. Pollen substitute is available in a powdered mix from your bee supplier. This feeding can cease when you see bees bringing in their own pollen.

Administering spring medication

A few weeks before the first blossoms appear, you need to begin medicating your bees. The list that follows contains a springtime medication regime that helps prevent diseases, control mites, and improve your bees' overall health:

✔ **To prevent foulbrood:** For each colony, mix 1 teaspoon of the antibiotic Terramycin with 2 tablespoons of powdered sugar (do not use granulated sugar). Sprinkle the sugar mixture on the *ends* of the frames' top bars. Don't allow the mixture to come in direct contact with open brood cells, because it's toxic to larvae. Repeat this "dusting" two more times at three- to five-day intervals.

✔ **For general health:** Add a teaspoon of Honey B Healthy to your sugar syrup solution during your spring feedings. It acts as a feeding stimulant and helps keep bees healthy even in the presence of mites.

✔ **For varroa mite control:** Place Apistan strips within the hive, using one strip for every five frames of bees. If two deep-hive bodies are used for the brood nest, hang Apistan strips in alternate corners of the cluster, utilizing the top and bottom hive bodies. Make certain each strip is placed between the frames, not on top of them. For best chemical distribution, use Apistan when daytime high temperatures are at least 50 degrees. Keep strips in the hive for at least 42 days (six weeks), but don't leave strips in the hive for more than 56 days (eight weeks). Honey supers may be put on the hive after the strips are removed.

Never, ever leave Apistan in the hive over the winter. Doing so constantly exposes the mites to the active ingredient, which becomes weaker and weaker over time. These sub-lethal doses increase the chance of mites building up a resistance to Apistan. This tolerance is then passed on to future generations of mites, and subsequent treatments become useless.

✔ **For tracheal mite control:** When the weather starts getting warmer, place a prepared bag containing 1.8 ounces of menthol crystals on the top bars toward the rear of the hive. Set the bag on a small piece of aluminum foil to prevent the bees from chewing holes in it and carrying it away. Leave the bag in the hive for 14 consecutive days when the outdoor temperature ranges between 60 and 80 degrees.

Creating room for your bees

Watch out for indications of swarming. Inspect the hive periodically and look for swarm cells. Later in the spring, before the colony becomes too crowded, add a queen excluder and honey supers.

Five to six weeks before adding honey supers to the colony, stop all medication treatments to prevent contamination of the honey that you want to harvest.

Reversing hive bodies

Bees normally move upward in the hive during the winter. In early spring, the upper deep is full of bees, new brood, and food. But the lower deep-hive body is mostly empty. You can help matters by reversing the top and bottom deep-hive bodies (see Figure 5-16). Doing so also gives you an opportunity to clean the bottom board. Follow these steps:

1. **On a mild day (50 degrees or so) with little or no wind and bright, clear sunlight, open your hive using your smoker in the usual way.**

2. **Place the upturned outer cover on the ground and then remove the upper deep-hive body.**

3. **Keep the inner cover on the deep and close the oval hole in the middle of the inner cover with a piece of wood shingle or tape.**

4. **Place the deep across the edges of the outer cover, so there are only four points of contact (you squeeze fewer bees this way).**

5. **Now you can see down into the lower deep that still rests on the bottom board.**

   It's probably empty, but even if you find some inhabitants, lift the lower deep off the bottom board and place it crossways on the inner cover that's covering the deep you previously removed.

6. **Scrape and clean the bottom board.**

Figure 5-16:
Reversing
hive bodies
in the spring
is beneficial
to the
colony.

7. **Stand the deep body — formerly the relatively empty bottom one — on one end, placing it on the ground; then place the *full* hive body onto the clean bottom board.**

8. **Smoke the bees and remove the inner cover, place the empty deep on top, and then replace the inner and outer covers.**

Repeat this reversal in about three to four weeks, restoring the hive to its original configuration. At that time you can put on one or more honey supers — assuming the bees are now bringing in their own food and you've ceased feeding and medicating.

Recipes for Sugar Syrups

You need to feed your bees sugar syrup twice a year, in spring and in autumn. The early spring feeding stimulates activity in the hive and gets your colony up and running fast. It also may save lives if the bees' winter stores of honey have dropped dangerously low. The colony will store the autumn sugar syrup feeding for use during the cold winter months. In either case, feeding syrup is also a convenient way to administer some important medications.

If you purchased your bees from a reputable bee breeder, you don't need to medicate your bees during your first season. But you still need to feed them medicated syrup twice a year (spring and autumn) in your second and subsequent seasons.

- ✔ **Basic sugar syrup:** Boil $2^1/_2$ quarts of water on the stove. When it comes to a rolling boil, turn off the heat and add 5 pounds of white granulated sugar. Stir until the sugar completely dissolves. The syrup must cool to room temperature before you can feed it to your bees.

- ✔ **Winter syrup:** This special syrup is for feeding bees that are going into the winter months. The thicker consistency of the recipe makes it easier for bees to convert the syrup into the honey they'll store for the winter. Boil $2^1/_2$ quarts of water on the stove. When it comes to a rolling boil, turn off the heat and add 10 pounds of white granulated sugar. Stir until the sugar dissolves completely. Let the mixture cool before feeding to your bees.

- ✔ **Medicated syrup:** For medicated syrup, prepare the basic sugar syrup recipe or the winter syrup as previously directed. Let it cool to room temperature. Mix 1 teaspoon of Fumidil-B in approximately $1/_2$ cup of cool water (the medication won't dissolve directly in the syrup). Fumidil-B protects your bees against nosema — a common bee illness. Add the medication to the syrup and stir. You also can add two tablespoons of Honey B Healthy to the syrup. This food supplement contains essential oils and has a number of beneficial qualities.

When making sugar syrup, be sure to turn off the stove before you add the sugar. If you continue boiling the sugar syrup, it may caramelize, and that makes the bees sick.

Book VI
Natural Health

The 5th Wave   By Rich Tennant

"Let me look at the recipe again. It was just supposed to cure the hiccups and settle your stomach."

In this book . . .

Given all the ads you see for medications and over-the-counter drugs, it's no wonder that many people feeling under the weather think the best solution is one that you buy from a pharmaceutical company.

But who says the best way to stay healthy is in a capsule? You can take several steps to stay healthy the natural way. Obviously, eating right is one. Couple that with the knowledge that certain foods and many common herbs can be used to prevent or alleviate certain health problems, and you have many more options for maintaining or recovering your good health.

Chapter 1

Healing Foods for Women and Men

*1*f you eat, this chapter is for you. Every time you choose one food over another, you make a decision that affects your health. As a nutrition-ist, I've witnessed the deterioration in health that poor-quality, empty-calorie foods can cause. I've also seen that a change in diet can produce a sometimes dramatic turnaround in how a person feels. So why not take advantage of the healing properties of foods? This chapter tells you how to use certain foods to ameliorate or prevent some of the aches, pains, and health conditions common to men and women, and it provides you with some great recipes, too.

Healing Foods for Women

Anatomy books 100 years ago showed the male body in detail but delicately omitted illustration of the female form and its more private parts. The female body was thought of as a sort of lesser version of male physiology. Some physical complaints were assumed imaginary or simply emotional.

Yes, we've come a long way since these Victorian times. Premenstrual syn-drome (PMS) is now acknowledged as an identifiable medical condition with various protocols for treatment. The word "menopause" can now be men-tioned in polite society, and it isn't the end of the world if people notice you perspiring from a hot flash. There's also a new respect for subtle differences in female anatomy; for example, women's arteries are more delicate than men's, requiring special care during heart surgery.

However, these are recent advances, and we still don't have all the answers. Fortunately, you can do much to ensure your well-being by choosing the right foods to eat. This section shows you how nourishing foods can support female health.

As a woman, you need certain nutrients in particular for hormonal health and normal reproductive function. Table 1-1 lists a variety of nutrients and the foods you can find them in. This list gives you a wide range of choices for everyday good eating.

Table 1-1	Top Nutrients and Best Foods for Women
Nutrient	*Best Foods*
B-complex	Meats, fish, and grains, such as brown rice and oats
Beta-carotene	Orange and dark green fruits and vegetables, such as butternut squash and collard greens, and organic liver
Boron (a trace mineral)	Apples, pears, dates, almonds, hazelnuts, broccoli, legumes, and honey
Calcium	Yogurt, kale, kidney beans, canned salmon and sardines with the bones, and chicken soup cooked with the bones
Choline	Egg yolks, organ meats, whole wheat, fish, and legumes
Copper	Organic liver, seafood, beans, and collards
Folic acid	Pork, organic liver, trout, yogurt, lentils, peas, avocado, asparagus, artichokes, beets, boysenberries, cantaloupe, and pistachios
Inositol	Whole grains, citrus, blackstrap molasses, fish, and legumes
Iodine	Seafood, seaweed, and iodized salt
Iron	Meats, fish, and grains, such as brown rice and oats
Lecithin	Egg yolks, organ meats, whole wheat, citrus, and nuts
Magnesium	Shrimp, halibut, whole grains, kale, lima beans, black-eyed peas, eggs, almonds, beets, plantains, bananas, and pumpkin and sunflower seeds
Niacin	Meats, poultry, fish, peanuts, brown rice, and dates
Phosphorus	Fish, meats, poultry, eggs, legumes, whole grains, and nuts
Potassium	Meats, whole grains, legumes, bananas, and sunflower seeds

Nutrient	Best Foods
Selenium	Brazil nuts, seafood, meats, eggs, whole grains, and sesame seeds
Vitamin A	Orange and dark green fruits and vegetables, such as butternut squash and collard greens, and organic liver
Vitamin B6	Meats, seafood, beans, peas, lentils, whole grains, and kale
Vitamin C	Sweet peppers, papaya, citrus, kiwi, alfalfa sprouts, and cantaloupe
Vitamin D	Fatty fish, such as salmon, sardines, and herring, and egg yolks
Vitamin E	Extra-virgin olive oil and other unrefined vegetable oils, whole grains, eggs, sweet potatoes, leafy green vegetables, nuts, and seeds

Book VI

Natural Health

PMS-friendly foods

An estimated 97 percent of females have PMS at some point in life. For about 40 percent of these women, symptoms are significantly intense, and for about 5 percent, PMS disrupts their usual routines for a day or two each month. Yet simple remedies for various symptoms of PMS abound. You can use food to balance hormones and increase or diminish their production, thereby taming monthly woes.

As many as 150 symptoms of PMS have been identified, covering a range from sugar cravings and crying spells to migraines and backache. These symptoms are commonly grouped into various categories, each associated with specific nutritional deficiencies that probably developed over a period of many years. Each group of symptoms can be treated with specific dietary changes. Take a look at some of the most common problems.

Irritability, nervous tension, mood swings, and anxiety

Irritability, nervous tension, mood swings, and anxiety are all symptoms characteristic of estrogen dominance, which occurs when your body makes too much of this hormone in relation to progesterone.

Your body may be producing excess estrogen, but estrogen can accumulate in the system in several other diet-related ways. If your body is lacking B-complex vitamins, for example, the liver can't perform its normal function of inactivating excess estrogen. If you're lacking fiber, estrogen in the process of being excreted via the intestines can be reabsorbed back into the bloodstream. And estrogen in the food supply — in meats and dairy products from animals raised with supplemental hormones — can add to your own supply of estrogen. If you're suffering from PMS, make sure to eat these foods only if they're organic.

What's going on in there?

PMS is triggered by an imbalance in sex hormones. These hormones direct a woman's monthly menstrual cycle. In the first half of the month, estrogen output is on the rise, and then it rapidly declines at ovulation. Then progesterone production kicks in and increases in the days leading up to your period. However, output can vary, and too much or too little of a hormone at the wrong time can trigger PMS symptoms.

Your hormone production may be off for many reasons, including taking birth control pills, gynecological problems such as endometriosis or fibroids, multiple childbirths, lack of exercise,

stress, and simply being over age 30. However, it's also more than likely that what you're eating is affecting your cycle.

Normal hormone production depends upon having a ready supply of certain vitamins, minerals, and, yes, fats — both essential fatty acids and saturated fats. When you consume saturated fats, such as those found in butter and animal foods, your body converts them into reproductive hormones. This is why women who diet or exercise themselves into a state of extremely low body fat stop having their periods, a medical condition known as *amenorrhea.*

Organic produce is also highly recommended. Regular produce may be sprayed with pesticides that mimic estrogen. While the body quickly metabolizes natural estrogens, the synthetic estrogen-like compounds that are byproducts of pesticides tend to accumulate in body tissue. These can be potent at even low levels, especially when several are present. Such compounds can upset your own hormone balance.

The emotional symptoms of PMS can also be triggered by rapid drops in blood sugar, as well as low levels of *endorphins,* brain chemicals that make you feel that all is right with the world. To help stabilize your blood sugar, eat a natural foods diet and give yourself sufficient protein. Such foods also provide B-complex vitamins, minerals, and fiber, and these ingredients are free of added hormones.

Go out of your way to eat foods that contain these nutrients: B complex, choline, inositol, magnesium, vitamin B6, vitamin C, and zinc. (Table 1-1, earlier in this chapter, lists foods that are high in these nutrients.) Foods that contain phyto-estrogens also help tame emotions. Puree of Green Soybean Soup is a delicious way to increase your intake. (The later section "Munching your way through menopause" explains phytohormones.) Flavonoids also help balance hormones.

Puree of Green Soybean Soup

In this soup, the mild flavor of fresh soybeans combines well with the more familiar taste of lima beans. Soybeans supply phyto-estrogens that help balance hormones, while lima beans, which are exceptionally high in magnesium, help quell PMS emotions. This soup makes a refreshing and slightly tart starter course.

Preparation time: *10 minutes*

Cooking time: *1 hour, 20 minutes*

Yield: *6 servings*

Book VI

Natural Health

2 cups fresh lima beans, or 1 cup dried lima beans

1 quart filtered water

2 cups green soybeans, removed from pod

2 ½ cups chicken broth

1 teaspoon lemon juice

½ cup buttermilk

Sea salt and freshly ground black pepper to taste

Seasoned Japanese rice crackers (optional)

1 Put the lima beans in a medium saucepan, and add water to cover. Cover the pan and simmer until tender, 15 to 20 minutes if using fresh beans, and 45 minutes to 1 hour if using dried beans.

2 In the meantime, bring 1 quart water to a boil. Add the soybeans, lower heat to simmer, and cook, covered, until tender, about 10 to 15 minutes.

3 Drain both pots of beans. Put the beans in a food processor and puree, adding some of the chicken broth if needed to facilitate the pureeing.

4 Put the pureed beans, remaining chicken broth, and lemon juice in a medium saucepan. Heat the soup on low heat for 10 minutes, until it just simmers. Remove from heat.

5 Stir in the buttermilk. Season to taste with sea salt and pepper. Pour into preheated individual soup bowls, and, if desired, serve with seasoned Japanese rice crackers.

Cravings for carbohydrates

In the five or ten days before you begin your period, you may be especially hungry for breads of all kinds, chocolate cake, and any cookie you lay eyes on. Elevated insulin levels may be the cause. Insulin is the hormone that enables your body to store sugar in your cells for ready energy later. Excess insulin causes your cells to rapidly absorb the sugar. Once this sugar is inside the cells, your blood sugar drops, sometimes suddenly if you've eaten a lot of sugar quickly. You feel fatigued, dizzy, shaky, and faint, and have a headache. This is the moment you decide that you can't live without lemon meringue pie.

When you crave sweets or carbs, have healthy ones, such as a couple of whole-grain crackers topped with nut butter, so that you give your system some protein and fat along with the carbs. This combination helps steady blood sugar and even helps prevent weight gain. Also, sometimes a craving for sweets masks a craving for protein. Give yourself a little chicken breast and some vegetables and then take note of whether you still have a strong urge for pie.

For carbohydrate cravings, focus on foods that contain these nutrients: B complex, magnesium, omega-3 essential fatty acids, and vitamin E. For foods that contain these nutrients, refer to Table 1-1, earlier in this chapter.

Fluid retention, swelling with associated weight gain, and breast tenderness

Forty percent of women with PMS experience some bloating. Reproductive hormones that are out of balance can hamper the kidneys' ability to manage sodium and fluid levels in the body. You can end up with swollen hands and feet or difficulty cinching your belt. High insulin levels and vitamin B6 deficiency can also cause fluid retention.

To reduce bloating, minimize your intake (or completely avoid) salt and concentrated sweets, including refined white sugar, honey, and maple syrup, as well as foods made with these. Increase foods rich in potassium, such as bananas, and take advantage of the diuretic properties of certain foods, such as parsley.

These three nutrients are especially helpful: magnesium, omega-6 essential fatty acids, and vitamin B6. (To find the foods you need, refer to Table 1-1, earlier in this chapter.)

Feeling blue and depression

In this group of symptoms related to depression, other possible complaints can include weepiness, confusion, insomnia, and forgetfulness. Such problems are again the result of hormone imbalance — in this case, a predominance of progesterone, which can act as a depressant. Low levels of certain neurotransmitters in the central nervous system and low blood sugar can also cause these problems.

Like your mother said, eat breakfast and regularly scheduled meals to keep your blood sugar steady. You also need these special nutrients to help decrease depression, plus phyto-estrogens and flavonoids: B complex, essential fatty acids, magnesium, and potassium. (For tips on what to eat, flip ahead to the section "Munching your way through menopause," or turn back to the food list in Table 1-1.)

Treating menstrual problems with food

Even if you have virtually no troubling symptoms of PMS, other medical problems can occur once menstruation begins. Like many women, you may experience abdominal cramping for the first few days of your cycle. Your menstrual flow may be particularly heavy or especially light. In these cases, a change in diet can greatly improve how you feel.

Book VI

Natural Health

Cramps and lower back pain

Cramps are a very common part of the package when you start having menstrual difficulties. Along with abdominal cramping, you may also feel pain in the inner thighs and lower back. In more severe cases, women also experience nausea, vomiting, diarrhea, and heavy bleeding.

These symptoms can be caused by an imbalance in a particular group of hormone-like compounds called *prostaglandins.* One sort of prostaglandin promotes expansion of blood vessels and muscles. Another sort, the Series II prostaglandin, promotes contraction. When Series II prostaglandins dominate, cramping can result as blood vessels within the uterus and the muscles surrounding the uterus contract. Sodium and fluid retention also do their share in causing menstrual pain.

Red meat and dairy foods promote the production of Series II prostaglandins. These foods contain arachidonic acid, which converts to the Series II prostaglandins. Beef contains the most arachidonic acid, lamb and pork somewhat less, and chicken and turkey the least of all. If you want to include meat in your meals but are suffering from menstrual cramping, eat poultry rather than beef. If your cramps persist, go vegetarian for a few days before you start your period and during it.

Choose protein sources such as fish, beans, and whole grains rather than red meat. Avoid milk products and processed cheese, which are high in sodium (sodium promotes fluid retention and adds to your discomfort). Use nondairy nut and soy milks instead. Eat fresh fruits and vegetables for fiber. Avoid refined sugar.

Be sure to eat sufficient amounts of the following nutrients, found in the foods listed in Table 1-1 earlier in this chapter: calcium, magnesium, and omega-6 essential fatty acids.

Heavy menstrual flow and related anemia

If your menstrual flow is infrequent or sporadic, you may experience heavy menstrual bleeding at times, which in turn may lead to anemia and iron deficiency, leaving you tired and pale. Besides iron, other important nutrients are vitamin C and the flavonoids, both of which help strengthen fragile capillary walls and thus prevent excess bleeding. You may also benefit from including flaxseed and flaxseed oil in your meals. Research shows that flaxseed can act as a menstrual regulator, restoring normal timing of the menstrual cycle.

To replenish your blood supply, you need the following nutrients: B complex, copper, iron, vitamin A, and vitamin C. (See Table 1-1 earlier in this chapter for recommended foods that contain these nutrients.)

Anemia can be a serious medical condition. If fatigue and pallor persist, consult a physician.

Eating for two

There's no better time to begin eating quality foods than during pregnancy, when what you eat also affects another's life. The first eight weeks of pregnancy are especially critical, when your baby's kidneys, heart, lungs, eyes, and mouth are beginning to form.

Begin by following these guidelines:

- ✔ **You need protein, essential fatty acids, and complex carbohydrates.** Eat natural, unrefined, and unprocessed foods, including grains, beans, eggs, nuts, seeds, fruits, vegetables, and meats, poultry, and fish as free of toxins as possible. Organic foods should be the rule rather than the exception.

- ✔ **Eat several small meals throughout the day.** Large meals can be more difficult to digest.

- ✔ **Avoid caffeine, sugar, and drugs.** Caffeine is found in sodas, teas, and chocolate. Eliminate all alcohol, tobacco products, and any over-the-counter drugs (other than those prescribed by a physician) or illegal drugs. If you use these, a miscarriage or a birth defect in your child can result.

Getting the right amount of calories

When you're pregnant, you need about 300 more calories a day than you're used to. This is what a growing baby requires. Of course, the extra calories should not come from candy, chips, pizza, or ice cream. Increase your protein intake significantly to at least 100 grams a day, well beyond the usual recommendation of 65 grams daily. Protein is the building block of body tissue.

Most women gain between 20 and 40 pounds during pregnancy. If, by your fourth month, you have already gained 30 pounds, you may need to cut back on your eating. But never, under any circumstances, go on a low-calorie diet when you're carrying a child. Your baby could have a low birth weight and be weaker and more susceptible to disease. Delayed physical and mental development can also result, and such a diet can leave you exhausted and unhealthy.

Always consult with your doctor before making radical changes in your diet while pregnant and before taking nutrient and herbal supplements.

Getting enough calcium

During pregnancy, you need about 1,000 milligrams a day of calcium, but most prenatal vitamin supplements contain only up to 25 percent of that. You'll probably need to take a supplement, as well as eat calcium-rich foods, including organic yogurt and other dairy products, almonds, and blackstrap molasses.

To increase your absorption of calcium, be sure to consume foods that supply vitamin D, such as fatty fish and egg yolks. Alternatively, get 15 minutes of sun exposure each day. Your body can use sunlight to manufacture vitamin D.

Feasting on folic acid

Folic acid helps prevent birth defects, especially those that affect the brain, spine, and nervous system. It also plays an essential role in the formation of DNA and RNA, the genetic material that controls cell division and replication and promotes the production of oxygen-carrying red blood cells. If you're pregnant or nursing, you need about 800 micrograms (mcg) of folic acid a day (1 microgram is one millionth of a gram). Fortunately, nature provides some delicious sources, which are listed in Table 1-1 earlier in this chapter.

You may also need to take a supplement, especially if you used an oral contraceptive before becoming pregnant, which can deplete folic acid.

Book VI

Natural Health

Artichokes with Mediterranean Garlic Sauce

Artichokes, an excellent choice of folic acid as well as other B vitamins, contain a wide variety of other nutrients important for female health — calcium, magnesium, iron, potassium, and some zinc. Even slowly nibbling one of these thistles at the end of an anxious day can be quite soothing.

Preparation time: *15 minutes*

Cooking time: *20 minutes, plus time to cool*

Yield: *2 servings*

2 medium globe artichokes

1 quart filtered water

2 tablespoons red wine vinegar

3 cloves garlic, 1 clove minced

2 tablespoons commercial mayonnaise, preferably free of hydrogenated oil

2 tablespoons plain yogurt

1 teaspoon lemon juice

1 Snap off the artichoke's tough outer leaves. Using a paring knife, cut off the stem and trim the bottom to an even round shape with a flat base. Cut 1 inch from the top of the remaining leaves.

2 Sit the artichokes upright in a medium saucepan. Add the water, vinegar, and 2 cloves unminced garlic.

3 Cook, covered, on medium heat for 20 minutes or until a leaf can be easily pulled out. Remove from heat and let cool to room temperature.

4 In the meantime, combine the mayonnaise, yogurt, lemon juice, and one clove minced garlic in a small bowl; whisk until well blended.

5 Remove the artichokes from the cooking liquid and drain well. Place each artichoke on a serving plate. Dip each artichoke leaf into the sauce and relax while you enjoy the slow-paced ceremony of artichoke eating.

Fiber

The female hormone progesterone, essential for providing an environment in which the fetus can thrive, has a tendency to relax the bowel muscles during pregnancy, which can result in constipation. Don't take a laxative. Instead, rely on prune juice and high-fiber foods. Consult a doctor if that doesn't work.

A wide range of foods contain fiber: apples, barley, beans, bean sprouts, berries, broccoli, brown rice, buckwheat, carrots, corn, kale, lentils, mangoes, oats, okra, papaya, pears, peas, popcorn, prunes, and whole wheat.

Essential fatty acids (EFAs)

Essential fatty acids, or EFAs, are the kind of fats that are good for you. They're critical for the normal formation of membranes, the outer part of every cell in the body. The brain of a growing fetus also requires EFAs, as they make up about 60 percent of brain tissue. The estimated optimal daily doses are 9 grams of omega-6 fatty acids and 6 grams of omega-3 fatty acids. A diet high in plant foods, including nuts, seeds, and unrefined vegetables oils, can provide what you need. Taking 1 to 2 tablespoons a day of flaxseed oil, especially high in the omega-3 fatty acids, is another good way to increase your intake.

As you increase your intake of EFAs, be sure to also increase your intake of antioxidants.

Iodine

Pregnancy requires at least 175 micrograms of iodine a day. (Take a look at the list in Table 1-1, earlier in this chapter, for food sources.) You can eat seafood and seaweed to obtain this. During pregnancy, limit your salt intake to 1 teaspoon a day.

Iron

The requirement for iron during pregnancy is 30 milligrams a day. Foods that contain iron include beets, blackstrap molasses, clams, legumes, liver, nuts, oysters, raisins, seaweed, and seeds.

Avoid drinking coffee and tea, caffeinated and decaffeinated, which increase urination and flush iron out of the system.

Magnesium

The recommendation for magnesium is about 350 milligrams a day. All green vegetables contain magnesium. (For specific suggestions, refer to Table 1-1, earlier in this chapter.)

Zinc

During pregnancy, you require 15 milligrams of zinc daily. Oysters are far and away the richest source of zinc. Enjoy these cooked. You can find other foods that contain zinc in Table 1-1.

Book VI

Natural Health

Medicinals for morning sickness

Ginger works as well for morning sickness as it does for seasickness. Grate a half-inch of ginger root into a cup filled with boiling water. Steep for 5 minutes before drinking. Have this tea every morning before breakfast. Eating little snacks throughout the day can also help a queasy stomach.

Foods to avoid during pregnancy

Certain foods that are relatively harmless when you're not pregnant can pose serious dangers to your body when you are. Stay away from foods that may carry various bacteria or parasites, such as

- ✔ Raw fish, including sushi and seviche
- ✔ Runny eggs
- ✔ Pâtés and soft cheeses such as blue cheese
- ✔ Unpasteurized milk, cheese, and juice

Also avoid cabbage, chilies, garlic, onions, red peppers, and other spicy or gas-forming foods if you're already sensitive to them.

In general, stay away from all herbal teas. Many can interfere with pregnancy.

After the baby arrives

Mother's milk is far superior nutritionally to baby formula. Of course, some of everything you eat or take into your body goes into your breast milk, and eventually into your baby. So if you're nursing, watch what you eat. It's a good idea to continue avoiding the foods, chemicals, and other substances that were dangerous for your fetus.

As a nursing mother, you also need to increase your calorie intake by about 500 calories a day compared to your pre-pregnancy calorie intake. And certain nutrients are especially important — all the B vitamins, including niacin, riboflavin, and thiamin, as well as calcium, iodine, and essential fatty acids.

Munching your way through menopause

Women who enter menopause with adequate reserves of vitamins, minerals, and other essential nutrients pass through this transition with fewer symptoms than do women who reach midlife physically depleted and poorly nourished. Even if menopause is years away, you'll thank yourself later if you improve your eating habits now.

Symptoms of menopause are most dramatic during the year or two leading up to menopause, the phase called *perimenopause.* As in PMS, symptoms are the result of hormone imbalances. You may have abnormally high levels of estrogen as compared with progesterone or vice versa. Symptoms such as irritability, anxiety, depression, and "menopausal rage" can occur. Lowered estrogen levels can also affect memory. In addition, the body's ability to regulate temperature may go on the fritz like a broken thermostat, triggering hot flashes.

Food is a powerful tool for dampening and even preventing these annoyances. And what you decide not to eat is just as important.

Vitamins E, A, C, and the Bs

Vitamin E, taken in through diet or as a supplement, is one of the most important vitamins for menopause. (Be sure to take the natural form.) The B vitamins and vitamins A and C, as well as a variety of minerals, are also essential. (You can find their food sources in Table 1-1, earlier in this chapter.)

Phyto-estrogens and flavonoids

Natural foods also provide other active compounds that recent research is showing are vital for your health. These include flavonoids and the group of compounds called *phyto-estrogens,* which function like hormones and help balance your own.

Phyto-estrogens

Phytohormones, popularly called phyto-estrogens, are found in dozens of plant foods. They work to help balance hormones and, as a result, help prevent symptoms of PMS and menopause that stem from the dramatic rise and fall of hormones. In some cultures, such plant foods may contribute as much as 50 percent of caloric intake. According to a 1990 study in the *British Journal of Medicine,* intake of phyto-estrogens at this level could potentially diminish menopause symptoms.

Soybeans contain especially potent phyto-estrogen, but many everyday vegetables, fruits, legumes, whole grains, and nuts exhibit some estrogenic activity. Add these to your shopping list:

- **Flavorings:** Licorice, anise, and garlic
- **Fruit:** Apples, cherries, citrus, and pomegranates
- **Legumes:** Chickpeas, red beans, soybeans, and split peas
- **Oils:** Extra-virgin olive oil, cold-pressed oils, and flaxseed oil
- **Seeds:** Sesame seeds and flaxseed
- **Vegetables:** Beets, broccoli, cabbage, carrots, cauliflower, celery, fennel, onions, parsley, potatoes, and radishes
- **Whole grains:** Barley, corn, oats, rice, rye, and wheat

Flavonoids

Flavonoids are a group of vitamin-like compounds with a chemical structure and activity similar to estrogen. Flavonoids help minimize estrogen highs and lows. Good sources of flavonoids include apples, lemons, onions green and black tea, and dark beer. (**Note:** Flavonoids are found in the pulp and pith of fruits and vegetables, so to get this nutrient, you need to eat these foods in their whole form.)

Buckwheat, which contains flavonoids, makes a good salad. In the following recipe, it substitutes for bulghur wheat in the traditional Middle Eastern dish tabbouli.

Turkish Buckwheat Salad

Buckwheat groats supply iron, niacin, and thiamin, nutrients that help you feel energized. Buckwheat is a source of flavonoids that help balance hormones.

Preparation time: *10 minutes*

Cooking time: *15 minutes, plus at least 1 hour to blend flavors*

Yield: *4 large servings*

2 cups unfiltered water

1 cup unroasted whole buckwheat groats

2 scallions, chopped

1 bunch fresh parsley, stems removed and leaves chopped (1 cup)

2 sprigs fresh mint, stems removed and leaves chopped

1 teaspoon ground cumin

3 tablespoons fresh lemon juice

2 tablespoons extra-virgin olive oil

Salt and freshly ground black pepper to taste

1 In a large saucepan, bring the water to boil over high heat.

2 Stir in the buckwheat groats and immediately lower heat to simmer. Cook, covered, for 15 minutes, or until all the water has been absorbed. Remove from heat and set aside.

3 Spoon the cooked buckwheat into a large bowl. Add the scallions, parsley, mint, cumin, lemon juice, oil, and salt and pepper.

4 Gently toss salad ingredients together until well blended. Cover and refrigerate for at least 1 hour to blend flavors. Serve as a side dish with grilled meats, such as lamb chops, and a cucumber-yogurt salad.

Healing foods for menopausal symptoms

Menopause involves far more than changes in hormone production. It is a shift in body chemistry that affects the adrenal glands, the nervous system, the skeleton, and the brain. You need to nourish your body with sustaining foods as your body adjusts. Foods that contain phyto-estrogens are especially important to include in your meals. Many symptoms of menopause are triggered by rapid changes in estrogen levels, and these phyto-nutrients help you avoid the extremes.

As your period becomes more irregular during perimenopause, you may experience PMS even if you didn't when you were younger. You may also experience heavy menstrual bleeding. Follow the dietary advice given earlier in this chapter for these conditions.

Hot flashes

If it suddenly feels like you're living in the tropics, you're having a *hot flash.* A small burst of heat begins in the chest area and quickly expands to the face and arms. You sweat and then feel quite chilled as the perspiration evaporates and your body temperature quickly drops. You may also feel some anxiety.

These special nutrients help with hot flashes: magnesium, selenium, and vitamin E. Vitamin E is considered the prime menopause nutrient, and selenium works with vitamin E to maximize its effectiveness. (Refer to Table 1-1 for food sources.) Flavonoids and phyto-estrogens are also important nutrients, because they both help balance hormones.

With all that sweating, hot flashes can leave you thirsty and depleted of minerals such as magnesium, potassium, and sodium, which you lose through the skin when you perspire. The same is true for *night sweats,* surges of heat that wake you from your sleep.

Avoid stimulating and warming foods such as caffeinated coffee and tea, chocolate, spicy foods, and alcoholic beverages, including beer. A large dose of sugar, such as a slice of pecan pie, can also bring on a flash.

Hot Flash Fruit Compote

Having a hot flash triggers your body to perspire in an effort to cool down. In the process of sweating, you lose fluids and several important minerals — magnesium, potassium, and sodium. At breakfast, replenish what you've lost with plenty of fresh filtered water and a mineral-rich fruit and nut compote. This recipe is a good place to start. Select from the following ingredients, making sure to include some juicy chunks of melon!

Preparation time: *10 minutes*

Cooking time: *None*

Yield: *4 servings*

4 cups diced fruit (apricots, bananas, black currants, cantaloupe, cherries, dates, guava, honeydew melon, kiwi, mango, papaya, and/or pears)

3 tablespoons pumpkin seeds

3 tablespoons nuts (almonds, cashews, and/or pistachios)

Sea salt (optional)

2 tablespoons yogurt (optional)

Unsulphured blackstrap molasses (optional)

Chopped fresh mint leaves (optional)

1 Put the fruit in a bowl and combine with the seeds and nuts.

2 Sprinkle the combination with a pinch of sea salt, if desired, and stir.

3 Spoon fruit mixture into individual serving bowls, and, if desired, top with yogurt and molasses and a sprig of mint. Dig in!

Fatigue

Fatigue is the most commonly reported symptom of menopause. Hot flashes can be draining. Anemia due to heavy bleeding may also cause fatigue, and iron-rich foods are needed. These special nutrients help reduce fatigue: B complex vitamins, iron, and vitamin C. (Refer to Table 1-1 for a list of food sources.)

Weight gain

With menopause, you may develop a rounded belly, due to changes in your output of reproductive hormones. It's in the lower abdominal tissue that you make some of your postmenopausal estrogen as production in your ovaries diminishes. Gaining about 5 to 10 pounds at menopause is normal. Fluid retention can also lead to a temporary increase in weight.

Resist going on a crash diet, which will rob you of needed vitamins and minerals. Instead, have moderate portions of whole foods. And avoid refined sugar, which is all calories and no nutrients.

Memory

Research has shown that estrogen improves verbal recall and the ability to acquire and remember newly associated thoughts. Estrogenic foods, essential fatty acids, antioxidants, lecithin, B complex vitamins, and the minerals potassium, magnesium, phosphorus, selenium, and boron all promote mental alertness. (Refer to Table 1-1 for a list of food sources.) In addition, maintaining stable blood sugar levels, getting sufficient rest, and exercising regularly to increase your oxygen supply can help.

Mood swings, irritability, depression

Follow the nutrient and food recommendations given for these symptoms earlier in this chapter under the sections on irritability and depression. Phyto-estrogens can also help balance hormones and steady mood swings. Avoid refined and processed foods, caffeine, and alcohol.

Sexual problems

While sexuality certainly continues post-menopause, there's no denying that as your supply of reproductive hormones declines, your sexual energy can alter and diminish. Vaginal tissue also goes through changes. However, the right diet can help you restore a once-vital sex life.

First, make a special effort to avoid symptom triggers such as caffeine, white sugar, and nutrient-depleted refined foods. Then boost your intake of whole foods, such as seasonal fresh fruits and vegetables, whole grains, seafood, nuts, and seeds. These foods supply nutrients that maintain vaginal health, keep tissues firm through the manufacture of collagen, and increase sexual response.

These nutrients help maintain healthy vaginal tissue: copper, essential fatty acids, vitamin A, vitamin B6, vitamin C, and vitamin E. The following nutrients help you maintain vaginal lubrication and sexual vitality: folic acid, niacin, and zinc.

Menopause and degenerative disease

Although you often hear osteoporosis and heart disease lumped together with the symptoms of menopause, these degenerative diseases aren't inevitable consequences of passing through the change-of-life. Lowered hormone levels can be a risk factor, and the likelihood of developing these diseases can increase as you pass middle age, but eating the right foods is a good way to help prevent these diseases.

Book VI

Natural Health

Healing Foods for Men

Some health issues unique to men — like enlarged prostate, prostate cancer, impotency, and faltering libido — can be affected by diet. The recommended way of eating for all these conditions is the same. Build meals based on natural, unrefined, and unprocessed whole foods. Avoid added hormones and toxins. Enjoy a wide variety of ingredients, from meats, poultry, and seafood to fruits of the field.

Many of the same nutrients listed for women (refer to Table 1-1 earlier in this chapter) are also recommended for various aspects of male reproductive health. Table 1-2 lists nutrients men especially need and the foods that contain them.

Table 1-2	Top Nutrients and Best Foods for Men
Nutrient	**Best Foods**
B1 (thiamin)	Pork, duck, lobster, egg yolks, pinto beans, potatoes, beans, grapes, and pistachios
B6 (pyridoxine)	Beef, chicken, tuna, brown rice, navy beans, broccoli, mangoes, walnuts, and sunflower seeds
Essential fatty acids	Unrefined vegetable oils, flaxseed, walnuts, organic eggs, and fatty fish, such as sardines, tuna, and salmon
Folic acid	Beef, chicken, trout, beans and lentils, whole grains, asparagus, beets, avocados, boysenberries, and pistachios
Manganese	Clams, bass, trout, lima beans, beans and lentils, whole grains, okra, pineapple, bananas, hazelnuts, almonds, and maple syrup
Magnesium	Shrimp, oysters, halibut, egg yolks, beans, whole grains, figs, plantains, avocados, Brazil nuts, cashews, walnuts, and seeds
PABA	Organ meats, whole wheat, yogurt, blackstrap molasses, and kale
Selenium	Brazil nuts, shellfish, tuna, herring, chicken breast, beef, lamb, whole wheat, carrots, cabbage, and mushrooms
Vitamin A	Liver, eggs, sweet potatoes, carrots, winter squash, and cantaloupe
Vitamin C	Citrus, cantaloupe, strawberries, broccoli, and green peppers
Vitamin E	Unrefined oils, eggs, whole wheat, organ meats, sweet potatoes, kale, and cabbage
Zinc	Oysters and other shellfish, sardines, beef, lamb, mushrooms, pumpkin seeds, sunflower seeds, and cheese

Prostate problems

The prostate is a small, walnut-shaped gland that sits at the base of the bladder. Its job is to produce part of the fluid that makes semen. With the first contractions of orgasm, prostatic fluid begins to flow. The gland also metabolizes the male hormone, testosterone.

There was a time when no one thought much about the prostate gland. But now that prostate tumors are the most commonly diagnosed form of cancer in men (excluding skin cancer) and the second leading cause of death among males, prostate disease is a common concern.

Enlarged prostate

About 60 percent of all men between 40 and 59 years of age have *benign prostatic hyperplasia* (BPH), or an enlarged prostate. The incidence has increased tremendously in the last few decades. Depending upon what portion of the prostate becomes enlarged, the gland can place pressure on the bladder, causing typical BPH symptoms. At first, a man may find he needs to urinate more frequently. Then, as BPH progresses, symptoms can include greater urgency of urination, increased frequency, especially at night, and difficulty completely emptying the bladder.

To combat BPH, you need to take advantage of several nutrients. (Refer to Table 1-2 for foods that contain these nutrients.)

- ✔ **Vitamin B6 and zinc:** Both play a role in the complexity of processes and chemical reactions that lead to hormone balance.

- ✔ **Vitamin E and selenium:** Both are essential nutrients for prostate health.

- ✔ **Essential fatty acids:** These acids have been used clinically to successfully reduce symptoms of BPH. Eat the equivalent of 1 teaspoon of essential fatty acids or 4 grams a day. Avoid processed and hydrogenated oils, and lower your intake of saturated fats.

Recent studies show that the herb saw palmetto can significantly improve the urinary difficulties associated with BPH and is useful in the prevention of BPH. Other herbal treatments include flower pollen, prescribed in Europe, and ginseng, which is used in China.

Pumpkin seeds are an excellent source of zinc, essential fatty acids, and certain amino acids, all helpful in reducing symptoms of BPH. However, these aren't the pumpkin seeds you find in the kind of pumpkin you carve and put a candle in for Halloween. Rather, they're long, flat, and dark green. They're sold in natural-food stores and in Latin markets, where they're called *pepitas*.

Two-Fisted Tuna on Toast

Fish is an excellent source of essential fatty acids. An easy-to-make fish sandwich for lunch is a great way to increase your intake. Choose a fatty fish such as tuna, salmon, or sardines, which gives you an extra dose of healing omega-3 essential fatty acids, important for prostate health.

Preparation time: *10 minutes*

Cooking time: *2 minutes for the toast*

Yield: *1 hefty sandwich*

1 6-ounce can tuna, packed in water	*2 slices tomato*
⅓ cup diced onion	*4 anchovies*
1 tablespoon red wine or balsamic vinegar	*Freshly grated pepper to taste*
2 slices crusty whole-grain bread, toasted	

1 In a small bowl, mix together the tuna, onion, and red wine or vinegar.

2 Lay the two pieces of toast on a work surface. Cover one slice with the tomato slices and spread the tuna mixture on top. Arrange the anchovies on the tuna. Season with pepper. Top with the second piece of toast.

3 With a sharp knife, cut the sandwich in half. Wolf down with potato salad and a glass of fruit juice mixed with club soda.

Healing foods for prostatitis

In prostatitis, the prostate gland is infected due to a urinary infection, a blood-borne infection, or venereal disease. If you have this condition, avoid spicy foods and refrain from caffeine, alcohol, and cigarettes, all of which are potential irritants of the prostate gland. Also avoid sugar.

Contaminants that can upset hormone balance

Pesticides and other contaminants present in food, some products, and the environment break down into compounds that behave like hormones. These substances include dioxin, polyhalogenated biphenyls, hexachlorobenzene, dibenzofurans, and diethylstilboestrol (DES). Such compounds may contribute to hormone imbalance in males. In one animal study, DES caused prostate changes similar to benign prostatic hyperplasia (BPH), or enlarged prostate. These are good reasons to eat only organic foods. And remember, nutrients such as carotenes, flavonoids, chlorophyll, magnesium, calcium, selenium, and zinc, as well as fiber, support the body's ability to rid itself of these contaminants.

Protective nutrients for prostate cancer

Age, family history, and race affect your risk of prostate cancer. African-American men have an especially high rate. Prostate cancer is related to diet in only about 10 to 20 percent of cases. However, recent research is discovering some nutrients that may be beneficial in lowering your risk.

- ✔ **Lycopene:** A phyto-nutrient found in tomatoes, lycopene is associated with a lower risk of aggressive prostate cancer.

- ✔ **Selenium:** An antioxidant, selenium is almost as effective as vitamin E in reducing the risk of prostate cancer. This mineral may block cell damage as well as protect the prostate from environmental carcinogens. (Nearly half the selenium a man carries in his body is in the testes and seminal ducts adjacent to the prostate gland.) Unfortunately, selenium deficiency is common. In addition, men lose selenium in their semen.

- ✔ **Vitamin D:** This vitamin appears to inhibit the spread of cancer. Sunlight allows the body to synthesize this important nutrient.

- ✔ **Vitamin E:** Taking a daily supplement of 400 IU of this antioxidant can help reduce the incidence of prostate cancer.

Regular consumption of red meat and dairy products is a risk factor. The Japanese, who consume a low-fat fish and vegetable diet, have the lowest incidence of prostate cancer in the industrialized world.

Quick and Easy Cajun Okra

You may stay away from okra because of its odd, slightly slimy texture, but that texture is just the reason you should be eating okra more than once every five years. In this recipe, the okra is cooked with tantalizing Cajun spices. Enjoy this dish with red beans and rice.

Preparation time: *5 minutes*

Cooking time: *20 minutes*

Yield: *4 servings*

½ pound young okra, stems removed and cut into 1-inch lengths if the pods are large

1 teaspoon unsalted, organic butter

1 tablespoon prepared Cajun Creole Seasoning

Salt to taste

1 Fill a medium pot with water to about 1 inch from the top. Bring to a boil, and add the okra.

2 Simmer, covered, on medium-low heat until okra is tender, about 10 minutes. Drain the okra when it's sufficiently tender.

3 Meanwhile, in a saucepan, melt the butter. Add the seasoning, and heat over low heat for 1 minute to develop seasoning flavors. Add the okra. Using a wooden spoon, toss the okra in the seasoned butter to evenly coat. Cook for 2 to 3 minutes to combine flavors. Salt to taste, and serve.

Tip: Spice Hunter is one brand of seasoning that makes Cajun Creole Seasoning.

Nourishing your sexuality

What you eat affects your sexual and reproductive anatomy just as much as any other part of your body. Problems such as impotence and lack of interest in sex can be brought on, in part, by poor food choices. The pituitary and testes produce sex hormones, and even the adrenals produce small amounts. These glands require specific nutrients to function properly. A change to eating healthier foods that supply certain vitamins, minerals, and healing fats can often help correct these conditions.

Erectile dysfunction (impotence)

The inability to achieve or maintain a full erection is known by the medical term *erectile dysfunction* (ED). If you've ever experienced ED, you're not alone. An estimated 30 million men in the United States — the majority over age 65 — have some degree of ED. (No, ED doesn't affect sexual drive or the ability to achieve orgasm.) Medications, stress, emotional problems, infection, and anatomical abnormalities can cause ED. In addition, certain medical conditions are often part of the picture (see the sidebar "Causes of erectile dysfunction").

To keep your heart and arteries healthy (which is necessary for sexual potency) and to reduce your risk of diseases or conditions that can cause ED, watch what you eat. Follow this way of eating to keep it all in tip-top condition:

- ✔ **Follow a heart-healthy diet.** A heart-healthy diet can normalize cholesterol levels, help prevent hypertension, and keep the vascular system healthy.

- ✔ **Avoid refined white sugar.** When eating sweets such as desserts, have only small portions. Eat regular meals, and when having a carbohydrate, also eat some protein — for example, apple pie and cheese.

- ✔ **Limit alcoholic beverages.** A small amount of alcohol stimulates blood flow, but alcohol also acts as a depressant and can be a downer. Caffeine can also interfere with performance.

- ✔ **Avoid estrogens and growth hormones in meat.** These hormones may interfere with your own hormone balance and reproductive health. Eat only meats that are free of hormone residues.

Take advantage of the special nutrients for potency. All the antioxidants — beta-carotene, selenium, vitamin C, and vitamin E — protect cells from free radical damage and help prevent tissues in the testes from degeneration. Zinc and the B vitamins are essential for the production of testosterone. Magnesium helps reverse hardening of the arteries in the penis. And manganese is typically low in body tissues of men who are impotent. (Refer to Table 1-2 for a list of the top food sources for these nutrients.)

Feeding your libido

Sexual drive, or libido, requires one nutrient in particular — zinc. If you want to boost your reserve, you'd best like oysters. These crustaceans are by far the most concentrated food source of zinc. While crab is a good source of zinc (3 ounces supply 5 milligrams), six medium oysters contain an extraordinary 76 milligrams! Oysters have long been used as an aphrodisiac, and now you know why!

TIP

Zinc and the mineral copper need to be kept in balance. Oysters also contain some copper, as well as small amounts of calcium and phosphorus, all minerals that increase the effectiveness of zinc.

Don Juan's Oyster Stew

To get your daily dose of zinc, try this recipe for oyster stew. It's delicious because it's buttery, the way oyster stew used to be. If you care only about what the oysters can do for you and you're watching your fat intake, skip the cream and make it just with milk.

Preparation time: *10 minutes*

Cooking time: *10 minutes*

Yield: *4 servings*

2 dozen fresh, shucked oysters

2 tablespoons organic, unsalted butter

1 cup oyster liquor or clam juice

½ teaspoon grated onion, or ½ cup sliced cooked celery

1 ½ cups milk, preferably without added hormones and organic

½ cup cream, preferably without added hormones and organic

Paprika, for garnish

1 Fill the lower portion of a double boiler with water and bring to a boil, making sure that the top pan doesn't touch the water. Put the oysters, 1 tablespoon butter, oyster liquor, and onion in the top half. Stir briskly and constantly until oysters are just beginning to curl, about 1 minute.

2 Add the milk and cream and continue stirring briskly just until it comes to a boil. Remove the double boiler from the heat, making sure not to allow the stew to continue boiling.

3 Pour the oyster stew into warmed individual soup bowls, dividing the oysters evenly.

4 Serve the stew piping hot, and garnish each serving with some of the remaining butter and a dash of paprika.

Tip: If you get a sense of accomplishment from shucking your own oysters, buy them in the shell, which should be undamaged and shut tight. Or have someone at your fish store shuck the oysters and make sure that he or she also gives you the juice from the oysters (the oyster liquor). Or buy oysters that are shucked, packaged, and marked with a "sell by" date.

Causes of erectile dysfunction

Normal sexual function depends upon having healthy arteries and nerves. Diseases that cause damage to these in the trunk of the body and limbs can also do harm in the genital area. Forty percent of men diagnosed with diabetes also experience some degree of impotency. High blood sugar levels, which occur in diabetes, limit the amount of oxygen the blood is able to transport to body cells. Sexual difficulties can result, especially because tissues in the penis need more oxygen than usual during sexual intercourse. In advanced diabetes, nerve damage occurs, which can affect sexual activity.

The arteries in the penis are vulnerable to atherosclerosis, or narrowing of the arteries,

preventing enough blood from entering the penis to cause sufficient hardness. Vascular disease can interfere with the delivery of oxygen and nutrients to cells. Hypertension, high total cholesterol, and low levels of HDL cholesterol are also risk factors for impotency.

Smokers, as compared with nonsmokers, are twice as likely to be impotent. Smoke injures arteries and disrupts blood flow. So if you smoke, quit!

Remember: Medications that promise to improve erection can't function if the blood vessels themselves are nonresponsive due to degenerative disease.

Nutrients for sperm production

Eggs are full of nutrients needed to launch new life, so it should be no surprise that sperm, too, are packed with vitamins and minerals. Sperm contains calcium, magnesium, zinc, sulfur, vitamin B12, vitamin C, and inositol, part of the B complex of vitamins. Whole grains, legumes, nuts, meats, liver, shellfish, and citrus are sources.

Zinc, in particular is essential for the production of sperm. Low levels can result in sperm that are infertile.

If you'd rather take a nap

Besides desire, sex requires energy. If you've been overstressed and aren't eating particularly nourishing foods, you risk adrenal exhaustion. Your body's stress coping mechanisms say, "No more." The adrenals cut back on energy production and insist that you rest. When these glands become exhausted, you're less likely to participate in your normal activities, including sex. Help your adrenals revive by staying away from sugar and caffeine. Increase your intake of foods that supply B vitamins and vitamin C.

You may also lack the desire and strength for sex if your thyroid gland isn't receiving essential nutrients. Your thyroid controls the rate at which you convert food to energy. A sluggish thyroid, or hypothyroidism, can also dampen desire. Foods that contain iodine, B vitamins, and especially thiamin, plus vitamin E are required.

Enjoy all sorts of seafood, whole grains, nuts, and unrefined oils to maintain your zest for life.

Chapter 2

Making Your Own Herbal Teas, Tinctures, Oils, and Elixirs

In This Chapter

▶ Stocking up on tools, equipment, and ingredients

▶ Finding out how to make herbal teas

▶ Blending your own aromatherapy scents and healing products

*H*arvesting wild or cultivated herbs and creating wonderfully scented aromatic balms and potions fulfill a basic human desire — to find allies for preserving health and vitality and promoting long life. A special bond exists between herbalists of all ages and those who feel the call to experience these colorful and aromatic potions, elixirs, and salves. This chapter tells you what you need to know to create your own herbal remedies.

A good way to find out more about creating effective herbal products is to visit herb shops, natural-foods markets, and even pharmacies to smell and taste their products, feel the texture, and observe the coloring. A salve maker who has made thousands of jars of calendula salve or a tincture maker who has created thousands of bottles of echinacea both know how to make a product that tastes good, looks good, and works well. And soon, you will too!

Getting the Gist of the Jargon

Most capsules, tablets, tinctures, salves, creams, and even herbal shampoos contain extracts. When you make a tea on your stove, for example, you're making an extract. When you simmer herbs in a pan of water, the active ingredients are released from the plant into the tea. The following definitions of terms related to extraction help explain this process:

- **The solvent:** When you make a tea, you add water to the herbs. The water is the *solvent,* also called the *menstruum.* A solvent is a liquid that can selectively remove certain active ingredients (often called *active compounds*), such as alkaloids, from herbs. Besides water, other solvents include alcohol, glycerin, and liquid carbon dioxide. The art of extraction is choosing the right solvent system for each herb to maximize its effectiveness.

- **The marc:** After a batch of herbs is extracted with water or another solvent, the liquid is thoroughly pressed from the spent herb. All the liquid is then collected and bottled or further processed. The dry, spent herb material is known as the *marc.* The marc is usually composted to make fertilizer for growing more herbs.

- **Maceration and percolation:** The process of soaking herbs in a solvent for a period of time, often about two weeks, is called *maceration.* Pouring or forcing a solvent through herbs packed into a large funnel in order to pull out the active ingredients is known as *percolation.* Herbalists use either of these two methods to make herbal extracts.

Looking at Tools of the Trade

To make herbal products at home, you need a few pieces of basic equipment, such as a blender, a coffee grinder or seed grinder, and a double boiler. You can often find these items in natural-foods stores, department stores, or kitchen shops.

Blender or grinder

Use a blender or grinder to reduce plant material (dry or fresh) to the smallest particle size possible. Doing so increases the surface area of the herb that's exposed to the solvent during the extraction process. In the case of expensive herbs like ginseng, you want to get as complete an extraction as possible, so blending and grinding are particularly important.

A good blender is one of the most important tools for the home herbal product maker. Although any high-quality blender will do, try to find one with a very high speed and a strong motor. A Vita-Mix has an extra-strong motor, which is reversible to help disentangle herb roots and stems that may get caught in the blade. The heavy-duty motor also gives a more complete breakdown of the plant material.

A small seed grinder or coffee grinder (available in many kitchen shops) is handy for reducing small quantities of dry seeds, root slices, and leaves to fine powders. A small grinder usually yields a finer particle size than a blender, but it can only process a small amount of herbs or other materials.

Any food processor can be useful for shredding fresh roots, seeds, and leafy material.

Book VI

Natural Health

Pots and pans

To simmer roots, barks, and flowers, you need a pot or pan. You may want to use different kinds of pots and pans, such as the following, for making different kinds of herbal products:

- **Quality stainless steel pot:** Works nicely for making herbal products. Use one with a heat-dispersing handle.

- **Pyrex glass:** Great for cooking herbs and herbal oils.

- **Coffee pots made of quality, heat-resistant glass:** Excellent for making tea because you can see the color of the tea and judge the strength of the tea by its color.

- **A double boiler (see Figure 2-1):** Useful for melting wax and other ingredients without overheating or scorching them.

- **A crockpot that allows the temperature to be set to about 100 degrees:** Good for making herbal oils because it keeps the oil warm, thereby increasing the extraction rate and concentration of the herbs in the final oil.

Jars and containers

You can find a wide variety of jars and containers for your herbal products. Think about obtaining the following types:

- **1- or 2-quart canning jars:** For extraction and storing herbs. The rubber seal keeps oxygen out, preserving the freshness of the herbs. (***Note:*** Some stores sell 1-gallon jars for larger extraction batches.)

✔ **1-, 2-, or 4-ounce Boston amber round bottles with droppers:** For tinctures. These bottles (shown in Figure 2-2) are available from pharmacies and herb shops.

✔ **1-ounce salve jars or tins:** For salves and creams.

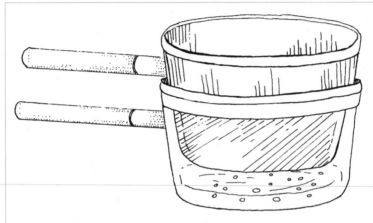

Figure 2-1:
A double boiler maintains the desired heat level when making infused oils and salves.

Figure 2-2:
Boston amber rounds are convenient for storing liquid herbal products.

You can make labels for your products by hand, on your printer at home, or by visiting a local printing shop. Labels for your laser or ink-jet printer are available in an amazing variety of shapes and sizes from an office supply store or paper-goods catalog.

A food dehydrator

A food dehydrator is a good investment for the home herbal product maker because you can

- Use it to dry flowers, leaves, root slices, and other herb parts quickly and still preserve valuable active plant chemicals and color.
- Make potent extracts of both dried and powdered teas.
- Dry kitchen spices, such as oregano and basil.

Miscellaneous tools

Following is a list of other useful items you may need to make herbal products:

- **Mortar and pestle:** A mortar and pestle is a traditional device used to grind small quantities of herbs into a coarse or fine powder by hand. Reducing herbs to a powder speeds up the extraction process (the process of removing the active chemicals from plants).

- **Muslin, linen, or cheesecloth:** You can use these fine-mesh cloths to filter tinctures or oils, separating the spent herbs (that have all medicinal chemicals removed) from the finished oil or tincture.

- **Funnel:** A funnel is helpful for pouring finished oils or tinctures into small-mouthed bottles, such as a 1-ounce dropper bottle.

- **Scale:** A weighing scale (in grams or ounces) is essential if you want to keep track of exactly how much herb you used to make a batch of tincture or oil. Knowing the weight enables you to make your next batch stronger or weaker by adding more or less herbs to the same amount of liquid oil or alcohol/water blend. Keep good records by writing these amounts in a small notebook.

- **Candy thermometer:** A candy thermometer helps you know just when to turn the heat off from a batch of herbal candy (like horehound candy for coughs) and pour it into the molds. If you pour the liquid candy too early, before all the water is removed, your finished candy will be sticky.

- **Candy molds:** Candy molds are available in a variety of different shapes from kitchen shops. Plain, round ones are good because candies of that shape are easy to wrap with a little waxed paper and put into a small box to carry in your pocket or purse.

Stocking Your Pantry

To make herbal products such as tinctures, salves, or creams, you need a variety of supplies both to create the extract and then perhaps to thicken it. Be sure to stock the items listed in the following sections.

Oils

For making herbal oils, salves, and creams, buy good-quality oils that won't go rancid quickly. Try to avoid polyunsaturated oils (canola, sunflower, and safflower oils) because they're sensitive to heat and light and degrade rapidly. Store your oils in the refrigerator to avoid rancidity.

- **Sweet almond oil:** A light oil, less greasy than olive oil, and a favorite for making medicated oils. Almond oil is especially soothing, and it helps relieve dryness and itching.

- **Apricot kernel oil:** A light oil more delicate than almond and often more expensive. Apricot kernel oil is blended with almond or other oils at about 10 to 50 percent of the total to lighten it up. This oil is excellent to use if you have sensitive skin.

- **Avocado oil:** A heavy, long-lasting oil for the skin. Avocado oil contains vitamins for the skin and adds a rich, dark green color to salves, creams, and other products.

- **Carrot oil:** A light oil that slows aging of the skin.

- **Castor oil:** A heavy, highly therapeutic oil. The oil contains toxic protein-like compounds called *lectins,* which when applied to the skin are absorbed and stimulate a local immune response to help break down a tumor or cyst. Use up to 20 percent in an oil blend.

- **Cocoa butter:** Obtained from the cocoa bean and used in lotion, cream, lip balm, and soap. Cocoa butter contains highly saturated fatty acids, so it's heavy and resists rancidity. It also smells of chocolate, which is good news to chocolate lovers.

   If you find the smell of cocoa butter overwhelming, use no more than 15 to 20 percent in your product.

- **Coconut oil:** Tropical oil that's semisolid at room temperature. Use it to thicken your creams and other skin products and to give them body. Coconut oil is one of the most stable oils and doesn't easily go rancid in your products.

✔ **Grapeseed oil:** An almost colorless, vitamin-rich oil that's easily absorbed. The oil is made from the seeds of the fruit. Grapeseed oil has a good texture, making it ideal for massage oils.

✔ **Olive oil:** The finest all-around oil for making medicated oils. What could be more natural than crushing the olives to release the nutritious and heart-friendly yellow-green oil? Many other oils require solvent extraction or heating during extraction, even when the product says *expeller-pressed* or *cold-pressed*. Olive oil stays fresh longer than other oils and is excellent for people with naturally dry skin.

Olive oil is a heavy oil that sometimes has a decided scent of olives. If the scent and oily feel are pleasant to you, fine — but they may make you feel like a walking salad.

✔ **Jojoba oil:** A wax that's traditionally used as a hair restorer but that's also an excellent moisturizer for dry skin. It's usually diluted by half with other oils for massage oils.

✔ **Palm kernel oil:** A heavy oil, containing mostly saturated fatty acids and a good quantity of vitamin A, which is a natural skin protector and cancer fighter. Add palm kernel oil to products to give them a thick, creamy feeling and to protect your skin.

Choose cold-pressed organic oils whenever they're available. Also, try using organic oils rather than commercial oils, which are made with harsh solvents that extract the oil from the seed mash.

Grain alcohol

Grain alcohol is absolutely the best solvent and delivery system to carry an herb's active constituents into the bloodstream. Vodka is the most effective distilled liquor for making tinctures or alcoholic herbal extracts. For home use, tinctures and elixirs can be made with 100-proof vodka, which is the most widely available. (Keep in mind that 100-proof vodka actually contains a little less than 50 percent ethanol by volume; 80-proof vodka contains a little less than 40 percent.)

Even better than vodka is pure grain alcohol, which is distilled from corn. Pure grain alcohol is 190-proof, or a little less than 95 percent pure alcohol. The reason it's not 100-percent pure is because absolutely pure alcohol always pulls some moisture from the air, and the solution stabilizes at 95 percent.

Other kinds of alcoholic beverages such as rum and brandy aren't ideal because they already contain coloring pigments, flavoring compounds, sugars, and other components.

Book VI

Natural Health

The proportion of alcohol to water is often adjusted in order to selectively pull out the desired constituents. For instance, resins such as bee propolis and the active constituents of milk thistle are only alcohol-soluble. Using a solvent with a high percentage of pure ethanol or grain alcohol yields the best extraction. For ginseng, which has active steroidlike compounds that are mostly water-soluble, you'd choose a solvent that contains a fairly low percentage of alcohol (45–50 percent alcohol to 50–55 percent water).

Glycerin

Good-quality glycerin from vegetable sources is widely available in natural-foods stores and pharmacies. Glycerin adds body and a little sweetness to herbal preparations such as cough syrups and elixirs. It's often added to creams and helps bring oils and tinctures together in a smooth, easy-to-apply blend. For folks who like taking a liquid herbal product but don't want alcohol, glycerin can dissolve certain plant constituents and act as a reasonably good preservative. Many flavored herbal glycerites, especially those for children, are available in natural-foods stores and herb stores. These products are helpful for parents who want a good-tasting, liquid preparation that's easy to disguise in juice. In these products, flavorful essential oils like orange or cinnamon are often added to the glycerin and herb blends.

On the downside, glycerin isn't as good a solvent or preservative as alcohol. Further, glycerin can be drying and irritating to the mucous membranes when used undiluted — as can alcoholic preparations. Finally, glycerin isn't as effective a carrier of the active herbal constituents into the body as alcohol.

All in all, glycerites are recommended only for children or for people who can't take any alcohol.

Beeswax

Beeswax is used to harden salves and creams and turn them into a suitable consistency. Here's what you want to look for when purchasing beeswax:

- ✔ Wax that's pure and free from chips of paint, dirt, rocks, and dead insect parts. (Hives may be painted with lead-based paint.)
- ✔ Wax that's a light amber color and has the delightful fragrance of honey with a slightly gluey smell.

You can buy beeswax at your local hobby shop, herb shop, or natural-foods store. Some grocery stores also carry it. Or you can try looking in the yellow pages of your phone book under "beekeepers" for sources of good beeswax.

Essential oils

You can achieve an appealing, inviting smell in your herbal body products through the use of *essential oils,* which are extracts of plants containing essential oils. Try the citrus family members (orange, lemon, and grapefruit), mints (peppermint and spearmint), wintergreen, and lavender.

Miscellaneous ingredients

Other items you may need for making herbal products include

- **Honey,** which is soothing to the throat and is a common ingredient in herbal cough syrups and throat lozenges.

- **Brown rice syrup,** which is available in natural-foods stores and is used in the same ways as honey. It's less sweet with more complex sugars. Brown rice syrup is a good choice if you have diabetes or another blood sugar imbalance.

- **Ascorbic acid,** which is also known as vitamin C powder. It acts as a mild preservative for herbal creams.

- **Borax,** which is a natural substance (commonly used for washing clothes) that you can use to help oily and watery ingredients mix together. It makes your herbal creams creamy.

Making Teas

Blending an herbal tea is a pleasant, healthy ritual that encourages you to slow down a little and smell the herbs — no capsule or tablet can do that! The next few sections show you how to prepare different herbal teas.

Infusions

Infusions are a simple way of preparing tea from leaves and flowers. To make an infusion, do the following:

1. **Pour boiling water over the herb and let it steep, covered, for 10 to 15 minutes.**

   Use 1 teaspoon herb per cup of water.

2. Pour the tea through a strainer into a teacup.

You can also store your herb tea in the refrigerator for two to three days.

Herbs commonly used for infusions include peppermint, chamomile, lemon balm, raspberry leaf, and red clover.

An Infusion of Calmness

This combination of herbs is formulated to infuse a feeling of calmness throughout your body and spirit. Drink a cup several times a day, or just before bed.

Preparation time: 20 minutes

Yield: 4 cups

4 cups boiling water	3 teaspoons passion flower
3 teaspoons linden flower	3 teaspoons orange peel
3 teaspoons chamomile herb	½ teaspoon stevia herb
3 teaspoons eleuthero root	

1 Pour the boiling water over the herbs, roots, flowers, and peels and cover the pan.

2 Let the brew steep for 15 minutes.

3 Strain the mixture and serve.

Elderflower Tea

Elderflower tea makes a good-tasting beverage with gentle cleansing power. Drink a cup or two several times a day to assist your body in getting rid of toxic waste products when you're going through a healing crisis or any time you want an easy yet efficient cleansing of your system.

Preparation time: 20 minutes

Yield: 4 cups

4 cups water	4 tablespoons dried elderflower

1 Boil the water in a covered pan.

2 Turn off the heat, add the elderflower, and allow it to steep (covered) for 15 minutes.

3 Strain the mixture and store what you don't use in the refrigerator.

Vary It! *Try adding a teaspoon of stevia (often referred to as "the sweet herb") to every 4 tablespoons of elderflower for extra sweetness.*

Decoctions

A *decoction* is a method of extracting the heavier and denser parts of plants such as roots, barks, and twigs. To make a decoction, do the following:

1. **Add 1 tablespoon of an herb or herb mixture (coarsely chopped or ground) to each cup of boiling water and simmer.**

   Thin barks, like willow bark, need only 15 or 20 minutes of gentle simmering. Thicker chunks of root, like ginseng, need 1 hour of simmering to extract all the active constituents.

2. **Turn off the heat and let the mixture steep for 15 minutes or so until it's cool enough to handle.**

3. **Pour the mixture through a strainer and add the herb residue to your compost pile.**

Herbs generally made as a decoction include licorice, yellow dock, dandelion root, and ginseng root.

Tonic herbs and herb formulas support and nourish your body systems. Take tonic teas for three to nine months to receive the full effects. Take the herbs daily for maximum benefits. Don't use tonic herbs during an acute infection. Begin again after the main part of the infection is over to bolster your immune system.

Decoctions are a time-honored way of using tonic herbs. In China, decoctions of the tonic herb dong quai are used as a base to make vegetable chicken soups. The vegetables, grains, and chicken take on the medicinal qualities of the herb. By eating the soup, you get all the benefits of the food *and* the medicinal effects of the dong quai, such as building the blood, increasing energy levels, and strengthening the uterus.

Immune Vitali-Tea

This decoction can be used daily for six to nine months to strengthen your natural defenses against colds, flu, and other diseases. Drink 1 cup, morning and evening.

Preparation time: *1½ hours*

Yield: *4 cups*

3 to 4 sticks astragalus root	*1 tablespoon burdock root*
1 tablespoon ligustrum	*1 teaspoon licorice*
3 to 4 roots codonopsis (about 4–5 inches long)	*5 cups water*

1 Simmer all the herbal ingredients in the water for 30 to 60 minutes.

2 Turn off the heat and let the tea steep (covered) for an additional 15 minutes.

3 Strain and pour into a quart jar for storage in the refrigerator.

Light decoctions

For lighter barks and hard leaves, or to remove heavier compounds from leaves and flowers, make a *light decoction* by doing the following:

1. **Place the herbs in water and simmer on the lowest heat possible, covered, for 10 to 15 minutes.**

   Use 2 tablespoons of the herb per 1 cup of water.

2. **Turn off the heat and let the mixture steep (covered) for an additional 10 to 15 minutes.**

3. **Strain the entire mixture and drink. Store whatever's left in the refrigerator — it keeps for up to three days.**

Pass-on-Gas Tea

This delicious tea is a favorite with many people for preventing gas after meals, as well as helping to ease gas pains and abdominal discomfort. Drink ½ to 1 cup of the tea after meals to help relieve that feeling of fullness.

Preparation time: *25 minutes*

Yield: *3 cups*

4 cups water	*1 teaspoon caraway seed*
1 teaspoon cumin seed	*1 teaspoon orange peel*
1 teaspoon fennel seed	*½ teaspoon licorice root*

1 Bring the water to a boil and add the herbs. Simmer in the water, covered, for 10 minutes.

2 Remove from the heat and steep the mixture (covered) for another 10 to 15 minutes.

3 Strain the mixture. Drink immediately, or store for later use.

Vary It! *After you turn the heat off, add 2 teaspoons of peppermint leaf.*

Mastering the Art of Tincture-Making

Tinctures are made by grinding up dry or fresh herbs in a solvent of alcohol and water or glycerin. Tinctures have several advantages over other types of herbal products. Their medicinal properties are easily absorbed by the body; they have a long shelf life (up to three years); they act quickly on your body; and they're easy to use — 1-ounce bottles fit in your pocket. The usual process for making a tincture is as follows:

1. **Place the herbs in a blender and add the solvent.**

   A tincture is made with five parts solvent liquid volume to one part herb by dry weight.

   See the earlier "Stocking Your Pantry" section for tips on choosing a solvent.

2. **Blend at high speed until smooth.**

3. **Place the mixture in a warm area that's out of direct sunlight.**

4. **Shake daily for at least two weeks.**

5. **Squeeze any liquid out through a linen cloth or press it out with a hydraulic press, such as a cider press.**

6. **Filter the remaining mixture, if desired.**

7. **Compost or discard the spent herb (the marc).**

You can add more dry herb to the solvent to make a stronger tincture. Keep adding the herb to the liquid and blend. After soaking, the herb settles out. Keep at least ½ inch of pure solvent over the herb. If the herb sticks up out of the solvent at any time, your tincture may ferment and produce an off flavor.

One teaspoonful (about 5 droppersful) of a tincture has approximately the same potency as one strong cup of tea. The average adult dose of most tinctures is about 1 to 3 droppersful, two to three times daily, for health maintenance and about twice that (4 to 6 droppersful, four to five times daily) for a therapeutic dose when you're treating a specific medical condition. Adjust the dose for children according to age and weight.

Store tinctures in amber bottles to minimize the adverse effects of sunlight on their important medicinal components. They can keep their potency for up to three years if you store them in a cool place away from heat and light.

Put 1 teaspoon of the tincture in 1 cup of warm water to make an instant tea — even when you're on the move and away from your kitchen.

Echinacea Leaf and Flower Tincture

This widely used tincture helps strengthen the body's natural defenses. Use it to prevent and help heal colds, flu, respiratory ailments, urinary tract infections, and other types of infections.

Preparation time: *10 minutes*

Yield: *6 ounces*

1½ ounces dried echinacea leaves (and flowers if available)

½ cup grain alcohol (or 100-proof vodka)

½ cup distilled water

1 Combine the echinacea, alcohol, and water in a blender.

2 Blend for about 1 to 2 minutes, or until smooth.

3 Pour into a quart canning jar or other suitable container.

4 Shake the blend vigorously for 1 minute every day for two weeks. Be sure to keep the mixture out of sunlight and in a warm place.

5 Press or squeeze the blend through a piece of linen or other fine cloth.

6 Transfer the finished tincture to an amber dropper bottle. Keep away from heat and light; refrigeration isn't necessary.

Vary It! *If you prefer a stronger echinacea tincture with more of a bite, add echinacea root to the leaves and flowers. Use the roots only for the most potent tincture; the leaves and flowers are potent enough for most situations.*

The best herbs to make into tinctures

Herbalists choose some herbs over and over again for use in making tinctures. These herbs are usually more potent in tincture form than in teas.

- **Orange peel, stevia, and licorice:** These are great flavoring herbs to add to any of your tinctures. Orange tincture eases digestive discomforts, helps relieve gas pains, and has a mildly calming effect. Stevia helps you manage an out-of-control sweet tooth. Licorice soothes your stomach and digestive tract.

- **Ginkgo:** It's used to improve memory, enhance mental function, and increase circulation to your legs.

- **Milk thistle:** Made from the seeds, milk thistle tincture has a protective and rebuilding effect on your liver.

- **Valerian:** It's probably the most popular herb for inducing sleep and relaxation.

- **Kava:** This herb helps to relax your muscles and improve sleep.

- **American ginseng:** It counteracts stress and helps support adrenal function.

- **Goldenseal/barberry:** Goldenseal is popular for easing infections of the sinuses, bladder, intestines, and respiratory tract. Goldenseal is endangered in some states because of overharvesting. For this reason, use only 10- to 20-percent goldenseal along with 80- to 90-percent barberry root, Oregon grape root, or coptis root (a Chinese herb). These herbs all have the same active principles as goldenseal.

- **Ginger:** This hot, spicy tincture helps to ease an upset stomach and promotes good digestion.

- **Dong quai:** One of the most popular herbs of all time, dong quai has a general strengthening effect on your energy and helps build healthy blood. For women, dong quai has a building effect on the uterus.

- **St. John's wort:** This is a popular herb for lifting your mood and helping to ease mild to moderate depression.

Do fresh or dry herbs make a more potent tincture?

Whether to use fresh herbs or dry ones is a debate that rages on among herbalists. Some contend that a number of herbs are more potent when tinctured fresh. This claim has been disproven by laboratory tests — most herbs make a more potent extract when extracted or tinctured freshly dried. *Freshly dried* means that the plants are harvested at the peak of perfection (in full flower, in the fall for roots, and so on), and then carefully dried in the shade. If these herbs are tinctured within two to three weeks of drying and are kept away from heat and light, they can be called freshly dried.

You can find exceptions, however — sensitive herbs (chickweed, gotu kola, cleavers, and the roots of *Echinacea angustifolia*) are best when tinctured fresh, not freshly dried. For tincturing fresh, undried herbs, add the plant material to the solvent and blend well until you have only about 1/2 to1 inch of clear liquid over the settled solid material.

Preparing Herbal Cough Syrup

Herbal cough syrups are sweet and thick and contain concentrates of herbs that help soothe inflamed tissues, calm coughs, fight infections, and eliminate thick, clogging mucus. You can buy a number of herbal cough syrups from your local herb store or pharmacy, but you can't find one that's as effective as the following classic: Horehound Hack-Free Cough Syrup.

Horehound Hack-Free Cough Syrup

Ever had a hacking cough that kept you up at night? This classic horehound recipe is similar to ones available commercially. But although commercial products contain horehound, sage, and wild cherry bark, they don't work nearly as well as this formula. They just don't have enough horehound or sage in them to do the job.

Preparation time: *1½ hours*

Yield: *2½ cups*

¼ ounce mullein	*¼ ounce wild cherry bark*
¼ ounce echinacea	*4 cups water*
⅛ ounce sage	*2 cups honey*
1/16 ounce horehound	*7 drops orange essential oil*
¼ ounce orange peel	*3 drops eucalyptus oil*
⅛ ounce licorice root	*3 drops peppermint essential oil*

1 Combine the herbs and water in a pot and simmer on low heat for 10 minutes.

2 Turn off the heat and steep (covered) for 20 minutes. Strain the mixture and return it to the pot.

3 Simmer the strained tea uncovered on low heat for 30 to 60 minutes, until approximately ½ cup of liquid remains.

4 Stir in the honey, orange oil, eucalyptus oil, and peppermint oil.

5 After the mixture cools, pour it into a bottle and store it in the refrigerator. Your syrup should last for a month or two.

Vary It! If the syrup tastes too strong for you or your kids, add another ½ cup of honey and more orange essential oil.

Producing Elixirs

Elixirs are a combination of an alcohol-based tincture and honey, raw sugar, maple syrup, or another sweetener. Good-tasting elixirs are made to help moderate the bitter taste of certain herbs for children and adults.

High-Energy Elixir

This herbal elixir combines some of the best energy herbs, nerve-support herbs, adrenal-support herbs, and antistress herbs, as well as, optionally, a small amount of a stimulant. Take 1 teaspoon twice daily to help increase energy and reduce stress.

Preparation time: *10 minutes*

Yield: *½ cup*

½ cup honey

½ cup barley malt

1 ounce eleuthero (Siberian ginseng) tincture

½ ounce red ginseng tincture

1 ounce gotu kola tincture

1 ounce wild oats tincture

Green tea (optional mild stimulant herb)

10 drops orange essential oil

1 Pour the honey and barley malt into a blender. Add the tinctures (and green tea, if you choose) and blend well.

2 With the blender running, add the orange essential oil.

Vary It! Substitute cinnamon, peppermint, or grapefruit oil for the orange essential oil.

If you can't find readymade tinctures, or if you find them too expensive, you can make your own (see the section "Mastering the Art of Tincture-Making" earlier in this chapter).

Concocting Creams

Creams are light and moisturizing and are made by blending distilled water or a water-based herbal extract (such as rosewater or a simmered-down tea concentrate) with oily ingredients (such as almond oil, cocoa butter, or beeswax) at high speed — just like you make mayonnaise. You can make a simmered-down tea concentrate by making a decoction of an herb (see the "Decoctions" section earlier in this chapter), filtering out the herb after simmering for 30 minutes to 1 hour, and simmering for another hour or two until the tea is reduced to about 10 percent of its original volume.

Creams can be astringent, moisturizing, antifungal, or antibacterial. They can also speed up healing of wounds, burns, abrasions, and cuts. To prevent contaminating a cream in the preparation process, wash your hands and all utensils in an antiseptic soap beforehand.

You can extend the life of homemade creams with these practical:

- ✓ **Prohibit mold growth through refrigeration.** Herbal preparations that are made with water are susceptible to mold growth after a few weeks (even less in a warm climate). Keeping your cream in the refrigerator extends its life by up to three times.

- ✓ **Add life-extending ingredients.** If your cream contains at least $1/2$ teaspoon of any of the following, it'll last up to six months without refrigeration:

  - Rosewater or other aromatic herb water

  - Tincture

  - A preservative such as grapefruit seed extract, citric acid, vitamin C, or vitamin E

- ✓ **Boost the vitamin content.** Vitamins C and E make a good preservative combination. They work well together to preserve both the oily and watery parts of the cream. Plus, vitamin C helps vitamin E extend its antioxidant properties, preventing the oils in your creams from going rancid.

Fabulous Moisturizing Cream

This cream adds moisture to the skin, preventing chapping and drying.

Preparation time: *30 minutes*

Yield: *8 ounces*

Oil-Soluble Ingredients (Oily Phase)

1 ounce coconut oil

4 ounces almond oil

1 ounce beeswax

10 to 20 drops essential oil, such as lavender or rose

Water-Soluble Ingredients (Watery Phase)

2 ounces distilled water, rosewater, or orangewater

2 ounces glycerin

1 teaspoon borax

½ teaspoon vitamin C powder

Eight 1-ounce salve jars

1 Melt the coconut oil, almond oil, and beeswax together in a pan. Set aside to cool. After the mixture cools for 15 minutes, add the essential oil.

2 In a separate pan, combine the water, glycerin, borax, and vitamin C powder and heat the mixture over low heat until warm.

3 Place the water mixture in a blender and blend at high speed for 30 to 60 seconds. Remove the small inset top from the blender cover and slowly drizzle the oil mixture (from Step 1) through hole while blending.

4 Blend until the cream is well-mixed; then pour it into the jars.

5 Let the cream cool before capping and labeling the jars.

*Tip: Keep the temperature of the oily phase and the watery phase as identical as possible —
160 to 175 degrees is about right. After pouring your cream into the jars, avoid capping until
the cream is completely cool; otherwise, the watery phase is more likely to separate.*

Book VI

Natural Health

Quick and Easy Aromatherapy Cream

If you don't feel inclined to start completely from scratch, try your hand at this cream. It's easy to make, and you can customize it by adding your favorite essential oils. Try substituting your favorite commercial facial or skin cream for the unscented cream to make a fragrant or healing herbal facial or skin cream.

Preparation time: *30 minutes*

Yield: *4 ounces*

4 ounces unscented cream

15 to 20 drops essential oil (rosemary, lavender, orange, myrrh, or cedar)

1 Place the container of unscented cream in hot water (about 100 degrees) until it becomes a liquid. Alternatively, you can spoon the cream into the top of a double boiler and slowly heat it until it turns liquid.

2 Add one or more of the essential oils.

3 Stir all ingredients together, allow to cool, and return the cream to the original container.

Vary It! *Try the following variations:*

  ✔ *Add thyme or tea tree oil for treating cuts, infections, and fungus.*

  ✔ *Stir in rosemary oil, ¹/₂ teaspoon St. John's wort oil, and vitamin E to protect the skin from sun damage.*

  ✔ *Blend in a little cayenne powder and rosemary oil for sore muscles.*

  ✔ *Add ¹/₂ teaspoon arnica oil and ¹/₂ teaspoon rosemary oil for strains and sprains.*

  ✔ *Blend in ¹/₂ teaspoon peppermint oil and 1 teaspoon St. John's wort oil to help cool the itching and burning of rashes, for example from poison ivy or poison oak.*

  ✔ *Add 2 teaspoons calendula cream to help protect your skin and prevent wrinkling.*

  ✔ *Blend in 2 tablespoons aloe vera gel to make a lotion from your cream that can help moisturize dry skin and help soothe and heal a sunburn.*

Creating Infused Herbal Oils for the Skin

Soaking — also called *macerating* — recently dried herbs in a vegetable oil makes a medicated herbal oil. The most popular herbal oils include arnica, St. John's wort, and calendula. Here's what you need to know about making and using these preparations for external use:

- ✔ Herbal oils are made by grinding the freshly dried herbs into a coarse powder and stirring them into an oil heated to about 100 degrees.

- ✔ The strongest oils are made by macerating the herbs for three to five days, stirring daily for a few minutes each day. If you don't have a crock-pot and are heating the oil on the stove, put the blend on first thing in the morning and take it off just before bedtime, giving the herbs a good 12 hours to macerate in the hot oil. Leave the burner on low, preferably on top of a heat diffuser. Stir the blend every few hours.

- ✔ Add essential oils with antibacterial, antifungal, and blood circulation–stimulating properties, such as rosemary, thyme, lavender, or tea tree.

- ✔ Herbal oils can be used to help soothe rashes, sunburns, and other skin irritation and to help ease the pain of strains, sprains, and sore muscles while speeding healing. Apply the oils liberally to the affected areas, twice daily. The oils have the added benefit of lubricating the skin and helping prevent it from drying out.

Herbal oils are a good place to start when making medicinal herbal products for external use because they're a key component in creams, lotions, salves, and ointments, and you can make them quickly and easily.

To make an herbal oil, first decide which of these medicated oils works best for your needs. Several are popular, and each has its own benefits.

- ✔ **St. John's wort oil:** A beautiful red oil that's effective for easing the pain and inflammation of burns, stings, rashes, bites, and scrapes. A recipe for making your own St. John's wort oil is given later in this chapter, or you can buy it at natural-foods stores.

- ✔ **Tea tree oil:** A strong antiseptic oil that helps quell infections of all kinds. Apply a few drops with a cotton swab. The preparation works well for athlete's foot.

Book VI

Natural Health

✔ **Ginger oil:** Add 2 or 3 drops of ginger and lavender essential oil to a teaspoon of calendula oil and apply to minor burns to help speed up the healing process and relieve pain.

✔ **Eucalyptus, pennyroyal, and citronella:** Add 2 or 3 drops of each oil to a teaspoon of calendula oil (which also repels insects) and brush lightly on clothing to repel mosquitoes and other biting insects.

Brush the repellant oil only on materials that the oil won't stain.

St. John's Wort Oil

The golden yellow flowers of St. John's wort appear at the height of summer, about June 24, which is traditionally St. John's Day. This oil has been made with similar recipes for more than 2,000 years.

This is a favorite oil to have in the medicine chest and to take along on trips for easing the pain and speeding healing of many kinds of injuries to the skin, joints, and nerves.

Preparation time: *20 minutes*

Yield: *8 ounces*

1½ cups St. John's wort flowers
2 cups olive (preferred), almond, or apricot oil

1 Coarsely grind up the flowers in a blender.

2 Add the oil and blend until smooth.

3 Pour the blend into a quart jar or other container and place in a warm spot out of direct sunlight.

4 Shake vigorously for 1 minute every day for two to three weeks.

5 Press out the oil through a fine strainer or cloth. If you want your oil to be completely clear, filter through an unbleached coffee filter. Bottle for use.

Note: If after two weeks of maceration, your St. John's wort oil is pink rather than a rich red color, set it in bright sunlight for one or two days to see whether it changes color. If it's still pale, press out the herbs and blend another batch of dried herbs with the oil. Let the new batch of herbs soak for another two weeks; then press the herbs out again through a fine strainer or cloth. If the oil still isn't red, then the flowers were of poor quality. Try to harvest or buy another batch of St. John's wort and repeat the process, or use the product anyway, with the awareness that it isn't as strong. The best flowers you can use are ones you harvest from your garden or local wild area. If you use fresh or freshly dried herbs (see the sidebar "Do fresh or dry herbs make a more potent tincture?"), you can make a deep red oil.

When you're short on time, you can easily create medicated herbal oils for your individual needs by buying readymade herbal oils such as arnica, calendula, and St. John's wort and adding a few drops of your choice of essential oils.

Muscle Pain Oil

Use this wonderful oil whenever you've overworked your muscles and need some relief.

Preparation time: 5 minutes

Yield: 1 ounce

¹/₃ ounce arnica oil   10 drops essential oil of wintergreen

²/₃ ounce St. John's wort oil

1 Combine all ingredients in a covered container and shake vigorously for 1 minute.

2 Apply as needed to aching muscles.

Book VI

Natural
Health

Making Massage Oils

If you can't afford regular massages, take a class on how to give them and trade massages with a friend. Massage shows you where you're holding tension and helps you let it go, thereby freeing up energy and reducing pain.

Create an aromatherapy massage by adding essential oils to a fixed oil such as sweet almond oil. An aromatherapy massage promotes circulation and is a popular, pleasant way to receive the healing and aromatic benefits of essential oils.

 After receiving an aromatherapy massage, you may want to wait three or four hours before showering in order to give the oils time for complete absorption.

Make your own massage oil by adding your choice of essential oil or oils to a carrier oil, such as sweet almond, grapeseed, or apricot kernel. Favorite oils for massage include vanilla, chamomile, rose, and lavender. Feel free to experiment and blend different oils to create your own special formulas.

 Ten drops of essential oils for every ounce of oil makes a mildly scented oil. If you add too much oil, your massage oil can have an annoying smell.

Heaven-Scent Massage Oil

If you don't have any specific ideas about your ideal essential oil massage blend, try this wonderful, relaxing massage oil to help reduce tension and the pain of sore muscles.

Preparation time: *20 minutes*

Yield: *4 ounces*

30 drops lavender essential oil	*15 drops rosemary essential oil*
25 drops chamomile essential oil	*3 ounces almond oil*
15 drops ginger essential oil	*1 ounce St. John's wort oil*

1 In a covered container, add the essential oils to the almond oil and St. John's wort oil; shake well.

2 Place a small amount in the palm, rub into both palms and fingers, and then massage evenly into the body.

3 After the massage, leave the therapeutic oil on the body for at least 30 minutes before showering or rubbing off with a towel. If you have the time, leave it on for up to 4 hours for complete absorption.

Aromatherapy Baths: A Stirring Experience

After a long, tiring day, few activities are as luxurious and relaxing as soaking in a hot bath — especially when you add healing essential oils. Bathing with essential oils is an effective method for opening up congested pores and easing muscle tension as you breathe the vapors and absorb the oils through the skin. Bathing with essential oils also relaxes your tired body, quiets your mind, and calms the spirit. Soak long enough, though, because you need approximately 10 to 20 minutes for essential oils to reach the bloodstream.

Customize your essential oil bath according to your desires at the moment. Whether you're feeling tense after a long day or having trouble sleeping, try taking a lavender bath, preferably by candlelight, just before you go to bed. Lavender is the premiere plant scent for relaxing and uplifting the spirits.

To avoid evaporation of the oils, add them when the tub is full, close the door and windows to keep the aromatic steam in, and then get right into the bath.

To dilute strong essential oils and help prevent hot water from drying your skin, mix your essential oils with a small amount of fixed oil before putting them in the tub. A good blend is 5 to 10 drops of one or more essential oils for every teaspoon of almond oil or apricot kernel oil. Mix it up in a tablespoon measure and add it right to the bath. You may want to make up 6 or 8 ounces of your favorite blend to have it ready and waiting.

Try these healing and relaxing aromatherapy baths:

- ✔ **Colds and flu:** Eucalyptus, thyme, lemon, and rosemary
- ✔ **Depression:** Lavender, basil, lemon balm, rose, neroli, patchouli, and clary sage
- ✔ **Nervousness:** Geranium, lavender, clary sage, lemon balm, and orange
- ✔ **Pain:** Rosemary, chamomile, cayenne oil, and ginger
- ✔ **Stimulating, energizing bath:** Rosemary, bergamot, and lime
- ✔ **Stress:** Neroli, lavender, and chamomile
- ✔ **Tense muscles:** Rosemary, marjoram, lavender, and chamomile

For a foot or hand bath, add 4 to 8 drops of oil to a bowl filled with warm water and stir the water to mix the oils. Soak feet or hands for 15 minutes and relax.

Bath Salts

Bath salts dissolve into the bath and help soften your skin while you enjoy the therapeutic benefits of an aromatic bath.

Preparation time: *5 minutes*

Yield: *3 cups*

¹/₂ cup Epsom salts	*¹/₂ cup powdered milk*
2¹/₄ cups sea salt or table salt	*¹/₂ teaspoon lavender or rosemary essential oil (or a combination of the two)*

1 Bottle the ingredients and let them stand for a week to ten days.

2 Add ¹/₄ cup of bath salts to your bath and enjoy!

Formulating a Hair Rinse

When you apply apple cider vinegar to your hair, you're using a time-honored rinse that removes excess oil, dust, and flakes of skin, while gently preventing bacteria growth.

Rosemary Hair Rinse

The rosemary oil in this recipe makes a rinse that improves the health and nutrition of the hair follicles while leaving your hair smelling inviting and fresh.

Preparation time: *5 minutes*

Yield: *4 cups*

2 cups apple cider vinegar	*10 drops rosemary essential oil*
2 cups distilled water	

1 Blend rosemary essential oil with the apple cider vinegar and water to make a hair rinse.

2 Work the rinse into your hair thoroughly after shampooing and then rinse with pure water.

Savoring Sprays and Mists

The scent of a fresh apple pie baking in the oven is an inviting scent that everyone appreciates. Other odors, like that six-day-old burrito forgotten in a corner of the refrigerator or certain bathroom odors you'd rather forget, aren't so pleasant. Commercial air fresheners, however, are often worse than the smell you want to cover — the heavy chemical smell of artificial flowers created in the laboratory does little to create a pleasant fragrance. Try making an herbal air freshener instead.

Nature Scent Freshener

You can easily make your own air freshener or spray disinfectant with a few essential oils, a spray bottle, and distilled water.

Preparation time: *5 minutes*

Yield: 6 ounces

4 ounces distilled water

1 tablespoon rubbing alcohol or grain alcohol

1 teaspoon orange essential oil

1 teaspoon grapefruit essential oil

1 teaspoon lemon essential oil

1 teaspoon lime essential oil

1 Combine the water, alcohol, and oils in a plant mister spray bottle and shake vigorously.

2 Spray the scented mist into the air to make a pleasant change in the atmosphere and give your nose a break.

Vary It! *Vary the Nature Scent Freshener in the following ways:*

> ✔ *Alter the proportions of the essential oils to produce different scents.*
>
> ✔ *For a more woodsy smell, add cedarwood or pine.*
>
> ✔ *Add antibacterial and antifungal oils such as thyme, eucalyptus, pine, juniper, sage, and tea tree oil (or a combination of these), to use around toilets, sinks, and other areas you want to disinfect.*

Book VI

Natural Health

Facial Mist

When traveling by air, try a spritz or two of this refreshing and uplifting facial mist after take-off or when you feel like you've been stuffed into a stale, oxygen-starved cabin too long.

Preparation time: 10 minutes

Yield: 2 ounces

1 drop rose essential oil

1 drop jasmine essential oil

2 drops neroli essential oil

1 ounce distilled water

1 ounce aloe vera

1 Combine the essential oils, water, and aloe vera in a small spray bottle.

2 Shake vigorously before use.

Vary It! *Try a combination of lemon, lavender, grapefruit, or rosemary for combating stale air and fatigue.*

Vary It! *For a cooling sunburn mist, try 9 drops lavender oil, 2 drops peppermint oil, and 1 drop spearmint oil with the water and aloe vera. Mist lightly over sunburned skin.*

Producing Potpourris

Potpourris are flowers and flower petals impregnated with aromatic oils. Potpourris are pretty to look at in dishes and pleasant to smell. Available in gift shops and department stores as well as natural-foods stores, scented potpourris are quite popular.

Creating your own potpourris is easy and fun and allows you the option of using pure essential oils. Make simple potpourris for your living room or bathroom by combining rose petals sprinkled with rose oil or lavender flowers sprinkled with lavender oil. Add ¹/₂ teaspoon essential oil for every 2 cups of flowers or herbs.

Rose Petal Potpourri

Here's a recipe for a brightly colored potpourri that you can vary to suit your individual taste. The orris root powder is used as a *fixative,* an herb that makes fragrances last longer.

Preparation time: *5 minutes*

Yield: *About 4 cups*

4 cups mixed dried herbs (choose from lavender, roses, calendula flowers, rosemary leaves, rose hips, lemon verbena leaves, and so on)	*4 tablespoons orris root powder*
	1 teaspoon essential oils of your choice (rose, lavender, geranium, orange, and so on)

1 Combine the ingredients in a zip-top plastic bag.

2 Shake the ingredients lightly for a moment.

3 Let sit for seven to ten days to allow the essential oils to be absorbed.

4 Pour the contents of the bag into a small, decorative bowl and place it on the toilet tank, bathroom counter, kitchen counter, bedroom nightstand, or any place that you want to create a special mood with scent.

When the scent of your potpourri starts to fade, repeat the process with the essential oils.

To occasionally freshen your carpet, mix ¹/₂ cup baking soda with 60 drops lavender, 20 drops orange, and 20 drops cedar. Allow to stand for 24 hours and then sprinkle the mixture over the carpet. Let it sit for 15 minutes before vacuuming.

Making a Compress

An herbalist reported having worked with an 80-year-old female patient who looked 60, took care of her health, but was suffering because of a knee joint that had been replaced two years before and was still swollen, sore, and stiff. She was a dancer who liked to go out on Saturday nights, and the knee was cramping her style. She had tried steroid anti-inflammatories and other modern medicines with no luck, and her doctor told her, "Get used to it." So she sought the advice of an acupuncturist and herbalist, who gave her one of the most simple yet effective remedies ever devised — the ginger compress. The next time the herbalist saw the 80-year-old patient, she was walking much better and had become a big fan of the ginger compress. As she left the office, she asked him, "Do you dance?"

Ginger Oil Compress

Use this ginger oil compress for easing pain, soreness, swelling, and stiffness of arthritis, injuries, and operations. The compress also works well for sprains, strains, and even bruises.

Preparation time: *30 minutes*

Yield: *4 cups*

¼ cup fresh ginger root (sliced)

4 cups water

5 drops ginger essential oil (optional)

1 Simmer the ginger root with the water in a covered pot for 20 minutes. Add the ginger oil if you want a more potent compress and stir well.

2 Soak a washcloth in the hot gingery tea and wrap it around a tender or sore area, resoaking the cloth and applying several times before the tea cools. Repeat several times a day as time permits.

Vary It! *Submerge a washcloth in a bowl of water containing 10 to 20 drops of your favorite essential oil to make other aromatherapy compresses. Hot compresses are useful for muscular pain and cramp relief; cold compresses are useful for treating swelling or headache. Try chamomile, rosemary, or juniper for muscle pain; lavender for headache; and ginger for swelling.*

Simmering Your Own Salves

Salves are medicinal ointments made from an herbal oil and beeswax. (The beeswax helps thicken the salve, makes it more spreadable, and increases the time that it lasts on your skin, allowing the medicinal action of the herbs to have a greater effect.) A salve can be thin and creamy, a form that's known as an *ointment* and is placed in tubes or squeeze bottles for dispensing. It can also be of a harder consistency, which is placed in a salve jar or tin. Salves don't contain many water-soluble components that fungi and bacteria can feed on, so they tend to be more stable than creams.

Protective and Healing Salve

This salve is designed to reduce inflammation, speed healing, and lessen the possibility of infection with cuts, scrapes, and other injuries.

Preparation time: *30 minutes*

Yield: *5 ounces*

4 ounces herbal oil, such as St. John's wort oil

³/₄ ounce (by weight) beeswax

10 drops essential oil of your choice (lavender, orange, mint, or thyme)

Eight ¹/₂-ounce or four 1-ounce salve jars

1 Pour the herbal oil into a saucepan or double boiler and heat gently to about 100 degrees.

2 Grate the beeswax with a cheese grater and add it slowly to hot oil, stirring it in well.

3 Turn off the heat and allow the salve to cool in the pan for 5 minutes or so, but not so long that it gets so thick that you can't easily stir in your essential oils. The consistency of a milkshake is about right.

4 Add the essential oil to the mixture and stir.

5 Pour the hot salve into salve jars or other suitable containers.

6 When cool, cap and label for use.

Tip: *When the salve is nearly set, a small crater may appear in the middle of the surface. To remedy, add a small amount of hot salve to the hole. When the salve cools, it should have a smooth surface.*

Vary It! *You can use herbal oils made of calendula, arnica, or yarrow rather than St. John's wort. You can purchase these herbal oils readymade at a natural-foods or herb store. Calendula and arnica oils may also be available at pharmacies.*

Preparing Liniments

A *liniment* is a liquid herbal preparation with a base of alcohol and oil for external application. Liniments are used for sore muscles to reduce pain and stiffness, increase blood flow, and accelerate healing. To increase blood circulation, vigorously rub the liniment into the affected area. Liniments aren't meant for internal use.

Ease-Up Liniment

Book VI

**Natural
Health**

This liniment can help your muscles loosen up. It's good for soothing the pain and stiffness of arthritis and for easing the pain of minor strains and sprains. It's even great for sports buffs to use before or after a run or workout. Apply as needed to the injured area.

Preparation time: *5 minutes*

Yield: *5 ounces*

3 tablespoons castor oil

1 tablespoon glycerin

1 tablespoon cayenne tincture

20 drops ginger essential oil

10 drops cinnamon essential oil

¹⁄₂ cup vodka

1 Combine all ingredients in a blender and blend at high speed for 2 minutes.

2 Bottle for use.

Chapter 3

A to Z Guide to Common Herbs

In This Chapter

▶ Exploring the medicinal usage of common herbs

▶ Reviewing dosage suggestions

*F*or thousands of years, herbs have been safe and effective medicines. Today, modern science is accumulating an impressive body of research on several healing herbs. Although the research is still preliminary to many hard-nosed scientists, even skeptics agree that herbs may just be *the* medicine of the next century. This chapter lists more than 100 herbs with medicinal properties, alphabetized by their common names. Their Latin names appear in parentheses.

The information in this reference isn't intended as a substitute for expert medical advice or treatment. Because each individual is unique, a professional healthcare provider must diagnose conditions and supervise treatments for individual health problems. If you're under a doctor's care and receive advice that's contrary to the information provided in this reference, follow your doctor's advice.

Alfalfa (Medicago sativa L.)

Add alfalfa to your supplement regime to help prevent elevated cholesterol. You can also use it as a gentle substitute for estrogen after menopause. The herb may also have cancer-protective properties.

Dosage: Take 3 to 5 grams a day as tea or in capsules (5 to 10 double-ought capsules with meals), or make a decoction by simmering 1 teaspoon of the herb in 1 cup of water for 20 minutes. Drink 1 cup, two or three times daily.

Aloe Vera (Aloe spp.)

Use aloe resin to relieve constipation and sluggish or dry bowel movements. The liquid gel cleanses the bowels and helps clear the skin of acne and rashes. Use aloe gel for burns. Aloe is also currently used as a mild antiviral for people with AIDS and HIV.

Dosage: Take 10 to 300 milligrams per day of the resin, before bed, in capsules or tablets. You can add orange peel or fennel seed to reduce cramping. Follow the label instructions for the liquid gel.

Aloe resin can cause bowel cramping and diarrhea when you exceed the manufacturer's recommended dose.

Angelica (Angelica archangelica L.)

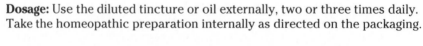

Use angelica to improve your appetite and assimilation of nutrients. Use the root and seeds for poor digestion and gas.

Dosage: Make a decoction with ½ to 1 teaspoon of the herb per 1 cup of water. Drink 1 cup three times daily, before meals, as a decoction, or take ½ to 1 teaspoon of the tincture in water, preferably before meals.

Avoid prolonged sunlight exposure and don't use during pregnancy.

Arnica (Arnica montana L.)

Use Arnica liniments and oils for joint and muscle inflammation, sprains, bruises, and varicose veins. Use arnica in homeopathic form for shock or trauma to body tissues, or after an accident.

Dosage: Use the diluted tincture or oil externally, two or three times daily. Take the homeopathic preparation internally as directed on the packaging.

Don't use on open wounds, because arnica can cause irritation. Don't use arnica preparations internally, except in homeopathic dilution.

Artichoke (Cynara scolymus L.)

Use artichoke leaf preparations for poor appetite, weak digestion, and weight loss. They're also good for gallbladder problems and high cholesterol.

Dosage: Make an infusion by simmering ½ cup of the dry or fresh leaves for every 2 cups of water for 5 minutes, then steeping for 15 minutes. Take ½ to 1 teaspoon of the tincture two to three times daily, preferably before meals. When using the dry extract, take 2 capsules before meals.

Astragalus (Astragalus membranaceus Bunge)

Astragalus, also known by its Chinese name, *Huang Qi* (pronounced *hwang-chee*), increases the body's resistance to disease. The root is an ingredient in many products targeting general immune weakness and digestive weakness with lack of appetite. It's also used as a supportive product — along with chemotherapy and radiation — for the treatment of cancer.

Dosage: You can chop up four or five astragalus sticks with a pair of scissors and decoct the herb for up to an hour in 4 cups of water, drinking 1 strong cup in the morning and 1 cup in the evening. Blend astragalus with other tonic herbs like poria to balance the herb's effects. Follow the directions on the bottle for capsules and tablets.

Avoid for about seven to ten days during an acute infection, such as the flu or a urinary tract infection. Otherwise, astragalus is safe. If you're taking astragalus for longer than two weeks, avoid the tincture form and instead take teas or dry extracts in capsule or tablet form.

Bilberry (Vaccinum myrtillus L.)

Use bilberry extracts to reduce capillary fragility, improve night vision, counteract diarrhea, and help relieve the pain and distension of varicose veins. Regular use of bilberry extract helps keep your eyes clear and youthful.

Dosage: Take 1 to 2 capsules of the standardized extract, twice daily.

Black Cohosh (Cimicifuga racemosa [L.] Nutt.)

Use black cohosh for hot flashes and menopausal depression; for rheumatism or sciatica; or as a muscle relaxant.

Dosage: Simmer 1 teaspoon of the cut and sifted herb for every cup of water and drink 1 cup decoction twice daily. Take 10 to 60 drops of the tincture two to three times daily, or 1 capsule or tablet of the standardized extract two times daily.

Avoid using this herb while pregnant or nursing without the advice of an herbalist. Don't use for a period longer than six months.

Black Walnut (Juglans nigra L.)

Use black walnut hull liquid tincture to prevent and slow diarrhea (especially the kind caused by intestinal parasites, such as giardia). Use black walnut preparations to help treat candida infections and gastrointestinal irritation.

Dosage: Take 1 to 3 droppersful of the tincture, or 2 to 3 capsules, three to five times daily, depending on the severity of your symptoms.

Don't use black walnut for more than a month at a time. Consult a qualified herbalist or physician if symptoms persist or are severe.

Bloodroot (Sanguinaria canadensis L.)

Use bloodroot to prevent plaque or treat gum problems. The rhizome extract is an ingredient in medicinal mouthwashes and toothpastes; it's also a component of many expectorants and cough syrups. The herb extract can treat skin cancers and fungal infections.

Dosage: Use ½ to 1 dropperful in 2 or 3 ounces of water as a mouth rinse, or follow the manufacturer's directions for using the mouthwash or toothpaste. Consult a qualified herbalist before attempting to use bloodroot to treat skin cancer. Apply a few drops of the tincture on a wart, or rub on ½ teaspoon of a commercial cream for athlete's foot.

Avoid using this herb during pregnancy. Don't exceed the recommended dose because doing so can strongly irritate the skin, throat, and intestines. Consult a physician for a diagnosis if you suspect you have a skin cancer lesion.

Blue Cohosh (Caulophyllum thalictroides L.)

Use blue cohosh for pain (especially the kind associated with menstruation, ovulation, and childbirth). Blend blue cohosh with black cohosh to help facilitate childbirth.

Dosage: Drink 1 cup of the decoction made by simmering ½ teaspoon for every cup of water, two to three times daily, preferably with a little orange peel or licorice to ease the harsh taste. Take 20 to 30 drops of the tincture three times daily in a little water or tea.

Avoid using this herb during pregnancy except in small amounts just prior to giving birth and under the supervision of a qualified health practitioner.

Burdock (Arctium lappa L.)

Use burdock (especially the seeds) for skin problems such as acne, eczema, and psoriasis. Use the root (called *gobo* in Japan) to help ease liver congestion and difficulty in digesting fats and to help protect against cancer. Use either the root or the seeds for rheumatism and arthritis.

Dosage: Make a decoction by simmering 1 teaspoon of the cut root, fresh or dried, for every cup of water for 30 minutes. Drink 1 cup of the decoction three times daily, around mealtimes. Slice one or two crisp, juicy fresh roots and add to a soup or stew. Take 3 droppersful of the tincture, two to three times daily.

Butcher's Broom (Ruscus aculeatus L.)

Use butcher's broom for varicose veins and hemorrhoids, as a liver regulator for jaundice, and for improving overall circulation and relieving edema.

Dosage: Make a light decoction by simmering 1 teaspoon of the herb for every cup of water for 15 minutes. Drink 1 cup, take 2 to 3 capsules with a little water, or take 20 to 40 drops of the tincture, two or three times daily.

Calendula (Calendula officinalis L.)

Use calendula internally (tea or tincture) for speeding the healing of ulcers in the digestive tract; easing gallbladder inflammation and enlarged, sore lymph glands; and treating measles and painful menstruation. Use calendula externally (cream or salve) to heal cuts, sunburns, skin cancers, diaper rash, sores, ulcers, varicose veins, chapped skin and lips, and insect bites. Calendula can also prevent infections after an operation.

Dosage: Use externally as needed. Drink 1 cup of the infusion made with a heaping teaspoon of the petals of chopped-up flower heads. Take 1 to 3 droppersful of the tincture in a little water, several times daily.

California Poppy (Eschscholzia californica Cham.)

Use poppy extracts to ease anxiety, nervousness, sleeplessness, stomach cramps, bronchial constriction, and toothaches. They can also be given to children with hyperactivity disorders rather than Ritalin; consult a qualified herbalist before using the herb for this purpose.

Dosage: Take 2 to 4 droppersful, or 1 teaspoon of the tincture in a little water or herbal tea as needed, up to three or four times daily.

Avoid using this herb while pregnant.

Caraway (Carum carvi L.)

Use caraway for easing colic, painful digestion, bloating, and a feeling of uncomfortable fullness after eating. Also use it to treat flatulence and diarrhea and to increase lactation. Caraway tea is safe for children and adults.

Dosage: You can make the infusion by steeping a heaping teaspoon of the seed for 15 to 20 minutes in freshly boiled water and drinking 1 cup, two or three times daily.

Cascara Sagrada (Rhamnus purshiana DC.)

Cascara relieves constipation and moistens the bowels for dry, hard bowel movements or nonmovements. It's also helpful as an addition to herbal formulas for gallstones and hemorrhoids.

Dosage: Take 2 to 4 capsules of the powdered herb, or 1 to 3 droppersful of the liquid tincture in a little water, before bedtime. For other kinds of extracts, follow the manufacturer's directions. You should experience a good bowel movement the next morning. If your cascara preparation doesn't work, try increasing the dose by 50 percent for a few days. If constipation persists, see your herbalist.

Avoid using this herb if you're pregnant, when you have persistent pain or obstruction of the intestines, or if you have a history of kidney stones. Children under age 12 should use the herb no longer than one week. Sensitive people who start with more than the recommended dose may experience diarrhea and bowel cramps. Reduce your dose by 50 percent and continue if you have persistent trouble with constipation, or consult your herbalist. To use cascara for the other uses mentioned in this section, consult with a qualified healthcare practitioner.

Book VI

Natural Health

Castor Oil (Riccinus communis L.)

Although castor oil is a favorite old-time remedy for constipation, its external use is more common today. The castor oil pack is popular for healing cancerous and benign tumors of all kinds, and herbalists often recommend the poultice for treating uterine fibroids and breast cysts.

Dosage: Take 1 to 2 tablespoons of the oil before bedtime, depending on your age and weight.

Don't take castor oil internally longer than one week. Also, don't use this herb if you're pregnant. Avoid using castor oil if you have intestinal obstruction or abdominal pain.

Catnip (Nepeta cataria L.)

Beyond being adored by cats, catnip makes a mild, aromatic tea for colds, flu, fever, and fussiness in children. The herb has mild calming, sweat-releasing, and digestion-promoting effects.

Dosage: Drink 1 cup of the strong infusion made with 1 tablespoon of the dried or fresh herb, two to three times daily.

Avoid using this herb during pregnancy.

Cayenne (Capsicum annum var. annum.)

Use cayenne powder or tincture if you have a cold, poor circulation, or weak digestion. In hotter climates, cayenne helps cool the body by promoting sweating. One of its active ingredients, capsaicin, is effective for blocking the transmission of the pain impulse in the body, and it's found in commercial over-the-counter and prescription products for shingles, arthritis, carpal tunnel syndrome, and sore muscles.

Dosage: Take 1 to 4 capsules powder, twice daily. Follow the manufacturer's directions for other products. (***Note:*** The burning sensation you sometimes feel after ingesting cayenne won't hurt you. In fact, studies show that cayenne can help heal an ulcer rather than aggravate one.)

Avoid getting cayenne near your eyes, because it can burn (but it won't cause damage).

Chamomile, German (Matricaria recutita L.)

Drink chamomile tea liberally to help ease intestinal cramps or irritation, indigestion, and nervousness. You can also use chamomile tea for colic, fever, and teething in children. Externally, you can apply a chamomile cream for soothing skin inflammation, burns, and bites.

Dosage: Drink 1 cup of the infusion, made with 1 tablespoon of the herb, three to five times daily. You can make a strong instant tea by adding @bf1/2 to 1 teaspoon of the tincture to a cup of warm water.

Allergic reactions to the pollen in the flowers are rare, but they do occur.

Chaparral (Larrea tridentata [DC] Cov.)

Chaparral promotes sweating; improves elimination of toxins from the liver and skin; and eases the symptoms of colds, flu, and bronchitis. A concentrated extract is sometimes used externally for skin cancer. Chaparral may have potent antioxidant properties.

Dosage: Make a light decoction with 1 teaspoon of the chopped herb for every cup of water and drink ½ to 1 cup of the infusion twice daily. Alternatively, take 2 capsules or droppersful of the tincture twice daily.

Don't use chaparral if you have a pre-existing kidney or liver condition, such as hepatitis. Don't use for more than two weeks except under the advice of your herbalist.

Cinnamon (Cinnamomum zeylanicum Blume)

Drink cinnamon bark tea to relieve the symptoms of colds, mucus congestion, and digestive problems. Cinnamon also has an astringent effect, and you may find it effective for easing diarrhea.

Dosage: Make a light decoction by simmering 1 teaspoon of the bark for every cup of water for 10 minutes; then steep for 15 minutes. Drink 1 cup, one to three times daily.

Cinnamon is a warming herb, so avoid the tea if you run hot all the time.

Cleavers (Galium aparine L.)

Cleaver (also known as bedstraw or goosegrass) cleanses the lymphatic system and shrinks swollen lymph glands. Consider using it if you have tonsillitis, psoriasis, or other skin conditions. It can also clear bladder infections, cleanse the urinary tract, and help prevent small kidney stones from forming.

Dosage: Drink 1 cup of the infusion, or take up to 1 teaspoonful of the tincture in a little water, two to three times daily.

Codonopsis (Codonopsis pilosula [Franch.] Nannf.)

Codonopsis strengthens digestion, the respiratory tract, and the immune system. Try using it for fatigue, poor appetite, chronic lung infections, shortness of breath, asthma, and general weakness.

Dosage: Make a decoction with about 9 to 25 grams of the roots to 3 or 4 cups of water; simmer down to 2 or 3 cups. Drink 1 strong cup, twice daily. Follow the manufacturer's recommendations for other products.

Comfrey (Symphytum officinale L.)

Comfrey helps heal burns, bites, stings, and cuts, as well as strains, sprains, and broken bones.

Dosage: Make a light decoction with the leaves and drink 1 cup two or three times daily for up to ten days. Blend the leaves or roots with a little water to make a slimy paste and apply to external injuries for as long as needed on unbroken skin and up to a week on broken skin, under the advice of an herbalist.

Avoid using comfrey if you're pregnant or nursing. Also, don't use comfrey leaf preparations internally longer than one week, twice a year, under the advice of a qualified herbalist.

Cramp Bark (Viburnum opulus L.)

Use cramp bark to ease menstrual and intestinal cramps.

Dosage: Drink 1 cup of the decoction made with 1 teaspoon of the chopped herb per cup of water, or 2 droppersful to 1 teaspoon of the tincture in a little water, two or three times daily.

Cranberry (Vaccinium macrocarpon Aiton.)

Cranberry juice helps cleanse your urinary tract and prevent bladder infections and kidney stones. Cranberry is also useful for incontinence.

Dosage: Drink 1 cup of unsweetened (if you *really* like sour) or lightly sweetened cranberry juice, one or two times daily. Increase to 3 to 5 cups to help eliminate a urinary tract infection. Or take 2 to 4 capsules of an extract in capsule or tablet form. Use cranberry for several weeks to get the best results.

Dandelion (Taraxacum officinale Wiggers.)

Use dandelion for liver-related problems, such as hepatitis, cirrhosis, and liver toxicity, as well as for poor appetite and constipation. The leaves are used to help retain water and increase lactation.

Book VI

Natural Health

Dosage: Make a decoction by simmering 1 tablespoon of the leaf or root for every cup of water. Drink 1 cup, two or three times daily, or 2 to 4 droppersful of the tincture, one to three times daily.

Don't use dandelion if you have bile-duct blockage, gallbladder inflammation, or intestinal blockage, except under the advice of an experienced herbalist. (*Note:* Don't confuse the ever-present dandelion with similar-looking plants, such as sow thistle or false dandelion. Dandelion is the only one of the three that has single flowering heads on hollow, unbranched stalks and hairless, large-toothed leaves.)

Dong Quai (Angelica sinensis [Oliv.] Diels.)

Commonly taken by women for strengthening the blood and female organs, dong quai is also useful for coronary problems and mild anemia in both men and women. Use dong quai for anemia, PMS, and menopause, and if you're experiencing general weakness, debility, and circulatory disorders, such as angina.

Dosage: Make a decoction by simmering 1 crown or 3 or 4 of the palm slices in 2 or 3 cups of water for 45 minutes. Drink 1 cup, two or three times daily. Take 1 to 3 droppersful of the tincture twice daily.

Avoid using this herb while pregnant.

Echinacea (*Echinacea purpurea*)

Echinacea possesses strong immune-stimulating activity. Use it to help prevent and treat all kinds of infections, especially colds, flu, urinary tract infections, and skin infections such as impetigo and boils. You can also use echinacea as a mouthwash for gum problems.

Dosage: Take 2 droppersful to 1 teaspoon of the tincture, three or four times daily in cycles of two weeks on and one week off. Make a tea by simmering 1 teaspoon of the chopped root or leaf in 1 cup of water for 10 minutes, and then steeping for 15 minutes. Drink 1 cup, several times daily. Follow the label instructions for other products.

Use echinacea cautiously under the advice of an herbal practitioner if you have an autoimmune condition such as lupus, or an immune-compromised condition such as AIDS.

Elder (*Sambucus spp.*)

Use elder to relieve colds, flu, and fevers; clear infections like acne, boils, skin rashes, and other forms of dermatitis; and strengthen resistance against infections. Herbalists sometimes also recommend elder for treating hay fever and sinusitis. The extracts can be an excellent remedy for chronic rheumatism, neuralgia, and sciatica.

Dosage: For colds and fever, take 2 to 3 cups of the infusion, two to three times daily to induce sweating. Soaking in a hot bath or wrapping up in a sheet and a sleeping bag or blankets helps bring on a good flow of sweat, thereby eliminating toxins and speeding the healing process. Follow the manufacturer's instructions for berry syrups and extracts in capsule or tablet form.

Eleuthero (Siberian Ginseng) (*Eleutherococcus senticosus* [*Rupr. ex Maxim.*] *Maxim.*)

Take eleuthero if you're feeling tired or run-down, facing major changes in your life, living under stress, or serious about sports. Studies show that you may have more energy, get sick less often, have better workouts, or let stress roll off your back more easily with eleuthero.

Dosage: Make a decoction with 1 teaspoon of the herb for every cup of water by simmering for 30 minutes. Twice daily drink 1 cup of the tea, or add ½ teaspoon of the tincture to a little water and drink. Follow the label directions for other kinds of products.

Evening Primrose (Oenothera biennis L.)

Use evening primrose to ease the symptoms of arthritis and skin problems (like eczema and psoriasis). Added to other herbal remedies like vitex, black cohosh, or skullcap, evening primrose may also help with PMS and breast tenderness.

Dosage: Take 250 to 500 milligrams of the oil daily, in capsules.

Eyebright (Euphrasia spp.)

Eyebright has anti-inflammatory and mild decongestant properties. Use it for eye infections such as pink eye and sties, as well as for eye irritation, sinus infections, and hay fever.

Dosage: Take 2 to 4 droppersful of the tincture, 2 to 3 cups of the infusion, or 3 to 5 capsules of the herb, two to three times daily.

Fennel (Foeniculum vulgare Mill.)

Use fennel for dyspepsia, flatulence, nausea, and stomachache and for easing the pains and spasms of colic and diarrhea in babies and young children. Fennel also helps mothers increase lactation after a child is born. An infusion of the seeds is used externally as a compress for conjunctivitis.

Dosage: Drink 1 cup of the light decoction or infusion, made by steeping 1 teaspoon of the herb for every cup of water. Alternatively, take 3 or 4 capsules, or 2 to 4 droppersful of the tincture, two to three times daily.

Fenugreek (Trigonella foenum-graecum L.)

Use a fenugreek poultice over boils and sores to help draw out waste products and speed healing. Fenugreek tea helps relieve atherosclerosis, bronchitis, and diabetes; it also increases lactation.

Book VI

Natural Health

Dosage: Simmer 1 to 2 tablespoons of the ground or crushed seeds in 4 cups of water for 15 minutes and let the decoction steep for another 15 minutes. Drink ½ to 1 cup, two or three times daily. To make the poultice, crush the seeds and simmer them to make a thick, slimy tea; then spread the mass onto a piece of cloth.

Avoid using this herb while pregnant.

Feverfew (Tanacetum parthenium [L.] Schulz-Bip.)

Use feverfew as a remedy for flu and other respiratory infections that are accompanied by a fever, as well as for migraine headaches and arthritis. When used as an herb in cooking, feverfew is an appetite stimulant.

Dosage: Take 1 to 3 droppersful of the tincture one to two times daily, or 2 capsules of the powder or standardized extract daily.

Avoid using feverfew if you're pregnant.

Flaxseed (Linum usitatissimum L.)

Use flaxseed to ease constipation, inflammation, and irritation of the stomach, intestines, and respiratory tract. Applied externally, it can draw out toxins, reduce inflammation, and speed healing. The regular use of flaxseed meal and some commercial oil products may help balance estrogen activity, reduce the risk of some cancers and heart disease, and benefit women who are going through menopause.

Dosage: Simmer 1 tablespoon of flaxseed or flaxseed meal in 2 cups of water and drink 1 cup, twice daily, as needed. Sprinkle flaxseed meal on cereals and other foods. Grind 1 or 2 tablespoons of flaxseed in a seed grinder or blender to a powder and soak in ¼ to ½ cup of hot water until a slimy mass forms. Spread the gel onto a small piece of cloth and apply to boils and sores.

Don't use flaxseed if you have bowel obstruction. Always drink plenty of water, about two 8-ounce glasses, when taking this herb.

Garlic (Allium sativum L.)

Garlic is an important antibiotic and antiviral remedy for colds, flu, bronchitis, pneumonia, and other infections. Garlic preparations can also help protect the blood and cardiovascular system. With regular use, the herb slightly lowers your high blood pressure, reduces high cholesterol, and helps prevent atherosclerosis. Garlic also kills and clears intestinal parasites.

Dosage: Take 2 to 4 perles of a garlic product daily, or follow the manufacturer's directions. The therapeutic dose of whole garlic is two to three cloves daily with meals, either cooked or raw.

Avoid using garlic if you're nursing. Raw garlic can sometimes irritate your stomach if you eat too much.

Book VI

Natural Health

Gentian (Gentiana lutea L.)

Use gentian root for weak digestion, poor appetite, and anemia. You can also use it if you're recovering from an illness.

Dosage: Make a decoction by simmering ½ teaspoon of the herb for every cup of water for 10 minutes, then steeping for 15 minutes. Drink ½ cup of the decoction, or take 10 to 30 drops of the tincture, two to three times daily in a little water before meals. (**Note:** Because the root doesn't contain tannins or other digestive irritants, it's recommended for daily use and can be taken for years.)

Avoid using this herb if you have an ulcer or gastric irritation or inflammation.

Ginger (Zingiber officinale Roscoe.)

Use ginger for nausea or to settle your stomach if you have morning sickness, motion sickness, or other intestinal problems; to help with poor circulation; and to ease and shorten symptoms of colds and flu. Use a hot compress of ginger tea for arthritis; sore joints after a joint-replacement procedure; and for strains, sprains, sore backs, and other injuries. Cool ginger tea is effective for easing the pain of minor burns and rashes.

Dosage: Make ginger tea by simmering several slices of the fresh rhizome or 1 teaspoon of the cut and sifted dried herb for every cup of water. Drink 1 cup of decoction, two or three times as needed, preferably around meal-times. You can also take 2 capsules of the powder, or 2 to 4 droppersful of the tincture, two to three times daily.

Avoid consuming more than 2 or 3 cups of ginger a day during pregnancy. The fresh rhizome is safer to use during pregnancy than the dried root.

Ginkgo (Ginkgo biloba L.)

Use ginkgo extract to improve memory, increase mental alertness, and slow the progression of Alzheimer's disease. The herb also restores circulation to your legs if you have blocked arteries and improves circulation to your eyes and ears, thus reducing ringing in the ears *(tinnitis),* protecting your eye-sight, and helping to prevent and treat macular degeneration. You can also use ginkgo for autoimmune conditions, such as some forms of hepatitis and asthma.

Dosage: Take 2 to 3 droppersful of the tincture for up to a month or two for daily prevention or mild to moderate symptoms. For longer-term use or for moderate to severe symptoms, use 1 capsule or tablet containing 60 milli-grams of the standardized extract, two to three times daily.

The highly purified extract containing 24 percent flavone glycosides can cause mild gastrointestinal irritation if you're sensitive.

Ginseng (Panax ginseng C. A. Mey.)

Take ginseng if you have digestive problems like gas or malabsorption, or if you commonly experience a feeling of fullness, even after eating only small meals. You can also use it for chronic fatigue, convalescence, lethargy, depression, and chronic infections related to immune weakness, especially if you're over age 45.

Dosage: Make a decoction by simmering 1 level teaspoon of the ground-up root for every cup of water and drink 1 cup, two to three times daily. Take 1 to 3 droppersful of the tincture, or 1 to 2 capsules of the standardized extract, two to three times daily.

Avoid using this herb if you have hypertension. Use American ginseng or eleuthero (Siberian ginseng) if you're under age 40, unless prescribed by a practitioner of Traditional Chinese Medicine.

Ginseng, American (Panax quinquefolius Meyer.)

Use American ginseng for adrenal fatigue, chronic fatigue, chronic rashes, arthritis, digestive weakness with inflammation, irritable bowel syndrome, certain kinds of insomnia, and nervousness.

Dosage: Take 2 to 4 grams daily as a decoction. Alternatively, you can take either ½ to 1 teaspoon of the tincture in a little water or 2 capsules or tablets containing a powdered extract that you consume with your morning and evening meals.

Don't use ginseng if you feel anxious — it's slightly stimulating.

Book VI

Natural
Health

Goldenrod (Solidago spp.)

Goldenrod stimulates kidney function and increases the flow of urine output. Use it with saw palmetto extract to strengthen the prostate gland and urinary organs and reduce inflammation. It's also recommended for varicose veins. For colds, blend goldenrod with echinacea and ginger.

Dosage: Make a light decoction with 1 teaspoon of the herb for every cup of water and drink ½ cup several times daily. Take 2 to 4 droppersful of the tincture, two or three times daily.

Avoid goldenrod if you have chronic kidney problems. See your herbalist and a physician if you suspect that you have a kidney infection.

Goldenseal (Hydrastis canadensis L.)

Internally, take goldenseal preparations to reduce inflammation, for bacterial infections of the upper respiratory tract and urinary tract, and for bacterial or amebic infections of the digestive tract, such as giardia and dysentery. The herb isn't as effective for viral conditions like colds and flu, gastritis, and sinus infections. Externally, use goldenseal tea as a wash for conjunctivitis and gum problems and as a douche for vaginal infections from candida or trichomonas.

Dosage: You can take 1 to 2 droppersful of the tincture, or 1 to 2 capsules, twice daily. Make a light decoction with ½ teaspoon of the herb for each cup of water and drink 1 cup, up to three times daily, as needed.

Don't use goldenseal if you're pregnant. Contrary to popular belief, goldenseal isn't effective for clearing drugs out of the body to help you pass a drug-detection test.

Gotu Kola (Centella asiatica [L.] Urban.)

Use gotu kola internally for improving your memory and supporting your mental functions and nervous system. Use creams and external preparations for healing eczema, wounds, and other skin conditions.

Dosage: Take 2 to 4 droppersful of the tincture made from the fresh plant, or 2 to 3 cups of the infusion made from the dried herb, two to three times daily.

Grapeseed (Vitis vinifera L.)

Grapeseed extract helps protect the skin and internal organs against the ravages of stress and environmental toxins. Regular use of grape skin and seed extracts may help protect you from developing cancer. The seed extract contains potent antioxidant compounds that some researchers claim may slow down the aging process.

Dosage: Follow the manufacturer's instructions on the packaging. Or, depending on your need, take 1 or 2 capsules of the extract, one or two times daily.

Green Tea (Camellia sinensis [L.] Kuntze.)

Green tea may protect you against heart disease, ulcers, and cancer. It can also help relieve diarrhea, reduce pain, and invigorate the mind and the nervous system. Use it as a mouthwash to prevent plaque formation.

Dosage: Make a cup of tea with 1 teaspoon of loose herb for every cup of water and drink 2 to 3 cups of the infusion daily. Follow the manufacturer's instructions for other products, but know that generally 1 or 2 capsules a day of the standardized extract is recommended.

Green tea contains 4 or 5 percent caffeine. Avoid using the herb if you have heart palpitations or experience insomnia or anxiety, or just use the decaffeinated varieties instead.

Hawthorn (Crataegus laevigata [Poir] DC.)

Take hawthorn for heart irregularity and palpitations, atherosclerosis, angina, hypertension, and nervousness, and to support and strengthen your heart. Used over months and years, you may find the herb has a pronounced strengthening effect on the heart and blood vessels.

Dosage: Take 2 to 3 droppersful of the flower and leaf tincture, 1 cup of the decoction, or 3 to 4 capsules of the powder, two to three times daily.

Hawthorn can make the effects of digitalis preparations (such as digoxin) more potent. See your doctor if you're taking digoxin or related compounds.

Book VI

Natural
Health

Hops (Humulus lupulus L.)

Use hops to relieve nervousness, insomnia, restlessness, excitability, excessive sexual excitement, nervous digestion, insufficient breast milk, and heart palpitations. It may also have weak estrogenic properties.

Dosage: You can take 1 to 3 droppersful of the tincture, two to three times daily, or 1 cup of the infusion made with 1 tablespoon of hops, as needed.

Avoid hops if you're depressed.

Horehound (Marrubium vulgare L.)

Use horehound to relieve coughs and ease congestion, wheezing, coughs associated with colds and asthma, sore throats, and fevers.

Dosage: Make an infusion by steeping 1 teaspoon of the dried herb in 1 cup of boiled water and drinking ½ to 1 cup, or 2 to 4 droppersful of the tincture in a little water, two or three times daily. To relieve coughs, you can suck on a horehound candy several times daily.

Avoid horehound when you're pregnant.

Horse Chestnut (Aesculus hippocastunum L.)

The two-inch nuts produced by the horse chestnut tree are harvested and extracted to produce liquid extracts and standardized capsules, as well as creams for external use. Use horse chestnut tinctures or standardized extracts for treating varicose veins, hemorrhoids, and sports injuries. Use horse chestnut creams for easing the pain and swelling of sports injuries, sprains, strains, bruises, and varicose veins.

Dosage: Take 5 to 20 drops of the tincture, three times daily. Follow the manufacturer's directions for other products.

Don't exceed the recommended dose. The raw, unprocessed nuts can irritate the gastrointestinal tract and are considered toxic. Commercial preparations are safe when you follow label instructions.

Horsetail (Equisetum arvense L.)

Take horsetail herb internally for treating cystitis or prostatitis and for strengthening and regenerating connective tissue. The herb is useful for strengthening bones, hair, and nails. In Europe, extracts of horsetail are used for easing inflammation and speeding the healing of rheumatism and arthritis. The tincture or tea is a diuretic and helps cleanse the urinary tract and remove excess mucus.

Dosage: Drink 1 cup decoction several times a day made by simmering 1 or 2 tablespoons of the cut and sifted herb for each cup of water for up to three hours to extract the organic silica. Take 2 or 3 droppersful of the tincture, two or three times daily. Follow the manufacturer's directions for taking the standardized extract.

Consult with an herbalist before taking horsetail if you have chronic heart or kidney problems.

Juniper (Juniperus communis L.)

Use the berries to ease the symptoms of urinary tract infections and for cystitis, gout, and weak digestion with gas. Rubbing the tincture on sore rheumatic joints helps to ease pain and inflammation.

Dosage: Make a tea by infusing 1 teaspoon of the berries with 6 cups of freshly boiled water for 20 minutes. Drink ½ cup of the tea, several times daily. Take 20 to 30 drops, or 1 to 2 capsules of the ground berry powder with a little water, several times daily.

Avoid using juniper berries when you're pregnant or if you have pre-existing kidney disease.

Kava (Piper methysticum G. Forster.)

Kava drinks and tinctures are good for fatigue, insomnia, tight muscles, and mild depression, as well as for bladder infections and prostate inflammation with decreased urination. Use the tincture for relaxing tight, tense muscles; use powdered extract or the tea for mental relaxation.

Book VI

Natural Health

Dosage: Take 2 to 4 droppersful of the tincture, or swallow 1 or 2 tablets or capsules of the standardized extract, two or three times daily with a little water. Make a decoction by simmering 1 teaspoon of the herb for every cup of water and drink 1 cup several times daily as needed.

Avoid using this herb if you're pregnant or nursing. Don't exceed the recommended dose. If you drink kava, be careful when driving. People have been cited — and fined! — for driving while under the influence of kava.

Lavender (Lavandula angustifolia Mill.)

Lavender is best-known for helping lift spirits, relax the body, and settle the stomach. Use lavender for nausea, depression, and colic. Use lavender oil topically for burns and add a few drops to baths for relaxation.

Dosage: You can make the infusion with 1 teaspoon of the flowers for every cup of tea. Drink 1 cup, two to three times daily.

Lemon Balm (Melissa officinalis L.)

Drink lemon balm tea to settle the stomach. Use lemon balm creams to treat genital and oral herpes sores. Use other lemon balm preparations to calm the nervous system, a nervous heart, and a nervous stomach; to ease tension and insomnia; and to relax spasms of the stomach and intestines. Combine it with other soothing remedies, like marshmallow root and licorice root, for ulcers.

Dosage: Make an infusion with 1 tablespoon of the dry leaves and tops for every cup of water and drink 2 or 3 cups during the day, as needed. Boil the herb for 30 to 60 minutes, let it steep for 15 minutes, and soak a washcloth in the warm tea for external application.

Licorice (Glycyrrhiza glabra L.)

Licorice has potent soothing, anti-inflammatory, and antiviral effects. Take licorice tea or other preparations for digestive weakness, ulcers, irritable bowel and bowel inflammation, bronchitis, coughs, and adrenal weakness due to stress or overwork.

Dosage: Make a decoction by simmering 1 teaspoon of the herb for every cup of water for 30 minutes. Drink 1 cup of the decoction, or take 1 or 2 droppersful of the tincture, two to three times daily. Follow the manufacturer's directions for DGL (*deglycyrrhizinated licorice,* an extract of licorice) products or standardized extracts.

Avoid using licorice if you're pregnant or have diabetes or hypertension. When taken for prolonged periods, licorice may potentially cause potassium depletion and sodium retention. Licorice is available in a deglycyrrhizinised form, which doesn't cause these side effects.

Ligustrum (Ligustrum lucidum Ait.)

Take ligustrum for chronic adrenal weakness due to stress and overwork, low back pain, ringing in the ears, and premature graying. Also use it to strengthen the immune system during cancer treatment.

Dosage: Make a decoction by simmering 1 teaspoon of the dried berries 40 to 60 minutes for every cup of water. Drink 1 cup, or take ½ to 1 teaspoon of the tincture in a little water, two or three times daily.

Linden (Tilia x europaea L.)

Use linden to bolster your immune system and induce sweating and elimination to relieve symptoms of colds and flu. The flowers, which have mild sedative properties, are often added to products for calming your nervous system and reducing blood pressure.

Dosage: Make an infusion by steeping 1 tablespoon of the herb for every cup of boiled water for 20 to 30 minutes and drink 1 cup, two or three times a day. Commercial extracts of linden are available but aren't as effective as the tea.

Ma Huang (Ephedra spp.)

Use ma huang to relieve temporary symptoms of asthma, colds with no fever or sweating, hay fever with nasal congestion, coughs, and earaches.

Dosage: Make a decoction using 1 tablespoon of the herb for each cup of water and drink ½ to 1 cup, two to three times daily. Follow the label instructions of other products.

Avoid ma huang when you're pregnant. Ma huang stimulates the nervous system and may cause anxiety, nervousness, or sleeplessness. Several people have died from using excessive quantities of this herb to stimulate energy. Regular use of ma huang products robs the digestive system of the energy it needs to properly digest and assimilate important nutrients and can adversely affect your energy and immune function, nervous system, and cardiovascular system.

Marshmallow (Althaea officinalis L.)

Marshmallow root reduces irritation and inflammation of bronchitis and other respiratory tract infections with sore throat. Use marshmallow to help soothe a urinary tract that's inflamed with cystitis or to relieve the effects of gastritis, ulcers, and colitis on your stomach and colon.

Dosage: An effective way to take the remedy involves blending 1 teaspoon of the root for each cup of cool water for 5 minutes, steeping for 30 minutes, and straining and drinking 1 cup several times daily. You can add plantain leaf or calendula flowers to increase the healing powers of the tea. Follow the label instructions for other kinds of products.

Strong marshmallow tea may interfere with the absorption of some pharmaceutical medications, so take them separately.

Meadowsweet (Filipendula ulmaria [L.] Maxim.)

Use meadowsweet for treating headaches, heartburn, fevers, rheumatism and arthritis, gastritis, or ulcers. Also use it to soothe the digestive tract and relieve nausea and hyperacidity.

Dosage: Make an infusion by steeping 1 or 2 teaspoons of the herb for 20 minutes for each cup of water. Drink ½ to 1 cup, two to three times daily. Or you can take 2 to 4 droppersful of the tincture, two to three times daily.

Milk Thistle (Silybum marianum [L.] Gaertner.)

Take milk thistle to protect your liver from toxins and drugs and build liver health. Use standardized seed extracts and tinctures for cirrhosis, hepatitis, and jaundice.

Dosage: Take 2 to 4 droppersful of the tincture, or 1 to 2 capsules or tablets of the standardized extract, two to three times daily. If you have a chronic liver condition such as hepatitis or cirrhosis, avoid using the tincture of milk thistle. Instead, take the standardized extract in tablets or capsules only.

Motherwort (Leonurus cardiaca L.)

Use motherwort for the cardiovascular system or as a heart tonic for easing palpitations, helping hypertension, strengthening the heart, and helping relieve the pain of mild angina. You can also use it for painful, delayed, or suppressed menstruation and premenstrual tension (PMS).

Dosage: Make an infusion by steeping 1 teaspoon to 1 tablespoon of the herb for every cup of freshly boiled water. Drink 1 cup, or take 2 to 4 droppersful of the tincture, two to three times daily.

Avoid using motherwort while pregnant.

Mullein (Verbascum thapsus L.)

Mullein leaves are one of the safest and most useful herbal lung tonics; they have a soothing action on the mucous membranes of the respiratory tract. Mullein can also be effective for relieving skin problems, such as psoriasis. Take mullein to ease the symptoms of asthma, chronic bronchitis, dry coughs, and laryngitis. Use the flower oil in your ears for inflammation; earaches; and infections of the Eustachian tubes, inner ear, and ear canal. See your doctor or herbalist if you have an ear infection.

Dosage: Make a light decoction by simmering 1 tablespoon of the herb for every cup of water for 15 minutes. Drink 1 cup, up to several times daily, as needed. Use 2 to 4 drops of the oil in the ear, morning and evening.

Nettle (Urtica dioica L.)

Nettle has diuretic, cleansing, antihistamine, and anti-inflammatory properties. Use nettle for hay fever, arthritis and rheumatism, anemia and weak blood, cystitis and water retention, and gout. Nettle rhizomes are increasingly used to reduce prostate inflammation and improve symptoms such as painful urination that occur with benign prostatic hyperplasia (BPH).

Dosage: Make a decoction with 1 tablespoon of herb or rhizome for every cup of water by simmering for 20 or 30 minutes. Drink 1 to 2 cups, two or three times daily. Follow the label instructions for other products.

Orange Peel (Citrus aurantium L.)

Orange peel is a flavorful herb for enhancing digestion and relieving symptoms such as nausea, vomiting, burping, and a feeling of fullness after eating even small amounts. You may find orange peel effective for assisting the body in removing excess mucus and relieving coughs and a feeling of fullness in the chest.

Dosage: You can make a light decoction of orange peel in a covered pan by gently simmering ½ cup of the fresh or ¼ cup of the dried peels in 5 cups of water. Drink 1 cup two or three times a day, after meals.

Oregon Grape Root (Mahonia aquifolium [Pursh] Nutt.)

Use Oregon grape root for cooling the liver, stimulating bile flow, reducing inflammation in the intestines, and benefiting symptoms of dermatitis. It can also clear skin disorders (such as acne, cysts, or psoriasis), gastritis and ulcers, vaginal yeast infections, and bowel infections.

Dosage: Make a decoction by simmering 1 teaspoon of the cut and sifted herb for every cup of water. Drink ½ to 1 cup, or 1 to 2 droppersful of the tincture, two or three times daily.

Avoid using this herb while pregnant.

Parsley (Petroselinum crispum [Mill.) Nym. Ex A.W. Hill.)

Parsley seed tea is a potent diuretic. The roots are less potent, but are also used. European herbalists and doctors recommend parsley fruit and root tea for relieving water retention and edema.

Dosage: Make a tea by steeping ½ teaspoon of the fruits or 1 teaspoon of the cut and sifted root for every cup of water for 15 minutes. Drink ½ cup of the preparation, two to three times daily.

Avoid using parsley root or fruits in medicinal doses during pregnancy. Don't use parsley fruit tea for more than two weeks at a time without consulting an experienced herbalist.

Passion Flower (Passiflora incarnata L.)

Use passion flower to ease anxiety and insomnia, especially the kind caused by hypertension, PMS, and neuralgia.

Dosage: Take 2 to 4 droppersful of the tincture in a little water, several times daily as needed.

Pau d'Arco (Passiflora incarnata L.)

Herbalists recommend pau d'arco for its proven antifungal and cancer-fighting properties and its possible immune-strengthening qualities. Consider using the bark for helping to prevent and eliminate candida yeast infections.

Dosage: Make a decoction by simmering 1 teaspoon of the dried bark for every cup of water for 20 minutes. Drink 1 cup of the tea, or 1 to 3 droppersful of the tincture in a little water, three or four times daily.

Peppermint (Mentha x piperita L.)

Peppermint is a favorite remedy for relaxing the intestinal tract; relieving gas pains; and easing nausea, vomiting, heartburn, morning sickness, irritable bowel syndrome, and colitis. Try peppermint tea for helping to relieve symptoms of the common cold, fevers, and headaches.

Dosage: Make an infusion by steeping a small handful of the fresh herb or 1 tablespoon of the dried herb for every cup of water and drink 1 cup, two to three times daily.

Pipsissewa (Chimaphila umbellata Nutt)

Use pipsissewa for bladder and kidney weakness, cystitis, arthritis, and rheumatism.

Dosage: Simmer 1 teaspoon for every cup of water for 20 minutes. Drink 1 cup, or take 2 to 4 droppersful of the tincture, twice daily.

Book VI

Natural Health

Plantain (Plantago lanceolata L.)

Internally, plantain leaves soothe inflamed and infected tissues of the respiratory, urinary, and digestive tracts. Take the tea liberally for relieving coughs, ulcers, irritable bowel, colitis, cystitis, and painful urination. Externally, the fresh leaves quickly reduce the pain of bites, stings, cuts, scrapes, and burns. Use a slimy wad of the herb inside the mouth for easing the inflammation and pain of infected gums, gum disease, and abscesses.

Dosage: To make a poultice for external use, blend fresh leaves with a little water to form a slimy paste. Apply to the affected spot, cover with a bandage or adhesive tape, and leave in place for an hour or two. Replace the poultice several times a day, keeping it wet, and apply before bedtime. Make a decoction by simmering ½ cup of the fresh or dried leaves in 2 or 3 cups of water for 30 or 40 minutes. Drink 1 or 2 cups of the tea several times daily. Juice the fresh leaves and add the juice to carrot, celery, apple, or other juices.

You can substitute plantain for comfrey during pregnancy or for long-term use because it contains similar active constituents and effects.

Psyllium (Plantago spp.)

Psyllium seed is used as a gentle bulk laxative to relieve constipation; it's also used for diarrhea, hemorrhoids, irritable bowel syndrome, Crohn's disease, and high cholesterol.

Dosage: Soak ½ to 2 teaspoons in 1 cup of warm water and drink 1 or 2 times daily, especially first thing in the morning and before bedtime. Follow the label instructions of any commercial products.

You must take psyllium seed with at least 8 ounces of water. When taking other drugs, wait an hour before taking psyllium.

Raspberry (Rubus idaeus L)

Raspberry leaf tea is the safest and least controversial tea to use during pregnancy. Use raspberry leaf for toning up the uterus and facilitating labor. When used regularly, the herb is also effective for easing painful periods and slowing diarrhea.

Dosage: Make a light decoction by simmering a small handful of the dried or fresh herb in 2 cups of water for a few minutes and steeping the herb for 15 minutes or so. Drink 1 cup, two or three times daily.

Red Clover (Trifolium pratense L.)

Red clover flowers can help eliminate toxins in the liver and bowels and stimulate immune function to assist the body in removing toxic waste products; they're also effective as a mild expectorant and cleanser for the respiratory tract for helping to heal lung problems, such as dry coughs, laryngitis, bronchitis, and whooping cough. Red clover can also help relieve skin problems such as eczema, psoriasis, acne, and other kinds of dermatitis. This herb is an important component in well-respected formulas that assist the body in its fight with cancer; red clover is also used to help prevent the disease.

Dosage: Make a tea by simmering 1 tablespoon of the herb for each cup of water for 15 to 20 minutes. Drink 1 cup, or take ½ to 1 teaspoon of the tincture in a little water, two or three times daily. Follow the label instructions of commercial capsules or tablets.

Avoid using this herb while pregnant.

Reishi (Ganoderma lucidum [Leyss. Ex Fr.) P. Karst.)

Reishi calms the nervous system, strengthens the blood and cardiovascular system, and supports the immune system, especially for people who have cancer and are undergoing western treatments such as chemotherapy and radiation therapy. Take reishi to help relieve the symptoms of anxiety, allergies, general weakness, heart problems, insomnia, and chronic fatigue syndrome.

Dosage: Make a decoction by first grinding the whole mushroom in a blender or food processor and then simmering 1 cup of the herb for every 4 cups of water for an hour. Drink 1 cup of the tea, or take 3 tablets or capsules, two to three times daily. Follow the label instructions for other products.

Rosemary (Rosmarinus officinalis L.)

Use rosemary if you have nervous system or cardiovascular weakness, your period is sluggish or stopped, or you want to slow the aging process and reduce your risk of heart disease and cancer. Rosemary also helps with headaches, chronic fatigue, poor appetite, low blood pressure, and weak circulation. For the elderly, rosemary invigorates the nervous system and digestion and helps preserve good health. Rosemary tea hair rinses are excellent for keeping your hair shiny and healthy. Add a pot of tea to your bath to make an invigorating and restorative rosemary bath.

Dosage: Make an infusion of rosemary by steeping 1 teaspoon of the herb for each cup of water for 20 minutes. Drink 1 cup of the tea, or take 10 to 30 drops of the tincture, two or three times daily.

Avoid using rosemary if you're pregnant.

Sage (Salvia officinalis L.)

Use sage for colds, especially with a sore throat or excessive perspiration. Sage is an ingredient of herbal preparations used externally in antiperspirant formulas to reduce body odor and as a gargle and spray to ease the pain and inflammation of a sore throat. Nursing mothers often use sage to help dry up the last flow of milk.

Dosage: Make an infusion by steeping 1 teaspoon of the herb for every cup of boiled water for 15 minutes. Drink 1 cup of the tea, or take 20 to 30 drops of the tincture in a little water, several times daily, as needed. Follow the label instructions for externally applied products.

Avoid using this herb while pregnant. Also, avoid long-term use and don't exceed the recommended dose.

Book VI

Natural
Health

St. John's Wort (Hypericum perforatum L.)

Take St. John's wort internally if you're depressed or have insomnia, or if you want to relieve chronic nerve pain caused by conditions such as peripheral neuropathy or trauma and injuries that involve nerve damage. St. John's wort can also be used for children who wet the bed. Used externally, the herb reduces inflammation and the pain of scrapes, bruises, strains, burns, and other trauma.

Dosage: The effective dose of St. John's wort is about 4 droppersful of the tincture in the morning and 3 in the evening in a little water, or 2 capsules of a standardized extract in the morning and 1 capsule in the evening. You can go up to 1 teaspoon of the tincture, or 2 capsules or tablets, morning and evening, as needed. You can make an infusion of St. John's wort if you want to, but that isn't as effective as the other preparations. Apply the oil, or any other external preparation, liberally as needed, preferably at least twice a day. (*Note:* A review of several commercial standardized extract products in capsules and tablets showed that the products actually delivered from 30 percent to 80 percent of the advertised levels of active constituents. For this reason, if you've tried capsules with no results, try taking a teaspoon of the tincture in the morning and ½ to ¾ teaspoon in the evening for a month.)

Avoid regular use of this herb when taking pharmaceutical MAO-inhibitors or if you have fair skin.

Saw Palmetto (Serenoa repens [Bart.] Small.)

Use saw palmetto for easing symptoms of prostate inflammation and enlargement (*benign prostatic hyperplasia,* or BPH). It also helps strengthen and improve the nutrition of the urinary and genital organs, helps prevent bladder infections, and relieves neurogenic and irritable bladder conditions.

Dosage: Take 2 capsules powdered extract twice daily, or 2 droppersful tincture twice daily. Consider taking a double dose of saw palmetto if you're on the verge of a bladder infection, especially if you get them frequently or have persistent prostate enlargement and restricted urine flow. See your doctor if symptoms persist.

Schisandra (Schisandra chinensis [Turcz.] Baill.)

Use schisandra if you have chronic coughs from lung weakness, incontinence from a weak bladder, or excessive sweating during menopause or during chronic infections (such as AIDS). Schisandra can also protect livers with conditions such as hepatitis.

Dosage: Make a decoction by simmering 1 teaspoon of the dried fruits for every cup of water for 30 minutes. Drink 1 cup of the tea or ½ teaspoon of the tincture in a little water, several times daily.

Book VI

Natural Health

Shiitake (Lentinus edodes (Berk.) Singer.)

Take an extract of this mushroom to help ease symptoms associated with high cholesterol, lowered immune function, hepatitis, environmental allergies, candida, AIDS, and cancer. Scientific studies show that shiitake is a potent immune booster, cancer-fighter, and antiviral herb.

Dosage: Take 3 or 4 tablets or capsules of a concentrated extract twice daily with meals. Take half that amount for prevention and general health-promoting benefits. Eating shiitake, which is widely available as a food in grocery stores and natural food markets, is a great way to get the benefit with the flavor.

Skullcap (Scutellaria lateriflora L.)

Native American Indians and herbalists have used the flowers and upper leaves of skullcap for more than 100 years to calm the nervous system and ease spasms. Use skullcap for insomnia, headache, nervous exhaustion, muscle spasms, and the nervous tension and irritability associated with PMS. This herb is also used to ease the discomfort of withdrawal from drugs or alcohol and is considered helpful in alleviating excessive sexual desire.

Dosage: Take 3 to 5 droppersful of the liquid tincture in a little water or tea, several times daily. To make a tea, simmer ¼ ounce of the herb for every 2 ounces of water for 5 minutes. Let the brew steep for 20 minutes; then strain and drink 1 cup, several times a day.

Slippery Elm (Ulmus fulva Michx.)

Take a slippery elm lozenge or warm tea when you have a sore throat or any irritation or inflammation of the digestive tract. Slippery elm can also ease diarrhea and soothe ulcers, gastritis, colitis, and coughs.

Dosage: Make a decoction of the bark by simmering 1 tablespoon for every cup of water for 15 minutes. Drink 1 cup, two or three times daily.

Strong slippery elm tea may interfere with the absorption of some pharmaceutical medications, so take them separately.

Thyme (Thymus vulgaris L.)

Drink a cup of strong, antiseptic thyme tea to help eliminate coughs, mucus congestion, or sore throat associated with colds or the flu. You can also take this herb for bronchitis or pneumonia. Use thyme sprays, syrups, or lozenges externally for soothing a sore throat and inhibiting infection.

Dosage: Make an infusion with 1 teaspoon of the dried herb or 1 tablespoon of the chopped fresh herb for every cup of water for 15 or 20 minutes. Follow the label directions for other products.

Turmeric (Curcuma longa L.)

Consider turmeric if you have an inflammatory condition such as arthritis, pain after an injury, gallbladder inflammation, liver inflammation associated with hepatitis, or menstrual pain. Additionally, turmeric is known to help protect against cancer.

Dosage: Make a light decoction with 1 teaspoon of the herb powder or cut and sifted herb, or 1 tablespoon of fresh slices of the rhizome, for every cup of water by simmering for 15 or 20 minutes. Drink 1 cup, or take 1 to 4 droppersful of the tincture in a little water, several times daily. Follow the label instructions on other products.

Avoid using this herb while pregnant. Don't use turmeric if you have an obstructed bile duct, gallstones, stomach ulcers, or hyperacidity without the advice of an experienced herbalist.

Usnea Thallus (Usnea barbata [L.] Wigg.)

Many lichens, usnea thallus included, produce strong antibiotic compounds. Use usnea when you have conditions such as strep throat, a staph infection (like impetigo), urinary tract infections, and pneumonia.

Dosage: Take 2 to 4 droppersful of the tincture, two to three times daily.

Uva Ursi (Arctostaphylos uva-ursi [L.] Spreng.)

Consider taking uva ursi if you have a bladder infection or mild kidney infection.

Dosage: Make a tea by simmering 1 tablespoon of the leaves in 2 cups of water for 30 to 40 minutes, until the water is reduced to 1 cup. Drink ½ cup of the tea twice daily. Add 1 teaspoon of the tincture to a cup of water and drink ½ of the cup in the morning and evening. For persistent infections, you may find a double dose effective, but consult an experienced herbalist first. Because uva ursi works better when the urine is acidic, take the tea or tincture concurrently with cranberry juice or tablets.

Avoid using this herb while pregnant. Don't use in cases of chronic kidney disorders or digestive irritation without the advice of an experienced herbalist.

Valerian (Valeriana officinalis L.)

Use valerian to calm the nervous system if you feel nervous, anxious, or upset, and to promote healthy sleep. Also, try the herb for menstrual cramps (with cramp bark), heart palpitations (with hawthorn or hops), or for pain (with Roman chamomile or Jamaican dogwood). (***Note:*** Don't use standardized extracts of valerian available in capsules or tablets because the active ingredients often break down when the rhizomes are so highly processed.)

Dosage: You have to take valerian in a strong dose for it to be effective. Start with ½ teaspoon of the tincture, several times daily in a little water, and increase to 1 teaspoon if this dosage isn't working. The tea is also effective. Make an infusion with 1 tablespoon of the cut and sifted herb for every cup of water. Steep the valerian for 30 minutes in a closed pot and drink 1 cup, several times daily.

Valerian has few side effects, but some people find the rhizome can cause stimulation rather than a feeling of calm. You can reduce the chance of this situation happening if you avoid valerian when you have chronic fatigue or depression (try California poppy or passion flower instead) or if you consult an herbalist first.

Vitex (Vitex agnus-castus L.)

Take vitex if you have symptoms associated with PMS and menopause. It's also effective for helping a woman ease off of birth control pills, increasing the flow of mother's milk, and reducing teen acne (although it doesn't work as well for teens with a strong family history of acne who are continuously broken out).

Dosage: Take 1 to 2 droppersful of the tincture daily, first thing in the morning, or 2 to 4 capsules containing the powdered herb, twice daily. You can try a double dose if the regular dose doesn't work after two or three months. Follow the label instructions for standardized extracts.

Avoid using vitex if you're pregnant or taking birth control pills, except under the advice of an experienced herbalist.

White Willow (Salix spp.)

Willow bark is an ancient medicine and a source for aspirin. Use willow bark tea if you have a headache, fever, pain, or an inflammatory condition such as carpal tunnel syndrome, rheumatism, or arthritis.

Dosage: Make a decoction by simmering 1 tablespoon of the cut and sifted bark for every cup of water for 10 minutes; then let the brew steep for another 10 minutes. Drink 1 cup, two or three times daily.

Wild Oats (Avena fatua L.)

Take wild oats if you have trouble with depression, nerve weakness from too much mental work, or an addiction (like smoking) that you're trying to beat.

Dosage: Make a tea by simmering ¼ cup of the spikelets for every cup of water for 20 minutes. Drink 1 cup of the tea, or take ½ to 1 teaspoon of the tincture in a little water, three or four times daily as needed. Best results come after taking wild oats for a few months; you can take the herb up to a year or more.

Wild Yam (Dioscorea villosa L.)

Use wild yam for easing the cramping of colic, intestinal and uterine spasms, and gallbladder pain. It's also an effective addition to herbal formulas for nausea, morning sickness, and chronic rheumatism. (***Note:*** You can find wild yam in bulk for making teas, but be careful not to try grinding it in your blender — it's so tough that it can break the blades! Buy the herb already cut and sifted.)

Dosage: Make a tea by boiling 1 teaspoon of the herb for every cup of water for 40 minutes. Drink 1 cup, or take 2 to 4 droppersful of the tincture in a little water, two to three times daily.

Witch Hazel (Hamamelis virginiana L.)

Consider taking witch hazel internally for hemorrhoids, varicose veins, or diarrhea. Externally, witch hazel is a favorite remedy for stopping the bleeding of cuts, removing spots and blemishes, and toning the skin.

Dosage: Use ¼ to ½ cup of the bark or dried leaves to make a light decoction by simmering for 20 minutes. Take ½ to 1 cup of the tea, two or three times daily, or apply the lotion externally as needed.

Use of witch hazel tea or tincture for more than a few days can worsen constipation in some cases.

Wormwood (Artemisia absinthium L.)

Use wormwood if you have a poor appetite, sweet cravings, stomach weakness, painful digestion, or worms. Wormwood can also help you regain strength after a prolonged or serious illness or operation. Wormwood tea is a popular healing drink in Europe for easing the symptoms of stomach irritation and gastritis, or for strengthening and lifting sagging digestive organs.

Dosage: Make an infusion of wormwood by steeping 1 teaspoon to 1 tablespoon of the dried herb for every cup of water for 20 minutes. Drink ½ to 1 cup of the tea, or 20 to 30 drops of the tincture in a little water, several times daily and before meals.

Avoid using wormwood if you're pregnant or nursing. Don't exceed the recommended dose and don't use the tincture for more than a few weeks at a time without first consulting an herbalist.

Yarrow (Achillea millefolium L.)

Take yarrow for a variety of conditions: to relieve mucus congestion, inflammation, and fever from colds, flu, and other upper respiratory infections; to regulate blood flow throughout the body; to relieve pain from arthritis and rheumatism; to relieve spasms and inflammation, irritable bowel complaints, colic, and intestinal and uterine cramps; to relax the bowels and improve digestion, as well as help prevent and treat gallstones and gallbladder inflammation; and to help with sluggish or painful menses, fever, delayed menstruation, poor appetite, and convalescence.

Dosage: Make an infusion by steeping ¼ cup of the bulk herb for every 2 cups of water for 20 or 30 minutes. Drink 1 cup of the tea, or 1 to 3 droppersful of the tincture in a little water, two or three times daily. Take yarrow for several weeks or months to experience the best results. (**Note:** The best form of yarrow is the fresh herb right from a wild place or garden, but a good quality dry herb works fine.)

Avoid using this herb while pregnant.

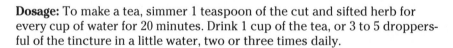

Yellow Dock (Rumex crispus L.)

Yellow dock is a common weed, but don't underestimate its powers. Its root is a magnificent bowel balancer and blood tonic. Use it to treat constipation, sluggish bowels, or loose stools. Consider adding yellow dock to formulas to help cleanse parasites and worms from the intestines and to perk up the appetite.

Dosage: To make a tea, simmer 1 teaspoon of the cut and sifted herb for every cup of water for 20 minutes. Drink 1 cup of the tea, or 3 to 5 droppersful of the tincture in a little water, two or three times daily.

Avoid using this herb if you have kidney stones.

Yerba Santa (Eriodictyon californicum [Hook. Et Arn.] Torr.)

Consider yerba santa if you have respiratory congestion, a cold, asthma, or a moist cough. Yerba santa is a warming expectorant that helps remove excess damp, cold mucus so you can breathe easier. The herb is especially useful during the cold, damp months of the year.

Dosage: Make an infusion by steeping ¼ cup of the dry herb for every 2 cups of water for 30 minutes. Drink 1 cup of the tea, or take 10 to 30 drops of the tincture, three times daily.

Index

D

E

O

P